PRAISE FOR *THE GREEKS*

"A monumental, sweeping history of the Greeks covering more than three thousand years right up to the present day. Authoritative, compelling, and beautifully written. A wonderful book."
  —Peter Frankopan, author of *The Silk Roads*

"A masterpiece, from a towering expert in all things Greek."
  —Gregory Nagy, Harvard University

"Roderick Beaton has given us a wonderful big picture of the Greeks, with a very generous cross-cultural, temporal, and geographical sweep. At the same time, the book's solid detail and careful distinctions—for example, between the Platonic and the Christian vocabulary for 'virtue'—should help in discouraging political exploitation of stilted, anachronistic ideas about Greek civilization."
  —Sarah Ruden, translator and author of *Paul Among the People*

"Over three millennia, the locus of the Greek spirit has shifted perpetually. In antiquity it darted about between the cities, harbors, and mountain valleys of the east Mediterranean, moving eventually through the swathes of North Africa, the Levant, and southwest Asia where Alexander and his successors held sway. In modern times, it has flowed between the footloose global diaspora and the two volatile states which embody Greekness. In a tour de force, Beaton has managed to tie this story together in a single compelling narrative, written with deep affection and hard-earned knowledge of all things Greek."
  —Bruce Clark, author of *Athens: A History*

"A remarkable and readable book: this single, masterful volume lays out the entire thirty-five-century history of the Greek-speaking peoples. From Minoan to modern times, their triumphs, their tragedies, and above all their endurance are all here. For anyone who wants to understand Greece today, this is the place to start."

—Ian Morris, author of *Why the West Rules—for Now*

"Histories of the Greeks have so far been written with a classical or a modern bias, but Beaton does not play favorites: with the vantage-point of a scholar enjoying a deep knowledge of Byzantium as well as all phases of Greek literature, he weaves together a vivid narrative reaching from the age of heroes and lore down to the present. The Greeks emerge not as a single nation but rather as a series of great civilizations. They were often at odds with each other but, in all phases of their long history, contributed cultural capital to the rest of the world. Beaton's Greeks are always on the move, self-reflexive, and surprising. Their story has not yet been told in a global fashion, as it is here."

—Anthony Kaldellis, Ohio State University

"Professor Beaton, already very well known as a formidable and distinguished exponent of modern Greek history, here expands exponentially his vision and chronological scope and turns his more than competent hand to composing a comprehensive history of Greeks, or rather Hellenes, from the Late Bronze Age BCE to the present day. His handsomely illustrated and fully documented text is a consistently illuminating encapsulation of the manifold achievements of one of the globe's most creative and inspirational peoples."

—Paul Cartledge, Cambridge University

THE
GREEKS

THE
GREEKS

A GLOBAL HISTORY

RODERICK BEATON

BASIC BOOKS

NEW YORK

Basic Books
Hachette Book Group
1290 Avenue of the Americas, New York, NY 10104
www.basicbooks.com

Printed in the United States of America

First Edition: October 2021

Published by Basic Books, an imprint of Perseus Books, LLC, a subsidiary of Hachette Book Group, Inc. The Basic Books name and logo is a trademark of the Hachette Book Group.

The Hachette Speakers Bureau provides a wide range of authors for speaking events. To find out more, go to www.hachettespeakersbureau.com or call (866) 376-6591.

The publisher is not responsible for websites (or their content) that are not owned by the publisher.

Print book interior design by Trish Wilkinson

Library of Congress Cataloging-in-Publication Data
Names: Beaton, Roderick, author.
Title: The Greeks : a global history / Roderick Beaton.
Description: First edition. | New York : Basic Books, 2021. | Includes bibliographical
    references and index.
Identifiers: LCCN 2021012414 | ISBN 9781541618299 (hardcover) | ISBN
    9781541618282 (ebook)
Subjects: LCSH: Civilization—Greek influences. | Greece—Civilization. | Greeks—
    Ethnic identity. | Greece—History.
Classification: LCC CB69 .B43 2021 | DDC 909—dc23
LC record available at https://lccn.loc.gov/2021012414
ISBNs: 978-1-5416-1829-9 (print), 978-1-5416-1828-2 (ebook)

LSC-C

Printing 1, 2021

This book is dedicated to all my Greek friends, acquaintances, former students, and colleagues, wherever they are in the world today, and to the memory of those who are no longer with us.

By so much has our city exceeded all mankind in matters of thought and speech, that her students have become the teachers of others; she has caused the name of Greeks to be understood, not in terms of kinship any more, but of a way of thinking, and people to be called Greeks if they share our educational system, rather than a common ancestry.

—Isocrates, *Panegyricus* (Athens, 380 BCE)

There one can see a western European acquiring his ABCs, a Russian learning Greek, a Byzantine studying the works of the ancient Greeks, and an unlettered Greek learning to spell the ancient language correctly.

—Anna Komnene, *Alexiad* (Constantinople, c. 1150)

The language given to me was Greek:
the poor man's home on Homer's sandy shores.
My language is my single care on Homer's sandy shores.

—Odysseus Elytis, *The Axion Esti* (1959)

I do not say that we are of the same blood—because I have a horror of racial theories—but we still live in the same country and we see the same mountains ending in the sea.

—George Seferis, speech accepting the
Nobel Prize for Literature (1963)

CONTENTS

Contents

LIST OF MAPS AND CREDITS

AUTHOR'S NOTE

IN THIS BOOK I use the abbreviation BCE (equivalent to BC) whenever the year or century referred to falls before the start of the Common/Current Era. BCE dates are counted *down*, so the fourteenth century BCE comes *before* the thirteenth century, and so on. There was no year 0 in this system, so the year 1 BCE was followed immediately by the year 1 CE (equivalent to AD). I use the abbreviation CE *only* where the context otherwise might cause confusion. So, whenever neither BCE nor CE is indicated, a date should be assumed to be CE.

FOR MORE THAN two and a half millennia, Greek names of people and places have been written in the Greek alphabet, described in Chapter 2. Various conventions have been used at different times to represent these names in the Latin, or roman, alphabet that we use in English. Because pronunciation has changed over the centuries, the sounds represented by several letters of the Greek alphabet are not the same today as they were in ancient times. There is therefore no fully consistent way to write Greek names in English. The problem is compounded because there is a long-established practice of representing *ancient* Greek names in the Latin forms adopted by the ancient Romans. These are usually far more recognisable in English today than a more rigorous transliteration direct from Greek:

'Thucydides', for example, is the *Latin* transcription for the name of the historian whose name was more accurately Thoukydides. Particularly well-known names, of both places and people, have long since acquired English equivalents: 'Athens', not 'Athenai' (ancient) or 'Athina' (modern); 'Plutarch', not 'Ploutarchos'.

I have tried to follow these principles in the pages that follow:

- Whenever a name has a reasonably well established English equivalent, I use that ('Thessalonica', not 'Thessalonike'; 'Jesus', not 'Iesous').
- Up to the end of Chapter 7, I use latinised spellings for most Greek names, with exceptions for place names which are today more familiar in their Greek form, so 'Mycenae' (latinised), not 'Mykenai'; but 'Knossos', not the latinised Cnossus.
- For the Byzantine period, I use the closest equivalent to the Greek letters of the name: so 'Anna Komnene', not 'Anna Comnena'; although older generations of scholars once did so, it makes no sense to latinise the names of people who lived *after* the end of the Latin-speaking Roman Empire.
- For the modern period, I adapt the same principle so as to reflect today's pronunciation (so, someone called 'John' in the Byzantine period will be 'Ioannes', but in the modern, 'Ioannis' or the more colloquial 'Yannis').

PREFACE

T HE GREEK LANGUAGE is one of only three, among those now spoken and written anywhere in the world, that can boast a continuous written tradition stretching back for more than three thousand years. The others are Chinese and Hebrew. The collective heroes and heroines of the story told in this book are all those people who have spoken and written the Greek language throughout the long centuries of its recorded evolution.

During that time, Greek was used at first to keep bureaucratic records, then to preserve for posterity the heroic epics, the *Iliad* and the *Odyssey* of Homer, that have been read with wonder by every generation since. It was the language of the world's first fully alphabetic system of writing. It was in Greek that the foundations for modern philosophy and science were laid and, later, that the apostles of Christianity would disseminate the new religion through the New Testament. The original Greek text of the Gospels is still read aloud in Orthodox churches around the world. Evolving as all human speech does over time, Greek in its present-day form is the official language of the Hellenic Republic and one of the two official languages of the Republic of Cyprus.

The Greeks of the title and the pages that follow are to be understood as *speakers of the Greek language*. The story of these Greek speakers will turn out to be a story about identity—or rather, about *identities*, in the plural. Greek speakers have been adept, ever since we first get to know them through their earliest writings, at asking questions and interrogating *themselves*. The answers they have come up with have differed greatly over the centuries, according to cultural changes and changing historical circumstances. Throughout history, Greeks have created types of societies and political systems very different from one another. If they have continuously inhabited the same southeastern corner of Europe and the eastern Mediterranean, they have also, at different times, put down roots in many different places. Again and again, they have proved resourceful at reinventing themselves. They have fought against different enemies, traded with different partners around the world, worshipped different gods, even called themselves by different names. We call them 'Greeks', and their land 'Greece', in English today because the ancient Romans first encountered a local tribe of Greek speakers whom they called, in Latin, *Graeci*. In their own language in ancient times, these people were known as 'Hellenes' and their land as 'Hellas', as they have been known once again since the early nineteenth century. But they have also, at different times, been *Achaiwoi* (Achaeans) and *Romaioi* or *Romioi* (pronounced *Romyí*), meaning literally 'Romans'.

This book asks: What can we learn from the accumulated experience of those who have spoken and written this language, during three and a half thousand years, about how identities are created, perpetuated, and modified or reinvented over time? We all rely on perceptions of the past to establish our own identity in the present. In a world ever more threatened by the clash of mutually exclusive, monolithic identities, we might all do well to reflect, on a more informed basis than we often do, on the ways in which these identities come to be formed and also adapted as the world around us changes. The story of the Greeks, based on their own words, that can be traced all the way back to the earliest period of recorded history, sheds light on this *process* rather than on any single identity, seemingly fixed and given at any one time.

The story that follows will be rather different from anything you have ever read about Greeks or Greece before. For one thing, it is not the story of a *place*. 'Greece', or 'Hellas', was only ever a rather imprecise geographical term in the ancient world. There was never a political entity of that name until 1821, when Greek subjects of the Ottoman Empire raised the flag of revolution and declared their independence. The frontiers of the Greek state as we know it today mostly date from as recently as 1913. To confine the story to these narrow geographical limits would be to leave out precisely the dimension of Greek history that this book is designed to highlight, namely, its global reach.

Also, it is not the story of a single 'Greek civilisation'. For most of us, unless we are booking a holiday or doing business, when we think of 'Greeks', what comes to mind first is likely to be the artistic and scientific achievements of a group of city-states led by Athens and Sparta around two and a half thousand years ago. The story of that civilisation, that we still call 'classical', has been told many times. And deservedly so—because it really was the origin of much of the arts, sciences, politics, and law as we know them throughout the developed world today. In these pages we will often observe this process in action, and sometimes also probe the mechanisms that enabled these achievements to penetrate so far beyond their starting point. Suffice it for now to remind ourselves how many words current in the globalised languages of today, particularly in scientific terminology, come from Greek and refer to things that the Greeks were the first either to create or to define: *democracy*, *politics*, *philosophy*, *drama*, even *crisis* and *epidemic*, to name just a few. Many more, based on Greek roots, have been invented in modern times to refer to inventions unknown to the ancients: *telephone*, *technology*, *photon* are examples. Another is *pandemic*—a

3

real ancient Greek word given an entirely new meaning in many languages in modern times.

But there is far more to the story of the Greeks than that. Rather than focus on a single civilisation, however foundational for the rest of the world, in this book I will be looking at a whole interconnected *series* of civilisations. Long before the classical period came the Greek-speaking civilisation that today we call 'Mycenaean'. The Mycenaeans were Bronze Age warriors. But they were also traders who amassed great quantities of gold and built fortresses that later generations thought could only have been the work of giants. Their world ended suddenly, about three thousand three hundred years ago. Nobody knows for certain why. But the modern theory of 'systems collapse', that has been devised to explain how this and other world civilisations came to disappear, is one that we will encounter again, in the rise and fall of later civilisations in which Greek speakers had an important part to play.

The 'classical' civilisation began many centuries after the Mycenaean had ended. That world of competing city-states, in its turn, came to an end when the city-states came under the control of the powerful Greek-speaking kings of Macedonia. The most famous of those kings, known to history as 'Alexander the Great', conquered the whole of the Middle East, as far as the frontiers of India today. With that conquest began a new era that we know as 'Hellenistic', when Greek first became a world language, in much the same way as English is often said to be today.

Later still, it was the turn of Greeks to be conquered, as the power of Rome expanded. Greek speakers living under the Roman Empire produced their own, quite distinct version of what we call Roman civilisation. Indeed, the whole eastern half of that empire, reaching from the Adriatic Sea in the west to the River Euphrates in the east and as far south as Aswan in Egypt, used Greek, not Latin, as its common language. After that came Christianity and with it an entirely new centralised, monotheistic Greek-speaking civilisation that for the best part of a thousand years was the envy of the West. Nowadays we call that civilisation 'Byzantine', or 'Byzantium'. Lastly, Greeks in more recent times have played distinguished and distinctive parts in forging the most complex society that has ever existed—the global civilisation that we enjoy today, with all of what the founder of psychoanalysis and devoted classicist Sigmund Freud once famously termed its 'discontents'.

When we look at Greek history through this perspective and tease out the multiple ways in which Greeks have interacted with all manner of outsiders over more than three millennia, we reach the remarkable conclusion that Greeks have got just about *everywhere*. Today, the Greek language, the art and archaeology of many different periods of the Greek past, Greek philosophy, literature, and the ancient Greek contributions to science, medicine, law, and politics are studied in schools and universities from Chile to China, from Norway to New Zealand, from Siberia to South Africa. All over the world, during the last three centuries, architects of grand buildings, both public and private, have given a new lease of life to the soaring marble columns and lofty pediments that the Greeks once devised for the temples of their gods. In different ways, the heirs of those ancient Greeks have been interacting, for centuries, with all manner of people, all over the known or accessible world of their time.

That is why this book is called a 'global history'.

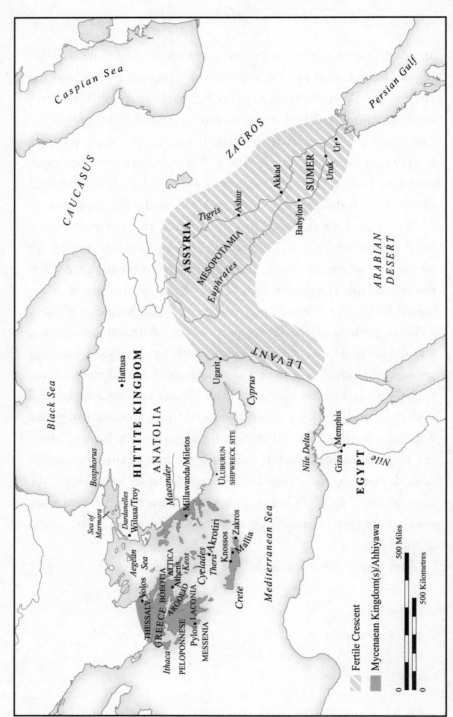

1. The eastern Mediterranean and the Fertile Crescent in the Late Bronze Age

1

OF LEDGERS AND LEGENDS

1500 BCE–c. 1180 BCE

LET US IMAGINE dawn coming up over the Aegean Sea in the year 1500 BCE. Far away to the east and south, the sun is already well above the horizon across the Fertile Crescent that stretches from the top of the Persian Gulf, along the course of the Rivers Tigris and Euphrates, and westwards all the way to the Mediterranean. Those were the lands where the domestication of crops and animals had first begun, many thousands of years before. Complex societies, or civilisations, have been flourishing in those regions for longer than a millennium: in succession, Ur, Akkad, Sumer, Babylon. In 1500 BCE, it is the turn of the Assyrians, ruling from their capital of Ashur on the banks of the Tigris. Recently, a new centre of power and wealth has been making its mark farther north, and closer to the Aegean, in the highlands of Anatolia.

This is the kingdom of the Hittites. Although over the sea it is still barely dawn, the sun rises upon Hattusa, the Hittite capital, which lies not far from the site of the future Turkish capital of Ankara. The Hittite king maintains an army that can field hundreds of war chariots—and another army of a different kind, less visible, that keeps and maintains immense numbers of records in a script known as cuneiform, devised in the Fertile Crescent during the previous millennium. At almost exactly the same moment, far to the south, the valley of the Nile is lit up. The sun first catches the tops of the pyramids of Giza, which are already some fifteen hundred years old. Egypt has been a stable kingdom, with a hierarchical society and a developed system of writing for all that time, and has as many centuries again ahead of it. The wealth and the fabled wisdom of the Egyptians are magnets that draw traders and military rivals from throughout the region.

Back in Anatolia, the light is starting to pour down the river valleys that lead westward from the plateau that is the Hittite heartland, towards the sea. The people of the coastal lowlands have their own languages, related to Hittite. But in 1500 BCE, they are not ruled directly from Hattusa. As the sunlight reaches the coast, it lights up a city near the mouth of the greatest of these rivers, the Maeander. The city is known to the Hittites as Millawanda and will later enter Greek history under the name Miletus.

Moments later, a couple of hundred miles to the north and slightly to the west, the strait known as the Dardanelles, or Hellespont, is beginning to catch the growing light. On the Asian side, and a few miles inland from the Aegean coast, the densely populated streets of an even larger city are waking up to the new day. Built in the middle of a fertile plain, this city is well placed strategically to profit from any traders moving from the Aegean through the straits into the Sea of Marmara or beyond, through the Bosphorus into the Black Sea. Its citadel is fortified with massive walls. Below them, the much larger lower city is home to some ten thousand people, a significant population for this part of the world at this time. What language the people here speak, or what name they give to the place, will not be recorded for posterity. It is called Wilusa by the Hittites and Wilios, later Ilios or Ilion, by the Greeks—eventually to become known by the alternative Greek name, which may be no less ancient, Troy (Troia).

The dawn light spreads across the Aegean. The first rays catch the peaks, one after another, of the three great mountain ranges that run from east to west across the island of Crete. Two hundred miles long, no more than forty wide, and with no other land of any size visible from its shores, Crete is home to an advanced civilisation that will be dubbed 'Minoan', after the island's legendary king, Minos, when its remains are discovered three and a half millennia later. Crete under the Minoans is a land of prosperity and plenty. As the sunlight reaches down to the coastal lowlands, on the roofs of buildings it picks out the characteristic, stylised representations of bulls' horns that look a little like medieval crenellations, though they have not been put there for defence. (The first archaeologists to uncover them, at the beginning of the twentieth century, will call them, rather portentously, 'horns of consecration'—and the name will stick.) Larger towns are grouped around tightly organised, complex structures that the same archaeologists will call, conventionally, 'palaces'. In reality, these are centres for the collection and redistribution of agricultural produce and craftwork. These processes are integrally linked to religious ceremonial and ritual activity that has been developing on the island over centuries.

To most outsiders, even from the perspective of 1500 BCE, the Cretan way of life must seem exotic. Neither the Minoan language nor their writing system is like any other that is in use, anywhere. Minoan architecture has an upside-down appearance: upper storeys are supported on columns that taper downwards from the top. Ceremonial rooms in these palaces are brightly painted, their interior walls covered with stylised frescoes in a range of vibrant colours. Men are depicted wearing short, pointed kilts or loincloths; women, in long, flounced skirts and short jackets that leave their breasts bare and prominent; on occasion they hold live snakes in their hands. Both sexes are shown with unnaturally slim waists.

Other scenes depict a public spectacle that must be part hazardous sport, part religious observance: acrobats take it in turns to grasp a running bull by the horns and somersault over its back, to land perfectly poised on their feet, facing the way they have come.

Inside the palaces, tucked away and lit only by lightwells from the upper storey, 'lustral basins' flanked by columns lead down into the earth and enable celebrants to communicate with the divine powers below. One of these is often represented in the form of a bull and is probably the forerunner of the 'Earthshaker', Poseidon, worshipped in later times. It is possible that the greatest deity of them all is the lithe-waisted, bare-breasted goddess often represented on top of a pinnacle of rock, while wild animals or male humans gaze up at her in adoration. Worship also takes place in sanctuaries high on mountaintops or deep in caves. It is not unknown—and this could even be a regular occurrence—for a young man to be ritually killed, or for child victims to be prepared for a cannibal feast, to propitiate those same gods.[1]

And the Minoans of Crete have good reason to fear them. The Aegean is a part of the world where the earth's crust is on the move. Often in the past, their palaces and towns have been laid low by earthquakes. So far, each time this happens, the Minoans have rebuilt them, more splendidly than before. Now, as the sunlight sweeps across the sea, it illuminates the group of islands to the north, that will come to be known as the Cyclades. Among this group, and closest to Crete, rises into the light an awe-inspiring monument to the destructive forces that lie deep within the earth. This is the ring of rocky islands surrounding a sea-filled, volcanically active caldera, that will later be known as Thera and later still as Santorini. The gently sloping coasts on the seaward side, away from the caldera, used to boast several thriving towns. People used to live here in two-storey houses and painted the interiors with brightly coloured frescoes in the Minoan style. There are probably some still living, in 1500 BCE, who remember the catastrophic eruption that hurled volcanic debris many miles into the upper atmosphere and buried every sign of human habitation on Thera under a layer of more than thirty feet of ash and pumice.[2]

The remains of Akrotiri, as it will come to be called, will lie undiscovered until 1967 (CE). All that can be seen in 1500 BCE are lifeless mounds of white ash, scored with the black streaks of pyroclastic flows whose temperature, at the time of the eruption, would have reached hundreds of degrees centigrade. No life at all on the island could have survived the destruction. Even after almost half a century, only the scrubbiest vegetation has regained a foothold. Sea winds scour the surface, creating treacherous, shifting ravines and blowing ash and grit far out to sea. It will be a long time before any daring mariner sets foot on Thera again. The inhabitants must have had warning, because the houses and streets that twentieth-century archaeologists uncover will be empty of people. Further afield, terrifying though these events must have been at the time, the eruption of Thera has caused less long-term disruption than might have been expected. The Minoans appear to have taken it in their stride, as they have previous disasters. It could be, though, that more insidious effects are at work and have yet to come to a head. Few signs of this may yet be visible, but it is possible that public faith has been shaken, among the people of Crete, in the deities they rely on for protection or in age-old rituals that may no longer seem sufficient to appease them.[3]

At the time of the eruption the winds were blowing from the west. Least affected would have been the people living between one and two hundred miles upwind of the catastrophe on the mainland, whose turn it is, at last, to greet the sunlight on this imagined morning. This is the land that after many centuries will come to be known by the names of *Hellas* and later *Graecia*, or Greece. Here, people live in scattered communities, year after year balancing risks of crop failure, drought, and flash floods. Apart from a few fertile coastal plains, land suitable for growing crops and grazing is broken up by mountain ranges that keep communities apart from one another. Subsistence farming and animal husbandry, mostly of sheep and goats, are the norm. The terrain is capable of feeding only so many mouths, human and animal. This is a constant that will never really change in all the centuries to come.

In 1500 BCE there are no buildings anywhere on the mainland to rival those of Crete, either in number or in scale. Until relatively recently, and especially when compared to Crete, the whole area has been a 'cultural backwater'.[4] But a change is in the air. This is especially evident at Mycenae, a hilltop settlement on the edge of the plain known as the Argolid, in the northeast Peloponnese, where a wealthy elite has begun to emerge. The people of the southern Greek mainland are on the way up. These are the people whose descendants, within a few generations, will come to dominate the whole Aegean region, eclipsing the power and wealth of Minoan Crete, and leave behind the earliest records written in Greek.

THE MORE DISTANT origins of the Mycenaeans, as we call these people and their civilisation today, and the Greek language that they spoke, are lost in prehistory. Greek belongs to the Indo-European group of languages, which in prehistoric times spread through many populations, from the Indian subcontinent to Iceland. It is often suggested that the first Indo-European speakers must have arrived in the Greek mainland from the north, sometime between 2300 and 1900 BCE (in prehistory, all dates are approximate). As they mixed with the people who had been there before them, the language that we know as Greek slowly emerged—distinct from others of the Indo-European group and incorporating elements absorbed from the older language, or languages, of the region.[5] Alternatively, it may be that a form of early Indo-European arrived with the first farmers, when knowledge of the techniques of agriculture first spread this far westward from the Fertile Crescent, some six thousand years ago. In that case, the distant origin of the Greek language may reach all the way back to the beginning of the period that we call the Neolithic, or New Stone Age.[6] Either way, Greek must have been taking shape as a distinct language in the southernmost tip of the Balkan Peninsula, during several hundreds of years, perhaps even thousands, before our imagined Aegean dawn in the year 1500 BCE.

It was at the imposing citadel of Mycenae that in 1876 the German archaeologist Heinrich Schliemann first found proof that a complex society had flourished on the European mainland in the Late Bronze Age, a whole millennium before the heyday of 'classical' Greece. Buried in what he termed 'shaft graves', Schliemann uncovered the remains of the families that had ruled there between about 1600 and 1450 BCE. The bones of the men still showed traces of the wounds and the deformations they had survived during battle-hardened lives. Buried with them was a fearsome array of swords, daggers, and spearpoints. Images represented on grave goods show scenes of fighting, lion and boar hunting, and trapping wild bulls. In six of the burials, the face of the dead man had been covered by a death mask of beaten gold. Women were accompanied by elaborate gold headdresses and finely worked jewellery. In one grave, a small child had been laid to rest encased entirely in gold leaf.[7]

Since then, many more finds have come to light, at Mycenae and elsewhere in the southern and central mainland of today's Greece. In 2015, American archaeologists working at the site of prehistoric Pylos in Messenia, in the southwest Peloponnese, unearthed very similar treasures of the same period in the grave of the 'Griffin

Warrior'.[8] Clearly, the elites of the sixteenth and fifteenth centuries BCE on the Greek mainland prided themselves on their strength and skill at arms.

The practice of burying so much wealth out of sight along with the dead has aptly been termed 'ostentatious waste'.[9] How these riches came to be in the hands of the Mycenaean warriors and the families buried alongside them is something of a mystery. Their immediate source, on the other hand, is not far to seek. It lies in Minoan Crete. The Minoans at this time had spread their influence right across the southern Aegean. Later traditions that King Minos of Crete had once ruled the seas probably have their origins in the same centuries that saw the beginning of the Mycenaeans' rise.[10] Minoan outposts had been established on many of the Aegean islands, on the west coast of Anatolia, and as far away even as Cyprus. Trade between Crete and fabulously wealthy Egypt had been going on for centuries. This was the route by which precious materials such as gold and ivory entered the Aegean. It was not only the raw materials that came from Crete. Many of the objects buried in the shaft graves of Mycenae are of recognisably Minoan workmanship. There are so many of these that archaeologists have concluded that craftsmen trained in Crete must have been engaged to work for the local Mycenaean rulers. As they did so, they would have adapted prized Minoan styles and decorations to the artistic tastes, or perhaps the different religious beliefs and customs, of the Mycenaeans.[11]

But what did the warrior chieftains of obscure places like Mycenae, Athens, Thebes, or Pylos on the mainland have to offer in return for all these rich goods and services? Archaeologists, attuned to modern patterns of exchange and trade, have noted that mining of copper, lead, and silver at Laurion (modern Lavrio) in Attica seems to have begun at about this time. Perhaps the Mycenaeans traded their surpluses for the exotic treasures that would end up buried along with their chieftains? Or were these riches perhaps the reward won by the very feats of arms that the graves were designed to commemorate?

An intriguing hint comes from a fresco found in a house in the Minoan outpost of Akrotiri on Thera. The house had been buried by the eruption that devastated the island some time before 1500 BCE. In one of the scenes shown in the fresco, a line of warriors emerges from the gate of a walled town and forms up, apparently ready to defend their livestock from attackers trying to land from ships, though they have also been interpreted as a raiding party.[12] Either way, the figures are immediately recognisable as Mycenaeans by their beehive-shaped helmets with rows of boars' tusks stitched to the outside, the enormous rectangular shields that cover the greater part of their bodies, and the spears that they carry, each twice as long as a man. Actual remains of these helmets, traces of the shields, and the points of the spears have all been found in mainland graves and would often be depicted by Mycenaean artists in years to come.

This evidence tells us that Mycenaean warriors were already a recognisable presence in the Minoan-dominated Aegean before 1500 BCE. But the Minoans seem not to have regarded them as a threat to their own way of life. Coastal towns such as Akrotiri had no defensive walls. At least two of the distinctive Minoan palaces in Crete, at Malia and at Kato Zakros, flourished on flat land right by the sea and were not fortified either. It may well be that Mycenaean warriors acquired their wealth by offering their services as paid enforcers for the Minoans in their Aegean possessions, on islands such as Thera.[13] In this case the communities of the mainland would have been exporting not only copper but also surplus manpower. It would have been a way of solving a demographic problem that the region would often have to confront, in not dissimilar ways, in the future.

Whatever the truth, one of the few things we can be sure of is that, beginning about a hundred years after the Thera eruption, a remarkable reversal took place. Around 1450 BCE, most of the palaces and towns of Minoan Crete were gutted by fire. Only Knossos, already the largest and in some sense the most influential of the palaces, survived intact. But telltale damage to some of the outlying buildings surrounding the palace suggests that the cause of the disaster on this occasion was not uncontrollable forces beneath the earth but human action. Who was responsible?

We have no way of knowing. But we do know who gained by it (which of course is not the same thing). Those who gained the most, in the short term and within Crete, were the rulers of Knossos. This one palace then controlled the greater part of the island, perhaps even all of it. But in the longer term, and over a much wider geographical area, it was the Mycenaeans who benefited.

In Crete itself, huge changes took place, seemingly very soon after the destructions. Most of the sinister lustral basins were filled in and no new ones would be built thereafter. On the remote northeast coast, in the town of Palaikastro, the destruction seems to have targeted objects of religious significance. A rare idol, made of ivory and other precious materials, was smashed and burned. Here and elsewhere, fragments of the ubiquitous sacred symbol, the horns of consecration, have been found thrown away or mixed with building material.[14] Things that the Minoans had once held sacred were now being trashed.

At the same time, parts of the Palace of Minos itself, at Knossos, were drastically remodelled and redecorated. The wall paintings in the Throne Room, that visitors still queue up to enter, belong to this period—though what you see today is an imaginative reconstruction created in the early twentieth century. Painstaking examination of the fragments of painted plaster has revealed that the original design adapted traditional motifs for a purpose not found in Minoan art before this time: to concentrate the attention of the viewer on the majesty of the king, sitting on his throne. Elsewhere at Knossos, tombs began to appear that closely resemble those of the Greek mainland. Minoan burial customs during the previous centuries had been for the most part communal and inconspicuous—it has been suggested that the Minoans paid little attention to their ancestors. By contrast, the ostentatious graves and rich displays, including many weapons buried along with the dead in the environs of Knossos between about 1450 and 1375 BCE, closely match the customs of the Mycenaeans on the mainland at the same time.[15] Archaeologists are now reluctant to conclude that there was anything so systematic as a Mycenaean 'takeover', or even an invasion of Crete, to explain these developments. But it does look very much as though the palace of Knossos, and therefore at this time most of the island, had come under the control of people with close ties to the Greek mainland.

It was not just in Crete that these changes were taking place. All over the Aegean, within a few decades either side of 1400 BCE, it was no longer Minoan customs and artefacts that were setting the trend but Mycenaean. In Crete itself, centralised arrangements for the collection and distribution of goods and the organisation of craftwork were now controlled by a single centre at Knossos. Crete became more prosperous than it had ever been.[16] And it was here, at the very heart of the Minoan system, that archaeologists found the equivalent of the smoking gun that proves the presence of Greek-speaking Mycenaeans at the top of the new hierarchy in Crete.

Minoan society had already developed more than one system of writing during the preceding centuries. From about 1900 BCE, the series of signs, each representing a spoken syllable, that we know today as Linear A had been used to keep the palace ledgers. Administrative records were incised into tablets made of soft clay. The documents created in this way were not intended to be permanent. But when fire ripped through the palaces, the clay became baked hard and, as a result, preserved for archaeologists to uncover almost four millennia later. This had happened on more than one occasion before the general destruction around the year 1450 BCE—enabling us to recover some of the day-to-day records of the destroyed palaces.

But when it was the turn of Knossos to experience a damaging fire, the clay tablets preserved in the debris were no longer being written in the Linear A script and in the Minoan language, which has never been deciphered. Within only a few decades after the upheavals of 1450 BCE, the writing system at Knossos had been adapted to produce its close cousin, known as Linear B. For half a century after the first discoveries of documents written in Linear B, by Sir Arthur Evans and his team digging at Knossos, no one could decipher this script either. The breakthrough came in 1952, when a young architect and amateur code breaker by the name of Michael Ventris, working alongside the Cambridge classical scholar John Chadwick, proved that the language of these ledgers was an early form of Greek. Since then, a total of almost six thousand Linear B tablets, more than half of them found at Knossos, have been deciphered and translated. The oldest of these, again from Knossos, are now thought to date from not long after 1400 BCE. Specialists have even detected, in their hesitant, scratchy handwriting, the traces of a new generation of scribes learning to adjust to the new system of writing. If this observation and this dating are correct, then the cache of documents found in the Room of the Chariot Tablets at Knossos represents the earliest surviving records in the Greek language ever found.[17]

Whatever happened in Crete during the decades that followed the destructions of 1450 BCE, the consequence was to install a Greek-speaking Mycenaean elite at the head of an island-wide bureaucratic system. It was in this way that the Greek language first made it into writing, and Greek speakers first found themselves running a complex economic and political system, which had already been developed by others before they arrived. No wonder, then, if the Greek language, along with the stories and some of the beliefs that would later come to be recorded in it, bear many traces of this formative period. Mycenaean civilisation was a fusion born out of the encounter between these two very different languages and cultures, of the Greek-speaking mainland and Minoan Crete.

AT THE SAME time as Crete was being transformed, the Mycenaeans began to build palaces of their own on the mainland. These were designed along different lines. But evidently, they were intended to function in exactly the same way. And it appears that they did—indeed, with as much success as the new Greek-speaking elite had begun to achieve at Knossos. For two centuries at least, and perhaps nearer to three, the Mycenaeans who ran these palaces were able to create an economic system that has been called a 'massive redistributive operation', sufficient to support a population far beyond anything that had been possible before or indeed would be again until modern times.[18]

Scribes were employed to keep detailed inventories, in just the same way as they were in Crete. Several fragments written in Linear B, discovered at a house outside the citadel of Mycenae, and another at the site known as Iklaina in southwest Greece, both excavated in the twenty-first century, confirm that the new technology of writing and its bureaucratic purpose had spread to the mainland by 1350 BCE.[19] Many more Linear B documents, most of them dating from the end of the following century, have also been discovered at the mainland sites of Pylos, Mycenae, Tiryns, Thebes, Volos, and Agios Vasileios near Sparta, as well as at other sites in Crete. The total number found on the Greek mainland is around two thousand five hundred. Between about 1300 BCE, at the latest, and shortly after 1200 BCE, the Mycenaean elite was sitting at the top of a rigidly defined hierarchy of offices run by micromanaging bureaucrats.

These documents enable us to understand many details of how the economy and administration of the Mycenaean palaces were organised. At the top was the king (*wanax*). At the opposite end of the scale, below a long list of named officials, the local village community was called the *damos*—forerunner of the later Greek *demos*, which would give us the word *democracy*, meaning 'power of the people'. But the Linear B records give us no insight into the thoughts and feelings of the rulers who commissioned them, still less of the small professional class of scribes who alone possessed the skill to create and read them. The Mycenaeans seem never to have used the art of writing for anything other than bookkeeping. It is possible, of course, that they preserved other kinds of records on perishable materials such as parchment or papyrus, as we know the Minoans did before them. But no evidence has yet been found to prove that they did.[20]

Stories and storytelling, on the other hand, must have played a large part in life in the Mycenaean palaces. We know from archaeology that the rulers went to great lengths to keep alive the memory of ruling families from the past. The shaft graves at Mycenae had always been marked by carved gravestones. Some two centuries after the last burials were made there, a ceremonial precinct was built to set apart and preserve the place where the illustrious dead and their treasures had been laid to rest. At about the same time, the fortification walls of the citadel were extended so as to enclose this cemetery. These elaborate and expensive projects would have had no meaning unless the people who commissioned them had had a highly developed method for handing down memories from one generation to the next.

After about 1400 BCE, monumental 'tholos' tombs began to appear all over southern Greece. These were excavated out of hillsides, with spectacular entranceways dressed with stone, and topped with stone-built vaults that rose above ground level and punctuated the landscape. The fancifully named Treasury of Atreus at Mycenae is the most architecturally ambitious of these. Long ago ransacked and emptied of the burials and goods it must once have contained, its shell has been admired by visitors since at least the second century CE. This was another way to remember and honour kings, heroes, and their families long after their lifetime. In some form or other, stories about them must have been just as vigorously perpetuated.

Signs of a taste for storytelling have often been noted in Mycenaean visual art, too. Surviving fragments of the frescoes that once covered the interiors of their palaces show vivid scenes of fighting or hunting. In the Palace of Nestor at Pylos, the frescoes covering the walls, as a visitor approaches the central hearth and the throne of the *wanax*, seem to mirror the solemnity of actual processions that would have passed that way in honour of the king. To the side, a white-robed man sits on a rock. His head is tiny in proportion to the five-stringed lyre he holds in his left hand while he plucks the strings with his right. Just in front of the lyre, and flying away from him, is a bird proportionally even larger. It is hard not to think of the stock phrase 'winged words' that would later be immortalised in the *Iliad* and *Odyssey* of Homer. There was a place in the bureaucratic system of the palaces for lyre players: a Linear B tablet from Thebes lists two as due to receive rations. Foreshadowing later times, the lyre player was surely not just a musician but also a 'singer of tales'.[21]

The functions of the palaces combined political and economic authority with religious ritual and belief, just as they had in Minoan Crete. Mycenaean religion overlapped with Minoan, but there seem to have been many differences too. These would only increase over time as the Mycenaean elites began to emerge from the shadows of the earlier civilisation of the Minoans. The tablets from Pylos, which date from the very end of the Mycenaean civilisation, between 1200 and about 1180 BCE, give us some snapshots of religious practice as it had evolved on the mainland by that time.

Gods were both male and female. It is evident from the tablets, as well as from remains of animal sacrifices found in the palace itself, that the most important deity was the bull god Poseidon, in later mythology associated with earthquakes, as he almost certainly had been previously in Minoan Crete. His name appears in the form *Po-se-da-o*. A warrior goddess not unlike the later Athena seems to have been worshipped at Mycenae, and the name *A-ta-na Po-ti-ni-i-ja* (meaning 'Lady Athena') occurs in a Linear B tablet from Knossos. Names or epithets found on the Linear B tablets can be matched with most of the Greek divine 'family' that in later centuries would be imagined as living on the cloud-capped peaks of Mount Olympus. But the fussy preoccupation of palace officials with making sure that each deity received its due, in full and on the prescribed date, tells us little about the nature of the rituals involved, still less of the beliefs of the people who carried them out.[22]

One thing the records do tell us, and which is abundantly confirmed by archaeology, is that these palace rituals would culminate in massive communal feasts. Just as in later times, the gods would receive their due portion of the animals slaughtered in their honour. But it was the sharing of meat among the mortal participants that affirmed the self-belief of the community. If we may judge by visual representations, those feasts were shared by women as well as men. Women feature prominently in Mycenaean art, as well as in Minoan. Frescoes show women riding in chariots and as spectators watching a battle. But they are rarely shown bare-breasted like Minoan women. It seems that aristocratic women did enjoy high status in the world of the Mycenaean palaces—in death, as well as in life, on the evidence of burials that have been excavated. But when women are mentioned in the Linear B tablets, it is almost always in menial capacities, quite possibly as slave workers. The only woman of high status who has so far been identified in the records was a priestess. There is no indication that any female Mycenaean ever exercised particular authority in a palace hierarchy. Not even a royal consort or female royal title is mentioned in the tablets.[23]

Mainland palaces were built in naturally defensible positions above the surrounding terrain. But, to begin with, they had no defensive walls. This had been the Minoan way, and indeed in Crete would remain so even when Mycenaeans seem to have been in charge. On the mainland, by contrast, the palace builders and pioneers of the new centralised economy soon found the need to protect the stored surplus produce and the high-value artefacts they had accumulated inside. First at Tiryns, in the Argolid just outside the modern port town of Nafplio, then at Mycenae itself, a few miles inland, mighty walls began to rise around the citadels. These are no ordinary fortifications. So massive are the stones of which they are built that later generations could not believe they had been raised into position by human beings at all but must have been the work of mythical one-eyed giants, called Cyclopes. The circuit walls of Tiryns and Mycenae in the Argolid and Gla in Boeotia are still called 'cyclopean'.

These fortifications bear witness to the power of the rulers to command the labour of many thousands of men. Labourers must have been recruited from a wide area. To house so many and to keep them fed for the duration of the work would have required both resources and organisation. Though hardly on a comparable scale to the much older pyramids of Egypt, the cyclopean walls of the Mycenaean citadels would have presented logistical and engineering challenges very similar in kind. Where did all this manpower come from? And why was such a stupendous expenditure of resources and effort needed at all? Some have wondered whether the purpose might have been simply 'to impress and confer great status on the rulers of the sites'.[24] If this was so, it would have been an even more remarkable case of ostentatious waste than burying such a quantity of gold in the shaft graves.

The first fortifications went up around 1375 BCE at Tiryns and 1350 BCE at Mycenae. A century later, at both sites, they were extended farther. This was when the shaft graves and their ceremonial precinct at Mycenae were brought inside the circuit of the walls. At the same time, the famous Lion Gate was added. Above its lintel can still be seen a monumental version of a design adapted from Minoan Crete. Two lionesses flank a central pillar that may once have been topped with the figure of a deity, most probably a goddess. In a final phase of fortification, considerable engineering ingenuity must have been required, as well as heavy lifting, to enclose access to underground springs at both Mycenae and Tiryns. The same thing was done on the Acropolis of Athens, where few other traces have been preserved to indicate that a Mycenaean palace must once have existed. These efforts cannot be put down to mere ostentation. Around 1200 BCE, when the palaces were about two hundred years old, the elites who administered their economy were expecting to have to last out a siege.

Not all the Mycenaean palaces were fortified, at least on anything like the scale of Tiryns, Mycenae, the Acropolis of Athens, or Gla in Boeotia. Where they were, they tend to be clustered close together. In the small area of the Argolid, there are no fewer than three, and all were walled in the cyclopean style. By contrast, palaces that according to the bureaucratic record controlled a larger territory seem to have required less elaborate defences. This is the case at Pylos and Thebes.[25] So it may be that those elites who chose to fortify their palaces did so for protection not against any external threat but from each other. If so, that rationale would be in accord with much of later Greek history.

Nothing in the archaeological record or in the written documents indicates whether administration or any form of mutual obligation extended beyond the territory controlled by each palace. These territories could be quite extensive, particularly when compared to the generally much smaller city-states of later times. It is rare to find references in the documents to transactions *between* regional centres. From Mycenae, we have a record of a consignment of cloth being sent to Thebes. Tablets from Thebes refer to 'Lacedaemonians', which ought to mean people from the region of later (and modern) Sparta in the southern Peloponnese. But there is nothing to give us a clue to how the separate palatial administrations interacted with one other. Nor is there any hint of a higher level of political authority than that of the *wanax* who ruled over the territory of each palace.[26]

The picture presented by the Linear B tablets is consistent with the evidence of archaeology. Overwhelmingly this is a picture of autonomous kingdoms, each managing its own affairs, but all of them doing so in much the same way, with common standards of language, writing, architecture, arts and crafts, and religious practice. Did all those things that they had in common ever lead to an overarching political structure, with a single geographical centre and a single overall ruler, as was the norm in other civilisations at this time? In the search for answers, we have to look beyond the Mycenaean world to see what outsiders looking in made of it.

The Hittites, with their capital far to the east in the highlands of Anatolia, came into contact with the Mycenaeans only when the latter began to impinge on their own side of the Aegean. Fragments of Hittite diplomatic correspondence covering the period between 1400 and 1200 BCE—the heyday of the Mycenaean mainland palaces—make reference to a maritime power on the western edge of the Hittite sphere of influence. At first this was named as Ah-hiya, later as Ahhiyawa. In approximately 1250 BCE, the reigning king at Hattusa wrote at length to an unnamed king of Ahhiyawa, addressing him as his 'brother' and equal. Some forty years later, another Hittite king, Tudhaliya IV, declared in the formal text of a treaty: 'the Kings who are my equals in rank are the King of Egypt, the King of Babylonia, the King of Assyria, *and the King of Ahhiyawa*.' The last phrase has been erased by the scribe, who seems to have recognised at once that he wasn't supposed to include it. But the fact that a professional scribe could have made such an error suggests that kings of Ahhiyawa had until very recently enjoyed this level of recognition at the Hittite capital. The same treaty places an embargo on 'any ship of Ahhiyawa' going to the king of Assyria, with whom the Hittites were currently at war. This could refer either to trade or to military reinforcements. In any case, it is evident that Ahhiyawa, by about 1220 BCE, had become a power to be reckoned with at sea, and indeed one of a handful of super-powers of the day.[27]

During the same centuries, the Egyptians, too, were in contact with the Aegean world. The Egyptians had long been trading with Minoan Crete, which they called 'Keftiu'. Then, shortly after the presence of the Mycenaeans began to make itself felt throughout the region, a new name enters the Egyptian records. The forty-second year of the reign of the pharaoh Thutmose III is usually reckoned to be equivalent to the year 1438 BCE, by our system of counting. In that year, the pharaoh accepted a diplomatic gift from a place called 'T-n-j'. Because Egyptian hieroglyphics record only consonants, not vowels, we can only guess at the exact sound of the name represented. But it was probably something like 'Tanaja' or 'Tanaju'. From the description of the gifts, which included a piece 'of Cretan workmanship', we can only suppose that 'Tanaju' is to be found somewhere in the Aegean—other than Crete, since the same text already mentions Keftiu. Almost a hundred years later, during the reign of Amenhotep III, who died in 1353 BCE, an Egyptian monumental mason recorded a list of regions that may have been destinations for an embassy or trade mission to the Aegean. This time Keftiu and Tanaju appear as separate headings. Several of the readings are uncertain, but the listed destinations clearly imply that the territory known to the Egyptians as Tanaju covered all of the Peloponnese, Boeotia (because Thebes is included), and perhaps some islands.[28]

It seems from this evidence that the Hittites and the Egyptians had different names for what we call the Mycenaean world. But the scribes and officials of both civilisations take it for granted that they were dealing with a *kingdom*, ruled over by a king whose status their own monarch was prepared to recognise. The Hittite texts are quite explicit about this. Even if we understand Tanaju as a geographical term, rather than necessarily the name of a political state, for an Egyptian pharaoh to accept a diplomatic gift implies that whoever ruled there was regarded as worthy to take part in this kind of formal exchange.

If there *was* a single kingdom that encompassed the whole Greek-speaking, Mycenaean world of southern Greece, the most likely candidate for its capital would be Mycenae, though Thebes has also been proposed. Or there may never have been a unitary kingdom at all, but rather some sort of confederacy of smaller states, whose different names might have confused outsiders.[29] Either way, the Hittite and Egyptian sources reveal a geopolitical dimension to the Mycenaean world that must have some basis in fact, even if we still don't know how to square this information with the evidence of archaeology and the Greek records.

But how did the Mycenaeans define themselves and the land where they lived, in their own language? *Both* the Hittite name, Ahhiya or Ahhiyawa, and the Egyptian, Tanaju, would find close echoes in Greek several centuries after the Mycenaean civilisation had ended. We find these in the epic poems of Homer, the *Iliad* and the *Odyssey*. There, the people who lay siege to the city of Troy are known collectively not by the later name of 'Hellenes' but as 'Achaeans' (echoing Ahhiya) or 'Danaans' (echoing Tanaju). The place name Achaea would continue in use for centuries, though not always attached to the same place, right through to the end of the Roman period. It seems most likely that, if the Mycenaeans did have a single name for all the lands they lived in, it was something like *Achaiwia*, an early form of Achaea. And those whom we call Mycenaeans most likely thought of themselves, as Homer's heroes would later do, as both Achaeans (*Achaiwoi*) and Danaans— because where else could the Hittite and Egyptian names have come from?

HOWEVER THEY ORGANISED their affairs in their homeland, the Mycenaeans increasingly made their presence felt far beyond it. On several occasions, the Hittite vassal states on the Aegean coast of Anatolia attempted to rebel. The first time this happened was around the year 1400 BCE. A revolt by some twenty cities or states in northwestern Anatolia was serious enough to require a military expedition led by King Tudhaliya himself to put it down. Among the rebels was Wilusa (Troy). Once it was over, among the spoils dedicated to the Hittite Storm God in his temple was a bronze sword, of Mycenaean type, that would be discovered by archaeologists in the twentieth century. The weapon bears an inscription in Hittite giving thanks for victory in putting down the revolt. Support for the rebels, then, seems to have come from Ahhiyawa—that is to say, from the Greek speakers across the Aegean.[30]

Not long after this, a Hittite inscription records a 'ruler of Ahhiya' making new trouble for Hattusa. The name of this ruler, Attarissiya, would be preserved by much later Greek legends as Atreus, the father of Agamemnon, king of Mycenae. Attarissiya is not dignified in the Hittite document with a royal title. Nonetheless, he was apparently capable of mustering a force of a hundred war chariots on the Anatolian mainland. Sometime later, this same Attarissiya took part in a raid on Cyprus, another Hittite vassal. This is the first clear indication that the Mycenaeans had at their disposal a significant naval force. It may also have been the first time that Greek speakers began to make their presence felt in Cyprus.[31]

The height of Mycenaean power abroad seems to have been reached between about 1350 and 1250 BCE. This was achieved not by feats of arms alone. The rulers of the Mycenaean palaces were also capable of exercising something resembling 'soft power', as we understand it today. Documents written in the Linear B script mention goods such as textiles and scented oils as being 'for export'. Trade will have taken the form of barter and exchange. It is presumed that the Mycenaeans also took part in ritualised exchanges of gifts between rulers, such as that recorded with Pharaoh Thutmose. Frustratingly, no comparable records of international transactions have so far been discovered on the Greek side.

Despite this absence of documents, we know from archaeology that Mycenaean traders at the time were exchanging goods all over the Mediterranean. Their ships travelled as far west as Sardinia and the coast of Spain, in the opposite direction to the ports of Egypt and the Levant, and through the straits of the Hellespont and the Bosphorus into the Black Sea. Specialist raw materials came from places even more distant. Amber, used to make necklaces, must have been transported partway by river or overland from the Baltic. Tin, an essential ingredient of bronze, most probably came from Afghanistan, via the Levant coast.

The cargo of a ship that sank in about 1300 BCE while on its way from the Levant via Cyprus towards the Mycenaean Aegean included ten tonnes of copper ingots together with quantities of tin, jars that would have contained olive oil and apparently resin-ated wine, coloured glass, raw ivory, and several precious objects. Personal items belonging to the crew or passengers also turned up on the seabed. These included tools, weapons, cosmetics, and jewellery, as well as the remains of what they ate onboard and a wax tablet that must have been used for writing—though sadly with no trace of anything that might once have been written on it. Some of the personal possessions reveal from their design that their owners were Mycenaeans heading for home when their ship foundered off the headland in southern Turkey known as Uluburun, which gives the wreck its name today. Objects recovered have been identified as 'Egyptian, Nubian, Assyrian, Babylonian, Cypriot, Mycenaean, Italian, Balkan, and Baltic'—showing what a truly worldwide network of exchange, relative to the possibilities of the time, already existed in 1300 BCE.[32]

Those early Greeks, and the ships they must have built to carry them and their goods in all these directions, were already a major trading force. This seafaring tradition, which has given Greeks their preeminent place in the modern world of shipping today, began early—though it is worth noting, this, too, was something that they must first have learned from their Minoan predecessors.

One other export, this time almost invisible in the archaeological record but destined eventually to become the most important of all, can also be traced back to the Mycenaean world of the thirteenth century BCE. This was the Greek language. Other than in Crete, no written records in the Linear B script have been found outside the Greek mainland. But it is a reasonable bet that wherever Mycenaean goods were exported, some knowledge of the language spoken by the manufacturers and traders would have reached there too. As a result, in places where the local people were not Mycenaean at all, it was becoming fashionable to give people names that we can recognise today as Greek.

Our best evidence for this comes from Crete. Within a few generations of the arrival of Greek-speaking rulers at Knossos, many of the individuals who appear in Linear B documents have Greek names. Those named go far beyond the ranks of the elite. Often they are humble shepherds and craftsmen, who must surely have been local people.[33] Possibly, these names were handed out by the bureaucracy—much as condescending colonial masters in more recent times would do with native servants. Or it might be better to think of something more like the practice traditional in Greece closer to our own day, whereby parents invite a wealthy or influential godfather to baptise their children, who then carry the name of a designated benefactor as their own. In this way, 'becoming Mycenaean' might have been a conscious choice made by individuals in a fluid and changing society.

A more surprising case was Troy. Culturally, archaeologists are agreed, Troy was an Anatolian city, on the fringe of the Hittite world. But during the reign of the Hittite king Muwattalli II, who ruled from 1290 to 1271 BCE, a treaty was drawn up with the ruler of Wilusa (Troy), who is named as Alaksandu.[34] This can only be the Hittite rendering of the Greek name 'Alexandros' (Alexander), which means, literally, 'defender against men'. In later Greek legends, Alexander would be an alternative name for the Trojan prince better known as Paris. There could be a connection between this Alaksandu and a dynastic marriage that had apparently taken place about a century before, between a king of Ahhiyawa and a princess of the confederacy that had rebelled against Hittite rule, and had included Wilusa.[35] Or perhaps Greek names were becoming popular here, too, during the heyday of the Mycenaean palaces? Royal outsiders as far away as Troy might have wished to adopt what they saw as a winning fashion—as indeed another dynasty of Alexanders would do almost a thousand years later, and end up conquering the whole of the known world.

THE MYCENAEAN ASCENDANCY came to an end during a period of only a few decades either side of the year 1200 BCE. As always in archaeology, the exact sequence of events across many different sites is hard to piece together. Establishing the causes of the Mycenaean collapse is even harder. Palaces and fortifications had been severely damaged before but had then been rebuilt. The Mycenaeans had proved themselves as capable as the Minoans before them of withstanding natural disasters and carrying on. But at a certain point, each of the great Mycenaean palaces was destroyed. Most were burnt out. Whether they were actively ransacked is less clear.

These catastrophes happened without warning. At Thebes, a routine list of barley rations, due to be handed out to a list of named individuals, had only just been completed. The clay had not yet had time to dry when the entire palace succumbed to fire. At Pylos, no human remains were found inside or near the palace, as might be expected if defenders had fought to save it from invaders or if an earthquake had trapped victims under the rubble. But archaeologists did find the bones of at least ten cattle. Evidently, a sacrifice had just taken place. The bones had been ritually burnt, then brought indoors, perhaps for the archivists to record the details. The expected feast would have been in full swing outside, in the open air. This was the moment when flames engulfed the palace.[36] Even today in southern Greece, summer wildfires frequently destroy homes and whole villages, sometimes with the loss of dozens of lives. It could have been an accident.

Any number of more dramatic explanations have been offered to account for this accumulation of disasters: invasion by sea, civil war, popular uprising, climate change, crop failure, or some combination of these. But none addresses the key question. This is not how or why each palace came to be destroyed, but why it was *never rebuilt*. And what can have caused other settlements to be abandoned at the same time, without any sign of destruction? Why, even at sites like Mycenae and Tiryns, where some reoccupation and rebuilding did take place, were the ruins of the palaces left untouched?

Since the 1970s and 1980s, systems-based theories have been developed to account for the collapse of an entire civilisation on such a scale.[37] *Systems collapse* will reappear several times in the course of this longer history as an explanation for catastrophic changes that affected Greeks at different times and in different historical circumstances. According to this theory, it is the very complexity of the system that brings about its downfall. Collapse is explained by an economic model that shows how an increase in complexity brings large benefits at first, then just about sustainable ones, until in a final phase the cost of maintaining the system outweighs the benefits. At this point, instead of gently falling back upon an earlier phase of the cycle, the system becomes vulnerable to increasing threats. Once upon a time, these threats would have been easily seen off. The steps taken would have brought a further increase in the complexity of the system. But with complexity already past its peak, the costs of further action outweigh the benefits and cannot be met.[38]

A good example of how this might have worked in practice can be seen in the fortifications of the Mycenaean palaces. Up to a certain point, it must have made sense to the rulers to mobilise vast resources and command huge workforces in order to bring more of the palace's essential functions and personnel within the area protected by the walls. Later, when the perceived threat became more acute, it still seemed worth the effort and expense to enclose access to the water supply within the circuit. But what do you do when the next threat appears, and this time the cost of meeting it is greater than the system can bear? At this point, following the theory of systems collapse, competing sections within society begin to doubt that their own interest is best served by the system that supports all. The mechanism of collapse now sets in. Unless a rival power is on hand to take over and incorporate the failing society into its own more viable system, collapse becomes inevitable.[39] The first of these possible outcomes would well account for what happened in Crete around 1450 BCE, when an internal collapse of Minoan civilisation seems to have been reversed by intervention from the rising power of the Mycenaean mainland. The second would account very well for the demise of the entire Mycenaean political and economic system around 1200 BCE.

It wasn't just in Greece and the Aegean that this happened. At about the same time, a similar fate befell Troy. All the other cities of the Anatolian coast went the same way. So did the entire Hittite empire and most other civilisations of the Levant. Egypt alone survived with its institutions intact, although only after several decades of upheaval. Much has been made of Egyptian records which refer to attacks on the coast of Egypt by 'Sea Peoples'. Certainly, large numbers of people must have been on the move around the eastern Mediterranean *after* the multiple collapses. But at least in the Greek-speaking world, these movements were a consequence, not a cause. Whatever happened elsewhere, seaborne invaders cannot account convincingly for the destructions in Greece, where most of the destroyed or abandoned sites were not on open coasts. The same must apply to the destruction and abandonment of the Hittite capital of Hattusa, which lies many hundreds of kilometres inland. In all probability it was the sheer weight of all these cyclopean fortresses, and of the top-heavy bureaucracy that had grown up around them, that brought them down.[40]

THE FIRST ATTEMPT by Greek speakers to emulate the more advanced complex societies (or civilisations) of the Near East had ended in failure. No more palace records seem to have been kept after about 1180 BCE. The Linear B script would soon be forgotten, except in faraway Cyprus. Despite this, stories about the Greeks' legendary past would continue to pass from generation to generation by word of mouth. To an extent that can be traced for few other prehistoric societies, the Mycenaean age gave birth to collective memories that would later take on a new life as a result of being *written down*. The stories that resulted—the myths and legends of ancient Greece as we know them today—would never subsequently cease to be read, copied, embellished, and commented upon.

Consider the legend of Theseus and the Minotaur. According to the story, the king of Athens is obliged to send a regular tribute of seven lads and seven maidens to King Minos of Crete to be devoured by a monster that is half-man, half-bull and lives in a 'labyrinth' beneath his palace. With the help of Minos's daughter Ariadne, Theseus kills the beast and escapes with his companions back to Athens. On the way, as well as ungratefully abandoning Ariadne on the island of Naxos, he destroys the Cretan war fleet, thereby putting an end to the tribute and, implicitly, to the supremacy of King Minos at sea.[41] We have abundant evidence that between about 1700 and 1450 BCE the Minoans did indeed enjoy such supremacy. Certainly, they exercised a great deal of cultural influence in all the mainland centres that have been excavated. There was a Minoan settlement on the island of Keos, which is about as close to Athens and the silver mines at Lavrio as you can get without coming ashore on the mainland. It is perfectly possible that Athens and its surrounding region, Attica, had once been a Minoan dependency.

If that were the case, Theseus's expedition and its successful outcome would be a distant reflection of the tussle for power that must have taken place in the Aegean, between the mainland and Crete, in the years either side of 1450 BCE. The non-Greek name 'Minos' may well reflect a dynasty or a royal title rather than the name of an individual. The 'labyrinth' in which the monstrous Minotaur was housed can be interpreted as a memory of the Palace of Minos at Knossos, the remains of which do indeed very much resemble the later metaphorical meaning of the term, as a maze. It has been speculated that 'Labyrinthos', or something like it, may have been the original name for the palace of Knossos in the Minoan language, and indeed a version of it occurs on a Linear B tablet.[42]

The Minotaur itself, supposedly the issue of a union between Minos's queen Pasiphae and a miraculous bull sent by the god Poseidon, similarly reflects the importance of the cult of the bull in Minoan worship and iconography. And the story's most shocking and memorable element of all, that the Cretans nourished their monster on the flesh of young human victims, has even found its counterpart in the butchered bones of children found together with cooking pots in a building close to the palace at Knossos. These bones date from shortly before the upheavals that led to the Mycenaean presence in Crete after 1450 BCE. Whatever grim ritual lay behind these remains, it would hardly be surprising if the memory of being at the receiving end had persisted for hundreds of years afterwards.[43]

Other features of these stories may also preserve distorted historical memories, unless they reflect fundamental human anxieties—or perhaps more accurately, *male* anxieties. It is partly thanks to the father of psychoanalysis, Sigmund Freud, that everyone has heard of Oedipus, who killed his father and married his mother (though without knowing who they were). Freud relied heavily on one version of this story, as told by the Athenian dramatist Sophocles in the fifth century BCE, as evidence to support his theory of the Oedipus complex. According to this, every male child at a certain stage of development experiences impulses that mirror the actions of Oedipus.[44]

These stories are full of powerful, feisty women. Think of Clytemnestra, who murders her husband Agamemnon on his return from war, and their daughter Electra, who eggs on her brother, Orestes, to kill their own mother in revenge. Or the enchantress Medea, who in the story of Jason and the Golden Fleece performs much the same role as Ariadne in the tale of Theseus; instead of being dumped on the way home, Medea becomes Jason's wife and the mother of his children—only to murder them later in revenge for his infidelity. The gorgon, Medusa, whose hair is made of snakes and whose gaze turns men to stone, has become literally a monster. Minos's insatiable queen, Pasiphae, was fairly monstrous, too, and her alleged sexual appetites gave birth to a monster: the Minotaur.[45]

It has sometimes been speculated that these stories reflect a dimly remembered Minoan society in which women had enjoyed a much stronger public presence, and quite possibly also more political power, than in any Greek society that we know about. The notion that Minoan Crete had been a form of matriarchy (that is to say, actually ruled by women) was popularised in the twentieth century and still has its adherents today—although it has been pointed out that no such society is known to have existed anywhere in the world. But it is a striking fact that Greeks of the classical age reserved prime positions for dominant females in their *stories*, while largely excluding women from public roles or positions of authority in real life. Is this the result of perennial male anxieties, of the sort proposed by Freud, or an enduring revulsion from a different type of society that Greek speakers had once been closely involved with and ever since were determined to shun?[46]

In some respects the most powerful—and dangerous—of all these legendary women was Helen. The most beautiful woman in the world, Helen was capable of arousing undying enmity among immortal goddesses and causing the great war that ever afterwards would become a focal point of all the interconnected web of myths and legends. This was the war between a combined force of Greeks and the city of Troy. When Helen deserted her husband Menelaus, king of Sparta, and eloped with the handsome Trojan prince Paris, also known as Alexander, the Greeks mounted a mighty expedition to bring her back. In later times, even Helen's name would be routinely held up as a warning by Greek authors who liked to pun on its first part, which can also mean 'destroyer'.

The war lasted ten years, so the story goes. In the end it would be won not by overwhelming force but by ingenuity. As famous as Troy or Helen is the stratagem of the Wooden Horse, or Trojan Horse. This was the device that enabled the besiegers to send a concealed advance guard inside the city to open the gates for the rest, while the Greeks pretended to give up the siege and sail for home. After totally destroying the city, murdering its inhabitants, and taking the women as slaves, the victors gained little from their triumph. Helen's return to the husband she had abandoned back in Sparta, and to a life of blameless domesticity, is an anticlimax. Most of the men who had led their contingents to the war would find only troubles on their return. Odysseus, who had devised the ruse of the Wooden Horse, would have to endure a further ten years of wandering upon the seas before reaching his home in Ithaca. Even then, he would have to fight to repossess his kingdom and be reunited with his faithful wife Penelope—whose constancy in the face of adversity would often be held up as a foil to the behaviour of the more flamboyant heroines of Greek myth.

Does this legendary war, too, derive from real events in the lost history of the Mycenaean age? Opinions have been divided ever since ancient times. At least one popular retelling of the story for the twenty-first century takes it for granted that there really was a Trojan War. Heinrich Schliemann, back in the nineteenth, had never doubted it. Schliemann's discovery during the 1870s, that great Bronze Age cities had flourished at Troy and at Mycenae, seemed to prove him right. But since then, any chance of locating Homer's sack of Troy in the archaeological record has seemed to recede. These days, most archaeologists are sceptical, if they do not dismiss the possibility altogether.[47]

If such a war did take place, the most likely context for it might be during the twilight of the Mycenaean world rather than during its heyday. By 1200 BCE, the Mycenaeans had been driven by the Hittites from the coast of Anatolia. But then the Hittites, too, disappeared suddenly from the scene. There must have been a power vacuum in western Anatolia during the first years of the twelfth century BCE. Troy may have been the richest city in the whole region still left standing, a prize quite literally 'to die for', in a time of failed and failing states. Excavations at the site reveal that Troy was violently destroyed, and probably also sacked, around 1180 BCE. It may be only coincidence, but according to one set of calculations made in the ancient world, the War of Troy was supposed to have lasted from 1194 to 1184 BCE, by our system of counting.[48]

During the same years, archaeology tells us that on the northern edge of the Mycenaean world, in the coastal part of Thessaly, a late arrival among Mycenaean palaces briefly flourished before it, too, collapsed a few decades later. This was the region where, according to legend, the young Achilles ruled. In later retellings of the story, much is made of the tussle between the king of Mycenae, Agamemnon—presented as higher in authority but a hopeless leader—and Achilles, who proves himself the greater hero. Perhaps the rivalry between the two dramatises a distant historical memory of a power struggle between a youthful offshoot of the Mycenaean world in Thessaly and the traditional centre, whose authority was failing, at a time when the Mycenaean system was crumbling and some of its survivors had set their sights on the glittering prize of Troy?[49]

If we were to think of the Greek expedition not so much as an organised show of strength by a united force in its prime but more like a desperate act of piracy by a warrior elite whose world back home was falling apart, we would not be all that far from the picture that emerges from the later written versions. It is striking that many of the heroes have no expectation that they will ever return home. Those who do have a hard time of it. And as the story would later be told, there is a lingering sense that the effort to conquer Troy had been the last gasp of a dying age.[50]

2

'HOMER'S WORLD, NOT OURS'

c. 1180 BCE–c. 720 BCE

AFTER THE PALACE of Nestor burned to the ground, no one ever again returned to build and live on the hilltop where it had stood. Only the name, Pylos, remained in memory—in due course to be transferred to a different place, some miles away on the coast. At Knossos, in Crete, the story was much the same. Here the name remained, but the new town that would grow up, in centuries to come, would never encroach on the ruins of the former palace. Mycenae and Tiryns, with their massive 'cyclopean' walls, continued to dominate the landscape of the Argolid. But at the highest points within their citadels, nothing remained but fire-gutted ruins. At both sites, humbler dwellings clustered in their shadows. All over the Mycenaean world, it would have been impossible to escape from the traces of the past. Ruined, deserted palaces and public buildings must have seemed like an ever-present reproach to the current generations that no longer possessed the means, or perhaps even the will, to build anything more than rudimentary shelters. Stone-built houses that still stood were used to bury the dead, while the living made do with makeshift mud huts. It must have been like living in a 'ghost world'.[1]

Within a single generation, in the towns and villages that had made up the kingdom of Pylos, as much as 90 per cent of the

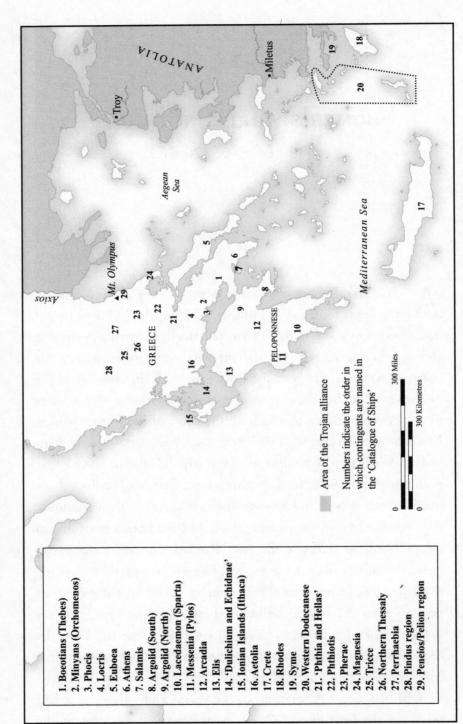

1. Boeotians (Thebes)
2. Minyans (Orchomenos)
3. Phocis
4. Locris
5. Euboea
6. Athens
7. Salamis
8. Argolid (South)
9. Argolid (North)
10. Lacedaemon (Sparta)
11. Messenia (Pylos)
12. Arcadia
13. Elis
14. 'Dulichium and Echidnae'
15. Ionian Islands (Ithaca)
16. Aetolia
17. Crete
18. Rhodes
19. Syme
20. Western Dodecanese
21. 'Phthia and Hellas'
22. Phthiotis
23. Pherae
24. Magnesia
25. Tricce
26. Northern Thessaly
27. Perrhaebia
28. Pindus region
29. Peneios/Pelion region

ANATOLIA

• Troy

• Miletus

Axios

Mt. Olympus

Aegean Sea

GREECE

PELOPONNESE

Mediterranean Sea

Area of the Trojan alliance

Numbers indicate the order in which contingents are named in the 'Catalogue of Ships'

0   300 Miles

0   300 Kilometres

2. The geopolitical world of the *Iliad*

population may have been lost. Whether from famine, from disease, or from warfare, people would have died by the thousand if this estimate is anywhere near accurate. Not all regions fared quite so badly. But long-term trends show that the sudden, catastrophic drop in population observed in the southwestern Peloponnese was no temporary blip. Over the next two hundred years, at a cautious estimate, the population throughout the Greek mainland fell to no more than half of what it had been in Mycenaean times.[2]

Many of those who survived abandoned their homes to find the means of subsistence elsewhere. Some took to the mountains of the interior of the Peloponnese to try to eke out a living from marginal land that had probably never been cultivated before. Others headed overseas while ships were still serviceable and crews could be found to take them. In this way, new settlements were established on islands in the Aegean and Ionian Seas, and farther afield in Cyprus. In Crete, but not on the mainland, coastal sites were abandoned and people moved inland, to higher ground.[3] Here and elsewhere in the eastern Mediterranean, where seaborne invaders brought disruption at this time, the threat may have been caused by displaced Greeks fleeing from disaster at home or even turning to piracy.

For those who remained where they were, life returned to the subsistence level of the days before the rise of the Mycenaean palaces. Once again people lived on smallholdings and in scattered settlements, growing and harvesting their crops and herding their sheep and goats. Everywhere, the Greek-speaking world fragmented into a patchwork of local communities. Not only had trade links across the Mediterranean all but vanished, but even those Greek communities that were relatively thriving seem not to have been on speaking—or at least on trading—terms with one another. No wonder, then, that the archaeologists who first began to uncover the Mycenaean civilisation in the nineteenth century chose to describe the centuries that followed its demise as a 'dark age'.

Today, thanks to excavations carried out during the last fifty years, we know that the 'darkness' was not quite uniform. Athens seems to have been spared the worst. The citadel of the Acropolis was probably never completely abandoned. And the first signs of recovery there can be detected as early as 1000 BCE. Not far from Athens, at about the same time, on the coast of Euboea on the other side of a narrow strait, something more surprising was happening at the site known by its modern name of Lefkandi. There, not long after 1000 BCE, the only building of any size to be put up anywhere in the Greek mainland in four hundred years, so far as we know, seems to have been designed to house the grave of a local 'hero'. The cremated remains of the man were accompanied by the body of a woman, decked out in sumptuous jewellery and accompanied by the knife most probably used to kill her. The remains of four horses, dispatched at the same time, were found in the next chamber. Even more unusually for this period, the people of Lefkandi during the tenth century BCE were benefiting from renewed links with the eastern Mediterranean. Archaeologists speak of a revival of trade. But at Lefkandi, it appears that the transactions were all in the one direction. Precious objects buried with the 'hero of Lefkandi' came from places as distant as Cyprus and Babylon. But there is no sign in the archaeological record elsewhere to indicate that local goods made in Euboea were being exported. Perhaps the Greeks of Lefkandi were still living as mercenaries, or as piratical raiders, two hundred years after the Mycenaean collapse?[4]

Everywhere, the centuries of darkness were a time of profound and irreversible change. People coped as best they could. There is no clear pattern or evidence of purpose in most of the changes that we can observe. About 1050 BCE, the new technology of smelting iron was first developed in Cyprus. From there it quickly spread throughout the eastern Mediterranean. The period of human development that archaeologists and prehistorians call the Iron Age had begun. The weapons that accompanied the hero of Lefkandi to the underworld were made not of bronze but of iron. Elsewhere, few communities had enough to spare that they could afford to bury anything much at all with their dead. In the Greek-speaking world, one of the most far-reaching technological changes in human history seems at first to have passed most people by.[5]

By 800 BCE, the darkness was beginning to lift. Populations were no longer declining. Indeed, they had begun to rise. Craftsmen were once again creating objects that were of more than essential utility. Communities began to exchange goods with one another again. Trading links were revived. Greek speakers once more found themselves rubbing shoulders with rival traders who spoke other languages. In one direction were the people they called Phoenicians, who traded from the cities of Byblos, Tyre, and Sidon on the eastern Mediterranean seaboard that would later be known as the Levant; in the other, the Etruscans of central Italy.

Greeks were once again on the move in large numbers. This time they were no longer fleeing chaos and collapse at home but seeking new and better opportunities across the sea. Later Greek accounts present a picture of an extraordinarily mobile population, both within and beyond the heartland of the Greek peninsula. Much about these mass movements of people remains obscure and the object of scholarly debate. There were still no written records. But of two things we can be reasonably certain. First, there was no significant influx of newcomers from outside the region. The idea of a series of invasions by 'Dorians' from farther north in the Balkans, that looms large in many twentieth-century history books, has not been confirmed by archaeology. All the ancient sources agree that those they call Dorians were Greek speakers and had migrated from no farther north than central Greece. In times to come, during later collapses, successive waves of new arrivals would leave permanent traces in all later forms of the Greek language:

Latin-speaking Romans, Slavs, French- and Italian-speaking Crusaders, Albanians, Turks. Nothing like this happened during or after the post-Mycenaean dark age.

Secondly, during the ninth and eighth centuries BCE, the centre of gravity of the Greek-speaking world shifted eastwards. By the middle of the eighth century BCE, we find Greek communities firmly established right across the islands of the Aegean, all the way down the Aegean coast of Anatolia, from the ruined site of Troy in the north down to Lycia in the southwest corner and far to the east in Cyprus. In anticipation of developments to come much later, some Greek speakers were reaching out in other directions too: northwards to form pockets on the coast of Macedonia, and westwards to Italy.

As Greeks became more geographically dispersed, their world was becoming more fragmented than ever. By the time the dark age came to an end, even the Greek language had split to form several distinct regional dialects.[6] We know this, as we know so much else about the Greek world from that time to this, thanks to the very first of those Greek inventions whose effects are still with us all over the world today: the alphabet.

THE ALPHABETIC REVOLUTION was every bit as transformative as the digital revolution of our own time. The invention would create its own version of an 'information age' for the ancient world—at a slower pace, to be sure, but with equally long-term effects for the ways that humans communicate with one another across space and time. The conceptual shift that made it possible was even simpler than the application of binary mathematics to electrical circuits. Indeed, it is so simple, and so much taken for granted throughout much of the world today, that we need to pause for a moment to grasp what was so revolutionary about it.

The basic technology of writing had been known for at least two thousand years already—nothing new about that. By the time the Greeks were beginning to emerge from their dark age, writing systems had proliferated all over the Middle East. In one corner of the Greek-speaking world, in Cyprus, Greek itself was still being written in a script closely related to Linear B. The Mycenaean writing system had long ago been forgotten, but the 'Cypriot syllabary', its close cousin, would remain in use in Cyprus right through the dark age and until long after it had ended.[7] Both these older systems for writing Greek share the same drawback. A syllabary is a system in which each syllable of the language is represented by its own sign. (One of the first Greek words to be recognised in Linear B was represented by the four characters: *ti-ri-po-de*, meaning 'two tripods'.) To make this work, you need around ninety characters. To learn to write in Linear B or the Cypriot syllabary meant acquiring a specialist skill. And the resulting written record still left a good deal of guesswork for the reader, as any expert on Linear B will tell you.

Instead, the Greeks looked elsewhere. The writing system that eventually caught their attention had been developed during the previous centuries by the Phoenicians living on the Levantine seaboard. The language of the Phoenicians, and the script they used to write it, belonged to the Semitic family that also includes Hebrew. The Phoenician script was in effect a syllabary. But by leaving out the vowels, it had the great advantage of reducing the number of signs to just over twenty. Here was the beginning of a system that anyone could learn. The Semitic signs were given names that served as mnemonics for the respective sounds: *alf, bet*, and so on. This is why, when the Greeks adapted this system for their own use, they called it the 'alphabet'.

But there was one vital difference between the Phoenician system and its adaptation by the Greeks. And here we aren't talking any more about 'the Greeks' in general. This can only have been the initiative of a single individual, because it happened only once, at a single point in space and time. As well as borrowing the symbols of the Phoenician script to represent similar-sounding consonants in Greek, this individual picked out four other symbols that represented Semitic consonants not needed in Greek and invented one new one, so as to represent the five basic vowel sounds that are still found in most alphabets today. Suddenly, it was possible, using hardly any more signs than the Phoenicians did, to write down fully and accurately the actual sounds of speech.[8] From now on, the 'winged words' addressed to each other by heroes on the battlefield, or by gods decreeing human destinies, even unspoken thoughts or the fleeting contents of the imagination, could be brought down to earth, preserved and transmitted far beyond the time and place of the original utterance. And within a few years, all over the sea routes that were once again being plied by Greek traders, this is what happened.

It wasn't just Greeks who adopted the new system. The alphabet was soon being adapted to write Phrygian, an Indo-European language of western Anatolia distantly related to Greek, and Etruscan, the largely undeciphered language of the Romans' northern neighbours in Italy. The invention was still new when Rome itself was founded, according to tradition in 753 BCE. Soon the Romans, too, would adopt a version of it to write their own language, Latin. The actual form of the letters used in each region and to write each of these languages varied enormously, particularly during the early centuries. The distinct Greek and Roman alphabets, as we know them today, would not become standardised until much later. But none of these was a separate invention. We can be sure of this, because the basic system and the equivalence between the Phoenician and the alphabetic signs remained everywhere the same.[9] This single invention—the addition to the existing Phoenician system of separate symbols to represent vowel sounds—lies at the root of the 'roman' alphabet in use all over the world today, as well as the Greek.

Exactly when and where the invention took place are the subject of much speculation. We will probably never know. If recent redating of some of the earliest inscriptions is correct, it must have happened between 850 and 825 BCE. This is a little earlier than the generally accepted date of the early eighth century. As for *where*, it must have been a place where Greek and Phoenician traders rubbed shoulders. One possibility is Crete. A Phoenician trading post had been established on the south coast of the island during the ninth century BCE, and a sample of Phoenician writing has been found in a tomb at Knossos, dating from the same period. Or it could have happened at Lefkandi, or another port town in southern Euboea, since the area was a centre for Greek trading networks at the time. Ancient traditions name Thebes, nearby on the mainland, and also link the first 'Phoenician letters' with the city's legendary founder, Cadmus. Other candidates that have been proposed lie at opposite ends of the Greek world at the time: either Cyprus or one of the Greek outposts in southern Italy.[10]

Wherever it started, to borrow a metaphor from the digital age, it very quickly went viral. At places hundreds of miles apart, owners of decorated drinking cups began to scratch messages onto their glazed surfaces. Often it was no more than the owner's name that was written, or a brief phrase of the type 'I belong to Philion'. Even this is revealing. There's no point in writing your name on a treasured possession if nobody but you can read it. Not long after the year 750 BCE, at the trading settlement of Pithecoussae on the island of Ischia in the Bay of Naples, the owner of a high-value painted cup went further and etched into its surface three lines of verse:

Nestor's hearty-drinking cup am I.
He who drinks this cup will soon take fire
with fair-crowned Aphrodite's hot desire.[11]

The anonymous writer playfully links together the joys of drink and sex (Aphrodite being the goddess of carnal love). And the use of verse links the very new technology of alphabetic writing with the rhythm and the mythological subject matter of what must have been a centuries-old tradition of storytelling in Greek before this time.

Within a few decades, makers of fine pots would begin to add captions to the images that they painted on them. This was done deliberately, before the clay was sent to the kiln for firing, and therefore as part of the manufacture. Once again, to make it worth anyone's while, there must have been an assumption that if you could afford to own such an object, you and your friends would be able to make the connection between word and image. Literacy would still not become widespread for several centuries. But writing was no longer the preserve of a specialised craft guild of scribes. Aptly it has been said that 'The early alphabet likes to declare ownership or belonging, and it speaks in the first person'. There had been nothing like this in the Mycenaean world, or anywhere else in the ancient Near East.[12]

Over the next few centuries, the alphabet would bring into existence the forms of communication that we know today as history, philosophy, and literature. All of these depend on the preservation and transmission of the spoken word by means of writing. The alphabet was now unleashing the full potential of the written word to generate and to replicate messages beyond the control of any single authority, be it political, religious, or commercial. This potential first manifested itself, on a scale that we still call epic for this very reason, in two monumental poems whose written versions are almost as old as the alphabet itself, and in all probability began to take the shape in which we read them today not long after the year 800 BCE.[13]

THE ILIAD AND the *Odyssey* of Homer bring to life the legendary world of the Trojan War and its aftermath. The *Iliad* tells, in almost sixteen thousand lines, of the quarrel between Agamemnon and the best of his fighters, the youthful Achilles, during a period of only a few days in the final year of the ten-year siege of Troy. The *Odyssey*, in over twelve thousand lines, takes as its subject the adventures and homecoming of just one of the heroes, Odysseus (also known as Ulysses), after a further ten years of wandering on the sea. Neither epic gives anything like the whole story. From passing allusions scattered throughout the texts, we realise that the audiences who would have heard these poems sung or recited were expected to be already familiar with the bigger picture.[14]

These stories have become so well known that it can be hard to grasp the sheer strangeness of the original Greek texts. One thing about them is their enormous length. Whether they were created on the page or in the course of an oral performance, the logistical challenge would have been extraordinary. Based on techniques that have been observed at work in modern oral traditions around the world, it has been estimated that the *Iliad* would have taken three full days to perform before an audience—much longer if the poet was dictating his words to a scribe.[15] On the other hand, if someone had sat down to conceive an entire epic poem in writing, in a world in which storytelling had for centuries been defined by the limits of an evening's entertainment and the patience of an assembled group of listeners, how could the result have ever reached an audience? No matter how you look at it, there's no getting away from a singularity almost as striking as the invention of the alphabet itself: How did the art of oral composition in performance ever make the quantum leap into writing? In some way, the new technology must have been the spur to a narrative experiment on a scale that would previously have been inconceivable. But how it was done, and why, we simply do not know.[16]

Then there is the language. Homer's Greek presents a notorious challenge to modern students. But this was the case in the ancient world as well. The language of the epics belongs to no single place or time. It can never have been the natural speech of any individual. Instead, the poems mix elements taken from dialects that in the eighth century BCE were spoken in different parts of the Greek-speaking world. At the same time, they preserve many linguistic 'fossils'—traces of earlier forms of Greek that, it has been argued, go back at least as far as Mycenaean times.[17]

Closely bound up with the language of the poems is their metre, or verse form. Verse is a way of organising language not just into sentences that make sense but also according to repeated patterns of sound, that resonate with the natural rhythms of the human body and so help to lodge them in the brain. (Those of us who were taught to memorise and recite poetry at school will recognise the process at once.) The metre known as dactylic hexameter was used for all the earliest Greek narrative poetry. It also appears in some of the oldest inscriptions that have survived from the eighth century BCE, among them the one incised on Nestor's Cup. It is now generally accepted that this system must have been the creation of generations of poets working in a tradition that functioned quite independently of the written word, long before the invention of the alphabet. Some would go further and see the hexameter verse form as another inheritance from the Mycenaeans, if not even from the Minoans before them.[18]

Neither the *Iliad* nor the *Odyssey* gives any indication of who its author may have been, when or where that person might have lived, or the circumstances in which these monumental narratives came to be born. The name 'Homer' begins to appear only around 500 BCE, more than two hundred years after the poems most probably began to circulate in written form. Various accounts, thereafter, imagine the epic poet as having been active somewhere on the coast of Anatolia—perhaps Smyrna or the nearby island of Chios. 'Homer' is not even a name but an ordinary noun which means 'hostage'. From the few and contradictory scraps that pass for information recorded in antiquity, it is evident that the Greeks of the classical period knew no better than we do whether there ever was such a person. The *Iliad* and the *Odyssey* may or may not have been the work of the same poet or poets. Opinions were divided in ancient times and remain so today. Though we still speak of 'Homer' (usually without quotation marks) as a form of shorthand, there is a growing acceptance that many different individuals, and indeed generations, must have had a hand in the creation of the epics that we read today. Behind the name 'Homer' we might do better to think not so much of an 'author biography' on the cover of a book but of the credits rolling at the end of a film.

Together with the earliest books of the Hebrew scriptures, these two poems are the oldest narratives in the world that have been continuously copied, read, commented upon, and used as a source of inspiration by creative artists in every genre and every generation from that time to this. After them a cycle of six other shorter epics came into existence, traditionally attributed to poets of whom we know even less than we do about Homer. These poems are known to us only through summaries and a few quotations by later authors. They seem to have been written to fill in the many gaps left by the two great epics. Possibly these 'cyclic epics', as they are known, represented more closely the living tradition that had preserved and enhanced these stories over the centuries. Or perhaps there was already a whiff of the library about them—conscientious attempts to capture whatever nuggets of the oral tradition their authors could come upon, and maybe even make up the rest. In any case, the cyclic epics never enjoyed the prestige of their towering counterparts attributed to Homer. Of the two, the *Iliad* always had pride of place, followed at some distance by the *Odyssey*.[19]

In the earliest years, performers called 'rhapsodes' (literally: 'stitchers of songs') had a special role in reciting the poems in public. But, as there were many rhapsodes, active in many different places, it seems that rival versions proliferated. None of these can have been exactly similar to the versions that we possess today. By the 540s BCE, the poems had already become so central to public life in Athens that the city's ruler, Pisistratus, decreed that definitive, authorised versions should be made. This may have been the time when the epics acquired the prestige throughout the Greek-speaking world that they would never lose thereafter.

Three centuries later, scholars in Alexandria in the service of the Greek dynasty, the Ptolemies, took it upon themselves to collate all the manuscript versions of the poems they could lay their hands on. They stripped out all the bogus, redundant lines that had crept in through successive retelling and copying. The result was the model texts that would ever afterwards be copied with great accuracy right down to the invention of printing in the fifteenth century. So anxious were the Alexandrian scholars to ensure that the epics could be read and reliably understood by future generations that they even introduced an innovation into the Greek alphabet. These are the accent marks written above all words of more than one syllable that have remained an essential part of written Greek ever since—allegedly devised for no other purpose than to assist the understanding of a form of the language that was already as distant from speakers in the third century BCE as Chaucer's

English is from us. Just so important had these epics become some six hundred years after they were first written down.

Over a period of almost a millennium after that, while Greek remained the language of education in Egypt, from the third century BCE to the seventh CE, more copies were made of the epics of Homer than of all other Greek authors put together. We know this from the many thousands of fragments cut or torn from scrolls of papyrus that were preserved by the dry conditions of the Egyptian desert and that have come to light in the last hundred and fifty years.[20] Many of these were school textbooks. In the ancient world, to be able to read and write, to be considered educated at all, you had to know your Homer. But the *Iliad* and the *Odyssey* were also read and studied as the nearest thing to a sacred scripture that the Greeks ever had. Historians, philosophers, anyone seeking moral guidance in the everyday world or seeking revelation about the true nature of the gods would turn as a matter of course to 'divine Homer'. Not even the coming of Christianity and the toppling of the statues of the old pagan gods would greatly change that. For another thousand years, devout Greek-speaking Christians would labour to expound the ways in which the ancient epics had prefigured the revealed truths of Christianity and devise ingenious interpretations that turned them into moral allegories.[21]

The *Iliad* and the *Odyssey* in later times would become a fixed point of reference for writers far beyond the Greek world. The Roman poet Virgil famously drew on both as the models for his *Aeneid*. Written at the turn of the first century CE, Virgil's epic links the Trojan story to the origin of the city of Rome and its still-expanding empire. In medieval and modern times, many nations have produced their own 'national epics'. In English, John Milton, writing in the aftermath of the English Civil War of the 1640s, drew on both Homer and Virgil to create the epic poem of

Protestant Christianity, *Paradise Lost*, first published in 1667. The twentieth century saw such literary experiments as James Joyce's Modernist novel *Ulysses* in 1922 and the modern verse epic of the Caribbean, *Omeros*, by Derek Walcott in 1990. In our own century, these quintessentially male stories have been memorably upended by leading women novelists: Margaret Atwood in *The Penelopiad* in 2006, and Pat Barker in *The Silence of the Girls* in 2018. And this is to confine examples to the English-speaking world and to the written word. Adaptations for cinema and TV go back to the early years of both these media and the creation of the 'swords-and-sandals' genre.[22]

It is not hard to see why the epics should have had such lasting appeal. Consider the moment in the *Iliad* when Hector breaks through the Greeks' defences to set fire to the ships beached on the shore:

> *Then glorious Hector burst in*
> *with dark face like sudden night, but he shone with the*
> *   ghastly*
> *glitter of bronze that girded his skin, and carried two spears*
> *in his hands. No one could have stood up against him, and*
> *   stopped him,*
> *except the gods, when he burst in the gates; and his eyes*
> *   flashed fire.*[23]

Or think of the ways that the homecoming of Odysseus has been adapted in later times to stand for a universal human experience. In many languages, today, we speak of an *odyssey* to describe either a long journey or a difficult quest. Near the beginning of the twentieth century, the Alexandrian Greek poet C. P. Cavafy wrote the poem 'Ithaca', which imagines Odysseus's journey as equivalent to life itself. Cavafy concludes:

To Ithaca you owe the splendid journey.
Had it not been for her you'd never have set out.
But she has nothing left to give you now.

And if you find her poor, Ithaca did not cheat you.
So wise as you've become, from your adventures,
you'll know at once the meaning of an Ithaca.[24]

This may be a far cry from the actual opinions of any Greek alive in the eighth century BCE. But Cavafy's much-loved poem testifies to the enduring power of the story. And there could have been no twentieth-century 'Ithaca' if there had not first been Homer's. What we now call 'world literature' effectively begins with the *Iliad* and the *Odyssey*.

THE ACTION OF the two poems is set in an age of heroes that was imagined as already long past before the stories came to be told. At four different points in the *Iliad*, a hero is said to pick up and hurl 'a stone, a huge thing which no two men could carry / such as men are now'.[25] The repeated expression betrays itself as one of the traditional building blocks of oral poetry, a ready-made 'formula' which the poet could adapt to fit different situations as his narrative developed. And this 'now', that is contrasted to the age of heroes, is not even fixed to any one point in time; it was already enshrined in the oral tradition before the *Iliad* ever came to be written down.

Specific details of the heroic age, particularly as it is described in the *Iliad*, often seem uncannily to correlate with objects or practices discovered by modern archaeology—but not consistently with those belonging to any one time. Some of these go far back into the Mycenaean Bronze Age. At one point we hear of a helmet made out of the tusks of wild boars stitched onto leather. Elsewhere a hero carries a rectangular shield large enough to cover his whole body. We know from the Thera frescoes, buried before 1500 BCE, and other finds of that period, that these types of armour had once been characteristic of the Mycenaeans. They were already becoming obsolete by the time the first palaces rose on the Greek mainland.[26] In another scene, the Trojans go out to battle sporting helmets crowned with a horse-hair plume and a horn. Helmets exactly matching this description appear on the long-nosed, rather bedraggled-looking warriors who march round the surface of the famous 'Warrior Vase' from Mycenae. But this vase dates from about 1150 BCE, at least four hundred years after the eruption that buried the Thera frescoes. Then there are the obsequies devised by Achilles for his dead friend Patroclus. The poet describes how female captives were killed above the hero's tomb, along with his favourite horses. Something very similar seems to have happened at Lefkandi but in a different historical period again, in the early Iron Age, not long after 1000 BCE.[27]

Armour and weapons, in the epics, are made of bronze, as they had been in Mycenaean times and for about two centuries afterwards, and not of iron, as they more often were in the eighth century BCE. Chariots appear regularly in the battle scenes in the *Iliad*. This was another feature of the Bronze Age that had disappeared from warfare long before the invention of the alphabet. But the poet seems unsure about how they might really have been used in the field—and the men in the audience, who can never have seen them in action either, appear not to have minded. Heroes in the epics, when they die, are invariably cremated on funeral pyres. The Mycenaeans had laid the bodies of warriors to rest in graves of varying types but almost always intact. The change to cremation had begun towards the end of the Mycenaean period and continued gradually until it became general during the dark age. Later, both methods for disposing of the dead would again coexist. But Homer knows only the practice of the dark age. Homer's age of heroes, then, cannot be a realistic depiction of any world that actually existed. Rather, it incorporates elements drawn from many different times, that range across a span of astonishing depth: from the sixteenth to the eighth centuries BCE.[28]

The same applies to what might be termed the geopolitics of the epic world. Halfway through the second book of the *Iliad*, the poet interrupts himself to call upon the 'Muses . . . who know all things' to tell 'Who . . . were the chief men and the lords of the Danaäns' (that is, the Greeks). The section that begins here has long been recognised as in effect a separate poem, embedded at this point. Most modern readers probably skip over the 'Catalogue of Ships', as it has come to be known, and with good reason. The story is held up while the poet lists the participants in the war on both sides. Alongside the names of places and their rulers, we also learn, for the Greek side, the size of each contingent, measured by the number of ships each leader has contributed to the expedition. The poet reveals a remarkable grasp of the physical geography of the Greek peninsula and the Aegean and describes it in terms that we would nowadays call political.[29]

No one in Homer's time, or for many centuries afterwards, could have seen anything remotely resembling a modern map. We have the advantage of being able to see the information contained in the Catalogue laid out in spatial form. But the 'singer of tales' had to spell it out in words. The act of telling brings in the dimension of time in the form of a sequence. This narrated 'map' begins in the centre, with Thebes and Boeotia, then spirals outwards to draw a circle that encompasses the Peloponnese and the southern part of the mainland to the north. (It may not be entirely accidental that this was almost exactly the area covered by the modern Greek state when its frontiers were first established in 1832.) The poet then reaches outside the circle to bring in a number of outliers: first moving in an arc from Crete northwards and eastwards to include several islands of the Dodecanese, including the largest, Rhodes. Then he jumps to the far north, where he starts with Achilles's homeland in Thessaly and rounds off with a rather vague account of even remoter places that mark the northernmost edge of his world.

This presentation gives a very clear sense of a geographical, and perhaps also political, centre and a periphery beyond it. Politically, the greatest concentrations of power, as represented by numbers of ships, are the Argolid, with a combined total of 180 from Mycenae and Tiryns, and Pylos with 90. Mycenae fields the largest single contingent, 100. Agamemnon, king of Mycenae, commands the entire expedition. Athens and Sparta, the cities that would emerge in classical times as the rival 'great powers' of the Hellenic world, are of middle rank, with 50 and 60 ships, respectively.

The opposing Trojan forces are presented rather more summarily, and of course they have no ships to be counted because they are defending Troy from the land. Effectively, and drawing on information given elsewhere in the poem, we learn that the defenders of the city have been recruited from the entire northern and eastern coastline of the Aegean, stretching from the Axios (Vardar) River, just to the west of modern Thessalonica, all the way round to Lycia, in the southwestern corner of today's Turkey. Some of the islands closest to the eastern mainland, including Tenedos and the much larger Lesbos, also lie within the Trojan sphere. The result is a world symmetrically split along an axis that runs through the Aegean Sea from northwest to southeast. On land, the two alliances are neatly separated by the highest mountain massif in the region, Mount Olympus, which is also the home of the gods who are the final arbiters of fortune in the war being waged between them.[30]

It has often been noticed that the picture presented in the Catalogue matches the archaeological record for the Greek-speaking world in the Mycenaean age far better than it does for Homer's time. But it is not an exact match for either. Many of the names listed refer to places that the Greeks themselves, in classical and Roman times, were unable to identify. Several of these names have now turned up in Linear B tablets and can be linked with Bronze Age sites known to archaeologists. By the eighth century BCE, on the other hand, the centre of gravity of the Greek-speaking world had shifted to the eastern side of the Aegean. Homer himself, according to tradition, and most probably his first audiences, too, on the evidence of the language used in the poems, actually belonged to that newly expanded *eastern* Greek world. Why are these things never mentioned?[31]

One answer must surely be that the political geography of the *Iliad* is inseparable from the great conflict that forms the background to the whole poem. The alliances and oppositions presented, according to the logic of the story, have been created by the unique event of the Trojan War. How the thirty-odd separate kingdoms that make up the Greek side relate to one another in peacetime we are never told. The Trojan alliance is an even more ad hoc affair. In other words, what divides the two sides and draws a line across the Aegean Sea in the *Iliad* is nothing but the Trojan War itself. This is not to say that Homer's world was simply invented. Rather, it must have been pieced together, probably over generations, if not over centuries, by people who had been brought up on stories handed down from different periods in the past. But the coherent whole that the *Iliad*, in particular, creates is an *imagined* age of heroes, not the faithful record of a historical reality.

In that imagined world, the people that we know as Greeks are never called by the name that would later become standard: 'Hellenes'. In the Catalogue of Ships, 'Hellas' is the name given to a local region in the kingdom of Achilles, in what would later become Thessaly. 'Hellenes' make up only a small group within one of the smaller contingents besieging Troy—though of course their leader

61

proves himself the most glorious of all, which may help to explain how the name would eventually come to be applied to everyone who spoke Greek. Instead, the combined forces that make war on Troy in the *Iliad*, and the survivors of the expedition in the *Odyssey*, are most frequently called 'Achaeans' (*Achaiwoi*). Sometimes they may alternatively be called 'Danaans' or 'Argives' (men of Argos). But so far as we can tell, all three of these names have the same undifferentiated meaning, equivalent to later 'Hellenes'. 'Achaeans', and probably also 'Danaans', had been current in Mycenaean times, as mentioned in the previous chapter.[32]

We have no means of telling how Greeks were in the habit of referring to themselves in the eighth century BCE. If anything like a 'panhellenic' identity is to be discovered in the Homeric poems, whether a distant echo from Mycenaean times or the beginning of something new in the eighth century BCE, it is curiously elusive.[33] It has been tellingly pointed out that there is nothing resembling what we would nowadays call a national consciousness on the Greek side in the *Iliad*. It is different for the Trojans: Hector speaks movingly of the honour and necessity of defending one's 'fatherland'. Among the Greeks, individual heroes are identified not as Achaean but by their place of origin—Mycenae or Argos, Ithaca or Phthia (Achilles's homeland). Achaeans, Danaans, and Argives only ever appear in a generalised plural.

Nothing in the epics marks out Trojan people as being different from Achaean people, except perhaps the detail that Priam seems to have many wives. Some of the Trojans' allies speak different languages, and the poet implies that this puts them at a slight disadvantage. We aren't told what language the Trojans speak among themselves (nor the Achaeans, either, for that matter). But both sides communicate with each other all the time, and without any hint of a language barrier, so we must presume in Greek. Neither the poet nor any of the characters, who often hurl defiance at each other in long speeches, expresses any sense of superiority for one side or contempt for the other on the grounds of being Achaean or Trojan.[34]

Both sides worship the same gods, whose home is on the cloud-covered peaks of Mount Olympus. Many scenes in the two epics are set there. Already in the first book of the *Iliad*, we meet Zeus, 'Cloud-Gatherer' and 'Thunderer', lording it over a dysfunctional family of nine other named gods and goddesses, who constantly conspire with each other or with favoured mortal heroes on one side or the other. The kingdom of Zeus among the clouds is as full of quarrels as the councils of men down below—with the difference, often wistfully invoked by poet and characters alike, that the Olympians live forever.[35]

Achaeans and Trojans approach these gods in identical ways. A hero begs a particular deity for a favour and promises rich sacrifices in return. Gods and goddesses are pleased or displeased by the amount of respect paid to them by mortals. Often, they intervene in person on the battlefield—either invisible to humans or in human disguise, penetrable only by the poet or sometimes by a hero at a heightened moment that brings a sense of frisson. Zeus has decided in advance that Troy is to fall and that Odysseus will be allowed to return home. But there is plenty of room for the scales of advantage to tip one way or the other through the ten years that elapse before either of these destinies can be fulfilled. There is never any suggestion that the 'Greek' gods show special or consistent favour to the Achaeans *because they are Greek*. There is nothing in Homer to compare with the 'chosen people' of the Hebrew scriptures.

On both sides, too, the heroes share the same code of values. It is honourable to die in battle and still more honourable to be remembered for your deeds long afterwards. Achilles knows that he has been given a choice:

Either,
if I stay here and fight beside the city of the Trojans,
my return home is gone, but my glory shall be everlasting;
but if I return home to the beloved land of my fathers,
the excellence of my glory is gone, but there will be a
    long life
left for me . . .

To run away to save your skin is dishonourable. And the greatest dishonour is for that, too, to be remembered after you are gone. Hector resolves to stand up to Achilles in the duel in which he will lose his life because he fears that if he does not:

        someone who is less of a man than I will
say of me:
    'Hektor believed in his own strength and ruined his people.'
Thus they will speak; and as for me, it would be much
    better
at that time, to go against Achilleus, and slay him, and
    come back,
or else be killed by him in glory in front of the city.

And shortly afterwards, when he realises that the gods have deserted him and he must die, Hector concludes:

Let me at least not die without a struggle, inglorious,
but do some big thing first, that men to come shall know
    of it.

For Achaeans and Trojans alike, in the bleak world of the Homeric poems, the generations of men are like generations of leaves that flourish, fall, and are forgotten.[36] The only compensation worthy of a hero is to win 'the fame of men' and to have his deeds commemorated long afterwards in song. What makes him a hero is neither his homeland nor the cause he is fighting for but the monumental song that preserves his memory.

And so in the end, the true heroes of this story turn out to be not the warriors, with their deeds of valour or ingenuity, but the poet and the Greek language in which he tells his tale. The *Iliad* and the *Odyssey* do not single out the deeds of Greeks and glorify them over the deeds of others. Anyone can win a place on the roll of honour if he lives up to a set of values that the poet assumes are universal. In many ways, the most sympathetically presented of all the heroes in the *Iliad*, on either side, is the 'enemy' champion, Hector.[37] Homer's world is a *Greek* world only because Homer's *words* are Greek. And that world is, above all, a world of the imagination. For all its multiple points of reference to a history that may reach back through hundreds of years, the real significance of that world lies in what it tells us about the Greek imagination, in or around the eighth century BCE.

IN BOTH EPICS, the main story of heroic words and deeds is punctuated by little vignettes drawn from everyday activities such as farming, hunting, or seafaring. These would have been part of the familiar experience of the poems' audiences. Known as 'epic similes', many of these vignettes seem to open up windows that enable us to look into the lives and experience of ordinary Greeks living in the eighth century BCE. Often extending to several lines of verse, there are almost two hundred of them in the *Iliad*. The *Odyssey* has far fewer. But one stands out because it brings home to the listener the horrors that await the inhabitants of a sacked town—seeming to imply that it could easily be your turn, and your family's, anytime:

> *. . . as a woman*
> *weeps, as she falls to wrap her arms around*
> *her husband, fallen fighting for his home*
> *and children. She is watching as he gasps*
> *and dies. She shrieks, a clear high wail, collapsing*
> *upon his corpse. The men are right behind.*
> *They hit her shoulders with their spears and lead her*
> *to slavery; hard labor, and a life*
> *of pain. Her face is marked with her despair.*[38]

Even in time of peace, in both poems a typical activity is to go rustling somebody else's livestock. In the *Iliad* the worldly-wise old windbag Nestor tells the story of how he first won his spurs in a glorified cattle-raid that blew up into a mini-war when things got out of hand. Odysseus, while still a boy, had been sent by his father from Ithaca to the mainland to reclaim three hundred stolen sheep. And at the end of the *Odyssey*, when he has killed the suitors who had been besieging his wife and depleting his stores, the hero knows only one way to begin to recoup his losses:

> *I have to go on raids, to steal replacements*
> *for all the sheep those swaggering suitors killed,*
> *and get the other Greeks to give me more,*
> *until I fill my folds.*[39]

Activities such as these seem to be taken for granted by poet and audience alike, because they elicit no comment. Another is trading by sea, something that we know Greeks were once again doing on a large scale by the eighth century BCE. Usually, in the *Odyssey*, sea traders are depicted as Phoenicians. They are usually also devious tricksters—though hardly worse in this respect than the hero himself, Odysseus 'of many wiles'. As in many other societies of later times, trade is presented as no occupation for a gentleman, still less for an epic hero. But Odysseus, that master of disguise, is several times permitted to *pretend* to be a trader—and even the goddess Athena is not above doing the same on occasion. Often the line between legitimate exchange of goods and piracy or plunder appears to be easily crossed. The Cyclops, the savage giant with one eye, shortly before he starts to eat his uninvited guests for dinner, suspiciously demands of Odysseus, newly arrived at his cave:

> *Where did you come from*
> *across the watery depths? Are you on business,*
> *or roaming round without a goal, like pirates,*
> *who risk their lives to bring disaster*
> *to other people?*[40]

Although heroes on the battlefield are expected to have higher motives, the force that drives ordinary people in the real world of the eighth century BCE is the brute reality of hunger and the fear of starvation. In another of his disguises, this time as a decrepit old beggar, Odysseus gives voice to a motivation that listeners to the poem would surely have had no difficulty in recognising:

> *There is no way to hide a hungry belly.*
> *It is insistent, and the curse of hunger*
> *is why we sail across the relentless seas,*
> *and plunder other people.*[41]

On the positive side, a special place in the world of the epic poets is reserved for song. In the *Iliad*, the great Achilles is not too proud to console himself by playing on the lyre and 'singing of men's fame', while sulking in his tent with only his companion Patroclus for company. But it is in the *Odyssey* that we encounter the 'singer of tales' at work. The suitors, who have taken over the hero's palace in his absence to pay court to Penelope, have conscripted the services of the local bard to entertain them while they plunder Odysseus's storerooms and feast to their hearts' content. And at the court of the imaginary kingdom of the Phaeacians, the blind singer Demodocus is loved and honoured by all—indeed, his name might loosely be translated as 'pillar of society'. Demodocus moves the hero to tears when he takes up his lyre and sings the story of the Wooden Horse and the sack of Troy, as vividly as though he could have actually seen these things. This episode in the *Odyssey* is probably the origin for the legend, often repeated in antiquity and since, that Homer himself was blind. Clearly no aristocratic feast would be complete without its 'singer of tales'.[42]

These vignettes in the *Iliad* and the *Odyssey* are not our only witnesses to what life was like for Greeks in the eighth century BCE. At about the same time as the great epic poems first made it into writing, or perhaps a little later, Hesiod of Ascra also took up his pen. Much shorter than the epics, and more personal too, Hesiod's two surviving poems are known today as the *Theogony* (or *Birth of the Gods*) and the *Works and Days*.

The first of these tells a story of origins. But in the course of telling this cosmic tale, a poet for the first time in Greek literature gives us his name and tells us how he had learned the art of song—directly, he would have us believe, from the Muses, the patron deities of the arts, on the slopes of nearby Mount Helicon.[43] More revealing of the realities of life in the eighth century BCE is the *Works and Days*. Here, we learn that Hesiod's father had migrated from the city of Cyme on the coast of Anatolia to the village of Ascra overlooking the Boeotian plain, where he had been born. It was there that Hesiod had inherited the plot of land that he was still cultivating for a living when he wrote his poem. The poet goes on to complain about his layabout brother, Perses, and the failure of the village authorities to deal fairly with Hesiod's complaints against him. All this is couched in the form of wise advice for fellow farmers, honed by bitter experience.

Much of what Hesiod has to say seems pretty strange to us today: 'Make sure you do not stand / Facing the sun when you piss'. (The wind, yes—but the *sun?*) His poem also brings vividly to our senses the sheer drudgery and hardship of eking out a living in what Hesiod, long before modern archaeologists, was the first to call an 'age of iron':

> *By day, men toil; night worries them with care,*
> *And the gods will give them troubles hard to bear;*
> *. . .   Lacking pity,*
> *With the rule of fist, one sacks another's city.*

It is the same bleak picture that we find in the similes in the epics, but this time with the added touch of authenticity that comes with Hesiod's individual voice. Life in Ascra is presented as a constant struggle against the elements and unscrupulous neighbours. Winter is so harsh that it 'bends an old man into the shape of a hoop'; the summer sun 'withers the skin'.[44]

But even while Hesiod was painting this grim picture of life in Boeotia, conditions in the Greek-speaking world were starting to change, and rapidly. As the eighth century BCE wore on, the population reached phenomenal proportions. It has been estimated that in Athens alone, by the year 720 BCE, the number of inhabitants had multiplied sevenfold over just two generations. (Ironically, it is from statistical evidence for burials of the dead that archaeologists have been able to base their estimates for the number of the living.) The Greeks were not the only people affected. Several populations around the shores of the Mediterranean seem to have experienced a similar increase at this time. We don't know the reason for this. But the ways in which Greeks responded would define the Greek world and its people for centuries to come and prepare the ground for the 'classical' civilisation that was still some way in the future. With good reason, the next three centuries would come to be known as an 'age of experiment'.[45]

3

INVENTING POLITICS, DISCOVERING THE COSMOS

c. 720 BCE–494 BCE

GREEKS WERE NOW taking to the seas as never before. From all over the Greek-speaking world, ships powered by sails and banks of rowers were heading westwards and southwards across the Mediterranean. Others passed through the straits of the Dardanelles and the Bosphorus and into the Black Sea. Once upon a time, according to legends which may go back to Mycenaean times, Greeks had first ventured into such remote seaways during the age of heroes. Jason, with his crew of Argonauts, had braved giants and monsters to bring back the Golden Fleece from today's Georgia. Odysseus, in the *Odyssey*, had travelled to fabulous lands in the west, often identified as Sicily and even, perhaps, the Strait of Gibraltar. But always, in those old stories, however far you travelled, your ultimate purpose was to return to your starting point—enriched if possible, but in any case to arrive *home* with a whole skin. The longing for *nostos*, the Homeric word for homecoming, was already deeply embedded as a concept in the Greek language—hence 'nostalgia', which means just that.

These new voyages were different. For most of those who embarked, there was to be no return. But this was not a repeat of the mass migrations of the 'dark age', either. People left their native

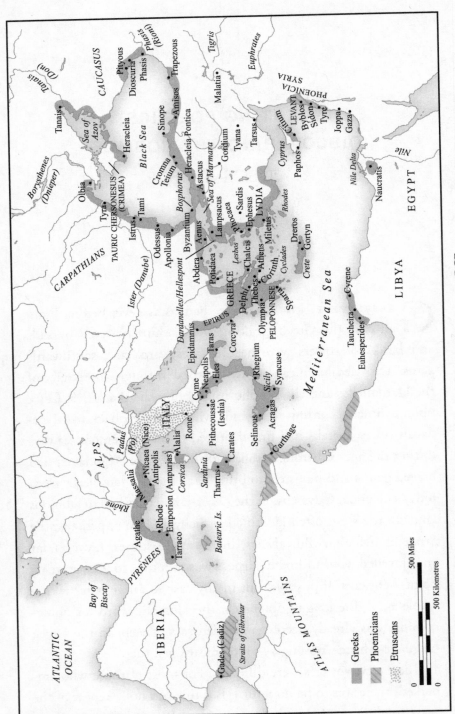

3. 'Like ants or frogs around a pond': Greek settlements in the seventh and sixth centuries BCE

land in small groups, determined to carve out new homes for themselves in distant lands. The Greek word for this kind of settlement abroad was *apoikia*. The word is closer in meaning to the English expression 'a home from home' than to the usual translation, 'colony'. These early Greek settlers were different from later Roman colonists, and still more from their successors in the age of European colonialism. Empire building would find a place in the Greek story in due course, but this was not it.

New Greek settlements sprang up all round the coasts of Sicily and southern Italy. Others formed a line along the southern shore of Europe, from Catalonia to just short of the French-Italian border. Modern names of towns and cities often still preserve the memory of their origins in a Greek settlement: in Italy, Naples (Neapolis) and Taranto (Taras) among many others; in Catalonia, Empúries, or Ampurias (Emporion); in France, Marseille (Massalia), Antibes (Antipolis), and Nice (Nicaea). On the coast of North Africa, there was Cyrene in what is now eastern Libya, Naucratis on the Nile delta of Egypt. To the east, beyond the Dardanelles, there were Greek communities to be found on all the shores of the Sea of Marmara and almost all the way round the Black Sea, including the Sea of Azov. All of these were in existence by around 600 BCE.[1]

Two centuries later, the philosopher Plato could put into the mouth of his teacher, Socrates, the assertion that 'we [Greeks] live between the River Phasis and the Pillars of Hercules . . . making our homes around the sea just as ants or frogs do around a pond'.[2] The River Phasis, now called the Rioni, flows through Georgia into the Black Sea near its easternmost point. The Pillars of Hercules were the Strait of Gibraltar. It was some pond.

As Plato had noticed, when Greeks left their homeland to establish communities abroad, they hardly ever ventured very far from the sea. (This has often been the case in the modern world, too.) Just like the Mycenaeans and Minoans before them, the Greeks of the 'age of experiment' had the sea in their blood. It was the sea, and their evident mastery of shipbuilding and navigation, that enabled so many groups of emigrants to keep in touch with one another and to prosper by moving goods from one part of that huge extended coastline to another. Even such notoriously stay-at-home landlubbers among Greek speakers as the Spartans, when they briefly joined in at the end of the eighth century, followed the same pattern as everyone else. At this time, it has been said, 'a new town was founded in south Italy or Sicily about every other year' by Greek settlers.[3]

What made them do it?

Various explanations have been offered, at different times and from different perspectives. Perhaps the strongest reason for this unusual pattern of migration was simply: *because they could*. Plato's analogy from the natural world brings to mind a different sense of the word *colony* from the historical one. Species, such as Plato's 'ants or frogs', colonise territory and maintain themselves there as long as no predators threaten to dislodge them. The analogy is surprisingly exact for what was happening all around the shores of the Mediterranean at this time. The only large, centralised, developed state with a Mediterranean coastline was Egypt. When Greeks went there, as they did both as mercenaries and as merchants, they did so by invitation of the pharaoh. That made the single Greek 'colony' in Egypt, Naucratis, a special case, the exception that proves the rule. Anywhere else on the coasts of the Mediterranean, the Sea of Marmara, the Black Sea, or the Sea of Azov, you could beach your ship wherever you could find a sandy shore, put up your tent, and start building your settlement, without having to ask permission of anyone.

Sometimes the founders of new Greek settlements abroad would have to fight to establish their territory or to maintain it afterwards.

But this happened surprisingly rarely, at least in the early stages. In the west, the earliest foundations seem not even to have been fortified. Instead, by moving into the marginal space between sea and hinterland, the new arrivals became the entrepreneurs—middlemen or intermediaries—whose presence and whose skills would enable goods, people, and technological know-how to pass from one part of the Mediterranean basin to another. For the time being, the newcomers could bask with impunity. In the absence of any serious predator, they became part of a new and thriving human ecology for the whole region.[4]

The Greeks were not alone in fanning out across the seas at this time. The Phoenicians had been setting out from their homeland on the Levant coast for longer and would reach even farther, as far as Cadiz beyond the Strait of Gibraltar. The Etruscans of the Italian peninsula also established settlements beyond their own shores. By the year 500 BCE, more than half the entire coastline of the Mediterranean would be dotted with the settlements of one or other of these three peoples. And it would be these rival settlers, rather than the native populations of each hinterland, that for several centuries would prove to be the Greeks' strongest competitors.[5]

All these new settlements naturally started out from small beginnings. More often than not, the dots they represent on the map do not even join up. Travel from one to another was invariably by sea, not by land. It may have been in these circumstances, rather than back home on the Greek mainland or on the coasts and islands of the Aegean, that Greeks first began to organise their communities in an entirely new way, one that would go on to command immense prestige throughout the Greek-speaking world for a millennium and whose legacy is still with us today. The Greek word for this kind of community was *polis* (*poleis* in the plural), usually translated as 'city-state'.

Typically, a *polis* would consist of an urban space, laid out around a sanctuary and an open area near the centre called an *agora*. The essential element of the sanctuary was one or more altars to the patron deity or deities of the city. Soon, more elaborate buildings would be built as the homes of these gods and goddesses. The Greek temple, built at first of wood and later of stone, with its rows of columns and pitched roof ending in a pediment at either end, was another innovation of the eighth century BCE. Many still stand as ruins today, and their architectural design would be copied again and again in later centuries. The *agora* was at first a meeting place for the citizens to assemble and only later took on the sense of 'market' (still the everyday meaning of the word in Greek). The city would be surrounded by an agricultural hinterland of varying size. Farming, trade, and the spoils of war were the principal sources of wealth.[6] City and hinterland together were ruled from the urban centre. Together, they formed the equivalent of a political state, as we understand the term today. The hinterland might include any number of villages or smaller settlements. But there was, more or less by definition, in each state only one 'city'.

It seems to have been a function of their size that in these city-states no institution or social group was consistently strong enough to impose its will on the rest. For the same reason, there was no given pecking order *among* city-states either. There was no equivalent to the Egyptian pharaoh or the 'Great King' of Assyria or, later, of Persia to rule by god-given right, whether within the limits of a single state or as overlord with authority over many. Later traditions held that *poleis* such as Athens and Thebes had once been ruled by hereditary monarchs. But in historical times, of all the Greek city-states, this was only ever true of Sparta, which was an exceptional case in many other ways, too. As for a single ruler with power to command all Greeks, that had only ever been possible in the distant, legendary past, when Agamemnon was supposed to have led the expedition against Troy. And even Agamemnon, according to Homer in the *Iliad*, had had a fractious time of it, his supremacy seemingly only a temporary response to circumstances and not immune to challenge or reproach from his peers.

In the absence of the principle of hereditary rule, the only other force that might have exerted a compelling authority over a *polis* would have been religion. The terrifying power of the Olympian gods was everywhere manifest in nature—in random 'acts of God', such as lightning strikes or earthquakes, for instance. When gods gave orders to humans, whether through oracles or omens, nobody doubted that they had to be obeyed. Offerings and sacrifices to the gods, and rituals both private and public, were an obligatory part of everyday life, as much for individuals as for whole communities. But in the ancient Greek world there was no religious hierarchy to dictate or regulate practice or belief. There was no equivalent to the role of prophet, such as had already emerged in early Judaism or would later in Islam. No section of Greek society, not even the priesthood, could command authority on behalf of the divine realm to compare with the power of popes or bishops or institutions such as the Inquisition during the Christian Middle Ages.

So, when a group of people came together to organise themselves into a *polis*, there was no one to tell them how to do it. They had to work it out for themselves. Suddenly, everything was up for negotiation and argument. And this is what Greeks began to do all over the Greek-speaking world both abroad and at home: to *argue*, to dispute with one another, to compete to find the best solutions that would work for the community as a whole, and then to persuade their peers to adopt them. Out of that combination of reasoned argument with persuasion would be born the world's first *politics* (literally, 'the affairs of the *polis*').

The philosopher Aristotle, looking back from the perspective of some four hundred years later in the 330s and 320s BCE, would tell his students in Athens that the *polis* represented both the natural and the best way for human beings to organise themselves into a functioning community. It existed to ensure for its citizens 'a perfect and independent life', 'that is to say, for them to live happily and well'.[7] In the minds of the ancient Greeks, it was the concept of the *citizen* that defined the state, rather than the other way round. Aristotle was clear that the *polis* was 'not a community of place'. Nor was it merely a means for people to come together for 'the reciprocal exercise of justice and exchange'. These things were *consequences* of the existence of the *polis*, not the reason for it, still less its essence. In official documents and proclamations, a *polis* would always define itself not by the name of the city but by the collective name for its citizens: 'the Athenians', 'the Spartans', 'the Thebans', and so on. For all these reasons it has been proposed in our own time that a better description than 'city-state' would be 'citizen-state'.[8]

On the other hand, the Greek word *polis*, in its everyday sense, has always meant simply 'town or city'. It is true that many of the elements of urban life as we know it today had not really developed in these early days. Even the largest *poleis* were very small by the standards of modern towns, let alone cities or states. Size was never a defining criterion; the smallest is said to have contained just 190 inhabitants.[9] But to belong to a *polis*, whether small or large, has always in Greek been tantamount to what a later age would call civilisation itself. Aristotle taught his students that anyone who lived far from cities or who had lived in times before the *polis* came into being must be like 'the man reviled by Homer for being "Out of all brotherhood, outlawed, homeless"'.[10]

It may be that the true essence of the *polis*, and what made it possible, was neither the place nor its people but the *rules* that were created specifically for each place and that bound all the citizens who lived there. It can be no accident that one of the earliest public uses of the alphabet in the ancient Greek world was to make laws. These were literally set in stone or bronze, inscribed in public places where all could see them—even if only a minority would have been able to read what they said. Probably the oldest that survives is a fragment preserved at the site of Dreros, in northeastern Crete, dating from about 650 BCE. Revealingly, the text from Dreros does not 'lay down the law' in the sense that we might expect today. A great deal of early Greek legislation was about *who* had the right to exercise particular forms of authority and in what circumstances. Preoccupations such as these would dominate the turbulent and often fast-changing lives of most *poleis* for the next three hundred years.[11]

Laws were created for just about every city-state and differed greatly from one *polis* to another. Because systems everywhere were being devised from the ground up, other rules also varied enormously. Names of months, systems for reckoning historical time, weights, measures, coins (when coinage was introduced from Anatolia in about 600 BCE), definitions of citizens' duties and privileges were different wherever you went. A modern traveller would have been bewildered passing through the boundaries of so many separate jurisdictions. And yet the *nature* of all these rules was remarkably consistent in all of them.

Out of these systems of rules emerged forms of government. Every *polis* had its own constitution, and every constitution was different in points of detail. One of the tasks Aristotle gave his students was to collect and write up some 150 of these that were in force in their own day (only the one for Athens survives). But from at least the first half of the fifth century BCE, the possible forms of government available to a *polis* could be reduced to three broad types: rule by one man, rule by the many, or rule by the few.[12] The standard Greek terms for these would soon become established as, respectively, *tyrannis, demokratia,* and *oligarchia*. Precise meanings have changed a good deal in the intervening two and a half millennia, but all three are immediately recognisable in the political vocabulary of our own time.

Back in the preclassical age of experiment, when all of them were first being tried out, *tyranny* meant rule by a single strongman, more of a dictator than necessarily a tyrant in the modern sense. Even tyrants could be assiduous legislators, sometimes indeed quite progressive by the standards of their time. By and large, they would abide by their own laws, having once made them, and often respected those that they had inherited. In an oligarchy, power was held by a self-chosen elite group, based on birth and wealth; in a democracy, by the mass of the male citizenry. Irrespective of the actual system of government, by the end of the sixth century BCE, the principle had become generally accepted that every citizen was equal before the law.[13]

Despite all this, we should not suppose that the ancient *polis*, as it began to develop from the seventh century BCE onwards, was everything that Aristotle and others would later claim for it, particularly when viewed by the moral and political standards of today. No ancient Greek state was ever prepared to give full privileges of citizenship to women or more than the most basic protections to slaves. This meant that those who were entitled to take part in public affairs could never make up more than between a quarter and a half of the total adult population. Everywhere, the buying and selling of human beings as merchandise was an accepted part of civilised life. Wars between states, more often than not, may have been fought not so much with the aim of seizing land but of acquiring human capital—in the form of captives who could then be put to work as slaves.[14] These grim realities were widespread, if not universal, at the time. But they seem never seriously to have been questioned by the Greeks of the age of experiment, who made it their business to question so much else about the world in which they lived and which they were shaping around them.

THESE WERE NOT the only limitations to the ancient *polis* as the system worked in practice. Its growth was piecemeal and never spread to the whole of the Greek-speaking world. So far as we can tell, every new settlement founded abroad from the end of the eighth century onwards soon adopted the *polis* model if it had not done so from the beginning. But many parts of the Greek mainland lagged behind. These were organised much more loosely into a type of state known as *ethnos* (*ethne* in the plural). This word had a range of meanings in the ancient language but did not yet signify what we could call 'ethnic' differences because all these communities were Greek-speaking. An *ethnos* has been described as 'a survival of the tribal system into historical times: a population scattered thinly over a territory without urban centres'.[15] Aristotle was not alone among ancient writers in regarding *ethne* as backward, precisely because they lacked the fabric and institutions that defined the *polis*. For this reason we know much less about how they ran their affairs.

In the southern half of Greece, most *ethne* would in due course coalesce into distinct *poleis* over the coming centuries. The farther north you went, the less likely that was to happen. One *ethnos* that never did adopt the *polis* system was Macedonia. There, hereditary monarchs belonging to a single dynasty would slowly consolidate their rule over an inland kingdom much larger than any city-state. The time would come for the kings of Macedonia to make their mark on world history, as Aristotle and his contemporaries had good cause to know. But in the meantime, it was the new kind of social organisation represented by the *polis* that would define the Greek world.

Among some one thousand five hundred Greek city-states that ever existed, at various times over a whole millennium, the most famous were Sparta and Athens. Neither was a typical *polis*. Sparta was not really a city at all but a collection of settlements along the banks of the Eurotas River, in the shadow of Mount Taygetos. Sparta ruled over the territory known as Laconia, or Lacedaemon, as well as neighbouring Messenia on the far side of the Taygetos range, which had once been part of the dominion of the Mycenaean kings of Pylos. All this added up to a Spartan state much larger than the hinterland of many other *poleis* put together, comprising roughly the southern half of the Peloponnese.

The people of Messenia, together with a portion of the native population of Laconia, were known as 'helots', a word which literally means 'captives'. The helots were the descendants of the indigenous inhabitants, who according to tradition had been enslaved by the incoming Spartans, presumably during the upheavals of the dark age. In historical times, the helots lived in a state of permanent subjection, working in effect as agricultural serfs. Thanks to slave labour on this scale, Sparta was the only city-state whose citizens were able to devote themselves full-time to soldiery. Indeed, a Spartan citizen was forbidden from exercising any sort of productive profession. Sparta has ever since been remembered as an intensely corporate, militarised society. One reason for this specialisation was an understandable fear among their ruling class that one day their oppressed subjects, who may have outnumbered them by as many as seven to one, would rise up and take their revenge—as indeed would come to pass eventually.[16]

Athens, by contrast, was first and foremost a *city*. Then, as now, the urban space was dominated by the imposing rock known as the Acropolis (the Greek word literally means 'high city', and in ancient times just meant a citadel). Athens controlled a hinterland much smaller than Sparta's and smaller even than the modern administrative region which has revived its ancient name, Attica (or Attiki in modern Greek). But in Athens, unlike in Sparta, every adult male born within the bounds of the state was a full citizen. Much of the menial work in and around the city was still done by slaves, either captured in war or bought in slave markets. But citizens farmed their own land, or else they earned their living as craftsmen or traders.[17]

In a Greek city-state, the law was supreme. And in this, at least, Sparta and Athens were no exception. Reverence for man-made laws that had been handed down from legendary figures of the past was as strong in the mind of an Athenian or a Spartan citizen as his awe (or dread) of the gods. The Athenian lawgiver Draco has bequeathed to us the word *draconian*; Lycurgus of Sparta most probably never existed, but his name would remain inseparably attached to the rigid Spartan system of laws. Beyond that common ground, the constitutional systems of the two states were about as different as it was possible to be.

Sparta was the only Greek *polis* to retain a traditional, hereditary monarchy. Even more unusual was that *two* kings, belonging to separate dynasties, always ruled together. Exactly where the balance of power lay in Sparta between the kings, at one end of the spectrum, and citizens' assemblies, at the other, is not entirely clear. Women in Sparta had a higher social status and more of a voice than women in most other city-states; unlike in Athens, they could even own property, though they had no voice in citizen assemblies. But in every other respect, Spartan society was intensely conservative. Having established their laws and their constitution in (probably) the seventh century BCE, the Spartans would resolutely stick to them for centuries thereafter. Whenever they looked beyond their own borders, the form of government they liked to see in neighbouring states was oligarchy. But the Spartans' own system was like no other.[18]

In Athens, on the other hand, the balance of power was continually shifting, and the Athenian constitution had to evolve to keep pace. By 500 BCE, Athens had experienced each of the three possible types of government that the *polis* system had thrown up: oligarchy at first, tyranny in the second half of the sixth century, and then finally an early form of democracy. The precise mechanisms that enabled the mass of the people (*demos*) to take power (*kratos*) have been much discussed. The information that has come down to us is incomplete and often distorted by later biases.

The last tyrant of Athens, Hippias, was expelled in 510 BCE—by an army from Sparta which seems to have been trying to meddle in internal Athenian politics. In the ensuing turmoil, one of the rival factions in Athens promised 'power to the people' in return for popular support. Quite how or why it worked we do not know for sure. But the fact is that it did. Cleisthenes, the leader of the winning faction, went on to introduce a far-reaching set of reforms. Another half century would pass before the Athenian constitution would become fully *democratic* and the word itself was coined. But however opaque its origins, the world's first functioning democracy is usually said to have been created in Athens during the years 508–507 BCE.[19]

EVERY *POLIS*, FROM Athens and Sparta down to the smallest, was fiercely jealous of its autonomy. The Greek word *autonomia* was coined in the fifth century BCE and originally referred to the freedom of the state to make its own laws. It also meant that no state could legislate beyond its own borders without encroaching on the autonomy of another. Relations among independent, self-governing *poleis* were as much open to competition, negotiation, and argument as were those among citizens and groups within each one of them. But the Greeks of the ancient world never did find a satisfactory way to regulate these relationships, one that would have been comparable to the invention of 'politics' within the *polis*.

On the occasions when city-states did work together, it was usually in temporary alliances for mutual self-protection. To justify these arrangements, Greeks liked to appeal to shared ancestry. But the evidence suggests that most, if not all, stories about distant ancestors were invented after the fact. Settlements that could trace their foundation back to a 'mother city' (*metropolis*) in the Greek heartland might draw on that city in later times for support—or commonly, in practice, vice versa. But this only highlights the remarkable degree of independence enjoyed by even small and far-flung *poleis*. There was never any expectation that a mother city would exercise any form of political control over 'its own' foundations abroad; whenever a *metropolis* tried, it usually ended badly. That is one more reason why the term *colony*, with its associations of wars of independence and twentieth-century decolonisation, is so badly suited to describe a Greek *apoikia*.[20]

A looser basis for alliances could sometimes be the three main dialects (strictly speaking, groups of dialects) that made up the Greek-speaking world. Western Greek dialects (also, confusingly, spoken throughout the southern Aegean, including Crete and the southernmost parts of the Anatolian coast) were known as Doric. On the eastern side of the Aegean, but also in Athens, the Ionic group was spoken. Aeolic was spoken farther north, mainly in the northern Aegean islands, the northern Aegean coast of what is now Turkey, and the Greek coast and its hinterland from Thessaly southwards as far as Boeotia. A convenient mythology identified the speakers of each dialect as the descendants of a common ancestor and gave them collective names: Dorians, Ionians, and Aeolians. It was among Ionic speakers that the first attempt at building a political confederacy was made, perhaps as early as the seventh century

BCE. A sanctuary called the Panionion (meaning 'All-Ionian', or 'Of All Ionians') served as a meeting point for representatives from a dozen city-states in western Anatolia. Not to be outdone, the Aeolians farther north seem to have set up something similar.[21] On the other side of the Aegean, the Spartans would often exploit their supposed kinship with other Doric-speaking states to claim a leading role among them.

Despite these partial exceptions, the default position for every city-state was complete autonomy for its citizen body, at all times and at all costs. Citizens expected they would have to fight to maintain it. 'The battlements of a *polis* are its fighting men,' memorably declared the poet Alcaeus, writing on the island of Lesbos in the late seventh century BCE. And Aristotle, three hundred years later, though he accepted that human beings could be enslaved, could not imagine the same for a *polis*. 'It would be unthinkable,' he said, 'to give the name of *polis* to something that was by nature enslaved, since a *polis* is independent and the condition of a slave is not.'[22]

And so, as rival states fought to maintain their much-prized freedom from each other, the *polis* system brought about a revolution in the Greek way of war. Homer's heroes had fought in chaotic hand-to-hand encounters between self-declared champions, who drove to and from the field in chariots. In the new kind of warfare, lines of heavily armoured infantrymen, known as 'hoplites', faced each other in phalanxes (we still use the same word). Each member of the phalanx was protected on one side by the shield of his neighbour. If you fought in a phalanx, your survival in battle would depend on the man next to you (unless you were unfortunate enough to be on the end of the line). It was a tactic that would dismay enemies whose forces were very much larger. And it worked because hoplite armies were above all *citizen* armies. At the same time, new, larger, and faster ships were being designed and built. These were crewed by banks of oarsmen who had literally to pull together in order to ram an enemy. Once again, in battle the survival of one depended on the combined actions of all.[23]

For hundreds of years, war was endemic among Greek city-states. Mutual suspicion was the norm. 'Autonomy' was the prize. These were all-or-nothing, zero-sum struggles, with no quarter given. And yet all these people spoke the same language. The differences among dialects were never enough to make one speaker incomprehensible to another. They all feared and begged favours from the same gods and in much the same ways (though there were plenty of local variations, too). By the sixth century BCE, the quarrelsome family of immortals described by Homer had expanded to become the 'twelve Olympians', whose names and attributes were now widespread, if not yet quite universal throughout the Greek-speaking world.

Zeus was king and often called the 'father' of the others—although Poseidon was his brother and Hera, his queen, was also his sister. Apart from Zeus, each had a special sphere of influence: Poseidon ruled over the sea and was responsible for earthquakes. Athena was the goddess of wisdom, Aphrodite of sexual love, Apollo of light and poetry, though the arrows fired from his bow were notoriously deadly. Ares personified war, Dionysus the emotions and intoxication, Hermes trickery. A city would boast a patron deity, in some ways the equivalent of a patron saint in later times; the best-known case is Athena as the protectress of Athens. But sometimes the worship of particular gods would become attached to places that were, politically speaking, in the middle of nowhere. And this is how a network grew up of religious sanctuaries that drew worshippers from every corner of the Greek world, in the process cutting right across the fragmented world of the *poleis* and the more loosely organised *ethne*.[24]

One of these was on the tiny island of Delos in the middle of the Cyclades, the birthplace, according to legend, of Apollo and his twin sister, the virgin huntress Artemis. Another, perched on a steep mountainside on the flank of the Parnassus massif in central Greece, was at Delphi. There, Apollo would answer the questions put to him by mortals through his infallible but often inscrutable oracle. Olympia, the third, lay on the bank of a shallow river among the wooded hills of the northwest Peloponnese and was dedicated to Zeus, the king of Olympus. From small beginnings, religious centres at all three would expand their influence over several centuries.[25]

Regular festivals dedicated to the gods worshipped at each of these sanctuaries provided a mechanism for the elites of city-states that most of the rest of the time were at war with one another to meet, argue and negotiate, display their prowess, and vie for prestige.[26] This was the origin of the ritualised tests of physical strength and skill that would become the forerunners of modern athletics (needless to say, another Greek word, from a root meaning originally 'to struggle' or 'to compete'). The games held every four years at Olympia were said to have been established in the year 776 BCE (according to our system of counting). From that time on, the Olympic Games would be a regular fixture in the ancient world for over a thousand years.

During the period of the Games, and for an interval on either side, an 'Olympic truce' was declared so that competitors and sponsors could travel freely. All states that sent competitors were obliged to respect this truce—the clearest indication, surely, that the organisers recognised these festivals as a benign surrogate for war.[27] Competitors and spectators travelled by sea from the ends of the Mediterranean and the Black Sea and by land from the mountainous hinterland as far north as Macedonia—then an outlandish place in the eyes of other Greeks. Numbers may have been modest at first. But when the stadium at Olympia was enlarged in the fifth century BCE, it could accommodate a crowd of forty thousand.

By that time, athletic contests had been established as part of regular religious festivals at other sanctuaries too. One of these, at Delphi, was known as the Pythian Games. Another was at Isthmia near Corinth, on the isthmus that joins the Peloponnese to the rest of the Greek peninsula; the fourth, at Nemea in the northern Peloponnese.[28] A Greek-speaking world was emerging that was at once thoroughly interconnected and deeply fragmented. What kept it fragmented was the autonomy of each *polis*. Delos, Delphi, and Olympia were the nodes through which connections were channelled.

It was from these religious centres, too, and hesitantly at first, that there began to spread the first stirrings of a shared sense of identity as 'Hellenes'. Originally, this had been the name of a small group living in the kingdom of the legendary Achilles. The name 'Hellas', which in the *Iliad* had defined a region within that small kingdom, expanded in meaning to cover everywhere that Hellenes, that is to say, Greek speakers, lived. But this kind of collective consciousness was most probably still in its infancy as late as 500 BCE. And in any case, it was a far cry from anything that could be called political cooperation, let alone unity.[29]

WHILE THE AGE of experiment lasted, Greeks were discovering themselves and their place in the world in a variety of other ways, too. New generations of poets composed and performed verses that for the first time brought into the public domain intimate aspects of what it *feels* like to be human. We know the work of these poets only through quotations by later writers or from chance finds of papyri in the Egyptian desert—which show that some of these poets, at least, were still being read a millennium after their lifetime. So far as we can tell, their poems were mostly short and designed

89

to be sung to the accompaniment of a musical instrument. This is why both the poems and their composers have come to be known as 'lyric', from the plucked lyre. Many of these poets evoke the joys of wine, the effects of age on hope and desire, the cattiness of envy, and the trading of insults—everyday concerns caught in language of sudden immediacy. In the middle of the seventh century BCE, Archilochus, from the island of Paros in the Cyclades, captured in elegant verse the anatomical details as well as the sensations involved in what sounds like a session of group sex.[30]

Most famous of all was Sappho of Lesbos. Her life seems to have spanned the decades on either side of the year 600 BCE. She it was whose evocations of love and sex between women and girls long ago gave the world the word *lesbian*. In many Greek city-states, male homosexuality, particularly between middle-aged men and adolescent boys, was an accepted adjunct to the education curriculum and often praised ahead of heterosexual love.[31] In Lesbos, the same applied to women. But it was not the local attitude to homosexuality, whether female or male, that made the island of Lesbos exceptional in the ancient Greek world. It was not even, probably, the fact that it was possible for women and young girls to come together in some kind of social setting, just as men did. What was extraordinary was that the poems Sappho composed and sang made it into *writing*, and so established a literary reputation that ever since has far outstripped the circle of her actual readers.

Sappho's poems radiate a sense of joyous self-discovery. For once, the preoccupations of warriors, male athletes, and the competing male citizens of the *polis* are put roundly in their place:

> *Some think a fleet, a troop of horse*
> *or soldiery the finest sight*
> *in all the world; but I say, what one loves.*

Observing a young girl flirting with a man, Sappho is so taken with the girl's beauty that she vicariously shares in the physiological response of her lover:

> *speech fails me,*
> *my tongue is paralysed, at once*
> *a light fire runs beneath my skin,*
> *my eyes are blinded, and my ears drumming,*
> *the sweat pours down me, and I shake*
> *all over, sallower than grass:*
> *I feel as if I'm not far off dying.*[32]

Still, for all the startling intimacy of these poems, written more than two and a half millennia ago, there is nothing in early Greek lyric of the private introspection that we often associate with 'lyrical' poetry in later times. So far as we can tell, these poets performed their works before an audience. Often this would be a close-knit group, gathered in a private house to eat and drink together, in what was called a *symposium*. Other occasions were more public, sometimes involving a whole choir of performers. Even if the circle of listeners was quite small, the physical presence of others and the act of performance were essential to the poem's conception and composition. So, too, must have been the responses, though of course these have not been recorded. The presence in the poems of real individuals, who may well have been part of the audience and who even had a 'right of reply' in their turn, anchors the intimate and the personal in an immediate, tangible community of equals.

In the visual arts, beginning a little before the lifetime of Sappho, Greek towns and cities became peopled with stone or bronze replicas of their citizens. Life-sized or slightly larger statues started appearing in great numbers in sanctuaries and graveyards all over the Greek-speaking world. A similar figure, erected inside a temple to represent the god or goddess worshipped there, might be up to four times natural size. But most represented ordinary citizens. In graveyards, the stone effigies of the dead stood tall, stark naked if they had been men, decorously draped if they had been women. Every one of them stared straight ahead at the viewer, as they still do in museums today, every one of them still smiling the same enigmatic smile, and always, eternally young.

The technology and the techniques of execution came from Egypt. The Egyptians had been raising monumental statues in their temples and royal palaces for centuries. But even if the earliest Greek statues 'look' Egyptian, the *uses* to which Greek sculptors put the newly learned technology were all their own. Human statues in ancient Egypt were made to overawe the viewer with the power of the pharaoh. But there was no one with that kind of status in a Greek *polis*. Not even a 'tyrant' could impose himself on his fellow citizens so blatantly. Greek gods, too, looked quite different from the strange hybrid forms of Egyptian gods: part human, part animal or bird. When the gods and goddesses of Mount Olympus began to take form in stone or bronze, they were always entirely human—just as they are described in the Homeric epics. Greeks worshipped superior beings who looked and behaved just like immortal versions of themselves. And their better-off citizens were prepared to go to great trouble and expense to have their own selves, and their loved ones, represented in the same way.[33]

Today, the statues that represent citizens are known respectively by the ancient Greek words for a boy or young man (*kouros*, plural *kouroi*) and for a girl or young woman (*kore*, plural *korai*). The poses are unnatural, the proportions derived as much from geometry as from anatomy. Even the famous 'archaic smile' has been explained in terms of the 'difficulties of carving the transition from mouth to cheek'.[34] Whether they were carved from shining white marble or from duller limestone or sandstone, the finish included paint for hair, eyes, and the drapery of the *korai* in colours that by modern standards would probably seem garish. Quite how the flesh of the naked males would have appeared is harder to tell. According to a very ancient convention, begun by the Egyptians and followed by the Minoans and Mycenaeans in their time, men's skin was represented by a reddish-brown pigment, women's by white. The assumption, in later times, that ancient Greek art had established an ideal of the *white* male body is sometimes still repeated. But it is not based in fact.

Neither the sculptors of this period nor the patrons who commissioned them as yet had any great interest in trying to reproduce the likeness of an individual—any more than the lyric poets spoke of truly private experience. On the other hand, behind the standardised poses and the fixed, enigmatic smiles, there *is* something individual about many of those creations. This is where the new technology of stone- and bronze-working meets the only slightly older technology of alphabetic writing. An early male figurine from Thebes, cast in bronze and evidently commissioned as an offering meant to stand in a temple courtyard, bears the words, in verse, carved into its legs:

> *Manticlus dedicated me to the far-shooter, silver-bowed god*
> *[i.e., Apollo],*
> *As a tithe. Phoebus [Apollo], provide a gift in return.*

There is something touchingly transactional about this attempt to negotiate with the divine, which the modern term *piety* doesn't come near to capturing. You give the god an expensive present— and you don't just hope or pray, you *ask* him outright for a favour in return.[35]

In a graveyard, it was the statue itself, and not the dead person it was supposed to represent, who was imagined as speaking in the inscription: 'Marker of Phrasikleia. I shall ever be called maiden, the gods allotting me this title in place of marriage: Aristion of Paros made me.' It is the *absence* of a loved person that the 'marker' perpetuates. The statue itself, standing dignified and holding between her breasts what appears to be a flower, perhaps the virginity that was never 'plucked', both speaks to us and looks at us.[36]

By the end of the sixth century BCE, then, Greeks were using both words and images to put down markers of who they were. And it wasn't only in solemn, public spaces that this was happening. Within the home, too, citizens were getting used to seeing images of their own kind reproduced—on the plates, cups, and mixing bowls that they handled daily. During the sixth century BCE, work produced by the potters and vase painters of two Greek cities, first Corinth and then Athens, was in demand all over the Greek-speaking world and even beyond. Some of the images displayed on these prized objects were of monsters or of fantastic hybrids, creatures of legend such as satyrs (half-man, half-goat), Egyptian sphinxes (a human face on the body of a lion), and centaurs (half-man, half-horse). But mostly they were images of male humans. Women are not absent but tend to appear only in the guise of goddesses or famous characters from legend. And the same dress code used on statues was usually, though not invariably, applied on painted pots.[37] It was the image of the Greek male, painted in profile with jutting chin, beard, and not infrequently, erect penis, too, that by the end of the century had become part of the furniture, in daily use all over the Mediterranean and Black Sea coasts.

This was an artform so taken for granted by everyone who ever dined and drank at a *symposium* that it earned barely a single mention in the work of any ancient Greek author.[38] For us today, these paintings in their thousands, recovered whole from graves or painstakingly reassembled by archaeologists from broken household crockery, offer fascinating glimpses into what it must have felt like to be Greek in the sixth century BCE and into the ways that Greek speakers of that time saw and thought about themselves.

In these images, naked athletes show off their prowess, flexing their muscles or wrestling an opponent to the ground, just as they did daily in exercise grounds in cities and sanctuaries all over the Greek-speaking world. Soldiers appear in full armour, topped by the forbidding bronze helmet of a type that survives in many museum exhibits today, with the prominent nose guard that leaves only narrow spaces for the wearer to see out. Another favourite type of scene shows animals being brought to sacrifice in a sacred grove or in front of a temple. Drinking vessels often show diners reclining and enjoying food, wine, and conversation at a *symposium*, the setting in which many of these objects would have been used.

More surprising to modern tastes, and shocking to earlier generations of classicists, are the scenes of courtship and sex. Some show gifts being offered as a preliminary to a tryst. Usually, these feature an older man and a younger man, though sometimes girls appear as well. Others depict sex acts between men, often with sufficient realism to suggest that the participants are thoroughly enjoying themselves.[39] It seems that the activities celebrated by poets such as Archilochus were in vogue as subjects to be represented on household crockery for use in smart homes. This was another way in which Greek society of this early period liked to look at itself—and successfully promoted the resulting images among not just its own members but outsiders too.

GREEKS AT THIS time were also looking outward at the world around them. The study of 'Nature' (*Physis*, giving us our word *physics*) would lay the foundation for much of modern science. Egyptians and Babylonians had already, for centuries, been probing the mysteries of the heavens and investigating the properties of numbers and shapes. Greeks who lived in cities on the Anatolian coast probably had the best access to these older discoveries. One of these cities, Miletus, was the home of the first Greeks to make a systematic study of them. Beginning about 600 BCE, Thales, Anaximenes, and Anaximander, all from Miletus, began to expound theories and discoveries of their own to explain the visible universe.

Before long, they and their successors in many different parts of the Greek world would come to be known by the Greek term *philosophoi*, which literally means 'lovers of wisdom'. They were the first philosophers. But they were also, because 'wisdom' was not compartmentalised in those days, the first scientists and the first mathematicians. Exactly how much they learned from the older civilisations of the Near and Middle East is debated today. What is not in doubt is that they invented an entirely new method, which lies at the root of all these disciplines as they have developed ever since. The method derives directly from the politics of the *polis*. In the same way that citizens argued about what we still call 'policy', philosophers constructed logical arguments that started from the evidence of the visible world in order to probe underlying causes. And in this way was born the concept, central to all mathematics and science, of *proof*.[40]

It can be hard to reconstruct in detail what these early philosophers thought and what they achieved; their writings have been preserved only in fragments, through the quotations of other, much later writers, who usually had their own philosophical axe to grind. The little we know about their careers shows that many of them took full advantage of the general mobility at the time. Pythagoras of Samos, in the later sixth century BCE, went all the way to Croton, in today's Calabria, to found what would become known as a 'school' of mathematics. Xenophanes, originally from Colophon, an Ionian city not far from Ephesus on the Aegean coast of Anatolia, is said to have travelled all over the Greek world from about 570 BCE during a life that spanned almost a century. Xenophanes was a poet as much as a philosopher and it is not clear how systematic his thinking may have been. He was the first Greek we know of to break with the traditional stories about the gods of Olympus and to argue instead that 'there is one god, greatest among gods and men, similar to mortals neither in shape nor in thought'. It was a very human error, he declared, to suppose that the gods look like ourselves: if cows, horses, or lions could draw shapes, he posited, they would draw their gods in the shape of cows, horses, or lions.[41]

Back on the Anatolian coast, Heraclitus of Ephesus was active during the decades either side of 500 BCE. He may have been the first to articulate the idea that the universe can be explained in terms of fixed laws, the natural equivalent of the laws that governed the Greek city-state. According to Heraclitus, the *cosmos* in which we all live had been created by 'none of the gods or men . . . but it always was and is and shall be: an ever-living fire, kindling in measures and going out in measures'. This is the earliest known use of the Greek word *cosmos* in the sense that it still has in many languages today, equivalent to 'the universe'. The original meaning of the word is 'order' or 'arrangement'.[42] Implicit in what Heraclitus says, then, is the idea that the natural universe is rationally ordered, even though no rational being created it. And its processes are governed by 'measures'—meaning, in Greek as in English today, a regularity that is capable of being measured. Modern science begins with Heraclitus of Ephesus.

FOR AS LONG as no serious predator existed to threaten them, the 'ants or frogs' remained perfectly content to thrive, prosper, and fight among themselves around their pond. This state of affairs lasted for almost two hundred years. But in the middle of the sixth century BCE, predators for the first time appeared on the scene. In the east, Croesus, the fabulously rich king of Lydia, from his capital at Sardis expanded the bounds of his kingdom until it drew in all the Greek settlements of western Anatolia during the decade between 560 and 550 BCE. In the west, Carthage, originally a Phoenician settlement in what is now Tunisia, had become the nucleus of a powerful local kingdom and was beginning to threaten the Greek cities of Sicily.[43] But those threats were as nothing compared to the sudden emergence of the empire of the Medes and Persians under its king, Kurash, known in Greek as Cyrus, who came to the throne in 559 BCE.

During a reign of thirty years, Cyrus extended Persian control from the Aegean Sea to the Caspian and far to the east into modern Afghanistan and Pakistan. His successor, Cambyses II, would conquer Egypt, the two-and-a-half-thousand-year-old kingdom of the pharaohs, to create the largest, most centralised empire the world had yet seen. And after Cyrus defeated the Lydians under Croesus in 546 BCE, one by one the Greek cities of Anatolia were brought under Persian rule.[44] A whole slice of the shore around the pond had been gobbled up. What were the Greek communities to do?

One solution was to remember past mobility and up sticks once more. According to the historian Herodotus, writing in Athens about a century after the events he describes, the people of the coastal city of Phocaea (today's Foça, in the Izmir province of Turkey), under cover of night:

> launched their galleys, put aboard their women and children and moveable property, including the statues and other sacred objects from their temples—everything, in fact, except paintings, and images made of bronze or marble—and sailed for Chios. . . . They also dropped a lump of iron into the sea and swore never to return to Phocaea until it floated up again.

The nearby island of Chios was only a temporary stopping place. The fleeing Phocaeans went on to build a new city, far away in Corsica. But after several decades, under mounting pressure from Carthaginians and Etruscans, they had to abandon it and moved to the toe of Italy instead, where many Greek settlements were already thriving. In the new world of the late sixth century BCE, the free-and-easy mobility of an earlier time was no longer a reliable solution.

Herodotus devotes several pages to the defiance of the Phocaeans. But he notes only one other example. Everywhere else, the Greek cities of Anatolia submitted to their new overlords.[45] Persian rule was devolved to regional potentates known as 'satraps' (soon to become a dirty word in Greek, as it still is to this day). The satraps, in turn, were content to allow the Greek city-states to manage their internal affairs, provided they stayed loyal. The Greeks who benefited the most from this arrangement seem to have been the elites. Prominent men and leading families vied with one another to secure the backing of the satrap, or of the Great King himself, in order to exercise the role of tyrant in their city. Some humbler Greeks even migrated in the opposite direction from the Phocaeans, to wind up as labourers or artisans in the Persian capital, Persepolis.[46]

First to wake up to the new threat, on the western side of the Aegean, was Sparta. At some point in the 540s BCE, while the Persians under Cyrus were seizing one Greek city-state in western Anatolia after another, the Spartans sent a delegation to the Great King: if he didn't desist at once, they would take it upon themselves to intervene to protect their fellow Greeks. As the story is told by Herodotus, Cyrus had never heard of Sparta and had to prevail on his Greek subjects to explain who these people were who thought they could threaten him. In any case, nothing more came of it. For the next half century, the Spartans concentrated their military efforts against other Greek city-states on their own side of the Aegean.[47]

By the final decade of the sixth century BCE, a combination of military conquest and asymmetrical treaties had brought most of the Peloponnese under the domination of Sparta. Spartan phalanxes began to venture across the Isthmus of Corinth. This was how the last tyrant of Athens, Hippias, came to be expelled from the city by a Spartan army. Two years later, the democratic reforms begun by Cleisthenes were proving even less to the liking of the Spartans than the tyrant had been. In 506, the Spartan hoplites were back at the gates of Athens, this time demanding the expulsion of Cleisthenes. In a moment of desperation, the Athenians turned to the new rising power in the east. The Great King of the Medes and Persians was now Daryaush, known to the Greeks as Darius I. Would *he* help them out?

It is once again Herodotus who tells the story. The satrap who interviewed the Athenian envoys was as bemused as Cyrus two generations earlier had been by the Spartans. The answer was only to be expected: 'If the Athenians would signify their submission by the usual gift of earth and water, then Darius would make a pact with them; otherwise, they had better go home.' By the time the envoys returned to Athens, having made the necessary act of submission, the Spartan troops had gone home, too. With the immediate threat withdrawn, the city's democratic rulers were not best pleased to be told what their envoys had done in their name. But nobody ever got round to rescinding the formal acknowledgement of Persian overlordship.[48]

Then, in 499 BCE, after almost half a century of subjection, revolt broke out in Miletus. Its immediate target was probably not so much the Persians directly as those local Greek elites who relied on Persian favour. Other Ionian cities of the Anatolian seaboard joined in. Thus began the one brief moment of glory for the confederacy known as the Panionion. The Ionians sent desperate messages for help to the free city-states on the western side of the Aegean. Sparta refused. But the Athenians offered a small contingent, even though Athens was not yet a naval power, had few ships to spare, and was still, technically, a Persian vassal. Support also came from the tiny city-state of Eretria in southern Euboea. Once the rebels and their allies had assembled at Miletus, they sailed north along the coast to Ephesus, disembarked, and marched upcountry to Sardis, the former capital of the Lydian kingdom and the present seat of the local Persian satrap. They failed to take the fortress but instead set fire to the city before retreating to the coast. There they were routed by a Persian counterattack. This was enough for the Athenians and the Eretrians, who abandoned the campaign and sailed for home.[49]

It seems that the rebels were poorly led and had no clearly defined objectives. Even so, the Ionians carried on, without external help, for five years. Defeat came finally in the sea battle of Lade, off Miletus, when the combined navies of the rebel city-states faced an even larger fleet of warships mustered by the Persians from their Phoenician subjects. The reprisals ordered by the Persian king, Darius, were horrific. As Herodotus tells the tale:

> Once the towns were in their hands, the best-looking boys were chosen for castration and made into eunuchs; the most beautiful girls were dragged from their homes and sent to Darius' court, and the towns themselves, temples and all, were burnt to the ground.

The last item is amply confirmed by the archaeological record, which shows that parts of Miletus were destroyed so thoroughly that they were never rebuilt.[50] By the time the 'Ionian Revolt' was over, in the summer of 494 BCE, Darius had thoroughly consolidated his grip on western Anatolia and was beginning to look farther afield. Already, Persian power was reaching across the Hellespont and would soon extend westwards through Thrace and into Macedonia.

The Athenians and Eretrians had achieved nothing by their intervention—other than to make themselves noticed. According to an anecdote reported by Herodotus, when news of the burning of Sardis reached Darius, he had first to ask who the Athenians were. On being told, the story continues, the Great King of the Medes and Persians reached immediately for his bow and shot an arrow into the air, crying aloud, 'Grant, O God, that I may punish the Athenians.' Like so many of Herodotus's stories, this one is probably too good to be true. The same can be said of the sequel—that from that time onwards, Darius had a servant repeat to him three times before he sat down to dinner each day, 'Master, remember the Athenians.'[51] But by 494 BCE, the new predator on their doorstep most definitely had the Greek city-states to the west of the Aegean in his sights.

4

THE FIRST WORLD WARS
AND THE 'CLASSICAL' AGE
494 BCE–404 BCE

I T IS ENTIRELY characteristic of the Greek world of independent city-states that during the very years when the Persians were preparing to move against them, both Sparta and Athens were engaged in bitter fighting on their respective doorsteps. In the summer of 494 BCE, at the same moment that the Persians crushed the last Greek resistance on the eastern side of the Aegean, the Spartans came the nearest they had done, yet, to knocking out the only rival that still stood out against them in the Peloponnese. This was Argos, the inheritor of the Mycenaean kingdoms of Mycenae and Tiryns, whose conical hill surmounted by a medieval castle is still a conspicuous landmark, not far from today's Nafplio. Spartan troops under King Cleomenes failed to take the city but killed most of its men of fighting age by setting fire to a wood in which they had taken refuge.

Athens at the same time had been locked for several decades in conflict with neighbouring Thebes to the north and with the island of Aegina to the south. Thebes, today a small market town, is less than an hour's drive from central Athens. Aegina can be reached in an even shorter time from the port of Piraeus. And yet in the early fifth century BCE, this island was home to a prosperous and

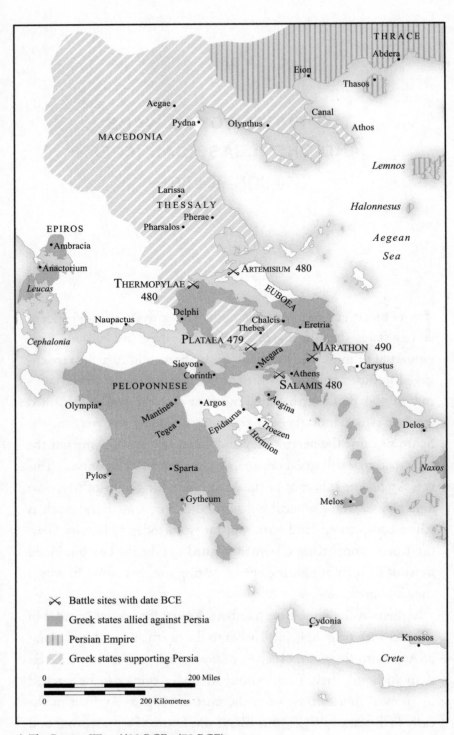

4. The Persian Wars (490 BCE–479 BCE)

proudly independent seafaring people, who were viciously at odds with the gentlemen farmers of Attica. Deadly though these local struggles were, their scale was tiny when set beside the looming threat from the largest empire in the world.[1]

As the fateful year of 490 BCE approached, both Athens and Sparta were also riven by internal dissensions. In the case of Sparta, these were serious enough to rock the very foundations of the state. The two kings, who according to Spartan custom ruled jointly, Cleomenes and Demaratus, had been at one another's throats for over twenty years. In 491 BCE, in effect, each moved to depose the other. The upshot was that Demaratus fled to Persian-controlled Anatolia. There, he was rewarded with a gift of lands and a position of trust by Darius. Within a year, Cleomenes had allegedly gone mad and is supposed to have committed suicide in prison, although it is more probable that he was murdered.[2] In Athens, tensions were not quite so high but still sufficient to threaten the stability of the state's new and still very experimental democracy. Memories of the deposed tyrants ran deep—and were perhaps also deliberately blackened by those who had most to lose should they return. Hippias was still alive; like his Spartan counterpart Demaratus, he was thriving under the protection of the Great King of Persia. For both cities, a Persian victory would be likely to bring back their own discredited rulers as compliant satraps.

In the same year, 491 BCE, Darius sent envoys to all the Greek city-states on the western side of the Aegean, inviting them to send the ritual gift of earth and water that would bind them as his vassals. Most complied. But at Athens the Persian emissaries 'were thrown into the pit like criminals. At Sparta they were pushed into a well—and told that if they wanted earth and water for the king, to get them from there'.[3]

After this defiance, a Persian fleet set sail from Anatolia in 490 BCE. In command were the satraps Datis and Artaphernes.

From Samos in the eastern Aegean, the ships headed west, through the archipelago. Eretria and Athens, the cities that had taken part in the Ionian Revolt, were among the first targets. Eretria was destroyed after a short siege. It was then to be the turn of Athens. The Persians were guided by local knowledge obligingly provided by Hippias, the former tyrant, who travelled along with them as an honoured guest. The expedition landed in the wide sandy bay of Marathon, on the coast of Attica nearest to Euboea. The plain of Marathon was ideal terrain for the Persian cavalry. Against them stood the Athenian citizen army, drawn up in a phalanx and supported by a small contingent from the Boeotian town of Plataea. When they knew that the Persian landing was imminent, the Athenians had sent a runner to Sparta to appeal for reinforcements. Pheidippides, the runner, covered the distance of almost 150 miles in under two days—despite which the Spartans found a pretext to delay their arrival until after the battle was over.[4]

Commanded by a general named Miltiades, who had seen service against the Persians during the Ionian Revolt, the Athenian hoplites charged the much larger Persian force at a run. By day's end, the Persians had retreated in disarray to their ships and were desperately pushing out to sea. Precisely 192 Athenians lost their lives in the battle, according to Herodotus. They were buried with full honours under a mound which today rises some forty feet above the plain of Marathon. A smaller number of Plataean dead were similarly honoured. An exact count of the Persian forces and their losses will never be known. Herodotus claimed six thousand four hundred were killed.

But the Persian fleet had escaped intact. The ships were already on their way round Cape Sounion. They could be expected to reach Phaleron, at that time the port of Athens, the next day. The entire Athenian army was camped at Marathon. If the Persians were to reach Athens first, there would be no one to stop them taking the city. There was nothing for it but a forced march over the shoulder of Mount Pentelikon, back to Athens. The hoplites covered the distance, reckoned at twenty-six miles by the shortest route, presumably still carrying their full kit, and arrived before the fleet was yet in sight. It was in emulation of this feat that the marathon race, named after the battle site, would be devised and run for the first time when the Olympic Games were revived in Athens in 1896.[5]

By the time the Persian ships reached Phaleron, it was too late for a surprise attack on Athens. They lay at anchor offshore for a few days, no doubt gazing at the temples crowning the Acropolis, clearly visible in the distance, and watching the manoeuvres of the Athenian hoplites on the plain between. Then Datis gave the order, and the ships set sail, back to the Anatolian coast. The first attempt by the Persian Empire to extend itself into the western side of the Aegean had ended ignominiously.

IT WOULD TAKE the Persians a full ten years to regroup and try again. Quite how the Spartan dual monarchy and the Athenian emerging democracy made use of the respite is a little mysterious. Sparta had two new, untried kings, who would have had their hands full rebuilding trust in the system after the debacle of 491–490 BCE. Leotychidas II had to live down the awkward fact that his predecessor and kinsman Demaratus was still alive and well, living in Anatolia as the guest of the Great King of Persia. Leonidas I, married to the daughter of the disgraced Cleomenes, would become a household name only at the very end of his ten-year reign. Along with the citizens' committees to which they were to some extent accountable, the Spartan kings would have been as watchful as ever of the domestic threat posed by the enslaved helots at home and their still defiant neighbours in Argos.[6]

In Athens, the new democratic institutions were struggling to cope with renewed internal tensions. A remarkable innovation, seemingly intended as a kind of safety valve, was tried out for the first time two years after the victory at Marathon. On a given day, every citizen was invited to inscribe on a discarded piece of broken pot the name of someone he wanted to see exiled from the city for the next ten years. The practice became known as 'ostracism', from the Greek word for the sherd on which the names were written or painted (*ostrakon*). Many of these primitive voting slips survive today, along with the evidence that vote rigging goes all the way back to the invention of the popular ballot itself. Out of a hoard of nearly two hundred sherds on which the same name was written, archaeologists have identified the handwriting of only fourteen individuals.[7] More striking still is the identity of the intended victim. It is one of the most famous names in all Greek history: Themistocles.

Described as 'a man of heroic features, as well as heroic temperament', Themistocles was not above manipulating the system of ostracism to clear the ground of rivals and reach the highest elected offices of the Athenian state. His own turn to fall victim would come later. But it was fortunate for Athens that this was the man who emerged, during the 480s BCE, to become one of the most far-sighted and effective political and military leaders that the city would ever have. It was Themistocles who persuaded the Athenians to settle their long-running differences with Aegina, to build a new fortified port at Piraeus (where several natural harbours were more defensible than the wide beach at Phaleron), and to raise a fleet of armed warships to match. All this happened between 483 and 481 BCE.[8]

By this time, Darius had died and had been succeeded as Great King by one of his sons, Xerxes. In 483 BCE, Xerxes turned his attention to his father's unfinished business in the west. This time, nothing was to be left to chance. The new invasion would be an amphibious operation. To prepare the way for the foot soldiers, a bridge was formed across the strait of the Dardanelles by lashing together hundreds of boats to link Asia to Europe. To ensure a safe passage for the ships in the notoriously stormy waters of the northern Aegean, a canal was dug through the isthmus that separates the promontory of Mount Athos from the mainland. The total strength of the expedition was reckoned by the Greeks at three million men under arms. Modern scholars dismiss these numbers as fantasy, as they also do Herodotus's implausibly exact figure of 2,641,610. But the number of warships, given as just over one thousand two hundred, has some corroboration and is enough to give a sense of war being mounted on a scale never before seen in the small world of the Greek city-states.[9]

As Darius had done before him, Xerxes sent emissaries ahead of the expedition. Cities and regions that voluntarily accepted Persian rule would not be molested. This time, too, most complied. But those that were determined to resist began to work on a concerted plan of action. A defensive league was formed, under the leadership of Sparta. Envoys were even sent to the distant Greek cities of Sicily and south Italy. But as luck would have it, this was just the time when that other predator, Carthage, was flexing its muscles in the western Mediterranean. In 480 BCE, decisive battles would be fought in Sicily, too, against the Carthaginians. So there was no help to be had from that quarter.[10]

In the end, only thirty-one city-states, out of several hundred that existed on the western side of the Aegean, formed the alliance that prepared to stand against Xerxes. Of these, no more than three were of significant size or strength: Sparta, Athens, and Corinth; Thebes would notoriously join the other side when it came to the final battle. Of the remainder, seven were based on small islands in the Aegean. The rest were about evenly split between small communities (some of them tiny) in the northern Peloponnese and the southern part of the Greek mainland, with a few outliers on the coasts of Macedonia and Epiros farther north.[11] Once it was known that the Persians were on their way, tension arose among the allies. Should the main line of defence be drawn at the Isthmus of Corinth, as the Spartans proposed? The Spartans had always been half-hearted about extending their influence north of the isthmus. And Spartan strategy was always based on land warfare. This was what their highly trained, full-time army of hoplites did best. It took an Athenian to point out that there was no point in fortifying the isthmus if the Persian fleet was left intact to sail round and take the infantrymen from the rear. And so it was agreed. A stand would be made farther north.

A first attempt to hold the coastal pass leading from Macedonia southward into Thessaly was abandoned—which was just as well, because Xerxes led his troops by an inland route instead. From Thessaly, the only way for an army to enter southern Greece was through the narrow pass known as Thermopylae, where the crags of Mount Oeta fell almost sheer to the sea, opposite the tip of Euboea. The name means 'hot gates', referring to a fortified position which contained thermal springs. Today, the sea has receded several miles, so it requires an effort of imagination for the visitor to grasp its strategic importance at the time. But back in 480 BCE, according to Herodotus, the passage between the mountainside and the sea was the equivalent of fifty feet wide, narrowing at some points to only the width of a cart track.[12]

The Spartans and their land-based allies dug in at one end of the pass, while a fleet led by the Athenians gathered a few miles to seaward. Neither the weight of Xerxes's infantry nor his cavalry could make any headway against the Spartan hoplites until a local Greek came forward and offered to show his men a way across the mountain to take the defenders from the rear. After this betrayal, the greater part of the army still had time to make its escape to the south. But Leonidas, the Spartan king, elected to stay, along with the remnant of his three hundred best fighters and a small contingent from Boeotia, to cover the retreat of the rest and fight to the end. The battle of Thermopylae, fought in August 480 BCE, has ever afterwards been remembered for the heroic self-sacrifice of Leonidas and the 'Three Hundred'. At the time, for Sparta and the few allied Greek states still resisting the Persian advance, it was a catastrophic defeat, because it left the route open to Athens, the Isthmus of Corinth, and beyond it, the Peloponnese.

During the days of the battle in the pass, several engagements took place at sea. These were indecisive. The invaders lost more ships to a sudden storm off the coast of Euboea than to action by the newly tested Athenian navy. As autumn drew on, Xerxes's forces began to converge, by land and sea, on Attica. In the face of this advance, the Athenians abandoned their city. Only a few diehards held out, sheltering in the sanctuary of the Acropolis. But then some enterprising Persians scaled the cliffs, opened the gates to the main force, 'and slaughtered those in the sanctuary'. Herodotus goes on, 'Having left not one of them alive, they stripped the temple of its treasures and burnt everything on the Acropolis.'[13] Many of the damaged sculptures, belonging to the old temple of the goddess Athena that was destroyed by the Persians on that occasion, and later buried in the rubble, can today be seen in the Acropolis Museum in Athens.

The Athenians had lost their city. In the eyes of their Peloponnesian allies, that meant also their right to command the allied fleet. It was time to fall back on the Isthmus of Corinth and defend the Peloponnese. But the Athenians still had two hundred warships at sea. Themistocles threatened to put the remnants of his people aboard and sail away with them to Italy. How, then, would the Peloponnese be defended? And so the decision was taken to engage the enemy at once, in a sea battle. Themistocles tricked the Persian commanders into thinking their huge fleet could trap the ships of the Greek allies in the narrow channel that separates the island of Salamis from the mainland of Attica. In the event, it was the invaders who became trapped, as the Greek captains were able to exploit the limited sea room to their advantage. The more unwieldy Persian galleys ended up ramming each other, while the Greek allies kept discipline. The battle lasted all day, with King Xerxes watching from the shore. When it was over, the remains of the Persian fleet limped back to its base at Phaleron.[14]

Salamis was the turning point. But it was not yet the end of the war. Xerxes himself returned to Persia, leaving his second in command, Mardonius, to last out the winter in Boeotia and try to put new momentum into the campaign come the spring. Before Mardonius left Attica, he sacked and burnt for a second time whatever had been left standing in Athens. The final battle was fought in September 479 BCE, near the Boeotian town of Plataea. Herodotus lists more than a dozen small Greek city-states whose troops fought alongside the Spartans and Athenians at Plataea. It was a long and closely fought battle. Mardonius was killed. The Persian retreat turned into a rout. On the same day, if Herodotus is to be believed, on the other side of the Aegean a Greek fleet under the surviving Spartan king, Leotychidas, went into battle against the Persians, who had been guarding their rear. At Mycale, near the island of Samos, the Greek forces won that battle, too.[15]

The 'Persian Wars', as the two campaigns of 490 BCE and 480–479 BCE have been known ever since, were over. Another thirty years would pass before the threat of a third would finally lift. But by the autumn of 479 BCE, the Greek-speaking world had been transformed out of all recognition. And although none of those who had fought could have had any inkling of this, the repercussions of what they had done would still be reverberating around the entire world two and a half thousand years later.

THE PERSIAN WARS have often, since, become a fixed point of reference and comparison. During the Middle Ages, when the Byzantine capital, Constantinople, was repeatedly threatened by Muslims from the east, and even after it had finally fallen to the Ottoman Turks in 1453, historians writing in Greek would regularly describe the enemy not as 'Arabs' or 'Turks' but as 'Persians'. Even though they were fighting for very different things, it would be self-evident to every Byzantine Christian that the struggles of their empire against the forces of Islam were a continuation of the struggles of Athens and Sparta in the fifth century BCE.

In modern times, those ancient battles have been invested with a significance that goes far beyond the limits of the Greek-speaking world. In hindsight, the Persian Wars have come to be seen as the first great conflict between a 'civilised' west and a 'barbarous' east.[16] The British philosopher and imperial civil servant John Stuart Mill, reviewing an influential history of ancient Greek civilisation, wrote in 1846:

> The true ancestors of the European nations are not those from whose blood they are sprung, but those from whom they derive the richest portion of their inheritance. The battle of Marathon even as an event in English history is more important than the battle of Hastings.[17]

It is often said that after the last of Mardonius's troops fled across the Aegean in their ships, or trudged across the bridge of boats that Xerxes had built to span the Dardanelles, the Persians would never again return to threaten the West. But this is a remarkably narrow understanding of the geopolitical history of the European continent. The truth is that Europe has been successfully invaded from the east many times since the Persian Wars—just not, as it happens, by direct descendants of the ancient Medes and Persians. It is not true, then, that the future history of Europe was secured by the Greeks at Marathon, Salamis, and Plataea in the first decades of the fifth century BCE. There must be something else.

The answer lies not in anything that was done on the battlefield but in the way the story came to be told afterwards. It was *Greeks* who told the story. Why else should these wars still, after so long, be called *Persian*? It was once again the invention of the alphabet that enabled the Greeks to tell the story in the way that they did and for it to be preserved ever after. For centuries before this time, victorious rulers had been proclaiming their achievements in writing—in ancient Mesopotamia, Egypt, Assyria, indeed in Persia. But the Greek world was different. This was in part because of the new writing system itself, in part because of the peculiar organisation of the Greek city-states. There *was* no supreme ruler to decree how victory should be commemorated, just as there was no top-down system to control the process. Nobody had a monopoly over the written word. Of all those Greeks who wrote down what they knew and what they thought about the Persian Wars, while the events were still within living memory, two were lucky enough to have their words spread and endure—to the extent that we can still read what they wrote today.

First into action was an Athenian by the name of Aeschylus. Aeschylus, as his epitaph tells us, had fought in the citizen army that defeated Darius's forces at Marathon. He had probably been an eyewitness of the battle of Salamis as well, although, aged about forty-five by that time, he may have been too old for combat. In 472 BCE, just eight years after the battle, Aeschylus's play *The Persians* was put on as part of the annual festival held in Athens in honour of the god Dionysus. What we still call 'drama' was nothing new in the Greek world at this time. From obscure beginnings during the previous century, the acting out of well-known stories in front of the assembled citizens had become an established part of religious rituals in several city-states, and nowhere more so than in Athens. Aeschylus wrote altogether about seventy plays. Only seven of these survive today. But the earliest of these to be written, making it the oldest Greek drama still in existence, was *The Persians*.

Aeschylus sets his drama at Susa, the Persian capital. The elders of the royal court are expecting any day to hear of victories over the Greeks. Instead, a messenger brings news of the disaster at Salamis. The ghost of the dead Darius lends dramatic effect. Then Xerxes himself arrives, humbled and in rags, to general lamentation (following the convention of the time, the play is after all presented as a 'tragedy'). *The Persians* not only preserves what is thought to be a firsthand account of the battle of Salamis. It also brings into being an entire moral and geopolitical universe that had not existed until the Greeks began to take stock, during the decade that followed the victories of 480 and 479 BCE.

The play presents Xerxes's overweening pride as an affront to nature and the gods. His punishment at the hands of the Greeks not only was deserved but also affirmed what was probably already a traditional Greek way of thinking about man's place in the world: pride goes before a fall.[18] But this is not all. Athens is presented in the play as the gateway to Hellas: if Xerxes had not been defeated by the Athenians, all Hellas would have been his. The Athenians of course come out of it well, in Aeschylus's rendering. But what his play celebrates, for the first time, is Hellas as a land and Hellenes as a distinct people. There is even a bond between the two: the 'land of the Hellenes' itself fights alongside its people, the chorus of noble Persians is informed. How can this be, they demand to know? 'It slays by hunger all those who are too numerous for it' comes the terse response, thereby articulating a permanent demographic reality as well as making powerful propaganda.[19]

And those Hellenes, small in number though they were by comparison with the might of Persia, are presented as fighting for something that, again, had probably never been articulated before but that would resonate down the centuries ever afterwards: their liberty. The Persians ask, baffled, How can such small forces stand up to them? What drives their soldiers into battle if they are free to speak their own minds and act on their own initiative? Why wouldn't they just run away? The answer comes in the 'great cry' that supposedly went up from the Greek ships at Salamis:

> *Sons of Hellenes, onward,*
> *set free your fatherland, set free*
> *your children, wives, the homes of your ancestral gods,*
> *and your forefathers' graves. For all of these the fight is on!*[20]

By 472 BCE, the Greeks had acquired a cause that was not just the cause of any one city or region. Retrospectively, it was a cause fit to die for. And an audience of Athenian theatre-goers, people whose ancestors had always been accustomed to put their own city first, was ready to hear that, this time, they had been fighting for something larger. Now they knew that they were not Athenians only but also Hellenes—unified by a shared identity and this common ideal: freedom. And because the play was popular at the time and was still being talked about and revived in Athens some seventy years later, we can be sure that the new way for Athenians to think about themselves had caught on.[21]

Aeschylus was the first. But a play is not history. What really set the seal on the way the Persian Wars would ever afterwards be remembered was another of those Greek inventions: the invention of history. To make this one possible, the new system of alphabetic writing had to make another leap forward and away from the traditional art of oral storytelling. This was the leap from verse into prose. A narrative written in prose would still, for several centuries after this, be more often read aloud to an audience than read on the page. But the divorce from the traditional techniques for remembering and delivering a story before an audience meant that any amount of information could be stored in a document that, for the first time, need not be memorised but could be retrieved whenever necessary.

This is where Herodotus of Halicarnassus comes into his own. He was not the first Greek writer to try his hand at prose. But he *is* the first whose work has come down to us complete. And so far as we can tell, it was *his* idea to use what was still quite an experimental medium, prose, for a new purpose. Herodotus was born within a few years of the battle of Salamis, perhaps in 484 BCE. Halicarnassus, today the fishing village and tourist resort of Bodrum in southwestern Turkey, was at the time part of the Persian Empire, so Herodotus began life as a subject of King Xerxes. If we are to believe his own account, he travelled widely, taking in most parts of the known world of his time. Later, he may have settled in Athens. Sometime around 450 BCE, he embarked on what he called the 'demonstration of an enquiry'. The task would occupy him for the rest of his life. The subject of this enquiry was to be 'what people had done' in the recent wars, its purpose to commemorate for all time the actions of both sides, along with the causes of the conflict.[22] The Greek word meaning 'enquiry' in Herodotus's Ionic dialect of Greek at the time was *historie*.

Herodotus's prose narrative is every bit as monumental in size and ambitious in scope as the Homeric poems. There are plenty of indications that the inventor of the new genre was looking over his shoulder at the venerated epics of the Trojan War and its aftermath. But unlike the elusive Homer, Herodotus the enquirer is a frequent presence in his own narrative—probing, prodding, weighing up one implausible explanation against another, and often genially withholding judgement, leaving it to the rational reader, or hearer, to decide. And for most of what he says, we have nobody else's word to compare with his. Historians working today on other parts of the ancient Mediterranean world often express frustration that they have only Herodotus, writing in Greek, from the Greek point of view, to rely on.[23]

Right from the beginning, Herodotus prepares us for a war between continents: Europe and Asia. On one side of the Hellespont and the Aegean Sea stand the Greeks; on the other, the Persian Empire. The idea of Europe as the seat of a civilisation that we now call 'European', and opposed to the 'barbarism' of Asia, has its origin in the pages of Herodotus. The Greek word *barbaros* at first just meant a foreigner who spoke a different language. It barely appears before the time of the Persian Wars. Afterwards, it was on everyone's lips, and of none more often than of Herodotus. The people of Asia (other than the Greeks who had settled all round its seaward edge) were *barbaroi*. This is the first time that the name 'Europe' acquires a geopolitical meaning. Indeed, in these pages, we can see the modern geopolitics of 'East' and 'West' being born. Throughout the nine books that follow, the clash between the 'barbarians' of Asia and the 'Hellenes' of Europe is played out.[24]

Herodotus rarely misses an opportunity to urge upon his hearers a sense of unity as Greeks in the face of a common enemy. But the details of his narrative constantly show up the opposite. With what must surely be deliberate irony, he puts into the mouth of the Persian general Mardonius this rueful piece of self-knowledge about his own people:

> The Greeks are pugnacious enough, and start fights on the spur of the moment without sense or judgement to justify them. . . . Now surely, as they all talk the same language, they ought to be able to find a better way of settling their differences: by negotiation, for

instance, or an interchange of views—indeed by anything rather than fighting.[25]

Not only were the Greek city-states notoriously at one another's throats, Herodotus knew perfectly well that the great majority of them had submitted to the Persians without a fight. This would have been common knowledge at the time when he was writing, and he makes no attempt to play it down. He acknowledges, too, that many of the ships and their crews that fought on the *Persian* side had been conscripted from Greek cities such as his own, in Anatolia. Themistocles, Herodotus tells us, had entertained hopes of persuading these Ionian Greek conscripts to turn against their masters, or at least to fight only half-heartedly. But he records no mass desertions. Of the mainland states, he tells us that Thebes actually sent troops to fight alongside the invaders at the battle of Plataea. Argos, the only surviving rival to Sparta in the Peloponnese, had maintained an ambiguous neutrality throughout but helpfully alerted Mardonius when Spartan troops were on their way to confront him in the same battle. Herodotus no doubt intended his narrative as an object lesson—on what Greeks *could* achieve when they settled their differences and acted together. But thanks to his candour, we know that in reality the resistance of 'Hellas' to the 'barbarians' had been a very patchwork affair, nothing like a united front.[26]

All the more impressive, then, the way Herodotus tells it, was the determination and the success against the odds of those who did resist. In yet another of the dramatic dialogues that enliven his history, the historian for the first time fleshes out the new understanding of what it meant to be Greek. While the alliance is forming that will confront the Persians at the final battle in 479 BCE, Mardonius sends an embassy to the displaced Athenians. They can have their city back, he tells them, on condition that they submit to

Xerxes. As told by Herodotus, it is a collective Athenian voice that rousingly rebuffs this offer. For good measure, the Athenians go on to explain for the benefit of their Spartan allies the reason for their solidarity at a time when self-interest might have tempted them to abandon the struggle. First of all, they say, they must avenge the destruction of their city and its temples. 'Politics' (the affairs of the city-state) still come first. But, secondly, the Athenians go on:

> there is the totality of the Greeks, made up of one blood and one language, and the sanctuaries of the gods which are shared, and sacrifices and practices carried out in the same way. All of these we Athenians would never betray.

The single Greek word *Hellenikon* which I have translated as 'totality of the Greeks' is often rendered in modern translations as 'Greek nation'. There has been much discussion of this passage as an early statement of what today we could call 'ethnic' or 'national' identity. All the more reason to look carefully at what Herodotus actually says. Elsewhere in his story, he uses the same word in contexts where it clearly refers to the Greeks, or the Greek city-states, all together.[27] It is not an abstract word, like *nation, race*, or the still more conceptual *Greekness* or *Hellenicity* of a later age. Here, it must mean very specifically *all* those people who share the things that are now spelled out by the Athenians in this imagined speech: genetic inheritance and language most immediately, and then, connected more loosely by Herodotus's syntax in Greek, what we would now term 'culture'.

By the time Herodotus wrote those words, probably in the late 430s BCE, the 'totality of the Greeks', in whose name the victory over Persia had been secured, was about to tear itself apart in a second great conflict, the repercussions of which are also still with us to this day. In truth, what Herodotus called the *Hellenikon* had never stood together, not even against the Persians. But the narrative of a common stand against invasion and the threat of tyranny, by an underdog fighting with great tenacity and at the cost of great sacrifice, was one that would go on to inspire many others in centuries to come—whether or not they thought of themselves as sharing the same 'blood', language, or culture as the Greeks of the fifth century BCE.

THE PERIOD OF almost fifty years that begins after the battle of Plataea in 479 BCE is generally reckoned to mark the high point of the civilisation that we now call 'classical Greece'. History books often give the impression that this, too, came about as a direct result of the Persian Wars. If it hadn't been for that cataclysmic upheaval, it's a reasonable guess that none of it would have happened in quite the way that it did. On the other hand, much of what was radically new in the Greek world after 479 BCE can be traced back to developments that had already been under way before the first Persian expedition set out. And the new achievements would spread out far and wide across the *whole* of that world. Whatever was going on, it was not limited to the thirty-one or so states that had actively resisted the invaders. So we might do better to think of the Persian Wars as a catalyst, rather than as a cause, of what came afterwards.

Between about 520 and the 440s BCE, lyric poets were bringing together words, music, dance, and ceremony to celebrate public occasions with ever more dazzling complexity. The career of Pindar, from Thebes, began in the decade before the battle of Marathon and continued for almost half a century afterwards. Pindar's 'odes' have been imitated by poets writing in many different languages, from that time to this. An ode, originally, was any kind of song. As it happens, the 'songs' of Pindar that have been preserved through the manuscript tradition are those that celebrated victors in the four 'panhellenic' contests, of which the most famous were the Olympic Games. The words, of course, are all that have been preserved, so we can only guess at the total multimedia experience that must have been involved.

Plays and performances, too, an artform that would later be especially associated with Athens, went back well before the Persian Wars. But almost all that we know about Greek drama dates from the decades that followed. Aeschylus continued to write plays for the best part of twenty years after the success of *The Persians*. He was followed by the tragedians Sophocles and Euripides, and the comic dramatist Aristophanes, among dozens of others whose works survive only in fragmentary form. Several complete plays by all four have remained in circulation ever since their lifetimes and have been frequently revived in theatres since the nineteenth century.

Tragedy, the genre that had been co-opted by Aeschylus to capture the new euphoria after the battle of Salamis, was more usually devoted to subjects drawn from mythology. But very often, Athenian dramatists would give a topical twist to their reenactment of a well-known story. According to Aristotle, writing a century after the heyday of 'classical' drama, the nature of tragedy was 'by means of pity and fear to bring about the purging of such emotions'.[28] Comedy was more overtly topical. On the comic stage it was a regular occurrence for prominent citizens and political issues to be caricatured, often with a hefty dose of obscenity as well as bravura. Among extravagant whimsies brought onto the Athenian stage, one that is still with us today is Cloud-Cuckooland (*Nephelokokkygia*)—still invoked, as it was then, to mean a never-never land of politicians' promises.

The main festival at which plays were staged in Athens was known as the Great Dionysia, held in spring each year. Somewhere between fifteen and twenty thousand spectators packed into the sanctuary of Dionysus on the slope below the walls of the Acropolis for several days on end to watch new plays performed one after the other, from dawn until dusk. The marble-lined Theatre of Dionysus, that occupies the space today, would not be built until the next century. Actors wore masks—so that even those in the audience close enough to have been able to make out facial expressions would have had to rely, instead, on observing the actors' gestures and, above all, on listening to every nuance of the words they spoke.

Action (the literal meaning of the Greek word *drama*) consisted only of dialogue or, on occasion, a monologue addressed to the audience. Almost everything that happens in a Greek tragedy or comedy happens offstage and is conveyed to the characters, as well as to the audience, by a lengthy report. A frequent exception to this rule was the appearance of a god or goddess, lowered from a gantry onto the stage, to wrap things up at the end. This type of intervention is still known by the Latin phrase *deus ex machina*, which translates the Greek for 'god from the machine'.

All parts were played by men, even though many of the most important dramatic roles were female. These ranged from goddesses and powerful figures of legend, such as Helen of Troy or the 'barbarian' enchantress Medea, to the fictional Lysistrata, who leads the Athenian women in a sex strike in order to force their menfolk to make peace, not war, in the comedy by Aristophanes named after her (performed in 411 BCE). A large part in both tragedy and comedy was played by the 'chorus' (the word actually means 'dance'), a group of actors who would sing and dance in a circular space, called the 'orchestra', in front of the stage. No less than the ceremonial odes of Pindar, Greek drama was a multimedia, multisensory experience, only one part of which we can even begin to recapture. Like so much else in the classical Greek world, writing plays was an intensely competitive business. Prizes were awarded by judges chosen by lot, so in effect the dramatists were competing for the approval of a public made up of their fellow citizens.

The Greek world after 479 BCE *looked* different, too. In the sanctuary at Olympia, a new temple, dedicated to Zeus, was built between 471 and 456 BCE. On the pediments, bodies carved from stone convey a sense of movement. The western pediment, now exhibited in the state-of-the-art new museum at Olympia, shows a scene from mythology. Brutish Greek tribesmen called Lapiths battle with centaurs (half-man, half-horse) to disrupt a wedding feast. In the centre a young god, probably Apollo, naked except for a cloak held over one shoulder and the opposite arm, with an expression of serene determination stretches out the other arm to quell the tumult. The message, if there is one, may not be quite as simple as Greek sweet reason overcoming subhuman barbarism. But it is there for the beholder, who might well have wished to see it that way when the temple was newly built. Some of the figures in this scene and elsewhere among the surviving sculptures of the Temple of Zeus at Olympia have been admired especially for their nuances of *individual* expression, including tension, fatigue, and pain.[29]

Life-size or slightly larger replica human beings were on the move in the fifth-century BCE Greek world in another sense, too. At the same time as sculptors were learning how to represent bodies in motion, the statues they made began to descend from the pediments of temples and to move out of cemeteries and sacred spaces into the everyday world of the city. Beginning in the fifth century BCE, and indeed continuing into the early Middle Ages, Greek civic spaces would become crowded with look-alike people made of stone and, increasingly, of bronze.[30] Because bronze has always been a valuable commodity, it is rare for a bronze statue to survive from the ancient world. Those that do most often come from ancient shipwrecks or were buried in antiquity, to be dug up by archaeologists in chance finds.

Our best clue to how these human-like figures would have looked in Greek cities in the years immediately after the Persian Wars comes from two stunning bronzes salvaged from the sea off the Italian town of Riace in Calabria in 1972. Slightly larger than life-size, they represent naked warriors with thick, curly hair and beards. Different materials and an inlay of semiprecious stones still give a shocking vividness to their staring eyes and preserve a strong colour contrast in lips, teeth, and nipples. Originally, the figures would have carried weapons, but these have not survived. The pair may well have formed part of a group, possibly even designed as a victory memorial for the Persian Wars, although of course there is no direct evidence for this. The two bronze men share a similar pose. But this is very different from the stiff full-frontal pose of the *kouroi* of the previous century. Unlike earlier statues and in common with most later ones, these warriors do not look directly at the viewer. They may not be true portraits, but they are individual human beings, each absorbed in his own world, a world that unsettlingly peeps into ours.[31]

Sculptors by this time had acquired the technical means and had developed enough understanding of human anatomy to create the likeness of real individuals. But this would turn out to be a 'road not taken'. How and why this came about has been revealed by the painstaking study of that most domesticated of the visual arts, the paintings produced on high-quality tableware destined for use within the home. Paradoxical though it may seem, just as sculptors were learning to capture bodies in motion, their peers working in two dimensions were cultivating, instead, stillness and composure in the human figures that they represented. By 450 BCE, a marked change had come about both in the style and the subjects chosen to decorate fine bowls, plates, and cups.

Instead of vivid scenes of battle, painters depict the young warrior, identifiable by his shield, saying farewell to his grieving wife and parents. Sexually explicit images disappear almost completely. Athletes exercising or competing naked in the gymnasium are caught in moments of stillness, to be admired for their beauty and composure, rather than actively competing as before.[32] Often described as idealist, rather than realist or naturalist, this was the perfect art for the citizen-state of the classical period. In this way, the aloof serenity of Apollo quelling the riot on the pediment of the Temple of Zeus at Olympia enters the home of every Greek—and also of the many customers of Athenian potters among the Etruscans of Italy, where so much of this intimate tableware would be unearthed by modern archaeologists.[33]

All these new trends would come together spectacularly when the Athenians began to rebuild their citadel, the Acropolis. They had waited more than thirty years since the Persian destruction. Then, starting in 447 BCE, no expense was to be spared. A massive complex of buildings called the Propylaea was designed as a ceremonial entrance to the sacred space. It cannot be an accident that the colonnade lining the entryway exactly frames the view of the distant site where the battle of Salamis had been won back in 480 BCE. The rebuilt Acropolis was to be the permanent memorial to that victory.[34] Inside, new temples arose, built out of marble quarried from nearby Mount Pentelikon. First to be completed, and largest of all, was the temple dedicated to the city's patron goddess, Athena the Virgin (*Parthenos*). The Parthenon, as it has been known ever since, was finished in just fifteen years. Now an empty shell, after its heart was blown out by a Venetian cannonball in 1687, its columns and pediments still dominate the skyline of central Athens. Usually framed against a sky of brilliant blue, with the humped back of Mount Hymettus in the background, the image of the Parthenon on the Acropolis of Athens must be the most widely recognised 'trademark' of Greece and Greek civilisation—just as it was in the century when it was built. And, of course, it was built to impress.[35]

As at Olympia, the pediments at either end of the building were decorated with sculptures. Less usual, and even more famous today, is the frieze in sculpted marble relief that ran round the top of the inner wall of the building, beneath the roof, some sixty feet above a viewer standing on the ground. Originally 160 metres long, the largest surviving portions of this frieze are exhibited in the British Museum in London and in the Acropolis Museum in Athens, which opened in 2009. It depicts a procession on foot, on horseback, and in chariots and culminates in an offering made in the presence of Athena, Zeus, and other gods and goddesses of Olympus, who are seated on simple thrones.

Opinions still differ as to what exactly is represented. But whatever its meaning in detail, there is no mistaking the solemn, collaborative sense of purpose of the celebrants (despite the liveliness of the horses) and the subordinate place of several hundred human figures as they approach, with deference and awe, their own larger-scale likenesses, the Olympians. For all the admiration that their 'classical' white marble has aroused in modern times, we should not forget that these sculptures, and probably large parts of the building that housed them, too, would originally have been painted in bright colours. And until they were taken down and placed in a museum, at eye level with most viewers, no one could have appreciated their finer points but the gods.

During the same decades, while on the Acropolis the Parthenon and other public buildings were rising, down at street level the philosopher Socrates would engage his fellow citizens in dialogues about the nature and purpose of human life. Socrates had been born in Athens in 469 BCE. His career would span the entire second half of the century. What we now call 'moral philosophy' begins with these dialogues, as they would later be reconstructed, often in highly fictionalised form, by his disciples Plato and Xenophon. In these seemingly artless conversations, the questioning of the *cosmos* that had begun more than a century earlier in Anatolia comes down to earth. For Socrates, the goal of all human beings was *arete*. Usually translated as 'goodness' or 'virtue', the Greek word has a sharper edge than these equivalents which derive from the Christian tradition. *Arete* also has the meaning of 'excellence'. It implies an element of competition, that was entirely characteristic of the Greek city-states of Socrates's time. In one of the few passages in which we probably do hear his words unalloyed, Socrates is reported as saying that it is 'the greatest good to man' to 'engage in discourse about *arete*'. The alternative—an 'unexamined life'— Socrates goes on, is 'not livable for a human being'.[36]

One of those who engaged with Socrates was Protagoras of Abdera, one of many itinerant philosophers, called 'sophists', who visited Athens during this time. Protagoras is credited with the doctrine that 'man is the measure of all things'. If we all live in a *cosmos* that is regulated by 'measures', as Heraclitus had believed, then it must follow that we ourselves are part of that universal 'order' or 'arrangement'. Similar thought processes were leading at the same time in a different part of the Greek-speaking world to the first systematic examination of the human body, what makes it work, and how its processes can be put right when we fall ill. On the island of Kos, in the eastern Aegean, the 'father of medicine', Hippocrates, was a contemporary of Socrates. He, too, is known to us only indirectly through the works of others. As a result, we cannot be sure which of the medical discoveries recorded against his name were really his.[37] But we know that the Greek world of the late fifth century BCE was becoming more than ever centred on the human. Among the pithy moral maxims that were probably first inscribed on a column in the Temple of Apollo at Delphi at about this time, the most famous of all must surely be *Gnothi seauton*: know your own self.

EVER SINCE THE end of the wars against Persia, the lifting of the external threat had not necessarily brought peace. Until the middle of the fifth century BCE, Greek forces continued to confront the Persian enemy, in Anatolia during the 460s BCE and in Egypt (less successfully) in the next decade. Sparta had withdrawn from the joint expedition to Anatolia after only a year, back in 478 BCE. From that time on, it had been left to the Athenians to organise an alliance of the liberated Greek cities to keep up the pressure against Persia.

Willing allies at the start, these states soon found themselves committed to doing the bidding of the Athenians, as well as contributing ships and, increasingly, money to a common treasury. At first, this was housed in the sanctuary of Apollo at Delos, neutral ground more or less at the geographical centre of the new alliance. For this reason, the alliance has become known to modern historians as the 'Delian League'. Then in 454 or 453 BCE the Athenians unilaterally moved what had become a massive accumulation of wealth to their own city. One of the reasons for starting work on building the Parthenon shortly afterwards was to create a secure home for it. But it was the contributions of the allies that, to a large extent, paid for the building along with the rest of the programme that over the next half century would turn the Acropolis and the Agora below into the glorious statement of self-assertion whose ruins we still admire today. What had started out as a defensive alliance against a return of the Persians had turned into Athenian rule over most of the Aegean.

Modern historians regularly use the word *empire* to describe this extension of Athenian power during the fifth century BCE. At the time, there was no equivalent word in Greek, so unprecedented did it seem that one Greek city-state should lord it over others (even though the Spartans had already achieved something similar in their immediate sphere of influence, the Peloponnese). In the earliest account of these events that we have, the *History* written by the Athenian Thucydides during the last three decades of the century, the Athenians are reported as justifying their 'rule' over other Greeks in terms that often make modern readers uncomfortable:

> We did not establish this rule by force. . . . We have done nothing surprising or contrary to human nature in accepting rule over others when it was offered to us and refusing to give it up, under the domination of the three most powerful motives—prestige, fear, and self-interest. . . . It has always been the way of the world that the weaker is kept down by the stronger.[38]

The Athenian empire was based on naval supremacy. This was the direct legacy of Themistocles's initiative to invest in the ships that had gone on to win the battle of Salamis. Sparta, by contrast, concentrated its power on land. As the century wore on, the Delian League was matched by the 'Peloponnesian League', led by Sparta. Of the entire peninsula, only Argos still held out doggedly against Spartan domination. The two leagues first clashed in 460 BCE, as each tried to expand its influence over the neutral territories that lay between them. Athens came off the worse. In 446 BCE, the Athenians agreed to give up the gains they had made on the mainland in return for keeping their maritime 'empire' intact. The peace agreement signed in that year was supposed to last for thirty years. It would hold for only half that long, during which time the rival power blocs eyed one another warily, each consolidating its grip over the allies it controlled.

In the meantime, during the 460s BCE, Athenian democracy had been radically overhauled. Exactly how the system had worked before this and, indeed, many details about these changes remain obscure. But it seems to have been only at this time that the word *demokratia* came to be coined and the fully fledged democracy began to function in the form that we know from later sources. The entire citizen body of some thirty thousand adult males was sovereign. In practice, around five to six thousand seem regularly to have attended the Assembly (*Ekklesia*), which met approximately once a month in the open air on the low hill facing the Acropolis, called the Pnyx. Executive authority was devolved to the *Boule*, or Council, of five hundred, chosen by lot each year from the total number of eligible citizens. Up to fifteen hundred officials, including the members of the Council, were chosen annually to fulfil all the offices of the state. Only those in the highest offices, in charge of finance and decisions on the battlefield, were elected. All the rest were picked at random by the drawing of lots.

This was very different from a modern democracy, in which the people elect representatives to make decisions on their behalf. In ancient Athens, the most important decisions were taken by a show of hands in the full Assembly. Every male citizen had the right to attend. And all officeholders, whether chosen by lot or elected, were held closely to account. It really was power (*kratos*) to the people (*demos*).[39] And the idea of increasing the wealth and power of their state appealed to the people enormously. The modern idea that democracies do not fight aggressive wars is certainly not borne out by the story of Athens in the fifth century BCE. Smaller states that were either conquered or brought within the Athenian sphere of influence would often be told to adopt a version of the same system themselves. The paradox of 'people power' being imposed by powerful outsiders, from above, in situations where it may not be wholly welcome, goes right back to the first decades when democracy began to spread from Athens across the Aegean.

It was under this system that Athenian political life, including the building programme on the Acropolis, came to be dominated by the charismatic orator Pericles, from the 450s until his death in 429 BCE. So influential was Pericles that he has often been hailed as the greatest Athenian statesman of all time, while Athens at its heyday is as often called 'Periclean'. It says a great deal for his personality and talents that Pericles managed to exercise as much influence as he did—since, like every other official, he had to be elected to office every year. The fact that he was, and over such a long period, gave continuity to a system that did not inherently value either experience in office or what we would today call efficiency.[40] Thucydides puts into the mouth of Pericles these often-quoted words in praise of Athenian democracy, supposedly delivered at the end of the year 431 BCE on an occasion when the historian had in all probability been present:

> We have a system of government that does not take its cues from the laws of neighboring states; we set the example and do not imitate others. That system goes by the name of democracy because it is administered on behalf of the many and not the few. Everyone enjoys equality before the law on matters of civil disputes. As to personal reputation, whoever wins esteem for some reason can advance in public affairs—not by turn, but through merit.[41]

This democratic Athens, for most of the second half of the fifth century BCE, was ready, sometimes even eager, to take risks. The Spartans, by contrast, holding rigidly to a system that had changed little over several centuries and permanently fearful of the threat from the helots, were by nature risk averse. Sparta still could field the most formidable citizen army in the Greek-speaking world. But qualifications for maintaining full citizenship were so strict, and so demanding, that fewer fighting men were available whose loyalty could be truly relied on. And when it came to resources, the Spartans never learned to be as unscrupulous as their Athenian rivals in extracting what was in effect protection money from the other members of the Peloponnesian League.[42]

Despite having led the resistance against the Persians in 480 and 479 BCE, the Spartans seem to have been the least inclined, or perhaps the least able, of all the Greeks to enjoy the fruits of their victory. No great new public buildings, no flowering of the arts or crafts, no poetry, history, philosophy, or scientific enquiry arose in Sparta during the fifth century BCE. By the 430s, if anything, the two great powers within the small world of the Greek city-states had come to define themselves by their differences from one another.

War broke out between them in 431 BCE. The Spartans started it, using a variety of pretexts. But the real reason, as Thucydides shrewdly noted, writing not long afterwards, was 'the growth of Athenian power and Spartan fear of it . . . when they could see much of Greece already subject to Athens'.[43] The war lasted much longer than the Persian campaigns—for twenty-seven years, on and off. Thucydides tells us at the beginning of his narrative that the conflict would spread to the entire Greek world, and even beyond—making it, for its time, the equivalent of a world war.[44] But what led to this second Greek war of the fifth century BCE being seen as truly global is once again not so much what happened on the battlefield but the way the story came to be told afterwards. The Peloponnesian War, as it is known today, is one case where history was *not* written by the victors. The Athenians lost. But Thucydides's meticulous, judicious account of causes and effects, of strategies and decision-making, of human brutality and human capacity for error has never ceased to be read since shortly after the war came to an end.[45]

IT STARTED OUT as a war of attrition. Each summer, Spartan hoplites would march northwards through the mountain passes of the Peloponnese, cross the Isthmus of Corinth, and invade Attica. They would stay for up to six weeks, burning and looting the crops, while the Athenians would be driven back inside their defensive walls. But, thanks to the initiatives taken by Themistocles in preparation for the second Persian invasion, the new port at Piraeus was linked directly to the city by two parallel lines of fortification, known as the Long Walls. This meant there was nothing the Spartans could do to prevent their enemies from being supplied by sea. Athens already relied on grain brought from the hinterland of the Hellespont and the Black Sea coast. For as long as their fleet ruled the seas, the people of Athens could still be fed.

It was probably as a consequence of overcrowding inside the city during the summer heat that plague broke out in 430 BCE. Over four years, as many as a quarter of the total population may have died from the plague. The veteran Pericles was among its victims. It was the first pandemic in recorded history. Thucydides, who himself became infected, treats his readers to a clinical and harrowing account of its symptoms and its effects on the population:

> The most dreadful aspects of the whole affliction were the despair into which people fell when they realized they had contracted the disease . . . and the cross-infection of those who cared for others: they died like sheep, and this was the greatest cause of mortality. When people were afraid to visit one another, the victims died in isolation. . . . The greatest pity for the dying and the distressed was shown by those who had had the disease and recovered. They had experience of what it was like and were now confident for themselves, as the plague did not attack the same person twice, or at least not fatally.[46]

While the Spartans were trying to throttle their enemy on land, the Athenians did the same by sea. They never came as close to

Sparta itself as the Spartans did to Athens. But they did manage to gain a toehold in the southwest of the Peloponnese, an especially sensitive spot for the Spartans, ever alert to the risk that the local helots there might rise against them. By 421 BCE, after ten years of campaigning in theatres all over mainland Greece and the Aegean, a stalemate was reached. Peace terms were agreed. It was to prove a phoney peace.

In the years 416 and 415 BCE, Athens had recovered sufficiently to embark on two of the most notorious episodes of the war—while still technically observing the armistice and defensive treaty with Sparta. The first was directed against the island of Melos in the Cyclades. Melos was a rare case of an Aegean island that had never joined the Athenian alliance and still remained loyal to Sparta. While the islanders waited in vain for a Spartan expedition to arrive and relieve them, the Athenians laid siege to their chief town. Thucydides presents at length the negotiations between the two sides. The passage in his history has ever since been known as the 'Melian Dialogue', and it has much in common with a scene from a tragic drama. It is here that the historian sets out most fully, and most chillingly, the foundations of what we now call *Realpolitik*. Just like a tragic dramatist, Thucydides himself declines to comment on the views expressed. When the Melians finally surrendered, without conditions, in January 415 BCE:

> Of the Melian population the Athenians executed all the grown men who came into their hands and enslaved the children and women. Later they colonized the place themselves, sending out five hundred settlers of their own.[47]

Three months later, back in Athens, the tragedy by Euripides, *The Trojan Women*, was staged at the Great Dionysia. The play focuses on the plight of female survivors of a deadly war and the cruelty of the victors. Whether the Athenian audience saw in this a moral condemnation of their own recent behaviour we do not know. The fate of Melos was by no means the only atrocity recorded by Thucydides during a war that increasingly brutalised all who participated in it. But thanks to the Melian Dialogue, it is the one that has remained the most remembered, ever afterwards.

The same year, 415 BCE, saw the Athenians overreaching themselves again. And this time it was they themselves who would pay the price. In June, an expedition set out from Piraeus that consisted of 134 warships, an unknown number of troopships carrying more than five thousand hoplites, with a small contingent of cavalry, and thirty supply ships. It was, says Thucydides, 'at that time the costliest and most magnificent Greek armada ever to sail from a single city'. It would be followed by a second, in response to a desperate plea for reinforcements, a year later.[48] Their destination was Syracuse, the most powerful Greek city of Sicily. Rather than attack the Spartan enemy on their own ground, and persuaded by the charismatic young general Alcibiades, the Athenian Assembly had voted to broaden the conflict by opening up a new front far to the west. There were, possibly, wealth and resources to be won that would tip the balance of power in favour of Athens. By the logic of the warmonger, in all times and places, Alcibiades had argued that 'if we do not rule others, others will rule us'.[49]

After a two-year campaign it ended in disaster. The entire fleet was lost. In the last of a series of land battles in Sicily, Athenian hoplites, tormented by thirst, fought among themselves to gulp down river water that was running with the blood of their comrades, while the enemy hacked and shot arrows at them from either bank. Some seven thousand survivors were taken prisoner and held for months in terrible conditions in stone quarries on the outskirts of Syracuse that can still be seen by visitors today. Other survivors of the defeated army fled into the Sicilian countryside and eventually made their way back to Athens to tell the tale. Two of the Athenian generals who surrendered were put to death by their captors. Alcibiades, one of the most colourful characters of his times, had already deserted the troops he was supposed to be leading, later to give his services to the kings of Sparta.

Astonishingly, despite the magnitude of their defeat, the Athenians set to work immediately building a new fleet. But the framework of their democracy had been weakened by the disaster. In 411, a group of oligarchs staged a coup d'état. That, too, would prove unstable, and democracy would be restored the next year. Two events had already happened that would decisively change the course of the war. In March 413 BCE, while the final stages of the Athenian collapse in the west were still unfolding, the Spartans returned to Attica. But this time, instead of merely disrupting the harvest and stealing the produce, as they had done before, they thought to fortify an outpost within the territory of Attica itself. Now the Athenians really were penned up behind their walls, and not just for a few weeks each summer but throughout the year. And then, the following summer, the Spartans revoked their long-standing hostility to the common enemy Persia and made a deal with representatives of the new Great King, Darius II.

So much, one might think, for the much-vaunted superiority of the Hellene over the barbarian and the collective self-confidence of the Greeks in the decades after Salamis and Plataea. The reality was that *both* sides had been trying to open negotiations with the Persians right from the first years of the Peloponnesian War. Up to this time, the Persians had kept these approaches at arm's length. For as long as the rival Greek city-states were doing their own dirty work for them, there was no incentive for the Persians to intervene. But after the collapse of Athenian sea power in the Sicilian campaign, Darius saw an advantage to be gained from supporting the Spartans.

According to the text of the treaty signed in 412 BCE, as reported by Thucydides, Sparta not only pledged itself to fight alongside the Persians for the defeat of Athens but acknowledged that 'All the territory and all the cities which are in the King's possession, or were in the possession of the King's forefathers, shall belong to the King.' In other words, all those Greeks living on the eastern side of the Aegean, who had been liberated at the end of the Persian Wars by the combined efforts of Athens *and* Sparta, were now to be returned by Sparta to the Persians. From the beginning, the Spartans had claimed to be fighting to 'liberate Hellas' from the overweening power of Athens. That claim was looking very threadbare now.[50]

At the same time, the Athenians were still trying to woo the old enemy to *their* side. Hopes of help from Persia lingered in Athens until 407 BCE. But in that year, Darius sent his son Cyrus to Anatolia as the new satrap. Cyrus worked closely with the new naval commander by the name of Lysander sent out by Sparta. Lysander was evidently an able strategist and, unusually for Sparta, of relatively humble birth. The Spartan state by this time had ships of its own. But it was the war fleet of the Persians, manned by Phoenician sailors and under the command of Cyrus, that gave this new alliance a commanding position in the Aegean.[51]

Even so, the Athenians were still putting up a convincing fight at sea. The battle of Arginusae, fought in 406 BCE in the strait between the island of Lesbos and the mainland of what is now Turkey, would be described later by the historian Diodorus of Sicily, writing in Greek, as 'the greatest naval battle in history of Greeks against Greeks'.[52] It was a resounding triumph for the Athenians. But victory was soured when a storm prevented the rescue of survivors from the ships that had been lost in the battle, or proper burial for the dead. On their return to Athens, six of the eight commanders were collectively put on trial by the Assembly for this negligence, condemned to death, and executed. It was not the finest hour of the recently restored Athenian democracy.

The Spartans and their Persian allies determined to cut off the supply of grain and other foodstuffs to Athens through the straits leading from the Black Sea to the Aegean. Another sea battle, fought the following year at Aegospotami in the Dardanelles, all but wiped out the Athenian fleet. The news reached Athens at night. The well-to-do Athenian Xenophon, who was probably in the city at the time, would later capture the moment:

> A sound of wailing arose and extended first from Piraeus, then along the Long Walls until it reached the city. That night no one slept. They mourned for the lost, but more still for their own fate. They thought that they themselves would now be dealt with as they had dealt with others.[53]

For several months, during the winter of 405–404 BCE, Athens and Piraeus were besieged by land and sea. In the spring, forced into starvation, the Assembly voted to accept the terms of peace laid down by Sparta. Thanks in part to the moderation of Lysander, then in command of Spartan forces on the ground, the Athenians would not have to share the fate that they themselves had meted out to the Melians and others. Their lives would be spared. But they must never again possess a war fleet of more than twelve ships. All Athenians who had been exiled (prominent among them being the oligarchs who had seized power in 411 BCE) were to be recalled. The Long Walls and the defences around Piraeus were to be destroyed. And Athens was henceforth to obey the will of Sparta in all military matters.

This part of the story is not told by Thucydides. His history breaks off in 411 BCE, although we have his word for it that he had seen the war through to the end and intended to tell the story in full. Instead, we have to rely on Xenophon, who is less judicious and far less reliable—and who, by the time he came to write up these events, had transferred his own loyalty to the winning Spartan side. It was in this spirit, and probably oblivious to the bitter irony of his words when set alongside the victorious conclusion of that other great conflict seventy-five years before, that Xenophon brings down the curtain on the Greek tragedy that was the Peloponnesian War:

> After this, Lysander sailed into Piraeus, the exiles returned, and the walls were pulled down among scenes of great enthusiasm and to the music of flute girls. It was thought that this day was the beginning of liberty for Hellas.[54]

5

CULTURAL CAPITAL
404 BCE–322 BCE

I T WAS A strange sort of liberty. Neither of the Greek rivals had proved strong enough to beat the other on a level playing field. Everybody knew that the power of Athens had been broken only thanks to the vastly superior resources of the old enemy, Persia. After the war was over, interstate politics in the Greek world continued to be as rancorous as before. There was one difference, though. After the Spartans made their treaty with the Persian Great King in 412 BCE, an external ringmaster was always involved in the affairs of the Greek city-states. For half a century after the end of the Peloponnesian War, that would be Persia—until another entirely unexpected player entered the ring.

On the Athenian side, losses in battle and from the plague during the war's early years had reduced the citizen body to little more than half of what it had been during the heyday of the previous century. On top of the humiliation of having part of their fortifications demolished and surrendering most of their remaining fleet, the Athenians had to submit to being ruled by a thirty-man junta, known ever since as the Thirty Tyrants. In reprisals against democrats, somewhere between twelve hundred and fifteen hundred Athenians were murdered under their regime.[1] Within months, civil war broke out. The Spartans then changed their

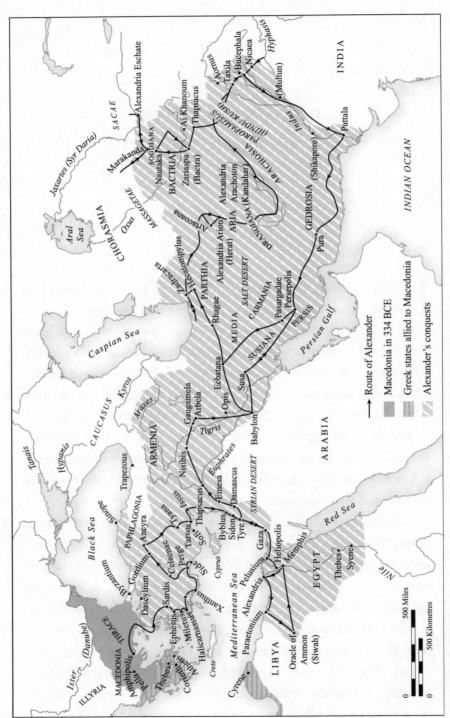

5. Alexander's expedition and empire

policy. After only a year, democracy was restored—for the second time in a decade. Slowly, a morally and financially depleted Athens began to rebuild something of what had been lost.

For Sparta, it was a classic case of 'winning the war but losing the peace'. It may have been because the *polis* system offered no rules on how to exercise authority over outsiders that Greek city-states, when they did find themselves in a position to do so, were so bad at it. The Athenians had failed in the fifth century BCE; now it was to be the turn of the Spartans. Victory over Athens simply replaced a much-resented Athenian empire with a Spartan one that would soon be resented, if anything, even more. By the time the Thirty Tyrants had been deposed in Athens, divisions had already deepened between the Spartans and the two most powerful states that had been allied with them in the war against Athens: Corinth and Thebes. The two-way rivalry of the past century and a half was giving way to a more complex set of relationships that would involve all four of these city-states and dozens of minor ones. This was the dynamic that would play out in the Greek-speaking world over the coming decades.[2]

Far away to the east, Darius II of Persia died in the same year as the Peloponnesian War ended, 404 BCE. The new Great King was Artaxerxes II. But his claim was contested by his brother Cyrus, the satrap in Anatolia who had proved such a good friend to the Spartans in general and to Lysander in particular during the final years of the war against Athens. The Greek cities of Anatolia, as well as Sparta itself, opted to back the man they knew, Cyrus, for the throne of Persia. A contingent of mercenaries from other Greek states, known ever afterwards as the 'Ten Thousand', joined in. But then Cyrus was killed in a battle on the banks of the Euphrates in 401 BCE. The story of the mercenary expedition is vividly told by Xenophon, who had left Athens to join it and ended up command-ing the remnant that made its way through many hardships to the

Black Sea coast and thence to the Aegean.[3] The Greeks had picked the wrong side after all. They found themselves up against the new satraps sent to the region by the victorious Artaxerxes. Sparta, still backed by the Greek city-states of the region, went on to fight a limited war against them for several more years.

To put a stop to this, the Persian satrap came up with a psychologically astute ploy. In 396 or 395 BCE, he sent bribes in gold to 'the leading men in various states on the understanding that they would make war on Sparta'. If Xenophon is to be believed, the Athenians disdained the money. They 'were ready enough for the war in any case, as they thought that empire was their own prerogative'. Another historian tells us that they took the cash anyway. So did the Thebans and Corinthians, and perhaps others.[4]

The Corinthian War, as it has become known, lasted until 386 BCE. On one side were the Spartans; on the other, a fragile alliance of Thebes, Corinth, Argos, and Athens, backed by Persia. Once the allies began to gain the advantage, the Persians shifted back to supporting Sparta. As a result, the Spartans emerged as marginally ahead of their rivals at home. The commander of their fleet, Antalcidas, who had once again defeated an Athenian naval force in the Hellespont, went all the way to Susa, the Persian capital, to negotiate terms of peace with Artaxerxes. So far as these concerned the Greek states, the terms were designed to benefit Sparta. But the author and principal beneficiary of the peace treaty was the Great King himself. For this reason, it would most often be called, then and later, the 'King's Peace'.

This time, Sparta really did have to hand back to Persia all the Greek 'cities of Asia' that had been liberated at the end of the Persian Wars—a promise that had been made during the later stages of the Peloponnesian War, but not fulfilled. In the event of the treaty being violated, the king reserved to himself the right to intervene with full military force. The King's Peace was understood to apply to *all* Greek states, whether or not they had formally ratified it. For those that did, including Athens, Sparta, Corinth, and Thebes, it was not quite an act of submission, such as the gift of earth and water that had once been demanded by Artaxerxes's predecessors. But it did surrender the unambiguous right to regulate relations among the Greek states. Their much-prized 'autonomy', meaning from each other, was guaranteed at the same time—but at the price of acknowledging the Great King as final arbiter among them.[5]

From the Persian point of view, the King's Peace worked extremely well. The Greek states continued to war among themselves, often using the treaty's terms as a pretext. The Peace would be renewed several times, and each time followed by new wars. Artaxerxes II, who reigned until 358 BCE, could be forgiven for thinking that the chronic boil on the western flank of his empire had finally been lanced.

In 378 BCE there came another shift in the balance of power among the Greek city-states. In Thebes, newly liberated from direct control by Sparta, a democratic regime brought to prominence two men who would go on to dominate politics on the Greek mainland until both were killed during the wars of the next decade, Pelopidas and Epameinondas. One of the few really decisive battles of this period was won by the Thebans, led by Epameinondas, over the Spartans at a place called Leuctra, not far from Thebes, in 371 BCE. The Thebans under Epameinondas pressed home their advantage. The Spartan homeland of Laconia had never been invaded by an enemy since, according to their oldest legends, their own Dorian ancestors had arrived to displace the native helots. Now, Theban troops advanced right up to the outskirts of Sparta itself. It seems to have been Epameinondas who thought of the killer blow. According to the terms of the King's Peace, every Greek *polis* was supposed to be autonomous. What better pretext could there be, now that Thebes had gained the upper hand, for joining forces with the enslaved helots of Messenia and compelling the Spartans to grant them their liberty as an autonomous city-state?

This was what the Spartans had most dreaded for centuries. Now it came to pass. Epameinondas has ever afterwards been remembered as the liberator of this oppressed population. His motive was probably less what we would call today humanitarian, and more a matter of political strategy. Once the Messenian helots had been liberated, Epameinondas encouraged them to build their own city. The walls and many of the public buildings of Messene, founded shortly afterwards, are still impressive today. The Spartans would never afterwards sign up to any treaty that included recognition of Messene as a free *polis*. As a direct result, once-mighty Sparta would become increasingly marginalised in Greek affairs from this time on.

But still the Greek city-states continued to wage war among themselves. Athens began to rebuild a set of maritime alliances that more cautiously mirrored the Delian League of a hundred years before. This time, though, the Athenians more often than not sided with their old rivals, the Spartans, to try to halt the rising power of Thebes. Matters came to a head once again in a battle fought outside the city of Mantinea, in the centre of the Peloponnese, not far from today's Tripoli, in 362 BCE. On one side were the Thebans, supported by all the Peloponnesian states that had benefited from Theban intervention against Sparta. On the other were the Spartans, their few remaining allies from the Peloponnese, and a contingent sent by Athens. As the now elderly Xenophon put it, writing not long after the event:

> Nearly the whole of Greece had been engaged on one side or the other, and everyone had imagined that, if a battle was fought, the winner would become the dominant power and the losers would be their subjects.

In the event, 'both sides claimed the victory', but neither side 'was any better off after the battle than before it'.[6]

Xenophon had already noted, a few pages earlier, writing about the Athenian contingent at Mantinea, 'Good men among them were killed and, very evidently, those whom they killed themselves were good men too.' The historian left it to others to record that his own son, Gryllos, had been among the Athenian dead. Epameinondas, too, died shortly afterwards of a wound he had received during the battle. One account even credits Gryllos with delivering the fatal blow. A statue of Epameinondas, erected in Thebes shortly afterwards, bore an inscription that commemorated his achievements in the Peloponnese. Thanks to him, it claimed, 'all Hellas' was now 'autonomous in freedom'.[7] The promise of local autonomy, that had been enshrined in the terms of the King's Peace, was now, thanks to Epameinondas, supposed to apply to the entire Greek world. One wonders what anybody thought the boast could possibly mean, in the circumstances.

Xenophon was not far off the mark when he concluded, in almost the last sentence of his history, 'There was even more uncertainty and confusion in Greece after the battle than there had been previously.' One modern commentator puts it more pithily: the city-states 'had reached a balance of impotence'.[8] The reality of what Greeks were *doing* during the first half of the fourth century BCE is depressing. But to hear them talk, you would hardly have guessed it.

AND WE *CAN* hear them talking. That, paradoxically, is their real achievement at this time—to enable us to listen in to what some of them, at any rate, were thinking and saying. In 399 BCE, the seventy-year-old Socrates had been prosecuted before an Athenian law court, charged with impiety and 'corrupting the city's youth'. This was only four years after the brutal regime of the Thirty

Tyrants had been overthrown and democracy restored. Several members of that junta, in their time, had been among the 'youth' allegedly corrupted by the accused. The charge of 'impiety' might well have resonated with a citizen jury still edgily looking for scapegoats after their city's defeat by Sparta.[9] Socrates was found guilty and condemned to die by drinking hemlock in prison. It is one of the best-known stories of classical antiquity. But its aftermath was to affect even more than the future course of Western philosophy.

Beginning quite shortly after Socrates's death, and continuing for half a century afterwards, two of his pupils determined to perpetuate his legacy. One of these was Xenophon, the historian, who was also a philosopher. The other, Plato, had been born in 427 BCE and would go on to lay the foundations for a whole philosophical tradition, including aspects of Christianity. Both men presented to a *reading* public a series of conversations that supposedly had taken place between Socrates and a host of interlocutors while he had been alive. Increasingly over time, it is thought, Plato relied on the dramatic device of the dialogue and the fictional voice of Socrates to expound ideas which were all his own.

The most ambitious of Plato's dialogues, known in English as the *Republic*, sets out a rather unworldly version of the ideal state. Although he was not averse to grappling with political issues— indeed, at one stage he gave advice to a 'tyrant' of Syracuse in Sicily—Plato's philosophy tended to advocate a withdrawal from the real, visible world altogether. Everything that we see and experience, Plato argued, is only a crude copy of the eternal and unchanging 'idea' or 'form' that it embodies. It is the task of the philosopher to reach out for knowledge of the real thing, even if it will always lie beyond our senses. Plato's idealism is a far cry from the Greek-on-Greek carnage of the Corinthian War, or Leuctra, or Mantinea, or the politicking that fed those conflicts. But thanks to Plato's artful handling of the written word, we never lose the impression that we are listening to the speaking voice of Socrates, in the constant to and fro of conversation.

At the same time, the art of public speaking flourished as never before, particularly in Athens, where citizens addressed the Assembly or the law courts. This was the art that in time would come to be known by the Greek word *rhetoric* and is still with us today. The English *oratory* derives from its Latin equivalent. In the world of a Greek *polis*, to able to speak well in public, and to persuade your hearers, was much more than an accomplishment. In a law court, it could be a matter of life or death; a speech in the Assembly could make the difference between peace and war.

Just like the informal conversations of Socrates, formal speeches, too, were beginning to cross over into the domain of writing and gain a new life far beyond their original context. By the time that Socrates was tried and condemned, it was becoming increasingly common for orators to compose their speeches in writing ahead of their delivery—just as politicians or their speechwriters do today. Not only that, but in Athens a lively market had grown up for ghostwritten speeches to be used in law courts. In a legal system in which there were no barristers and every citizen had to plead his own case before a jury that might be made up of five hundred fellow citizens, there was a market for ready-made speeches written in advance and memorised for the occasion. If you lacked the spontaneous brilliance of a Socrates but could afford the expense, your chances of winning your case would be greatly enhanced when you hired a professional to write your speech for you.

No doubt the same thing went on in other cities too. But it was in recently defeated Athens that the art of speech*writing* really caught fire. This was how Isocrates (no relation to Socrates) started out in his thirties around the year 400 BCE. But soon Isocrates went one better. On his own admission, he lacked the physical stamina to stand up before an audience of six thousand in the Assembly or the five hundred that made up the city's Council or a citizen jury in a court of law. Instead, Isocrates created a name for himself as, in effect, the world's first political columnist—more than two thousand years before the first newspapers. Always couched in the form of a spoken address before a live audience, his speeches were carefully composed in the study, on a papyrus roll, and then circulated in manuscript copies, the equivalent of publication in a preprint age. If Socrates had been the greatest philosopher who never wrote a word, his near-namesake is remembered as the greatest speechmaker of the ancient world who never made a speech.[10]

In 380 BCE, Isocrates published his *Panegyricus*, or *Festival Speech*. The King's Peace had been handed down six years before. Isocrates makes out that he is addressing a crowd assembled from all over the Greek world to celebrate one of the great 'panhellenic' festivals, such as the Olympic Games. Now, he argues, is the time for the Greek city-states to sink their differences and win new glories in 'an expedition . . . gathered together in the cause of the liberty of our allies, dispatched by all Greece, and faring forth to wreak vengeance on the barbarians', that is to say, on the Persians who had twice invaded their homeland a century before.[11] That the Greeks could unite at all for such a purpose was scarcely credible in 380 BCE. But Isocrates draws on the imagined setting for his speech to invoke the spirit of collective euphoria that had been new in the time of Aeschylus and Herodotus. He urges his fellow Hellenes to go beyond identifying with their own particular city-state or region and identify, instead, with Hellas as a whole.[12]

On the face of it, Isocrates was promoting the same idea of Greek unity as Herodotus had once done. But there is a difference. The historian from the Ionian mainland had been even-handed in giving each of the city-states (more or less) its due. Isocrates writes as an Athenian. His whole argument is designed to create a leading role in the proposed expedition for his own city. Athens, he declares, now leads the rest of the Greek world in the art of fine speaking—indeed, in the very sort of verbal dexterity that is on display in the *Festival Speech*:

> By so much has our city exceeded all mankind in matters of thought and speech, that her students have become the teachers of others; she has caused the name of Greeks to be understood, not in terms of kinship any more, but of a way of thinking, and people to be called Greeks if they share our educational system, rather than a common ancestry.[13]

At a stroke, Isocrates had redefined what it meant to be Greek. No longer primarily a matter of kinship or biological inheritance, identity is to be understood as a set of values that anyone can aspire to attain, given sufficient goodwill and effort. In all probability, long before this, outsiders had been attracted to Greek ways of doing things and had adopted Greek customs and even the Greek language. There were signs of something of the sort having happened as far back as Mycenaean times. But to spell it out like this, and to propose it in writing as a principle that applied to all Greeks, now and in the future—that was entirely new. And, against the grain of political probability or the military realities of the time, it was to prove a self-fulfilling prophecy. How this would come about, no one alive in 380 BCE could possibly have foreseen. But both Isocrates and Plato, with their mastery of the written word masquerading as oral speech, would play their parts, both in and beyond their lifetimes. More than two thousand years before there was ever any question of Athens becoming the real capital of Greece, the city that had been humiliated in the Peloponnesian War and that still struggled to project its power on the battlefield was on its way to becoming the world's first *cultural* capital.

WHEN ISOCRATES SENT out his *Festival Speech* to be copied and circulated, Philip II, King of the Macedonians, as he would come to be known, was just two years old. Twenty years later, and two years after the Greek city-states had fought themselves to an impasse at Mantinea, the death of his brother in battle brought Philip to the throne. The year was 360 BCE.[14] The battle had been fought between Macedonians and Illyrians, far away on the northern fringe of the Greek world. At the time, the news was barely noticed among the city-states. But this was the event that would herald the arrival, within a very few years, of a new and decisive force in interstate Greek politics.

Contemporaries recognised even in his lifetime that 'Europe had never produced a man like Philip son of Amyntas'. It was a two-edged assessment. Tales of Philip's drunkenness and debauchery abounded in the ancient world. But at the same time, according to one later account, he had been 'possessed of eloquence and a remarkable oratorical talent'. Wounds sustained in battle at different times in his life had left him with one eye and a pronounced limp. But much of Philip's later success would be the result of astute diplomacy rather than the brutality of which he was also capable. A modern biographer credits him with creating the 'first nation state in Europe' and suggests that it was Philip, far more than his more famous son Alexander, who truly laid the foundations for the conquests and the new Greek civilisation to come.[15]

This was the man who wasted no time in pulling together the ramshackle kingdom he had inherited. Next, he began to enlarge it at the expense of its neighbours. The nearest of these were the settlements that Greeks from the southern Aegean had been building on the coastline of Macedonia and Thrace for several centuries. All of these had been established on the *polis* model and were technically autonomous. But from the early years of the Peloponnesian War, Athens and Sparta had competed for the allegiance of these settlements; each, at different times, exercised varying degrees of control over them. Now, Philip began a series of campaigns to take control of his own coastline and gain access to the sea. With a mixture of guile and brute force, one by one he annexed these settlements to his kingdom or else obliterated them.

With Macedonia well on the way to becoming a regional power, it was only to be expected that the next time war broke out among the Greek city-states, Philip would be drawn in. In 355 BCE, a spat began over the custodianship of the sanctuary of Delphi. A 'sacred war', as conflicts of this type were conventionally known, dragged on for almost ten years. The immediate protagonists were Thebes and a number of very small states indeed, in central Greece, that traditionally had worked together to administer the sacred site. But as usual, the conflict widened through a network of shifting alliances. It was an appeal to Philip by one of the states involved, in 353 BCE, that brought the Macedonians for the first time into the fray. By 346 BCE, when terms of peace were hammered out, Philip was in a position to dictate them. And despite face-saving formulas all round, it was he who emerged as the only real victor—the new master of the ring.[16]

For the Greeks of the most powerful city-states, the immediate challenge was political and military: How to respond to this new threat to their own ambitions? But thanks to the Athenian habit of preserving their political debates in writing, we can see that a deeper perplexity held the southern Greeks in its grip. The argument was not only about politics. It was also about *identity*. Who *were* those Macedonians who had suddenly arrived on the doorstep of the Greek city-states and seemed poised to take over? For Demosthenes, the statesman whose passionate oratory would dominate the Athenian Assembly from the 350s to the 320s BCE and be admired ever since, Philip was a monster bent on the destruction of everything the Greeks had ever held dear. 'Not only is he no Hellene,' thundered Demosthenes in a speech delivered at a time when the peace of 346 BCE was already beginning to unravel, but also

> he has nothing to do with the Hellenes. He is not even a barbarian from a place that one could speak well of, but a pestilence of a Macedonian, from a place that used not to be able to provide even a slave worth buying.[17]

One Athenian's idea of a 'pestilence' could be another's golden opportunity. Isocrates was ninety years old in 346 BCE but as active an opinion-former as ever. He had never given up on his long-cherished idea of a united Greek expedition against Persia. Here, in Philip, was a force capable of filling the gap at the top and providing the leadership that had eluded both Athens and Sparta for so long. In a wordy and often obsequious open letter, written in May 346 BCE, Isocrates addresses Philip directly and lays out for him his destiny. This is to be nothing less than to unite all the Greeks and lead them in avenging the wrongs inflicted by the Persians a century and a half before.[18]

Isocrates was writing as much for home consumption as to flatter the man he addressed. For the benefit of his Athenian readers, he played up the traditional claim made by Macedonian monarchs that their dynasty was directly descended from the demigod of legend, Heracles, and had come originally from the city of Argos in the Peloponnese. As a descendant of the most 'Hellenic' hero of all time, argued Isocrates, Philip was ideally suited to lead the expedition against the Persian 'barbarians'. His subjects, the Macedonian rank and file, on the other hand, Isocrates rather carefully describes as 'a kinship group not of the same race'. Greek speakers would have to rethink the simple division of the world into 'Hellenes' and 'barbarians' that went back to the Persian Wars. From now on, and for as long as it continued to matter, 'Macedonians' would become an in-between category, sometimes opposed to 'Hellenes', sometimes grouped along with them in opposition to 'barbarians', depending on the point of view of the person speaking.[19]

The question of Macedonian identity, that so preoccupied Athenian opinion-formers and politicians in the middle of the fourth century BCE, has continued to divide scholars in our own day. The truth must surely be that the Macedonians living in the time of Philip II were as 'Hellenic' as they chose to be—and *when* they chose to be. Often, they seem to have prided themselves on their differences from the Greeks of the city-states.[20] Macedonia was, in Greek terms, an *ethnos*, meaning a more or less tribal society ruled by a hereditary monarch. Society was hierarchical, with the king at the top and surrounded by a competitive military elite, known as *Companions*. City-dwelling Greeks, accustomed to diluting their wine with water, were routinely horrified that Macedonians drank theirs neat. For us today that might not seem so terrible—but the stories of both Philip and his son Alexander indulging in binge drinking and drunken violence with their Companions are too frequent and too well-attested to ignore. These were not so much individual character traits as part of the culture of the Macedonian court.

On the other hand, there is good evidence that the Greek language had been spreading northwards from Greek-speaking Thessaly since the eighth century BCE. By the time of Philip II, not only the Macedonian royal house but also their elite, at the very least, had been giving their sons and daughters Greek names for several generations. Many of the most characteristic Macedonian names are transparently formed from Greek words. Among them are some of the most famous: Philip ('Horse-Loving'), Cleopatra ('Father's Fame'), Ptolemy ('Warlike'). Whatever languages or dialects may once have been spoken among the people over whom they ruled, the highest levels of Macedonian society were thoroughly

Greek-speaking by the mid-fourth century BCE. And wherever the elite led, the rest could be expected to follow. Macedonia, in other words, was rapidly *becoming* Greek.[21]

Philip led the way more vigorously than any Macedonian king had done before him. Under his rule, Macedonian centres of population began to *look* like Greek cities. At Aegae, the old capital now used for mostly ceremonial purposes, at Pella, that by 400 had replaced it closer to the coast, and at Dion on the lower slopes of Mount Olympus, colonnaded temples began to rise, built in the manner found throughout the Greek-speaking world. At Aegae, as well as a sumptuous new palace, Philip had a huge semicircular theatre built right in front of it, in the Greek style. Athenian drama had been appreciated in Macedonia since at least the end of the fifth century BCE, when the elderly Euripides had retired there. During Philip's reign, painters, sculptors, and philosophers from the southern city-states, and especially from Athens, were recruited in large numbers. The most famous of these was Aristotle, who had studied philosophy under Plato in Athens and would later return there to found his own school. Aristotle's home city of Stageira had been one of those Greek settlements on the coast of Macedonia recently razed by Philip. But this was to prove no bar to Philip recruiting Aristotle to become private tutor to his son, Alexander— nor to Aristotle accepting the post.[22]

Most striking of all is the earliest evidence for the public use of writing in Macedonia. This was another innovation which took place under Philip. Along with written documents and the first public inscriptions on stone came a choice, one that would have far-reaching implications. Once upon a time, in the days when Greek-speaking settlements were being founded all over the Mediterranean, each one would develop its own distinctive version of the alphabet and proudly display its own local form of speech on stone. But no longer. As literacy had become widespread, standardisation had set in. By the mid-fourth century BCE, writing was reaching far beyond the bounds of any one city-state. If you wanted your words to be intelligible and to be read by as many people as possible, you would need to write in a way that people would be familiar with, wherever they happened to live and irrespective of how they spoke at home. It is not clear whether the initiative came from Philip himself, but when Macedonians began to put pen to papyrus and to carve words into stone for public consumption, they did so not in their own dialect but in the Greek of Athens, known as Attic.[23]

THE PEACE BROKERED by Philip in 346 BCE would prove short-lived. During the next five years, most of his energies were directed eastwards, towards conquering Thrace. Apart from city-states on the coastline that had been founded centuries earlier by Greeks from the Aegean, Thrace lay outside the Greek-speaking world, as its people had their own language. But once the Macedonian army had subdued all of Thrace and reached the straits that separate the continents of Europe and Asia, whose shores had been thoroughly 'colonised' by Greeks, Philip's interests came directly into conflict with those of Athens. This was because the Athenians were dependent, as ever, on supplies of grain from the Greek settlements on the Black Sea coasts. A hostile power in control of the straits had starved Athens into submission twice before and could well do so again. Amid this crisis, in 341 BCE, Demosthenes even urged an alliance with the old enemy, Persia, to head off the new one, Macedonia.[24]

War broke out the next year, in 340 BCE. Attempts led by Demosthenes to recruit an Athenian-led alliance against the Macedonians met with only a lukewarm response. Once again, the city-states of central Greece were at loggerheads over the custodianship of Delphi. Philip had acted as arbitrator before. Would he do so again? Appeals by rival contestants gave him the excuse he may have been waiting for to divert his armies from Thrace and bring them south. Panic broke out in the Athenian Assembly when news arrived that an army of Macedonians and northern Greeks thirty thousand strong, with two thousand cavalry, had already reached the borders of neighbouring Boeotia. For once, so great was the emergency, Demosthenes was able to persuade his city's age-old rivals, the Thebans, to fight alongside Athens to preserve both their homelands. The decisive battle was fought at the beginning of August 338 BCE on the banks of the Cephisus River in Boeotia, below the town of Chaeronea. On one side were the Macedonians and their northern Greek allies. On the other, more or less matching them in numbers, were the combined forces of Athens and Thebes, with small contingents from a few other city-states. Sparta, as so often now, stood aloof.

Philip won the day. As many as half the Athenians and Thebans were either killed or taken prisoner. Demosthenes himself fought among them and survived to deliver the public oration on the fallen back in Athens shortly afterwards. In another speech that has been often quoted since, the up-and-coming Athenian politician Lycurgus pronounced the obituary in 330 BCE, not only for those who had lost their lives but also for the 'liberty of Hellas' that had been extinguished along with them. Even today, there are many who date the end of 'classical' Greek civilisation to the battle of Chaeronea in 338 BCE.[25]

It all depended on what you meant by *liberty* and *Hellas*. It had been in the crucible of the Persian Wars that these concepts had been forged in the first place. But Demosthenes had been prepared to cut a deal with the Great King of Persia. The 'liberty' of the Greek city-states by now meant little more than the right to annihilate one another on the battlefield in a cycle of mutual attrition in which no one could ever win. So deeply ingrained had the mentality of the autonomous *polis* become in the Greek heartland, it was the idea of their *autonomy from one another* that held the deepest claim on the loyalty of Greek citizens, trumping by some margin their shared identity as Hellenes. 'Hellas' was barely even a pretext.

In any case, Philip's actions during the weeks and months after the battle hardly lived up to the apocalyptic tones of a Demosthenes or a Lycurgus. Thebes was punished by having its democracy replaced by an oligarchy and a Macedonian garrison installed to ensure good behaviour. But Athens was spared, even though its leaders had been far more outspoken against the Macedonians, and for far longer. Those states that had not already promised allegiance to Philip quickly did so. Only Sparta refused. A brief punitive expedition by Macedonian troops into Laconia had the effect of isolating the Spartans in their heartland while leaving their city and its institutions untouched. All the other Greek city-states were then required to send representatives to a conference convened by Philip at Corinth. This was where the new political settlement was handed down. It established a military alliance and a 'Common State (*Koinon*) of the Hellenes', with rules for its governance. Modern historians refer to this as the 'League of Corinth', a name which rather misses the point of the original Greek. In effect, the settlement prescribed a kind of federation, governed by a representative council but with all members owing allegiance to the 'Leader' (the Greek word *hegemon* gives us the word *hegemonic*). Needless to say, the Leader was to be the king of the Macedonians—meaning not just Philip but also his heirs in perpetuity.[26]

Perhaps curiously, and a source of dissension to come, Macedonia itself remained outside the federation. Politically and culturally, Philip chose to mark a separation between his own kingdom and the wider 'Hellas' that for the first time acquired a semblance of political existence under his leadership. For long afterwards, people would continue to talk of 'Greeks' and 'Macedonians' as distinct groups, even though both together would soon make up the nucleus of a rapidly expanding Greek-speaking world.

A second meeting of delegates, summoned from the city-states, took place at Corinth in the spring of 337 BCE. Philip announced his intention of leading an expedition to liberate the Greek cities of the Anatolian seaboard from Persian rule. This was exactly what Isocrates had been preaching in vain for so long: a united, 'panhellenic' expedition against the old, common enemy. Among the last words that Isocrates ever wrote, before his death at the age of ninety-eight, were these, addressed to the victor of Chaeronea. If you can 'force the barbarians into servitude to the Greeks', he wrote to Philip, 'there will be nothing else left for you but to become a god'.[27]

PHILIP BY THIS time controlled a territory that included almost all of today's Greece, much of Bulgaria, Albania, the Republic of North Macedonia, and all the European part of Turkey.[28] No one except Xerxes—and he only very briefly—had ever before held so much power in this region or over so many Greeks. True to his word, a year after his announcement to the Greek representatives assembled at Corinth, Philip despatched the advance guard of the promised all-Greek expedition into Persian-held territory. In the spring of 336 BCE, three of his generals led a force across the strait of the Dardanelles from Europe to Asia.

Presumably Philip still intended, as he had announced at Corinth, to place himself at the head of the main force that was to follow. But he seems to have been in no hurry. First, there was to be a royal wedding celebrated at Aegae, the old, ceremonial capital of Macedonia. The previous year, Philip had married for the seventh time, though several of his previous wives were still living. Now, he was marrying off his daughter, Cleopatra, to a close relative who was the ruler of neighbouring Epiros. All of Philip's own marriages, with the possible exception of the most recent, had been strictly strategic. So was this one for his daughter. A dynastic alliance with Epiros would neutralise a potential threat to his rear while he was away campaigning in Asia.

It would also neutralise a threat closer to home. His estranged fourth wife, Olympias, was not only the mother of the bride and sister of the groom but also belonged to the royal family of Epiros. This mattered because Olympias was the mother of Philip's chosen heir, the twenty-year-old Alexander. Philip and Alexander had quarrelled violently during the past year, apparently over Philip's own latest marriage to a girl closer to his daughter in age. The quarrel had been patched up, at least on the surface, by the summer of 336 BCE. But Alexander, who had led one of the charges at Chaeronea when aged only eighteen, had not been included in the expedition that had been sent across the Dardanelles. Philip was laying his plans carefully. While he had been away on a previous campaign, he had appointed his young heir to manage the kingdom during his absence. This was the role he seems to have been planning for Alexander once again.

The wedding took place at Aegae (modern Vergina) in either July or October 336 BCE. It was in every sense a state occasion. Guests were invited from every corner of the Greek world and beyond. The morning after the ceremony, the recently completed theatre was packed—which implies an audience of many thousands—for the entertainment that had been promised. Despite hard drinking the night before, the festivities were due to begin at sunrise. In procession, statues of the twelve gods of Olympus were wheeled or carried into the circular space in front of the tiered seats. Along with them came a thirteenth, representing Philip himself. Whatever exactly was meant by this, it was the kind of statement that up to this time Greeks, however vainglorious, had always stopped short of making. To traditional ways of thinking, there was a line between mortal men and the immortal gods that no mere human, no matter how powerful, could safely try to cross. Behind the procession came Philip's son and heir, Alexander, walking with the bridegroom, then Philip himself, dressed all in white. The royal bodyguard, ordered by Philip to hang back for the occasion, followed at a discreet distance.

What followed must surely qualify for the most theatrical murder ever staged. As Philip entered the open space in front of the assembled spectators, a former member of his bodyguard rushed up to him, drew a concealed dagger, and plunged it into the king's chest. Philip died on the spot. The assassin ran for the city gates, where there were horses waiting. He would have got away, so the story goes, but he tripped over a trailing vine as he was trying to mount. Three of the king's guards caught up with him and killed him before he could speak.[29]

Philip had been murdered in broad daylight, in front of witnesses numbered in the thousands. No one could doubt the identity of the murderer. His name was Pausanias. The official story was that he had harboured a grudge, not directly against his king but against one of his courtiers, and Philip had refused him redress. But Pausanias did not act alone, as the detail of the getaway horses proves. The convenient vine that tripped him as he was preparing to mount suggests that he was never meant to get away. Even Alexander entertained no doubts that Pausanias had been part of a plot. Those would be the very grounds on which the new king would have several potential rivals for the throne executed in the next few days or weeks, as supposedly complicit.[30]

Speculation has been rife ever since. Ancient authors suspected Alexander's mother, Philip's estranged wife Olympias. Some also, circumspectly, even though they were writing hundreds of years after the event, thought that Alexander himself might have been implicated. Modern historians have returned to the issue—a classic murder mystery with a trail that had already gone cold more than two thousand years ago. Many of them entertain the possibility that Olympias, or Alexander, or both, may have given Pausanias his instructions. No one doubts that the chief beneficiary of Philip's death, at that particular time, was the twenty-year-old who would very shortly afterwards be crowned Alexander III, King of the Macedonians—later to be known the world over as 'Alexander the Great'.[31]

No new evidence is ever going to come to light that would prove the matter one way or the other. But the *manner* of the crime has Alexander's fingerprints all over it. Everything we know about Alexander's life and deeds, both before and after the event, shows an audacity that is still, after so long, breathtaking. Time and again, he would respond to a challenge that everyone else thought impossible and succeed—through ingenuity, physical endurance, sheer delight in risk for its own sake, as well as, surely, an extraordinary run of luck. This is the well-rehearsed story of the most audacious military commander, probably of all time, who spent most of his short life on campaign and never lost a battle. Everything that Alexander did, from his taming of the unbreakable horse Bucephalas in his early teens to the legendary cutting of the Gordian knot and innumerable exploits against towns and fortresses built in remote and inaccessible places, betrays the same ruthlessness and the same determination to succeed at any cost, whether to himself or to others.[32]

Almost everything that Alexander ever did was done in *public*, more or less explicitly performed for show. This was as true of his most celebrated triumphs as it was of those acts that even his most devoted biographers, ancient and modern, have deplored. He would develop a track record for eliminating some of the individuals who had been closest to him and to whom he owed the most.

A comrade who had saved his life in battle would be rewarded by being run through with a pike during a drunken brawl, in front of an assembled company. Others, after serving with him for years, would be judicially murdered, often horribly and always in public, on the flimsiest of pretexts.[33] To commit the ultimate crime in Greek eyes, the killing of one's own father, in a public place, onstage before a huge audience drawn from all over the Greek world, while also being physically present, with his own hands perfectly clean—and to get away with it. . . . Was not that the ultimate test and proof of the psychopathic genius that Alexander would go on to display throughout his life?

In Aegae, a very public wedding had turned into a very public funeral. Philip's body was cremated, then the remaining bones were washed in wine, wrapped in a purple cloak, and placed inside a casket of solid gold emblazoned on the lid with the Macedonian emblem of the sunburst. When the tomb was opened by the archaeologist Manolis Andronikos in 1977, with all its treasures intact, forensic examination of the remains inside the casket revealed that they had belonged to a man in his forties (Philip died at forty-six), with signs of trauma around the right eye and one leg shorter than the other. These details are consistent with the injuries that Philip is known to have suffered in battle. Although doubts have been cast by some archaeologists, it is almost certain that the 'Tomb of Philip', that lies beneath the reconstructed 'Royal Tumulus' on the edge of the Greek market town of Vergina, is indeed the last resting place of Philip II. Alexander himself must have been present at the obsequies and have overseen every detail of what has been preserved.[34]

The new king was now ruler over all the lands and peoples that had been subdued by his father. But to secure his position, it was not enough to eliminate those members of Philip's inner circle who could possibly present a threat in future. Alexander lost no time in making his mark and facing down any actual or potential revolts on several fronts. His first move was to forestall any reassertion of independence by the Greek city-states. The Athenian delegation to the wedding at Aegae had unctuously given an assurance that there would never be a safe haven in their city for anyone who dared to plot against Philip. But no sooner was Philip dead, and the news arrived in Athens, than Demosthenes led jubilant celebrations in the Assembly.[35] And it was not just in Athens that this happened. Other states were restive too. So Alexander's first move was to reconvene the conference at Corinth. His father's tomb had probably only just been sealed when he headed south. But this was to be more than a diplomatic mission. Or rather, it would define Alexander's future ideas of diplomacy. He travelled south at the head of a large Macedonian army.

The Thebans and the Athenians panicked when they found the victors of Chaeronea back, in strength, on the borders of their territory. But Alexander had made his point. So long as they obeyed his orders and sent their representatives to a new meeting at Corinth, their citizens were in no danger from his army. Once the delegates from all the city-states had assembled, he reaffirmed the settlement that his father had handed down two years before and his own position as *hegemon*. Only the Spartans continued to sulk. They sent no delegates nor recognised the terms. Alexander ignored them. The expedition against the Persians would still go ahead, he announced. All the Greek city-states were to contribute troops. They should make preparations and be ready. In the meantime, Alexander had another war to wage, against the Illyrians, Macedonia's northern neighbours. And so he headed north again with his army in the spring of 335 BCE.[36]

Then, a few months later, came news that he was dead, killed on campaign. Once again, rejoicing flickered through the Greek states like wildfire. This time it was Thebes that took the lead, declaring a struggle in the name of 'liberty' and a mission to 'throw off the Macedonian yoke'.[37] But Alexander was not dead. He arrived outside Thebes, at the head of an army, with characteristic swiftness. In the event, the Thebans stood alone in their defiance, although they had many sympathisers, including Demosthenes and most of the Athenians. When the defenders refused to back down, Alexander's troops took Thebes by storm. Once the battle was over, Alexander determined to make an example of Thebes. The warning was all the more effective because it was carried out in the name of the 'Common State of the Hellenes', whose representatives had to sign up to it. The citadel of Thebes was razed to the ground. Only the house that had once belonged to the poet Pindar was spared, as a mark of respect. Some six thousand Thebans were killed and thirty thousand sold into slavery. Once again, the Athenians were fearful that they would be next; once again they were spared. Alexander would never greatly trust the Athenians—and with good reason, as later events would prove. But at this point he needed them as more or less willing allies if he was to justify his invasion of Asia as revenge for the depredations of the Persian Wars.[38]

By the spring of 334 BCE, everything was ready. All through the preceding winter, contingents summoned from the Greek city-states had been mustering in Macedonia. The advance guard of Macedonian troops, that had been sent to Anatolia by Philip, was coming under increasing pressure from the new Great King of Persia. Darius III had come to the throne at about the same time as Philip's assassination, and was very effectively beginning to assert his authority. If the Macedonians were to stay in the field against him, they would have to be reinforced soon. Alexander led his army from Amphipolis, in Macedonia, to the Dardanelles in just twenty days. Then, while the whole army and its baggage train were being ferried across the straits, he took time to visit the site of ancient Troy. It suited his purpose to present himself as the new Achilles, the 'best of the Achaeans', according to Homer in the *Iliad*. His would be the destiny to carry forward the age-old conflict between Europe and Asia that (according to Herodotus, not Homer) had begun with that legendary war.[39]

The full force of Greeks and Macedonians that came together on the Asian side of the Dardanelles may have reached as many as fifty thousand men. It included an elite cavalry numbering about five thousand. Compared to estimates of the amphibious forces that Xerxes had once led in the opposite direction, the size was quite modest. Alexander would soon get used to his forces being heavily outnumbered in each of their major battles. But this was the largest army that had ever come together under Greek command.[40] The greatest adventure in the whole of Greek history, and surely one of the greatest in the history of the world, was about to begin.

THE PERSIANS HAD moved too slowly either to hinder the crossing of the Dardanelles or to prevent Alexander's forces from joining up with the Macedonians already on the Asian side. But they were not far away. Battle was joined a few miles inland from the southern shore of the Sea of Marmara. A steep-banked river then called the Granicus presented a natural obstacle that the Persians could exploit to halt the Greek advance. This was the first of four set-piece battles fought during the next eight years that would determine the course of the campaign. At one point, Alexander came close to losing his life. But in the end the Persians were pushed back across the river. Their retreat turned into a rout. The invaders had won the day.

After it was over, Alexander sent a trophy to Athens, to be dedicated to the city's patron goddess, Athena. Accompanying it was the inscribed legend, 'Alexander, son of Philip, and the Hellenes, excluding the Lacedaemonians, dedicate these spoils, taken from the barbarians who dwell in Asia'.[41] It was the old opposition writ large: between Hellenes and barbarians, between Europe and Asia. But there was a barb, too. The 'Lacedaemonians'—the Spartans—were the only Greeks who had refused to join Philip's 'Common State' or to subscribe to the expedition. The Spartans had also, not long before, been the bitterest rivals of the Athenians. And the trophy itself consisted of precisely three hundred captured suits of armour. This had been the number of Spartans killed during the defence of the pass of Thermopylae in 480 BCE, remembered ever since as the most heroic act of self-sacrifice during the Persian Wars. Alexander's dedication to the patron goddess of Athens was the ultimate snub to Sparta. The military machine that had humbled Athens in the Peloponnesian War had become simply irrelevant.

In the same spirit, though far more chilling in modern eyes, was the savagery shown to the sizeable force of *Greek* mercenaries who had fought in the battle on the Persian side. During the battle itself, Alexander had given orders for this contingent to be surrounded and 'butchered to a man'. Despite this, some two thousand survived to be taken captive. To make an example of them, Alexander had them sent back to Macedonia in chains and put to hard labour. The conference at Corinth had expressly forbidden citizens of member-states from enlisting in foreign armies.[42] So Alexander's behaviour could still be seen as the legitimate actions of the *hegemon* of the Common State of the Hellenes. Even the harshness of the methods was scarcely out of the ordinary by the standards of traditional Greek interstate warfare. But the episode also dramatically highlights how far Alexander's expedition was from being anything like a Greek 'crusade', as is often claimed. More Greeks actually fought on the *Persian* side against him than under his banner. Often disparagingly called 'mercenaries', these paid soldiers were in many cases exiles from their own cities or, like the survivors of the destruction of Thebes, implacable enemies of the Macedonians by conviction. The Common State was very far from being able to claim the allegiance of all Hellenes.[43]

By the autumn of 334 BCE, Alexander's army had traversed the entire Aegean seaboard of Anatolia and had reached the south coast. The work of liberating the Greek cities was already done— even though some of them, notably Miletus and what had been Herodotus's hometown of Halicarnassus, had put up resistance and had to be 'liberated' by force. At the end of the year, Alexander turned inland and made for the heart of Anatolia. It was at the ancient Phrygian city of Gordium, not far from today's Ankara, that he is supposed to have 'cut the Gordian knot'. Centuries before, this knot had been tied so intricately that no one could undo it; anyone who succeeded, according to a local prophecy, would become master of the entire Persian Empire. Alexander's solution, so the story goes, was to slice through the ropes with his sword. The places he was passing through, by this stage of the expedition, had previously lain on the outer fringes of the Greek world. As he resumed the march next spring, Alexander was leading his troops ever farther from that world and from the political arrangements that his father had set up for its governance.

The second great battle was fought in November 333 BCE on the south coast of today's Turkey at a place the Greeks called Issus. Darius III led his troops in person this time. When he fled the battle, his camp followers and much of his baggage train fell into the Macedonians' hands. In this way Alexander took captive Darius's mother, one of his wives, and two of his daughters. For centuries afterwards, he would earn praise for his treatment of these royal captives, which a later age would have called 'chivalrous'. Darius then offered peace terms, but Alexander rejected them. He himself was the new 'King of all Asia'. 'Everything you possess is now mine,' he wrote back haughtily. If Darius disagreed, he would have to come back and fight another day.[44]

That day would come two years later, when the two armies once again faced each other, this time on the plains of today's Iraqi Kurdistan, not far from Mosul and the site of the ancient city of Nineveh. By this time, Darius was prepared to hand over to Alexander the entire western half of his empire, up to the River Euphrates, as well as his daughter in marriage and an enormous ransom for his other captured family members.[45] But Alexander was not interested in making peace. His expedition had already crossed the Euphrates, and the Tigris beyond it, to reach Gaugamela, where the battle would be fought. Alexander had used the time in between to win two famous sieges, of Tyre and Gaza, and massacre most of the survivors among those who had resisted. He had also annexed from Persia the whole of Egypt, with the willing support of its people, and paid a visit to an oracle at the remote oasis of Siwah in the Libyan Desert. There, the priest may or may not have told him that he was the son of Zeus, whom the Egyptians worshipped under the name of Amun. Before leaving Egypt, it is said that he laid out the ground plan for a new city on the Mediterranean coast to be named after him—Alexandria.

At Gaugamela, on 1 October 331, Alexander faced his largest opposing force yet. This was the first time that the Greek cavalry encountered war elephants, recruited from Darius's easternmost provinces. But once again, the enemy was routed. Darius escaped with his life but would soon be treacherously murdered by his own side. Alexander's way was now open to Babylon, one of the greatest cities of the ancient world, and Susa, the administrative capital of the Persian Empire. In both cities he seems to have been acclaimed as the new, legitimate Great King of Persia.[46] He then fought his way south to Persepolis, the Greek name for the empire's old ceremonial centre. Before Alexander was done there, his troops set fire to the sumptuous palace of the Persian kings and a large part of it was destroyed. According to one version of events, the fire was started by Alexander himself, by accident during a drunken rampage. Another presents it as a calculated act of revenge for the burning of Athens by Xerxes and Mardonius. Shortly afterwards, Alexander dismissed from his command all the troops from the Greek alliance that had followed him thus far. Those who wished to enlist for further conquests were invited to do so as mercenaries. And some did. The rest went home.[47]

In the eyes of those who continued to follow him, Alexander's goals from this point on became harder and harder to understand. The historians on whose words we rely for our information, most of them writing in Greek several hundred years later, were just as puzzled, as indeed are we today. Was it an insatiable desire for conquest that led Alexander on, now that all his readily understood objectives had been achieved? Or was there a rational plan? Was his undoubted tactical military brilliance harnessed to a strategic *political* mind and a longer-term purpose?

Alexander left Persepolis in May 330 BCE. For the next four and a half years, he led his armies north and east to the shores of the Caspian Sea and far into modern Afghanistan, then south, to cross the River Indus into the Punjab. The last of the great battles of the campaign was fought on the banks of the River Jhelum, in today's Pakistan, in May 326. The enemy this time was the rajah of the Pauravas, a gigantic figure of a man whom the Greeks called Porus. His army included the largest contingent of war elephants that the expedition had yet faced. Despite the elephants, Porus lost; Alexander allowed him to keep his kingdom in return for his future allegiance.

Shortly afterwards, the expedition reached its farthest point. Camp had been pitched on the bank of the River Hyphasis, now the River Beas, in northwest India, probably not far from Amritsar. All the ancient sources agree on what happened next. Alexander wanted to go on. There was more rich land to be conquered, between here and the next even greater river, the Ganges. Beyond that, Greeks believed at the time, must lie the river called Ocean, that marked the ultimate boundary of the inhabited earth. Alexander urged his men to follow him onwards, to create an empire that 'will have no boundaries but what God Himself has made for the whole world'.[48]

If Alexander did in fact utter those words, or something similar, it was the only time in his life when he failed to get his way. As the story continues, the men were implacable. They would go no farther. After sulking in his tent for three whole days, Alexander agreed to turn—not quite back, but aside, to follow the course of the Indus downriver to the Indian Ocean. Along the way he fought more battles, brutally imposing his authority against anyone who dared to stand against him. Once at the coast, he divided his forces, sending one half by sea up the Arabian Gulf and into the strait of Hormuz, while he himself led the land force by a punishing route through the deserts of Baluchistan.

This is the Alexander of legend, the world conqueror who would never have stopped unless he had been forced to. The story may well be true. No ancient source contradicts it, and most modern historians take it at face value. But it has been suggested that Alexander's motivation may have been more calculated. According to this alternative view, the path of Alexander's conquests followed the traditional boundaries of the Persian Empire at its greatest extent—so far and no farther. His strategic and political objective would therefore have been to assert his personal authority over all the far-flung domains of the empire that he had conquered with the defeat of Darius. If this was so, then his one and only reported defeat, by his own subordinates on the banks of the Hyphasis, was no such thing, and the return via the Indus and Baluchistan had already been part of the plan.[49]

Alexander arrived back at the Persian capital, Susa, in the spring of 324 BCE. Apart from a brief campaign against a rebel movement the following winter, he concentrated on the administration of his empire. Evidently, it had never been his intention simply to put his own people in charge of the lands they had conquered, still less to impose Greek or Macedonian ways upon them. To some extent like the Persian kings before him, and very much as the Romans would later do on an even larger scale, Alexander went out of his way to win over the local ruling class in each region and to exercise control through them.

A constant complaint by contemporaries and by later Greek historians was that their hero demeaned himself when he conferred titles and responsibilities on defeated 'barbarians', and himself adopted 'barbarian' ways of dressing and behaving. But what looked like 'going over to the enemy' and the self-aggrandisement of a 'tyrant' or an oriental despot (all traditional terms of abuse in the ancient Greek world) have seemed to modern historians more like the signs of a far-reaching programme for cultural and political fusion.[50] The empire that Alexander was busy consolidating in 324 BCE was not conceived as a *Greek* empire. It may well have been a first—ever—attempt at global supremacy, deliberately transcending the boundaries of ethnicities, cultures, and identities. But, even though Alexander had probably never had any such intention, the *effect* of his conquests was already, visibly, to carry Greek ideas, Greek ways of doing and making things, and above all the Greek language far inland from the places where they had started out, across the Asian landmass as far as today's Uzbekistan, Afghanistan, Pakistan, and the northwestern corner of India.

The result can be compared to the spread of 'global English' since the nineteenth century of our own era—and it came about for very much the same reasons. Just as English is spoken and written all over the world today by millions of people of very many different backgrounds and ethnicities, so the *Koine* (or 'Common Greek') of Alexander's day, based on the prestige dialect of classical Athens, was already taking root as a universal language of government, commerce, and culture.

MEANWHILE, BACK IN Athens itself, the years when Alexander was storming through the east were a time of remarkable *cultural* investment. Ever since the exemplary destruction of Thebes in 335 BCE, the world of the Greek city-states had experienced an almost unprecedented interval of peace. The settlement laid down by Philip after the battle of Chaeronea seemed to be working well. True, there had been a revolt by Sparta in 331 BCE. But no other state joined in, and the Spartans had never been part of the Common State of the Hellenes anyway. The role of *hegemon* had been taken by Antipater, the regent left behind by Alexander to rule over Macedonia. Antipater had put down the Spartan rebellion within a year. In 324 BCE, the peace was still holding throughout the entire Greek peninsula and the islands of the Aegean.

Peace brought renewed prosperity. Athens was not the only city-state whose treasury had been emptied by decades of interstate warfare. Now revenues were flowing again. The citizen body of democratic Athens was receptive to the big-spending ideas of their most accomplished orator and administrator, Lycurgus. New public works were designed to impress citizens and visitors alike. One of these was a marble stadium for the games that were part of the regular Panathenaic Festival, the city's local answer to the Olympic Games. Another was the splendid new theatre, also built of marble, on the southern slope below the Acropolis. Plays had been performed there, in the sanctuary of Dionysus, for more than 150 years. But, remarkably, Athens had never boasted a permanent theatre until this time. The Theatre of Dionysus that we see today took thirty years to build and was not finished at the time of Lycurgus's death in 324 BCE. It seems to have been part of a deliberate drive to establish the dramatic repertoire of the previous century as a distinctively Athenian 'brand', a legacy to the whole Greek-speaking world.[51]

These were the years when the philosopher Aristotle moved to Athens and taught students in a school, known as the Lyceum, built in a shady grove on the banks of the Ilissos River. Alexander's former tutor would always remain an outsider in Athens, denied the rights that came with citizenship. Shortly before he arrived there, Aristotle's experiments with living organisms in a lagoon on the island of Lesbos had laid the foundation not only for biology as a subject of scientific enquiry but also for the experimental method which is today the basis for every branch of science.[52] In Athens, in his class on philosophy, Aristotle told his students that the goal of human life is 'so far as possible to become immortal and to strive in every way to live according to the finest thing that is in us', that is, according to reason. Alexander may really have believed he was a god and seems to have claimed divine honours from his subjects; but his more humane master argued instead that godhead lies within the grasp of every human being—and without having to kill, conquer, or destroy anyone or anything.[53]

At the same time, the public spaces of the Agora and the precinct of the new Theatre of Dionysus were becoming populated on a scale never before seen by men and women made of bronze and marble. Sculptors had devised techniques to create a more fluid impression of bodies in motion. A softer sensuousness was replacing the austere formality of the previous century. The greatest Greek sculptor of the age, the Athenian Praxiteles, is reputed to have been the first to create a female figure entirely nude—and she was no less a personage than Aphrodite, the goddess of love. His *Aphrodite of Cnidus* caused a scandal when it was first seen, perhaps around the year 330 BCE. The explicit sensuality of the pose has provoked conflicting responses in viewers ever since.[54]

There must have been a sense of unreality during those years, as Athenians and other Greeks went about these peaceful pursuits while news kept arriving of more and more battles fought and won hundreds of miles to the east. It was one thing to speculate about the nature of human happiness, to catalogue and promote classic works of dramatic art, or to celebrate the languid pleasures of the human body. But even as we still celebrate these achievements today, it takes an effort to remember that at the time these must have felt like stolen pleasures. Nobody in the Greek world knew when, or whether, Alexander would return, or if he did, what he might do next.

AFTER HE HAD dismissed their contingents from his army at Persepolis, Alexander seems to have given little thought to the Greek city-states that he had left behind. Back in Susa, early in the summer of 324 BCE, it was time for him to take stock. The centre of gravity of his newly conquered empire lay in Mesopotamia, not the Aegean. But then Alexander decided it was time for the Greeks to learn where they belonged in the new order of things. The settlement that his father had reached with them a dozen years earlier, after the battle of Chaeronea, had been made for a different world. The four-year cycle of the Olympic Games was about to come around again. The full moon on 4 August would bring the great festival to its climax.[55] The sanctuary of Zeus at Olympia would be packed not only with athletes but also with spectators and political actors drawn from the whole Greek-speaking world. Alexander had a shock in store for them.

When his envoy arrived at Olympia, he read out a document that has been known ever since as the 'Exiles' Decree'. On the face of it, the decree looked innocuous, even humanitarian. But its political implications were to prove far-reaching. Alexander announced that every citizen who had been deported from his home state or had lost citizen rights must now be allowed to return. The decree also gave Antipater authority to impose its terms by force if necessary.

To understand the full significance of this measure, we have to imagine a world in which it was not only thinkable but also normal practice to use deportation and deprivation of civic rights as a routine legal sanction. The Greek world of the fourth century BCE was full of deportees. Some would have been criminals convicted of an offence. But the great majority were either mercenaries who had forfeited their rights back home, political exiles who had fallen foul of the ruling faction in their city, or sometimes a whole population that had been displaced by an act of conquest. A particularly notorious case concerned the island of Samos, whose people had been deported en masse to the Anatolian mainland by Athens some four decades previously. In the summer of 324 BCE, as many as twenty thousand of these displaced persons had found their way to Olympia for the sacred festival. When the decree was read out, their jubilation was predictable.

For everyone else, it seemed like a recipe for chaos. What would be the rights of people living in property confiscated from owners who had been deported? Where were the returnees to be housed? Most shocking of all, the decree cut right across the terms of the settlement for the Greek city-states that had been handed down by Philip fourteen years before and subsequently renewed by Alexander himself. There was no question of consultation among delegates to the Corinth conference or of reconvening that notional governing body of the Common State of the Hellenes. In effect, the Common State was dead. In the words of one modern historian, this was 'the language of autocracy'.[56] It also had a very specific purpose. By this simple stroke, Alexander could ensure that every Greek city-state, however tiny, would in future be home to a sizeable proportion of citizens who owed their rights not to their own government but to Alexander personally. Autocracy, indeed.

No Greek state dared defy the ruling. But several, including Athens, did their utmost to drag their feet while they tried to negotiate exceptions. This was still going on the following summer when news arrived in Greece: Alexander was dead. This time, it was true. He had been taken ill in Babylon and died there on 10 June 323 BCE, a month short of his thirty-third birthday. The cause, despite the inevitable rumours that began to circulate shortly afterwards and have never quite been laid to rest, was almost certainly natural.

Far from mourning the loss of the most successful military leader the Greek world would ever know, or even celebrating his short life, the Athenians were as jubilant as they had been at the death of Philip before him. Secret preparations to throw off the 'Macedonian despotism' began as soon as the first rumours reached the city. Once the news was confirmed, the Assembly resolved 'that the *demos* (people) should take thought for the common liberty of the Hellenes'. Envoys were sent to potential allies to remind them how in the past the Athenian *demos* had stood up for the freedom of 'Hellas as the common homeland of the Hellenes' and to urge them to fight again, now, for their 'common deliverance'.[57]

It is a reliable measure of feeling among the Greek states that at least twenty of them responded to this call. In response, Antipater led a Macedonian force south into Greece. For a time, the Macedonians were besieged by the rebels in the town of Lamia— hence the modern name for the conflict, the 'Lamian War'. But after the arrival of reinforcements from Macedonia, the Greek states were roundly defeated at the battle of Crannon, in Thessaly, in September 322 BCE. Antipater then imposed a separate peace on each of the allies. The penalty for Athens was to have a Macedonian garrison imposed. The democratic constitution was abolished and replaced by an oligarchy. Only a cabal made up of the wealthiest citizens would be allowed to vote in the Assembly.[58] Demosthenes, whose power of oratory and whose passionate opposition to Macedonian expansion had dominated Athenian civil life for three decades, fled the city, only to take poison as Antipater's men came after him.

The story of Athens as a political and military power was finally over. But the cultural investment by Lycurgus and his contemporaries would prove its worth in the long run. Athens from this time on would fulfil the prophecy of Isocrates to become the *cultural* capital of a whole new, vastly expanded Greek-speaking world. So new would that world turn out to be, and so different the civilisation it would go on to produce, that today we call it not 'Hellenic' but 'Hellenistic'—from a Greek word that originally meant 'adopting Greek ways' or 'becoming Greek'.[59]

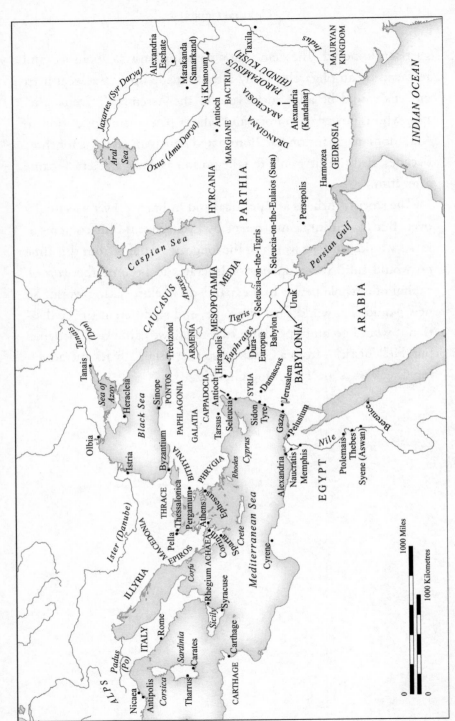

6. The Hellenistic world

6

'BECOMING GREEK'

322 BCE–27 BCE

I F ALEXANDER HAD ever intended to create a 'new world order', those who came after him failed spectacularly to see the project through. For thirty years after his death in Babylon, his former commanders fought among themselves—much as the Greek city-states had been doing for hundreds of years, only on a much larger geographical scale. Indeed, everything about the new Greek world that was emerging was gigantic compared to anything that had gone before—from the egos of its rulers to the monumental buildings they created and the millions of non-Greeks who were now their subjects. Eventually, three relatively stable new kingdoms emerged, one in each of the continents that made up the known world: Asia, Africa, and Europe. Each kingdom would be ruled by a dynasty founded by one of those 'successors', as the former commanders came to be known.[1] But the Greek-speaking world that we call 'Hellenistic' extended even farther, both to the east and to the west.

Starting in the east, wherever the Macedonian armies had passed and Alexander had left behind garrisons to protect their gains, a Greek-speaking population remained. Almost immediately, the easternmost of these regions was won back by the Indian king Chandragupta (Sandrakottos to Greek historians). The dynasty he founded, the Mauryans, would go on to dominate much of the Indian subcontinent. Those Greeks and Macedonians who lived in the territories reconquered by Chandragupta would be absorbed into the kingdom of his grandson, Ashoka. This king was an enthusiastic convert to Buddhism. An inscription from Alex-andria-in-Arachosia, today's Kandahar in Afghanistan, announces the success of the new religion, written in two languages, one of which is Greek. Evidently, Greek speakers were among those con-verted. And indeed one by the name of Menander would play a part in the development of Indian Buddhism a century later.[2]

As the Mauryan Empire in turn crumbled, new petty kingdoms emerged in the area of today's Pakistan. Known as 'Indo-Greek', the last of these seems to have survived for a little over three hun-dred years. So Greek rule in that part of the subcontinent lasted longer than the British Raj of modern times, that ended in 1947. No one ever wrote a history of these kings or their subjects, or if they did, their words have not come down to us. Often, the only evidence that they had once existed lies in the coins they minted. These are Greek in style and are stamped with the names and stylised images of the rulers. For a time, the city of Taxila, not far from the modern capital of Pakistan, Islamabad, was home to Greek-speaking kings and a distinctive style of sculpture that mixes Indian with Greek techniques and motifs. Known as Gandharan, from the name of the wider region, this art could still produce some remarkable hybrid forms, even after the last of the Greek kingdoms had disappeared.[3]

We know slightly more, but still tantalisingly little, about the Greek speakers of Bactria. This was a region geographically equiv-alent to today's Afghanistan and the southern part of Uzbekistan. Conquered by Alexander, Bactria would maintain its political in-dependence as a minor Macedonian kingdom on the fringes of the Hellenistic world for at least a century and a half. During that time, Kandahar and Samarkand were flourishing Greek cities. In 1966, the remains of another were discovered in eastern Afghanistan, on the border with Tajikistan. The site is known by the modern name of Ai Khanoum. Some of the buildings uncovered there by archaeologists are in the Persian style; others are immediately recognisable as Greek.

Carved on a monument at Ai Khanoum are several of the famous moral maxims that had first been displayed in the sanctuary of Apollo at Delphi, more than two thousand miles distant. The author of the inscription identifies himself as one Clearchus, probably to be identified with Aristotle's former student of that name who had gone from his native Cyprus to study in Athens before winding up in this far corner of the Greek-speaking world. Clearchus describes how he had 'conscientiously transcribed' the words in their original setting so that they would 'shine light even from so far away'. In another Greek inscription from Afghanistan, a businessman who had made good after many trials tells his story on his tombstone. 'Sophytos, son of Naratos', is unlikely to have spoken Greek as his mother tongue because neither his own nor his father's name is Greek. But whoever composed his epitaph had a sophisticated grasp not just of the language but of literary conventions too. Whether the words are his own or not, it was the dead man's express desire to turn his life into 'a speaking monument upon the road'. Greek, at this time and in this place, was the natural medium for doing so.[4]

Then, tracking westwards, there was Mesopotamia, the 'land between the two rivers', the Tigris and the Euphrates. Lying at the centre of the Fertile Crescent, where agriculture is believed to have begun, this had been one of the world's most densely populated regions for several millennia already. Susa, built on a tributary of the Tigris, had been the administrative capital of Persia. Babylon, on the Euphrates, had once ruled over an empire of its own and boasted one of the wonders of the ancient world, the Hanging Gardens, supposed to have been built by its king, Nebuchadnezzar, of biblical fame. Alexander had moved his headquarters from Susa to Babylon shortly before his death. Uruk, farther south on the Euphrates, had an even older history. Once the wars of succession were over, all three of these historic cities would continue to flourish as the main centres of power of the largest of the great Hellenistic kingdoms. Known as 'Asia', this kingdom reached westwards all the way to the Mediterranean and across Anatolia to the Aegean. The rulers of Asia were the Seleucids, the name of the dynasty founded by Seleucus I, who proclaimed himself king (*basileus*) in 305 BCE.

Archaeology shows us that these historic Mesopotamian cities changed remarkably little under the new dispensation. Babylon seems to have had only a small Greek community, possibly restricted to its own quarter. Older Uruk preserves no sign of Greek presence at all—other than the telltale ubiquitous tax receipts pressed into clay, which leave no doubt about who was in charge. Susa now had a new Greek name: 'Seleucia-on-the-Eulaios', but life there seems to have carried on much as before. Greek speakers must have been very much in the minority in such a populous region. But as if there were not cities enough already, Seleucus went on to build new *Greek* ones. In this he was followed by his son, Antiochus I. Most of these cities were named after either Seleucus or Antiochus (Antioch-on-the-Orontes, today's Antakya in southern Turkey, would become the most famous).

The nearest thing the Seleucid kingdom had to an official capital was another new foundation, Seleucia-on-the-Tigris, not far from Babylon at the point where the two rivers come closest together and were linked by a canal. Seleucia-on-the-Tigris very quickly grew to become home to a hundred thousand people—between two and three times the population of Athens in its classical heyday. All these new cities were laid out on the same rectangular grid plan.

Said to have been the brainchild of one Hippodamus of Miletus, back in the fifth century BCE, this system of town planning was now the hallmark of every new city throughout the Greek-speaking world.[5]

The language of the former Persian administration, Aramaic, continued in use alongside Greek for official purposes. Local people adopted Greek names, often in tandem with their original non-Greek ones. Many, perhaps even the majority, would have been able to function in several languages—as indeed they had been doing for centuries before this. The difference was that the *prestige* language was now Greek. It was in Greek that the Babylonian historian Berossus wrote what has been described as a 'sophisticated history' of the ancient city and its civilisation. Not enough of his work survives for us to form any idea of his motives. But we must wonder whether the impulse to write history at all did not come with Berossus's adopted language. At the same time, following the example of Alexander, the Seleucids were at pains to present themselves as the legitimate successors to the Persian rulers they had displaced. To this end, they embarked upon a generous programme of temple building in the traditional style in honour of the old Babylonian gods. The first Seleucus even married a Persian queen, Apama (and named several cities after her, too), though this would prove the exception rather than the rule.[6]

Out of these meetings of Greek with Babylonian minds, during the first century of Seleucid rule came a far-reaching innovation that would ever afterwards affect the way in which history is written and people everywhere think about the distant past. The ancient Babylonians had measured time by the reigns of kings. An event was recorded as having happened in the tenth year of the reign of Nebuchadnezzar, for example. With the accession of each new king, the clock started over. Similar systems were in use all over the ancient world. Greek city-states measured time by the names of the highest officials elected in each year. But after Seleucus I was assassinated in 281 BCE, the record keepers in Babylon kept the clock running. Time, from then on, was measured not by the year of each new reign but by the years that had passed since Seleucus had first gained control of his kingdom. This was in 312 BCE (seven years before he took the title of king). It was the first ever universal system for measuring historical time.[7]

FIFTEEN HUNDRED MILES to the west, and stretching far to the south into Africa, lay the second in size of the three great 'successor' kingdoms, Egypt. It was also by far the richest. This time, there was no question about where the centre of power lay. From its foundation by Alexander in 331 BCE to the time when his former general, Ptolemy, took the title of king in 305 BCE, Alexandria had grown exponentially to become a brand new, purpose-built capital city, comparable to Saint Petersburg in the eighteenth century or New Delhi or Brasilia in the twentieth. In size and in commercial importance relative to the rest of the country, Alexandria for the first thousand years of its existence far outstripped such modern equivalents as Washington, DC, Canberra, and Ankara.

Egypt had been a prosperous, developed, and relatively stable kingdom for some two millennia before this time. The land and its people were intimately connected with the Nile, whose annual flooding brought both fertile silt and the means of irrigation to make agriculture productive. But Alexander's decision to build a city on the coast, close to the westernmost mouth of the river, suddenly turned the geography of the kingdom on its head. The new Macedonian rulers built a canal between the river delta and the sea, in this way connecting the ancient Egyptian artery of trade with Greek networks that reached across the Mediterranean.[8]

Before long, the city's population would rise to about a million, making it one of the largest anywhere in the world at the time.

The Ptolemies could command wealth to lavish on public projects that had been unimaginable in the straitened conditions of the mountains or islands of the Greek heartland. The new fashion for enormous size was spectacularly manifested in the lighthouse built during the first half of the third century BCE on the island of Pharos, overlooking two newly constructed harbours. Named after the island and rising to something over three hundred feet in height, the lighthouse remained for centuries one of the tallest buildings in the world—topped only by the Great Pyramid at Giza.[9] But unlike a famous monument to a long-dead pharaoh, this new skyscraper had a practical function: to guide ships safely to port. Safer trading would be more lucrative, making the huge investment in manpower and resources also an economic one. The Pharos would stand for almost a millennium and a half until an earthquake caused much of it to fall into the harbour, where divers would discover the remains in the 1990s. Long before that, what was left on land was reused in the fifteenth century to build the Qaitbay fortress that dominates the seaward skyline of Alexandria today.

On the mainland, on the seafront opposite the lighthouse, an extravagant complex of buildings housed the royal palace. It used to be thought that the foundations of these must lie beneath the modern city, which still preserves much of the original street plan. But thanks to excavations that began in the 1990s, we now know that the sea level and shoreline have changed dramatically since the time of the Ptolemies. The monumental architecture of their palace and other public buildings has begun to yield treasures from beneath the sea.[10] Included in the palace complex was a sanctuary dedicated to the nine Muses, the divine powers that had once inspired Homer and Hesiod and that were credited by the Greeks with being the source of every form of imaginative creativity—in the sciences as well as the arts. The name of the sanctuary, *Mouseion*, has passed into many of today's languages with the sense of 'museum'. But the colonnades of the original *Mouseion* seem to have been empty of exhibits. In modern terms this creation of Ptolemy I was more like a research institute or a learned society.

Alongside the *Mouseion* was the famous Library of Alexandria, the first of its kind in the world. Scholars based there invented the discipline of establishing authoritative texts from among the dozens, or even hundreds, of competing versions available, commenting on them, elucidating their obscurities—and above all, cataloguing them. Alexandrian scholarship has ever since been caricatured as being as dry as the sand of the Egyptian desert. There was much more to it than that. But it is true that Alexandrians had a passion for making lists and classifying things. And it is also true that everything they collected, preserved, and catalogued was written in *Greek*.

What can have been the motive behind such an exclusive, and indeed expensive, fixation upon things Greek? Why invest on such a scale in commemorating and promoting *cultural* achievements that were not even native to their own kingdom of Macedonia but that belonged to the much more widely diffused Greek-speaking world? A rather crude but not unreasonable answer might be that Macedonia, world conqueror though it had proved itself to be, had nothing comparable of its own to offer. In any case, it was an astute move. And it brought results. Just as the famous lighthouse served as a beacon for trading ships, so the *Mouseion* and the library together performed the same function, for centuries, as a beacon to attract talent from every part of the Hellenistic world. And the research that went on there was by no means confined to what we would call the arts and humanities.[11]

Eratosthenes of Cyrene, a polymath and one of the first directors of the library, came from a long-established Greek-speaking city on the coast of today's Libya, that had been absorbed into the Ptolemies' kingdom. Eratosthenes was the first to use a scientific method to calculate the circumference of the earth by comparing the angle of the sun's shadow measured simultaneously at two points on the same longitude but separated by the length of the kingdom, from Alexandria to Aswan. And the answer that he came up with was very close to being right.

From the Asian shore of the Bosphorus came Herophilus of Chalcedon; from the Aegean island off the coast of Attica, Erasistratus of Keos. Working at the Library of Alexandria under the patronage of the first two Ptolemies, these two Greek speakers were the first anatomists to base their research on the dissection of human bodies. Exactly what they learned remains unclear. But they certainly added to the accumulation of medical knowledge that would be bequeathed to the modern world—along with issues of medical ethics that are still with us. Cutting up dead people for research would soon, once again, become taboo until well into the nineteenth century. And it seems that not all of the bodies cut up by these early anatomists, with the blessing of their royal patrons, were dead.[12]

The Ptolemies proved remarkably successful in progressively establishing Greek as the chief (though never the only) language of culture and communication throughout Egypt for a thousand years—long after their dynasty had been extinguished. This was the climate in which an Egyptian priest by the name of Manetho, during the reign of one of the early Ptolemies, wrote the history of his own people in Greek, just as Berossus would do in Babylon. Although his work has survived only through later excerpts and summaries, it remains today an invaluable source of information about the much older history of Egypt under the pharaohs.

And it may have been under the patronage of Ptolemy II that the *Torah*, the sacred scriptures of the Jews, began to be translated into Greek. This was the beginning of the corpus that would later become known to Christians as the Old Testament and that is today the oldest surviving witness to the ancient Hebrew scriptures. Some believe that the translations were made for the benefit of Jews who had settled in Alexandria and were rapidly adopting the Greek language, while keeping faith with their own distinctive religion. But there is also a story, dating from the second century BCE, that Ptolemy wanted a version that would be accessible to his own scholars working in the Alexandrian library. If this is true, it would show an openness to other cultures not otherwise in evidence in the activities of the library that we know about. But whatever the original motivation for these translations, their existence testifies to the unassailable position of the Greek language in Hellenistic Alexandria.[13]

Not that the Ptolemies were indifferent to the people who made up the great majority of their subjects, or their traditions. Beginning with Alexander himself, and just like the Seleucids in Mesopotamia, the Macedonian rulers of Egypt went to great pains to present themselves as the legitimate successors to the native rulers whose role they had usurped. In this case, that meant the pharaohs, whose dynasties were traced by Manetho back to the time of the first pyramids. Some of the best-preserved temples of the Egyptian gods, carved images, and inscriptions in hieroglyphics, the oldest form of Egyptian writing, that can still be seen along the course of the Nile today were in fact either first built or newly restored during the centuries of Macedonian rule.

Alexandria was something of a special case: native Egyptians, like the Jews, had their own quarter in the city and were clearly a minority. Egyptian antiquities and ancient Egyptian rituals seem to have been given less prominence in the capital than elsewhere. But they had their place even there. We know this from some of the finds made by archaeologists working in recent decades on the seabed in the Eastern Harbour of Alexandria. These include statues of Egyptian gods that were already more than a thousand years old before anyone ever lived on this bare stretch of desert shore. They had been brought by barge down the Nile from temples hundreds of miles away to adorn the royal palace of the Ptolemies.[14]

All this added up to a curious blend that was neither quite 'cultural apartheid' nor cultural fusion. Entirely typical was the practice first established by Ptolemy II when he married his own sister, Arsinoe, and made her his queen in 274 BCE. Marriage between royal brothers and sisters had been part of the ancient mystique of the pharaohs. For Greeks, on the other hand, incest of any kind had only ever been allowed for the gods of Olympus, who could do anything, even those things that they punished in mortals—as witness the story of Oedipus, hounded by the gods for marrying his mother, even in ignorance. But learned Alexandrian courtiers took the incestuous royal marriage of Ptolemy Philadelphus ('Sibling-Loving') in their stride. From that time on, most of the Ptolemies would marry within the family—at a stroke burnishing their credentials as true Egyptian rulers while actually ensuring the exclusivity of their Macedonian bloodline.[15]

By comparison with the regularly planned wide boulevards of Alexandria, bustling with horse-drawn wheeled traffic, Athens in the middle of the third century BCE was described by a contemporary visitor as having 'narrow and winding' streets, 'as they were all built long ago'. The water supply was poor and food scarce unless you could afford exorbitant prices. True, the same visitor concedes, in the city you will also 'see the most beautiful sights on earth', among them the temples on the Acropolis and the recently completed Theatre of Dionysus. But even so, he warns his readers, 'a stranger would find it hard to believe at first sight that this was the famous city of Athens'.[16]

Indeed, despite the grandeur of its public buildings, Athens had been reduced to a shadow of its former self. Inexorably, political power was draining upwards, towards the third of the successor kingdoms, Macedonia. There, the descendants of another of Alexander's commanders, Antigonus Monophthalmus ('One-Eyed'), were in charge and known as the Antigonids. The actual arrangements in force at any one time and the precise relationship between the city of Athens and whichever king was in power in Macedonia were in a constant state of flux, particularly during the early years of the century. Outwardly, the *forms* and the locutions of democracy, abolished after the defeat at Crannon in 322 BCE, had soon been restored and would more often than not be maintained thereafter. We know this from the many decrees and proclamations that were inscribed on stone for all to read. But how truly democratic was Athens at this time? The reality seems to have been that the self-determination of a few thousand citizens, acting (theoretically) as a body, was no longer a political force capable of directing events except at the most local level. The dynamics of a citizen assembly, galvanised by a charismatic individual such as Themistocles or Pericles, that had guided Athens through the Persian and Peloponnesian Wars, had become an anachronism in a Greek-speaking world that operated on the scale of the new kingdoms. Athenians still went through the motions. But that is all they were.[17]

In the face of these realities, Athenians continued to talk and to write down what they said and thought. Very little of what they wrote during the third century BCE has survived—in part, no doubt, because decisions about what was worthy to be preserved for the future were now being taken by the librarians of Alexandria. The most influential innovation of the time was a new style of comedy. In place of the bawdy humour and topical satire that had been the staples of Aristophanes and the earlier Athenian comic dramatists, New Comedy was tightly plotted. The action of these plays is built around a limited number of stock situations and characters. Romantic young lovers overcome all obstacles to win through to a happy ending. In melodramatic twists, long-lost family members turn up and are recognised. Along the way, the audience would be entertained by running repartee between masters and their wise-cracking slaves. From its beginnings in Athens, New Comedy would spread during the third century BCE right across the Greek-speaking world.[18]

In philosophy, too, Athens continued to lead. The schools that had been founded by Plato and Aristotle in the previous century were still flourishing, while new ones emerged to rival them. These were 'schools' in the double sense of institutions that involved an element of instruction, and 'schools of thought', which perpetuated the ideas of the original founders. But the quest for universal truths, or the highest purpose of human life, gave way to a more utilitarian approach. The new philosophy that emanated from Athens was designed to teach people how to make the most of their lives in the situations in which they found themselves. According to Epicurus, active in Athens until his death in 270 BCE, the secret was to make the best of life's good things. Zeno, from Citium in Cyprus, would gather an audience in the Painted Stoa (a kind of shopping arcade) in the Athenian marketplace during the same years and tell them, on the contrary, to minimise the worst. The followers of these two men would be known respectively ever afterwards as Epicureans and Stoics (after the arcade).

Both alike envisaged a world ruled by gods who are remote and indifferent. Both agreed that any kind of concerted action by groups or by society as a whole is ultimately futile. Instead, the key to happiness and fulfilment lies in what we would call a psychological attitude on the part of the individual. Crucially, they believed, this can be acquired by teaching and practice. Modern stereotypes brand Epicureans as seekers after sensual pleasure, often associated with the motto, 'Eat, drink, and be merry, for tomorrow we die'. By contrast, the word 'stoical' has entered the languages of today to describe patient endurance in the face of suffering. In reality, the teachings of both schools, as we know them from later times, were a great deal more nuanced than those stereotypes. Stoicism, in particular, would become hugely influential in the ancient world for the next eight hundred years. Some Stoic beliefs and practices would even lay the foundations for aspects of Christianity. But unlike a religious faith based on revelation, both philosophies were founded on a principle that was deeply ingrained in all ancient Greek philosophy: the way to truth was through the exercise of *reason* and rational judgement.[19]

Athens and the Greek peninsula marked the western limit of the three great Hellenistic kingdoms that had come into existence in the wake of Alexander's conquests. But the Greek-speaking world of the third century BCE did not end there. Farther west, Greek cities were still thriving on the coasts of Sicily and all over the toe and heel of Italy. Beyond Italy, Massalia (today's Marseille) was still very much a going concern and a Greek one at that. The greatest of the Greek cities in the western Mediterranean was now Syracuse. Not to be outdone by the new kings when they divided up the domains that had been won by Alexander, in 304 BCE the 'tyrant' of Syracuse also took the title of king (*basileus*).[20]

Ever since the time of the Persian Wars far to the east in the early fifth century BCE, the Greek city-states of Sicily had been fighting off their rivals, the Carthaginians, with varying success. Carthage, in modern Tunisia, had grown from its origins as a Phoenician settlement on a par with many others scattered throughout the western Mediterranean to become the most powerful state in the region. By the time that Syracuse became officially a monarchy on the Hellenistic model, Sicily had been effectively divided between the Greeks in the east of the island and the Carthaginians in the west.

During the century that followed, Syracuse would become the birthplace of two of the leading figures in Hellenistic poetry and science. Both of these men also benefited from the patronage of the Ptolemies and worked for part of their lives in Alexandria—a reminder of how interconnected the Hellenistic world was, even across political boundaries. The poet Theocritus single-handedly invented the genre of literature that we now call (from its Latin equivalent) 'pastoral'. His dialogues in verse, known as 'idylls', were very often set in an idealised Sicilian landscape of shepherds and pastures. The story of Daphnis, the singing shepherd who dies of unrequited love and is lamented by all of nature, is perhaps the best known of these.[21]

Archimedes of Syracuse, a friend and kinsman of the ruling dynasty, has been described as 'one of the greatest creative geniuses that Greek science produced'. He is still remembered for Archimedes's principle—a means to determine the specific gravity, and therefore something of the chemical composition, of an object submerged in water—as well as for the story that he made the discovery in his bath and emerged naked to proclaim to all who would listen, 'Eureka!' ('I have found it').[22]

It was during the lifetime of Archimedes, and on this western edge of the Greek-speaking world, that a new power began to rise, one that would soon create an empire to eclipse even Alexander's. Indeed, the final exercise of Archimedes's ingenuity would cost him his life, in 212 BCE, after he had devised anti-siege engines to keep this enemy at bay for two years encamped outside his city. The new world power, and the enemy laying siege to Syracuse, was Rome.[23]

ONCE UPON A time, Rome was no more than another city-state on the outer fringe of the Greek-speaking world. For hundreds of years, the borders of the Roman state had extended no farther than

Latium, the city's immediate hinterland in west-central Italy. Early Rome had developed as many a Greek city-state had done before it. The Romans had expelled their last king in 509 BCE. Since then, the Latin expression that defined their state was *res publica*, literally 'the thing belonging to the people', and the origin of the modern term *republic*. By the time of Alexander's conquests in the east, the Roman Republic had established a nominal balance of power between the Senate—in effect an oligarchy made up of the wealthiest citizens—and the majority of the people. This balance was enshrined in the initials SPQR, representing the Latin phrase 'the Roman Senate and People'. But it was a very unequal balance. By Greek standards, the Roman Republic was an oligarchy, though technically it was a hybrid that included some elements of democracy, such as the popular franchise for certain offices of state.[24] Of the Greek city-states, the one that Rome in its early years most closely resembled was Sparta. The Roman state was highly militarised. For its citizens, the highest goal was invariably to win honours in battle against the state's enemies. Eventually, this became a recipe for aggressive growth.

As the ambitions of Rome reached southwards towards the toe of Italy and Sicily, they were bound to collide with those of Carthage, expanding in the opposite direction. When that happened, the Greek city-states would find themselves caught in the middle. The First Punic War (so called from the Latin word for 'Carthaginian') began in 264. Until this time, Rome had been a formidable power on land but had no navy to speak of. With great risk, the Romans took to the seas. After a series of closely fought battles on both sea and land, many of them in and around Sicily, the war ended in 241 BCE. The Romans won and claimed Sicily as their prize. In this way, not just the Carthaginian cities of the island but the Greek ones too lost their independence to Rome.

That was only the beginning. Hostilities were renewed in 218 BCE. The Second Punic War is best remembered for the daring exploit by the Carthaginian general Hannibal bringing an army supported by war elephants all the way from Spain, through southern France and over the Alpine passes through winter snow and ice, to take the Romans from the rear and defeat them in a series of bloody battles fought in central Italy. Rome's survival hung by a thread. In the course of a dozen years of mutual attrition, the Romans slowly regained the upper hand. Hannibal was forced back to Africa and defeated in 202 BCE at the battle of Zama, fought not far from Carthage itself.

The Greek historian Polybius, writing a little over half a century afterwards, was the first to notice that with the outbreak of that war, history had become what today we would call global. Up till that time, as Polybius expresses it, events and their causes had been limited in their impact to the part of the world where they happened. But from then on: 'History works like an organism; actions taking place in Italy and North Africa are interconnected with those in Asia and Greece and the direction of all is towards a single end.' That end, as Polybius saw it, was the supremacy of Rome. He wrote his history for the express purpose of making sense, for his fellow Greeks, of how this had come about within, as he put it, the space of 'just fifty-three years'.[25]

The Second Punic War again drew in the Greek cities of southern Italy and Sicily. Several of them picked the wrong side to win—tempted by Hannibal's offer to ensure the 'liberty of the Hellenes'—and as a result shared the fate of Syracuse. From the other side of the Adriatic, the Antigonid kingdom of Macedonia also made an alliance with Hannibal. This had the effect of bringing the Roman legions into the southern Balkans once the Carthaginians had been dealt with. Some of the Greek city-states sided with the Macedonians led by Philip V, others with Rome. When Philip was decisively defeated in Thessaly in 197 BCE, it fell to the Roman Senate to settle the affairs of the Greek states. A commission arrived at Corinth headed by the victorious Roman general Titus Quinctius Flamininus. If we are to believe the word of Polybius, Flamininus persuaded the Senate that

> if [the Romans] wished to gain universal renown among the Greeks, and to convince the country as a whole that the Romans had originally crossed the Adriatic not to advance their own interests but to secure the liberty of the Greeks, they must withdraw from every place and set free all the cities which were now garrisoned by Philip [V].

When this settlement was announced, at the panhellenic festival of the Isthmian Games, held near Corinth in 196 BCE, the crowds went wild with excitement. Flamininus was mobbed. His herald had to make the announcement twice before he could even be heard. 'Every factor', wrote Polybius, who would have been a babe in arms at the time:

> combined to produce this crowning moment, when by a single proclamation all the Greeks inhabiting both Asia and Europe became free, with neither garrison nor tribute to burden them but enjoying their own laws.[26]

Flamininus was as good at his word. The legions departed. It was now up to the Greek city-states to manage their own affairs once again, and to keep the peace among themselves.

But five years later, the Romans were back. This time it was the Seleucid king Antiochus III (the Great), who had detected an opportunity to aggrandise his kingdom and sent troops across the

Hellespont, apparently in an attempt to win over the Greek states to his own cause. This was too much for the Senate in Rome. In a series of battles, the legions under Scipio Africanus, the victor in the war against Carthage, pursued Antiochus back to Anatolia. There they inflicted a final defeat at Magnesia (today's Manisa, not far from Izmir) in 188 BCE. It was the first time that Roman soldiers had fought on the Asian landmass.

From that time on, Rome became increasingly confident, some would say arrogant, in its dealings with the Greek-speaking world. The last king of Hellenistic Macedonia was called Perseus. He seems to have harboured ambitions to live up to his mythological namesake, who had slain the monstrous gorgon, Medusa, and founded one of the oldest Greek dynasties. The army mustered by this new Macedonian Perseus, in 171 BCE, according to the Roman historian Livy, was the largest since the time of Alexander.[27] Once again, the Greek city-states took different sides, some supporting Macedonia, others, including Athens, supporting Rome. All of Perseus's plans came to grief in the battle of Pydna, fought on the coast of southern Macedonia in June 168 BCE.

A year later the former king would be paraded through the streets of Rome among captives led in chains in the public spectacle that the Romans reserved for such occasions and called a 'triumph'. By that time, defeated Macedonia had been split into four subject states, all directly answerable to the Roman Senate. Thousands of those who had fought alongside the Macedonians were sold into slavery. To ensure good behaviour, prominent citizens of other Greek states were shipped off to Rome as hostages. Among them was Polybius, who would spend the next twenty years of his life there, writing the greater part of his *History* and trying to make sense of it all.

After the battle of Pydna, on the other side of the Mediterranean, the latest in a series of 'Syrian Wars' between the Macedonian kings of Asia and Egypt had just ended with the defeat of Ptolemy VI at the hands of Antiochus IV, the son of his namesake who had lost the battle of Magnesia to the Romans. A large portion of Alexander's former empire was poised to be reunited under the Seleucids and to become all-powerful. Once again, the Roman Senate decided to take a hand. Just as Antiochus was about to seal his victory, leading his victorious troops into Alexandria, a high-level envoy arrived by ship from Rome.

Caius Popilius Laenas had not even brought a significant military force with him. Instead of returning the king's greeting, as Polybius tells it, the Roman handed him a sealed wax tablet and told him to open it and read it on the spot. When Antiochus complied, he found himself instructed by the Senate to give up the war and return home empty-handed. When he tried to prevaricate, the Roman drew a line around him in the sand with his stick 'and told him to give his reply to the message before he stepped out of that circle'.[28] Antiochus had no choice. The episode is the origin of the phrase we still use, 'a line in the sand'. The 'day of Eleusis', as it has been known ever since, after the suburb of Alexandria where the meeting took place, marked a turning point. From that moment, the grateful Ptolemies and their Egyptian kingdom would be under the protection of the most powerful state in the world.

Rival Greek states now appealed to Rome as they had once done to Persia. In a last-ditch effort to assert their political independence, the cities of the Peloponnese had revived a cooperative venture that they called the 'Common State (*Koinon*) of the Achaeans'. Better known as the 'Achaean League', the name given to it by modern historians, the attempt has been hailed as 'one of the great constitutional innovations of the Hellenistic world' and has even been credited with inspiring the federal Constitution of the United States.[29] The historian Polybius was also a fan, as his father had been one of the leading lights in its formation. But if the Achaean

League represented a real constitutional breakthrough by the Greeks, it was too little and it came too late. The trouble with this latest attempt at confederation was the same as it had always been. How much autonomy could be allowed to individual members? What forms of coercion did it take to get them to work together? Sparta, in particular, had never wanted to be part of any federal state and violently resisted being dragged into this one. Others followed the Spartan lead. And so, as the year 146 BCE approached, the Romans had all the excuse they needed to intervene once more.

The timing was the worst possible for the Greeks. Quite why Roman policy should have taken such a savage turn that year was already a puzzle in the ancient world and remains so today.[30] But it seems that drawing lines in the sand was no longer enough for the senators. Even the humbling of Carthage at the end of the Second Punic War had not been decisive enough. Nothing less than total destruction would do. And so, without much regard for pretexts, a Third Punic War followed in 149 BCE. Three years later, Carthage was razed to the ground.

At almost the same time, during the summer of 146 BCE, an army fielded by the Achaean League was defeated outside Corinth by the Roman consul Lucius Mummius. The Greek city was singled out for the same treatment. Many of its people had already fled. Of those who remained, most of the men were killed, the women and children sold into slavery. Public buildings were torn down and set on fire. Art treasures were pillaged and shipped off to Rome. By order of the Senate, no one was allowed to return to the ruins or ever live there again. A hundred years would pass before the decree would be rescinded and Corinth would begin to rise once more, this time as a colony for settlers from Italy. In the meantime, at Corinth just as at Carthage, the wrecked houses and temples would be left as an empty wilderness—and a terrible warning to any other would-be enemies of Rome.[31]

Rome was not yet the capital of an empire, ruled by an emperor. That still lay more than a century in the future. But all the time that the Roman Senate and Roman legions were wresting political influence and military power away from the Greek-speaking world and into their own hands, the future Roman civilisation was being formed. The process of 'becoming Greek' could work just as well through *being conquered* as through conquering others.

Most Greeks had not taken a great deal of notice of Rome until they had been forced to by events. Romans, on the other hand, had always been aware of the stories and the art of the Greeks. Even before the foundation of Rome itself, as we know from archaeology, large numbers of Greek painted pots had found their way onto tables and into graves throughout western Italy. Romans spoke a different language, of course—Latin—though it still belongs to the same Indo-European family of languages (unlike Etruscan, the language of their neighbours). The gods they worshipped had different names. But Jupiter, his wife Juno, and the rest of the quarrelsome tribe of gods and goddesses worshipped in Rome bore strong family resemblances to Zeus, Hera, and the Greek gods of Olympus. According to a story that had been current since at least the fifth century BCE, the ultimate ancestor of the Romans was Aeneas, a hero from the *Iliad*, who had led the remnant of the defeated Trojans to make a new home in Italy. Through the myths about their gods and the legends of their heroes, the Romans from an early stage had been inserting themselves into older narratives that already existed in Greek.[32]

But it was during the third and second centuries BCE, at exactly the time when the Roman state was bursting out of its central Italian heartland and making conquests abroad, that Romans most obviously went out of their way to emulate the culture of this one group among the many peoples they conquered. Roman writers began to compose history, epic poetry, and tragedies, not only in the

Greek manner but also very often actually in Greek. Theatre came to Rome in the year 240 BCE. During the next century, the Latin comedies of Plautus and Terence, based closely on the plot devices and stock characters of Athenian New Comedy, would establish a tradition that would last for centuries. And while Latin established itself as what a later age would call a 'language of culture', most of those who made up the Roman elite were thoroughly bilingual in Latin and Greek.[33]

Writing in Latin not long after the Second Punic War, a Roman author commented that it was the very violence of Rome's conquests abroad that had brought the Muses, those divine patrons of the arts according to Greek mythology, to impose themselves 'on the fierce inhabitants of Rome'. And a century and a half after the destruction of Corinth by Lucius Mummius, one of the greatest of all Roman poets, Quintus Horatius Flaccus, better known as Horace, would famously acknowledge: 'Captive Greece took captive her fierce conqueror, and introduced her arts into rude Latium.'[34]

FARTHER EAST, IN places still beyond the reach of Rome, a double process was going on. On the one hand, the once-vast Seleucid kingdom of Asia was being steadily whittled away. On the other, all round the edges of what remained, new independent states were springing up, but still modelling themselves on the Hellenistic kingdoms and their Greek ways.

Beyond the Tigris, a nomadic people, the Parthians, annexed the Iranian heartland of the old Persian Empire and in time would become the principal rival in the region, first to the Seleucids and then to Rome. But Parthian rulers minted coins in the Greek style. They had their names inscribed on them in Greek, along with the Greek title *basileus* (king), and sometimes for good measure, 'philhellene' (literally, 'Greek-loving'). A Parthian palace on the eastern shore of the Caspian Sea, a place never reached even by Alexander, was designed in the Greek manner, with statues that imitated classical Greek originals.[35] On the other side of their kingdom, the Seleucids were losing their grip over Anatolia to breakaway rivals. In the northwest, the city of Pergamum, not far from the Aegean coast opposite Lesbos, became the capital of a newly independent kingdom. The rulers of Pergamum, the Attalids, were Macedonians and the region had been Greek-speaking for centuries. But farther east along the Black Sea coast of Anatolia, Bithynia was now ruled by Thracians, the non-Greek-speaking people from the European side of the Dardanelles; Pontus, by a Persian family whose name in Greek became Mithridates. Inland and to the south, another Persian family set up a dynasty in Cappadocia, yet another in the tiny enclave of Commagene on the borders of today's Turkey and Syria.

Some of these dynasties intermarried with the Seleucids. But in origin none of them, other than the Attalids of Pergamum, was Greek-speaking. Greek would have been a foreign tongue to most of their subjects. And yet, in all these places, the Greek language and the trappings of the Hellenistic kingdoms were seized upon by rulers and filtered through to their people. The elites of these non-Greek kingdoms seem to have vied with one another to show how 'Greek-loving' they could be—not in terms of political alignment, but culturally. And a common language that could be used across great distances must have had a practical appeal, too, particularly in Anatolia where none had existed before. 'Becoming Greek', quite simply, was the fashion everywhere during the second century BCE.

Only in one place, and by one group of people, was the trend seriously resisted. And even there, resistance had its limits. The exception that proves the general rule is the story of the Jews. Before the coming of the Macedonians, the people of the former kingdoms of Israel and Judaea had for several centuries maintained a form of 'extreme ethnic separatism'. Key to this was their worship of a sole god who was not only the creator and 'saviour' of this one people but also the only god who had existed or *could* ever exist anywhere. Among peoples who worshipped many gods, it could be an easy matter to recognise equivalences, as had happened with the Roman Jupiter and the Greek Zeus. There are many such examples throughout antiquity. But the Jewish belief in a single god, or monotheism, explicitly forbade the worship of any other.[36] The trade-offs that allowed the polytheistic religions of the ancient world to rub along together were not possible in the case of a different type of religion altogether.

While their lands had formed part of the Persian Empire, the Jews had been ruled by the high priest of the Temple at Jerusalem, the chief city of Judaea, without much interference. At first, the same arrangement continued after Alexander's conquest. But in 301 BCE, at a crucial moment during the wars of succession, according to later Jewish sources, Ptolemy I sacked Jerusalem and took thousands of Jews from Judaea back with him to Egypt as prisoners of war. For the next hundred years, most of what was then called Syria remained under the control of the Ptolemies of Egypt, not the Seleucids of Asia. In Egypt, the captives were given their freedom and encouraged to settle. This marked the beginning of the Jewish community of Alexandria. Before long, other Jews came of their own accord to join those already there. Just as Egypt under the Ptolemies proved a magnet to Greeks from elsewhere, so it seems to have been for Jews. By the middle of the third century BCE, substantial Jewish communities existed in Ptolemaic Egypt as well as in their traditional homeland.[37]

Back in Jerusalem, after the upheaval caused by the first Ptolemy, the high priests seem to have been left once more to rule over their people in the traditional way for a century. Then in 200 BCE, Antiochus III ousted the Ptolemies from Syria and took over. At first it seemed as though little would change. The new ruler reconfirmed the rights and privileges of the high priests. The separate laws and customs of the Jewish religion were once more to be protected. Nonetheless, whatever had been the practice before, it seems that now candidates for the high priesthood would be expected to pay for the privilege.

In 175 BCE, on the accession of Antiochus IV, the brother of the reigning high priest outbid the incumbent and obtained royal patronage to depose him. The usurper was probably named Joshua but seems to have chosen to be known by the Greek name of Jason. Jason's first act was to establish a *gymnasium* in Jerusalem. This was a traditional Greek complex of indoor and outdoor spaces combining something of the modern gym, gentlemen's club, and sixth-form college. Another innovation was an *ephebeion*: a cadet corps for young men. Both of these were modelled on institutions that had long been established in Athens and other Greek cities. We know nothing of Jason's motives, because we have only the word of his opponents. Currying favour with the patron to whom he owed his position no doubt played a part. But he may also have aspired to bring his people into line with a fashion that was sweeping the world around them.

For seven years, under Jason as high priest, the traditional Jewish rituals of the Temple seem to have coexisted with these innovations. Young men enrolled at the gymnasium and volunteered for the cadet corps. Jewish athletes were to be seen exercising wearing wide-brimmed sunhats called *petasoi*. In Athens and other Greek cities, of course, athletes wore nothing at all. The *petasos* was a Macedonian addition. Whether the young men of Jerusalem wore anything else when they exercised we are not told by the anonymous Jewish historian who wrote up these events, in Greek, some decades afterwards. But the author was not shy of expressing his opinions. The sense of outrage to Jewish sensibilities comes through loud and clear. As the writer sums it up, 'It was prime-time for "becoming Greek" (*hellenismos*) and for the rise of adopting alien customs (*allophylismos*)', both terms used for the first time in Greek, so far as we know. All this was due to the 'overweening and abominable wickedness' of the 'impious Jason,' who, behaving 'quite unlike a High Priest', had set about 'transforming the people of his own race to [conform to] the Hellenic character'.[38]

The last of the Syrian Wars, that ended in 168 BCE with Antiochus IV trapped by the line in the sand drawn by the Roman envoy Popilius Laenas, had shocking consequences for Jerusalem. Exactly what happened, and in what sequence, has been much debated. Jason lost office when an even higher bidder went over his head to Antiochus. The deposed Jason then led a rebellion against the new high priest, who had also adopted a name out of Greek mythology: Menelaus. Fighting broke out in Jerusalem between supporters of Jason and supporters of Menelaus. It may have been on the way to his humiliation in the Alexandrian suburb of Eleusis or on the way back that Antiochus diverted, with his army, to Jerusalem to quell the violence there. If the intention had been to restore order, the effect was to prove the exact opposite. Whether or not they were acting on orders, the royal troops ransacked the city and desecrated the Temple. To compound matters, shortly afterwards, Antiochus issued an edict which has no known parallel in the whole Hellenistic world but which chillingly prefigures any number of stories of religious persecution in much later times.

Thanks to a second Jewish chronicler, again anonymous, whose words would later be translated into Greek, we can read this summary of the edict: 'The whole of his kingdom . . . should all form one people and they should each give up their own customs.' Not content with that, according to the same chronicler, Antiochus went on to build an 'abomination of desolation' on Temple Mount. By this was probably meant an altar dedicated to the Syrian god

Baal. The writer does not say that Jews were compelled to worship at it. But the sacrilege in such a place was obvious. And it does appear that throughout the Jewish provinces sacrifices to pagan gods became compulsory. Some Jews even considered them a price worth paying in return for peace and royal favour.[39]

All this was the very opposite of what Alexander, or any of his successors, had done in the lands he had conquered. What could account for such a departure? No doubt Antiochus was still smarting from his humiliation by the Romans. The instinct of the bully, in such circumstances, to turn on an inferior might have been part of it. But there could have been a subtler calculation, too. What could be the secret of Roman power, Antiochus may have been asking himself, that his own still-powerful kingdom lacked? If Seleucid Asia were ever to stand up against a unified and homogeneous 'Roman Senate and People', maybe there would be no better place to start homogenising than with this recalcitrant group of subjects in Jerusalem?

In Judaea, the effect was incendiary. A revolt was led by a family known to history as the Hasmoneans, and also by the nickname of 'Maccabees' or 'Maccabaeans' (from the Hebrew word for 'hammer'). Antiochus himself died on campaign far to the east in 164 BCE, just when the revolt led by Judas Maccabaeus had succeeded in defeating the Seleucid garrison in Jerusalem and restoring the Temple. This is the event still celebrated in the Jewish festival of Hanukkah. Shortly afterwards, a decree issued in the name of the new king, Antiochus V, revoked the earlier one.[40] The persecution was over—though it could be said that its long-term effects are still with us, more than two thousand years later.

The consequences of these actions would prove very different from anything that could have been intended by Antiochus IV. In 140 BCE, another of the Maccabees would take the Greek title of king (*basileus*), effectively making Judaea independent. Over the next eighty years, under the Hasmonean dynasty, the boundaries of the Jewish kingdom would expand to include all the geographical area of Palestine west of the River Jordan, reaching to the Mediterranean coast. The revolt of the Maccabees had been directed not only against the *political* power of a Hellenistic kingdom but also against the *cultural* penetration of Greek ideas and Greek ways of doing things. It was probably the only time, in the whole history of the period, when this happened.

But even here, the rejection of 'becoming Greek' would only ever go so far. The Hasmoneans, like every other breakaway dynasty in the east, whether originally Greek-speaking or not, ran their kingdom along Hellenistic lines. Their rulers adopted Greek names along with Jewish ones. Their coins were inscribed in three languages: Greek, Hebrew, and Aramaic. And for the next three hundred years, the history of these and subsequent struggles of the Jewish people for self-determination would be written and disseminated in Greek. Indeed, it is only through the surviving Greek sources that we know about them at all.[41]

THE WAY THE story has been told ever since, the period of a little over a century after the destruction of Carthage and Corinth in 146 BCE saw the most rapid and continuous expansion of Roman power that would culminate in the establishment of Rome as an 'empire without limit'.[42] But for anyone alive during those years, and particularly in the Greek-speaking east, it cannot have seemed like that. While the Hellenistic dynasties were collapsing into internecine warfare, and breakaway kingdoms fought against one another, Rome was just one of many players in a crowded and bewildering field. Not even the Romans could be relied on to win *all* their battles. And even when the legions did carry the day abroad, at times the Roman *res publica* itself seemed on the verge of internal collapse. The abrupt rise from city-state to world power during the previous century had hollowed out the venerable institutions of the Republic. Over a sixty-year period, from 91 BCE to 31 BCE, at the same time as fighting external enemies, Rome was frequently at war with itself.

It began with a vicious war in Italy. By 91 BCE, the whole of the Italian peninsula was subject to laws made in Rome. But only citizens of the citizen-state could vote or have any say in the making of these laws. The misleadingly named 'Social War', that broke out in that year, was fought between the city of Rome and its 'allies' (*socii* in Latin) in the rest of the Italian peninsula over their respective rights. The original aim of the allies may have been to break away and regain their independence. Most of those in the south, after all, had originally been Greek-speaking city-states; plenty still were and kept up their cultural and economic links with the rest of the Greek world. Their citizens may still have been susceptible to the lure of the 'liberty of the Hellenes'. If that had been the aim, the outcome was the exact opposite. The Senate, threatened with losing the war, granted Roman citizenship and some of its traditional rights to almost all the inhabitants of Italy in 88 BCE. There would be no more talk of breaking away. And at the very time when the Roman elite was still becoming Greek *culturally*, the mass of the Greek-speaking population of southern Italy overnight became Romans *legally*. A precedent had been set.

Of greater concern to most Greeks than upheavals in Italy was the war that dragged on for almost half a century between Rome and Mithridates VI, the part-Greek, part-Persian strongman ruler of Pontus. During its heyday in the early first century BCE, this kingdom had expanded from its base in northern Anatolia to draw in the Greek settlements all the way round the Black Sea, and then to dominate the entire Anatolian subcontinent. In a single year, 89 BCE, Mithridates defeated Roman armies no fewer than four times. The following spring, he instituted a new kind of warfare that would reverberate down the centuries.

Secret orders sent to every Greek city in Anatolia orchestrated a massacre of 'Romans and Italians, together with their wives and children and freed slaves, everyone of Italian descent'. Modern historians draw the obvious parallels with genocide and 'ethnic cleansing'. Somewhere between eighty thousand and one hundred and fifty thousand people were killed on a single day throughout Anatolia. Horrific as it is, this story also highlights how many civilians must already have followed in the path of the Roman legions to make a home and livelihood for themselves in these eastern possessions, that had now fallen under the sway of Mithridates. Some will have been officials, such as tax gatherers, others former soldiers who had been granted land in return for service, others again engaged in business and trade. Those who carried out the order, concluded a Greek historian writing almost two centuries later, can have been motivated only in part by fear of Mithridates. They must also have 'hated the Romans enough to behave towards them in this way'.[43]

Many Greeks who followed these events from across the Aegean shared the same balance of sentiments. For all the savagery of his methods, might Mithridates be the best prospect, in the new circumstances, for the still-cherished 'liberty of the Hellenes'? Some thought it was worth taking a chance. Even Athens, which had traditionally been careful to cultivate close ties with Rome, switched sides. Retribution was swift and deadly. Now it was the turn of Athens to suffer as Thebes and Corinth had done in previous conflicts. The Roman general Sulla laid siege to the city and its port, Piraeus. The siege lasted until the spring of 86 BCE. By this time, some of the citizens had been reduced to cannibalism. When Sulla's forces broke in, there was a great and pitiless massacre: for the inhabitants were unable to escape because they were starving, neither was there any pity shown to children or women. Sulla ordered the killing of anyone who was found.

Archaeology cannot confirm the sufferings of the defenders. But clear signs of the devastation done to buildings came to light during twentieth-century excavations in the Athenian Agora.[44]

It would take another twenty years after this for the Romans to defeat Mithridates. In the meantime, in a sure sign of a growing power vacuum in the Aegean and the eastern Mediterranean, maritime communities were putting to sea and taking the law into their own hands, seizing goods and slaves on their own account. In 69 BCE, a raid on the island of Delos all but obliterated this thriving, multicultural, polyglot centre of the international slave trade. The perpetrators are invariably called 'pirates' in the ancient sources. But modern historians suspect that behind these upheavals must have lain deeper causes, rooted in widespread disaffection and the decay of law and order during a time when Macedonian power was collapsing and it was not yet clear whether Rome would prove strong enough to replace it.[45]

It was not until the 60s BCE that Rome convincingly began to regain the upper hand in the Greek-speaking east. Gnaeus Pompeius Magnus (the Great), better known in English as Pompey, was sent into the Aegean by order of the Senate in 67 BCE with five hundred ships and over a hundred thousand troops. Not only did he destroy the pirates' bases, Pompey went on to roll up what little was left of the Seleucid kingdom of Asia three years later, and the Hasmonean kingdom of Judaea a year after that in 63 BCE.

When Pompey returned to Rome to celebrate his 'triumph' in 61 BCE, it must have seemed as though he had brought the

Greek-speaking east back with him. Thousands of captives from almost every part of the empire that had once been conquered by Alexander were paraded behind Pompey's chariot through the streets of the city. The victor himself wore a shirt which he claimed had once belonged to Alexander. The title 'Magnus', that he had granted himself some years earlier, further placed the victorious Roman general in the shoes of the Macedonian conqueror. Statues of Pompey that still survive show him with the quiff or forelock that had long been the trademark of Alexander's public image.

A more lasting testimony to the same effect was the complex of buildings that Pompey commissioned at the same time in the centre of Rome. Pompey's Theatre opened its doors in 55 BCE. It was quite possibly the largest permanent theatre ever built on the standard Greek pattern. Its capacity is said to have reached forty thousand. And the complex housed more than the traditional semicircular auditorium. Anterooms and side halls accommodated a dazzling range of exhibits mostly trawled from the east. So opulent and capacious were the buildings that when the Senate House burned down in a riot shortly afterwards, the Senate took to meeting in one of the theatre's halls. The unmistakable trappings of Hellenistic kingship were coming to Rome.[46]

Rome now ruled the southern Balkans up to the River Danube, the whole of Anatolia and the Aegean, and in the east had become embattled against the Parthians for the spoils of what had once been the Seleucid kingdom of Asia. In the west, Roman power had spread even farther, and even faster, to take in Spain and Gaul (all of France, plus parts of Switzerland and Germany up to the Rhine). The conquest of Gaul and the first, brief landing by Roman legionaries on the coast of Britain had been the work of Pompey's younger rival, Gaius Julius Caesar. Military leaders who could command the loyalty of hundreds of thousands of soldiers and leave their mark on the urban landscape of Rome itself were carving up the world among them, while the traditional institutions of the Roman Republic were visibly struggling to contain their ambitions.

Civil war broke out in 49 BCE. From then on, the battles of Romans against Romans would all be fought in the Greek-speaking east. The last survivor of the great Hellenistic kingdoms, Egypt, found itself caught fatefully in the middle. For more than a century, the Ptolemies had relied on Rome for the external protection of their kingdom. Latterly, different branches of this incestuously ramified family had been at one another's throats, and Rome had become the arbitrator in these quarrels, too. Ptolemy XII Auletes ('the Oboe Player') had held his throne thanks to the patronage of Rome until his death in 51 BCE. Pompey had taken good care to nurture this relationship while he had been in the east. So when Caesar routed his army at the battle of Pharsalus in Thessaly in 48 BCE, it was to Alexandria that Pompey fled.[47]

Egypt was now ruled by the most famous of all the Ptolemies. This was the Oboe Player's daughter, Cleopatra VII. But the young queen was locked in a deadly struggle against her brother, Ptolemy XIII. The kingdom was in chaos. One faction murdered Pompey on his arrival in hopes of currying favour with Caesar. Caesar chose, instead, to back Cleopatra and secured her position on the throne, while her youngest brother, aged only twelve, became nominally the fourteenth Ptolemy—until he disappears from the record, presumed murdered, a few years later. Shortly after Caesar left Egypt, Cleopatra gave birth to a son, who would be nicknamed 'Caesarion' or 'little Caesar' because he was reputed to be Caesar's son.

Then came the murder of Caesar, while the Senate was meeting in a hall in Pompey's Theatre, on the Ides of March 44 BCE. The murder and its sequel make up one of the best-known stories of the ancient world, thanks in large part to the two plays that

Shakespeare based closely on the biographies of the protagonists written in Greek by Plutarch a little over a century after the events: *Julius Caesar* and *Antony and Cleopatra*. Violence once more tore through Rome and the Roman world of the east. It took two years before the armies of Brutus and Cassius, the principal conspirators in the murder, were defeated outside Philippi, the city in Macedonia that owed its name to Philip II. The victorious legions on that occasion were led by Mark Antony, a former supporter of Caesar who had whipped up the Roman crowd to a frenzy at his funeral, together with a distant relative of Caesar who had been only nineteen years old at the time, by the name of Gaius Octavius.

A decade later, a new power struggle broke out between these two. By the time battle was joined, in 31 BCE, Antony had made common cause (and a bigamous marriage) with Cleopatra of Egypt. Each side had a powerful claim to Caesar's legacy. Cleopatra ruled jointly (at least in name) with Ptolemy XV, who was none other than Caesarion, her teenage son whose father was generally supposed to have been Caesar. But the former Gaius Octavius could go one better. Caesar, in his will, had adopted him as his only legitimate son and heir, in the process changing his name to Octavian and adding to it the family name of Caesar. Cleopatra's son had (in all probability) much the closer relationship by blood. But in those days there was no way of proving it. Legitimacy counted for much in ancient Rome.

The decisive battle, this time, was fought at sea. But the nearest land was once again Greece: the cape on the west coast, near the modern town of Preveza, by the name of Actium. The outcome could have gone either way. If Antony and Cleopatra had won, Plutarch's account of a pageant held in Alexandria not long before gives a tantalising glimpse of what might have been. In sumptuous surroundings, the couple's three infant children and Caesarion were paraded before the people. Each was assigned a set of kingdoms in the east. Antony's twin sons by Cleopatra were proclaimed 'kings of kings'.

The scene would be reimagined almost two thousand years later by the Greek poet C. P. Cavafy, writing in the same city, Alexandria. With characteristic wistful irony, Cavafy suggests that the Alexandrians present 'knew of course that this was words and play-acting'. But the day was warm and the sun was shining, so they went along with the spectacle, even though 'they knew what these things were worth, what empty words these kingdoms were'.[48] Shorn of the hindsight enjoyed by a Plutarch or a Cavafy, this was simply Hellenistic kingship on show, in all its fantastical glory. There would have been a role for Rome, too, surely, as the greatest kingdom of all. In the event, it was Octavian's side that won at Actium. But the outcome, in the long run, minus the fantasy and dressed in a more brutal sort of glory, was perhaps not so very different.

Antony and Cleopatra fled back to Alexandria, where both committed suicide in the summer of 30 BCE. Caesarion, or Ptolemy XV, aged just seventeen, ruled alone for only a few weeks before being executed on the orders of Octavian. The Hellenistic kingdom of the Ptolemies was no more. Egypt became a Roman province at once. 'Achaea', meaning most of today's Greece, followed in 27 BCE. In the same year, Octavian proclaimed himself sole ruler in Rome. The mantle of Alexander, coveted by so many, had finally fallen on the shoulders of this man, who at the age of thirty-six took for himself yet another name: Augustus, or 'Revered One'. What we now know as the Roman Empire had begun.[49]

7

ROME'S GREEK EMPIRE

27 BCE–337 CE

P EACE HAD BEEN imposed on the entire Greek-speaking world by force of arms. Others before Augustus had tried, but the peace had never lasted. This time it did. Indeed, throughout the greater part of that world, it would last for a good two hundred years. The period is still summed up, even today, by the Latin phrases *pax romana* (Roman peace) or *pax Augusta*. Greeks had never experienced anything like it.

With peace went a political stability that was also without parallel in earlier Greek history. This was the underlying reality behind the stories of the lurid lives, sordid deaths, and intrigues of the first dynasty of emperors to succeed Augustus in Rome. These and many other such stories first went into public circulation towards the end of the first century CE and have lost nothing of their power to horrify or titillate ever since. Tiberius died a paranoid recluse in his seventies in 37 CE after instituting a reign of terror among the highest levels of the Roman elite; his successor, Caligula, probably did not, in reality, appoint his horse as consul but would still be murdered by his own guards in broad daylight in the centre of Rome. And the infamous Nero, the last in line, we will meet again.

But it has been argued that for most of the empire's subjects, during those two hundred years, the personality and private vices

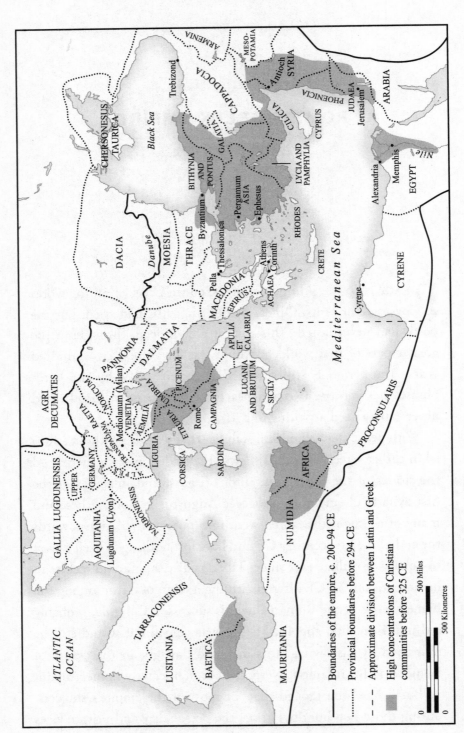

7. The Roman Empire in the late third century CE

ARMENIA

MESO-
POTAMIA

Trebizond

CAPPADOCIA

SYRIA

Antioch

ARABIA

CILICIA

PHOENICIA

JUDAEA

Jerusalem

CHERSONESUS
TAURICA

Black Sea

BITHYNIA
AND
PONTUS

GALATIA

CYPRUS

LYCIA AND
PAMPHYLIA

Byzantium

Pergamum

ASIA

Ephesus

Memphis

Alexandria

Nile

EGYPT

DACIA

Danube

MOESIA

THRACE

Thessalonica

Pella

MACEDONIA

EPIRUS

Athens

ACHAEA

Corinth

RHODES

CRETE

Mediterranean Sea

CYRENE

Cyrene

AGRI
DECUMATES

PANNONIA

DALMATIA

APULIA
ET
CALABRIA

NORICUM

RAETIA

GERMANY

Mediolanum (Milan)

TRANSPADANA

VENETIA

PICENUM

UMBRIA

LUCANIA
AND BRUTTIUM

SICILY

CAMPAGNA

UPPER

AEMILIA

ETRURIA

Rome

LIGURIA

CORSICA

SARDINIA

PROCONSULARIS

GALLIA LUGDUNENSIS

Lugdunum (Lyon)

AQUITANIA

NARBONENSIS

AFRICA

NUMIDIA

ATLANTIC
OCEAN

TARRACONENSIS

LUSITANIA

BAETICA

MAURITANIA

Boundaries of the empire, c. 200–94 CE

Provincial boundaries before 294 CE

Approximate division between Latin and Greek

High concentrations of Christian
communities before 325 CE

0   500 Miles

0   500 Kilometres

of the reigning emperor made little difference to their lives. The system of government laid down by Augustus during his forty-year reign would prove both stable and durable.[1] And although the right of a particular emperor to rule would frequently be contested in times to come, for as long as the empire lasted no one would ever challenge the imperial system itself—an extraordinary contrast to the constant political experimentation and turmoil of the old Greek city-states.

By the time Augustus died in 14 CE, the Roman Empire stretched from the Atlantic coasts of Portugal, Spain, and France in the west to the Euphrates in the east and Aswan in southern Egypt. It included all the islands in the Mediterranean and nearly all the coastline of what Romans were already calling *mare nostrum* (our sea). Around the eastern fringes of this empire, some smaller kingdoms that had broken away from the Seleucids maintained a notional independence for a little longer. Within a few decades they, too, would be fully absorbed. The Roman Empire would reach its largest extent a hundred years after the time of Augustus, in the reigns of the emperors Trajan and Hadrian. All the lands between the Euphrates and the Mediterranean, where the process of 'becoming Greek' had been going on ever since the time of Alexander, would once again be brought together into a single political entity.[2]

Everywhere, the language of imperial administration and in the highest courts of law was Latin. But throughout the eastern provinces, Greek had either been spoken as a first language for centuries or had long ago been adopted as the normal written medium for business, education, and local administration. Roman officials, no doubt for pragmatic reasons, accepted the situation as they found it. There was never any kind of formal recognition that the eastern half of the empire actually functioned in a different language from the official one. But much of the later history of Europe would be founded on an informal division that seems to have become tacitly accepted during or shortly after the time of Augustus—between a Latin-speaking west and a Greek-speaking east.

Nobody ever thought to draw this linguistic division on a map. Allowing for a few exceptional enclaves on either side, it follows a straight line drawn from north to south through the strait that separates the toe of Italy from the island of Corfu. In modern terms, Austria (up to the Danube frontier), Croatia, and parts of the western Balkans belonged to the Latin side, as did the North African coast from Tunisia westwards. To the east of that line, and south of the River Danube, the everyday form of Greek known as *Koine* continued to be the common language of speech and of most written records below the highest levels of the imperial administration.[3]

This line of division marks a subtle but important change to the shape of the Greek-speaking world. Long-established Greek settlements in Sicily, southern Italy, southern France, and the Mediterranean coast of Spain *were* assimilated. Romans still used the geographical term *Magna Graecia* (Great Greece) to describe the southern half of their own landmass, Italy. But they did so in Latin. Some memories of the language, customs, and the earlier history of these former Greek settlements would persist until at least the end of the second century CE, possibly for even longer. But despite these occasional survivals, effectively, 'Great Greece' had been absorbed into the Latin-dominated west by the time of Augustus. The dispersed Greek-speaking world of 'ants or frogs around a pond' had become consolidated, in a way never seen before, upon the islands and continental hinterlands of the *eastern* Mediterranean.[4]

Throughout the Greek east, the largest cities prospered and became even larger. The paved streets, long colonnades, elaborate fountains and bathhouses (relying on water brought by Roman engineering) of Gerasa (Jerash) and Gadara (Um Qais) in Jordan or Ephesus and Aphrodisias in Turkey can still be seen and admired by visitors today. Farther west, Crete, now the capital of a province that extended to include Cyrenaica in North Africa, prospered under a central administration as it had never done since Minoan times. On the Greek mainland, Corinth had been reestablished as a Roman *colonia* for settlers from Italy, after lying desolate for a century. The revived city was flourishing. So was Nicopolis ('Victory City' in Greek). This was originally another colonial project, built on the orders of Augustus on the coast of Epiros, close to today's town of Preveza, to commemorate his victory over Antony and Cleopatra in the sea battle of Actium not far offshore. But by the second century CE, the distinction between Roman 'colonies' and Greek cities established earlier had been all but forgotten. The process of assimilation, that in Sicily and southern Italy had seen Greek replaced by Latin, here worked in the opposite direction. The descendants of Italian settlers in the east now spoke and wrote in Greek.[5]

Roman rule lay lightly on these cities. The empire had been built on the formidable power of armies controlled from the centre. But in peacetime it was maintained by the absolute minimum of bureaucracy possible. Very much as the Persians had used to do, and as Alexander had done in the wake of his conquests, the Romans relied on the elites of the cities and regions they had conquered to do the business of ruling for them. The wealthier citizens of a traditional Greek *polis* could be relied on for their loyalty because Roman rule protected their interests and guaranteed their status within their communities. Increasingly, as time went on, more and more members of these elites would be rewarded with the gift of Roman citizenship. With it came privileges and rights not granted to the majority of the empire's subjects.[6]

Under these arrangements, many of the trappings of Greek civic governance continued long into the period of Roman rule. Larger cities still minted their own coins, even if currency values and the alloys used were standardised across the empire. Local officials could still be elected. City councils still operated and took decisions at the level of the municipality, even if the criterion for office was now wealth. Wealthy citizens vied with one another more than ever for the honour of hosting (and paying for) grandiose public works, festivals, and games. Their reward would be the privilege of seeing their likeness publicly displayed in a statue of stone or bronze. Ever afterwards, passers-by would be able to read inscribed upon the base on which the statue stood an account of how generous the donor had been. Increasingly, wealth was becoming concentrated in fewer and fewer hands. All these trends can be traced back to the period of the Macedonian conquests—that is to say, to the very beginning of the age of 'becoming Greek'. Under Rome, they only intensified. On these grounds, it has been argued, we can rightfully speak of a 'long Hellenistic age' that began with the campaigns of Alexander in the east and lasted well into the second century CE.[7]

Greek speakers had probably never at any time in their previous history been so numerous, so prosperous, or lived such comfortable lives as they did now. And throughout the eastern empire they continued to do what they had always done best, which was to talk and write in their own language. Writers in every genre that had so far been devised put pen to papyrus. They also invented new ones: biography, the novel, satirical sketches. Philosophy continued to flourish, particularly in Athens and Alexandria. Historians still did their best to understand and interpret the past—particularly, and with an evident nostalgia, the achievements of Alexander the Great. The writers of this period have never won the level of admiration that they themselves heaped upon their long-dead predecessors of the classical period. But far more of what they wrote has survived. Much of what we know about earlier centuries has come to us filtered through the perceptions of Greeks who lived and wrote under the rule of Rome.

In other branches of knowledge, writers in Greek during the same two centuries have been credited with achieving the 'culmination of ancient science'. Ptolemy of Alexandria, during the first half of the second century CE, studied the movements of the stars and planets. His treatise on astronomy, written in about 150 and known by the name of its translation into Arabic, *Almagest*, would represent the furthest extent of human knowledge on the subject until the discoveries of Copernicus in the early fifteenth century. A generation after Ptolemy, Galen of Pergamum was a practising surgeon and anatomist. His surviving medical writings fill twenty-one substantial volumes in the standard modern edition, much the largest output of any ancient writer in Greek. And that is believed to be only about a third of all that he wrote. Volume, of course, is not everything, in either literature or science. But Galen's understanding of the anatomical structure of humans and animals and his experimental method would set the benchmark for medical knowledge until modern times.[8]

ALL THESE WERE the dividends of peace. But they came at a price. Greek speakers no longer held their destinies in their own hands, except at the most local level of city government. Plutarch, writing towards the end of the first century CE, put into words what many must have thought. Advising a young man who was thinking of running for office in his city, Plutarch warned him that he would face responsibilities once borne by the great Pericles. But you should never forget, either, he goes on, that 'you who rule are also ruled over by others; you rule in a city subjected to [Roman] proconsuls, the functionaries of the emperor.' You must not take your authority too seriously, 'since you can see the *calcei* above your head'. (*Calceus* is the Latin word for 'shoe', the foreign word tactfully injected to suggest something more like the hobnailed boot of the Roman soldier.) Better, for that reason, says Plutarch, to behave like an actor and keep within the limits of your allotted role. In the present 'weakened condition of Greek affairs', the advice continues:

> the best course for those who think wisely is to enjoy a life of peace and harmony, since fortune has left to them no prize worth striving for. For what authority do you have . . . or what power, when a minor edict from a proconsul can dissolve it at a stroke or hand it over to someone else? Even if it should last, what is the point of it?[9]

The answer that Plutarch and dozens of others like him gave, spread over thousands of pages written during the first centuries of the Roman Empire, was an oblique one. More often than not, they would avoid even mentioning the existence of the political system under which they all lived, still less the compromises that living in it required. Plutarch, in all that he wrote, under his Greek name as a citizen of Chaeronea in Boeotia and latterly as a priest of Apollo at Delphi, chose never to mention that at some point in his life he had acquired another public identity, as the Roman citizen Lucius Mestrius Plutarchus.[10] Plutarch was proud enough of that second identity to see it inscribed on the base of a statue of the emperor Hadrian erected at Delphi. But it had no place in his work as a *Greek* writer. To have alluded to it would have been a lapse of taste, or what today we might term a 'category error'.

A far more congenial topic was the glory days of the past. Within a couple of generations of the death of Augustus, all over the Greek-speaking east a network of private educators had established a curriculum that inculcated a knowledge of ancient Greek history and culture. For this informal, unofficial system to flourish as it did, there must have been demand for what it offered. At the highest level, students learned to write elaborate speeches in the manner of Isocrates and Demosthenes, who had lived in the heyday of

Athenian democracy. Those who graduated as professional speech makers went on to tour the provinces and even gave command performances in Rome itself. They became known as 'sophists', after the itinerant philosophers who had made a name for themselves in the fifth century BCE. But these new sophists were celebrated, not for their ideas but for their *words*. The days when an Alcibiades or a Demosthenes would address the Athenian Assembly and the lives of thousands would depend on whether the motion was carried or not were long gone, and everybody knew it. This was speech making as an art form, even a medium of entertainment.

It was not enough for the members of this new educated elite to write *about* a better past. They even made a virtue of trying to imitate the very language and style of their great predecessors. This meant turning back the clock on the many changes that had been quietly happening in everyday speech since the conquering Macedonians had adopted a form of the Athenian dialect as their own official language. 'Common Greek', or *Koine*, had evolved a good deal in the four centuries that had gone by since then. But sophists vied with one another to re-create the dialect of Athens, known as Attic, as it had been in the time of the orators they most revered. The craze lasted for a full two hundred years, from the middle of the first century CE to about 250. Around that time, the descriptive label, the 'Second Sophistic', began to appear and the name has stuck ever since.[11]

Fascination with the Greek culture, history, and language of times long gone reached right to the very top of the Roman Empire. Augustus, even before he became emperor, had paid homage to the tomb of Alexander in Alexandria, as his adoptive father, Julius Caesar, had done before him. The victories that had brought supreme power to Augustus had all been won in the Greek east. During his reign as emperor, he went on to take a personal interest not so much in the Greek-speaking regions of his empire as in the historical heartland of what Romans began to term 'true' Greece (*Graecia vera*). Augustus lavished expensive buildings on Athens, Sparta, and other cities of the Greek mainland, as well as on his own huge new settlement of Nicopolis. It may have suited Roman policymakers to promote past Greek achievements as a way of defusing any sense of resentment on the part of their Greek-speaking subjects. It could even be that the obsession with past glories that marks the Greek writers and orators of the Second Sophistic was something subtly—or not so subtly—foisted upon them by their rulers. Whatever the case, both sides seem to have gone along with it. Signs of open discontent are remarkably few.[12]

Politically speaking, neither 'true Greece' nor the wider Greek-speaking empire was of any strategic importance to the emperors, except on those occasions when they waged war on the eastern frontiers. Greece itself, in the form of the provinces of Achaea, Epiros, and Macedonia, had no military significance. No legions were stationed there. But after Augustus, Nero in the first century and Hadrian in the second were particularly fascinated. Both emperors made tours of the east and drew extravagantly on the imperial treasury to grace selected Greek cities with new buildings and public spaces. The cities in their turn were extravagantly grateful.

Nero is mostly remembered today as the psychopath who supposedly 'fiddled while Rome burned'. But even after his memory had been well and truly damned everywhere else, he still had his admirers in the Greek-speaking east. Nero it was who made the first attempt to cut a canal through the Isthmus of Corinth, a project not completed until 1893. And in a fit of generosity, after having been allowed to win contests in all the great 'panhellenic' games, which had to be specially rescheduled to fit in with his visit, Nero granted exemption from all taxes to the entire province of Achaea. 'Other princes have liberated cities,' he declared in a speech at the Isthmus of Corinth on 28 November 67 CE, but 'Nero alone has freed a province'. One enthusiastic beneficiary, echoing a refrain that had long ago become meaningless, went so far as to thank the emperor for restoring 'the freedom of the Greeks, which from the beginning of time has been indigenous and autochthonous, but had been taken away'.[13] Even the very limited 'freedom' that Nero had granted, from liability to pay taxes, would soon be taken away again by another emperor, and this time for good.

No Roman emperor took a greater interest in what he called 'Greece' than Hadrian, who spent an entire winter in Athens on no fewer than three occasions during a reign that lasted from 117 to 138 CE. His particular fondness for the city would result in a building programme that seems to have been intended to rival those of Pericles and Lycurgus before him. The results can still be admired today. Among them was the Odeon of Herodes Atticus, since the mid-twentieth century a prestige venue for open-air concerts and theatrical performances. Hadrian's Library was designed to rival the more famous Library of Alexandria, founded by the Ptolemies. The Arch of Hadrian and the surviving Corinthian columns of the Temple of Olympian Zeus, completed on Hadrian's orders on the banks of the Ilissos River, still stand in the centre of Athens, serenely rising above the traffic-filled urban highway that replaced the riverbed in the last century.

Under Hadrian, Athens was declared the capital city of a new organisation called the *Panhellenion*. Vaguely modelled on the leagues or temporary alliances of classical times, the *Panhellenion* was meaningless politically. It was mostly about appearances. But it did set the seal of imperial approval on the supreme *cultural* position of Athens in the Greek and indeed the Roman world. In other ways, Hadrian's innovation was an anachronism. Membership of the *Panhellenion* depended on candidate cities providing proof that their founding fathers had had Greek *ancestry*.[14] Cities that stood to gain from the emperor's largesse made ingenious efforts to qualify.

But further afield, the majority of Greek speakers, and certainly the erudite speech makers whose words we read today, seem to have taken little notice of Hadrian's initiative. It is easy to see why. A world in which so many people of different backgrounds and languages had been 'becoming Greek' for the best part of five hundred years could no longer be meaningfully defined in terms of imagined family trees.

By this time, instead, the view of Isocrates had long ago prevailed in the Greek world: it was not birth that made a man a Hellene but his participation in a type of education that had begun in Athens in the fifth century BCE and that was now enjoying such a vigorous revival. Among the most admired Greek writers of the age were the satirist Lucian, from Samosata on the Euphrates (now Samsat in southern Turkey, close to the Syrian border), and the novelist Heliodorus of Emesa (today's Homs in Syria). The first described himself (in elegant Greek) as Syrian by birth, the second as Phoenician. Even Plutarch, born and bred in Boeotia, in the old Greek heartland, thought that being Greek was less a matter of race or birth than of *moral* qualities that could be learned from reading the best ancient authors.[15]

Beyond the cosmetic and short-lived *Panhellenion* confected by Hadrian, the larger Greek world of the eastern empire enjoyed a kind of unity that would never have been possible while the Greeks still possessed their political 'liberty'. Isocrates had urged his contemporaries to raise their sights above the level of the city-state and learn to think of the whole of Hellas, instead, as their *polis*. In the scattered, embattled world of the fourth century BCE, that could never have been more than a dream. But now, in 155 CE, seventeen years after the death of Hadrian, a sophist from Anatolia by the name of Aelius Aristeides went further in a show speech he delivered in Rome itself.

The whole Roman Empire, Aristeides informed his listeners, was now one single *polis*. The thousands of cities scattered across its length and breadth were the equivalent of suburbs to imperial Rome.[16] In other words, the highest praise that a devoted disciple of Isocrates could think of, for a world empire founded on military might, was to make out that it was really just an inflated version of a Greek *polis*. It is not recorded what Aristeides's Roman audience made of this. Romans had been accustomed, for centuries, to think of their *res publica*, as they still called their state, as a proud and unique creation of their own. No matter, Aristeides was speaking in Greek, and a very erudite sort of Greek at that. For those who wished to hear, in Rome in the middle of the second century, the process of 'becoming Greek' had expanded to encompass the whole of Rome's vast empire.

Six years after that speech was delivered, the emperor Marcus Aurelius came to the throne. He was a Roman, like all the emperors before him, and had been brought up in the capital. But, again like many of his predecessors, he had benefited from a Greek education. For once, when an emperor took an interest in the Greek world, Marcus's motive was neither political nor antiquarian. He had very little opportunity, in the course of a reign that would last until 180 CE, to spend time in the Greek-speaking east. Much of his energy had to be devoted to waging the first of Rome's defensive wars, fought against Germanic tribes along the Danube frontier. What attracted Marcus was Greek *philosophy*. In particular, he was drawn to the ideas of the Stoics that went back to Zeno of Citium, who had taught in Athens in the early third century BCE. Stoic ideas had been widely disseminated and adopted by the Roman elite well before this time. So there was no reason why Marcus could not have expressed his own philosophical thoughts and kept his private diary in his own language. But instead he chose to do so in Greek.

Why he did and whether his *Meditations*, as they have come to be known, were really intended for himself alone has been debated by scholars. Whatever the truth, Marcus's introspective candour shows an insight into the mind of an emperor such as is rare, if not unique, in world history. 'Do not expect Plato's ideal commonwealth', he warns himself at one point.[17] What more touching recognition could there be of the limits to imperial power? He is *emperor*, after all. And here, perhaps, lies the key to Marcus's choice of language. In Latin and in public, Marcus Aurelius Antoninus Augustus was the supreme commander of armies, ruler of the known world, god incarnate, recipient of public prayers and sacrifices in temples everywhere from Hadrian's Wall in Britain to the Euphrates in today's Iraq. But in private and in Greek, the same man faced his own self as a unique, fallible human being, humble in the face of nature and of a divine power in which he was not sure he believed, while he struggled to put into words the consciousness of his own individual humanity.

THE QUESTIONS THAT exercised Marcus Aurelius towards the end of the second century CE were by no means confined to his own exalted circles. Indeed, the philosopher-emperor was giving voice to anxieties and to a type of introspection that were also very much products of the age. The roots of these can be traced quite far back into the Hellenistic period.[18] But it was under the Roman Empire that they reached their fullest expression. Part of what was new can be summed up as the discovery of the human individual. Another, closely related, was the yearning of each individual, whether great or humble, to be in some sense 'saved'. The world of the traditional Greek *polis* had been intensely corporate. The highest good had been the survival and prosperity of the citizen body. This was what public rituals and worship of the traditional gods had been designed to secure—and always for the whole community.

Since then, the newer philosophies of the Stoics and Epicureans, among others, had encouraged their adherents to think about the meaning and purpose of their own individual lives. But philosophy, for the great majority of the population, would take you only so far. Minimising pain and making the most of pleasure were all very well in principle, but thinking about it wouldn't make you better if you were ill or save your life when you were in danger. Worst of all was what happened to you when you died. Lucretius, the Roman follower of Epicurus back in the first century BCE, had said it didn't matter because you wouldn't be there to worry about it.[19] But what if you still worried in the meantime? This is where a new element, one that had no real equivalent in the vocabulary of formal Greek or Roman religion, appears in the thoughts and words of those who wrote in Greek, namely faith. Faith means something more than sharing stories and participating in rituals that express the hopes and fears of a whole community. Faith is personal. Faith means not only that you believe but also that you place all your trust in a divine force that can do something *for you, personally*. Already, by the time of Augustus and for several centuries thereafter, people were looking for a power beyond themselves that they could trust in this way.

Alongside official religion and public ceremonies, individuals had begun entrusting their welfare to new deities and the cults devoted to them. The bull god Serapis and the goddess Isis had become the objects of empire-wide cults that had originated in Egypt under the Ptolemies. In these cults, elements of older Greek and Egyptian beliefs and ritual practices seem to have been deliberately fused together to serve the new needs of the age. During the second century CE, in the same way, the cult of the Persian sun god Mithras spread through the ranks of the Roman legions to reach into every corner of the empire. Asclepius, originally a minor Greek deity associated with healing, came to be worshipped at sanctuaries which by the Roman period had become more like nineteenth-century sanatoria or the health spas of today. Patients went through elaborate rituals and slept in the sanctuary. If they were lucky, the god would visit them in a dream and they would wake up cured of their ailment. Thousands of inscriptions survive from all over the Greek-speaking world apparently testifying to the success of such cures.[20]

But not even Asclepius could save you when you died. For this need, too, ritual and some form of religious faith had to be invoked. Initiation by secret rituals into cults that were called 'mysteries' was nothing new. The most famous of these, the Eleusinian Mysteries, held at Eleusis outside Athens, had for centuries been a prestigious rite of passage from adolescence to manhood, not just for Athenians but for Greeks from elsewhere too. Now, mystery cults were proliferating. It became a matter of personal choice whether or not to become an initiate, and if so, into which cult. The secrets of these rituals in the ancient world were remarkably well kept. But a good indication of what was *expected* of them comes from the mid-second century CE, when a would-be initiate into the 'mysteries' of the goddess Isis was told to prepare for 'a kind of voluntary death and salvation through divine grace'.[21]

Among the Greek-speaking elite of the eastern empire, an attempt was made to address this need in a secular way. This is how the literary genre that we know today as the novel came to be born in the form of the 'ancient Greek novel', or 'romance', which flourished between about 50 CE and (probably) the early third century. In these stories, boy and girl meet by chance, fall in love, are separated, and then endure extreme ordeals in the most exotic places, before they can be reunited and married, to live happily ever after. Hero and heroine both face the threat of death. Each is willing to die for the sake of love. In set-piece episodes that lend themselves to the kind of melodrama characteristic of later horror movies, each appears to be violently killed, only to be 'resurrected' in an apparent miracle.

The most elaborate and technically experimental of these novels is known as the *Aethiopica*, or *An Ethiopian Story*. Its author was Heliodorus of Emesa, the self-confessed outsider to the Greek-speaking world who was also a master of elegant Greek prose. Heliodorus in his fiction frequently plays with a numinous sense of a 'divine providence' that ultimately oversees the happy outcome of the hero's and heroine's trials. But the salvation found in the fulfilment of heterosexual love—itself an innovation in Greek literature, which had largely preferred homosexuality up to this time—is purely secular. Through this and other stories, the human self discovers a purpose for its existence and ultimate salvation in the love of another in its own likeness.

At the time, and for many centuries afterwards, the exploration of the condition of the individual self and its search for salvation in the works of these early Greek novelists would remain a dead end. Too many of these fictional stories were couched in the old-fashioned language and grandiose style of the Second Sophistic, accessible only to those with an advanced education. The novel would have to wait a long time before it could come into its own, eventually to be hailed in the twentieth century, among many other things, as a 'secular scripture'.[22] But in the meantime, the road to salvation for the newly discovered individual would lie through the growth of an entirely new religion. The scriptures of this religion, too, would be written first in Greek.

DESPITE THE FACT that the near-universal system for reckoning historical dates today was first created by Christians who counted from the birth of their religion's founder, it is now generally accepted that the birth of Jesus of Nazareth took place in or shortly before 4 BCE. That was the year when King Herod 'the Great',

in effect a vassal of Rome, died, and the kingdom of Judaea was
split four ways. Most of Jesus's life was spent in Galilee, where the
long-running process of 'becoming Greek' had scarcely penetrat-
ed.[23] It is generally supposed that he and his disciples must have
spoken Aramaic among themselves. This had been the common
language of the Persian Empire before the conquests of Alexander
and was still widely used by ordinary Jews. Jesus himself is said
never to have written anything down. If his immediate followers
did, nothing of what they wrote in their own language has ever
come to light.

Jesus's short life took him to Jerusalem, at the time the capital of
the Roman province of Judaea. There, Greek ways and the Greek
language had been resisted in the past. But by this time, Herod's
former capital had acquired more than a Greek veneer. Greek was
widely spoken there, and written too, as we know from inscriptions
found by archaeologists. It was in Jerusalem that Jesus was accused
of sedition and crucified, the standard Roman punishment for
slaves and criminals who did not enjoy the benefits of citizenship. It
was in Jerusalem, too, during the twenty years or so after his death
in about 30 CE, that his former followers began to disseminate
the message he had taught. This message first makes its mark in
the written record when a Jewish preacher embarked on a mission
to spread the new beliefs beyond the geographical heartland of the
Jewish people and to make converts among the gentiles. To reach
this new audience, the message had to be delivered in a language
that everybody could understand. The obvious choice was Greek.
And so Jesus's message was first, rather modestly, announced to
the wider world as the 'Good News', or 'Gospel': *Euaggelion*, from
which come our words 'evangelist' and 'evangelical'.[24]

The preacher's name was Paul. No one could have been more
different than Paul from the writers of the Second Sophistic, who
were beginning to set the literary agenda for the eastern empire

during his lifetime. His origins were humble. Originally called Saul, or Shaul, he was born in the city of Tarsus in the province of Cilicia (today part of southern Turkey) and brought up there as a Jew; his parents may have been freed slaves. Later Paul went on to spend time in Jerusalem, where he probably arrived not long after the crucifixion of Jesus. It was there that he met the surviving disciples and learnt firsthand about Jesus's life and teaching. All this would have taken place in Aramaic. But along the way, Paul had learnt to read and write in Greek, probably in his home city as a young man. This must have brought him into some degree of contact with older Greek texts and the ideas expressed in them. But that was all. The Greek language, for him and for all the earliest Christian writers whose work we possess, was a means to an end. Paul's Greek is the Greek of every day. He used it to write letters, the most direct means to present information or ideas in permanent form. Communication by letter was part of the daily life of the Greek-speaking eastern empire by this time—not a literary genre at all. This was the form that the great majority of the earliest Christian writings would take.[25]

Paul's letters are the oldest Christian texts that we possess. They are addressed to the embryo Christian communities around the eastern Mediterranean that he helped to establish. What he writes in them is extraordinary by comparison with anything that had ever been written in Greek before. From the earliest of them, written within a few years either side of 50 CE, we learn that the writer, who introduces himself by name, is 'an apostle (not of men, neither by man, but by Jesus Christ, and God the Father, who raised him from the dead)'. 'Apostle' is the English form of the Greek word *apostolos*, which means 'missionary'. Jesus had died, the self-declared apostle reminds his readers, 'for our sins, that he might deliver us from this present evil world'. Here was the promise of salvation indeed. The way to reach it lay through the cultivation of virtues that must have seemed at the very least strange to most Greek speakers of the time, quite possibly incomprehensible: 'love, joy, peace, longsuffering, gentleness, goodness, faith, meekness, temperance'. 'Thou shalt love thy neighbour as thyself', declares Paul in one of his most frequently quoted sentences.[26]

Paul's letters have almost nothing to say about Jesus as a historical figure, about his life, or about the content of his teaching. The stories that we know from the four Gospels must have been in circulation in some form during Paul's lifetime, but the Gospels as we know them had yet to be written. For Paul, what matters most about Jesus is that he is 'the Christ' (*Christos*). This was originally not a name in Greek but a title. It translates the Hebrew 'Messiah', meaning 'the anointed one', and refers to the coronation rituals of the ancient kings of Israel. As with so much in the New Testament, if the language is Greek, the concepts conveyed in it belong to a different tradition entirely, that of the ancient Jews.

What defines the Christ for Paul is the fact that he 'died for our sins . . . was buried, and . . . rose again the third day'. Christ's resurrection, the way Paul tells it, signals a victory over death itself. 'O death, where is thy sting? O grave, where is thy victory?' he writes in one of his most famous passages. It is also, for Paul, a guarantee of what would later be termed the 'Second Coming'.[27] The first generation of Christians actually believed that Jesus would come again during their lifetime. When that happened, the world would end in a fiery conflagration, and God would sit in judgement on the living and the dead.

By the year 64 CE, the 'good news' had spread as far as the empire's capital, Rome itself. We know that there was already a Christian community there, because Paul had addressed its members in a letter written a few years earlier and, according to one early account, went on to preach in the city for two years.[28] In July of that year, fire broke out in Rome. It raged for nine days.

The entire centre of the city was burned down. To the city's Jewish population who had been exposed to Christian teaching, as well as to the smaller community of committed Christians, it must have seemed as though the prophecies of the Second Coming were being fulfilled. Although the connection is made by none of the ancient sources, it may have been this that inspired the emperor Nero to lay the blame for the catastrophe on the still obscure Christian sect. The historian Tacitus, writing about fifty years later, reports:

> The confessed members of the sect were arrested; next, on their disclosures, vast numbers were convicted. . . . And derision accompanied their end: they were covered with wild beasts' skins and torn to death by dogs; or they were fastened on crosses, and, when daylight failed were burned to serve as lamps by night.[29]

Tacitus surely exaggerated the numbers. But the ferocity of Nero's scapegoating set a benchmark for cruelty that resonates through later accounts of a type of persecution that would come to be known by the term 'martyrdom' (from a Greek word meaning 'bearing witness'). According to tradition, both Paul and Jesus's former disciple Peter were executed in Rome as part of this pogrom.

By the time Tacitus came to write up these events in Latin, Christians had begun to produce their own written narratives of Jesus's life and death. All of these, like Paul's letters and everything else that in due course would go to make up the Christian New Testament, were written in Greek. First came the *Gospel According to Mark* in the early 70s CE. Matthew and Luke followed not long afterwards, probably during the 80s. These three are often grouped together and called the 'synoptic' Gospels because they share much material and tell broadly the same story. The *Gospel According to John* came later. It is usually dated to between 90 and 110. The attribution of each Gospel to an 'evangelist' was a later invention.

By the time that any of the Gospels came to be written, it is most unlikely that any eye witnesses to the life and death of Jesus would still have been living.

Mark's language is the simplest of the four. Luke is at home with a more 'middlebrow' style of Greek and shows some familiarity with the culture that went with it. John goes much further, grafting onto the story not only the divinity of Jesus as the Christ (an element which emerges only slowly in the development of early Christianity) but also the identification between Christ and the divine *Logos* (meaning 'word', 'reason', or 'account'). This was a Christian extension of an idea that had been explored in a long philosophical tradition that went back via the Stoics to Plato, and ultimately to Heraclitus seven hundred years earlier.[30]

During the second century CE, Christianity attracted very little attention among the elites of the eastern empire. For those who noticed it at all, such as the philosopher Celsus, who in the second half of that century wrote a treatise demonstrating its 'errors', the crux of the matter lay in the choice between faith and reason.[31] Faith-based Christianity was very much a bottom-up movement. Converts seem at first to have been drawn from the lower classes of society in cities and larger towns—though noticeably not from the lowest and probably also the largest: the ubiquitous population of slaves. There is some evidence that the new religion may have attracted more women than men. And although Paul's view of women was no more enlightened than the traditional Greek one, the Roman Empire already granted considerably more rights to its female subjects than most Greek states had done. The early Christian church seems to have been more welcoming to them still.[32]

Except for a few notorious instances, Christianity during the first two and a half centuries of its existence spread largely below the radar of the Roman authorities or the civic institutions of the empire. Individual Christians could be imprisoned, tortured, and if they refused to recant, executed with the usual Roman relish for public suffering inflicted upon the outcast. This was the fate of several prominent Christian leaders and preachers during the second century. But there was still nothing like a systematic attempt to persecute the new religion, still less to stamp it out altogether. Martyrs would remain a tiny minority within a group that in most parts of the empire was itself, in modern terms, not yet statistically significant.[33] Martyrdom had to be actively sought because most Roman authorities followed the practice attributed in the Gospels to Pontius Pilate, the governor of Judaea who had condemned Jesus; like Pilate, they would give the accused every opportunity to avoid the extreme penalty. In official eyes, Christianity was a mere *superstitio.* What its adherents believed was of no importance, so long as they gave proof of their loyalty to the state. It was political subversion that governors feared and punished, not private belief.

Later Christian tradition would give prominence to the extreme sufferings of martyrs. For centuries, the fate of these men—and, later, women too—who had been willing to face a horrific death for their faith, would be held up as the highest example of Christian virtue.[34] But these stories obscure for us a reality that must have affected far more people at the time and that would play no less formative a role in the subsequent evolution of Christianity into the world religion that it has since become: right through the second century and well into the next, in the Greek-speaking east there were actually more signs of convergence than of confrontation between Christianity and the mainstream.

Christians were not the only ones to question whether the ritual killing of large numbers of animals in the open air was really the best way for humans to make their peace with a higher power. Galen, the pioneer of medicine and anatomy who had worked with

Marcus Aurelius and died not long after 200 CE, was speaking for the new mentality of the age when he justified his own scientific study as

> a sacred book which I compose as a true hymn to him who created us: for I believe that true piety consists not in sacrificing many hecatombs of oxen to him or burning cassia and every kind of unguent, but in discovering first myself, and then showing to the rest of mankind, his wisdom, his power and his goodness.[35]

At about the same time, the citizens of a minor city in southwest Anatolia called Oenoanda chose to display these lines, couched in the ancient verse form of Homer, in a prominent position on the outer wall of their city:

> *Self-born, untaught, motherless, unshakeable,*
> *Giving place to no name, many-named, dwelling in fire,*
> *Such is God: we are a portion of God, his angels.*

The inscription goes on to explain that this had been the response of the god Apollo himself, given through an oracle, when questioned 'about God's nature'.[36] Statements like these, two hundred years after the lifetime of Jesus, are not proof that Christian teaching was directly influential on the wider Greek-speaking world at this time. Rather, the new religion, and the new language of faith that had come into existence along with it, addressed concerns that were also widely shared by non-Christians.

On the other side of the divide, leading Christians were now more likely than before to have benefited from an education in Greek rhetoric and philosophy. As the second century gave way to the third, when Christian writers came to compose the letters, sermons, and treatises in which they set out their beliefs and argued over the true interpretation of the Gospels, they did so in a much more elevated language and style than would have been thinkable for Paul or the evangelists. Starting a little before 200 and continuing into the middle of the next century, first Clement and then Origen, both of Alexandria, promoted and discussed the Christian faith in a language and style that were scarcely less rarefied than those of the Second Sophistic. These Christian thinkers also brought to their task a profound knowledge of earlier Greek philosophy, and especially the ideas of Plato, which at this relatively early stage became permanently grafted onto the Christian tradition. Before the third century was well advanced, the new religion had made its accommodation with mainstream Greek education.[37] The effects of this convergence would be slow to manifest. But when they did, they would transform what could be said, or imagined, in Greek ever afterwards.

ACCORDING TO THE English historian Edward Gibbon, whose classic account was written in the 1770s and 1780s, the 'decline and fall of the Roman empire' began with the death of Marcus Aurelius and the accession of his son Commodus. These events took place in 180 CE. Commodus today enjoys an unexpected degree of name recognition in the English-speaking world, thanks to his portrayal in two blockbuster films, *The Fall of the Roman Empire* in 1964 (with Christopher Plummer playing the emperor) and *Gladiator*, starring Russell Crowe, in 2000. Much of what these popular portrayals say about Commodus seems to have been true, including his assassination in the amphitheatre while dressed as a gladiator.[38] But on the scale of personal vices, Commodus may not have been much worse than Nero. The difference was that, after Nero committed suicide in 68 CE, the civil war that followed lasted only a year before the stable system that had been established by Augustus reasserted itself. After the death of Commodus in 192 CE, civil war and empire-wide chaos lasted, on and off, for almost a century.

During the third century, the Roman Empire underwent a series of profound shocks. The *pax Romana* was at an end—even though in the Greek-speaking east it would return. Emperors came and went, raised to power by the legions they commanded, and as often as not assassinated by the same soldiers a few months later. The legions, especially those stationed on the empire's frontiers, became more important than they had ever been, as the empire found itself fighting defensive wars on all sides: on the Rhine, on the Danube, and in the Middle East.

In 224 CE, a new Persian dynasty, the Sassanids, came to power. Within a few decades they had taken over Rome's old enemy in the east, the Parthian kingdom, and reconstituted much of the former strength of the Persian Empire that had once threatened the Greeks and then been conquered by Alexander. In 260 CE, the emperor Valerian was taken prisoner, along with much of his army, while campaigning against them. The great Hellenistic city of Antioch-on-the-Orontes, which at one time had been the chief city of the Seleucid kingdom, fell briefly into Persian hands. On the Balkan front, not long afterwards, a roving band of Goths crossed the Danube and laid siege to Thessalonica. They went on to ravage the coast of Anatolia as far south as Ephesus, where they set fire to the famous Temple of Artemis in 262. Another tribe, called Herouloi, from the area of the Crimea, sailed through the straits from the Black Sea and into the Aegean. Once there, they caused devastation in Athens and other cities of the Greek mainland and islands.

People living in places that had not seen warfare for more than two hundred years found themselves catapulted into a violent and uncertain world. To compound matters, the empire ran out of money. In order to mint sufficient coins to pay the legionaries, the amount of precious metal contained in them had been declining for years. Suddenly, the monetary system seemed on the edge of collapse. Prices of everyday commodities soared. Wealthy benefactors no longer funded new buildings or expensive games—or if they did, they could no longer afford to pay a sculptor to commemorate the fact in stone. What has been called the 'epigraphic habit', the gift to modern archaeologists that had flourished in the cities of the Greek east for centuries, came to an abrupt end.[39]

Beyond the obvious measures, such as doing what they could to defend their frontiers, different emperors turned to different, more or less extreme remedies. In 212 CE, during the early years of the third-century 'crisis', the emperor Caracalla took everyone by surprise when he decreed that all subjects of the empire, other than slaves, would from then on be full Roman citizens. It may have been nothing more than a short-term expedient to raise revenue— by vastly extending the tax base. Caracalla did not live long enough afterwards to explain his reasons. But the effect was permanent and would profoundly change the character of the Roman Empire. Up to this point, citizenship had been a prized privilege. According to one modern estimate, no more than a third, and perhaps as few as a fifth, of all Roman subjects had been full citizens before this. The change affected over thirty million people. It has been called 'one of the biggest single grants of citizenship—if not *the* biggest—in the history of the world'.[40] But Caracalla's supposedly tax-raising stunt would have an even more far-reaching consequence. From this time on, almost everyone who spoke Greek anywhere in the world was entitled to be called a Roman citizen. The time would come when Greek speakers would no longer think of themselves as 'Hellenes' at all, but rather as 'Romans' (*Romaioi* in Greek)—as the great majority of them would continue to do until the nineteenth century.

As the crisis went on, other emperors tried another type of extreme remedy for their ills. This was to turn back to the corporate mindset of traditional religion. If things were going so badly for the empire, it must mean that the gods had been offended. Who could be at fault? Who could you punish, and be sure that the gods would look kindly on you as a result? So began the first systematic persecution not just of individual Christians who fell foul of the Roman authorities but of an entire religion. The first attempt, by the emperor Decius in 249, seems to have been intended not so much to create martyrs as to turn Christians back to the official forms of worship. Many times more sacrificial animals than Christians lost their lives during the two years that it lasted. But later stories made much of the horrific sufferings of those Christians who had refused to perform the prescribed sacrifices. It was an unprecedented intervention by the Roman state.

After Decius was killed in battle in 251 (the first Roman emperor ever to suffer this fate), the persecution eased. But it was back with a vengeance a few years later. The new emperor, Valerian, as he prepared to confront the Persians who had overrun the easternmost provinces, once again decreed that all citizens must make animal sacrifices to the gods. In 258, Valerian went further and ordered the execution of all Christian leaders. Once again, it was the defeat of the emperor in battle, and his subsequent death in captivity, that brought about a reprieve two years later. We only know about these events from later Christian sources, so we have no independent evidence for what may have been the emperors' motives.[41] After Decius and Valerian both met their ignominious ends, several decades would pass before another emperor was ready to repeat the experiment.

It is generally agreed that the crisis experienced throughout the Roman Empire came to an end with the series of military and economic reforms instituted by Diocletian, who ruled from 284 to 305. But, for the Christian minority, the respite would not last long. In March 303, according to Eusebius, the bishop and historian of the early church who lived through these events:

> an imperial decree was published everywhere, ordering the churches to be razed to the ground and the Scriptures destroyed by fire, and giving notice that those in places of honour would lose their places, and domestic staff, if they continued to profess Christianity, would be deprived of their liberty.[42]

Once again, those at the receiving end had no interest in recording what might have been the reasons for these measures. And we have no other source of information. In 303, the empire was not under threat—far from it, a decisive victory over Persia had been won only five years before. And if Christians were not, this time, being offered up as scapegoats, what other purpose could there have been to the persecution? Across the empire as a whole it is likely that by the year 300 CE, Christians amounted to no more than between 7 and 10 per cent of the population on average. So they can hardly have been a threat in themselves.[43]

Whatever the reasons behind the measures taken, their effects would be to propel Christianity from being a fringe sect and minor social and administrative irritant to being within a very few years the biggest political issue to face the Roman state. And once that challenge had been thrown down, it was Christianity that would emerge triumphant.

AMONG THE REFORMS instituted by Diocletian was the curious, and in the event short-lived, innovation of dividing imperial authority four ways. Two senior and two junior emperors ruled simultaneously, each with responsibility for a different part of the empire. The 'tetrarchy', as this system was called, could in hindsight be seen as the first tentative gesture towards the empire's future division, roughly along the line of the language division between Latin and Greek. For the time being, though, it was not to last. The four-way succession to Diocletian was excessively complicated. The son of one of the previous tetrarchs, by the name of Constantine, became co-emperor in 306. Probably from the start, Constantine determined to restore one-man rule. It would take him the best part of twenty years.

Constantine was born in today's Niš in southern Serbia. His mother, Helen, may have come from a Greek-speaking family. But his own first language was Latin. Benefiting from the usual upper-class education, Constantine would have learned to read Greek, but was apparently never very fluent in it.[44] His first imperial responsibility was for the empire's most westerly provinces. Indeed, it was at York, in England, that the troops who had been loyal to his father proclaimed him co-emperor. Despite this, it would be in the east that Constantine would leave by far the greater legacy. Exactly what role Christianity played in Constantine's early life has been hotly disputed ever since. All we know for certain is that in 313, with the tetrarchy now reduced from four to two, Constantine and his last remaining co-emperor, Licinius, issued a joint proclamation that officially ended the persecution of Christians throughout the empire.[45]

In Christian circles, stories were soon circulating about a vision that Constantine had seen while he had been preparing for a campaign to eliminate one of his imperial rivals. The campaign had ended in a spectacular victory that gave Constantine control of Rome in October 312. In the fullest account of this vision, circulated by Eusebius in a biography of Constantine written shortly after his death and allegedly reported on oath:

About the time of the midday sun, when day was just turning, he said he saw with his own eyes, up in the sky and resting over the sun, a cross-shaped trophy formed from light, and a text attached to it which said, 'By this conquer'.

The following night, so the story went on, Constantine had dreamed that 'the Christ of God' came to him and ordered him to fashion a military standard in the form of the Christian cross.[46] So far, so traditional. Constantine had found a new divine patron. Greek and Roman history is full of such portents. Commanders of armies had set great store by them since at least the time of the Persian Wars. Still within the bounds of tradition, during the next few years, as co-emperor with responsibility for the western half of the empire, he paid appropriate respects, in return, by paying for the building and adorning of Christian churches in Rome.

What made it political was that at the same time, Licinius, now Constantine's only remaining imperial rival, began a new persecution of Christians in the east. This meant going back on the agreement that the two men had reached and their joint proclamation. Now, one co-emperor was backing the new religion in one half of the empire, the other trying to eliminate it in the other. So the stage was set for the final struggle for supremacy between the two. Constantine defeated Licinius in September 324 in a battle fought on the Asian shore of the Bosphorus. Whether intended or not, his campaign to make himself sole emperor had turned into a war of liberation on behalf of the Christian minority. In a letter to Eusebius, written shortly after his victory over Licinius, Constantine explained it like this:

But now, with liberty restored and that dragon driven out of the public administration through the providence of the supreme God and by our service, I reckon that the divine power has been made clear to all, and that those who through fear or want of faith have fallen into sins, and have come recognize That which really Is, will come to the true and right ordering of life.[47]

From this point on, there could be no going back. Politically, Constantine had won his supremacy as the champion of an oppressed minority—and of the God that they worshipped. He now had no choice but to deliver. The traditional two-way transaction between gods and favoured mortals would never work again. Perhaps by this time, more than a century after Marcus Aurelius, Galen, and the Oenoanda inscription, no one really believed in it anyway. You couldn't negotiate with the one god of the Christians. Nothing less than total obedience would do. It was the perfect religion for an autocratic political system.

The price for Constantine was to forgo the divinity that had been the traditional entitlement of Roman emperors while alive and formal deification after death. Instead, when the time came for him to die, in Nicomedia (today's Turkish city of Izmit) in 337, shortly after celebrating the newly instituted festival of Easter, Constantine became the first Roman emperor to be 'initiated by rebirth in the mysteries of Christ' when he received the Christian rite of baptism. Eusebius describes the dying emperor as transfigured, as he 'put on bright imperial clothes which shone like light, and rested on a pure white couch, being unwilling to touch a purple robe again'.[48]

Constantine's personal motives and the nature, or sincerity, of his conversion have been the subject of controversy in modern times. Was he essentially a traditionalist who realised too late how radical a revolution he had started? Or was he perhaps a realist who recognised a new spirit of the age and decided to make a virtue of the inevitable? Maybe he was one of those rare, true innovators who are willing to risk the challenge of the new in the knowledge that they cannot possibly foresee where it might lead? The dedicated champion of the faith depicted by Eusebius is too one-dimensional to be credible—unless one believes, with Eusebius, that battles and military campaigns are won by faith alone. Constantine was a canny and successful ruler over a still-mighty empire, one of very few in three centuries. Devout Christian or not, he was not above putting his own son and first wife to death for reasons of cold politics. It may be that what mattered most to Constantine was to restore order to a disordered empire and that he saw in Christianity the means to do it. Whether he was right or not may still be an unanswered question almost two thousand years later.[49]

In any case, at the time of Constantine's baptism and death, Christianity was not yet the official, still less the only, religion of the Roman Empire. But the adoption of the new religion by the most powerful man in the world had consequences for Christianity, too. Overnight, a bottom-up movement had become top-down. One of Constantine's first acts after defeating Licinius and becoming sole emperor was to convene a conference of Christian bishops at Nicaea (today's Iznik), in northwest Anatolia, to decide between the rival interpretations of the faith that were in circulation at the time. It has aptly been observed that the intention behind this and later 'ecumenical councils', as such meetings came to be called, was not to encourage debate but to quash dissent.[50]

The official definition of the Christian faith that came out of that meeting is known as the 'Nicene Creed'. The same Greek text, translated into many different languages, is still recited by congregations in Christian churches around the world. It begins, 'I believe . . .' The Nicene Creed establishes belief as an *act* of public declaration. And as such it has remained the basis of the Christian faith ever since. For the first time, it mattered what people, collectively and individually, declared in front of their peers that they *believed*. In this way, private belief or opinion (*doxa* in Greek) was drawn into the public sphere, where it could potentially be regulated or controlled. Religion was political, from that time on, in a way that it never had been before. A word that had barely existed up to this time had to be pressed into service to give expression to the novel idea. This was *orthodoxia*, meaning 'correct belief'. Christianity as a *state* religion begins not with Jesus of Nazareth or with Paul the Apostle but with the Council of Nicaea in 325 CE. At the same moment, too, begins the history of the world's troubled relations between religion and politics.

Another decision by Constantine would have almost as great an effect on later world history. Once again, the sequel would be quite out of proportion to anything that Constantine himself could have intended. It had been a common practice, going back at least as far as Alexander, for victorious Hellenistic kings and Roman generals or emperors to found new cities or reestablish old ones and to name them (in Greek) after themselves: well-known examples are Philippopolis (Plovdiv in today's Bulgaria) and Hadrianopolis (Adrianople in English, now the Turkish city of Edirne). Often, the location would be chosen close to the site of a spectacular victory. Constantine decided to be no different. More or less opposite the place where he had beaten Licinius, on the European side of the Bosphorus, was a small, half-ruined Greek city, built on a promontory between a long inlet and the Sea of Marmara. This city was already a thousand years old—if it is true that its first settlers had come from Megara, near the Isthmus of Corinth, in the seventh century BCE. It was a good strategic site, surrounded by water on three sides and overlooking the straits that separate Europe from Asia. Its name was Byzantium.

The inauguration of the refounded city took place with much pomp and circumstance on 11 May 330 CE.[51] The new city was an imperial foundation; one of the first institutions to be created for it was a Senate, modelled on the traditional aristocratic assembly of Rome. But it was not yet a capital. Constantine would make his home there for most of the years that remained to him. It was, of course, in Greek that the emperor named his city: *Konstantinoupolis*, or Constantinople, meaning 'city of Constantine'. For the first time ever, and almost by accident, the Greek-speaking world had acquired a political centre, one that would remain unchallenged for almost eight centuries and would never entirely lose its symbolic resonance for Greeks thereafter.

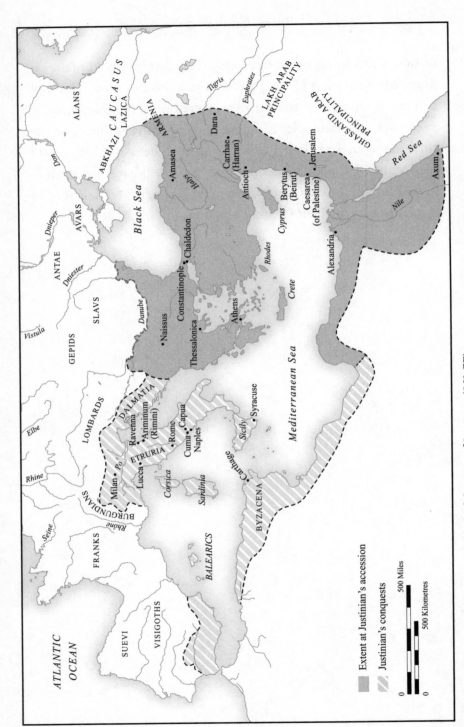

ATLANTIC OCEAN

ALANS

ABKHAZI · CAUCASUS · LAZICA

ARMENIA

Tigris

Euphrates

LAKH ARAB PRINCIPALITY

GHASSANID ARAB PRINCIPALITY

Dniester

Dnieper

Don

AVARS

ANTAE

SLAVS

Vistula

GEPIDS

Elbe

LOMBARDS

Rhine

BURGUNDIANS

FRANKS

Seine

Rhône

SUEVI

VISIGOTHS

Black Sea

Danube

Naissus

Thessalonica

Constantinople

Chalcedon

Athens

Amasea

Iris

Dara

Carrhae (Harran)

Antioch

Berytus (Beirut)

Jerusalem

Caesarea (of Palestine)

Cyprus

Rhodes

Crete

Alexandria

Nile

Red Sea

Axum

DALMATIA

Ravenna

Ariminum (Rimini)

Milan

Po

Lucca

ETRURIA

Rome

Capua

Cuma

Naples

Corsica

Sardinia

Sicily

Syracuse

Carthage

BYZACENA

BALEARICS

Mediterranean Sea

Extent at Justinian's accession

Justinian's conquests

0   500 Miles

0   500 Kilometres

8. Extent of the Roman Empire at the end of the reign of Justinian (565 CE)

8

BECOMING CHRISTIAN

337–630

A T THE TIME of Constantine's deathbed baptism in 337, the overwhelming majority of his subjects were still pagans. That is to say, they worshipped the traditional Greek and Roman gods in the traditional ways. Civil life still revolved around temples and sanctuaries as it always had done. Even the emperor's new city on the Bosphorus had its share of those. Indeed, while the building had been going on, Constantine had sent his agents to scour the precincts and public spaces of the eastern empire for bronze and marble statues to be shipped to Constantinople. Many of these ended up adorning the Hippodrome, newly built for the popular sport of chariot racing and long to remain at the civic heart of the city. Some of these monuments even survive today in the open space opposite the Blue Mosque that preserves the shape of the ancient race course. Eusebius would have us believe that Constantine's purpose in gathering all these ancient art objects had been to force the unconverted 'to renounce their error, when the emperor held up the very objects of their worship to be the ridicule and sport of all beholders'.[1] Sometimes the bishop protests too much.

In fact, Constantine and the three of his sons who succeeded him moved cautiously in imposing Christianity on the empire. There was no attempt to repeat the excesses of their predecessors against Christians and create a new round of martyrs. To begin with, there was little even in the way of legislation. Instead, people were nudged towards the new religion by the exercise of high-level patronage. In Constantinople and the cities of the east, cash donations from emperors, generous tax breaks to Christian individuals and institutions, and state funding to build churches all had their effect, cumulatively, over several decades. But change was gradual. And perhaps even more important were grassroots movements from below. Even now, Christianity had not lost the bottom-up momentum of its earliest years.

This was particularly evident in some of the empire's provinces: in Egypt, Syria, and Mesopotamia. Far more numerous than the martyrs who had preceded them, new generations of religious pioneers would once again prominently include women as well as men. And they would come from all walks of life, including the humblest. These were the people who would soon come to embody, in the minds of millions, the purest expression of the Christian life.

Some set out alone for deserts or mountains, to emulate the episode reported in the Gospels when Jesus retreated to the wilderness for forty days and was tempted by the Devil. Known variously as 'hermits' or 'ascetics', these individuals subjected themselves to ferocious conditions and privations, deliberately tormenting their bodies so as to perfect the soul within and prepare it for a better life after death. Just as Christ had fought against Satan, so these ascetics saw themselves as engaged in a cosmic struggle. The hermits who proliferated throughout Syria and Mesopotamia have been described as 'wild vagrants dressed in skins, their matted hair making them look like eagles'. 'Men of fire', they 'amazed and disquieted the Greco-Roman world by their histrionic gestures'. But they were not just loners. Turning their backs on society, the ascetics found that society came to *them*. People sought them out for moral guidance, to cast out demons, or just to gape and marvel at their endurance. A century after the time of Constantine, crowds would gather near Aleppo to gaze up at the top of a tall column where Saint Symeon Stylites lived for thirty-seven years perched on a small platform, sustained by food supplied by the local faithful and drawn up in baskets. Men and women such as these were the popular heroes and heroines of the day.[2]

Others created whole communities with similar aims. In Egypt, a villager by the name of Pachomius, who had converted to Christianity while serving in the Roman legions, seems to have been one of the first to establish a system of communal living for segregated groups of men and women, under strict religious rules and keeping their distance from towns and cities. By the time that Pachomius died in 346, nine of these 'monasteries', as they came to be known, were in existence in Egypt. Those who submitted to the rule of a monastery were known as 'monks'. The Greek word *monachos* literally means 'one all alone', a description that better fits the hermits and solitary ascetics than members of the communities founded by Pachomius and others. A hundred years later, there may have been as many as fifteen thousand monks living in Egypt, including at least four hundred nuns.[3] Many of those would have spoken Coptic, a form of ancient Egyptian that was also gaining ground as a written language among Christians. But the lives of the founders were written in Greek and widely read throughout the eastern empire. It was to the monks and hermits of their own localities that ordinary people looked for an example of how to live as Christians, as much as to distant emperors laying down the law in Constantinople.

And yet, during an extraordinary period of twenty months, beginning in November 361, it looked as though the whole process might be about to go into reverse. On the death of his last surviving son, Constantius II, Constantine's thirty-year-old cousin Julian, who had already proclaimed himself co-emperor in the west, became master of the entire Roman world. Posterity would remember Julian as the 'Apostate' or (in Greek until today) the 'Transgressor'. On his father's side, he was descended from the same Latin-speaking Balkan family as Constantine. Like Constantine, he had a Latin name. But his mother tongue, literally, was Greek. Julian was born and spent his earliest years in Constantinople. From there, he went on to study philosophy, grammar, and rhetoric in Athens. His military honours and ranks were all won in the west, where he commanded the legions in battle against German invaders from across the Rhine. But despite this, Julian's heart and mind would always remain rooted in the Greek-speaking east.[4]

Even among Roman emperors, Julian was an oddball. Bearded in the manner of ancient Greek philosophers, he could boast of an intellectual training unmatched by any previous emperor, except Marcus Aurelius (whom he greatly admired). He came to the throne determined not just to suppress the new religion of Constantine but to replace it with something that in its way was almost as much of a novelty. Julian's project went further than restoring the old practices of animal sacrifice and festivals in honour of the traditional gods (many of which were still continuing anyway). Julian was *religious* in a sense that would have been incomprehensible to most Greeks in the heyday of the classical Athens that he held in such esteem. He shared with the Christian ascetics a revulsion for the flesh. He had been brought up to be a Christian, after all.

Devoted though he was to Greek philosophy, it was faith in a supernatural higher power, not the power of human reason, that inspired Julian. What the new emperor demanded of his subjects was uniformity of *belief*. The idea of *orthodoxia*, that had entered the language of official religion with the Nicene Creed, was now to be applied to the ancient myths and legends about the Greek gods. Conceding that Greek literature possessed nothing of its own to match the divine revelation contained in the sacred texts of Christians or Jews, Julian called for the old stories to be interpreted anew.[5] Soon the religion he was promoting began to look and sound less like the old one it was supposed to restore and more like Christianity itself.

The task that Julian set himself was to turn the curriculum of a traditional Greek education into the basis for a religious faith. Those who shared in that education had long been proud to call themselves 'Hellenes'. This was merely a reflection of the deeply embedded acceptance that it was education, not birth, that defined a person as 'Hellenic'. Now, in Greek, the word 'Hellene' began to be used in the sense of 'pagan'. It may even have been Julian himself who first used it in this new sense. A long-term consequence of his 'apostasy' was that it would stick. Until the end of the eighteenth century, it would be standard practice in Greek to restrict the meaning of 'Hellenes' to those who either stood out against Christianity or had lived too long ago to be able to share in the salvation it offered—in other words, *ancient* Greeks.

It all came to an end suddenly on 26 June 363. While leading an expedition against Sassanid Persia, Julian was struck by a spear and died shortly afterwards. Had he succeeded, he might have turned the eastern empire into something resembling a *Greek* state, defined by its culture and religion, as well as language. His failure also helps to explain why the Greek-speaking Christian empire that would soon become independent of Rome would ever afterwards continue to identify itself and its people not as Greeks (Hellenes) but as Romans (*Romaioi*). In hindsight, a newly rebranded 'Hellenic' religion could only ever have appealed to an elite, while Christianity was proving that it really *was* for everyone.[6]

Despite this, the eastern empire would never turn its back on the language and the educational curriculum that were also called 'Hellenic'. Greek was after all the language of Christianity too. If the earliest Christian writers had been little versed in the Greek classics or the art of rhetoric, the deficiency had been made good long before this. In Julian's day, the leading Christian theologians had been through exactly the same education in the Greek language and the Greek classics as he had. Indeed, two of the bishops still remembered as 'Fathers of the Church', Saint Basil the Great and Saint Gregory of Nazianzus, had been Julian's fellow students in Athens. Together with Basil's brother, Saint Gregory of Nyssa, and Saint John Chrysostom in the next generation, these men would go on to exercise an enormous influence to ensure that Christians would not forsake a system of learning that had served their own teachers so well for so long.[7]

THE CAMPAIGN THAT cost Julian his life was part of a series of wars on the empire's eastern frontier that would drag on inconclusively for most of the next three centuries. On other fronts, too, the empire that had been founded on conquest was being forced onto the defensive. Germanic tribes had been crossing the Rhine into today's France—indeed, it had been in battle against them that Julian had first won his spurs before he became emperor. In the Balkans, others were coming across the Danube and settling in large numbers in Roman territory. In 378, an army of Goths defeated the Roman legions outside Adrianople (today's Edirne), only one hundred and fifty miles from Constantinople. The emperor Valens was killed in that battle. But the Goths failed to follow up on their victory. Gradually, and for the time being, the immediate threat to the eastern parts of the empire receded. But as the fourth century came to a close, the reality could no longer be denied: the foundations of the thousand-year-old Roman state were starting to crack.

Holding the vast structure of the empire together under these pressures was proving too much for emperors, senators, and dispersed military commands. For what happened next, the model of systems collapse has often been invoked by modern historians.[8]

First of all, in 395, the empire was formally divided when Theo-dosius I, on his deathbed, split the succession between his two sons. Almost immediately, the western half began to disintegrate. Rome itself was sacked by a Gothic army in 410, then again by another Germanic invader, the Vandals, in 455. Nominally, the western empire would limp on until 476, when the last emperor of Rome would be unceremoniously deposed and replaced by a German who took the Latin title of *rex*, or king, that to Romans had long been taboo. By that time, the Roman Empire in the west had al-ready broken up into a patchwork of petty kingdoms. This would remain the reality for centuries to come.

Constantinople was now on its own—no longer *an* imperial capital but *the* capital of the only Roman Empire that still existed. And it still *was* an empire, of perhaps thirty million people. Its ter-ritory stretched from the Danube in the north to the first cataract on the Nile at Aswan in the south and from the Balkan shoreline of the Strait of Otranto in the west to the Euphrates in the east. All the mechanisms remained in place for taxes to be raised and for grain to be shipped from Egypt to the capital and the empire's other great cities. In most of the eastern provinces, levels of popu-lation and prosperity were once again on the rise.

This meant there was plenty of manpower to supply the ranks of the legions and to build and to crew ships. Since the time of Constantine, a new source of gold had been found far away in the Caucasus—a discovery that seems not to have been shared with the 'twin' empire in the west but provided the basis for a currency that would keep its value undiminished for hundreds of years.[9] Un-der Theodosius II, who reigned from 408 to 450, the empire could mobilise the resources required to build the massive series of forti-fications for the capital, known as the 'Theodosian Walls', that are still an impressive part of the cityscape of modern Istanbul. For the next century and more, while the remains of the Roman Empire in the west continued to fragment, the fortunes of the eastern empire were set to rise still further.

Officially, when the empire had been divided, the line had been drawn between administrative regions. But the real division was the long-standing one of language and culture that had existed since the time of Augustus. It was during the reign of Theodosius II that the Greek-speaking east began belatedly to acquire a political existence of its own. Even so, it was still not quite a *Greek* empire. Latin continued to be spoken and written at the very top—by the emperor, by his immediate family, at the highest levels of the administration, and by the most senior ranks in the army. And in both halves of the empire, ever since Caracalla's grant of Roman citizenship almost two hundred years before, people had become accustomed to think of themselves as 'Romans'. The difference in the east was that they did so in Greek, not Latin. They were *Romaioi*, not *Romani*. 'Hellenes', of course, had been given a bad name by Julian. Only those who still hankered after his failed project might still describe themselves in that way. With the collapse of the empire in the west, its eastern counterpart became, in reality, an entirely new and independent state, at once Greek by language and Roman in name: 'a Greek Roman empire'.[10]

By the time of Theodosius II, it was also well on the way to becoming a *Christian* empire. New ecumenical councils were convened as new controversies erupted over the interpretation of matters of doctrine. The most contentious of these was how to understand the double nature of Jesus Christ as at once human and divine. Another was to define the Trinity, consisting of God the Father, the Son, and the Holy Spirit, in such a way as not to seem to dilute the principle of 'one God', or monotheism—a complaint levelled by nonbelievers from that time to this. These debates may seem arid and abstract, even abstruse, today, but at the time the issues were capable of arousing the passions of large sections of the population. On the distinction between defining the nature of Christ as either *homoousios* (of the same substance) or *homoioousios* (of similar substance) as God the Father, the allegiance of whole provinces could be won or lost.

In Egypt and the Levant, the overwhelming majority of the faithful preferred a more rigorously monotheistic definition to the one that had been officially adopted at Nicaea in 325. But the double nature of Christ was reaffirmed in 451 at the council held at Chalcedon, on the opposite side of the Bosphorus from Constantinople. The finest intellects of the day were at once trying to keep pace and to guide the passions of the faithful. They also bickered shamelessly among themselves. Only the dogmatic determination of an emperor, in this case the successor to Theodosius II, Marcian, could push through a resolution and try to enforce it, as Constantine had done. But time and again, a single 'correct belief' (*orthodoxia*) would prove hard to foist upon unwilling subjects, even while Christianity was steadily gaining ground to become the majority religion and pagans were pushed more and more onto the defensive.[11]

The tipping point seems to have come around the start of the fifth century. But that still left a sizeable population of pagans, or 'Hellenes', who either remained unconverted or actively resisted conversion.[12] Even before the empire's division, the first Theodosius had begun legislating to ban pagan practices. Under Theodosius II, pagans were banned from serving in the highest ranks of the civil service and the judiciary. It is often hard to tell how thoroughly these and other sanctions were enforced, or how effective they were. There was never a policy of systematic persecution of pagan 'Hellenes'. But there was little, either, to prevent outbreaks of spontaneous violence against individuals, institutions, or buildings. Usually, these would be spurred on by local leaders. On occasion, even an emperor would turn a blind eye.

In Alexandria, in 391, bands of zealot thugs, loyal to one of the least-tolerant bishops of the time by the name of Cyril, burnt down the vast temple complex dedicated to the Egyptian bull god Serapis, known as the Serapeum. It was the same Cyril who a few years later decided to round up and expel all the city's Jews—probably one of the largest Jewish communities anywhere in the world at this time. This was in 415. In the mayhem that ensued, a Christian mob targeted one of Alexandria's most prominent and respected 'Hellene' ladies. Hypatia was a teacher of philosophy and mathematics at the *Mouseion*, the institute of learning founded by the Ptolemies some seven hundred years before. The story of what happened next we owe to a horrified contemporary, himself a Christian and a historian of the church:

> They dragged her from her carriage, took her to the church called Caesareum, where they completely stripped her, and then murdered her with tiles. After tearing her body in pieces, they took her mangled limbs to a place called Cinaron, and there burnt them.[13]

Episodes such as this have invited comparison with the terrorist acts of Islamist extremists in the twenty-first century. Palmyra in Syria, whose well-preserved remains were targeted by ISIS fighters in 2015, had been attacked and had sustained similar damage in 385 while still a living city—on that occasion at the hands of militant *Christians* from the desert.[14] But it is worth noting that (again, like Islamist terrorism today) these were the acts of extremist individuals and groups. They were not ordered by the state. Most emperors, until well into the sixth century, seem to have been content to promote a policy of gradual assimilation rather than sudden coercion.

As a result, throughout this time, pockets of pagan beliefs and customs continued to coexist with a now dominant Christian culture. The last Olympic Games had been held at Olympia in 393, before the festival was closed down by order of Theodosius I. But their namesake at Antioch would keep going until 520. At some point along the way, athletes no longer exercised naked. Soon, it seems that nobody was exercising at all. The Greek word for physical exercise, *askesis*, had already been conscripted by the 'ascetics' of the new faith.

Theatrical performances involving singing, dancing, and slapstick comedy had been popular all over the Greek east for centuries. Called 'mimes' or 'pantomimes', these seem to have been the last gasp of the venerable tradition of Greek drama. Christian preachers weighed in against the 'dishonourable' profession of the 'laughter-maker' and 'the man of many disguises, the unstable man, the easy man, the man who becomes all things'. Just so far had the mentality of the Greek-speaking world moved on from Homer's Odysseus 'of many wiles' and certainly of many disguises. If ever there was a definitive 'closure of the theatres', like that of Puritan England in the seventeenth century, we don't know when it happened. But along with less innocuous forms of entertainment, such as gladiatorial fights and wild beast shows, the Greek theatrical tradition certainly came to an end. Play texts were read and studied as part of an education that was still considered suitable for Christians—but for their language and style, no longer as living drama.[15]

Everyday life was changing, too. Constantine had given new secular powers to the highest local authorities of the church, the bishops. The Greek word for 'bishop', *episkopos*, from which the English is derived, literally means 'overseer'. Charismatic and often highly educated, these men were elected for life, unlike municipal officials or provincial governors. By the fifth century, it was more often to bishops than to magistrates or imperial appointees that people looked for leadership in towns and cities. In the past, prominent citizens had vied with one another to pay for games, spectacular shows and buildings, and in this way to earn the gratitude of their poorer peers. Now, bishops channelled spare wealth to create hospices for the needy and the sick. Christian charity had become a civic duty by the fifth century. Bishops were not themselves either poor or humble. But they did preach the virtues of compassion, humility, and forgiveness, virtues which had no counterpart in older Greek thinking or behaviour. Above all, they preached the worth of every human being. And they preached the possibility of eternal salvation for the individual soul.[16]

The physical appearance of cities was being transformed at the same time. Ancient temples, with their long colonnades, still stood. But those that had not been converted into churches lay abandoned or in ruins. Worshippers no longer congregated in the open air in front of them. Outdoor altars no longer smoked with burnt offerings meant for the gods. Massed male citizens no longer feasted on the edible parts of ritually slaughtered animals. Worship had moved into the enclosed spaces of interiors which had never featured much in pagan worship. Perhaps this was a reflection of the movement from the extrovert and communal towards the inner world of the experiencing individual that marks the whole transition towards Christianity.

But there was one aspect of urban life that no amount of pious exhortation by the 'Fathers of the Church' could suppress. In Constantinople and in every large city of the eastern empire, crowds still flocked to the Hippodrome to watch their favourite riders race chariots against each other. Perhaps it was because so many other forms of public entertainment were being shut down, or withering away, that this one not only bucked the trend but actually grew in the numbers it attracted and the intensity of the passions it aroused. Originally, there had been four teams, all named after colours. But, by the end of the fifth century, just about everyone, from the emperor downwards, was a supporter of either the Blues or the Greens—and not just at Constantinople but in all the larger cities, such as Thessalonica or Antioch.

Since at least the time of Theodosius I in the late fourth century, rioting between supporters of the rival teams had often led to bloodshed. From today's perspective, these public convulsions have been compared to football hooliganism. For once, it seems they had little or nothing to do with religion. The fans of the Blues and the fans of the Greens were nothing like political parties or even, probably, factions with a consistent political agenda. But by the start of the next century, in Constantinople, they were operating as political pressure groups powerful enough to make or break an emperor.[17]

WHEN THE EMPEROR Anastasius died in July 518 at the age of eighty-seven, no plans had been put in place for the succession. The next highest authority in Constantinople lay with the Senate, that had been established by Constantine along Roman lines from the beginning. Unlike the original Senate, though, this one had never much say in the governing of the empire—except in a situation like this. It was supposed to be for the senators to name the new emperor. But power to control the streets lay elsewhere. The Hippodrome, built to accommodate a hundred thousand people, filled up with a chanting crowd. No doubt there had been work behind the scenes. It would be claimed afterwards that money had changed hands. The commander of the palace guard, a grizzled old soldier by the name of Justin, was certainly well placed to work the crowd. Before the day was over, Justin had entered the royal box in the Hippodrome and was being hailed as emperor by supporters of both Blues and Greens. This was to be the way for power to be transferred from one emperor to another on several occasions during the remainder of the century and well into the next.[18]

Justin was already in his seventies when he took office. When he died nine years later in 527, he had already appointed his nephew and adopted son, Justinian, to succeed him. The younger man was then aged about forty-five. According to a pen portrait written towards the end of his reign, almost forty years later:

> In appearance he was short, with a good chest, a good nose, fair-skinned, curly-haired, round-faced, handsome, with receding hair, a florid complexion, with his hair and beard greying.

Most of these details can be confirmed from surviving images made out of mosaic in the Italian city of Ravenna during Justinian's lifetime. The writer, a loyal civil servant from Antioch by the name of John Malalas, adds, perhaps dutifully: 'He was magnanimous and Christian'. The historian of Justinian's reign, Procopius of Caesarea, who had an axe to grind, although we do not know why, shows both sides of the man he certainly knew personally:

> He showed himself approachable and affable to those with whom he came into contact; not a single person found himself denied access to the Emperor, and even those who broke the rules of etiquette . . . never incurred his wrath. . . . He never gave even a hint of anger or irritation to show how he felt towards those who had offended him, but—with a friendly expression on his face and without raising an eyebrow—in a gentle voice he would order tens of thousands of quite innocent people to be put to death, cities to be overturned and the confiscation of all their money by the Treasury.[19]

Justinian is probably best remembered today for commissioning the monumental codification of the entire corpus of Roman law that still bears his name. Announced within a year of his accession, in 528, its several stages were completed in only five years. Wherever legal systems today are said to be based on Roman law, it is the work of Justinian's legal teams that is meant. This massive compilation was of course made in Latin, the language of the much older original documents that were edited and harmonised in the process. But as well as tidying up the corpus of lawmaking that his officials had inherited, Justinian would soon become a prolific lawmaker himself. Beginning in the 530s, new laws would be drafted not in Latin but in Greek. By the decision of an emperor who was himself a Latin speaker, Greek had at last reached all the way to the top to become the language of imperial legislation.

Along with all this legal activity, it is hardly surprising to see the full force of the law directed against the last outposts of pagan beliefs and practices that still existed in the empire. Right at the beginning of Justinian's first compilation of laws, issued in 529, comes this directive:

> All people who are ruled by the administration of our clemency shall practice that religion which the divine Peter the Apostle transmitted to the Romans. We command that those who follow this law shall embrace the name of Catholic [i.e., universal] Christians.

Other laws for the first time prohibited homosexual practices, overturning centuries of tolerance—even, in the case of classical Athens, celebration—of same-sex relationships. Also in 529, according to Malalas:

> There was a great persecution of Hellenes. Many had their property confiscated. . . . The emperor issued a decree and sent it to

Athens ordering that no-one should teach philosophy nor interpret the laws; nor should gaming be allowed in any city, for some
gamblers who had been discovered in Byzantion had been indulging themselves in dreadful blasphemies. Their hands were cut off
and they were paraded around on camels.[20]

The philosophers seem at least to have been more humanely
treated than the gamblers. A few decamped for a time to Persia.
But the ease with which a pious civil servant could equate the great
philosophical schools that went back to Plato and Aristotle with
the gambling dens above the Bosphorus is revealing of the attitude
of the time. Athens would never again be a centre of learning until
the nineteenth century. At Alexandria, the teaching of philosophy
would continue for a hundred years more—but with Christian
teachers.[21] The eastern empire was not only becoming more Greek,
under Justinian it was also becoming more uniformly Christian,
more centralised and autocratic than ever before.

But it soon turned out that Justinian was not yet secure on his
throne. Trouble began, once again, with the fan clubs of the chari-
ot-racing teams, the Blues and the Greens. Nobody could be above
the fray. Justinian himself, according to Procopius, was a Blue supporter. In January 532, a flashpoint came when popular charioteers
fell foul of the authorities. Soon fighting broke out in the Hippodrome in front of the emperor. Crowds massed in the centre of
the city. True to form, the confrontation was rapidly becoming
political. When supporters of the Greens demanded the dismissal
of three of the emperor's highest officials, Justinian gave way. But
even this was not enough to quell what Procopius called the 'mob'.
Massed voices called on the emperor himself to resign. Chanting
'Win! Win!' (*Nika* in Greek), as they must have done regularly to
cheer on their favourite charioteers, some began to hail one of their

own ringleaders as emperor. Ever since, the event has been known to historians as the Nika riot.

According to Procopius, it was the emperor's wife, Theodora, who stiffened Justinian's resolve at this moment of crisis. By the time that imperial troops had restored order several days later, some thirty thousand citizens lay dead in the Hippodrome and the surrounding streets. Much of the centre of the city had gone up in flames, including the cathedral Church of the Holy Wisdom (Hagia Sophia in Greek).[22]

The sequel would change the geopolitics of the entire Mediterranean for the better part of two centuries and the cityscape of Justinian's capital to this day. The emperor had come very close to being deposed by the power of the mob. He had been saved by the resolve of his empress and the bravery and resourcefulness of the commander of his guard, a general by the name of Belisarius. Justinian now had to prove himself in the eyes of his subjects. What he needed was a war. And he needed to *win*. The chants hurled at him by the rioters in the Hippodrome must still have been ringing in his ears.

A campaign against Persia had been going badly. But suddenly, in 533, a new opportunity presented itself in the west. Peace was hastily patched up with the Persians, and that June, Belisarius sailed out of the Bosphorus at the head of a fleet of six hundred warships, bound for the Mediterranean. Their objective was North Africa. For the past hundred years, the former Roman provinces there had been under the control of the Vandals, the Germanic tribe that had sacked Rome for the second time in 455.

On 15 September, Belisarius entered Carthage, the Vandals' capital. Within a year, the entire North African coast had been brought once again under Roman rule. Belisarius himself returned to the capital to celebrate in a manner that has the ring of an old

Roman triumph, being carried aloft through the streets by Vandal captives on New Year's Day 535. But this was only the beginning. A second expedition that same year wrested Sicily from the Ostrogoths, who controlled all of Italy and part of the northern Balkans. A new campaign began on the Italian mainland. Rome itself opened its gates to Belisarius in December 536. The Ostrogoths withdrew their troops to defend their capital, Ravenna, farther north on the Adriatic coast. Three years later, Belisarius had Ravenna under close siege and finally took the city in May 540.[23]

It had been an astonishing run of victories. Justinian gave orders for a column to be erected near his palace. Plated with brass, it was topped by a gigantic equestrian statue of himself holding a globe in his hand to symbolise his conquest of the entire world. The column and the statue would stand for close on a thousand years.[24] As the decade of the 530s ended, Justinian and his generals had everything to celebrate. Modern historians usually call it a 'reconquest'. But none of the territories 'reconquered' had ever previously been ruled from Constantinople. The shape of Justinian's new empire on the map looks quite different from any state that had existed previously. This new 'Roman' empire was a maritime one, unlike the old. It had been achieved by sea, very much as the earliest expansion of Greek speakers into the western Mediterranean had been more than a millennium before. For the first time since the heyday of the Hellenistic kingdoms, the centre of power in the Mediterranean world now lay in the Greek-speaking east.

In the meantime, on the home front, Justinian had mobilised the empire's architects and builders. As soon as peace had been restored after the Nika riot, the task of rebuilding the centre of the imperial city began. The destruction offered Justinian the opportunity, and perhaps also the motive, to build on a scale that had never been seen before. To replace the destroyed church of Hagia

Sophia, he adopted a design that was just then being pioneered. It was based on a rectangular space with a square at its centre and topped by a dome. Many centuries would pass before a version of this form of church architecture would find favour in the West. But it has ever since remained the basic design of most eastern Orthodox churches in the Balkans and Russia and would soon be adopted by Muslim architects as the template for the mosque.

Justinian's church, the greatest of all the many building projects commissioned during his reign, was completed in five years—only a third of the time taken to build the Parthenon in Athens, with which it is often compared. It was dedicated in December 537, twelve months after Belisarius's troops had reclaimed Rome for the empire. For a thousand years after that, Hagia Sophia would remain the largest religious building anywhere in the world. Its nave is eighty metres long. The top of its dome still rises fifty-five metres above the pavements of modern Istanbul. The creation of two Greek architects from Anatolia, Isidore of Miletus and Anthemius of Tralles, Hagia Sophia successfully marries the old Greek science of theoretical geometry to Roman skills of practical engineering. Light filters into the huge open space through windows placed high under the dome in such a way as to create a perfectly enclosed world that also seems capable of encompassing the whole universe, under God's overarching heaven.[25]

Created out of the wreckage caused by the riot of only five years before, Justinian's Church of the Holy Wisdom was the visible, monumental proof of how the Greek-speaking world had changed in the two hundred years that had passed since the death of Constantine. The triumph of Christianity was visible for all to see. And the new Greek-speaking empire, with its capital at Constantinople, was carrying all before it on the battlefield. Justinian could have been forgiven for believing, as he celebrated his victories at the end of the 530s, that the words addressed by Eusebius to Constantine had come true at last:

> The image of the higher kingdom is reflected in the emperor who, beloved of God and in imitation of the Superior Being, by his governance steers the helm of all the world's affairs.[26]

AND YET, FAR away, beyond the serene dome of Hagia Sophia, forces were already at work whose effects would severely disrupt the cosmic order that Justinian's armies and generals, craftsmen and architects seemed to have created. Even while the great church was reaching towards the sky above Constantinople, volcanic eruptions in East Asia were hurling vast quantities of ash and debris into the upper atmosphere. The consequence, in modern terms, was a 'dust-veil event', that caused temporary disruptions to the climate over large parts of the world. No one alive in Europe or the Middle East at that time, of course, could have had any inkling of this. Modern scientists infer it from evidence contained in ancient tree trunks that reveals changing weather patterns far back in the past. Nomad horsemen from central Asia, who depended on the 'delicate grassland ecology' of that vast region, burst westwards and southwards towards Europe and the settled lands of the Middle East. In 539, great numbers of them, called 'Huns' by Procopius, crossed the Danube and broke through the undefended Balkans to devastate all of mainland Greece north of the Peloponnese. Their raiding parties even reached close to the walls of Constantinople itself.[27]

Farther east, and probably from the same environmental cause, the balance of powers was shifting, too. A new king of Persia, Khusro I, known in Greek as Chosroes, accused Justinian of being in league with the nomads who were pressing hard against his own northern flank and aimed a preemptive strike westward towards the Mediterranean. In 540, a string of cities in the Greek east was sacked and burned to the ground. At the very time when Belisarius was accepting the surrender of Ravenna in the west, in May, the great city of Antioch was razed by Chosroes's troops and its people killed, taken into slavery, or forced to flee their homes. Belisarius had to be brought back hastily from Italy to confront the new threat. Procopius, recording these events at the time, vividly expressed the perplexity felt by his contemporaries:

> It makes my head spin to write of such suffering. . . . I cannot understand what God can possibly be thinking of, to allow a man or a country to rise to great heights, only to throw them down so soon afterwards and obliterate them without the slightest visible cause.[28]

But worse was still to come. It has been suggested that those same climatic conditions that had brought the nomad horsemen sweeping out of the steppes may also have affected the rodent population in the regions bordering the Red Sea, bringing them into closer contact with humans. The first cases of bubonic plague, probably carried by rat fleas, were recorded on the Nile delta in 541. By spring the next year, the plague had spread throughout the Middle East and reached Constantinople. Over the next few years, it would rampage across all of Europe and the Middle East. In Constantinople alone, out of a population of some four hundred thousand, modern estimates put the number of deaths at around 20 to 25 per cent. The impact on daily life, as recorded by Procopius, resonates uncannily with the worldwide pandemic of Covid-19 that began in 2020:

> No one was to be seen out buying anything. Everyone sat at home, those who were well enough either caring for the sick or keening

for the dead. All work stopped, craftsmen laid down their crafts, and each person set aside whatever he was doing.

During a four-month peak in the spring and summer of 542, Procopius tells us, the plague claimed between five and ten thousand lives each day. The rational historian can only record, with horror, what he sees:

> Some died immediately, others after many days. Those whose bodies broke out in black pustules, the size of a bean, would not see out the day, but died in short order. Many began spontaneously to vomit blood and died soon after.

What especially perplexed Procopius—and again he cannot have been alone among the sophisticated citizens of Constantinople—was the 'absence of any cause for the disease that could be grasped by human reason'. Almost as bewildering was the unpredictability of outcomes. Doctors were as confounded as everyone else. People survived who had been given up for dead. Treatment that had seemed to help one patient might have the opposite effect on another. There was no precaution you could take, and of course no cure. 'Suffering would strike without warning; recovery would happen all by itself'.[29]

Many saw the affliction in literally apocalyptic terms. The end of the world and the return of Christ in judgement were at hand. Malalas, a devout Christian, wrote not long after it was over: 'The Lord God saw that man's transgressions had multiplied and he caused the overthrow of man on the earth, leading to his destruction in all cities and lands.' A hymn by the great religious poet of the age, Romanos the Melodist, like Malalas a Syrian writing in Greek, sums up a sense of mingled doom and fulfilment that seems to have been widespread in Constantinople during the latter years of Justinian's reign:

> *The last day is nigh,*
> *Now we behold those things . . .*
> *Nothing is lacking of which Christ told . . . : famines and*
> *   plagues and frequent earthquakes.*
> *Nation has risen up against nation,*
> *Within all is frightful, without all is filled with strife.*[30]

Even the plague, terrible though it was, brought one unexpected benefit: the Persians found themselves hit just as hard, and in 545 made peace. This left Justinian free to turn his attention back to the west. Over the next decade, his forces went on to conquer the rest of Italy and all the islands of the western Mediterranean, as well as a slice of the southern coast of Spain captured from the Visigoths.

In Ravenna, the newly built church of San Vitale was dedicated in 547, seven years after Belisarius's triumph over the Ostrogoths. The mosaics which decorate the apse are among the finest surviving examples of Christian art of this period. Among them are the side panels that depict Justinian and Theodora surrounded by elegant courtiers, churchmen, and ladies-in-waiting. The costumes, particularly of the ladies, are magnificent and flowing. The empress wears a diadem from which pearls hang down over her breast; the emperor, a jewelled crown. The heads of both the imperial figures are surrounded by golden haloes. Much of the background, too, is made of up glass tesserae coloured by real gold leaf. Curtains swing and part, a fountain plays. Although the expressions of the faces are sombre, the background, particularly behind Theodora and her attendants, is a riot of colour. All this is subordinated to a religious purpose, of course. The human figures are the servants of Christ, depicted high above them, and Justinian is holding a bowl of money which may represent his contribution to the adornment of the building.[31] There is no sign, here, of the apocalyptic gloom that some were expressing in the capital at the very same time.

Farther afield, during the 540s and 550s, we get glimpses into a wider world that was still very much open to the future, indeed open for business. Throughout the Mediterranean, the effect of Justinian's conquests was to give a new lease of life to long-distance trade routes that had languished since the collapse of the empire in the west. In a different direction, Greek-speaking traders were reaching out from Egyptian ports on the Red Sea into the Arabian Gulf and the Indian Ocean to reach the coasts of Africa and India.[32]

In the 550s, one of these traders wrote a book based, in part, on his experiences. The main aim of Cosmas Indicopleustes (Sailor-to-India) was to prove, even against the better-informed scientific opinion of his time, that the earth was after all flat and that every inhabited part of it conformed to a divinely ordained pattern derived from the Bible. But Cosmas was also a curious observer of the places and people he encountered. He had travelled far outside the Roman Empire and had seen for himself how very much larger was the world beyond. He had encountered rhinoceroses and giraffes, though the hippopotamus he knew only from its name and its teeth, which he had traded. He had seen pepper and coconuts growing. His voyages had taken him as far as Sri Lanka (called Taprobane in Greek). He demonstrates the mentality of a truly global trader when he describes that island as being 'in a central position'—obviously not in relation to his own homeland, still less its capital city, but rather to a maritime network that reached westwards to Africa, north to India and Persia, and eastwards to China, which he calls Tzinitza.

By the time Justinian died in 565, aged over eighty, not only had the empire expanded in new directions but the world itself had become wider too. Cosmas the Sailor-to-India may have been badly wrong about the place of our world in the universe, but his earthly geography was based on experience and remarkably sound. Cosmas appears to have been the first writer in Greek to know, at least roughly, where China is and how far distant. And however wishful his thinking, the confidence of this pious and presumably not unsuccessful Greek shipowner, writing in the 550s, in the aftermath of plague, warfare, and natural disasters, would seem to confound the more dire predictions of imminent doom that were circulating in Constantinople:

> The empire of the Romans thus participates in the dignity of the Kingdom of the Lord Christ, seeing that it transcends, as far as can be in this state of existence, every other power, and will remain unconquered until the final consummation.[33]

MODERN HISTORIANS FREQUENTLY dismiss Justinian's conquests in the west as a mere flash in the pan. The empire's dwindling resources had been disastrously overstretched, so the story goes; the 'regained' provinces in the west could never have been sustainable in the long term. Procopius, writing in darkly satirical mode during the last years of Justinian's reign, foreshadowed that modern interpretation when he caricatured the emperor and his wife Theodora as 'blood-thirsty demons' who had taken on human form for no other purpose than 'to find the easiest and swiftest means of destroying all races of men and all their works'.[34] But some modern historians take a more upbeat view. Most of Justinian's conquests were still holding up, come the turn of the next century, and some would last for much longer. By the year 600, although more ground had recently been lost in the Balkans, many towns and cities in the east, including Antioch, that had previously fallen to Persia, had been regained. Yet another peace treaty with the Sassanids had been concluded as recently as 591.[35]

The architect of that treaty was a former general by the name of Maurice, who had become emperor nine years before. At the start of the seventh century, Maurice led a series of campaigns to win back territory in the Balkans. By the end of the campaigning season in 602, the troops had had considerable success. But when the emperor gave the order to keep up the pressure on the tribesmen during the Balkan winter, this was too much for the legionaries and they mutinied. The leader of the mutiny, a junior officer by the name of Phocas, led them towards Constantinople. So far, so traditional. It was a legacy of the earlier turmoil during the third century that emperors could be made, and also unmade, by the men they led into battle. But this was different.

As rumours of the troops' approach swirled through Constantinople, the emperor announced a chariot race and everybody poured into the Hippodrome to watch their favourite champions. It is doubtful whether the fans of either the Blues or the Greens in the Hippodrome that November day had any coherent political objective at all. The same probably goes for the charioteers, though their managers had links to high places and probably did have an agenda of their own. Maurice's calculation must have been that if he could secure the backing of *both* factions, as Justin had done a century before, he would have sufficient support in the city to face down the rebel army.

What followed was in many ways a rerun of the Nika riot. Fighting broke out in the Hippodrome and then spread through the city. It was not the soldiers gathered outside the walls who forced Maurice and his immediate family to flee for their lives, but the populace, whipped up to a frenzy by the cheerleaders of the rival sporting factions. Order was not restored until the emperor and four of his five sons had been apprehended and their severed heads displayed to the crowd in the Hippodrome.[36]

With the deposition of Maurice, the treaty he had negotiated with the Persians under Khusro (Chosroes) II came to an end. The eight-year reign of Phocas saw the start of the last and deadliest of all the wars between Persia and a European power since the time of Alexander. In its first phase, it has also been described as a civil war between the army and the civilian elite within the Roman Empire. We only have one side of the story, but the accounts that have been preserved all portray Phocas as presiding over a series of purges, a brutal ruler who never managed to gain legitimacy in the eyes of his subjects.[37]

Matters came to a head in 610 when a fleet from the North African provinces, that had been annexed under Justinian, arrived off Constantinople. The ringleaders this time seem to have belonged to the senatorial class. But they must have been efficient at mobilising the cheerleaders of the Blues and the Greens. While the new emperor, Heraclius, was receiving his crown, the dismembered corpse of Phocas was displayed to a baying crowd in the Hippodrome, and the severed head of one of his advisers was thrown into a public furnace. Others may have been burnt alive.[38]

Heraclius's reign began with a series of disasters. One by one, the great cities of the east were either sacked by the Persians or surrendered: Jerusalem, Alexandria, Damascus, Antioch (again). Almost all of the Balkans had already been overrun by groups of Slavs, Avars, and Bulgars by the time that Heraclius took charge. Thessalonica, the gateway to mainland Europe from the Aegean, held out almost alone—thanks to the massive circuit walls that had been built in the reign of the Theodosius II, though an anonymous chronicler of the time would give the credit, instead, to a series of miracles performed by the city's patron saint, Demetrius.[39] Now the decision was taken to abandon the defence of the European provinces altogether and move all available troops to the eastern front. But not even this was enough to prevent a Persian expeditionary force from fighting its way through Anatolia towards the capital in 615. The enemy pitched camp on the Asian shore of the Bosphorus at a distance from Constantinople that today is spanned by three suspension bridges. In desperation, Heraclius made a humiliating offer of peace. If it had been accepted, it would have turned the Roman state into a Persian vassal. But Khusro contemptuously rejected the terms and murdered Heraclius's ambassadors.

For the next ten years, the fortunes of war went to and fro. For a time, the Persians were pushed back into Anatolia. Then, in the spring of 622, Heraclius embarked on a daring plan. Determined to take the fight to the enemy, he left Constantinople to lead an army in person through the foothills of the Caucasus in today's Azerbaijan. The strategy had not yet proved its worth when a Persian force once again appeared on the Asian side of the Bosphorus. This time a combined body of Avars and Slavs had massed on the European side beneath Theodosius's great walls. It may not have been by pre-arrangement among the besieging forces, but Constantinople was surrounded. And now, if not before, the Persians began seriously to coordinate their efforts with those of the Slavs and Avars on the opposite shore. The siege began on 29 July 626 and lasted for ten days. The Persians had no boats to ferry their infantrymen across. But the Slavs did, and volunteered their services. The vessels must have been quite small, because the attackers had apparently carried them overland from the Danube (the Greek sources contemptuously call them 'canoes' or 'punts'—*monoxyla*). So when the Slavs began to ferry the Persian troops across the Bosphorus, the fleet putting out from Constantinople was able to sink them.

Five days later, the Slavs made another attempt, this time to land their own men from farther down the coast. But the defenders got wind of the plan in time and lured the invading boats into an ambush in the narrow waterway known as the Golden Horn. It was the decisive moment in the siege. The two attacking forces had been prevented from joining up. Both had stretched their supply lines to the limit. On the night of 7–8 August 626, the Avars and Slavs set fire to their siege engines and retreated northwards into the Balkans. The Persians, unable to do anything but watch from the hills and shore of the Asian side, soon turned tail. Constantinople had been saved, and with it the Greek-speaking Roman Empire.[40]

When Themistocles had famously triumphed over the Persian fleet using a similar tactic in the battle of Salamis in 480 BCE, the experience of deliverance had inspired the Greek city-states with a new sense of their own identity and the self-confidence to create the civilisation that we still call 'classical'. Aeschylus and Herodotus had inaugurated the resonant and long-running cause of the 'liberty of Hellas'; Socrates and the philosophers had championed the power of human reason. Now, in 626, the victory was attributed to the Virgin Mary, whose icon had been carried round the walls during the siege. The Church of the Mother of God at Blacherna overlooked the battle site on the Golden Horn, and she herself, it was said, had intervened to protect the Christian capital.[41] If the aftermath of that first Persian war had brought out a spirit of unity among Greek speakers *as Greeks*, this victory, eleven hundred years later, was bringing them together as never before in their new identity *as Christians*.

An unprecedented kind of warfare was developing. Today, we call it 'holy war'. The idea was made explicit for the first time when Heraclius launched his expedition through Transcaucasia to strike at the Persian heartland. On that occasion, the emperor urged his troops to 'keep in mind the fear of God and struggle to avenge insults to Him'. Once upon a time, Greek city-states had fought to avenge damage and destruction to the citizen body, to cherished public buildings and sacred temples. But Heraclius's enemies were the enemies of God himself. And however great the odds, the troops could rest assured that 'Our danger is not without reward but is the harbinger of eternal life'.[42]

It was a risky venture. But it worked. Less than two years after the siege of Constantinople had been lifted, Heraclius entered Persia from the north and the Sassanid Empire imploded. Chosroes was murdered by his own side early in 628. The whole of the Middle East, up to the River Tigris, was returned to Roman rule. So was Egypt, which for centuries had provided most of the grain that had once fed the people of Rome and until recently had done the same for Constantinople. For a few short months, it even looked as though the next king of Persia would become a Christian and be baptised with a Greek name. It would have been the ultimate vindication for a political state that now defined itself by the religious faith of its citizens. According to the Book of Genesis in the Old Testament, God had created the world in six days and rested on the seventh. In the same way, it was said at the time, Heraclius had laboured for six years on campaign. In the seventh, he returned to his capital—to commemorate his victory not with the parade of strength and riches that had marked a traditional Roman triumph but rather with a 'mystic celebration', presumably under the heavenly dome of Hagia Sophia.[43]

Shortly afterwards, Heraclius set out for Jerusalem. Part of the 'True Cross', on which Jesus had supposedly been crucified, had been venerated as a relic in the Church of the Holy Sepulchre there, ever since it had come to light three centuries earlier. When the Persians sacked the city in 614, they had taken the prized relic back with them to Ctesiphon, their capital on the Tigris. Now, with the terms of peace, it had been returned. Heraclius determined that he would be there in person to oversee its formal restoration to its rightful place and in this way to mark the symbolic triumph not of Roman arms but of the Roman faith.

But first, before he left Constantinople in 629, Heraclius adopted a new imperial title. His predecessors had always styled themselves, in the Roman manner, either 'emperor' or 'Augustus' (*Sebastos* in Greek). In their Greek forms, these titles would have many centuries of life left in them yet. But alongside them, Heraclius became the first ruler of a 'Roman' empire to revive the long-disused Greek word for 'king', *basileus*.[44] From then on, this would remain the official title, in Greek, of every ruler to rule from Constantinople, even after Christian emperors had been replaced by Ottoman sultans, until the end of the eighteenth century.

The significance of this is not just religious. It is often pointed out that *basileus* had been the title of King David in the Greek version of the Old Testament, and Jerusalem had been his royal city. But for a far longer period, *basileus* had been the title of the ancient Macedonian kings and of the Hellenistic dynasties that had come after them. In styling himself 'faithful *Basileus* in Christ', Heraclius at a stroke redefined the empire over which he ruled: as the inheritor not only of God's chosen kingdom but also of the great Hellenistic kingdoms that had preceded the power of Rome. What had once been a pagan empire was now to be a Christian kingdom, defined by faith and (although the second was only implicit) by the Greek language.

When Heraclius entered Jerusalem on 21 March 630, at the head of a solemn procession, and carried the fragment of the True Cross to the church that had been built over the site of Jesus's crucifixion, it must have seemed to many of those present that something momentous had been fulfilled. Among the many prophecies about the end of the world that were in circulation by this time was one that imagined the last emperor of the Romans, or according to another version, 'King of the Greeks', setting up the Holy

Cross on the site of the crucifixion, placing his crown on top of it, and 'hand[ing] over the kingship to God the Father'. These events would be a sure sign that the Second Coming of Christ, the Last Judgement, and the Kingdom of Heaven were at hand.[45]

Needless to say, Heraclius did not lay down his crown in Jerusalem and the world did not end. But with the change of royal title, in a sense Heraclius *was* the last emperor to rule over the people who still called themselves 'Romans'. In hindsight, we can see that an era really was about to end, though not even the most apocalyptic of prophets could have imagined how. During the three hundred years since the inauguration of Constantinople, the Roman Empire had been transformed. Greek speakers had reinvented themselves once more, this time as Christian Romans. Their state was once again ruled by a *basileus*. And the city that Constantine had founded, now nicknamed the 'second Rome' or 'new Rome', had first eclipsed and then replaced the old one in the geopolitics of the Mediterranean and the Middle East.[46]

9

'THE EYES OF THE UNIVERSE'
630–1018

H ERACLIUS MAY HAVE invented holy war, but it was the Arab successors of the prophet Muhammad who perfected it and for the first time gave it a name: *jihad*. The emperor had not long been back in Constantinople when far to the south, beyond the limits of his rule, Muhammad died in June 632. For the past ten years, this charismatic leader had been uniting the tribes of Arabia in the name of a new monotheistic religion: Islam. Beginning in 635, a Muslim army led by Muhammad's successor, Caliph Omar, swept through the entire region. Damascus was the first city to fall. The next year, an army sent out from Constantinople was decisively beaten at the point where the gorge of the River Yarmuk emerges into the plain of Galilee beneath the Golan Heights—today at the meeting point, and closed borders, of Jordan, Israel, and Syria. By 638, Jerusalem had a new master and was about to become a holy city of Islam, as well as of Judaism and Christianity.

Heraclius's hard-won victory over the Persians had proved, in so short a time, to have been the most hollow of triumphs. Modern historians have concluded that the age-old adversaries of the ancient world had fought themselves to a state of exhaustion. Both had become so weakened as to create a power vacuum throughout the Middle East. The Arabs simply seized their moment. Heraclius

ATLANTIC
OCEAN

VIKINGS

SCANDINAVIA

North
Sea

BRITAIN

•Aachen

GERMANY

MAGYARS

TURKS

FRANKS

Black Sea

Constantinople

Caspian
Sea

•Rome

SPAIN

Sicily

Crete

Cyprus

IRAN

SARACENS

Mediterranean
Sea

Baghdad

•Damascus

IRAQ

EGYPT

Persian Gulf

||| Western Christendom (papal authority)

▓ Eastern Christendom (Byzantine empire)

▨ Muslim

0   1000 Miles

0   1000 Kilometres

9. The new geopolitics in the centuries after the Arab siege of Constantinople in 717–718. The solid line shows the division between Christendom and the Muslim world in the mid-eighth century.

died in 641, just as news reached Constantinople that Caesarea, on the Mediterranean coast, had been taken. Alexandria was next. Within five years, all of Egypt was in Muslim hands. The once-mighty Persian Empire fared no better. By the start of the next decade, the whole of Persia had submitted to Arab rule. The three-hundred-year-old Sassanid dynasty was at an end. The entire Middle East became the Muslim Caliphate, ruled from its new capital in Damascus.

Constantinople had lost ground before and bounced back. But this time, the changes would prove permanent. Islam had come to stay. So had the Arabic language, which eventually would take the place of Greek in all the conquered Roman provinces. Along with more than half the empire's territory had gone the manpower, the tax revenues, and the greater part of the food supplies that had sustained its cities and their institutions for centuries. The remaining Greek-speaking heartland, in Anatolia, was now open to Arab raids from the south and east. Renewed outbreaks of plague would sweep through the region, roughly once in each decade. Under these continued onslaughts, cities that for centuries had been rich and populous shrank to a fraction of their former size. This was the case with Ephesus, where the Temple of Artemis had been counted as one of the Seven Wonders of the Ancient World, Pergamum, Ancyra (modern Ankara), Aphrodisias, and dozens more. Less well-known cities and smaller towns throughout Anatolia were abandoned altogether as the surviving population moved to smaller, defensible sites.[1]

In the Balkans the situation was even worse. Settlement by speakers of a Slavonic language seems to have begun in earnest in the southern Balkans during the 570s and 580s. While the nomadic Avars had been briefly powerful enough to mobilise the local Slavs and mount a full-scale assault on Constantinople in 626, they would disappear from the historical record soon afterwards.

But the Slavs would remain, even if at first their communities were small and widely scattered. The Slavs were never an organised force at this time, rather a symptom of the fragmentation that was taking place. Then in the 680s a new group of Turkic-speaking Bulgars established their own state, the distant ancestor of today's Bulgaria, more or less on Constantinople's northern doorstep.

In most of what is now Greece, urban life all but disappeared during the seventh century. Thessalonica continued to hold out within its massive walls, a mere outpost reachable from Constantinople only by sea. Farther south, most of the great cities of classical times shared the fate of their counterparts in Anatolia. Athens somehow limped on as little more than a provincial town huddled at the foot of the Acropolis. Even in Constantinople, by the year 700 the population may have fallen from its peak of around four hundred thousand to just forty thousand. If that estimate is anywhere near correct, it matches the drop in population in southwest Greece after the Mycenaean palace of Pylos had burned down almost two millennia before, heralding a 'dark age' of several centuries.[2]

This period, too, is often described as another such dark age. Theophylact Simocattes, the last of the historians writing in the tradition of Herodotus and Thucydides, fell silent shortly after 630. The historical record does not pick up again until a monk by the name of Theophanes completed his *Chronicle* shortly before his own death in 818. No one any more was asking the kind of question that Procopius had asked about the causes and effects of the plague back in the time of Justinian. When everything is falling apart around you, you either concentrate on the immediate needs of survival—or you turn to faith in a better life beyond this one. That is what Greek writers did during those years, and indeed for long afterwards. Almost all that they wrote is devoted to religious topics, including hymns, the lives of saints, and the continuing disputes about Christian doctrine.[3]

Historians since the nineteenth century have become accustomed to label the civilisation that emerged at this time as 'Byzantium' and its people as 'Byzantines'. In the language of today, the Greek-speaking Roman Empire after the death of Heraclius in 641 had turned into the Byzantine. Out of this process a new Greek civilisation was emerging. From this point on, we, too, must bow to modern usage and call the people who created this new civilisation Byzantines—even though they themselves never did, and their descendants would continue to think of themselves as Romans for more than a millennium to come.[4]

THROUGHOUT THE SECOND half of the seventh century and well into the next, successive Arab caliphs kept up the pressure on the Byzantine Empire. In 653, once again an enemy force pitched camp on the Asian shore of the Bosphorus. By this time, the Arabs had built a war fleet and launched it into the Mediterranean. Early the next year, their land forces facing Constantinople were joined by the first hostile navy to appear in the Sea of Marmara since long before the city had been founded. The threat was even greater than it had been in 626 because the attackers were able to move by sea as well as by land. This time it really was only an 'act of God' that saved the day. While the emperor 'stripped off his purple [robes], put on sackcloth, sat on ashes, and ordered a fast to be proclaimed', a sudden storm blew up and destroyed the enemy fleet. Without transport across the water, once again the attacking force was powerless and had to withdraw. A little over a decade later, they would be back. This time a new siege lasted for two years, from 667 to 669, with blockades in the Sea of Marmara continuing until 678.[5]

By 700, the Byzantines had been forced back upon the western regions of what is now Turkey, together with their capital and its immediate hinterland on the southeastern tip of Europe. Beyond that core, Constantinople still controlled scattered islands and strips of coastline in the Aegean, several pockets of the Italian mainland, including Ravenna on the Adriatic coast, and Sicily. It was on the last of these that the citizens of the capital had come to rely for their food supply (a further justification, in hindsight, for Justinian's war of 'reconquest' almost two centuries before). Once again, ships and the sea were proving to be the main lifeline for Greek speakers. Added together, these scattered territories barely made up a viable state, let alone an empire. Only one thing held them together, and that was the imperial city, with its centralised institutions. The key to survival would be Constantinople.[6]

As Muslim forces advanced ever closer to the Bosphorus, emperors came and went with increasing rapidity. Most of these were military men, raised to the highest office by their fellow commanders and deposed again by the same means. Between 711 and 717 no fewer than five emperors held the imperial throne. Given little time to prove his worth while in office, a deposed ruler would be lucky to be allowed to retire to the obscurity of a monastery. Justinian II and his son were murdered in 711, Philippikos, who had ousted him, was blinded two years later—a new and effective way of ensuring that there could be no comeback. In such extreme circumstances, even loyalty could become expendable. In 716, Anastasios II appealed to the approaching Arab commander for help against the latest usurper in Constantinople, though the appeal received short shrift. This was collapse from within and from the top.

In March 717, after yet another rebellion in the military, the commander of the eastern division was crowned in Hagia Sophia with the imperial title of Leo III. The third and final Arab siege of Constantinople began five months later, on 15 August. Arab warships crowded into the strait of the Bosphorus. The following spring, a new fleet of transports from Egypt landed troops on the European shore. The city was surrounded, by land and sea.

We have no eyewitness account of the siege. It lasted for a whole year. Leo seems to have been an astute tactician and made the best use he could of his limited resources. His predecessors had prudently concluded an alliance with the Bulgar kingdom to the north. That meant there would no repeat of the siege of almost a century before, when the Persians on one side of the Bosphorus had come so close to linking up with the Avars and Slavs on the other. Bulgar troops even joined with the Byzantines in mounting counterattacks against the enemy. And the defenders had a secret weapon. It had been invented, probably in the 660s, by a Greek called Kallinikos, from Arab-controlled Syria. Westerners would later call it 'Greek fire', but in Greek it was known as 'liquid fire'. It seems to have been an early form of artillery. A lighted petroleum-based liquid was projected from a tube, to burn on the surface of the water and engulf an enemy ship. Its effects on the Arab fleet proved deadly— and the secret would be so well kept, down the centuries, that even today no one knows for sure how it worked.[7]

After a year, it was the besiegers, not the besieged, who were starving. If Theophanes, writing almost a century later, is to be believed, the Arabs were reduced to eating their own faeces and the corpses of their comrades. Whether or not that was the cause, it does seem to be true that their ranks were decimated by disease. By August 718, a new caliph had come to power in Damascus and ordered his forces to withdraw. For centuries thereafter, in Muslim histories, the failure to take Constantinople in 718 would be reckoned as one of the greatest defeats for the forces of Islam. Muslim leaders from that time on would have to come to terms with the existence of the Byzantine Empire, which they continued to call 'Rome' (*Rum* in Arabic). It would not be until the coming of the Ottoman Turks, in the fourteenth and fifteenth centuries, that a Muslim army would once again set its sights on the 'city of the world's desire'.[8]

BY THE FIRST half of the eighth century, the geopolitics of the entire western part of the Eurasian landmass had been transformed. From the Atlantic to the Hindu Kush, from the edge of the Sahara Desert to the Arctic Circle, the overriding division among the human population was no longer between east and west but between north and south. And for the first time in history, it was not a division between competing *states* (or between a centralised state and the absence of one beyond its borders) but between competing *religions*. On one side stood Islam, on the other an entity that had no single political existence but that now came to be known as Christendom.[9]

To the south of an arc drawn through the Mediterranean and extending to the Pyrenees in one direction and the Caucasus in the other, Islam was the official religion and Arabic the dominant language. For the time being, all political power across this vast region lay with the Arab Caliphate. North of that line, wherever Rome had once ruled and where Constantinople still did, Christianity was by now all but universal. The only exceptions were regions where incoming 'barbarian' peoples had settled in large numbers and had yet to be converted. This was the case at opposite ends of Europe: in the British Isles and in much of the Balkans, including large parts of today's Greece. On the Christian side of the line, the long-standing division between a Latin-speaking west and a Greek-speaking east was now more marked than ever. Knowledge of Greek had disappeared from the west, knowledge of Latin from the east. In the west, Latin would continue to be the written language of western kingdoms for several centuries yet and remains to this day the official language of the Roman Catholic Church. East of the old line of division and allowing for intrusions by Slavonic and Arabic in particular regions, the equivalent language remained Greek—with the difference that, unlike Latin, Greek would also continue as the *spoken* language of the majority.

In the western part of Christendom, in the absence of any political centre of power, the bishops of Rome had already begun to
acquire a spiritual authority that would not be seriously challenged
until the sixteenth century. In Byzantium, on the other hand, the
special status of the Pope, the official title of the bishop of Rome,
was never recognised. There, because the political role of the emperor continued without a break, the highest ecclesiastical authority
would remain the Patriarch of Constantinople, who was usually
an imperial appointee. It was probably inevitable, given such fundamental differences, that sooner or later the two halves of Christendom would come into conflict, even while both fought to resist
the expansion of Islam on their borders and to reverse it when
they could.

After 718, the enemy had retreated from beneath the walls of
Constantinople, but Arab raids deep into central Anatolia would
continue for several decades. It was not until 740, the last full year
of the reign of Leo III, that a Byzantine army scored a decisive
victory, and the tide began to turn.[10] During this time, the forces
of the Caliphate were not the only existential threat, as Byzantium
struggled to reassert itself. In the summer of 726, the subterranean
volcano beneath the caldera of Thera exploded in what was probably the largest eruption since the one that had buried the Bronze
Age town of Akrotiri more than two millennia earlier. Smoke, 'as
if from a burning oven, arose from the depths of the sea,' wrote the
chronicler Theophanes, who had not yet been born at the time.
Out of the 'fiery combustion', 'great lumps of pumice like hilltops'
were projected high into the air and fell on coasts hundreds of miles
away. The 'whole face of the sea' was covered with floating pumice.
By the time the eruption subsided, a new island had emerged from
the seabed inside the caldera.

Other natural disasters followed. In 741, Constantinople was
rocked by a severe earthquake. Churches and fortifications were

damaged throughout Anatolia. Tsunamis swept the Aegean. Shortly afterwards, in 747, came another outbreak of plague. This was the worst since the first one, that had been described so vividly by Procopius, two hundred years before. The dead were piled high in makeshift wagons. Orchard gardens within the city walls were dug up to bury them. But there was not enough ground; corpses ended up in wells and cisterns, which can hardly have been good for public hygiene. After this, as it turned out, the plague would not come again until the Black Death of the fourteenth century. But, of course, no one was to know that at the time.[11]

Modern societies and governments, faced with threats like these, turn to 'experts'—technologists and scientists. The experts who were in greatest demand in Byzantium in the eighth century were theologians. Christianity was now so deeply embedded that imperceptibly, in public consciousness, it had taken on something of the mantle of the old religion that it had replaced. Once upon a time, in the Greek-speaking world, success in war and protection from unpredictable forces of nature had depended on propitiating the gods. Ever since Heraclius had successfully mobilised his troops in a holy war against an enemy of unbelievers, that role had become attached to the Christian God. But there was a vital difference. If the whole universe was ruled by a single, all-powerful God, you had only the one chance to get it right. Constantinople had been saved in 718, but only just. What was it about the Muslim Arabs that made God seem to favour *them* and not the Christian 'Romans'? If emperors and their subjects were being punished with pestilence, fire, and earthquakes, what could they possibly be doing wrong?[12] So began a controversy that would occupy the best minds and the highest authorities of the Byzantine church and state for almost a century and a half and remains today one of the most lasting legacies of Byzantium to the modern world.

TODAY WE CALL this controversy 'iconoclasm', which is Greek for 'breaking images'. The Byzantines themselves called it, more accurately, *eikonomachia*, or 'iconomachy', which means 'battle over images'.[13] Much of the detail of what happened remains obscure and has been hotly debated by historians since the eighteenth century. All we can be sure of is that during two periods, totalling a little over sixty years, from 754 to 787 and from 815 to 843, it was forbidden throughout the empire to produce or to display images of Christ, the Virgin Mary, angels, or saints in human form. To do so, it was declared at a Church Council held in 754, was to violate the commandment in the Old Testament against worshipping 'idols' or 'graven images'. The iconoclasts, as the champions of the change became known, had noticed that their Muslim enemies interpreted the same sacred text in this way, as indeed has been the practice in Islam ever since. Just as mosques contain no representations of human figures, so it was decided that Christian churches could be decorated only with the symbol of the cross. Anything else would be blasphemy and offensive to God. Unwittingly, the Christian empire had strayed into the sin of idolatry. No wonder its people were being punished.

This radical new policy provoked the first serious disagreement between the churches of Constantinople and Rome—since the western church saw no problem and pointedly refused to sign up either to iconoclasm or to the eventual solution that would be found to replace it. It is hard to tell how much artwork was actually destroyed. Examples have been found of mosaics in which the telltale signs of alteration can still be seen, with glass tesserae removed and replaced by others in the approved design—though this may not have happened as frequently as used to be thought. After it was over, lurid stories began to circulate in Greek about wanton desecration of holy pictures and the persecution, even martyrdom, inflicted on priests and monks who had stood up in their defence.[14]

The ebb and flow of the controversy can be mapped fairly precisely onto the fortunes of military campaigns to secure and stabilise the borders of the Byzantine state. Revival had begun in the last years of the reign of Leo III, who would later be remembered (probably wrongly) as an instigator of iconoclasm. It went much further under his son, Constantine V. During a reign that lasted from 741 to 775, Constantine made military gains in the east and in the Balkans, against Slavs and a now hostile Bulgar kingdom. Even his later detractors had to give Constantine the credit for restoring the water supply to Constantinople by repairing the fourth-century aqueduct (part of which still stands near the centre of Istanbul) that had been out of commission since the siege of 626. These are indications that the city's population was once again on the rise, and resources were becoming available again for public works. When the first period of iconoclasm ended, in 787, the Byzantine throne was occupied by an empress, Irene, who held it as regent for her young son, Constantine VI. Irene's reasons for reversing the policy on images have been much debated. Probably they were more political than religious. The empress may have seen it as a priority to patch up relations with the Church of Rome in the west.[15]

Irene went on to become the first woman to rule the Byzantine Empire in her own right after her son plotted against her and she had him blinded. But the experiment did not last long. In 802, she was ousted in a bloodless coup organised by her senior ministers and died shortly afterwards in internal exile. The new emperor was Nikephoros I, a former treasury official. Nikephoros seems to have been the architect of a far-reaching reform of taxation and military organisation known as the 'theme' system. This created incentives for local communities to take responsibility for their own defence, while saving precious resources for the central treasury. The logic behind the reform was surely defensive, and it would stand the Byzantine state in good stead for at least the next two centuries.

Not content with the defence of his realm, Nikephoros also went on the offensive. A series of campaigns during the first decade of the ninth century brought much of today's Greece back under Byzantine control. By extending the theme system into the Greek mainland, Nikephoros ensured that the pagan, Slavonic-speaking communities, that had been scattered throughout the region for several centuries, would quickly be assimilated to become Christian, Greek-speaking 'Romans'. The emperor's name means 'Victory-Bearer'. But Nikephoros's run of victories was brutally cut short when he was killed in battle against the Bulgars in 811, and his skull allegedly used as a drinking cup by the Bulgar king.[16]

Two years later, another usurper, Leo V, needed urgently to consolidate his grip on the throne. The 'breaking of images' was back on the agenda. After the disaster at the hands of the Bulgars, the new emperor was not the only one to look back with nostalgic admiration at what had been achieved during the reign of the iconoclast Constantine V. Surely, God could not, after all, favour religious images and was punishing the empire accordingly? So a new Church Council, in 815, reversed the previous reversal. Images were prohibited for a second time.[17]

But a quarter of a century later, as the reign of the emperor Theophilos was coming to an end, evidence for divine favour was becoming harder and harder to find. Crete had been lost to Arab raiders from Spain in 827. The Arabs had begun their conquest of Sicily at the same time; inexorably, year by year, more ground was being lost there. What remained of Byzantine control in the southern Italian mainland was being whittled away. In 838, on land, an Arab army advanced far enough into Anatolia to sack Amorion, near today's Afyonkarahisar in western Turkey. When Theophilos died in January 842, once again an empress, Theodora, held the throne as regent for their young son. This time, too, the motives behind what happened next have been much debated. The outcome was that, after yet another Church Council, on the first Sunday of Lent, 4 March 843, a solemn procession made its way to Hagia Sophia to celebrate what has ever since been commemorated as the 'Triumph of Orthodoxy'. Iconoclasm was over, this time for good.

In a later icon which represents the scene, the painted image of the Virgin and Child has pride of place, with the holy figures represented to a slightly larger scale than the worshippers below them. The experiment of banning religious images had spectacularly backfired. If some among the theological 'experts' had thought the way to win God's favour was to ape the rival Muslims, the latest gathering of bishops had resolved that the Christian state of Byzantium was going to be as *different* from them as possible. After this, the face of Christ would be displayed on every imperial coin minted.[18] Every interior space in a Byzantine church would be covered with frescoes depicting holy figures and scenes from the Old and New Testaments. High above all would float the severe figure of Christ Pantokrator (Almighty) looking down from the central dome. The Greek word meaning 'image' (*eikon* or icon) came to be particularly attached to portable images of the saints that could be carried in procession and would be routinely kissed by the faithful on entering church.

A careful theological distinction had been devised to explain that the 'veneration' of images was not the same as worship, or idolatry. Under the firm guidance and control of the ecclesiastical authorities, sacred images were recognised as a precious channel of communication between the worshipper and the divine. 'Holy images' were 'the eyes of the universe', in the memorable words of the Patriarch Photios, the most learned man of his day, preaching in Hagia Sophia on Easter Saturday 867. And in the presence of the reigning emperor and his heir apparent, Photios called on God himself to:

protect [such images] like the pupil of an eye, keep them above any evil, make them seem terrible to their foes and keep them, as well as us, worthy of you and your endless and blessed kingdom.[19]

As the dangers to Byzantium and its citizens receded, so had the spectre of God's displeasure. 'Roman Christians' could now take comfort, as their patriarch also assured them, in the knowledge that they were the divinely Chosen People, as the Israelites of the Old Testament had once been.[20] Like the ancient Israelites, they might still be punished for their misdeeds. But once chosen, they could no longer be cast off entirely, as many must really have feared might happen to them while they endured the shocks of the first half of the eighth century.

With the end of iconoclasm, the Byzantine state had defined itself anew. But it was entirely characteristic of the novel way of thinking that no Byzantine, either then or later, would ever willingly admit just how new it really was. The Triumph of Orthodoxy was celebrated, and is still commemorated by the Orthodox Church today, as the vindication of beliefs and practices that supposedly go back to the very dawn of Christianity. Every Byzantine writer who refers to the controversy describes its conclusion as a 'restoration'; the attempt to suppress religious images had been that most heinous of things, an 'innovation'. But the theology that gave a special place to religious images as intermediaries between the human and the divine was not traditional at all. Challenged and honed by the intervening bouts of iconoclasm, it had been worked out in Constantinople over the two centuries that had passed since the start of the Arab conquests.[21]

UNTIL THE END of the battle over images, most emperors had been content to follow a policy that has been labelled 'defensive imperialism'. Nikephoros I had been the exception; his fate, if anything, only reinforced the general rule. Throughout this time, the overriding priority of successive emperors was to consolidate within existing borders rather than to expand the state and lord it over others. Indeed, it has been argued that this was always the default option for the Byzantines and that they were not warlike by nature.[22] Ever since the parting of the ways between the eastern and western empires at the end of the fourth century, the bureaucracy in Constantinople had developed its own distinctive approach to handling outsiders and rival powers—not by war but by diplomatic means.

Diplomacy had never been a strong point for the ancient Greeks; Rome, throughout its heyday, had been blunt in its dealings with outsiders. But the eastern empire, during its transition from Roman to Byzantine, had been well served by the subtle patience of its diplomats. At the heart of Byzantine diplomacy lay an assumption of innate superiority. The trick was to persuade foreign rulers that the emperor possessed riches and powers such as they could only ever dream of; in return for services to the Byzantine state, a token portion could be theirs. And for many centuries, it worked. More often than not, the inducement would take the form of official titles. These cost nothing to grant and no doubt sounded grand in the foreign languages of the recipients. More crudely, whenever the imperial treasury could afford it, potential enemies were simply bought off. In the most favoured cases—and in later centuries routinely—a marriage alliance into the imperial family might be brokered.[23]

Elaborate rituals were devised to impress ambassadors or princes from abroad. A manual of ceremonial practice, dating from the tenth century, describes the intricate hierarchy and dazzling spectacle of the Byzantine court that would be on display. Visitors would be cowed by the emperor's apparent power to command even nature, seated upon a golden throne that could be raised up into the air, while mechanical lions roared and mechanical birds sang.[24] It was no doubt because the Byzantines managed to flatter and bamboozle outsiders for so long that the adjective 'Byzantine' would acquire the connotations that it has today: of deviousness and bureaucratic impenetrability.

By the middle of the ninth century, ambassadors were being dispatched from Constantinople to states and kingdoms across vast distances, in every direction. To the east they had extensive dealings with the Chazars, who controlled much of central Asia, and farther south, with the Arab Caliphate, first in Damascus and later in Baghdad. The first embassy from Byzantium may have reached China as early as the mid-seventh century; in later Chinese accounts, Constantinople was called 'Fu-lin', equivalent to the familiar Greek abbreviation *Polis* or *Poli* ('City'). In the opposite direction, Byzantine missions negotiated with popes in Rome and even, after some reluctance, with the German king of the Franks, known to history as Charlemagne, who on Christmas Day in the year 800 had been crowned by the pope to rule over a rival Roman empire in the west.[25]

In the case of the Slavs, the diplomatic offer took an unusual form, which is still with us today. Methodios and his younger brother Constantine grew up in Thessalonica, where their father was serving as a senior army officer. There, they learned to speak the language of the Slav settlements that surrounded the city. The linguistic talents of the pair were recognised early. While Methodios gained advancement through the church, Constantine was taken to Constantinople to receive the highest level of education available in his day. Before long, he was undertaking diplomatic missions to central Asia. In the 860s, when the Patriarch Photios devised a new mission to convert the Slavs of central Europe to Christianity and bring them into the orbit of Constantinople, he called upon the brothers for the task. Constantine devised a modified form of the Greek alphabet, that for the first time made it possible to write in

Slavonic. Methodios went on to translate the Bible into this newly written language.

Even though the original mission failed, its longer-term consequence would be to convert most of the Slavonic-speaking populations of the Balkans, as well as the ancestors of today's Russians and of many Ukrainians, to the eastern, Orthodox form of Christianity. The modern states formed by the descendants of these peoples still use the alphabet devised for the mission and named 'Cyrillic' after Cyril, the monastic name taken by Constantine after he became a monk in his last years. The conversion of all these previously pagan peoples was another achievement of patient diplomacy and ingenious innovation. This was in marked contrast to the wars of conquest that had brought about the spread of Islam in the seventh century or the practice of western rulers such as Charlemagne, who had imposed Christianity on the peoples of today's Germany at the point of the sword in the last years of the eighth.[26]

But soft power had its limits. Byzantines were soldiers, too. And they still maintained a formidable navy, even if by the middle of the ninth century they had lost control of most of the Mediterranean except for the Aegean and the Adriatic. With the battle over images finally resolved and the Abbasid Caliphate in disarray, it would soon be time to match soft power with hard. The first signs of a decisive turn of the tide came with the arrival of a new emperor, and a new, unusually long-lasting dynasty, on the Byzantine throne.

THE EMPEROR AND heir apparent who had been present in Hagia Sophia on that Easter Saturday in 867, when Photios delivered his sermon about holy images, were Michael III and Basil I. It was quite usual, by this time, for a reigning emperor to appoint his successor in his lifetime. The designated heir would share the imperial title but have no power or authority of his own. Normally, this would be a son or another close family member. But Michael had no legitimate children. Instead, he had chosen to elevate an older man to this coveted role. If, as seems probable, there was a sexual element to the relationship, this would have been strictly taboo in Christian Byzantium and would have had to be concealed.

Basil had risen from obscurity on the strength of his exceptional physique and his prowess at taming horses. Six months after that sermon in Hagia Sophia, the relationship had soured. Michael was apt to drink himself into a stupor. His public reputation was beginning to suffer as a result. And Michael could see that Basil was poised to take advantage of his role as heir apparent. By September 867, each was plotting to murder the other. Basil got in first. While the emperor was in his cups, Basil opened the imperial bedchamber to a gang of assassins who first hacked off Michael's hands, then stabbed him fatally in the back.[27]

Under Basil's rule, the Byzantine state began to expand once again. Its fleet regained control of the Adriatic and the southern Italian coasts. Although the Muslim hold on Sicily would prove too strong to break, the whole of the Italian mainland south of Naples was regained by the 880s. Two new military districts, or 'themes', were created in Italy and would last for close on two hundred years. The origins of the Greek-speaking communities that still exist in Calabria and Puglia are thought to lie in this period of Byzantine reconquest. At the same time, Byzantine land forces pushed farther east in Anatolia than they had been able to penetrate for more than a century. After Basil died in 886, his successors held on to the gains that had been made in the west and continued to push the bounds of the realm outwards in all the other directions of the compass.

To the south, beyond the Aegean, Crete was recaptured in 961. Four years later, Cyprus, which had been jointly administered with the Arabs for almost three centuries, became fully a 'Roman' possession once more. Byzantine armies had been reaching from Anatolia into Syria since the 930s. Antioch and Aleppo were regained in 969; once again the eastern frontier was pushed back to the old Roman line of the Euphrates. To the northeast, beyond the Black Sea, Georgia and much of Armenia were brought within the imperial fold, through a combination of hard and soft power that would continue to yield dividends into the 1060s. These lands were largely Christian, but their peoples spoke their own languages, as their descendants still do today (and Armenians were spread out across a much wider area than the republic that now bears their name).

It was to the north, and closest to their own doorstep, that the Byzantines experienced the greatest difficulties. The Rus, centred on the city of Kiev and the political forerunners of both modern Russia and Ukraine, would never accept Byzantine rule, even though their ruler Vladimir embraced Orthodox Christianity in 989. Neither would the Bulgars, whose kingdom had long since moved on from being a pliant ally during the last Arab siege of Constantinople. The original founders of the Bulgar state had been Turkic nomads from central Asia. But by the time of their greatest confrontation with Byzantium in the early eleventh century, the ruling Bulgars had long since adopted the Slavonic language of the majority. They, too, were now Christians and, like the Rus, celebrated the Orthodox liturgy using the Slavonic translation of the Bible by Methodios and the Cyrillic alphabet that had been devised for the purpose by his brother.

Basil II, whose reign from 976 to 1025 was the longest in all Byzantine history, made it his mission to conquer the independent Bulgar kingdom and bring its Slavonic-speaking people within the Byzantine fold. The campaign seems to have lasted, on and off, for almost twenty years. The decisive battle took place in 1014, in a narrow pass called Kleidion, today close to the meeting point of the borders of Bulgaria, North Macedonia, and Greece. After his victory, later historians would claim that Basil had ordered some fifteen thousand Bulgar captives to be blinded and sent back to their king in batches of a hundred, each led by an officer who had been spared the sight of a single eye for the purpose. When Tsar Samuel of Bulgaria saw his troops returning in this condition, the story goes on, he was himself struck blind and died of grief shortly afterwards. The truth of this horrific tale has been questioned. But, with or without this added atrocity, Basil's victory earned him the bloodthirsty title of *Boulgaroktonos*—the Bulgar Slayer—by which he has been known in Greek ever since. By 1018, four years after the battle, the whole of the Balkans, to the south and west of the Danube, had been brought back under 'Roman' rule—something that for many of these regions had not been the case for five centuries or more.[28]

To celebrate this achievement, Basil II did something that no other emperor of Byzantium had done before or ever would again. He led his entourage on a long detour south to Athens. The depleted city had been a backwater for hundreds of years; it had no political or strategic importance to the empire. But the fifteen-hundred-year-old Parthenon, that the Athenians had dedicated to the patron goddess of their city, Athena Parthenos (the Virgin), had long ago been converted to a Christian church and dedicated to the Virgin Mary. Since the settlement of the controversy over religious images two centuries before Basil's time, the interior walls would have been densely painted with images of the Virgin, Christ, and other holy figures. This was the setting that the emperor chose for his act of public 'thanksgiving for his victory to the Mother of God', whose church he also endowed with precious gifts.[29] Once upon a time, the Athenian democracy, led by Pericles, had given

305

thanks to the virgin protectress of the city for victory over the Persians, and the roof-high gold and ivory statue of Athena had dwarfed the viewer. Now a very different kind of Greek-speaking ruler made his devotions and gave his thanks to a different divine virgin for victory over a different enemy beneath the gaze of the 'eyes of the universe'.

1. Gold funerary mask from Grave IV (Grave Circle A) at Mycenae, 16th century BCE, discovered by Heinrich Schliemann in the 1870s.

2. Detail from a fresco found at Akrotiri, Thera (Santorini), dating from before 1540 BCE (including conjectural restorations on the right). The warriors forming a line in the foreground have been identified as Mycenaeans.

3. Lyre Player and Bird Fresco from the Throne Room of Nestor's palace, Pylos, c. 1300 BCE. Watercolour reconstruction by Piet de Jong.

4. Clay tablet inscribed in Linear B from the palace of Pylos, c.1200–1180 BCE. The text describes a tour of inspection made by an official named Alxoitas to check plots of agricultural land not far from the capital.

5–7. *Kore* (Phrasikleia) c. 550–540 BCE, with conjectural restoration (*centre*), and *kouros* from Anavyssos, Attica, c. 530 BCE.

8. Scene of courtship painted on a vase by the Amasis Painter, c. 540 BCE.

9. Bronze statue, c. 460 BCE, found on the seabed off Riace, Calabria, Italy, in 1972.

10. The monumental gateway to the Acropolis of Athens (the Propylaea) frames the distant view of the island of Salamis, where the Greeks defeated the Persians in the naval battle of 480 BCE.

11. Marble relief (Block V) from the East Frieze of the Parthenon. Seated deities receive offerings from mortals depicted to a smaller scale.

12. (*left*) Head of Philip II, King of the Macedonians. Portrait in ivory from the Royal Tomb, Vergina.

13. (*above*) Head of Alexander III ('the Great', 356–323 BCE), found at Giannitsa (c. 325–300 BCE).

14. Alexander (on horseback, left) confronts Darius III in his chariot (centre) at the Battle of Issus in 333 BCE (mosaic from Pompeii, 1st century CE).

15. Gandharan art from Pakistan, dating from about 500 years after Alexander's conquest: the princess Cassandra tries to prevent the Wooden Horse from entering Troy.

16–17. (*above*) Portrait bust of Cleopatra VII of Egypt (c. 40–30 BCE) and (*right*) Sphinx discovered in the submerged palace of Alexandria, believed to represent her father, Ptolemy XII.

18. Athens: The Temple of Olympian Zeus, completed by the emperor Hadrian (reigned 117–138 CE), with 'Hadrian's Arch', photographed c. 1869.

19. A street in Jerash (Jordan).

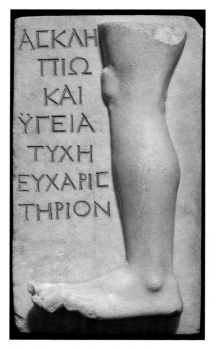

20. (*above*) Marble relief with an inscription dedicating it to Asclepius and Hygieia (Health) as a thank offering for a cure.

21. (*above*) An early papyrus (c. 175–225 CE) containing part of Saint Paul's First Letter to the Corinthians.

22. (*left*) Monumental head of Constantine, the first Christian emperor (reigned 306–337 CE).

23. The interior of Hagia Sophia, Constantinople, completed on the orders of Justinian in 537.

24. Mosaic portrait of Justinian (S. Apollinare Nuovo, Ravenna).

25. Mosaic panel depicting the Empress Theodora and her retinue (S. Vitale, Ravenna, 547).

26. Mosaic cross from the period of iconoclasm, apse of the
Church of St Irene, Constantinople.

27. Late Byzantine icon (c. 1400) showing the 'Triumph of Orthodoxy', detail. The divine
figures represented on the painted image (centre) are larger in scale than the human worshippers.
Compare image 11.

28–30. The three emperors of the Komnenian dynasty who ruled from 1081 to 1180, *left to right*: Alexios I, John II, Manuel I.

31. The sack of Constantinople by the Fourth Crusade in April 1204 (15th-century miniature, detail).

32. Theodore Metochites, mosaic donor portrait in the Kariye Camii (Church of the Chora), c. 1316–1321.

33. Frankish warriors in the Peloponnese (from an illustrated manuscript of *The Chronicle of the Morea*, c. 1393).

34. George Gemistos Plethon, detail from fresco, *The Cavalcade of the Magi*, by Benozzo Gozzoli, 1459.

35. Sultan Mehmed II, the Conqueror (portrait attributed to Nakkas Sinan Bey), 15th–16th century.

36. Candia (modern Heraklion, Crete) under siege from 1648 to 1669 (c. 1680, detail).

37. A Phanariot in Constantinople, 1818–1820.

38. The 'Caryatid' porch of St Pancras New Church, Euston Road, London, built 1819–1822, imitating the Erechtheion on the Acropolis of Athens.

39. *The Reception of King Otto in front of the Theseion, Athens,* by Peter von Hess, 1839.

40. Greek Independence Day (25 March), Sydney Opera House, Australia.

41. Cartoon by Andy Davey for *The Sun*, May 2012, at a time when the Greek financial crisis threatened the future of the Eurozone.

42. (*left*) Street art, Athens, 2013: 'I wish you could learn something useful from the past'. Artist: Dimitris Taxis.

43. (*right*) The new National Library of Greece, Stavros Niarchos Foundation Cultural Center, Athens, opened 2017.

10

'CITY OF THE WORLD'S DESIRE'

1018–1204

THE MEDIEVAL STATE that we call Byzantium was very close to the height of its power and extent when Basil II died in 1025. Only a few short-lived gains still remained to be made, in eastern Anatolia and in Sicily, over the next forty years. Constantinople was now the largest and richest city in Europe, quite possibly in the entire world. Its population may once again have reached four hundred thousand, a level not seen since the onslaught of plague during the reign of Justinian, in 542. Controlling the land routes that led across Asia to China, emperors and their officials were enriched by the proceeds of worldwide trade. A Jewish visitor from Muslim Spain, Benjamin of Tudela, writing more than a century after Basil's death, marvelled:

> The Greek inhabitants are very rich in gold and precious stones, and they go clothed in garments of silk with gold embroidery, and they ride horses, and look like princes. Indeed, the land is very rich in all cloth stuffs, and in bread, meat, and wine. Wealth like that of Constantinople is not to be found in the whole world.[1]

This reputation acted as a magnet to soldiers and traders from far and wide. The elite Varangian guard, which protected the imperial

307

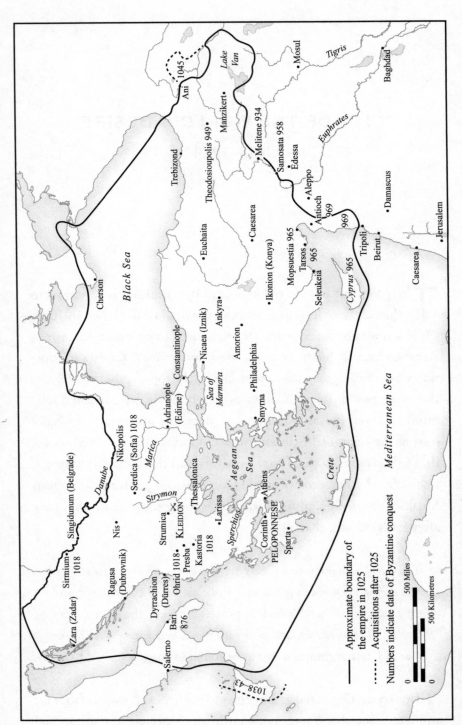

Tigris

Mosul •

Baghdad •

Lake
Van

1045

Ani •

Manzikert •

Euphrates

Melitene 934 •

Theodosioupolis 949 •

Samosata 958 •

Edessa •

Trebizond •

Aleppo •

Damascus •

Caesarea •

Antioch
969

969

Euchaita •

Tripoli
Beirut •

Mopsuestia 965 •

Tarsos
965

Caesarea •

Jerusalem •

Black Sea

Cherson •

Ikonion (Konya) •

Seleukeia •

Cyprus 965

Constantinople •

Nicaea (Iznik) •

Ankyra •

Amorion •

Sea of
Marmara

Philadelphia •

Adrianople
(Edirne) •

Smyrna •

Mediterranean Sea

Nikopolis •

Marica

Serdica (Sofia) 1018 •

Aegean
Sea

Singidunum (Belgrade) •

Danube

Nis •

Strymon

Thessalonica •

Crete

Sperchios

Sirmium •
1018

Strumica •

KLEIDION ✕

Larissa •

Corinth •

Athens •

Ragusa
(Dubrovnik) •

Presba •

Kastoria •
1018

PELOPONNESE

Sparta •

Zara (Zadar) •

Dyrrachion
(Dürres) •

Ohrid 1018 •

Bari •

876

Salerno •

1038–43

—— Approximate boundary of
the empire in 1025

······· Acquisitions after 1025

Numbers indicate date of Byzantine conquest

500 Miles

0

500 Kilometres

0

10. The Byzantine Empire in the mid-eleventh century

palace, recruited Russians, Vikings from as far away as Scandinavia and Iceland, Normans, and Anglo-Saxons. From Italy, merchants began arriving from the rival trading centres of Venice, Genoa, and Pisa. Soon, there would be so many of them that they would be granted their own quarter, where they could make permanent homes with their families, on the opposite side of the Golden Horn from the city proper, in the area known as Galata. The Byzantine capital that Benjamin saw must have been one of the most cosmopolitan places on earth. The scholar and teacher Ioannes Tzetzes, writing at about the same time as that visit, boasted of his familiarity with half a dozen languages that he would hear spoken daily in the streets around him: Latin, Persian, Georgian, Arabic, Slavonic, Hebrew, as well as his native Greek. Eustathios of Thessalonica, the city's bishop and famous for his commentaries on Homer, was struck by the exotic speech and costumes of visitors he encountered at the imperial court in the capital. From the names that Eustathios gives them, we can identify steppe nomads, Hungarians, Serbs, Turks, Armenians, Indians, sub-Saharan Africans, northern Europeans, and Italians—while others, he says, were 'so remote and outlandish that even their names were unpronounceable'.[2]

From the middle of the eleventh century until very nearly the end of the next, Constantinople was at the centre of a new flourishing of the arts and a renewed engagement with the intellectual achievements of the ancient world. The most brilliant all-round man of letters of the age was Michael Psellos. Born in 1018, Psellos served several emperors in high positions in the imperial bureaucracy and went on to write a scathing history of the fourteen reigns he had lived through, from the accession of Basil II in 976 down to the eve of his own death in 1078. The *Chronographia*, as this history is called in Greek, is full of psychological insights and the wry observations of an insider. Deeply versed in ancient Greek philosophy, Psellos also wrote treatises on many branches of science.

More than five hundred of his elegantly written personal letters have survived. After a gap of many centuries, Psellos and several of his contemporaries wrote as self-aware individuals, anxious to explore (and indeed to promote) their own place in the secular world in which they found themselves. Psellos has often been called a forerunner of modern humanism. The remarkable explosion of literary creativity in Constantinople that followed during the century after his death has invited comparison with the better-known achievements of the Renaissance in the West that would not begin for another two hundred years.[3]

Secular genres that had been neglected or forgotten since the days of the Second Sophistic, under the Roman Empire, suddenly came back into fashion. Novels (or romances) once again explored the redemptive possibilities of human love. Satires mocked the pretensions of real individuals or parodied well-known types from ancient literature. There was even an attempt at epic poetry based on oral narratives that must have circulated in the badlands of eastern Anatolia and Mesopotamia during the centuries of conflict against the Arabs. Freelance writers vied for commissions from the imperial family or other highly placed officials. To judge from the sheer volume of their work that has come down to us, there must have been careers to be made from reciting the praises of living patrons and the obituaries of their deceased relatives—even if those careers were also precarious.[4]

Elegant, erudite, sometimes witty, and on occasion scurrilous, these new practitioners of the art of rhetoric could turn their hand to any literary style and write in any type of Greek, from the long-obsolete idiom of the *Iliad* and the *Odyssey*, via the 'high style' of classical Athens, to the plainer manner of everyday bureaucratic exchanges and even, for the first time since Aristophanes in the fifth century BCE, the language of the contemporary street. The most prolific poet of the twelfth century, Theodoros Prodromos, was also the most versatile. It is to Prodromos that we owe some of the earliest recorded cadences of the Greek language as it is still spoken today. We hear them in this famous rant, addressed to no less a person than the emperor himself. The poet's skills have gone unrewarded for too long, he complains; now he has had enough:

> *Letters be damned, dear Christ, and all who've any truck*
> *with them,*
> *damn the time and damn the day when I was sent to school*
> *to learn my letters—fat chance, that, to earn a living!*[6]

During the same two centuries, the building of new churches and monasteries went on as never before. By the time that Benjamin of Tudela visited, there was a church for every day of the year in the capital alone. The huge monastery of the Pantokrator, overlooking the Golden Horn, was built in the 1130s to house the tombs of emperors, and it survives today as the Zeyrek Mosque. Contemporary rulers, who were often the Byzantines' enemies, competed with one another to emulate the architecture and decoration of their churches and palaces, possibly also recruiting craftsmen trained in Constantinople for the purpose. Some of the best-preserved church interiors in the Byzantine style are to be found in Sicily, at Cefalù and at Monreale outside Palermo, where the Palazzo dei Normanni is also the nearest thing to a Byzantine palace that survives anywhere. All of these were commissioned by the island's Norman rulers in the twelfth century. Churches of this period, designed and painted in the Byzantine style, can also be seen in today's Ukraine and Russia, in Kiev and Novgorod.[6]

THESE ACHIEVEMENTS ARE all the more remarkable when set against the political and military realities of the time. A mere forty years after the death of Basil II, Byzantium found itself faced with new and aggressive enemies on all sides during the 1060s: Seljuk Turks in the east, Normans in the west, and in the north the latest nomadic groups to arrive from the steppes, known as Pechenegs and Cumans. From this time on, every Byzantine emperor would be forced back to the policy of defensive imperialism that had been the hallmark of the first centuries after the Arab conquest: a combination of limited, defensive wars with proactive diplomacy on several fronts simultaneously.

After a period of messy court intrigue, described in forensic detail by Psellos, in 1068 the empire once again had a military man on the throne. Romanos IV Diogenes set out for eastern Anatolia to take the war to the Seljuks, who had conquered Baghdad in 1055. At first he seemed to be having some success. Then, in August 1071, at a place called Manzikert, close to Lake Van, a disastrous error of tactics led to the emperor being taken prisoner by the Seljuk sultan Alp Arslan ('the Lion'). The emperor was treated much more generously by his captor than he would be by his own people after his release. In the early stages of the ensuing civil war, that would last for almost a decade, Romanos was blinded and despatched to a monastery, where he died shortly afterwards. There were no rewards for failure in the Byzantine system.[7]

The Seljuks pushed westwards to capture Smyrna on the Aegean coast and Nicaea (today's Iznik), only ninety kilometres to the southeast of Constantinople. Anatolia, and not the European provinces, had long since become the heartland of the Greek-speaking world. Now, between 1071 and the mid-1090s, the centre of gravity of that world was forcibly shifted back to where it had started out, in the southern Balkans and the Aegean. On the Byzantines' opposite flank, beyond the Adriatic, the Normans had come a long way from their small kingdom on the north coast of what is now France to become a powerful new force in the Mediterranean. In the same year as the battle of Manzikert, 1071, they captured Bari, the last remaining Byzantine possession in southern Italy. Over the next twenty years, the Normans went on to complete the conquest of Sicily from the Arabs, something the Byzantines had never managed to do. Ten years after that, a Norman expedition crossed the southern Adriatic to land on the west coast of Epiros. Led by Robert Guiscard, one of the most formidable soldiers of the age, this was a direct threat to the integrity of the Byzantine state in the Balkans. Meanwhile, on the northern frontiers, Pecheneg tribesmen were making repeated raids across the Danube.

In Constantinople, the civil war ended just in time for a robust response to these emergencies. On 1 April 1081, Alexios Komnenos, an aristocrat from a military family in Anatolia, seized the throne in a well-organised coup d'état. For the first time in Byzantine history, this emperor would go on to establish his own family as a kind of ruling caste, to the point that in time the family name would come to signify a distinguished rank—much as the name 'Caesar' had once done in ancient Rome. We are exceptionally well informed about the character and achievements of Alexios thanks to his daughter Anna, who several decades after his death would become the first female historian to write in Greek—indeed, quite possibly in any language. Anna's account of her father's reign is written in a revival of the grand style of Herodotus and Thucydides; as a stylist and historian, she makes a worthy successor to Psellos. But the title of her work gives due warning of her purpose: the *Alexiad* of Anna Komnene, with its overt nod towards Homer's *Iliad*, also foreshadows the modern genre of celebrity biography.[8]

The new emperor found formidable difficulties in his way. By this time the theme system that Nikephoros I had devised almost three centuries before had largely broken down. Local communities no longer contributed the manpower for their own defence.

Instead, the Byzantine state had come to rely on mercenary soldiers, often recruited, like the Varangians, from outside its borders. The loyalty of these troops was not always reliable. And the money had to be found to pay them. Alexios inherited a treasury that was seriously depleted and a currency that had been repeatedly debased over the previous decades. Reading Anna's history, and indeed modern accounts too, one wonders how so many foreigners could have continued to believe for so long in the fabulous wealth of Constantinople. Evidently, these things were relative. But establishing a new stable currency and filling the imperial coffers were among the first challenges to be faced by Alexios.

By the early 1090s, he had defeated Guiscard and the Normans in northern Greece and the Pechenegs in Thrace. On the Seljuk front in Anatolia, it looked for a time as though diplomacy, in the form of lavish gifts and hospitality, was going to be successful. But by the middle of the decade, a series of upheavals in the Seljuk sultanate turned all these plans upside down. The impregnable fortress of Nicaea, on its lake, remained in the hands of implacable enemies, while others controlled much of the hinterland of Anatolia. From his base in Smyrna, the emir Çaka, or Tzachas, was in control of the coast and harried Byzantine shipping in the Aegean. As one modern account puts it, 'The situation facing Byzantium in the mid-1090s was not so much desperate as catastrophic.'[9]

From those unlikely beginnings arose an event that in its way would leave almost as great a mark on subsequent world history as the Muslim conquests of half a millennium before. We know it as the First Crusade, although the term would not become current until a good deal later. Among its long-term consequences would be the collapse of the empire that it had first been conceived to protect. What Alexios needed was manpower. In particular, given the very specific demands if Nicaea were to be retaken by force, he needed siege engines. The western kingdoms were ahead in this kind of military technology at the time. What Alexios seems to have had in mind was simply another call-up of mercenaries from abroad. But with money so short, they could be paid in a different currency—not cash but faith.

Envoys sent by Alexios caught up with Pope Urban II while he was attending a church council in the northern Italian city of Piacenza in March 1095. In the emperor's name they begged the pope to raise troops in the western kingdoms for 'the defence of this holy church, which had now been nearly annihilated in that region by the infidels who had conquered as far as the walls of Constantinople'. The pope was shrewd enough to see the benefits to his own office from taking up this diplomatic challenge. The 'holy church' of which the envoys spoke had been officially split for the past four decades—ever since the patriarch in Constantinople and the emissaries of a previous pope had excommunicated each other in 1054. Though it seems to have created little stir at the time, that event is still remembered as the 'Great Schism' that marked the irrevocable split between the churches that we now know as Roman Catholic and Eastern Orthodox.[10]

Four decades after the schism, the appeal by Alexios opened up the possibility not only of a reconciliation but also of papal authority being extended to the eastern church and its clergy. At the same time, a groundswell of anti-Muslim sentiment in western Europe had been growing, partly because the coming of the Seljuks had made it much more difficult for Christian pilgrims to make the journey to the Holy Land. The time was ripe to declare a holy war. Alexios, for his part, was seeking reinforcements to protect his empire from invasion by the Muslim Seljuks. But the clarion call that was heard in the west was the more symbolic one: to 'liberate' Jerusalem and the holy places of Christianity.

After a summer spent sounding out potential leaders, Urban formally announced what would become the First Crusade in the town of Clermont Ferrand in central France in November 1095. The response was beyond anything Alexios or his advisers could possibly have imagined. Noblemen and knights from all over western Europe rushed to join up. Urban had been determined to oversee an organised military expedition. And this was what Alexios was expecting. But once the torch had been lit, there was no way of controlling the fire. While preparations were still going ahead under Urban's careful supervision, a spontaneous movement sprang up in northern France and parts of Germany. Inspired by a charismatic individual known as Peter the Hermit, but without any organised leadership, the 'People's Crusade', as it came to be known, set out through Germany and the Balkans for Constantinople on their way to Jerusalem. Before they even reached Byzantine territory, they had begun their holy war by massacring or forcibly converting the Jewish populations of the German towns they passed through. Anna Komnene, who was writing with the benefit of half a century of hindsight, chose to suppress altogether the fact that the father whom she revered had brought this invasion upon his own head. She describes their arrival like this:

It was as if he [Peter the Hermit] had inspired every heart with some divine command. Kelts assembled from all parts, one after another, with arms and horses and all the other equipment for war. Full of enthusiasm and ardour they thronged every highway, and with these warriors came a host of civilians, outnumbering the sand of the seashore or the stars of heaven, carrying palms and bearing crosses on their shoulders. There were women and children, too, who had left their own countries. Like tributaries joining a river from all directions they streamed towards us in full force.

Adroitly, if cynically in the eyes of some western observers, Alexios had the whole contingent shipped over the Sea of Marmara to the advance base he had prepared for the main expedition on the Asian shore. Against his advice, they then went on to attack the nearby Turks with horrific ferocity, only to be butchered in their turn. Peter was one of the few to make it back to Constantinople—saved, according to Anna, by the timely intervention of her father.[11]

The arrival of the contingents that made up the main force was managed rather better. Alexios had laid elaborate plans to keep them supplied with provisions. He also sent military escorts to stop them plundering the countryside while they made their way overland to the Bosphorus from their various landing points on the western coasts of today's Albania and Greece. Their numbers must have been far beyond anything that Alexios could have expected. Modern estimates suggest that as many as eighty thousand may have taken part in the First Crusade.[12] It was never a unified army, and from the start Alexios was determined to keep it that way. He ensured that the troops were kept well away from Constantinople. Only their leaders were allowed inside the city and, so far as possible, he dealt with each of them separately.

Alexios's objective was to extract from each an oath of allegiance. All cities and territories that the crusaders captured on their expedition were to be handed over to the emperor, as their rightful ruler. Many of the leaders demurred. The full panoply of Byzantine diplomacy, and the targeted channelling of ostentatious bribes in gold, had to be deployed. Alexios was playing for high stakes. But from his point of view, far from being recruited by the crusaders to serve their cause, *he* was recruiting *them* as a 'Byzantine imperial army'. Whether they would ever make it as far as Jerusalem was not his concern: properly handled, these people were to be the means of restoring Anatolia to 'Roman' rule. It must have seemed worth it. And in any case, now that the crusaders were there, and in such numbers, Alexios had little choice.[13]

After several months of haggling in Constantinople, all the leaders agreed. Even Bohemond, the son of Robert Guiscard, who had fought against Byzantium before and would again, found it expedient to comply. By early summer 1097, all the crusader forces were in place, encamped outside Nicaea. Alexios himself crossed over the Bosphorus with a force of his own and two of his most trusted generals and directed operations from not far away. The 'impregnable' fortress fell on 19 June. But the manner of its taking explains a great deal about the different aims and methods of the Byzantines and the crusaders.

The westerners brought superior technology. The crossbow doesn't seem to have played a role at Nicaea but was still enough of a novelty that the normally contemptuous Anna felt it necessary, half a century later, to give her readers an admiring account of how it worked and how deadly it was. Siege engines were built by both Byzantines and crusaders, and there seems to have been some disagreement about whose were the more effective. If the western advantage in this field had been Alexios's first motivation in drawing them in, it was not directly decisive in the outcome.[14] Nicaea was not taken by storm. It says something for the way sieges were conducted in this part of the world at the time that Alexios's trusted aide and general, Manuel Boutoumites, was able to enter the city and negotiate with the defenders, not once but twice. On the second occasion, a relieving army sent by the sultan had just been wiped out by the crusaders; Alexios had arranged for a fleet of boats to be carried overland from the Sea of Marmara and launched on the lake in front of the fortress. The defenders could no longer be supplied by that route. Without these military pressures, no diplomacy could have been effective. But with them, in classic Byzantine manner, Alexios was spared the effort and expense of a debilitating siege.

The Turkish commanders agreed to surrender in return for a guarantee of safety, signed by Alexios himself, and the promise of money and honours if they would serve him in future. (Characteristically, Anna, who evidently relishes the story, tells us nothing about what was to happen to the rank and file.) But first, the crusaders had to be duped into thinking that the city had been won by force and that the decisive breakthrough had been made by the Byzantine army. So the defenders allowed an advance guard from a Byzantine siege tower to climb over the walls. Victory was proclaimed, and the Turks surrendered to Boutoumites. Only once the whole city was secure were any crusaders allowed inside—and then only in groups of ten, a precaution, according to Anna, against their overwhelming numbers and 'their fickle nature and passionate, impulsive whims'.[15]

After that, the crusaders were to proceed to Antioch. The emperor would join them there, having in the meantime subdued the western parts of Anatolia—as his forces were now able to do, thanks to the terror instilled in the Seljuk defenders by the presence of the crusaders farther east. It was during the siege of Antioch, which was finally taken a year after Nicaea, that the alliance between the crusaders and the Byzantines began to fall apart when Bohemond seized the city for himself. In the meantime, Alexios's generals campaigned successfully against the Seljuks in western Anatolia, but he himself remained in Constantinople. There could be no prospect of a reunion in Antioch now that Bohemond had gone back on his oath.[16]

From Antioch, the crusaders went on their way to Jerusalem to seize the city and massacre everyone in it on 15 July 1099. Against enormous odds, and at terrible cost in human life, they had won their 'holy war'. Most of them, by that time, had become convinced that Alexios and the 'Greeks' were not to be trusted. These Greeks did deals with infidels. They failed to keep their promises—though this was a complaint heard only after large amounts of Byzantine gold had already changed hands.

The truth must be that both parties had quite distinct agendas in the first place. No Byzantine emperor, for hundreds of years, had ever seriously thought of trying to recapture Jerusalem. A crusade, from the Byzantine point of view, would make no strategic sense. The very idea of holy war, that had begun with Heraclius, had long ago become outdated in Byzantium. Alexios had been prepared, no doubt with great misgivings, to ride the tiger of crusader religious passions for pragmatic reasons. But he also recognised the danger he had unleashed. Before he died in 1118, he would exhort his son and chosen heir, John II, to

> ponder and keep in mind the recent commotion from the West, lest there arise a time of need which will chasten and humble the lofty dignity of New Rome and the majesty of its throne.[17]

Alexios's deathbed warning was to prove prophetic—but not for some time yet, thanks to the capable stewardship of his son and his grandson, whose reigns, together with his own, would add up to a full century.

IN THE EVENT, John II would be spared another such 'commotion' during his reign. Instead, he had to find a way to deal with a proliferation of new Christian states in the Levant, that had been created in the wake of the First Crusade. Their rulers were Catholic princes who, like Bohemond before them, still refused to recognise the 'emperor of the Greeks' as their overlord. By 1143, John II had made up his mind to take control of the crusader states by force. But as his army was passing through southern Anatolia, the emperor was killed in an accident while hunting. Suspicions about the nature of this 'accident' have surfaced from time to time, not least because the campaign had to be immediately aborted. The new emperor, Manuel I, needed to have his army near the capital to secure his own position.[18]

If the crusader states in the east had been spared attack from Byzantium, they were now coming under a sustained onslaught from the Seljuks. The County of Edessa, which included a sizeable part of today's Syria, fell in 1144. Three years later, a new crusade set out from western Europe to try to win it back. This time the expedition was led not by mere noblemen and minor royalty but by two of the crowned heads of western Europe: Louis VII of France and the German emperor, Conrad III. They passed by Constantinople in 1147 on their way east, and again the next year on their return, having failed to regain Edessa. The arrival of huge foreign armies, uninvited this time, outside Constantinople once again raised the same jitters as before. But Manuel dealt with the crusaders as his grandfather had done. He kept the rank and file of the soldiery well away from the capital, and his coffers were full enough that he could afford to lavish generous hospitality on the expedition's leaders.

Both royal guests, as a result, spent several months in the vicinity of Constantinople. Although we know tantalisingly little about how they spent their time, their courtiers must have had plenty of opportunity to exchange ideas with their Byzantine counterparts. By the time they left again, without serious incident, it seems that mutual animosity between the western knights and the Byzantine elite was much less than it had been during the First Crusade, or would be again. It may even be that the literary genre we know as the 'medieval romance', that first began to flourish in French during the following decades, owed something to these encounters with the Byzantine court during the passage of the Second Crusade. In the early 1170s, in northern France, it was possible for

Chrétien de Troyes to devise a historical fiction in which a prince of Constantinople travels to Britain and saves the kingdom for King Arthur, while in the next generation, King Arthur himself prepares an expedition to defend the legitimate heir to the throne of 'Greece' in Constantinople.[19]

On the Byzantine side, too, attitudes were changing, at least at the very top. Manuel, throughout his long reign, was known to be pro-western. Both his first and his second wife came from western royal families and had been brought up in the Catholic branch of the Christian faith. Famously, Manuel imported from the west the sport of jousting—to the bemusement of conservative-minded Byzantine spectators.[20] This was a far cry from the icy contempt of Anna Komnene, whenever she wrote about 'Franks', 'Latins', or 'Kelts', the names by which western Europeans were commonly known in Greek at this time. Whatever the rank and file of his subjects thought, here was an emperor who was prepared to take these 'barbarians' seriously. It was Manuel's diplomacy, not force, that eventually brought the rulers of the crusader states in the east to accept Byzantine supremacy in the 1060s, even if it was only nominal. This was how long it had taken to fulfil the terms that Alexios had tried and failed to impose more than half a century before. Manuel worked hard, too, to advance the cause of union between the eastern and western churches—a prospect that once had been held out by Alexios but had stalled after the First Crusade.

By the 1170s, all this was beginning to provoke a backlash at home. Then in 1176, the Byzantine army suffered a catastrophic defeat at the hands of the Seljuks, at the battle of Myriokephalon in west-central Anatolia. Manuel's prestige at home and abroad never recovered. He died on 24 September 1180, at the age of sixty-one. And from that moment, everything that had been achieved during the Komnenian century began to unravel. In the space of a little over two decades after Manuel's death, the Byzantine Empire collapsed from within.

HISTORIANS EVER SINCE have struggled to explain what happened and why, and exactly what was its impact on the course of later history. But Niketas Choniates, who lived through these events and rose through the ranks to become head of the Byzantine civil service during the crisis years at the beginning of the thirteenth century, was merciless in his diagnosis of the symptoms of what today we can call 'systems collapse'. Choniates is regarded as one of the most accomplished of all Byzantine historians. His position as an insider ensures that what he tells us is most likely to reflect the opinions of the Constantinopolitan elite at the time. His specific diagnoses sometimes reveal the prejudices of the man himself or his class. Choniates's contempt for the 'mob', for instance, is as visceral as his dislike of Franks or Latins. And we must allow for the possibility that he and those who thought like him may at times have been part of the problem. But the facts speak for themselves.[21]

Once again, in 1180, a widowed empress was left as regent for an underage heir. But this time, infighting within the ruling Komnenos family, and between the Komnenoi and powerful aristocratic rivals, led to a power vacuum that would last for more than twenty years. Reigning emperors were deposed, and in most cases blinded, or murdered, or both, in 1182, 1185, 1195, and no fewer than four times in a little over a year, between 1203 and 1204. On each of these occasions, the populace of Constantinople played a noisy, and often violent, part. Indeed, it is worth wondering whether something rather like today's populism was beginning to run out of control at the heart of the Byzantine body politic.[22]

In the course of the upheaval of 1182, seemingly spontaneous hatred of Latins spilled over into the streets. The communities of merchants from Italy—particularly, at that time, from Pisa and Genoa—living on the opposite side of the Golden Horn from Constantinople, were targeted, and hundreds were massacred. The killing was on nothing like the scale of the massacre of Roman settlers in Anatolia that had been organised by Mithridates more than a thousand years before. But the spectre of what a future age would term 'ethnic cleansing' was once again raising its head in the Greek-speaking world. Three years later, and partly in reprisal, the Normans of Sicily invaded the northern Greek mainland yet again. This time they succeeded in sacking Thessalonica before they were turned back. In 1189, a third crusade reached Constantinople in a doomed attempt to win back Jerusalem after the city had fallen to the Kurdish leader Saladin. The emperor Isaac II Angelos proved to be no match for the crusade's leaders, in a battle of wits with the German emperor Frederick Barbarossa, King Richard ('the Lionheart') of England, and Philip II of France. There even came a moment when they threatened to turn on Constantinople itself.

Similar things had happened often enough before, and the empire had recovered. But now they all came on top of one another. And a new trend was gathering momentum in the closing years of the twelfth century. In the past, whenever a rebellion had broken out in the provinces, its leader would either end up being swept to power in Constantinople or his movement would be crushed. It had been all or nothing. But no longer. By 1200, local members of aristocratic families, including the Komnenoi, had set up separate fiefdoms in places as far apart as Cyprus, Trebizond, the city of Philadelphia in western Anatolia, and the Peloponnese. At the same time, the Slavs of the Balkans broke away to create the separate kingdoms of Serbia and Bulgaria, at a stroke undoing the conquests of Basil the Bulgar Slayer. The authority of the capital over the provinces had collapsed, just as imperial authority was collapsing in the city itself.[23]

At the same time, in the west, momentum was gathering for a new attempt to regain Jerusalem. Inspired by Pope Innocent III, who came to the papal throne in 1198, this would become known as the Fourth Crusade. Unlike previous expeditions, this one was to be undertaken by sea. Ships provided by the maritime republic of Venice would convey the knights to Egypt. The final assault on the Holy Land would be launched from there. The pragmatic Venetians were more interested in trading than crusading. The doge of Venice, the ninety-five-year-old Enrico Dandolo, agreed to the crusaders' terms, on condition that they paid for the services of his fleet.

Led by the doge himself and Boniface of Montferrat, a relative of the French king, the expedition set out from Venice in October 1202. But almost from the first, it became evident that the crusaders had not enough money to pay the Venetians what they owed. A providential solution came in the form of a young Byzantine prince called Alexios. This was the son of Isaac II Angelos, who had been deposed back in 1195 when the throne had been usurped by his uncle, Alexios III. If only the crusaders would divert their expedition to Constantinople and restore him to his rightful position as emperor, the younger Alexios promised to repay them out of the imperial treasury with all that they needed.

Despite allegations that would first be made soon after the event and that have resurfaced frequently ever since, neither Pope Innocent nor the leaders of the crusade had any deep-laid plan to conquer Constantinople. Indeed, it seems to have been only at a late stage that it even occurred to them that they *could*. From accounts written by crusaders afterwards, it is evident that they looked with awe on the city, its defences, and the military might that the emperor could command.[24] Along with those, of course, went the lure of its fabulous wealth, which nobody doubted would be enough to repay their debt to the Venetians and cover the costs of the crusade many times over. It was the Byzantines themselves who played into the crusaders' hands, as the deepening power vacuum at the city's heart inexorably drew them towards it.

The expedition arrived with the Venetian fleet in the Bosphorus in June 1203 and set up camp on the Asian shore. The pretender Alexios proved much less welcome among his own people than he had led the crusaders to expect. In a bid to enforce his claim, Venetian ships fought their way into the narrow waterway that gave access to the heart of the city, the Golden Horn. Once inside, they overwhelmed a much-reduced Byzantine navy and took control of the shoreline below the walls. In the face of this pressure, the desired regime change took place: the crusaders' young protégé was crowned in Hagia Sophia as Alexios IV Angelos. In the meantime, the Venetian ships stayed inside the Golden Horn. Others ferried the crusaders across the strait, from their camp on the Asian shore. The expedition was now ensconced right under the walls of Constantinople. In every previous emergency, the Byzantine fleet had kept control of the waterways that surrounded the city on three sides. Now, with their ships beached or captured, there was no chance of launching the deadly 'Greek fire' that had ensured Byzantine supremacy at sea for centuries.[25]

All that was needed, at this point, was for the imperial treasury to pay up, as the new emperor had promised, and the crusaders would be gone. But even at this moment, when the danger should have been obvious, the prevailing opinion within the city seems to have reverted to the traditional one, that went back to the time of Alexios I: these 'Franks' were barbarians. Their brute strength existed to be exploited to serve Byzantine ends; savage and unpredictable as they were, they could always be managed through the age-old diplomatic techniques of bribery and division. The more nuanced approach of Manuel I seemed to have been forgotten. Under the influence of this way of thinking, Alexios dragged his feet. Attitudes inside the city were hardening too—perhaps a further sign of the growing influence of populism on decision-making.[26]

By the start of the new year, 1204, the patience of the crusaders was wearing thin. But so was the anger on the streets of Constantinople. Alexios was overthrown on 25 January and murdered shortly afterwards. The new emperor was Alexios V Doukas, known by the nickname Mourtzouphlos ('Bushy', apparently because his eyebrows were joined in the middle). There was still time to buy off the crusaders. It was what any competent ruler in the centuries-old Byzantine tradition would have done. And apparently Mourtzouphlos did have the means to pay. It is not clear to what extent the emperor was a free agent; most likely, his hands were tied by powerful advisers or by the ever-growing power of the mob. Instead of paying, Mourtzouphlos haughtily handed down an ultimatum to the crusaders: he gave them just a week to sail away.[27]

The decision to take Constantinople by force seems not to have been reached until February. During March, plans were drawn up by Dandolo, Boniface, and the other leaders of the crusade for a division of the spoils. Then on the morning of Monday, 12 April 1204, the Venetian galleys inside the Golden Horn carried siege engines mounted precariously on their decks and brought them right up against the walls at their weakest point. The first groups of crusaders leapt onto the ramparts in this way. Others, under cover of the siege engines, broke through a bricked-up postern gate. Fighting continued in the streets for the rest of the day. Mourtzouphlos fled that night. Yet another emperor was chosen, but by the next morning no one was willing to fight on, and he too abandoned the city. Within twenty-four hours, Constantinople had been overrun. On 13 April, the never-silenced mob was back on the streets, this time chanting the name of Boniface as their *basileus*. But nothing, now, could stop the pent-up rage of the crusaders. As Choniates, who had experienced it, wrote shortly afterwards:

> Thus it fell out that the fair city of Constantine, the shared delight of all peoples and famed by all, was blackened by fire and obliterated, conquered and emptied of all its riches, whether public, private or dedicated to God, by the scattered tribes of the west, a feeble rabble for the most part and without a name.[28]

What we now call the 'Byzantine Empire' would limp on for another two and a half centuries after this. But it would never again be a significant political force. And from that April day in 1204, the overwhelming majority of Greek speakers would have to get used to living under rulers who shared neither their language nor their religion, a state of affairs that would last until 1923.

11

HOPEFUL MONSTERS

1204–1453

T HE DESTRUCTION OF the greatest Christian city in the world by Christian crusaders was not universally welcomed even in western Europe. Pope Innocent III, who had called for the crusade to set out in the first place, denounced the soldiers of Christ for betraying their vows to liberate the Holy Land. The savagery of their behaviour in the conquered city would only make them hated by their Orthodox co-religionists, he complained.[1] Byzantines belonging to the educated elite, such as Niketas Choniates, or Anna Komnene before him, had been convinced from the start that the ultimate goal of the crusading movement had been not the Holy Land but the far richer pickings of their own. The events of the Fourth Crusade seemed to prove them right. And for many in the Greek-speaking world, thereafter, this view would become deeply ingrained.

In reality, the crusaders and the Venetians had probably surprised themselves as much as anyone else by what they had done. Afterwards, the victors found themselves in a weaker position than they might have expected. The plans drawn up by the leaders in March 1204 had been for a division of the spoils, not a takeover of a functioning empire. Even Constantinople had to be divided— with Hagia Sophia and the ecclesiastical jurisdiction that went

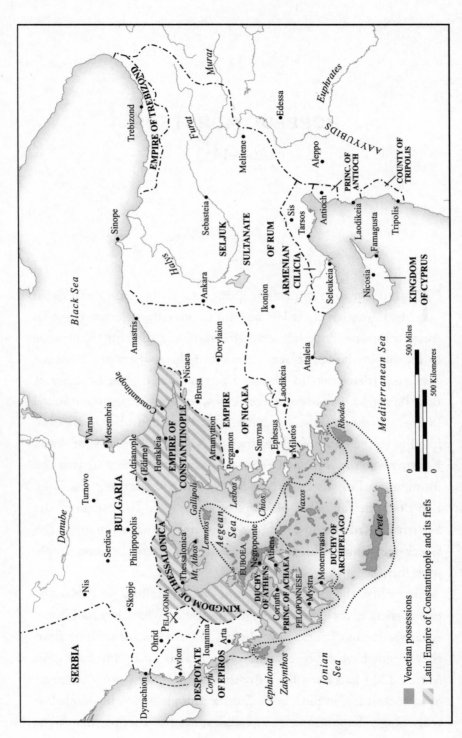

11. 'A kaleidoscope of petty fiefdoms, principalities and kingdoms', c. 1214

Legend:

- Venetian possessions
- Latin Empire of Constantinople and its fiefs

with it going to the Venetians, while a new 'Latin' emperor, the former Count Baldwin of Flanders, ruled from the Blacherna palace at the other end of the Golden Horn. Boniface of Montferrat, who had been the nominal leader of the crusade but missed out on the imperial title, became king of Thessalonica instead.

Within the next few years, the Venetians went on to secure their hold on islands and coastlines that would become the basis for a commercial, maritime 'empire' in the eastern Mediterranean. Other islands, and parts of Constantinople itself, would fall to Genoa, Venice's bitter trading rival. On the Greek mainland, former imperial provinces were parcelled out among leading crusaders, who then ended up fighting to claim them from the local inhabitants, or sometimes from each other. Wherever they succeeded, the new rulers went on to organise their territories according to the western, feudal system. In theory, this meant that each of them owed allegiance to their overlord in Constantinople. But in reality, the 'Latin Empire', as it came to be known, ended up as no more than a city-state consisting of the capital, its immediate hinterland in Thrace, and a small wedge of territory on the Asian side of the Bosphorus between the Black Sea and the Sea of Marmara. Its supposedly feudal vassals went their own way.

The effect of all this was to shatter the highly organised, centralised Byzantine state into a kaleidoscope of petty fiefdoms, principalities, and kingdoms. Some of these would change hands, swap allegiances, and shift their boundaries many times, as the kaleidoscope continued to turn. During the next three centuries, Greek speakers living on the European side of the Aegean and on the islands, from the Ionian Sea to Cyprus, would find themselves under the sway of a bewildering variety of rulers at different times and in different places: French, Venetians, Genoese, Florentines, Catalans, Aragonese, Navarrese, and (recruited from all over western Europe) the Knights Hospitaller of Saint John.

Athens, for instance, would be ruled throughout the thirteenth century by a French baronial family from Burgundy, then for much of the fourteenth by the descendants of Catalan mercenaries who had briefly run amok through the Greek mainland before settling there, and finally in the fifteenth by Italian dukes from Florence. At some point during this time, the Parthenon was converted from an Orthodox church to a Catholic cathedral; the massive entrance gateway to the Acropolis, the Propylaea, into a ducal palace. A hundred-foot tower was built to guard it, in the style of the towers that still define the skyline in Italian cities and towns such as Bologna and San Gimignano. The 'Frankish tower', as it became known, would remain the tallest building in Athens until it was demolished in the 1870s. This was the Athens that would find its way into the pages of the *Decameron* by Boccaccio (written in the 1350s), *The Knight's Tale* by Chaucer, and Shakespeare's *A Midsummer Night's Dream*.[2]

The duchy of Athens was just one among many such states left behind in the eastern Mediterranean as the tide of the crusades ebbed. Modern historians often see these states as the precursors of western European colonial ventures around the world in later centuries.[3] From the perspective of colonial history this makes good sense—there are many continuities in the behaviours of the rulers. But, with the exception of the Venetians, the new masters were not acting in the name and interests of a colonial power. Rather, they were high-ranking adventurers setting up on their own account. Perhaps a better way to understand what was happening in much of the Greek-speaking world at this time is to compare it to developments in the home countries of the 'colonists', back in western Europe. There, during the same centuries, the foundations were being laid for what would later become *national* identities, as allegiances, identities, and political loyalties began to coalesce into the patterns familiar today.[4] In the Greek-speaking east, while the remnants of the old Byzantine Empire broke apart, we can see comparable signs of new political and cultural identities being formed and tried out.

In evolutionary biology, mutations that never made it to become successful species are known as 'hopeful monsters'. The eastern Mediterranean had its share of those during the centuries after 1204—and not only among the supposedly colonial western possessions. Even in those places where Greek speakers were still (or were once again) in charge, a very similar process seems to have been at work.

AT THE EASTERN end of what had once been the Byzantine state, facing the southeastern corner of the Black Sea, the port city of Trebizond and its hinterland had increasingly become cut off from the rest of the empire, both by geography and by political choice. Descendants of the Komnenoi had asserted their independence from Constantinople even before 1204. The mini 'Empire of Trebizond' had now become the endpoint of the silk roads that led overland all the way to China. By making their own arrangements with the Turkish Muslims to their south, and with the Venetian and Genoese merchants whose galleys connected Trebizond with the Mediterranean and western Europe, the canny Byzantines of this region would keep their state going until 1461.[5]

At the other end of the geographical spectrum lay Epiros, in the mountainous west of the Greek peninsula, beyond the formidable barrier of the Pindos mountains. Here, the grandiosely named Michael Doukas Komnenos Angelos made the most of his (illegitimate) descent from no fewer than three formerly imperial families to set up another mini empire, this time with its capital at Arta. In due course this was to become the 'Despotate of Epiros'. The rulers of Epiros soon had some success against the Latins in the north of today's Greece and in 1224 captured Thessalonica, bringing them within striking distance of Constantinople.[6]

Midway between these geographical extremes lay the largest swathe of their former territory that still remained to the Byzantines. Beginning a few kilometres east of the Bosphorus and some way south of the Sea of Marmara, this included much of the Aegean coastline of Anatolia, with its hinterland. Within this territory, a new provisional capital was established not far from Constantinople at Nicaea. Ironically, this was the impregnable fortress-city on its lake that Alexios I had retaken from the Seljuks, thanks to help from the First Crusade. It was there, in 1208, that a relative of the Angelos dynasty, Theodore Laskaris, was crowned emperor. From that time on, the newly reconstituted imperial court at Nicaea would be single-minded in its aim: to recapture the capital city and reestablish the authority of the emperor as it had been before.[7]

But in the fragmented Greek world of the thirteenth century, there could be no question of the three Byzantine successor states making common cause to achieve this. It is entirely characteristic that the decisive battle, whose outcome would determine the course of the empire's final centuries, was fought not between Byzantines and Latins but between the rival Greek 'emperors' of Nicaea and Epiros over which of them was to repossess the imperial capital. The battle of Pelagonia was fought in July 1259 near the modern town of Bitola, in North Macedonia, between proxies for Michael II Doukas, based in Arta, and a new usurper who had been crowned in Nicaea, Michael VIII Palaiologos. The Nicaean side won. And so the way was open for the last great dynasty of Byzantine emperors, the Palaiologoi, to rule from Constantinople.[8]

By this time, it was evident that the capital was ripe for the taking. A Latin emperor, Baldwin II, still ruled at the Blacherna palace. But deprived of the revenues of its hinterland, cut off from all its previous sources of food and wealth, and without material support from western Europe, Constantinople was quite literally falling into ruin under its Latin rulers. The Greek-speaking Orthodox population had melted away. In the capital, streets and houses were deserted. The city authorities had been reduced to stripping timber and lead from the roofs of churches to raise cash. Baldwin II even had to sell off some of the most priceless assets of all in that intensely religious age: those relics of the saints that had not already been looted in the sack of 1204.[9]

The reconquest, when it came, was an anticlimax. A small expeditionary force sent out from Nicaea to keep watch on the city walls from the European side of the Bosphorus received a tip-off. The Venetian fleet and most of the defending Latin troops had gone on a raiding expedition into the Black Sea. The city was practically undefended. With the aid of some local people, the Nicaean contingent was soon inside. Michael VIII Palaiologos was able to enter his capital city for the first time, in triumph, on the day of the Feast of the Assumption of the Virgin Mary, 15 August 1261.[10]

FOR THE NEXT twenty years, it must have looked to many observers as though the old times were back. Everything could go on as it had before. Evidently, Michael Palaiologos thought so. And he had the personality and the ruthless determination to make it come true if anybody could. Michael did all the same things as the Komnenian emperors had done before him. The geopolitical situation he inherited, once the capital had been restored, though grave, was after all familiar. The Byzantine state was surrounded by actual or potential enemies: it had been ever thus, since the beginning. So Michael rebuilt the war fleet whose last remnants had been destroyed by the Venetians inside the Golden Horn in the summer of 1203. Taking to the seas once again, Byzantines began to regain control of the Aegean. Michael recruited mercenary soldiers and sailors from the ranks of rival powers—still a risky policy, as it had proved for Alexios I and his successors, but with the empire's territory so diminished there was no alternative source of manpower or (in the case of the navy) expertise. He negotiated trade deals with the rising city-states of Italy, mainly Venice and Genoa, and exploited the bitter rivalry between them. This was an even riskier policy, as the sequel would prove; but it had worked in the past, and if the Byzantines were to keep the upper hand, it might work again.

Michael exercised the art of diplomacy as skilfully as any Byzantine emperor, before or after—indeed, so skilfully that no one has ever been able to determine how much of a hand his agents had in organising the massacre of French forces that had gathered at Palermo, in Sicily, for the purpose of destroying his empire in 1282. This was the episode known to history as the 'Sicilian Vespers'. Like most of his predecessors, ever since the formal schism between the eastern and western churches, Michael VIII made overtures to successive popes. If the Orthodox Church were to accept the jurisdiction of the papacy, rival powers in the west would no longer have the excuse that the Byzantines were 'heretical' and therefore fair game. And once again it might be possible to recruit armies of western Christians to prop up the front against the Muslim Turks in the east. In this direction Michael went further than any of his predecessors. In the French city of Lyon, a Byzantine embassy signed an act of union with the western church at a council held in 1274.[11]

But the world had changed. Not one of these initiatives, that had worked so well in the twelfth century, proved sustainable in the new world of the thirteenth. It had taken nothing less than a 'reign of terror', waged against Orthodox churchmen at all levels of the Byzantine hierarchy, to force through the union between the churches. One of the first acts of Michael's son and successor, Andronikos II, after his father died at the end of 1282, was to bow to near-universal pressure at home and repudiate it.[12] The battle between supporters and opponents of church union would continue for as long as the Byzantine state lasted. And it would be fought with all the passions that had once fuelled the 'battle over images', iconoclasm. This time the issue was insoluble. On the one hand, the secular state depended for its survival on good relations with the rising powers of the west; on the other, to submit to the alien authority of the pope in Rome, even if only in matters of the spirit, was seen by most Orthodox, Greek-speaking 'Romans' as a betrayal of their very identity.[13]

In the meantime, more and more ground was being lost to the Turks in Anatolia. There should have been a golden opportunity for the Byzantines when the Seljuk sultanate collapsed during the second half of the thirteenth century under pressure from the Mongols in the east. But neither Michael VIII nor Andronikos II managed to capitalise on the chaos that ensued. Instead, a patchwork of new and unstable states emerged under rival Turkish emirs, who from this time began to encroach ever farther into former Byzantine territory. In its traditional heartland of Anatolia, there seems to have been little nostalgia for the Byzantine Empire among the Greek-speaking Christian population. Of those who found themselves newly subject to Muslim Turks, large numbers converted to Islam rather than resist, and they appear to have been willingly absorbed into these emerging Muslim societies. Why this should have happened, when elsewhere resistance to western Catholicism was so visceral and strong, remains to be explained. In these regions, too, hopeful monsters were emerging out of the mixing of Greek speakers and incomers. But since the converts would usually lose their language within a generation or two, they disappear from the historical record as Greeks.[14]

Then there was finance. The kind of diplomacy that Michael had deployed so effectively had always been expensive. So, too, was the work of restoring and rebuilding the capital, after the depredations and neglect of the crusaders. Revenues were drying up. Disastrously, Andronikos disbanded the Byzantine navy to save money. This not only left Constantinople undefended by sea; taken together with the concessions already made to Venetian and Genoese traders, it placed all maritime trade and the revenues that came with it in the hands of Italian entrepreneurs and bankers. By the time Andronikos died in 1328, the shrunken Byzantine state had once more plunged into a civil war that lasted on and off for seven years and weakened it still further.

The one sphere in which the Palaiologan restoration looked at all convincing was in the arts. The historians George Akropolites, George Pachymeres, and Nikephoros Gregoras followed one another in bearing eloquent and unflinching testimony to their times. The first of these, a confidant of Michael VIII Palaiologos who had led the Byzantine delegation at the Council of Lyon in 1274, also played a leading role in restoring the system of formal education in the capital. Highly educated theologians, called 'philosophers', continued to probe the boundaries between the interpretation of Christian doctrine and the ancient philosophical tradition. Beginning with the scholar and monk Maximos Planoudes during the second half of the thirteenth century, scholars in Constantinople, for the first time in seven centuries, learned to read what the greatest minds of western Christendom had been writing in Latin, from Saint Augustine in the fifth century down to Saint Thomas Aquinas in their own time.[15]

The art of mosaic church decoration made a spectacular comeback when the church known in Greek as the Chora (today the Kariye Camii) was redecorated at the personal expense of the polymath, author, and senior civil servant Theodoros Metochites, between 1315 and 1321. The cycle of images depicting the life of the Virgin Mary has been much admired since the mosaics were rediscovered in the twentieth century. But some art historians have detected the rigidity and artificiality of an overly self-conscious revival. The same can certainly be said of the education curriculum restored under the direction of Akropolites. Essentially, this was still the system that went back to the time of the Second Sophistic, more than a thousand years before. Elite Byzantine writers cultivated an unchanging form of Greek that was more remote than ever from everyday speech, since the spoken language had moved on during the intervening centuries.[16]

The artistic and intellectual quality of the 'Palaiologan Renaissance', as it is sometimes called, is all the more astonishing when set against the terminal impoverishment of the state that produced it. But its very qualities perhaps reveal a reluctance or inability to adapt to a changing world. A detail in the Chora mosaics gives a hint of this. In one panel, the donor, Metochites, is depicted on his knees, offering a miniature replica of the church as a gift to Christ, who is seated on a throne. The concept and the composition are entirely traditional. What is not is the donor's hat, which has the appearance of a turban. The exotic piece of headwear is several times the size of the wearer's head and slightly larger than the model church he holds in his hands. Court fashions evidently *were* changing, and it mattered enough to this highly placed official to have the dignity of his office recorded in its full glory by the anonymous artist. Among the splendours of a revived artform, that all round the walls of the church seems to look backwards, the hat is a rare breath of fresh air.

THE GREATEST OF all the failures of the restored empire was its inability to halt the breakup of the Greek-speaking world that had been the root cause of the disaster of 1204. Even after the restoration, it seems that wherever Greeks still ruled outside the capital, they no longer wanted to buy into the empire that their ancestors had helped to build. And where Latins ruled, despite intensely felt differences between their respective churches, some, at least, among their Greek subjects now looked to new beginnings rather than hanker after a lost past.

The Peloponnese, at this time better known by its colloquial Greek name, 'the Morea', had been awarded jointly to two French knights from Champagne in northern France: Geoffrey of Ville-hardouin and William of Champlitte. The story of how they conquered the territory and how Geoffrey ousted his partner to found a dynasty of Villehardouin princes was told a century later in a remarkable narrative called the *Chronicle of the Morea*. The tale would be retold and updated in several different languages over the next two centuries. But in its oldest version in Greek, the *Chronicle* breaks new ground. Unlike all previous histories, this one is written not in the 'high style' favoured in Constantinople but in a language much closer to the spoken Greek of today. To some extent this must reflect the way that people actually spoke in the Peloponnese at the time. And it is written in verse, in a style which may reflect a local tradition of oral storytelling.[17]

Running to almost ten thousand lines in its longest version, the *Chronicle* brings to life a world in which French-speaking 'Franks', adherents of the Latin, western church, make common cause with a portion, at least, of their Greek-speaking, Orthodox subjects. Near the beginning, the anonymous author seems to mimic an oral performer, who explicitly addresses both groups together:

> *Hearken all, both Franks and Romans [i.e., Greeks]*
> *all ye who trust in Christ and bear the mark of baptism*
> *gather round and hearken to a great matter.*[18]

The *Chronicle* promotes a strong sense of a shared, *regional* identity. The two peoples and the two unreconciled branches of the

Christian faith are brought together under the label 'Moreots'—the people of the Morea. A key passage is the imagined speech of Prince William of Villehardouin to his knights on the eve of the battle of Pelagonia in 1259. They are about to fight *alongside* the Greeks of Epiros and *against* the Greeks of Nicaea (led by Michael VIII, who would soon restore Byzantine rule to Constantinople). The Morea, their homeland is far away, William tells them. But they must fight to retain their good name in the world. Entirely skipping over the awkward fact (for the many Greeks among them) that the forces ranged against them are those of the legitimate Byzantine emperor, William stresses instead that the Byzantine army is made up of mercenaries who speak a ragbag of different languages. A few lines later, he makes the contrast:

> *For even if we are few against them,*
> *we all share a bond as men of one substance,*
> *and so like brothers you all must love one another.*[19]

The odd term that intrudes here, 'substance', seems to be borrowed from the language of theology, as indeed is the echo of the commandment in Saint John's Gospel, to 'love one another'. There is something almost sacred about the bond that unites these troops, loyal to their Peloponnesian homeland and its ruler, and that trumps any residual loyalty that some may have felt towards the resurgent Greek-speaking state of Byzantium.

It is hard to tell how accurate a picture the *Chronicle* gives of conditions in the thirteenth-century Peloponnese. Its author celebrates the great aristocratic families (both French and Greek), who lived in the castles that still dominate the landscape in many parts of the region today. But the local peasants and craftsmen whose labour must have built these castles are passed over in silence. So, as a rule, are the townspeople, foot soldiers, farmers, and herders on whom the whole system must have depended. Compared to the civic institutions of the Byzantine Empire, the world of the Frankish-ruled Morea, as portrayed by its anonymous chronicler, sounds more primitive, heroic, one might almost say Homeric.[20]

Indeed, the leading actors in that world seem positively to have relished their links to the legends of a long-distant age. Soon after the conquest, the first Villehardouin ruler adopted the title 'Prince of Achaea', resurrecting a name that went back to the Roman Empire, and before that to the 'Achaeans' of Trojan War fame. Stories woven around that legendary ancient conflict once again began to circulate in the Morea—and like the *Chronicle*, these, too, were written both in French and in the spoken Greek of the time. New tastes were being cultivated. Rulers and ruled alike, it seems, could find role models for themselves among the Greek and Trojan warriors of legend. In the Morea, until it all began to go into reverse in the second half of the fourteenth century, a distinct, hybrid *Moreot* culture and identity were emerging.[21]

AT THE EASTERN end of the Mediterranean, back in the 1180s, Cyprus had been one of the first Greek-speaking regions to break away from Byzantine control; in 1192 the island ended up under the rule of French crusaders even before the Fourth Crusade. By the time the Kingdom of Cyprus and Jerusalem, to give it its full title, came into existence, Jerusalem had already been lost to the crusaders for good. For just short of three hundred years after that, until 1489, Cyprus would be ruled by the French aristocratic family of Lusignan, which had previously ruled in Jerusalem. There, the Greek-speaking, Orthodox majority was more obviously treated as second-class citizens than in the Morea. But they were not persecuted; attempts to convert them forcibly to the Latin church were few, and successfully resisted.

During the centuries of Lusignan rule, Cyprus enjoyed a stable political system. New institutions emerged and new loyalties formed. Once again, local people must have been conscripted in huge numbers to build the Gothic cathedral of Nicosia, the abbey of Bellapais in the hills above Kyrenia, the towering castles of Saint Hilarion and Buffavento nearby, or 'Othello's tower' in Famagusta, that would later be imagined as the setting for Shakespeare's play. The great churches of late medieval Cyprus were all built and consecrated by the rulers for the western, Catholic faith; the native population had to make do with the humbler buildings whose exquisitely decorated interiors can still be admired in villages tucked into folds of the Troodos mountains in the island's south.

Even in these less than favourable circumstances, Greek speakers had a role to play in Lusignan Cyprus at most levels below the very highest. By the time they found a voice that we can still hear, in the 1430s, the fragmentation of the Greek world had extended even to the language. For the first time since the post-Mycenaean dark age, Greek had once again split up into recognisably different regional dialects. A hundred years after the anonymous chronicler of the Morea had broken new ground by writing in a form of Greek that resembles the language of Greece today, Leontios Machairas in Cyprus began to write the history of his native island, in prose this time, and in a form of the dialect that still marks out Greek Cypriots from other Greeks.[22]

Machairas was an Orthodox subject of the Lusignan kings. By his own account, he had served as secretary to a local member of the French nobility. In July 1426, when King Janus Lusignan was preparing to defend Cyprus against a Mamluk force that had landed from Egypt on the south coast, Machairas found himself in charge of the provision of wine for the defending army. The battle that followed, at a place called Choirokoitia, on the road that leads inland from Limassol on the coast to Nicosia, the capital, marks a climactic point in the narrative that he would soon afterwards begin to write. The king was taken prisoner, his army was routed, and towns were pillaged. Once the invaders had left, the Greek-speaking Orthodox subjects of the kingdom rebelled. But the king returned after a ransom was raised for his release. The pretender Alexios, who had raised the standard of revolt, was executed on the same day. Writing of these events during the reign of Janus's son, John II Lusignan, Machairas is clear about where his loyalties lie. The native Greek rebels had been 'accursed peasants', their actions 'evil'; their leader, the self-proclaimed 'King Alexios', only merits a few lines in his narrative. For the historian writing in Cypriot Greek, the Lusignan kings are the guarantors of stability and the best interests of their subjects. Whenever there is dissension or rebellion, he comes down on the side of the king.[23]

But the word Machairas uses for 'king' is a recently coined one in Greek—*regas*, derived from the Latin *rex*. The older Greek title, *basileus*, he reserves for the emperor in Constantinople. By the time that Machairas was writing, the days of the imperial capital were already numbered; the Orthodox king-emperor (*basileus*) had precious little empire left to rule. But the historian writes with wistful respect of this remnant of an old order whose day is almost done. Just as the *Chronicle of the Morea* created a new category of people called 'Moreots', so Machairas, for the first time on the historical record, speaks consistently and with evident solidarity of 'Cypriots'. Quite clearly, these Cypriots are made up of both rulers and ruled.[24] It was the *Cypriots*, collectively and all together, who had suffered defeat and humiliation on the battlefield of Choirokoitia in July 1426—from King Janus Lusignan and his French-speaking knights, down past their wine steward and future chronicler, all the way through the ranks to the Greek-speaking peasants who would rebel in the aftermath. In its own way, although very different from the shorter-lived 'Principality of Achaea' in the Peloponnese, the Kingdom of Cyprus and Jerusalem, by the middle of the fifteenth century, had progressed even farther down a comparable evolutionary path.

These developments in different corners of the Greek-speaking world were perhaps not so very different from the gradual amalgam of peoples, cultures, and languages that a little earlier had been completed in England, two and three centuries after the Norman conquest of 1066. The Morea and Cyprus are the best documented examples of this process at work in the Greek-speaking world. But they are not the only ones.[25] And the process would not be exhausted even by the fifteenth century. The most hopeful monster of them all, Venetian Crete in its heyday, was still some way in the future.

ALL THIS TIME, the little that was left of the Byzantine Empire was steadily whittled away. In 1347, the Black Death ravaged Constantinople on its way westwards to wipe out as much as a third of the population of western Europe. By then, only a handful of towns, islands, and disconnected stretches of coastline remained under Byzantine control. Almost the whole of today's Greece was divided between Latins in the south and an expanded Serbian kingdom that had taken control of most of the north. Constantinople, with its Thracian hinterland, was once again in effect just another city-state, distinguished only by its massive city walls and an exaggerated sense of its own importance. But the truth was that the 'queen of cities' now lagged far behind Venice or Genoa in military or commercial strength.

The diminished nature of the prize proved no bar to rival candidates who on several occasions mustered armies to fight for the imperial title. In 1346, no fewer than three self-proclaimed 'emperors of the Romans' reigned simultaneously. That struggle ended in 1347 with a victory for John VI Kantakouzenos over the supporters of the underage John V Palaiologos, that would prove pyrrhic. When the new emperor was crowned in Constantinople on 21 May, the crown and the jewels in which he was invested were cheap fakes, because the real ones had been pawned to Venice by the opposite faction four years before. They would never be returned. Even Hagia Sophia was in such a state of disrepair that the coronation could not be held there, but in a church next to the Blacherna palace.[26]

Worse was to come. For several decades, now, successive emperors had tried to exploit the divisions among their neighbours to the east and south, the Turkish emirates. If there was no longer any serious prospect of regaining territory lost in Asia, Turkish troops could still be hired as mercenaries. One emir would be recruited as a tactical ally to help weaken a rival. John Kantakouzenos enjoyed a particularly warm relationship with Orhan, son of Osman, the emir of Bithynia, and had even given him his daughter in marriage. Orhan's territory included the entire southern coast of the Sea of Marmara, which meant that his emirate was the closest of all to Constantinople. The emperor could not know to what heights the Osmanli, or Ottoman, dynasty would rise in times to come. But he should perhaps not have been surprised when, the next time he summoned Turkish mercenaries across the Hellespont to Gallipoli, to help him in a renewed bout of civil war in 1352, Orhan's son Suleiman simply refused to go home afterwards. Suleiman's occupation of a number of small towns on the Gallipoli peninsula in that year marks the first permanent Turkish settlement on European soil.

John VI Kantakouzenos, dubbed the 'reluctant emperor' by his only modern biographer, had unwittingly paid a high price for his ascendancy. It would bring him very little gain, either, as he would shortly afterwards bow to pressure and abdicate in favour of the rival he had previously defeated, John V Palaiologos.[27] By the end of the century, the Ottomans had moved their capital from Bursa on the Asian shore of the Sea of Marmara to Adrianople in Thrace, and they had overrun the kingdoms of both Bulgaria and Serbia. Constantinople itself was placed under siege by the Ottoman ruler, Bayezid, who had in the meantime been elevated to the title of Sultan, in 1394.

Faced with these pressures, whole sections of Byzantine society, and individuals in a position to do so, turned in contradictory directions in a desperate search for solutions. One initiative came from monks and monasteries. During the fourteenth century, a movement began which combined mystical contemplation with private prayer and an attitude of resignation towards the things of the world. Hesychasm, as the movement became known, at least superficially shares common elements with the Sufi tradition in Islam, and in today's terms with yoga and Transcendental Meditation. The word means more or less 'the art of stillness'. In a world in which the political order was visibly failing, it could make sense to withdraw as far as possible. But politically, hesychasm was bound to breed a form of resignation, bordering on fatalism.[28]

A very different approach came from those more pragmatic members of the Byzantine ruling class who still pinned their hopes on saving the *state*. This was to work for a diplomatic compromise with the western church in return for military reinforcement from the west. To this end, in the course of a long reign after the abdication of his rival, John V Palaiologos paid a humiliating visit to the pope in Rome. He arrived there in October 1369 and stayed five months. The upshot was that the most a Byzantine emperor could promise was a purely personal submission to the authority of the pope. Whether from conviction, or more likely from a desperate attempt at expediency, John V was received into the Latin church. In ecclesiastical terms it was too little because he could not even pretend to bring the clergy of his own church along with him, as his predecessor Michael VIII had tried to do almost a century before. And strategically, even if he had been able to offer more, by this time there were limits to the power of a pope to mobilise a crusade in the way that Pope Urban had done back in the 1090s. So nothing practical came from John's mission to Rome.[29]

His son and successor, Manuel II, tried a different tack. Manuel set out for the west in December 1399. The siege of his capital by Bayezid's forces had still not been lifted. There had never been a more critical moment if the last bastion of Christendom in the east was to be saved. Manuel wasted no time with popes or ecclesiastical councils, and for once held out no promises of an elusive unification of the churches. Described as 'an urbane and scholarly man with a finer and more commanding presence than his father', this emperor traversed Europe to pitch his appeal for military support directly to Charles VI of France and Henry IV of England.

In the course of a tour that lasted three years, Manuel was received with honour in London at the end of 1400 and entertained to Christmas dinner and a tournament at Eltham Palace. Less than eighteen months had passed since Henry had deposed his predecessor, Richard II, and taken the crown for himself—a far less common occurrence in England than it was in Byzantium. Manuel would have been overjoyed to learn that his host had every intention of leading a crusade to the east, probably not realising that Henry was only hoping to distract attention from his own illegitimacy so as to quell dissent at home. In the event, as every student of Shakespeare and English history knows, Henry IV would spend the rest of his reign fighting civil wars in his own kingdom, while his son Henry V would direct his efforts against neighbouring France. Despite the raised hopes of Manuel, the crusading spirit in this corner of western Europe was dead.[30]

As things turned out, the reprieve for what was left of the Byzantine Empire came not from the west but from the east. In July

1402, while Manuel was still in Paris, in a battle fought outside Ankara in July 1402, a Mongol army led by Timur-lenk, known in English as Tamburlaine, defeated the Ottomans and took Sultan Bayezid prisoner. For the time being, the Turks were at the mercy of the Mongols. In Europe, and particularly in Constantinople, it looked as though the Ottoman state was about to fall apart, as the Seljuk sultanate had done before it. The effect, instead, was to grant the Byzantines another fifty years to argue among themselves about the means to their salvation.[31]

So FAR, AT least explicitly, there had been only two broad strategies on the table—the one designed to uphold the integrity of the Orthodox Church; the other directed towards preserving the state and its institutions. But in the second decade of the fifteenth century came for the first time an explicit and highly articulate plea for a *part* of that state to go it alone, and in a way that was unprecedented in all the earlier Byzantine centuries. It originated from a provincial centre that had been steadily regaining ground during the past hundred years. This was the Morea, or Peloponnese. The Frankish Principate of Achaea was long gone. By 1430, the whole of the Peloponnese was once again in Byzantine hands. But in the spirit of the times, the 'Despotate of the Morea', as it was known, was ruled not directly from Constantinople but from the provincial capital at Mystra, the medieval town built on a steep hilltop overlooking the Eurotas valley and the long-abandoned site of ancient Sparta. The 'despot' was appointed by the emperor, usually from among his closest relatives, but was able to exercise a good deal of autonomy on the ground.[32]

Throughout the first half of the fifteenth century, the court at Mystra functioned as a political and cultural centre in its own right. The traces of this can still be seen in the ruined palaces and churches, some of them now restored, that rise in terraces punctuated by winding streets that afford sudden glimpses of the olive groves of Laconia in one direction and the rocky peaks of the Taygetos range in the other. It was here that one of the most brilliant and original thinkers of the day, George Gemistos, who preferred to be known by the name of Plethon, came up with nothing less than an entirely new way for Greeks to reinvent themselves in the new conditions of the time.

Not much is known for certain about Plethon's life. He was born shortly before 1360, probably in Constantinople; he enjoyed the benefits of a Byzantine education at the highest level and went on to occupy a number of administrative positions, first in the capital, and then, from about 1400 onwards, at Mystra. Today, Plethon is best remembered for his attempt to rehabilitate the ideas of the ancient philosopher Plato, whose name he seems deliberately to echo in the choice of his own, and for his later influence on the Italian Renaissance. But the political programme he set out in two memoranda, one addressed to Despot Theodore II in Mystra and the other to the despot's father, Manuel II Palaiologos in Constantinople, was also deeply grounded in the political realities of the Peloponnese at the time when he wrote them (probably between 1416 and 1418).

The Morea, Plethon argued, is large enough and fertile enough to produce enough for the needs of its people. Separated from the mainland except for the narrow Isthmus of Corinth, it is 'simultaneously an island and a continent' and 'with minimal preparation has adequate means to defend itself'. Moreover, 'It appears that this land has always been inhabited by Hellenes, who have been the same for as long as humans can recollect'. As Plethon put it to the emperor in an often-quoted line: 'We whom you lead and over whom you rule are Hellenes by descent, as our language and our traditional education bear witness.'[33]

This was to reverse the terms that had been used by Plato's contemporary Isocrates almost two thousand years before, in 380 BCE, and all but universally accepted ever since: that it was language and education, rather than ancestry, that defined a person as Greek. In Plethon's formulation, language and education are still there, but 'descent', or kinship group (*genos* in Greek, the same word that Isocrates had used), now takes first place. Byzantines before Plethon had very occasionally revived the old term 'Hellenes' to describe themselves, but never as seriously as this. Plethon's blueprint for the Morea in many ways anticipates the concept of national identity as it would develop in much of Europe in later centuries.[34]

Having established the case for a 'Hellenic' Morea, self-sufficient and effectively independent of Constantinople, Plethon went on to set out detailed proposals to reform its administration along lines derived from Plato. Some of this sounds distinctly totalitarian by our standards today. Plethon was an admirer not only of Plato but also of the ancient counterpart to Mystra, the corporate state of Sparta that had once flourished in the valley below. Private land, he writes to the emperor, is to be confiscated and redistributed to those most able and willing to cultivate it. Plethon reserves some of his harshest criticism for monasteries and monks ('a swarm of drones'). Their wealth and the privileges accorded to them (this is also a sideswipe at the influence of hesychasm) uselessly drain the resources that should be available to the state and in this way benefit only the Turkish enemy.[35]

In political terms, Plethon's proposal for the governance of the Peloponnese was by a long way the strangest of all the evolutionary dead ends, or hopeful monsters, thrown up by these centuries. But this one only ever existed on paper. Neither Despot Theodore nor Emperor Manuel took any notice. In his later years, released from the pragmatic necessity of persuading an imperial patron to adopt and implement his ideas, Plethon would extend his theoretical blueprint even beyond politics. His last book, the *Laws*, would be discovered after his death in the early 1450s. It seems that he had shared its contents only with a close circle of trusted friends and pupils at Mystra. In the *Laws*, Plethon parts company not only with the Byzantine Empire but with Christianity too, to propose a return to worshipping the ancient Greek gods, rather as Julian the Apostate had done a little over a millennium before. But this most radical experiment of all didn't even survive on paper—except for a few tantalising passages, preserved only so as to show how heinous it was. The manuscript itself was publicly burned on the orders of the patriarch of the Orthodox Church.

BY THE SECOND half of the 1430s, the survival of Constantinople once again hung by a thread. On the throne was Manuel's son, John VIII Palaiologos. The only policy left to the Byzantine state to pursue was a full union between the churches. Even that might not succeed, and the emperor and his advisers were well aware of the strength of opposition at all levels of the Orthodox faithful. Everything seemed to be coming together when Pope Eugenius IV agreed to a long-standing Byzantine precondition that had never previously been met: only a council of the *whole* Christian church, with eastern and western branches fully represented, could finally settle the terms of union. Not on the table, of course, was the supremacy of the papacy. That would have to be conceded.

In March 1438, a delegation some seven hundred strong representing the entire Orthodox communion arrived in the northern Italian city of Ferrara for the promised ecumenical council. It was headed by the emperor and the patriarch. All the intellectual and ecclesiastical luminaries of Constantinople, its outlying territories, and the Despotate of the Morea seem to have been present. Plethon, now well into his eighties, was dutifully among them—even though secretly, in all probability, he had already turned his back on both the contending parties. The council dragged on at Ferrara until an outbreak of plague in the city forced a move to Florence instead. A modern historian describes 'trained theologians on either side of the debate, brandishing their bones of contention with all the passionate intensity of obsessed academics'.[36]

Eventually, the formal union of the churches was proclaimed in Florence on 6 July 1439. The quid pro quo was that Pope Eugenius would now announce a crusade to save Constantinople from the Turks. And despite the changed political climate in Europe, an expedition did in fact set out, five years later. The Crusade of Varna would turn out to be the last. An expedition recruited from Burgundy and Venice in the west and from Serbia, Hungary, and Wallachia in the east was ignominiously crushed near the town of that name, on the Black Sea coast of Bulgaria, on 10 November 1444. The hope of some form of western military support for the Byzantines had not quite vanished. But there was little chance, now, of intervention on a comparable scale again. Constantinople stood alone.[37]

Two things made it inevitable, as the decade of the 1450s began, that the 'city of the world's desire' would fall to the Ottomans: geography and gunpowder. Ottoman rule already extended through much of the Balkans, reaching hundreds of miles to the west and north on the European mainland. Protected by its immense walls, Constantinople was an island entirely encircled by an enemy intent on conquest. The walls that had been built in the reign of Theodosius II in the early fifth century had stood against any and every kind of assault for a thousand years. Provided only that the Byzantines kept control of the waterways that surrounded them and could keep an enemy out of the safe harbour of the Golden Horn, their city was impregnable. It had been taken only twice before:

in 1204 after the Venetians had forced a way for their ships inside the Golden Horn, and then in 1261 while it had been practically undefended, allowing Michael VIII to oust the last Latin emperor.

But the young and determined Ottoman sultan, Mehmed II, known ever since in Turkish as *Fatih*, 'the Conqueror', had a new weapon. Once upon a time, the Byzantines had been ahead in military technology: the mysterious 'Greek fire' had saved them on numerous occasions in the past. This time, they had been left behind. Gunpowder, originally from China but now combined with the technology of cannon that the Ottomans had imported from the Christian west, became the clinching factor. As Mehmed assembled his forces in the autumn of 1452, fifth-century defences were up against the newest and most deadly invention of the fifteenth.

The final siege began on 6 April 1453. It was the week after Easter. Daily, Turkish cannon bombarded the walls. In overall command of the defence was Constantine XI Palaiologos. Forty-eight years old (more than twice the age of his adversary, Mehmed), Constantine had served his elder brother John VIII ably as Despot of the Morea before becoming emperor in 1449. The last 'emperor of the Romans' had received his title and regalia in Mystra but would never be formally crowned in his own capital. So visceral was the opposition of the Orthodox clergy to the union of the churches that no patriarch could be found to perform the age-old ceremony in Hagia Sophia. Indicative of the attitude of many among the defenders was the often-quoted assertion attributed to one of Constantine's senior commanders, which may well be apocryphal: 'better a Turkish turban than a popish mitre'.[38]

Despite this, the defence of the city was reinforced by contingents from Genoa and Venice. A war fleet from Venice was eagerly awaited. But by mid-May, a vessel that had broken the siege to reconnoitre returned to report that none was on the way. An official, sent to make a tally of the fighting men present in the city, would later record that he had personally counted 4,773 imperial soldiers and 200 foreigners. Other sources put the number of the defenders at somewhere between six and seven thousand, facing an Ottoman army at least eighty thousand strong.[39]

On 21 May, Mehmed sent an embassy offering terms of surrender. If it had been accepted, it would have saved the city from the traditional three days of plunder and massacre. Constantine rejected it out of hand. A final vigil was held in Hagia Sophia on the night of Monday the twenty-eighth. For once, everyone who could be spared from duty on the defences took part, Latins and Orthodox alike. The Turkish assault began before dawn the next day. The walls had been seriously weakened by weeks of cannon fire. Now, under cover of the Turkish guns, wave after wave of the Ottoman elite force, the janissaries, charged forward. By the time the sun rose, the first of them had scaled the ramparts. For hours there was hand-to-hand fighting inside the city. Many of the Venetians and Genoese managed to escape on their ships. The city's inhabitants were left to their fate. Constantine himself was last seen fighting on the ramparts among the common soldiers. His body was never found. Later, the legend would circulate that the 'immortal emperor' had been spirited away by an angel to a secret place deep within the city walls and turned to stone, there to await the moment when he will emerge in triumph and reclaim Constantinople for the Orthodox faithful.[40]

Once the city had been taken, the killing and looting began. Some four thousand of the city's inhabitants were probably cut down during the first twelve hours. As many as fifty thousand may have been taken as slaves. By early afternoon, Mehmed entered the city in a ceremonial procession. According to a Venetian eye witness, the sultan rode a white horse, while 'blood flowed through the streets like rainwater after a sudden storm'. The procession made its way at once to Hagia Sophia, where the Christian liturgy had been celebrated for the last time the night before. A priest went up into the pulpit and chanted the Muslim call to prayer.[41] Justinian's great cathedral of eastern Christianity, that had already stood for the best part of a millennium, had now become the greatest mosque in the Muslim world.

From a Greek point of view, the second sack of Constantinople in 1453 is often seen as the culmination of a process of dissolution that had been set in motion by the crusaders and Venetians two and a half centuries before. But from a broader perspective, the consequence of the Ottoman conquest was actually to *reverse* that process. The imperial centre had been progressively sidelined from the late twelfth century onwards, as the Greek-speaking world fell apart, and the rump Byzantine Empire found itself increasingly left high and dry by the tide of history. Of all the speculative new political projects, or hopeful monsters, that had sprung up from small beginnings during the chaos of the thirteenth century, the one that finally made it to dominate the human ecology of the whole region turned out to have been the tiny emirate founded in Bithynia by Osman, that had been nurtured—and exploited—for his own ends by the Byzantine emperor John VI Kantakouzenos back in the 1340s and 1350s. Osman's descendant Mehmed II, by his conquest, simply restored Constantinople to its former position, under the new name of Istanbul, as the capital city of a world empire, as it would remain for the best part of the next five hundred years.

12

BETWEEN TWO WORLDS

1453–1669

AFTER THE LOSS of Constantinople, Greeks remained in charge of their own destinies only in the Despotate of the Morea, with its capital at Mystra, and in the 'Empire of Trebizond' at the far end of the Black Sea. Mehmed wasted no time in mopping up these last outposts. Mystra fell in 1460, Trebizond the year after. For the next three hundred years, everyone who spoke Greek as a first language would be a subject of either the Ottoman sultan or a western European, and usually Roman Catholic, administration. For most, it wasn't a matter of choice but of where you happened to live. For those who did opt to leave the land of their birth, and had the means to do so, the choice was stark.

Survivors of the imperial family and the Byzantine elite fled westwards to Italy, often by way of Crete or other islands that were still under Latin rule. But despite occasional heady talk of renewed crusades against the Turks, there was never any prospect of a political revival for the Byzantine Empire on foreign soil. The last emperor had died childless. The final descendant of the Palaiologoi with a legitimate claim to the Byzantine throne would wind up penniless in Rome. Having nothing else to live on, he would surrender all his titles, first to the king of France, and then to the Catholic Monarchs Ferdinand and Isabella of Aragon and Castile.

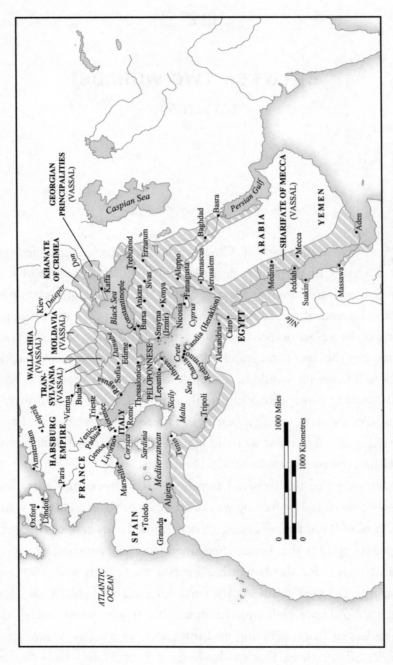

12. The Ottoman Empire at the time of the death of Süleyman I ('Süleyman the Magnificent') in 1566

Not even this would be enough to save Andreas Palaiologos from dying in poverty in Spain in 1502.[1] The Greeks who would make their mark on western Europe during the decades after the fall of Constantinople were not soldiers or political leaders but scholars and men of learning. Through these fugitives, Byzantium, at the last, would bequeath to the rest of the world its highly prized system of education that was still based on a thorough knowledge of Homer and the classic Greek authors of the fifth and fourth centuries BCE. This was the gateway through which knowledge of the Greek language and access to ancient Greek thought returned to western Europe after an absence of almost a thousand years.

The ground had been well prepared, not least during informal encounters that had taken place on the fringe of the church council in Ferrara and Florence back in 1438 and 1439. More lasting in its effects than any of the council's resolutions would prove to be a series of fringe encounters between individuals on the opposing sides. The maverick ideas of a Plethon or the manuscripts of ancient Greek history, poetry, and philosophy assembled by Plethon's pupil Bessarion, who would go on to become a cardinal in the Roman Catholic Church, would prove to be of more interest in intellectual Italian circles at the time than any amount of argument about the procession of the Holy Spirit.

This was because, for some time before this, enquiring minds in Italy had been seeking out the lost or forgotten arts and ideas of antiquity. The intellectual and artistic movement that reached its peak during the decades after the fall of Constantinople is now known as the Renaissance.[2] Naturally enough, the rediscovery had begun with ancient Rome. But as soon as Italians once again were reading and rereading ancient Roman authors such as Cicero, it became obvious how much they, in their turn, had learned from the Greeks. If the ancient Romans had been 'held captive' (in the often-quoted line of the poet Horace, in the first century CE) by the Greek civilisation they had conquered, so too could Italians, a millennium and a half later.

Elite immigrants from Constantinople or Mystra, steeped in the classical Greek education they had acquired there, were eagerly made welcome by their Italian hosts. The city-states of the Italian peninsula were, after all, republics. Just like the ancient Greek *poleis*, they were constantly in a state of war against one another. Their leaders were more than ever preoccupied with the questions of governance and civic responsibility that had first been debated in the ancient Greek city-states and had found a permanent record in the pages of Plato and Aristotle. Italians, and in due course other Europeans, too, were avid to find out firsthand what these long-lost treasures, hitherto known only through summaries and comments preserved in Latin, had to say on issues that were pressing in their own time and place. In this way was born the political philosophy now conventionally known by the name of 'civic humanism'—a very specific legacy of the ancient Greek *polis*, that came via the Italian Renaissance to the modern world.[3]

During the second half of the fifteenth century, university chairs in Greek began to proliferate at Italian universities. Many of the first and second generations of professors were Greek émigrés— provided they were willing to part company with their own Orthodox Church and adopt Roman Catholicism. In Rome, Pope Nicholas V began to establish a collection of Greek manuscripts in the Vatican Library in 1448; for the rest of the century, Rome would become a centre of Greek scholarship, attracting many more high-profile Byzantine converts. These highly educated migrants can never have been very numerous. Nor were they the *originators* of the Renaissance; they were more like a catalyst that made it possible. And essential though their contribution undoubtedly was, what counted with their hosts was their knowledge of the *ancient* language and its treasures, from the poems of Homer and

Hesiod down to the sermons of the Fathers of the Church, written in the fourth and fifth centuries CE. Few western Europeans in the fifteenth century wanted to learn to *speak* the Greek of their own time, still fewer to learn about the recent past or future prospects of the communities their teachers had left behind.

On the other hand, the impact of these teachers and the learning that they brought with them went well beyond secular scholarship and the arts. Before long, the skills acquired through a humanist education, and particularly the knowledge of Greek, would exercise a profound influence on the course of Christianity in the west. For the first time in many centuries, churchmen in western Europe could learn to read the original Greek text of the New Testament. Erasmus of Rotterdam, one of the leading figures in the Protestant Reformation in the early sixteenth century, had studied Greek at the University of Padua. This was what enabled Erasmus and others to challenge the authority of the 'Vulgate', the Latin translation of the Bible on which the western church had always had to rely. After that, it was not long before Protestants were translating the Christian scriptures directly from Greek and Hebrew into the modern languages of Europe—and the full fury of the Reformation, the Catholic Counter-Reformation, and Europe's 'wars of religion' would be unleashed.

In a very different sphere, among the newly rediscovered books translated from Greek was the *Geography* of Strabo, that had been written in the first century CE. It was from two passages in this work that the Genoese explorer Christopher Columbus learned that it must be possible to sail westwards from Europe to reach India, at least if we accept the later testimony of his son. Ironically enough, according to the Byzantine system of reckoning historical time, the year 1492, when Columbus made his first voyage across the Atlantic, would have marked the end of the seventh millennium since the Creation. Generations of Orthodox Christians had been brought up to believe that the Last Judgement and the end of the world would come about in the year 7000.[4] In Constantinople, the apocalypse had been premature, but only by a matter of a few decades. As one world ended, another was about to begin. Just at the time when the political self-determination of Greek speakers had been extinguished in their own lands, an outward movement was beginning that would spread their language, together with the ideas that had once been expressed in it, not just to the rest of Europe but right around the world.

FOR THE VAST majority, though, the realities of daily life meant accepting the new conditions in which they found themselves. One of these was peace. Ever since the Byzantine Empire had begun to break up two and half centuries before, wars had been fought more or less continually in most of its former territories. Some modern historians speak of a *pax ottomanica*, the equivalent of the *pax romana* that had once been imposed by Rome. The Ottoman state was Islamic and theocratic, but at the time of the conquest, Muslims still made up only a minority of its subjects. Ways had to be found to bind the subject Orthodox population into the new status quo.

Constantinople had been a ghost city when Mehmed first declared it his imperial capital. Almost at once, he set about repopulating it. It seems to have been a deliberate policy to import *Greek* families, forcibly moved from other conquered regions, so as to fill the empty streets and houses. Twenty-five years after the conquest, almost a third of the city's approximately sixty thousand inhabitants were Orthodox Greeks. This was a far cry from the heyday in the time of Justinian, when it had been home to some four hundred thousand. But it was a start. And as the city grew over the centuries to come, so would the number of Greek-speaking Orthodox Christians.[5]

The contrast is often drawn between the apparent tolerance of the Ottomans towards their non-Muslim subjects and the religious persecutions that were notorious in the west at this time and for long afterwards. There was to be no equivalent, as the Ottoman Empire expanded, to the expulsion of Jews and Muslims from the Iberian peninsula after the last Muslim kingdom in Spain fell in 1492, or to the excesses of the Holy Office, or Inquisition, in Catholic Europe during the centuries that followed. Matters of private conscience were of no interest to the Ottoman authorities—any more than they had once been to the Romans back in the early years of Christianity. What mattered was loyalty to the state. Mehmed's masterstroke was to turn the Orthodox Church into an institution of the Islamic Ottoman Empire.

His choice for the man to run it was a monk by the name of Gennadios Scholarios. Known as an outspoken critic of the Latins and a leading figure among those Byzantine clergy who had stood out against the abortive union of the churches, Scholarios could be expected to steer the Orthodox faithful away from any lingering nostalgia for the rival religious authority of the papacy or for military interference from the west. It had taken some trouble to find him, because the monks of his monastery had already been sold off as slaves. Eventually, Mehmed's agents ran him to earth where he was working in a household in Edirne and brought him back to Constantinople. There, Scholarios was duly invested by the sultan as Gennadios II, Ecumenical Patriarch of the Orthodox Church, according to the ritual that had been performed by Byzantine emperors for centuries.

From that time on, the highest office of the Christian church in the Ottoman state would be in the personal gift of the sultan. The arrangement was as much as anything a financial one: the patriarch and his officials were given responsibility for the collection and payment of taxes by the Christian community (a role that of course they had never been called on to fill before). Given how numerous were the sultan's Christian subjects, this was a far more lucrative proposition than persecution would have been. These policies had little to do with what a later age would term tolerance. Mehmed had made a political calculation. And it worked. As early as 1466, the sultan was being addressed in Greek by the old Byzantine title of 'Basileus of the Romans'. And at about the same time, Kritovoulos of Imbros, one of the last Greek historians to write in the Byzantine tradition, flattered his new sovereign by comparing him favourably to 'Alexander the Macedonian'.[6]

On the other hand, there was no getting away from the fact that Greeks, in common with all other non-Muslims, were second-class citizens. They had to pay discriminatory taxes. An institution that was much feared by Christian families throughout the rural districts of the empire's European provinces was the notorious *devshirme*. This was a regular levy that forcibly removed Christian male children from their homes to be converted to Islam. Forbidden to marry, they would be pressed into a lifetime of service in the elite corps of janissaries. Not all of these recruits ended up as soldiers. Some would be selected for high-ranking positions in the civil administration or the personal service of the sultan. In this way, for all its arbitrary cruelty, the system did bring spectacular opportunities to some of the poorest of the empire's subjects. And paradoxically, the *devshirme* could not have existed without the Christian communities to keep it supplied with young recruits. At an early stage, Ottoman administrators had concluded that these converts, who by definition could have no family loyalties to compete with their loyalty to the sultan, would be more trustworthy than the high-born Muslims who vied with one another for status at the imperial court.[7]

These were some of the mechanisms that enabled Greek-speaking communities, and therefore the Greek language, to survive in their homelands after the Ottoman conquest. But inevitably, the initiative lay with the conquerors. Greeks themselves had no say. This is why it is not enough to repeat the commonly heard assertion that Greeks were held together during the centuries of Ottoman rule by their language and their church. Yes, they were—but only because the political self-interest of the Ottoman state made it possible. The fate of the Jews and Muslims of Spain is a stark reminder of what could have been.

That said, Greek individuals and whole communities were not slow to make the most of the opportunities that the system allowed them. One route to preferment was always conversion, whether forced, as in the case of the *devshirme*, or voluntary. And some Greek converts to Islam could become very powerful within the Ottoman state. Before the end of the fifteenth century, at least two grand viziers (a role roughly equivalent to the sultan's prime minister) had started out as members of the Byzantine elite before the conquest.[8] But in most areas of the empire, and certainly in the capital, those who converted would soon be lost to the Greek language. It was *as Christians* that Greeks continued to be a visible and fully accepted presence in the Ottoman Empire. Non-Muslims could be employed in many different roles, without being expected to convert. Ottoman armies, for instance, recruited large numbers of Orthodox Greeks and allowed them the privileges that went with their rank. This meant that, over the years, probably as many Greek speakers fought *within* the Ottoman ranks as fought against them in the armies of western-ruled Christian states.[9]

For several centuries after the conquest, there was little sign of Greek resistance or active defiance. Revolts were rare, local, and swiftly put down. Even the phenomenon of 'neo-martyrs'—Christians who refused to convert and who died for their faith, as the early Christian martyrs had once done—was small in scale, though their stories also bear harrowing witness to the brutality of

Ottoman punishments. More often than not, the victims were former Christians who had at first given in to pressure and converted to Islam and later reverted—thereby calling upon themselves the traditional Islamic penalty for apostasy.[10] For the great majority of Greeks who were Ottoman subjects throughout the sixteenth century and beyond, it made sense to find an accommodation with an empire that was vigorously expanding in all directions, gobbling up both Muslim and Christian states in its seemingly unstoppable progress.

DURING THE REIGN of Selim I, between 1512 and 1520, the Ottomans defeated the Mamluk rulers of Syria and Egypt, extended their power right through the Arabian Peninsula as far as Yemen, took control of the Muslim holy sites of Mecca and Medina, and made inroads against the newly established Safavid dynasty of Persia. The Ottoman sultan was in a position to claim the title of Caliph, the supreme ruler over Muslims, wherever they might live. The next sultan, Süleyman I, was poised to inherit all the riches that came with control of the trade routes of the Mediterranean and the Middle East and would extend the empire's conquests even farther afield. Remembered in the west as 'the Magnificent' and by Muslims as 'the Lawgiver', Süleyman pushed farther into the European continent and farther west into the Mediterranean than any sultan had done before him.

Belgrade fell in 1521, followed by much of Hungary and today's Romania, Moldova, and Ukraine. In 1529, Süleyman's forces laid siege to Vienna, though the Habsburg capital would prove to be a prize too far. In the meantime, in the Greek-speaking world, the Knights Hospitaller of Saint John had been forced to surrender their stronghold on the island of Rhodes in 1522. During the next two decades, the Ottoman fleet for the first time outstripped that of Venice, to become the strongest in the Mediterranean. By 1540, almost all the islands of the Aegean were under Ottoman control. Then in 1565, the fleet laid siege to Malta, the new headquarters of the Knights of Saint John, but failed to take it. Süleyman died the next year on an abortive campaign into Hungary. Even if Ottoman power was no longer quite invincible, Süleyman's forces still managed to take the island of Chios from the Genoese in the spring of 1566.[11]

That left the 'Most Serene Republic of Venice' as the only rival to the Ottomans in the eastern Mediterranean. Venice had acquired control of Cyprus when the last Lusignan king died in 1489, leaving his kingdom to his widow, who happened to be a Venetian. Since then, the chief bulwarks of Venetian power abroad had been Cyprus and Crete. It was on Cyprus that the next sultan, Selim II, set his sights. In the summer of 1570, a massive Ottoman force landed on the south coast of the island, not far from today's Larnaca. The capital, Nicosia, was besieged and sacked in September. A Venetian garrison held out in Famagusta for almost a year longer, but soon the whole island was in Ottoman hands. For the local Greeks, there was gain as well as loss from the change of masters: one of the first acts of the new Ottoman administration was to abolish the Catholic hierarchy and allow the Orthodox Church to appoint its own bishops again. This was a calculated policy, and it was applied wherever the Ottomans supplanted a Catholic administration: the Catholic church they saw, not wrongly, as a political arm of the papacy and the powerful courts of western Europe, while the Orthodox hierarchy was under their own control.[12]

In the battle for Cyprus in 1570 and 1571, there must have been many Greeks in arms fighting on both sides. This would be the case once again only a few months after the fall of Famagusta, when the Ottoman fleet came up against the combined ships of Venice, Spain, and the Papal States at the entrance to the Gulf of Patras, off the fortified town of Nafpaktos, also known by the

Italian name of Lepanto. The Ottoman fleet, 230 galleys strong, was almost completely destroyed. The battle of Lepanto, fought on 7 October 1571, can be seen in hindsight as the decisive turning point that halted the expansion of the Ottoman Empire into Europe by sea.[13] But from the point of view of most Greeks, it merely consolidated a reality that their parents and grandparents had been living with for more than a century. After 1571, apart from isolated coastal garrison towns, the only places left where Greeks still lived under western, Venetian rule were the Ionian Islands off the west coast of the Greek mainland and Crete. And it is only after the loss to the Venetians of Cyprus that the story of Venetian Crete really comes into its own.

CRETE WAS A late developer among the hybrid cultures, or hopeful monsters, that had sprung up in the wake of the Fourth Crusade. This was because Venice had begun by imposing a strictly colonial system on its overseas possessions. Policy was made and directed from the metropolitan centre. The highest officials, including the *Provveditore Generale*, who reported directly to the Venetian Senate, were sent out for tours of duty that lasted only two years at a time. In the beginning, land, property, and privileges in Crete had been handed out to settlers who belonged to Venetian noble families. A rigid separation had been created between these Venetian nobles and the native Cretans of all classes, including the local aristocracy who claimed descent from a nobility that went back to Byzantine times. And at least in theory, this segregation would be maintained for several centuries, based on the religious divide. The very rigidity of the system fuelled a series of rebellions, and these continued into the sixteenth century. All of them were put down with a ferocity more usually associated in Greek collective memory with the Ottoman Turks. But their effect over time was to win some limited concessions from the Venetian authorities for the Orthodox population.[14]

Even in such a polarised society, and despite repeated efforts emanating from Venice, the permanent settlers soon began to 'go native'. Intermarriage between Venetians and the local aristocracy was frequent. Although those on the highest rungs of the social ladder were obliged to reaffirm their Catholic faith in each generation as a condition of renewing their titles, many minor branches of the same families soon quietly adopted Orthodoxy, or at least reached an easy accommodation with the majority religion. This came the more naturally because everyone who lived permanently in Crete had taken to speaking Greek within a few generations after the Venetians' arrival in 1211. In Crete, as elsewhere during those centuries, a regional dialect soon began to diverge from the Greek spoken elsewhere, in this case incorporating words and some characteristic sounds from the Italian spoken in Venice.[15] By the middle of the fifteenth century, poets were cultivating a written form of their regional dialect of Greek as a medium for sophisticated literary expression, the equivalent of Dante's Italian, Chaucer's English, or the Spanish of Cervantes.

The decisive change came around the middle of the sixteenth century. The threat from the Ottoman Turks was growing. After the fall of Cyprus, it became acute. The Venetian state was determined to invest heavily in strengthening this last bastion of its maritime empire abroad. At the most literal level, this meant a drastic reinforcement of the fortification walls surrounding the capital, known at the time as Candia or Kastro, today's Heraklion. One of the greatest military engineers of the age, Michele Sanmicheli, was drafted in from Venice to create a system of bastions, earthworks, and carefully cleared fields of fire to proof the town against the heaviest artillery that might be brought against it. Venetian Crete would be defended by the very latest technology that was available; there was to be no risk of Candia going the way of Constantinople in the previous century. The outlay for the Venetian treasury must have far exceeded any direct revenues that could have been expected to flow in the other direction. Modern historians see a transition at this time from a colonial relationship to one between a capital city and a province.[16]

The investment didn't stop at stones and mortar. The Venetians also set about, belatedly, winning over hearts and minds. The results would be spectacular—but of course, in Venetian Crete, just as in the Ottoman Empire, there were no Greeks in the very highest positions of power. The initial push came from above, from the rulers, even though it would be Greeks, for the most part writing and working in their own language, who would create the little-known miracle that today we call 'Renaissance Crete'.

Religious segregation was no longer enforced. The proselytizing Catholic order, the Society of Jesus (also known as the Jesuits), was expelled from the island shortly before 1600, once the authorities understood how far their activities were alienating the native population. A growing middle class in the thriving Cretan towns—Candia, Rethymno, and Chania—was gaining an ever greater share of overseas trade, which until this time had been jealously reserved for merchants from Venice. Education was largely in the hands of private tutors, rather than a matter for the state. But there seems to have been no lack of suitably qualified teachers in the Cretan towns. Legal documents that survive in the Venetian archives testify to an impressive level of literacy, for the time, among the island's townspeople.[17]

In this new climate, Cretan painters in the sixteenth and seventeenth centuries cultivated a subtle fusion of traditional Byzantine religious imagery with new elements, such as perspective, learned from Renaissance painters in Italy. Their work travelled far beyond the island to monasteries and churches in the Ottoman Empire and sometimes even to Venice. Domenikos Theotokopoulos, born in Candia in 1541, learned the art of painting in his native island and was already earning eyewatering prices for his work there before he left to seek his fortune in Italy. First in Venice, and then in Rome, Theotokopoulos developed his own idiosyncratic version of the high Renaissance style. But people found his name too much of a mouthful, so they called him 'il Greco' (the Greek) instead. Adapted to the hybrid Spanish-Italian form 'El Greco', this would become the name by which one of the greatest of all the religious painters of the Renaissance would become known to posterity, after he moved in 1577 to the city of Toledo in Spain. From the contents of his library, we know that El Greco had acquired a sound education in ancient Greek, as well as Latin and Italian. And to the end of his life, he would sign his works, in Greek script, with his given name, to which he would add 'the Cretan'.[18]

But to appreciate the fullest extent of the cultural fusion between east and west that was taking place in Venetian Crete around the turn of the seventeenth century, one has to turn to the poetry and drama written in the contemporary Cretan dialect of Greek. Plays had not been regularly performed in Greek anywhere for more than a thousand years. Now, new works were being written and staged in Candia, from at least the 1580s until the very last years of Venetian rule, when the town was under siege and Turkish cannonballs were falling inside Sanmicheli's fortification walls. Many of these works have been lost because no one ever thought to bring a printing press from Venice. Most of them circulated only in manuscript. Only a handful made it as far as the metropolis to be published there. But from manuscripts that survive, we learn yet another curious aspect of that fusion. Instead of writing in the traditional Greek script, authors who wrote in the contemporary Cretan dialect used the roman alphabet, giving the letters the same sound values as they have in Italian. Words on the page *look* at first sight like Italian, but as soon as you hear them spoken you recognise the distinctive sounds of Cretan Greek, as they can still be heard in Crete today.

The dramatist Georgios Chortatsis was only a few years younger than El Greco. His plays were probably written and first performed during the 1590s, at the very time when his younger contemporary, William Shakespeare, was embarking on his career in London. In Chortatsis's tragedy *Erophile*, a king's daughter falls in love with one of her father's courtiers and they are married in secret. The king, balked of his ambition to marry her off to royalty and in this way to establish a blue-blood dynasty, takes a terrible revenge. Pretending forgiveness, he invites Erophile to open the wedding present he has prepared for her. It turns out to contain the dismembered body of her beloved. By the end, almost everybody is dead—even the king, who in a rather daring move on the part of the dramatist is despatched, onstage, by the chorus of Erophile's serving maids.

Cretan comedies, by Chortatsis and others, follow conventions that had been revived by the Italian Renaissance and that go back, via Roman comedy, to the New Comedy of fourth-century-BCE Athens. Thwarted lovers overcome implausible obstacles, long-lost family members are reunited, and stock characters raise predictable laughs.[19] One of those is the schoolmaster, who in several plays has a lewd eye for his young male pupils and constantly shows off his proficiency in Italian and Latin. In *Katzarapos* by Chortatsis, and *Fortounatos*, written by Markos Antonios Foskolos half a century later in the 1650s, this character's learned utterances are constantly mistaken by other characters for hilariously inappropriate, or even obscene, statements in Greek.

For readers today, these word games are not merely a source of recondite amusement; they give us the best clues we could hope for to the background that these dramatists must have shared with their audiences. In the imagined world of Cretan comedy, just as in reality, Italian is the language of the highest social class, Latin of the educated. But it has been pointed out that not a single joke of this sort plays on *ancient* Greek.[20] Cretan dramatists seem to know of the ancient Greek world and its achievements only through the medium of Italian and Latin—that is to say, filtered through the prism of the Renaissance, which had already reinterpreted them in its own way. Plenty of Cretans in Chortatsis's day were capable of reading Aristotle or Aeschylus in the original, and we know that works by these authors were in circulation in Crete. But it seems that those who had been educated in the ancient language moved in different circles from the writers who brought the fresh air of the vernacular into an age-old tradition—exactly as Shakespeare and his contemporaries, also with a limited classical education, were doing at the same time in England.

The literary masterpiece of Venetian Crete, the romance, or novel in verse, *Erotokritos* by Vitsentsos Kornaros was probably completed within a few years either side of 1600. The author's name reveals him as one of the very numerous Cretan descendants of the famous Venetian aristocratic family of Correr. Sometimes wrongly called an 'epic', *Erotokritos* is a story of romantic love stretched out to some ten thousand lines and divided into the equivalent of the five acts of a stage play. It is at least as good as *The Old Arcadia* by Sir Philip Sidney, written at almost exactly the same time in Elizabethan England, and which it rather resembles. But unlike Sidney's prose romance, *Erotokritos* has never ceased to be read. Not only that, but from the seventeenth century to the twentieth, the poem would enjoy an afterlife that its author could surely never have imagined—sung all over the Cretan mountains by 'rhymesters' of little or no education, who have kept favourite passages alive as part of the oral tradition of the island. Today the name of the poem's male protagonist, Erotokritos, is revered in Crete as much as that of King Minos. There is probably still scarcely a Cretan alive who cannot recite, or at least recognise, the lines in which the hero bids farewell to his beloved Aretousa through the bars of her prison.[21]

The story is set 'in times of old, when Hellenes ruled', before the coming of Christianity; the action takes place:

> *in Athens which was the nursemaid of learning,*
> *the throne of power and fount of knowledge.*

Whatever Kornaros actually knew about ancient Athens, he is content to leave it at that. The characters worship the sun and moon rather than any actual ancient gods. But it soon turns out that the imagined world of *Erotokritos* is not so remote from the author's own time and place after all.[22]

In the second 'act', a tournament (still at that time a popular sport in Crete, and of course imported from the medieval west) brings together contestants from all over the *contemporary* Aegean. Among them are a 'prince of Byzantium' and a Cretan, who between them steal much of the action until eventually the prize in the contest goes to the story's hero, as it must. Charidimos, the Cretan, is pitted against a ferocious Turk who, we are told, 'was like a wild beast . . . and had great enmity toward the isle of Crete'. The rules of chivalry are cast aside as these two fight to the death. All in the crowd hold their breath, fearing for the life of the Cretan, whose 'virtue and wisdom and grace of speech' make him everyone's favourite.[23] Supposedly taking place in ancient Athens, the mortal combat between the Cretan and the Turk, and the bloody victory of the Cretan, seem to reflect in microcosm the conflict between Venetian Crete and the Ottoman Empire. The sympathy of the crowd for the knight Charidimos in turn implies solidarity between the Greek speakers for whom the story was written and the Venetian state in its struggle to survive.

For many Cretans, particularly those who lived in the towns or owned property in the country, that solidarity was evidently real and deep. Writing when it was all over, in exile in the Italian city of Padua, one of their number recalled at length the world he had known for the first fifty years of his life. Zuanne Papadopoli (Ioannis Papadopoulos in Greek) came of a landowning family of possibly Byzantine origin, which had at some point converted to Catholicism. He himself had served as an official in the Venetian administration. He writes in Italian, for the benefit of his new countrymen—who, he expects, will find much that he has to tell 'extraordinary', if not 'pure fiction . . . even though everything described . . . is perfectly true'.[24]

The Crete that Papadopoli remembers is a land of plenty. He fondly recalls the great variety of fish and meat, available in all seasons. Even turkeys were farmed in Crete, he tells us—evidently an early import from the New World—'as large and as fat as pigs', while snails were so plentiful that no one would sell them, and the poorest had available to them an abundance of a delicacy that is still much appreciated by Cretans today.[25] Malmsey wine, so called after the Malevizi winegrowing district close to the capital, was in demand as far away as England. So many sweet things were exported from Crete at this time that the name 'Candia', often used for the whole island as well as for the town, is the origin of the American English word 'candy'.

Papadopoli's nostalgia is evident and understandable; but he was well aware of the cracks beneath the foundations of the society that he so lovingly describes. At the top of the social pyramid, the blue-blooded descendants of the original colonial families he remembers as lazy, incompetent landlords who sat on their vast, accumulated wealth and made poor use of the yield of their estates. Their hired bodyguards, known as *bravi*, were notorious for the murders committed in the service of their masters, more often than not with impunity. Papadopoli's account of hot summer evenings in the capital, when bands of musicians sang and played and noble youths strutted around with their armed gangs, all too often looking for a fight, sounds exactly like a scene out of Shakespeare's *Romeo and Juliet*.[26]

At the base of the pyramid, and far more serious, was the plight of the rural peasants:

> The death-warrant for peasants in the Realm was galley service, because the villagers were obliged to be ready to serve as rowers, each time the Provveditor Generale wished to equip galleys by order of the Senate. For this purpose they would make a roll or census of all the villagers, drawing by lot two or three per village.[27]

This was no more humane than the Ottoman levy, the *devshirme*. Life expectancy of those taken for this service, again according to Papadopoli, would be no more than two or three years. And unlike those taken to serve the sultan, there was no chance of preferment, even for a lucky few. A century earlier, in Crete, similar levies had been used to raise the manpower needed to build the fortifications for the towns. One enlightened *Provveditore Generale* had warned his masters in Venice, back in 1589, that 'these unfortunates raise with their sweat and their blood those very walls which will shut them out in time of need and they will be left to the disposal of the enemy'. The same observer had also made the point that in Cyprus the Ottoman invaders had only been helped by the disaffection of a peasantry that had nothing left to lose.[28]

The warning would prove prophetic. But even though the Venetians were aware of the problem, neither the Senate in Venice nor the authorities in Candia would ever find a way to overcome it. The Venetians desperately needed the manpower drawn from the peasants of Crete. Although they had eventually conceded rights and privileges to the higher levels of Cretan society, it seems never to have occurred to their legislators to do the same for the peasants. Or perhaps they were simply afraid to put weapons into the hands of people whose forefathers had so often in the past risen up against them. As a result, the largest part of the population, outside the fortified towns, was not only deprived of protection but also of any incentive to buy into the state system. This was the fundamental reason why this most hopeful of hopeful monsters, which had far outstripped every previous attempt at fusion between Greek east and Latin west, was doomed, like all the others, to extinction.

BY THIS TIME, Greeks were on the move again—probably more than they ever had been since ancient times. Beginning in the fifteenth century, many had made new or temporary homes in Venice. In 1478, already some four thousand Greeks had settled in the city. A century later, that number had almost quadrupled. These were nearly all of them much humbler people than the professors who had brought the benefits of a Byzantine education to the west. Among trades recorded as being exercised by Greeks in Venice in the early sixteenth century, we find tailors, swordsmiths, barbers, carpenters, and builders, as well as mercenary soldiers, seamen, and merchants. Women are represented in the records by seamstresses and wet nurses, as well as, inevitably, 'housewives'.[29]

Arriving in such numbers, these artisans and traders were able to form their own community. Solitary teachers had been obliged to embrace Catholicism in order to practise, but this much larger group successfully petitioned to be allowed to build an Orthodox church for its members. After many delays, San Giorgio dei Greci opened its doors to its first congregations in 1573. Today, its belfry leaning slightly towards the canal that flanks it, the Greek church remains a well-known landmark in the Castello district of the city.

In an age when Europeans were setting out by ship to explore the entire globe, for some Greeks Venice served as a springboard to adventures much farther afield. Pedro de Candia, as his name suggests, came from Crete and was one of the thirteen companions of Francisco Pizarro who conquered Peru in the 1530s. Ioannis Phokas, born on the Venetian-ruled island of Cephalonia in the same decade, also took service with a king of Spain, Philip II this time. Phokas served on several voyages of exploration, sailing east by way of the Cape of Good Hope, across the Indian Ocean to China and then across the Pacific to the western seaboard of the Americas. Known in Spanish as Juan de Fuca, he was apparently the first European to navigate the channel that separates Vancouver Island, in Canada, from the northwestern tip of Washington State in the USA and which bears his name today.[30]

When the exceptionally well-travelled Nikandros Noukios, from Corfu, arrived in England in 1545 as part of an embassy from the Holy Roman Emperor Charles V to Henry VIII, he thought he was breaking new ground—and it is true that Noukios was the first Greek to record an account of a visit to the British Isles that we can read today. But not the least impressive aspect of his narrative is his encounter with a squad of Greek mercenaries serving in the English army, whose leader, one Thomas of Argos, he befriended. In the high-flown style that Noukios borrows from Herodotus, he attributes to his friend these rousing words as he prepared to lead his troop, in the service of the English king, into battle against the French:

We are sons of Hellenes and do not fear a swarm of barbarians. . . .
Let everyone say that men from Greece, finding themselves in the
remotest parts of Europe, showed themselves valorous in combat.

This speech is most unlikely ever to have been made, and certainly not in such terms as these. But Noukios shows a certain dogged determination in trying to revive the two-thousand-year-old distinction between 'Hellenes' and 'barbarians'—and to put it into the mouth of an army captain rousing his compatriots to fight for one lot of 'barbarians' (the English) against another (the French) in a distant land.[31]

These were evidently exceptional individuals—though it seems that mercenaries like the ones encountered by Noukios could be found in armies all over western Europe in his day. By far the greatest number of new journeys made by Greeks, during the sixteenth and seventeenth centuries, were trading voyages. The epicentre of this new burst of activity was not Venice, nor even Candia, but Constantinople. By the early 1600s, the total population of the Ottoman capital had risen to something between two and three hundred thousand. Of those, it has been estimated that a remarkable 40 per cent were Greek Orthodox. Constantinople was once again 'the capital of the Greek world'.[32]

At the very time when enterprising Greeks living under Venetian rule were winning the right to own their own ships and to buy and sell their own cargoes, their compatriots in Constantinople had acquired a near monopoly on seaborne trade in the Ottoman Empire. The Ottomans had long ago cancelled the privileges that the Byzantines had given away to their Italian commercial rivals. Steadily, ever since, it was Greeks who had moved in, to fill the vacuum left behind. New trading networks were being established by highly mobile Greek families, whose branches would spread out so as to straddle the great divide between east and west, between Islam and Christendom. Merchant houses based in Constantinople would work with family members strategically placed in Venice, Candia, or Corfu to control the exchange of goods over great distances. On the Aegean coast of Anatolia, the rise of Smyrna (today's Izmir) to become one of the great commercial centres of the eastern Mediterranean began spectacularly during the first decades of the seventeenth century, with a huge influx of Greeks, along with Armenians and Jews, who among them ran the burgeoning European trade. The time would come when Orthodox Greek speakers would outnumber the Muslim population of the city nicknamed in Turkish 'infidel Smyrna'.[33]

While the 'Cretan Renaissance' was enjoying its heyday under Venetian rule, Greek trading networks were once again spreading out across the Mediterranean and the Black Sea. Once more the Greek language could be heard from end to end of the maritime trade routes that had first been opened up some two thousand years before by the pioneer founders of Greek city-states during the 'age of experiment'. Greeks were learning to find advantages to living between two opposing worlds. And in the process, the foundations for the great Greek shipping dynasties of the nineteenth and twentieth centuries were already being laid.

THE FINAL ACT for Venetian Crete began almost by accident. In the summer of 1644, an Ottoman ship carrying pilgrims on their way to Mecca was captured in the Aegean by a flotilla sent out from Malta, the headquarters of the Knights of Saint John. The Ottomans were determined to punish this act of blatant piracy. But the last time they had sent a fleet against Malta, almost a century before, it had ended badly. Malta, lying so far to the west, would be of little use to them in any case. Crete, on the other hand, was much closer and had long been coveted. Technically, the Venetian authorities in Crete were implicated, since the prize and its captors had stopped off briefly at Candia on their way home. No one in either Crete or Venice was expecting it when the Ottoman fleet put ashore a huge fighting force in western Crete at the end of

June 1645. Chania capitulated after a siege that lasted two months. Rethymno was next, the following year.[34]

Exactly as wiser counsels had predicted, there was little resistance to the invaders on the part of the local peasantry. As a result, by 1648, the whole island, with the exception of Candia and a handful of fortresses, was under Ottoman control. The new rulers moved swiftly to install an Orthodox archbishop and an Orthodox hierarchy. At a stroke, the restrictions that the Venetians had maintained for four and a half centuries were swept away. For the Orthodox peasants who had resented for so long the 'popish mitre', the 'Turkish turban' was definitely to be preferred. There were some who went even further: so great was their pent-up hatred of the Venetians that many Cretan villagers embraced Islam and chose to fight alongside the invaders who now laid siege to Candia, and against their former masters. According to one contemporary western account, by 1657, sixty thousand Cretans had converted—almost a quarter of the island's total population before the war, and far more than had ever been prepared to give up their Orthodox traditions for the rival Catholic branch of their own religion.[35]

Everywhere outside the capital, the 'Cretan Renaissance' was already at an end. But the fortifications of Candia, that had been reinforced by Sanmicheli in the previous century, were proving their worth. For twenty-one years, every assault failed. And since the Ottoman navy was never able to impose an effective blockade, the defenders could be supplied by sea, even though they were completely cut off from their own hinterland. By the end, most of the Catholic powers of Europe had rallied to the defence of this last outpost of western influence in the eastern Mediterranean. Spain sent money and supplies; several French contingents arrived at different times and were either killed or departed again. At one point the Venetians even entertained hopes of help from Protestant

England. Mercenary 'soldiers of fortune' from all nations, including English and Scots, found their way to Candia to aid the cause.[36]

Native Cretans fought bravely alongside them. Overwhelmingly, these were the townspeople, those who had most fully invested in the Veneto-Cretan way of life. The chronicler of the war, Marinos Tzane Bounialis, writing up the story in verse in Cretan Greek shortly afterwards, went out of his way to emphasise the loyalty of those native 'Romans' (Orthodox Greek speakers) who made common cause with the 'Franks' (Catholics, whether Venetian or from elsewhere). But even he could not gloss over the defection of some highly placed individuals as the pressures of the siege took their toll. And the besiegers evidently found it worth their while to invest large sums in bribes to encourage more.[37]

The final act was not a battle but a negotiation. The Turks could not break through the walls. The defenders had just been weakened by the departure of the latest contingent that had recently arrived from France. They had had enough. At the end of August 1669, two representatives from each side met in secret to hammer out terms of surrender. In command of the defence was the last *Provveditore Generale*, Francesco Morosini; the besiegers were led by the formidable grand vizier, Fazil Ahmed Köprülü. Representing Morosini were a Scotsman and a Greek from the local Cretan aristocracy; representing the vizier were a Turk and another Greek, this time from Chios, by the name of Panagiotis Nikousios.

Sharing the same language and interpreting between the Scotsman (presumably in Italian) and the Turk, the two Greeks seem to have done their utmost to advance the interests of their respective sides. Without that bridge of language and the negotiating skills that had been honed by generations of doing business right across the divided Mediterranean, there could have been no peaceful end to the siege. What the Greek speakers representing each party thought of those on the other is much harder to gauge. Bounialis, for instance, has nothing but contempt for those on his own side who defected to the enemy. But he writes with the greatest respect of the Greek representative of the Ottomans at these negotiations ('Panagiotakis the Roman', he calls him), even while he harbours not the slightest doubt that this fellow Greek is the bitterest of enemies.[38]

And so, in the last days of September 1669, the Venetians sailed away in their galleys. With them went the foreign fighters who had remained and most of the population who had stayed in the town to the last. Many would find new homes in the Ionian Islands, in Venice itself, or elsewhere in Venetian territory in Italy, as Zuane Papadopoli did in Padua. The Greek Orthodox population of Venice would grow yet again, by many thousands. The boundaries between the Islamic east and the Christian west had shifted. Greek speakers remained as deeply embedded as ever in each of those opposing worlds and would soon find new ways to exploit their unique facility for moving between them.

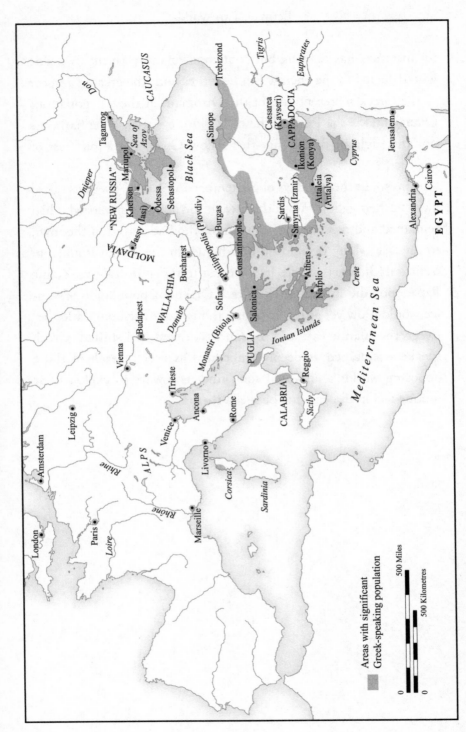

13. The Greek world in the late eighteenth century

13

'GREEK REVIVAL'

1669–1833

VENETIAN CRETE WAS no more. But the last of the great armed struggles between the Ottoman Empire and the Christian states of Europe still had another half century to run. Almost every Greek speaker who lived through them must have been affected by these convulsions. Once again, we find Greeks in arms serving in the ranks of opposing sides, whether forcibly conscripted or as paid mercenaries. And once again the best Greek minds of the age would be tested by the challenge of negotiating peace—on behalf of masters who belonged to a different faith and language.

Fourteen years after the surrender of Candia, in 1683, emboldened by their success in Crete, Ottoman land forces struck northwards and westwards through the Balkans to lay siege to Vienna for the second time. For two months, during the late summer of that year, it looked as though the Habsburg capital would go the way of Candia. But once again, reinforcements from other Catholic states arrived just in time, and on this occasion their intervention was decisive. The retreat from Vienna and a string of defeats in the Balkans during the years that followed mark the turning point of Ottoman fortunes in mainland Europe.[1]

The Venetians were quick to take advantage. Although Crete proved too distant and too strong to take back, Venetian forces, once again under the command of Francesco Morosini, seized control of almost all the southern mainland of Greece, including the whole of the Peloponnese, between 1685 and 1687. Athens was briefly taken at the end of the latter year—though not before a cannonball, fired into the Parthenon from a Venetian battery, had ignited gunpowder stored inside. The resulting explosion blew off the roof and caused much of the two-thousand-year-old building to collapse.

Venice had never before possessed so much of the Greek mainland. But the native Greek-speaking population had no enthusiasm for this enforced change of masters—since the Catholic Venetians were far less tolerant of their Orthodox faith and practices than the Ottomans had been. No one, now, was talking of union between the Catholic and Orthodox Churches. The indifference of the local Greeks is probably the main reason why the fortunes of war soon swung back the other way. When hostilities broke out again in 1714, the Venetians were forced to abandon everything that they had gained and, the year after, left the Greek mainland for good. Venice would never recover from the demands of its last, short-lived campaign in Greece.

The Ottoman Empire, too, was changing. The centuries of conquest were over. And as the empire changed, its rulers found themselves in need of skills that had not been much prized before this time. This was where the most highly educated among the Greek-speaking Orthodox Christians in Constantinople came into their own. Panagiotis Nikousios, who had served as one of the two negotiators for the Ottoman side in the closing stages of the siege of Candia, had studied medicine at the University of Padua. It was as a physician that Nikousios had first gained the confidence of the grand vizier whom he served. Like many sons of wealthy Greek families in the capital, Nikousios was also proficient in half a dozen languages, ancient and modern, as well as Ottoman

Turkish. His reward was to be promoted to the newly created office of Grand Dragoman, or interpreter. From then on, the grand dragoman would become the senior diplomat in the Ottoman service. For more than a century, this office would be held exclusively by wealthy and highly educated Greek-speaking Orthodox subjects of the empire.[2]

It fell to Alexandros Mavrokordatos, the second grand dragoman, to represent the sultan in a still more demanding diplomatic task. In 1688, the Ottomans were losing badly to the Austrians and Hungarians. Negotiations failed on that occasion. But eleven years later, Mavrokordatos deserves a large share of the credit for the first peace treaty ever to be signed between the Ottoman Empire and an alliance of European powers at Karlowitz (today's Sremci Karlovski, in Serbia) in 1699. With consummate skill, Mavrokordatos gained the confidence of the representatives of Russia, Austria, and France, as well as of his own side. It has been speculated that the grand dragoman may have been acting as a quadruple agent; on the other hand, just as Nikousios had done in Crete, Mavrokordatos did at least secure the best possible terms for his Ottoman masters.[3] The treaty of Karlowitz would soon be broken. But a precedent had been set. And after the Ottomans had defeated the Venetians in the Peloponnese, and in turn had been beaten by the Austrians in the Balkans, a second treaty was signed at Passarowitz, today's Požarevac, not far from Belgrade, on 21 July 1718. And this time the peace would hold (more or less) for half a century.[4]

NOW THE STAGE was set for other highly placed Greeks to follow where Nikousios and Mavrokordatos had led. Learning, usually gained at a university in the west, was the passport to success. Soon, not only the role of grand dragoman but also other trusted positions in the Ottoman administration would become effectively Greek prerogatives. In this way a semiofficial Greek-speaking aristocracy arose within the Ottoman elite. These people would become known as 'Phanariots', from the name of the district in the capital where the Ecumenical Patriarchate was (and is still) housed—Phanari in Greek, today the Fener quarter of Istanbul. Orthodox Christians were of course still excluded from the very highest levels of government (Greeks could only reach those by converting to Islam); but as the eighteenth century progressed, the tight-knit Greek-speaking community of Phanariots would become an increasingly indispensable part of the Ottoman system.[5]

Individuals rose to prominence through a combination of successful commercial enterprise, state privilege, and a foreign education. It was a self-perpetuating cycle. The profits of trade could be invested in the education of the next generation. Education and wealth together would open the door to a privileged position in the service of the state, which had to be bought. Offices of state would bring still greater profits to the holder, and these could be ploughed back to renew the cycle. For this Greek-speaking aristocracy, mobility was the key to success. Theirs was an often precarious existence: tenure of the most coveted positions tended to be short, and many an illustrious career would end in impoverishment or execution. But it was not a closed system. As some fell from grace, there was always scope for new entrants to climb up from below.[6]

The centre of gravity for the Phanariots was naturally the capital. But from early in the eighteenth century, many of these families found themselves exported northwards, into the buffer zones that separated the Ottoman from the Habsburg and Russian Empires. The provinces of Wallachia and Moldavia, which together make up two-thirds of today's Romania and lie immediately to the north of the Danube, had remained technically Ottoman territory after the treaty of Passarowitz. But because their populations were almost entirely Orthodox Christian, successive sultans delegated the task of ruling them, not to the native population, the ancestors of today's

Romanians, but to members of the Greek Phanariot aristocracy. In this way, throughout the eighteenth century, not just the ruling families but also a whole supporting network of Greek-speaking bureaucrats came to be transferred from Constantinople to Bucharest and Jassy (modern Iaşi) and to put down roots there.

At the same time, Greek speakers in humbler walks of life were becoming more mobile than ever. Opportunities for trade brought more and more of them to move beyond the bounds of the Ottoman Empire. In London, the first coffee houses were opened in the 1660s by 'Nicholas the Grecian' and one Georgios Konstantinos, whose shop was known as 'The Grecian'. Soon the nucleus of a community had grown up in the Soho district of the capital, where the name 'Greek Street' remains to this day. The first Orthodox church in London opened its doors in Greek Street in 1681. During the next century, others would follow in most of the great commercial centres of Europe—Vienna, Trieste, Livorno, Marseille, Paris, Amsterdam. By the end of that century, communities would be established as far away as Calcutta and Dacca in Bengal in one direction, and Argentina in another.[7]

The closing decades of the century saw huge new opportunities open that would set in motion an even larger migration of Greek-speaking Orthodox Christians. The century of relative peace between the sultans and their western neighbours also saw the start of a series of wars against Russia. One of these conflicts, fought between 1768 and 1774, for the first time brought a Russian fleet from Saint Petersburg, by way of the Atlantic, into the eastern Mediterranean. Encouraged by Russian propaganda, the Greek-speaking regions of Crete and the Peloponnese rose up in revolt in 1770. These were the first really serious rebellions against Ottoman rule—more than three hundred years after the conquest of Constantinople—and they were brutally suppressed. No Russian troops landed to make common cause with their Orthodox co-religionists. But Russia still came off best and succeeded in annexing from the Ottoman Empire the whole northern shore of the Black Sea and its hinterland.

It then became the policy of Catherine the Great, the Russian empress, to populate 'New Russia', as these territories became known, with Christians from the Ottoman Empire. Many thousands of Greeks had been compromised with the Ottoman authorities during the recent revolts, whether they had actively participated or not. The offer of grants of land to farm in a new, Orthodox homeland proved irresistible. For the first time since the 'Empire of Trebizond' had capitulated to Mehmed II in 1461, Greek speakers had the possibility to live under a Christian Orthodox administration, as subjects of the Russian tsars. It has been estimated that a quarter of a million answered the call.[8] Urban communities grew up in Taganrog on the Sea of Azov and in the newly founded cities of Odessa, Mariupol, and Sebastopol (the last two with lightly Russianised Greek names). The rich grain-growing country of New Russia, after centuries of neglect, once again became a source of prosperity, just as it had been in ancient times.

The immigrant Greeks started out as farmers, but most soon gave up the land and went into trade. In this they were immeasurably assisted by the family networks that many maintained, whether back in the Ottoman Empire, farther west in Europe, or both. These networks would go on to dominate the international trade in Russian grain until the late nineteenth century. By the end of the eighteenth, Greek-owned merchant ships made up the largest fleet in the eastern Mediterranean, with a thousand 'deep-seagoing' vessels trading, mainly under the Ottoman flag.[9] The map of Greek mercantile communities flourishing by that time—from the Sea of Azov in the east to Marseille in the west—by a quirk of history seems almost to re-create the pattern of the seventh century BCE. The historical circumstances, of course, were completely different, as the Greek language itself tacitly acknowl-edges. The term used for these modern communities established abroad is not *apoikia* ('home from home' in the ancient world) but *paroikia*, which means roughly 'a home in a foreign land'.

This time, it was not just by sea that trading activity was becom-ing concentrated in Greek hands. The great rivers of southeastern Europe and Russia—the Danube, the Don, and the Dnieper—were opening up to the movement of ever more goods by water. Greeks, originally from Crete and the Aegean islands, traded wine as far north as Poland. At the same time, if probably on a smaller scale, overland trade was growing, too, both inside the Ottoman Empire and beyond its borders. From urban centres in the north of today's Greece, caravans of camels set out to cross the mountain ranges of the Balkans to connect with the great artery of the Danube.[10]

By THE SECOND half of the eighteenth century, Greek elites of varying size, wealth, and political influence were established in Constantinople, in the Danubian principalities (as Wallachia and Moldavia were collectively known), in the Ionian Islands, and in southern Russia, as well as in many cities of western and central Europe. Of all these places, only the Ionian Islands, which at the time still belonged to a now-fading Venetian Republic, would even-tually become part of the Greek state as we know it today; most lie far beyond its borders.

Indeed, the Greek-speaking world of the eighteenth century was nothing like a modern state. Even the relatively settled majority—the peasant farmers, herders, and fishermen who rarely make it into the history books—lived spread out across a wide geographical area. Beginning in the west with the Ionian Islands, this took in the Greek peninsula, an arc of the Balkan mainland bordering the northern Aegean, all of the islands as far south as Crete, parts of the western Anatolian seaboard, and detached enclaves in Cyprus,

Cappadocia in central Anatolia, and Pontos in the northeast. In many of these areas, and particularly outside the towns, Greek speakers undoubtedly made up the largest part of the population. But there was no single heartland where *everybody* spoke Greek as a first language. Wherever you went in all those regions, you would hear other languages being spoken in the street, see other languages and scripts in use in public signs. Most people must have been able to function with a smattering of one or more languages other than their own.

The wider Greek world that was taking shape during the eighteenth century has often been described as a *diaspora*—a Greek word meaning 'dispersal', which had first been applied to the Jews. But the idea of a dispersal presupposes the existence of a corresponding centre. In the case of the Greeks in the eighteenth century, there *was* no centre.[11] This was a world that rather more resembled the Hellenistic one created by the conquests of Alexander—with the difference that this time Greek speakers were not the rulers but the ruled.

There was another similarity, too, though once again the historical reasons for it were quite different. Education in the Ottoman Empire was left to the different religious communities to organise for themselves. Schools had been established by the Orthodox Church in Constantinople since shortly after the conquest. The eighteenth century saw a massive expansion of education aimed at the Christian population, directed by the church, in urban centres wherever there was a community large enough to make a school viable. From the beginning, the language of instruction was Greek. Essentially, this was a more modest continuation of the old Byzantine programme of education. The Greek language had never lost its prestige; it remained the bureaucratic language of the Ecumenical Patriarchate, and therefore of the higher clergy throughout the empire. As schools began to proliferate in the eighteenth century, those who were destined to become merchants or doctors, bureaucrats, priests, or sometimes even high officials in the Ottoman system would learn to read and write in Greek—even if the family spoke a Slavonic language, or Albanian, or Wallachian (Romanian) at home.[12] *Becoming Greek* was once again in fashion in the European provinces of the Ottoman Empire, and once again it brought practical as well as intellectual benefits.

IN MANY PARTS of Christian Europe, too, Greek ways of thinking and doing were in fashion as never before. The eighteenth century was the era of Neoclassicism in the arts and of the Enlightenment in philosophy and the sciences. The century of the Enlightenment has also been called the Age of Reason because the new ideas that were being pioneered and promoted, particularly in France, were systematically based on rational principles. These, too, went back to the earliest years of Greek philosophy.

Although the actual business of government in most of the larger European states was conducted along autocratic lines, educated individuals began to exchange ideas about what might be the best, and most *rational*, form of government for human societies—just as once upon a time had happened in the ancient Greek city-states. Inevitably, this brought many of the new thinkers, either implicitly or explicitly, into conflict with the Catholic church—an institution that of course had no equivalent in the ancient world. Out of this ferment of ideas came the 'social contract' of Geneva-born Jean-Jacques Rousseau, who first began to articulate the concept of the nation as a voluntary association of individuals and groups who surrender some of their liberties in return for corresponding rights. These ideas would transform the political landscape of large parts of the world during the next three centuries.[13]

The *Encyclopaedia, or Systematic Dictionary of the Sciences, Arts, and Crafts*, published in Paris in multiple volumes between 1751 and 1772, became an extended manifesto for the Age of Reason. *Encyclopaedia*, as the editor in chief Denis Diderot explained, was a modern word based on ancient Greek, intended to mean 'joined up knowledge'. The avowed aim of the project, he went on, was nothing less than to 'change the common way of thinking'. Elsewhere in the *Encyclopaedia*, *civilisation*, another new and still rare word in French, was presented as the gift of 'the illustrious dead, the sages of antiquity . . . sacred shades, the objects of veneration'. First among those, in a long list of philosophers and lawgivers drawn from the ancient Greek world, comes Socrates, who 'braved the fury of tyrants, without fearing for his life, without fearing death, knowing no other masters than the sacred laws of enlightened reason'.[14]

Those words were published in 1765. A year earlier, the German art historian Johann Joachim Winckelmann had brought out his *History of the Art of Antiquity*. This extraordinarily influential work set out the bold new claim that the greatest heights of European art and the human spirit had been reached not by the ancient Romans but by the Greeks before them. According to Winckelmann, who had never been there, this was because Greece was blessed with a perfect climate. As a consequence, he maintained, not only the arts but political liberty, too, had been perfected in the Greek city-states. 'The only way for us [moderns] to become great', he famously asserted, 'is to imitate the Ancients.' As the emerging modern civilisation of Europe began to define itself and to gain confidence, the intellectual, artistic, and political inheritance from the ancient Greek city-states, along with republican Rome, became deeply embedded in the entire project. From now on, the building of a modern, 'Western' civilisation would be founded on the rediscovery—as well as, often, the distortion or reinvention—of the legacy of the Greeks of antiquity.[15]

During the decades that spanned the turn of the nineteenth century, the craze for things Greek was beginning to make its mark on the appearance of cities, not only in Europe but also wherever Europeans were establishing their presence as colonists on other continents. In town planning, the grid plan that went back to Hippodamus of Miletus in the fifth century BCE and that had been adopted for all the new Greek cities founded in the wake of Alexander's conquests, was revived in places as far apart as the 'New Town' of Edinburgh, begun in the latter part of the eighteenth century, and a few decades later, in several cities in North America and in Melbourne and Adelaide in Australia. In the early years of the nineteenth, the Scottish capital even began to pride itself on being known as the 'New Athens' or the 'Athens of the North'.[16]

At the same time, the neoclassical trend reached a late peak in a 'Greek Revival' that would soon leave its mark on the monumental architecture of several continents. When a new parish church was built for what was then a suburb of expanding London between 1819 and 1822, its design faithfully reproduced features of the temple on the Acropolis of Athens known as the Erechtheion—including a 'Caryatid' porch, in which the columns take the form of draped female figures. Now grime-stained from decades of London pollution, the Caryatids of Saint Pancras New Church stare severely over the heads of pedestrians and traffic too busy to take much notice of them as they pass by on Euston Road. Winckelmann's injunction to 'imitate the ancients' had fallen on fertile ground.

Wealthy connoisseurs of art from all over western Europe competed with one another to bring back prized examples of ancient Greek sculpture to their own countries. However shocking to modern sensibilities, this was a practice as much taken for granted at the time as the establishment of European colonies abroad. In the case of antiquities, it was driven by a new and emerging sense of the cultural value of the objects acquired. The most notorious of these collectors, Thomas Bruce, Seventh Earl of Elgin, removed about half of the sculpted blocks that make up the frieze of the

Parthenon between 1801 and 1803. At first, Elgin had intended to use them as a prestige adornment for his country seat in Scotland. It was only unforeseen circumstances that led to the sculptures being put on public exhibition in London and, eventually, in 1816, being acquired by the British Museum.

Elgin's actions were highly controversial at the time and have continued to arouse competing passions ever since. But it was the arrival of the 'Elgin Marbles' in London and the artistic judgements of the connoisseurs of the day that finally set the seal on Winckelmann's bold claim. For the first time, the most intricate artwork that had once formed part of the rebuilding of the Acropolis of Athens in the 530s BCE could be seen in its original form in a Western city. And enough people were convinced that, yes, this was indeed superior to the best productions of ancient Rome, that the opinion has never seriously been challenged since. The marbles had passed to a dull climate in a distant land, but the prestige of their homeland and the people who had produced them had never been higher since at least the time of the Roman emperor Hadrian.[17]

Travellers, in increasing numbers, returned to northern Europe from seeking out the traces of Greek civilisation in the Ottoman Empire and published accounts of what they had seen and experienced. The young George Gordon, Lord Byron, suddenly became the most famous of these when he published his travelogue in verse, *Childe Harold's Pilgrimage*, in 1812. Byron speculated whether it could be possible for an ancient civilisation to come back from the dead, reincarnated by its modern heirs. Less poetically, other travellers were asking themselves and their readers the same question.[18] And thanks to the astonishing success of his youthful work (Byron was only twenty-four when his poem was published), the speculative possibility of a literal Greek revival reached into households not only throughout Great Britain but also, in translation, in every corner of the European continent. By 1821, a vaguely undefined

'Greece' was at the forefront of public consciousness all over Europe, as well as in the young United States of America.

CONTEMPORARY GREEKS WERE well aware of these developments, whether they lived in the Ottoman Empire or in communities scattered across Europe. With the rapid spread of Greek schools and the movement of goods by Greek entrepreneurs, ideas travelled far and fast. As literacy increased, there was ever more demand for printed books. There were no printing presses in Constantinople (except for brief, short-lived experiments) before the nineteenth century, and elsewhere in the Ottoman Empire only in Wallachia and Moldavia, where they were sponsored by the Phanariot rulers and the Orthodox Church. But Greek publishing houses flourished in many European cities. Chief among these was Venice, where printing in Greek had begun at the turn of the fifteenth century. By the end of the eighteenth, Greek presses had been established in Vienna, Leipzig, Budapest, Trieste, Moscow, and Saint Petersburg. Among them, these presses produced some 120,000 volumes during the century before 1821, most of them translations from Western languages. Books were not prevented from circulating in Ottoman territory; many, if not most, of the readers of these ones would have been Ottoman subjects. In this way, the new secular ideas of the European Enlightenment found their way to the hearts and minds of Greek speakers, wherever they were to be found. And in response, a 'Greek Enlightenment' grew up during the second half of the century.[19]

Educated Greeks were now reading the same books as their Western counterparts. If Socrates and a dozen other 'heroes' of the intellect and of battles such as Thermopylae and Salamis could inspire the veneration of the editors of the *Encyclopaedia*, they had never been forgotten, either, by those who continued to speak and write in a form of their own Greek language. Knowledge of the ancient 'classics' had, after all, never been lost in the Greek-speaking east. If the nations of Europe were starting to define their own identity in terms that went back to the ancient city-states, was it not time for enlightened Greeks to claim a portion of that inheritance for themselves?[20]

This was not as simple a proposition as it might sound. Greek speakers still overwhelmingly thought of themselves as 'Romans': in the language of the time, *Romioi*, pronounced *Romyí*. To be a *Romios*, or (in the feminine) *Romia*, meant above all to be an Orthodox Christian. In the Ottoman Empire, the spread of secular education had been very largely sponsored by the Orthodox Church. This meant that in the Orthodox east there was none of the tension between established religion and the new ideas of the Enlightenment that was so characteristic of the movement in the West—at least until the very end of the eighteenth century. On the other hand, when foreigners wrote about 'Greece' and 'Greeks' in their own languages, they did so in a purely secular sense. And to confuse matters further, they applied these names equally to both ancient and modern times. This was impossible in Greek because the ancients were still known by the ancient name of 'Hellenes'. But ever since the time of Julian the Apostate in the fourth century CE, this name had signified not just an *ancient* but a *pagan* people. Modern Romans and ancient Hellenes may have been united by their language, but bonds of religion went just as deep, and in those terms, the pagan Hellenes were almost as alien as the Muslim Turks or the western Catholics or Protestants.

The idea of a bloodline had counted for little during most of the intervening centuries (Plethon, in the fifteenth century, had been the exception). But now that those long-dead Hellenes were being lionised in ever more exalted terms in the foreign books that Greeks were reading and translating into their own language, it was time for this to change. The solution that they came up with was to begin to think of themselves as the sons, or the children, of the Hellenes of old. It helped that the phrase that most naturally expressed this idea in the semiformal written Greek of the time was identical to the war cry of the Greeks at the battle of Salamis, as reported in Aeschylus's drama *The Persians*: 'Sons of Hellenes, onward.' It was becoming a matter of pride that the Hellenes of old had been the *ancestors*; today's Romans were their descendants.[21]

And because so many of those books written in other languages described the ancient Greeks as a nation, could not the same be said of the moderns, too? In the 1780s, the essayist and educational reformer Dimitrios Katartzis, writing in Greek at the Phanariot court in Bucharest, could urge: 'We can become once again a nation, civilised and envied, to the extent that we are able to approach the education of our ancestors.' A few years later, a book called *Modern Geography*, published in Greek in Vienna in 1791, gives the ancient name of 'Hellas' to the southern Balkan peninsula and the islands of the Aegean, while the people who live there are described as 'modern Hellenes' and the descendants of an ancient 'nation'.[22]

This was the beginning of a process that within three decades, between 1790 and 1820, would transform the way that many, if not yet most, Greek speakers thought about themselves. From 'sons of Hellenes' or 'modern Hellenes' it was a small step for *contemporary* Greeks to become simply 'Hellenes'. At the same time, Orthodox Greek Christians began giving their children ancient names alongside their baptismal ones. Names like Themistocles, Pericles, Odysseus for boys and Penelope, Calliope, or Aspasia for girls begin to appear in the record. New family names were coined in the ancient way, by adding the suffix *-ides* or *-ades* to a personal name, just as in the *Odyssey*, Odysseus the son of Laertes had been known as Laertiades.

This was the surest sign that ordinary people, and not just intellectuals, were beginning to think of the ancients as part of the same *family* as themselves. The 'hellenizing of the *Romioi*', as it has been called, was the biggest reinvention by Greek speakers since the much more gradual one that had taken place under Roman rule some fifteen hundred years earlier. It was fuelled by ideas that came from western Europe. And it went hand in hand with another series of changes that were literally revolutionary.[23]

In July 1776, on the far side of the Atlantic, the American Declaration of Independence set out the 'self-evident truths' that 'all men are created equal' and enjoy an 'inalienable' right to 'Life, Liberty and the pursuit of Happiness'. Seven years later, the United States of America won recognition as an independent republic after defeating the colonial power, Great Britain. Then in 1789, again in July, the storming of the Bastille fortress in Paris set in train the events we now know as the French Revolution. Under the slogan *Liberté, Egalité, Fraternité*, revolutionaries went on to overturn the centuries-old autocratic French monarchy, abolish the role and privileges of the Catholic church, and turn France into a 'republic' made up of 'citizens'. Some of the political organisation of the French revolutionary republic, while it lasted, and much of the rhetoric associated with it, were deliberately based on names and rituals revived from republican Rome. If the revolutionary French could be heirs to one ancient republic, perhaps similarly minded Greeks could revive the glories of another—in their case, democratic Athens? In some quarters, particularly among the expatriate communities of merchants abroad, and in the intellectual circles of the Danubian principalities, enthusiasm was spreading fast enough to alarm the Ottoman authorities and the highest echelons of the Orthodox Church.[24]

In the Ionian Islands, it reached fever pitch in the summer of 1797. At the end of June, a French expeditionary force landed to take possession. Napoleon Bonaparte, at the time 'first consul' of the French Republic, had recently forced the submission of Venice and despatched a fleet of French warships to take over the foreign dominions that had belonged to the now defunct 'Most Serene Republic'. For two years after that, the Greek Orthodox population of the Ionian Islands experienced what it was like to be called 'citizens' and to be given rights, at least notionally. Elsewhere, idealistic intellectuals, educated in the Enlightenment tradition—Rigas of Velestino in Vienna, Adamantios Korais (also known as Coray) in Paris—set about imagining in philosophical terms what a newly liberated Greece might look like. Theirs were among a chorus of voices, many of them anonymous, urging their fellow Greeks, in patriotic poems and pamphlets, to rise up against their Ottoman masters and break free. In parts of the Ottoman Empire, as well as in European cities, Greek revolutionary anthems began to be composed and sung to the tune of the French 'La Marseillaise'.[25]

Not all Greeks were so enthusiastic. In 1798, the Ecumenical Patriarchate of the Orthodox Church issued a stern encyclical that condemned 'the much-vaunted political programme of liberty'. God himself had 'raised up out of nothing the mighty empire of the Ottomans' so as to rule over the Orthodox faithful for their own ultimate good and to guarantee the 'salvation of the chosen peoples'.[26] While some Greeks looked eagerly to the west and saw themselves as 'new Hellenes' and potential citizens of a modern state on the French revolutionary model, the majority of Orthodox Romans, from the patriarch of Constantinople down to the humblest goatherd in the mountains or fisherman in the islands, had far more to lose than to gain from revolutionary change.

But, whatever might have been the preference of the majority, among Greeks as elsewhere in Europe, something that had been born during the French Revolution had come to stay. This spirit survived almost twenty years of the Napoleonic Wars, during which the French Republic became the French Empire, and the first consul Napoleon became emperor. No part of Europe was left untouched by these wars. After Napoleon was defeated, for the first time in 1814 and then decisively at the Battle of Waterloo in June 1815, the representatives of the European powers gathered in Vienna to determine the future shape of the continent. The French Revolution and its aftermath were at an end. Nothing like this must ever happen again.

So was born the 'Concert of Europe', an alliance of predominantly autocratic states that determined to establish a new international order, from the Atlantic to the Urals. But the ideas that had fanned out across the continent were not to be so easily suppressed; across the Atlantic they had already taken hold. Between 1811 and 1825, the Spanish and Portuguese colonial possessions in South America followed the example of their counterparts farther north and won their independence through wars of liberation. Even within Europe, undercurrents were swirling just beneath the surface. By 1820, secret societies had sprung up in many countries; clandestine activity was rife. In the summer of that year, first in Spain and then in Naples, capital of the 'Kingdom of the Two Sicilies', bloodless revolutions compelled monarchs to grant parliamentary constitutions to their subjects. A full-scale uprising in northern Italy, much of it at the time ruled by Austria, was planned for early in 1821. In France, the elderly Marquis de Lafayette, a veteran of both the American and the French Revolutions, noted at the time: 'The friends of liberty were never in such perfect sympathy as in this moment of European crisis.'[27]

Every one of these revolutionary projects would prove abortive. But Greek speakers had been forming societies, too. Most of these were ostensibly cultural rather than political. Their members made good use of the Greek printing presses that existed in several cities of Europe to exchange and disseminate views which could broadly be described as liberal. But one of these societies operated underground, and its aims were avowedly violent: the Friendly Society, also known in English by its Greek name, *Philiki Etairia*, was a secret society dedicated to a war of liberation. It was said to have been founded by Greek merchants in the (then) Russian city of Odessa in 1814, though this often repeated story has been questioned. The Friendly Society may actually have begun life in the Ottoman capital, and not until three years later.

Like all these clandestine societies, this one derived its rituals from Freemasonry. From the records of its activities, it seems that the members of the Friendly Society relished the secrecy and mystification of their ceremonies almost as much as the extreme means by which they prepared to pursue their goal. During the last months of 1820, an ambitious scheme was hatched: to strike at the heart of Ottoman power by setting fire to the fleet in the Golden Horn and simultaneously starting fires in the streets of Constantinople. In the ensuing general panic, the Orthodox population was to rise up and take over control of the capital.[28]

Events would turn out very differently. But by the beginning of the 1820s, revolutionary fervour was running high in at least some parts of the Greek-speaking world and through some sections of the population—both inside and outside the Ottoman Empire. Few people alive anywhere at the beginning of the 1820s, probably, would have bet on a Greek revolution being any more successful than so many others that had failed, still less on what the outcome might be if by any chance it did succeed. There is little sign that the secretive leadership of the Friendly Society had much of an idea. But a revolution carried out by men and women who now thought of themselves as *Hellenes*, in the name of an ancient nation in which so many progressive Europeans, and indeed Americans, believed that they, too, had a stake—that would turn out to be another proposition entirely.

It BEGAN ON 6 March 1821 (or 22 February according to the calendar in use in southeastern Europe at the time). A senior officer in the Russian imperial service slipped across the River Pruth, with a handful of retainers, from Kishinev (today's Chişinău, capital of Moldova) in what was then Russian territory into Ottoman-controlled Moldavia. Like many high-ranking Russians in those days, his native language was Greek. His name was Alexandros Ypsilantis, and he had recently become leader of the Friendly Society. Two days later, in Jassy, the Moldavian capital, Ypsilantis issued a proclamation headed 'Fight for Faith and Fatherland':

> The hour has come, o Men of Hellas! . . . The enlightened peoples
> of Europe . . . full of gratitude for the benefits bequeathed by our
> Ancestors to themselves, eagerly await the liberty of the Hellenes.

A month after that, in Kalamata, near the southern tip of the Peloponnese, a 'manifesto addressed to Europe by Petros Mavromikhalis, Commander-in-Chief of the Spartan Troops, and the Messenian Senate', announced that the 'unhappy Greeks of Peloponnesus' had taken up arms against the 'insupportable yoke of Ottoman tyranny' and went on:

> We invoke therefore the aid of all the civilized nations of Europe,
> that we may the more promptly attain to the goal of a just and
> sacred enterprise, reconquer our rights, and regenerate our unfor-
> tunate people. Greece, our mother, was the lamp that illuminated
> you; on this ground she reckons on your active philanthropy.[29]

For the first time in centuries, Greeks were ready to seize their political destiny and take their future into their own hands. During March and April 1821, all of the Danubian principalities, most of what is now mainland Greece, from Thessalonica in the north to the southern Peloponnese, and many towns and islands across the Aegean rose up in response to this call. Nothing on such a scale had ever happened before. The Ottoman state had been facing internal challenges to its authority for a number of years, not least from Muslim warlords in the Balkans, who had tried to break away on their own account. But these had been essentially local upheavals; none would have any lasting effect on the integrity of the Ottoman Empire. The Greek Revolution, as those proclamations show, was different—because it was never intended to be a matter for Greeks alone.

Even so, during the first months, fearsome Ottoman reprisals came close to stamping it out. In Moldavia and Wallachia, despite initial successes, the thousands of Greek and other Balkan volunteers who had rallied to Ypsilantis's call were routed by an Ottoman army in June. Ypsilantis himself sought refuge in Austrian territory, where he was interned for the rest of his short life. Many of his supporters fought to the death or were captured and executed. Farther south, in Macedonia, in Thessaly, and on the seaboard of Anatolia, the revolt was ruthlessly suppressed. Despite the ambitious plans of the Friendly Society, there was no outbreak in the capital. But this did not save the Phanariot aristocracy from near annihilation.

Within a few weeks in April and May, just about every Phanariot who had not managed to escape from Constantinople in time was rounded up and publicly beheaded. Gregory V, the seventy-five-year-old patriarch of the Orthodox Church, was seized at the end of the liturgy on Easter Sunday, 22 April, and hanged from the gate of his own precinct. It made no difference that Gregory had been one of those who had condemned the very idea of liberty or revolution more than two decades before and had recently excommunicated every Orthodox Christian who had dared to rebel against the legitimate *basileus*, the sultan. Similarly, in Cyprus, where there had been no uprising, the archbishop and leading members of the clergy were put to death anyway, apparently just to set an example.

But in one part of the Greek-speaking world, the revolution did take hold. This was the Peloponnese. The well-known story that the standard of revolt was raised by the bishop of Old Patras at the monastery of Agia Lavra, above the town of Kalavryta, on the day of the Christian festival of the Annunciation, 25 March, is almost certainly apocryphal. But once violence had broken out all over the peninsula in early April (or late March, according to the calendar in use there at the time), there was no going back. Local leaders, backed by former brigands and irregular bands of their armed followers, seized the initiative and swept across the country.

Those Muslims who survived the onslaught took refuge with the Ottoman garrisons that remained in the larger towns and in a series of strongholds that had been built in the time of the crusaders or the Venetians. A decisive moment came in October, when the chief town of the Peloponnese, Tripolitsa (today's Tripoli), was starved into submission and most of its inhabitants massacred, despite being promised safe conduct by the victorious Greeks. From the Peloponnese, the action spread to some of the nearby islands, notably Hydra and Spetses just off the northeast coast and Psara on the other side of the Aegean. Among them, these small islands boasted the lion's share of Greek-owned shipping in the eastern Mediterranean. Armed merchantmen began to achieve successes against the Ottoman navy. Other, larger islands joined in, including Samos and Crete, though many did not.

At the end of the year, a first 'national assembly' brought together representatives from all the areas that had been liberated to draw up a constitution. The site chosen, in the northeastern Peloponnese, lay close to the remains of the ancient theatre and sanctuary of the healing god Asclepius at Epidaurus. The first provisional constitution that emerged has ever since been known as the Epidaurus Constitution. This document drew heavily on the short-lived constitutions of revolutionary France. From the Constitution of the United States it derived the strict separation of powers between the legislature and the executive. It also established for all time that the newly liberated realm was to be known by the ancient name of 'Hellas', and its citizens as 'Hellenes'. So effective has that collective act of reinvention been that it requires an effort of imagination, today, to realise what a radical innovation it was at the time. Many Greeks would continue to think of themselves as Romans (*Romioi*), in everyday contexts and informally among themselves, for at least a century and a half after that. But the *official* designations, revived from the ancient world and adapted to the new political reality that was then being shaped, have never since been questioned.

It was one thing to talk of national assemblies, political rights, and the separation of powers, but the realities of liberation on the ground looked rather different. The majority of those who took up arms did so in the name of their Orthodox Christian faith. The enemy, usually called simply 'Turks' in Greek, were identified by their religion, not by what we might term their ethnicity. At the grassroots level, it was a war of religion.[30] The new talk of Hellenes, Hellas, and the heroes of Marathon and Thermopylae had yet to filter through to villagers, or even chieftains, who had never learned to read. When it did, it would remain only a thin veneer for some time. The most popular slogan under which people fought was 'Liberty or Death'.

But 'liberty', once it began to be achieved, meant rather different things to the architects of the first constitution, on the one hand, and to the warlords, who now vied with one another and with the official provisional government to impose their will upon the local areas they had liberated. During a relative lull on the external front, in 1823 and 1824, the Greek Revolution faced its first *political* test.

On the one side was Alexandros Mavrokordatos, who had chaired the national assembly and was elected the first president of the executive—in effect, president of independent Greece. This was the descendant of his namesake who had served as grand dragoman at the end of the seventeenth century and had founded one of the most successful dynasties of Phanariots. The younger Alexandros, one of the few men in revolutionary Greece to sport a western European frock coat, cut an unheroic figure, standing not much more than five feet tall, stout, and wearing thick-lensed spectacles for his myopia. But Mavrokordatos was a consummate politician, master of eight languages, committed to the humanitarian and secular ideas of the European Enlightenment, and deeply versed in the political theory and geopolitics of the day. He had been primarily responsible for the final draft of the Epidaurus Constitution and had successfully steered its provisions through the assembly.

On the opposing side, the most powerful among the warlords in the Peloponnese was Theodoros Kolokotronis, a former brigand and paid soldier of successive foreign governments in the Ionian Islands. Nicknamed 'the Old Man of the Morea' (he was fifty years old when the revolution began), Kolokotronis was a formidable guerrilla chieftain. By the second year of the revolution, he had a string of victories to his credit. Among them was the annihilation of an Ottoman army that had tried and failed to relieve the besieged garrison in Nafplio and had then been trapped by Kolokotronis's men in the narrow pass of Dervenakia, near Corinth, in June 1822. The Scottish historian George Finlay, an eye witness to many of the events he described and the author of one of the most definitive early histories of the Greek Revolution, gives this pen portrait:

A large head, a bold countenance, a steady eye, and a profusion of black hair, gave some dignity to an aspect that did not conceal looks of cunning and ferocity. . . . Nurtured as a brigand, he could never distinguish very clearly right from wrong, justice from injustice; and he had an instinctive aversion to order and law.[31]

Conflict between two such different individuals was inevitable. And, of course, it was a conflict not just between individuals but between whole concepts of what liberty was going to mean for the Greeks ever after. Armed conflict broke out between the provisional government and an alliance of warlords led by Kolokotronis on two separate occasions during 1824. On both occasions, government forces came out on top, with decisive consequences for the shape of the future Greek state. But both the conflict and the character of the protagonists have left a profound legacy that has never entirely gone away since and that would resurface as a fault line in many different later crises in Greek history.[32]

By THIS TIME, events in Greece were beginning to make an impact abroad. Those first appeals to Europe had fallen on predictably deaf ears. But if governments still shunned the insurgents, the same could not be said for individuals and pressure groups in many countries. Volunteers came from every corner of the European continent and from as far away as America. They were known as 'philhellenes' (lovers of things Greek). The most famous of them all was Lord Byron. A high proportion of them died in Greece, whether in action or, like Byron in April 1824, from disease. Often these volunteers had to evade the surveillance of their own governments, which did their best to try to stop them from going. Altogether about twelve hundred arrived in Greece between 1821 and 1827. But far more numerous, and in the end a great deal more influential on the outcome of the revolution, were those philhellenes who stayed at home to organise committees, pressure groups, and press campaigns in their own countries to lobby governments and to raise funds in aid of the Greek cause.[33]

It was very much as a result of these activities that governments abroad slowly, and usually reluctantly, began to reassess their position towards Greece. Great Britain was the first to break ranks among the 'Concert of Europe'. Early in 1823, George Canning, who had recently been appointed Foreign Secretary, recognised the captains and crews of Greek ships on the high seas as legitimate belligerents (rather than as pirates). At the end of the same year, in the USA, President James Monroe came close to recognising Greek independence in a famous speech to Congress. Mainly remembered for setting out the Monroe Doctrine, which defined respective spheres of influence for Europe and the New World, the presidential address of 2 December also included these words: 'There is good cause to believe . . . that Greece will become again an independent nation. That she may obtain that rank is the object of our most ardent wishes.' A little over a year later, a bill was introduced to Congress that, if it had passed, would have had the same effect. Even though it failed, public support in America remained strong enough to allow the fighting frigate *Hellas* to be built in a New York shipyard and delivered to the Greek government at the end of 1826.[34]

In Europe, no government was yet prepared to go so far. In 1824, Tsar Alexander secretly sounded out the British and French about carving out 'zones of influence' for each of them in an autonomous Greece which would still be nominally subject to the Ottomans. When the tsar's proposal was leaked, most of the Greek leaders saw this as a betrayal and turned instead to Great Britain. Although the British government refused to take the insurgents under its protection, and while rival Greek factions put out alternative feelers to both France and Russia, a diplomatic dialogue was beginning. Greece was firmly on the agenda of the chief maritime powers of the day.

From the point of view of the Greeks, it was not a moment too soon. By the time the plea to the British government was issued, on 1 August 1825, the Ottoman counterattack had begun. Ottoman land forces from the north were matched by a newly modernised fleet from Alexandria, commanded by Ibrahim Pasha, the son of the sultan's vassal, Muhammad Ali of Egypt. Ibrahim landed on the south coast of the Peloponnese in February 1825. Over the next two and a half years, the Ottoman army and the Egyptian fleet between them reversed nearly everything that the Greeks had gained since 1821. By the early summer of 1827, liberated Hellas had all but disappeared.

But too many Greeks had struggled for too long to think of going back now. Ibrahim Pasha, who had been promised the Peloponnese as his reward, was threatening to kill or enslave the remaining population and people the entire region with Muslims transported from North Africa. It was not only Greeks who were galvanised by these threats. Philhellenes throughout the world had been mobilised by the conviction that this was not just a distant squabble in a foreign land but that something fundamental to their own civilisation was at stake. It was becoming more difficult for governments to ignore them—and this at a time when the fate of Greece was increasingly becoming a matter of hard-headed geopolitics.

From the spring of 1826, the three Great Powers that had interests in the eastern Mediterranean—Great Britain, France, and Russia—had embarked on a delicate series of negotiations, not with the Greeks but with each other. If Ottoman power was going to be seriously weakened in Europe, it mattered a great deal to each of the three that neither of the others should gain a geopolitical advantage from the outcome. This was the diplomatic dilemma that would in due course become known as the Eastern Question;

it would not finally be resolved until after the First World War. A year later, in 1827, while Canning was briefly prime minister of Great Britain, the three powers agreed to send a joint naval task-force into the Aegean, charged with enforcing a truce between the belligerents. Not surprisingly, the Greeks welcomed this sign of military intervention; the Ottomans repudiated it as an unjustifiable interference in their internal affairs. The unintended consequence was a naval engagement in Navarino Bay, off the southwest coast of the Peloponnese, on 20 October 1827. The combined Ottoman and Egyptian fleets were all but destroyed, and Ibrahim was forced to abandon the Peloponnese shortly afterwards.

The success of the Greek Revolution, in some form, was now assured. But the eventual settlement had been taken out of Greek hands. It was now up to the three Great Powers to find a resolution—though this did not happen immediately. In the meantime, it was the provisional government of Greece, and not any external agent, that appointed an interim head of government for the state that still had no formally recognised existence. His name was Ioannis Kapodistrias, also known as Count John Capo d'Istria. Originally an aristocrat from Corfu, he had joined the Russian service and risen to become joint foreign minister of Russia from 1814 to 1822. Kapodistrias arrived in the Peloponnese early in 1828, with the title *Kyvernitis*, which exactly translates the Latin-derived term 'governor'.

Kapodistrias was at once an outsider—he had never been to mainland Greece before—and a Greek. His appointment was accepted by the representatives of the Great Powers, who were now in charge of the negotiations for Greece's future, though for different reasons he was distrusted by the governments of all three. But at least, from their point of view, they were dealing with a statesman whose credentials were widely recognised—Kapodistrias had after all helped to represent Russia at the Congress of Vienna. His arrival was another significant step towards the emergence of Greece onto the European stage.

The new governor set about establishing the institutions of the future nation-state and did his best to negotiate the most favourable terms for Greece with the representatives of the three Great Powers. But the decisive breakthrough seems not to have been due to Kapodistrias but rather to the defeat of the Ottoman Empire by Russia in yet another Russo-Turkish war in September 1829. The war had been fought mainly in the Caucasus; the future of the Greeks had not been its main cause. But when Russian troops came as close to the Ottoman capital as Edirne (Adrianople), even the Duke of Wellington, at the time prime minister of Britain and no friend to revolutions in general or to the Greeks in particular, suddenly saw the force of the Greek point of view: with the Ottoman Empire in decline, only an independent Greece could serve as a counterweight to Russia in the Balkans and the Aegean. The decisive moment came on 3 February 1830. A protocol signed in London on that day, on behalf of the governments of Great Britain, France, and Russia, declared for the first time, and under their joint guarantee, that: 'Greece will form an independent State, and will enjoy all those rights—political, administrative, and commercial—attached to complete independence.'[35]

In October 1831, Kapodistrias was assassinated by two political opponents as he was entering church in Nafplio. The powers had already decided that the new state must be a monarchy, not a republic as its provisional constitution had declared. In May 1832, a new treaty determined that Prince Otto, the second son of the philhellene king of Bavaria Ludwig I, would be the first king. Frontiers for the kingdom were drawn up at the same time. They included only the Peloponnese, less than half of mainland Greece as it is today, and those islands closest to it in the Aegean. The remainder was still part of the Ottoman Empire, except for the

Ionian Islands, which had been awarded to Great Britain to rule as a protectorate in 1815. Neither the Greeks nor the Ottomans had any say in these decisions.

At the time and for long afterwards, even today, many Greeks have felt sore at this outcome. What had been won fell some way short of the absolute ideal of 'Liberty or Death' that so many had fought and died for. On the other hand, the revolution had begun with those appeals to the conscience of Europe. And if the outcome had little to do with conscience and everything to do with geopolitical calculation, it also firmly integrated the newly independent state into the evolving geopolitics of the continent, and indeed of the wider world. When the future king, Prince Otto, arrived at Nafplio aboard a British warship on 6 February 1833, Greece ('Hellas' in Greek) was ready to take its place among the political states of Europe—for the first time in all the long history of the Greeks.

14

EUROPEAN STATE, GLOBAL NATION

1833–1974

NOT ONLY WAS Greece a new *state* on the map of Europe; it was a new *kind* of state, the first of many to be created in the name and in the image of a *nation*. The model was already being tried out in the New World, in both North and South America. In Europe, it had been pioneered, abortively, in France during the Revolution. The idea of what we now call national self-determination had been around since the Enlightenment. Europeans everywhere were aware of its possibilities; its day would dawn later in the century, in the national 'unifications' of Italy and Germany. But Greece, formally recognised as independent in 1830, was the first experiment in making it work in the Old World.

Ten years would pass before the new kingdom would be granted a parliament or a constitution. But even during the ten years of 'Bavarocracy', when Otto and his German advisers were accountable to no one, unless it was to Otto's father back in Munich, most of the portfolios in the government and most administrative positions were filled by Greeks. These were the people who now began to build the foundations of a state that would be truly modern, European, and above all *national*.[1]

To be national meant: to be 'Hellenic'. As a starting point they took the 'Greek Revival', whose example had done so much to

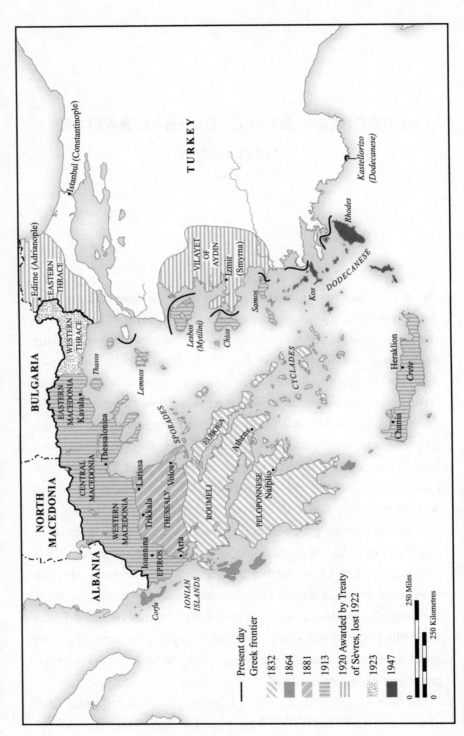

14. The expansion of the Greek state (1832–1947)

bring the state into existence in the first place. Within months of the arrival of Otto and the formation of his first government, the decision was taken to move the capital from Nafplio to Athens. The ruined citadel of the Acropolis, crowned by the Parthenon, still dominated the plain of Attica, as it had done ever since the time of Pericles. The modern town at its foot was home at the time to no more than twelve thousand people. But in the eyes of any classically educated foreigner, the ruins and the ancient reputation of Athens encapsulated the very idea of Greece. Athens must become a city once again, and a fitting capital for a modern state.

A whole new street plan was laid out during the 1830s. Its straight lines and geometric patterns followed Enlightenment principles, which in turn went back to Hellenistic models and ultimately to Hippodamus of Miletus. Over the decades to come, the wide straight boulevards of central Athens, that today are choked with traffic, were driven through derelict houses and open country. The focal point was to be the Acropolis high above, the new city laid out in homage to the old. And just about every sign of human activity during the centuries that separated the decline of the ancient world from the establishment of the new state was systematically obliterated—including all the medieval and later buildings on the Acropolis. Almost every new building, in Athens and many other parts of Greece, too, was built in the neoclassical style, reviving and perpetuating architectural details from the time of the ancient city-states. The new Greece was to be seamlessly welded onto the ruins of its ancient predecessor.[2]

But there was nothing ancient about the institutions that made all this possible, and enabled the state to function, even if some of them *were* given ancient names. With great vigour, during the 1830s, state institutions were created that were quite unlike anything that had ever existed before in this corner of the world. A national army was created. At the top of the national judicial system was a supreme court, named the Areopagus, after a rather different institution in ancient Athens. A national currency was introduced and called the drachma, after an ancient coin, but the monetary system was organised along entirely modern lines. A blueprint was drawn up for a national education system. The University of Athens opened its doors in 1837, named at first after the monarch and then, from 1862, as the National University. The Hill of the Nymphs, overlooking the site of the ancient Agora, was crowned in 1842 by the National Observatory on its summit—the claims of modern science were made early. There was even a national version of the Orthodox Church. The Autocephalous Church of Greece for a number of years cut all its ties with the patriarchate in Constantinople, which of course was obliged to remain an Ottoman, as well as a Christian, institution.

The obstacles to making all this work were formidable. The new state had only about six hundred thousand inhabitants, no natural resources, and an agricultural economy that had been ruined by more than ten years of conflict. It was already heavily in debt to the guarantor powers. Back in 1827, the provisional government had defaulted on two loans that had been raised from private speculators on the London stock market to keep the provisional government afloat in 1824 and 1825. None of the centres of Greek education that had flourished during the previous century lay within its borders; few of its citizens, beyond the elite, could read or write. Hardly a building, in most towns and villages, had escaped damage during the revolution; many lay derelict.

Given these challenges, it is all the more remarkable how much was achieved during the three decades of Otto's reign. Endemic problems remained. Many 'national' institutions still had the appearance of a European veneer laid over traditional ways of behaviour that would take decades, yet, to change. Brigandage was rife in the countryside. Outside the centre of Athens, far more people still dressed in the traditional Ottoman style than *a la franka* (meaning, in the European way). A telling detail is that the national currency, the drachma, did not fully oust the Ottoman piastre until the 1870s. The constitution belatedly granted in 1844 was way ahead of its time, at least in theory, in the breadth of the franchise it offered to citizens.[3] But much of this would remain a dead letter until its successor came into force twenty years later— and women would have to wait until 1952 to vote in parliamentary elections in Greece. New foreign debts incurred at the time of independence, as well as the sometimes blatant interference of the 'protector' powers, would severely curtail the sovereignty that had been promised by the founding treaties until well into the twentieth century.

Otto loved his adopted country, but his subjects only occasionally warmed to him. They deposed him in a second coup d'état in 1862. King Otto I (and last) of Greece departed, as he had arrived, aboard a ship of the British Royal Navy, to live out his days back in Bavaria. But despite the frustrations of Otto's reign, the Greek state had proved itself a 'new model kingdom in the east', in the words of its second monarch, the Danish prince who would be crowned as King George I of the Hellenes in the following year.[4]

A form of vindication came a generation later. In the 1890s, the Olympic Games were revived as a modern international athletic contest. The initiative came not from Greece but from a French sports enthusiast and educational reformer by the name of Baron Pierre de Coubertin. But with strong support from the Greek royal family (who of course were not ethnically Greek either) and leading Greek intellectuals, the city chosen to host the first modern Olympics was Athens. In April 1896, contestants and spectators from all over the world were won over by the splendid neoclassical buildings and wide-open spaces. The Panathenaic Stadium, originally built in the time of Lycurgus in the fourth century BCE, was restored in gleaming new marble, cut from the same quarries that had been used for the original construction. An additional boost to Greek morale came in the final event, the marathon race, which had been devised specially for the occasion, to re-create the twenty-six-mile forced march of the Athenian army after the battle in 490 BCE and was won by a Greek former soldier called Spyridon Louis.[5]

BUT GREEKS KNEW very well, as the nineteenth century drew towards a close, that the kingdom in which many of them took such pride was only one part of a far wider Greek-speaking world. At the time of independence, at least three times as many people who could be reckoned as Greeks had been living outside Greece as lived within it. Since then, the state had modestly expanded. The Ionian Islands had been ceded by Great Britain in 1864; Thessaly and part of Epiros, by the Ottomans in 1881. The population had quadrupled in the same period, to just under two and a half million in 1896. But the number of those living in the Ottoman Empire, in southern Russia, and in emigrant communities on four continents, although no precise means existed to count them, was probably between three and four million.[6]

Even though the state now had a national capital of its own, many both inside and outside Greece throughout the nineteenth century continued to look on Constantinople, not Athens, as the true capital of their nation. One way of resolving the dilemma would be a much more ambitious expansion of the state. And so was born what came to be known as the 'Grand Idea'.

Often said to be the brainchild of Ioannis Kolettis, a veteran politician who had played a leading part in the Revolution, in a speech delivered in 1844, this 'Idea' was in fact as old as the Greek state itself, and indeed inseparable from its very existence. Exactly what it might mean in practice and by what means it might be achieved were the subject of endless debate; many competing versions existed. In its fullest form, the Grand Idea envisioned a restoration of the Byzantine Empire, with its capital at Constantinople. But at its heart lay the aspiration to expand the borders of the Greek state so as to bring as much as possible of the nation within them. In one form or another, this aspiration became the basis for almost all the foreign and much of the domestic policy of every Greek government from the late 1830s to the beginning of the 1920s. And it was not confined to the elite; the Idea seems to have been very widely shared by Greeks in all walks of life, at least among those living in Greece.[7]

Beyond the borders of the state, attitudes varied. In Crete, and some other islands that had a majority Greek population, union with the Greek kingdom across the sea was a goal worth dying for. Revolts in Crete broke out in every decade of the century, from 1821 onwards, under the banner of 'Union or Death'. But elsewhere, Greek communities seem to have been more ambivalent. In Macedonia and Epiros, which bordered the kingdom to the north, and farther east in Thrace, Greek speakers lived cheek by jowl with speakers of Serbian, Bulgarian, Romanian, and Albanian, as well as Muslim Turks. Disentangling these mixed populations would prove a long and sometimes bloody business; in the nineteenth century, what we now call 'national consciousness' was only just beginning. Farther afield, if you lived in Trebizond or Caesarea (modern Kayseri) in Cappadocia, you would learn in a Greek school that you and your family were 'Hellenes' and belonged to an ancient nation whose fortunes were now reviving. But the simple facts of geography must make it very improbable that your homeland would ever become part of a political state governed from Athens.

We have all too little information on the opinions of rank-and-file Greeks living in the Ottoman Empire during this time. But we do know that throughout the nineteenth century, individual Greeks and family networks, based far outside the kingdom, were making their mark on the world, quite independently of the Greek state. Greek shipping and trading networks, whose origins can be traced all the way back to the explosion of activity in Constantinople, Smyrna, Venice, and Crete during the sixteenth century, had expanded hugely during the eighteenth and now began to reach out even farther. It has been argued that their methods, and their business model, would play a formative part in shaping the international trading systems that today we call 'global'.[8]

Typical of a new breed of entrepreneurs were the three Vagliano brothers, born on the Ionian island of Cephalonia. With one based in Taganrog on the Sea of Azov, another in London, and the third in the French Mediterranean port of Marseille, they oversaw a commercial network that exported goods from Russia and central Asia by way of the Russian ports on the Sea of Azov and the Black Sea right across the Mediterranean and as far as Paris, Rotterdam, London, and Manchester, bringing back manufactured goods on their return. By the time the last of the brothers died (Panagi Vagliano, in London, in 1902), the combined value of their estate was equal to almost half of the total gross national product of Greece.[9]

Other family-run firms reached even farther. The five Ralli brothers, born into a family originally from Chios, had set up operations in London during the Greek Revolution in 1823. Pandia Ralli, described as the 'brain' of the firm, remained in London; in later life he would become Sir Pandia, known with affectionate awe as 'Zeus'. With offices on four continents during the middle years of the century, the Ralli family became the most prominent among some sixty well-to-do Greek families established in London, all of them originating from Chios. Their island had been devastated in 1822 during the Revolution; most had set out on their business careers with almost nothing. Throughout the latter part of the nineteenth century and beyond, these families formed a close-knit community, many of them living within a few hundred yards of each other in London's Finsbury Park, frequently intermarrying, but also integrating to an unusual degree for an immigrant community into British high society. Their graves in West Norwood Cemetery in South London, many of them in grand mausolea designed in the neoclassical style, are a permanent and moving testimony to the public successes and private griefs of a world that has otherwise vanished.[10]

Fortunes were being made elsewhere, too. In Constantinople, during the second half of the century, out of a city population of just over one million, approximately a quarter were Greeks. Only a generation after the liquidation of the Phanariots in 1821, sweeping reforms in the Ottoman Empire had brought new opportunities for non-Muslims to take part in public life, to organise the education of their own communities, and, for the Greeks in particular, to build even further on the commercial successes of earlier generations. By the 1870s, Constantinopolitan Greeks had largely created the Ottoman banking system; even the sultan banked with Greek firms. Greek financiers based in Constantinople were the main source of inward investment in the Greek state during the latter part of the century. One of their number, Andreas Syngros, would later be remembered as a benefactor and philanthropist in Greece after he moved to Athens in 1870s. But Syngros was the exception; the majority preferred to stay where they were—which was where the opportunities lay.[11]

Another success story at this time was Egypt. Since the beginning of the century, Greek entrepreneurs had begun moving there in large numbers to exploit the possibilities of the cotton trade that was then opening up. When the American Civil War in the 1860s closed the Atlantic trade in cotton, these Greek businesses, based in Alexandria and Cairo, began to make money on a scale unimaginable in the constrained conditions of independent Greece. One of the most famous Greek businessmen in Egypt was Emmanuel Benakis, who presided over the community in Alexandria at the beginning of the twentieth century. Like Syngros, Benakis is better remembered today than most of his peers because he elected to move with his family to Athens, where he became the city's mayor in 1914. Benakis's son, the art collector Antonis, would give his name and his collection to today's Benaki Museum in Athens.[12]

It wasn't only in business and finance that Greeks outside the kingdom were achieving things that few of its citizens would even have dreamt of doing at home. At the turn of the twentieth century, and for some decades afterwards, some of the most influential literary periodicals that circulated in the Greek-speaking world were published in Alexandria. It was there, between the 1890s and his death in 1933, that Constantine Cavafy honed the unique poetic voice that would establish him as by far the best-known and the most frequently translated of all the poets of 'modern Greece'.

Cavafy was born in Alexandria, into a Greek family from Constantinople, whose fortune had been made, but subsequently lost, in the cotton trade. He rarely visited Greece and didn't greatly like what he saw when he did. Indeed, part of his youth had been spent in Liverpool and in London, close to the heart of the community dominated by Sir Pandia Ralli. Cavafy's achievement was to imagine a Greek world centred upon his native city, that had been founded by Macedonians on Egyptian soil more than two thousand years before. More than half of his published poems evoke moments snatched from that history, during periods when the Greek language and Greek culture had been diffused right across the eastern Mediterranean and the Middle East. Cavafy's take on this whole sweep of history is quintessentially at odds with a national narrative that, ever since the 1820s, has given priority to the Greek state. Imaginatively, in his verse, he celebrates and with self-deprecating irony participates in a narrative of Greek *cultural* superiority that goes all the way back to Thucydides and Isocrates.

The often-quoted pen portrait of Cavafy, drawn by the English novelist E. M. Forster, who met him in Alexandria in 1917, goes to the heart of an identity that must have been shared by very many educated Greeks of the time. Their mental horizons had been shaped far from Greece, but they would still take a deep, indeed a patriotic, pride in belonging to a much more broadly based Hellenic nation:

> He was a loyal Greek, but Greece for him was not territorial. . . .
> Racial purity bored him, so did political idealism. And he could
> be caustic about the tight-lipped little peninsula overseas. . . . The
> civilisation he respected was a bastardy in which the Greek strain
> prevailed, and into which, age after age, outsiders would push, to
> modify and be modified.[13]

IN THE SPRING of 1897, Greece went to war against the Ottoman Empire. For a heady few weeks, enthusiastic crowds in Athens cheered the accomplishment of the Grand Idea. The Greeks would take back Constantinople; the emperor 'turned to marble', Constantine XI, who had died fighting on the ramparts of his capital, would return to life and lead his people to victory; the Turks would be despatched back to central Asia where they had come from. What happened was very nearly the opposite. Within a month, the Greek army was in full retreat, pursued by Ottoman forces that could well have reached Athens if the guarantor powers had not stepped in to enforce the terms of Greek independence. The humiliation of this defeat was felt throughout the kingdom. Even the well-respected King George and the royal family came in for unprecedented abuse. But then, as one apologist for the campaign insisted shortly after it was over, 'It was the *state* that had been defeated and not the *nation*.'[14]

The Grand Idea now had to be rethought. Which mattered more: to preserve the integrity of the state, or to liberate the nation? The issue had become more complicated now that all the other inhabitants of the Balkan Peninsula had begun to emulate the Greek example and create new nation-states of their own. Romania, Serbia, and Montenegro had gained formal recognition in 1878; a Bulgarian principality was on the way to statehood, fully achieved in 1908; Albania would soon follow. All these new states had their own versions of the Grand Idea, because communities speaking their respective languages lived deeply interspersed throughout the southern Balkans. Meanwhile, the contested regions, known by their ancient names of Epiros, Macedonia, and Thrace, were all still part of the Ottoman Empire. So the stage was set for a three-, four-, or even five-way tussle.

The First Balkan War broke out in October 1912. Greece had a new prime minister, a lawyer who had cut his teeth in his native Crete, where the long-prized goal of union with Greece had still not been achieved. His name was Eleftherios Venizelos, and he would prove to be one of the most successful and also divisive leaders in modern Greek history. An admirer who met him shortly before this time would later record his first impressions:

> He seemed to shine, he was transparent, like alabaster, with the complexion of a young girl from northern climes, strangely framed by a beard with the first sparse white hairs. The spectacles added to the brightness, but still more the two blue-green phosphorescent eyes, which seemed to come out from behind the glasses and look directly at you.[15]

Venizelos was perhaps the only Greek politician of modern times to gain respect abroad as a statesman of world stature. At home, for his supporters he was nothing short of a Messiah. To his enemies (and they were many) he was a 'false prophet', inspired by the devil himself. Many, at the time and ever since, have held Venizelos personally responsible for the greatest disaster ever to befall the Greek state.[16]

After he became prime minister for the first time in 1910, Venizelos applied himself to making the Grand Idea a reality, despite the setbacks of the decade before. Under his stewardship, the economy recovered strongly and investments could be made in the armed forces, as well as in infrastructure and public services. New diplomatic overtures among the competing nation-states of the Balkans at the same time brought about an unexpected alliance against the Ottoman Empire. The first blow was struck by tiny Montenegro, on the Adriatic coast, on 8 October 1912. Within days, Greece, Bulgaria, and Serbia had joined in. A Greek army led by Crown Prince Constantine entered Thessalonica on 8 November, only hours ahead of a Bulgarian force that had been racing to reach the same goal. The Ottomans were driven back to within a few miles of their capital.

Less than a year later, the fragile alliance fragmented. A Second Balkan War, fought in July 1913, rearranged the pieces on the board: Greece and the Ottoman Empire both made gains at the expense of Bulgaria, which had come out as the biggest winner in the first round. By the end of 1913, the frontiers of Greece had been extended to the north, east, and south (to include Crete), almost to where they lie today. The land area of the kingdom had increased by more than half; its population had almost doubled to 4.8 million. Was the next stop to be Constantinople?[17]

But then, in 1914, came yet another war. This one, too, began in the Balkans, with the assassination of the heir to the Austrian throne while on a visit to the Bosnian capital, Sarajevo, on 28 June. In early August, wider hostilities were declared. This latest Balkan conflict was about to become the Great War, or the 'war to end all wars', later to be known as the First World War. On one side was the Triple Entente, consisting of the empires of Great Britain, France, and Russia; on the other, the Central Powers, namely, the German Reich, the empire of Austria-Hungary, and from October the Ottoman Empire, too.

What was the Greek government to do? If Greece were to enter the war on the side of the Entente, an estimated two million Greeks, living in Ottoman territory as Ottoman subjects, would be effectively held hostage. On the other hand, if the Entente were to win, and if Greece had contributed to the defeat of its arch enemy, these Ottoman Greeks could be liberated and their homelands incorporated into a greater Greece. Venizelos, the prime minister, was for joining the war on the side of the Entente; the former crown prince, who was now Constantine I and married to the sister of Kaiser Wilhelm of Germany, was for staying neutral.

In 1915, Great Britain and France began to force the issue by landing troops in Thessalonica so as to defend their Balkan ally, Serbia. Further violations of Greek sovereignty followed. Greeks in all walks of life were more bitterly divided than they had ever been since the days of the internal conflicts during the Revolution. These divisions were so bitter because the argument was fundamentally not about international alliances or the world war at all, but between the interests of the nation and the interests of the state. The old fault line from the 1820s had emerged in a new guise to pit one version of Greek patriotism against another.

In September 1916, Venizelos defied the king and set up an alternative government in Thessalonica. He justified his actions with the declaration:

The *Nation* is called, in the absence of the *State*, to answer a national emergency. . . . Whereas the *State* has betrayed its obligations, it remains to the *Nation* to act in order to achieve the task assigned to the *State*.[18]

For the next eight months, the country had two rival governments, one led by the king in Athens, the other by Venizelos in Thessalonica. Under this pressure, open civil war broke out on the streets of Athens in December 1916. Six months later, with the support of French troops, Venizelos finally prevailed. King Constantine was forced into exile, Venizelos returned to Athens to head a government of reunified Greece, and Greek troops contributed to the final battles on the Macedonian front that helped to bring the war to an end in 1918.

Once the war was over, and the Entente had indeed won, Venizelos exercised all his considerable talents as a statesman at the ensuing Peace Conference in Paris. The result was to be two huge gains for Greece. The first was the right to land troops in Smyrna and to occupy the surrounding administrative district in May 1919. Then the Treaty of Sèvres, signed in the French town of that name in August 1920, awarded to Greece large swathes of Ottoman territory in eastern Thrace and western Anatolia. With the longer-term future of Constantinople still to be resolved, it was even possible that one day the capital city founded by Constantine, which had never ceased to be the symbolic capital of the Greek-speaking world, might again be ruled by Greeks.

It was a tragic miscalculation. Venizelos and his policy suffered a double defeat: at home, in a parliamentary election held in November 1920, but more critically in Anatolia at the hands of the newly created Turkish Nationalist movement led by Mustafa Kemal, later known as Atatürk, the founder of the modern Republic of Turkey. The election result in Greece brought the exiled King Constantine back to his throne. Because of the king's stance during the world war, Britain and France withdrew all the diplomatic and financial support they had been giving while Venizelos remained in charge. The new government would have to go it alone. In 1921, Greek forces in Anatolia pushed eastwards in a preemptive strike against Kemal's provisional capital, Ankara. When that failed, the stalemate that followed lasted for a year. Then in September 1922, the Turks broke through the Greek lines, the Greek army withdrew to the coast and was evacuated to Greece. The Greek population of Anatolia was now left to its fate. The city of Smyrna, where Greeks had made up the largest part of the population for several decades, was devastated by fire within days of the arrival of Kemal's army.

The defeat of the Greek army in Anatolia, after a three-year campaign, has ever since been remembered by Greeks as the 'Asia Minor Catastrophe' (after the ancient name of the subcontinent, still current in Greek), or simply the 'Catastrophe'. The Greek *state* had expanded its borders, but to an extent far less than had been envisaged by enthusiasts for the Grand Idea. The price had been the permanent uprooting of the Greek *nation* from eastern Thrace, from all round the Sea of Marmara, from the Black Sea coast of Trebizond and its hinterland, from the Aegean coast as far south as Smyrna, and from Cappadocia in central Anatolia. These 'lost homelands', as they are still remembered by Greeks today, had been home to Greek speakers for centuries, if not for millennia, and had once made up the heartland of the Byzantine Empire.[19]

Over the next few months, uncounted thousands of Greeks were either killed or taken prisoner. In the aftermath, between 1.3 and 1.4 million Orthodox Christians, almost all of them Greek-speaking, permanently lost their homes. Those who had not already fled during the last months of 1922 were evacuated to Greece as part of a compulsory exchange of populations that was negotiated under the auspices of the League of Nations at the Convention of Lausanne in January 1923. The task of housing and assimilating so many refugees, with assistance from international bodies such as the League and the Red Cross, has often and justly been reckoned as one of the outstanding successes of the Greek state in its two-hundred-year history. But it was also, inevitably, a story of human loss, tragedy, and bitterness. If the immediate crisis was largely over by 1930—when, even more surprisingly, a government once again led by Venizelos was able to normalise relations with Kemal's new Turkey—it would take another five decades, at least, for the incomers to be fully assimilated.[20]

IN THE AFTERMATH, artists and intellectuals agonised over the nature and meaning of what they called 'Greekness', or 'Hellenicity'. A generation of poets, novelists, painters, philosophers, and historians grappled with the challenge: How was it possible, in this new world, to be at once *Greek* and *modern*? 'Greece is travelling, always travelling', wrote the poet George Seferis in 1936:

> *and we do not realise, do not realise we're all of us sailors*
> *   turfed ashore*
> *do not realise how bitter is the port when all the ships*
> *   put out to sea;*
> *we laugh at those who do.*

Seferis, who was himself an exile from his native Smyrna, took exception to the very term 'Hellenicity', which he saw as a form of stereotyping. In an essay published in 1938, he urged future generations 'to seek the truth . . . not by asking *how* to be Greek, but with the conviction that since they *are* Greek, the work that they will truly produce cannot be anything other than Greek'.[21]

The novel by Nikos Kazantzakis, written in the early 1940s and known in translation as *Zorba the Greek*, addresses the same question (though it is about a great deal else as well). 'Lots of people are patriots for what they can get out of it,' says the title character. 'I'm not a patriot, and too bad if I get nothing out of it. . . . If I hear the Greeks have taken Constantinople, it's the same to me as if the Turks have taken Athens'.[22] The fictional Zorba is anything but a typical 'modern Greek', as generations of readers of the novel in translation have supposed. Kazantzakis in his fiction, like Seferis in his essay, was casting about to discover a *new* Greek identity, and in the process helping to create one.

Successive governments during the 1920s and 1930s were much less successful in what was, essentially, the same quest. With the exception of the four-year administration of Venizelos, from 1928 to 1932, governments came and went, as often installed by one or other faction of a divided military as by the ballot box. Politically, the divisions of the previous decade obstinately refused to heal. Even the normally statesmanlike Venizelos was not above stoking them as his grip on power weakened in the early 1930s. The monarchy had been replaced by a republic in 1924, but was then reinstated eleven years later. In 1936, a political impasse enabled a former general, Ioannis Metaxas, to establish a dictatorship. During the next five years, the cult of the state became a fetish. The rhetoric of the Metaxas regime often echoed that of Hitler's Third Reich and Fascist Italy under Mussolini. A 'Third Greek Civilisation' was proclaimed, and young Greeks were told to emulate the attitudes and achievements not of democratic, arts-loving Athens but of the tightly controlled militarist state of ancient Sparta. As Europe stumbled towards a second world war, some speculated that Metaxas might even join the German-Italian Axis.[23]

EVEN AFTER THE Catastrophe of 1922, and despite the rhetoric of some in government at home, the story of the Greek state could never be the whole story of the Greek *nation*. For all the brutal simplicity of the compulsory exchange of populations, there remained untidy edges, and therefore unfinished business, in parts of the Balkans and the eastern Mediterranean which for centuries had been part of the Greek-speaking world. Exceptions had been allowed for the Greeks of Istanbul, who at the time numbered approximately one hundred thousand, and the small communities on the islands of Imbros and Tenedos (Gökçeada and Bozcaada) which strategically guard the strait of the Dardanelles and had been demanded by Turkey as part of the settlement. In return, a Muslim and mostly Turkish-speaking community had been allowed to remain in the Greek province of western Thrace—and to this day is the only officially recognised ethnic minority in Greece.

Elsewhere, in regions that had passed out of Ottoman control before the exchange, Greeks still remained the majority population and of course were not affected by it. This was the case with the Northern Epirots who lived (as do some of their descendants to this day) in the southern part of Albania. The islands of the Dodecanese had been annexed by Italy in 1912 and would have to wait until after the Second World War to become part of the Greek state. Largest, and in the event the most politically significant, was Cyprus. Administered by Great Britain since 1878, the island became formally a Crown Colony in 1925. The 80 per cent of its population who were Greek Orthodox and spoke the Cypriot dialect of Greek had long cherished the notion that Cyprus would one day become part of Greece. But maintaining good relations with Britain counted for more with successive Greek governments, and the issue would remain sidelined in Greece until the Cypriots themselves took the initiative in the 1950s.

In the meantime, Greeks who had been branching out to establish communities in other parts of the world were consolidating their position. In Egypt, effectively under British rule from 1882 until after the Second World War, the Greek community reached its peak in the 1930s, when it numbered about a hundred thousand. Not only from their prominent role in the cotton trade but also as pilots for ships using the Suez Canal, the 'Egyptiots', as Greek Egyptians are known in Greek, have been credited with contributing significantly to modernizing their host country. Their status there was somewhere in the middle between the British rulers and the native Arab-speaking Egyptians, and to some extent they were in a position to act as mediators between them.[24]

Beyond Europe and the Mediterranean, Greeks had been setting out to create new homes and new lives for themselves in the United States since the last decade of the nineteenth century. By the time that US legislation put a stop to large-scale immigration in the early 1920s, just over half a million Greeks had crossed the Atlantic. The great majority of those were young single men; many hoped to make a quick fortune and return home to marry and settle down, back in Greece. But soon Greek brides-to-be were taking ship to join husbands they had never seen in marriages that had been arranged by relatives through letters and photographs. While many did return, sometimes after a whole working life spent in the United States, many more stayed and made their homes in their new country. Almost all of these immigrants had started out in manual trades, often as miners or railroad workers. But within a generation they were proving themselves remarkably upwardly mobile and would soon be found mostly in cities or larger towns, running their own businesses and making the most of the educational opportunities offered by their new homeland.[25]

America was also the latest continent on which multinational Greek-owned businesses flourished during the first half of the twentieth century and beyond, despite the upheavals back home. The First World War and the revolution in Russia in 1917 had changed the focus of their operations, away from the Black Sea and the Mediterranean into the Atlantic. By the end of the 1930s, Greek-owned cargo shipping was working its way up the world league table and had reached ninth place, ahead of such great shipping nations as Japan and Norway.[26]

By that time, a new figure had entered the closed and competitive circles of Greek shipowners: the legendary Aristotle Onassis. Displaced to Greece from his native Smyrna in 1922, the young Onassis moved on quickly to the other side of the world. The foundations for his business empire were laid in Argentina, where a Greek immigrant community had been growing for more than a century. Later, he would move the base of his operations to the United States, then to Monaco—but not to Greece. His was to prove the most spectacular rags-to-riches story of them all. And, like so many other Greek success stories in the world of business and particularly of shipping, it had very little to do with the Greek state. In the twentieth century, no less than in the nineteenth, Greek fortunes were being made elsewhere.

GREECE ENTERED THE Second World War on 28 October 1940. The Italian dictator, Benito Mussolini, had annexed Albania the year before. Now, allied with Hitler's Germany, which had just overrun most of mainland Europe, Mussolini sent a telegram to Metaxas demanding unhindered access to Greece for his troops. When it came to it, Metaxas was more patriot than fascist (though he was both). In the early hours of that morning, he said 'no': *ochi* in Greek, an event still commemorated in the national holiday known as Ochi Day. After that, for six heady months, the deep divisions within the Greek state were set aside. Fighting in terrible conditions in the snow and freezing temperatures of the Albanian mountains in winter, the Greek army and air force pushed the Italians back. By March 1941, they had won the first victory over the Axis in the whole course of the Second World War. But in April, Hitler came to the help of his struggling Axis partner. Unable to stand against the German Third Reich, the Greek army surrendered. Greece was parcelled out among the occupying forces of Germany, Italy, and Hitler's Balkan ally, Bulgaria.

Metaxas, in his seventies and in failing health, had died three months earlier. What was left of the Greek government, headed by King George II, escaped into exile, first in London and later in Cairo. The Occupation authorities appointed an army general to head a puppet government in Athens; but it was powerless to prevent the Nazis from looting the country while almost the entire apparatus of the state collapsed. The whole house of cards, as it had been built up, painstakingly, since the disaster of 1922, came crashing down. Markets, the currency, and mechanisms for distribution and supply collapsed. During the first winter of the Occupation, as many as forty thousand civilians may have died from starvation in Athens and Piraeus alone. Between 1941 and 1943 the victims of famine are estimated to have reached a quarter of a million, close to 5 per cent of the total population.[27]

With the breakdown of civil society came a return to extreme violence, of a kind that had not been seen in Greece since the days of the Revolution in the 1820s. Organised resistance began in the mountains of the mainland in 1942. But almost from the beginning, it was not just a matter of fighting against the invaders. The Hellenic Popular Liberation Army, known by its Greek initials ELAS, by 1944 had as many as fifty thousand men under its command. The political leadership behind the movement belonged to the Communist Party, which had been outlawed by Metaxas. But not everyone who determined to take up arms and fight for freedom was prepared to sign up to this agenda. Just as had happened in the 1820s, incompatible ideas of liberty brought rival passions into conflict. Competing guerrilla groups took to the mountains, too.

Terror tactics were used by all parties, against the occupiers and against each other, while summary executions and the destruction of whole villages on the orders of Italian and German commanders intensified the cycle of violence still further. In a bizarre twist towards the end of 1943, thousands of Greeks took up arms *against* the resistance organised by ELAS and ended up taking orders from the Nazis. They then attacked fellow Greeks on the grounds that they were communists. Denounced at the time as 'fascists' and 'collaborators', these people can surely have been no more ideologically attracted to the doctrines of Hitler and Mussolini than most of the rank-and-file ELAS knew or cared about communism. All sides were simply fighting to survive in a failed state and to preserve what they could of what they valued, when even the forces of occupation could barely keep order outside the major cities, and only by terrorizing the citizens with arbitrary arrests and mass executions.[28]

The last German troops left mainland Greece in October 1944. The government in exile returned, but even with British military support proved incapable of governing a divided country. Civil war erupted on the streets of Athens in December. For half a century after that, the old fault line running through Greek society became aligned with the new geopolitical division of the postwar world, into a capitalist West and a communist East. The Greek communists were forced to lay down their arms in January 1945, but the 'battle for Athens' had been closely fought, with horrific atrocities on both sides. Not even the end of World War II later that year was enough to stave off a full-scale civil war in Greece. On one side was a communist-led Democratic Army that was the successor to ELAS; on the other, government forces backed by Britain and then, from 1947 onwards, by the USA.[29]

It ended in October 1949, when the last strongholds of the Democratic Army were overrun in the mountain ranges bordering Greece's newly communist neighbours Albania and Yugoslavia. The government in Athens had won largely thanks to American firepower and economic support. The consequence was that instead of following the rest of eastern Europe into the Communist bloc dominated by Soviet Russia, and somewhat in defiance of geography, Greece became part of the 'West' for the duration of the Cold War, joining the NATO alliance (along with Turkey) in 1951.

During the 'traumatic decade' of the 1940s, it has been reckoned that some two hundred thousand Greeks may have lost their lives or been forced into exile—a number that does not include the eighty thousand Jewish victims of the Holocaust, citizens of the Greek state deported and murdered by the Nazis in 1943 and 1944.[30] In the final stages of the civil war, thousands of Greeks, many of them children, either fled or were forcibly taken across the country's northern border. Branded as communists back home, they and their children would have to make new homes behind the Iron Curtain in eastern Europe. Many who ended up in Russia would be resettled by the Soviet authorities in Tashkent, in Uzbekistan. Some of their descendants remain in all these countries to this day.

Once it was over, many more left Greece voluntarily to seek new opportunities and security as far from home as it was possible to go—in the Southern Hemisphere. Some joined an already thriving community in South Africa. The largest number, about a quarter of a million, set out for Australia. Most of those settled in the states of New South Wales and Victoria. It is as a consequence of the Greek Civil War that, since the 1950s, the third largest Greek city in the world has been Melbourne.[31]

As THE 1940s drew to a close, the Greek state lay in ruins. Everything would now have to be rebuilt, from the ground up. And, remarkably, it was. Much of the credit for this, initially, must go to the programme for economic recovery in Europe approved by the US Congress in April 1948 and known as the Marshall Plan. During the next four years, more than one billion dollars were disbursed in aid to Greece. Seen as a bulwark in eastern Europe against the Communist bloc in the Cold War, the country benefited enormously from military and economic aid from America until the 1970s. During the 1950s and 1960s, new industries were established, while old ones, including the staple, agriculture, were modernised. Gross domestic product increased by an average of 6.5 per cent per year. The initial impetus might have been American, but this was very much a success story built by Greeks themselves.[32]

It was during those decades that Onassis and a new generation of shipowners came into their own. The Second World War had completely decimated the worldwide Greek shipping fleet. Vessels had been requisitioned, or sunk, or both. By 1946, when Greece was on its knees and about to embark on the final, bloodiest round of its civil war, the Greek shipowning firms were in scarcely better shape. What saved them was the offer of loans from a US government keen to offload a fleet of cargo ships that had been cheaply mass-produced during the war. The result was an investment that would pay off many times over. But Onassis was aiming higher still. In the 1950s, he launched a fleet of some of the largest tankers in the world.[33]

Within a few years, not only had Onassis become the 'King of Tankers' and one of the world's richest men, but in 1968 he married the widow of US president John Kennedy, and she became Jacqueline Kennedy Onassis. Now based in Monaco, but with a string of homes around the world, Onassis owned a private islet in the Ionian group of islands, Skorpios, where he would be buried when he died in 1975. Together with another new entrant to the Greek shipowning fold, his brother-in-law and most bitter rival, Stavros Niarchos, Onassis built upon business practices that had been developed by Greek dynasties over several centuries to create a trading empire that was at once global and, in its own distinctive way, Greek.[34]

Ships would more usually fly other flags than the Greek blue-and-white cross and stripes. This was a legacy that went back to the days before there was such a thing as a Greek national flag—not just to the immediate origins of these shipping dynasties in the eighteenth century but all the way back to the time, back in the sixteenth, when Greek merchants and captains had begun to negotiate their way between the two opposed worlds of the Ottoman Empire and Christian Europe. Onassis was by no means alone among Greek shipowners after the Second World War in flagging his vessels in low-tax states around the world, particularly Panama and Liberia.

On the other hand, just like the poet Cavafy in Alexandria, early in the century, these were 'patriotic Greeks', proud of their Hellenic heritage. Businesses with a global reach and a huge annual turnover were run on strictly family lines. Positions of trust were limited to close family members, and outsiders carefully integrated through arranged marriages. Management and ships' crews would include a high proportion of Greeks, often recruited from the island where the family had originated. The loyalty of employees to the Onassis firm was as enduring a part of the legend as the flags of convenience and the giant tankers. Once upon a time the Vaglianos, who rarely set foot there, had provided for an entire, unofficial system of social security in their native Cephalonia in the days when the state could offer nothing like it. On neighbouring Ithaca, several generations owed their employment and their prosperity to Onassis. This was the result of a visceral and deeply traditional sense of belonging to a community. But the community was a very different thing from the *state*. Greek shipping fortunes have always been securely banked offshore, well beyond the reach of the Greek state.[35]

CULTURALLY, GREECE WAS booming, too, during the 1960s. A new homegrown film industry, based on small-scale private enterprise, produced low-budget, mass-market films, shot mostly in black and white. The number of films produced rivalled the output of Hollywood at the same time when measured in proportion to the size of the population. Summer outdoor cinemas became so popular that the rate of cinemagoing in Greece was the highest in Europe. Many of these films are still treasured as classics by Greek TV viewers and buyers of DVDs today. Two that were made partly in English have kept their place in the international repertoire: *Never on a Sunday*, directed by American-born Jules Dassin with Melina Mercouri in the lead role, and *Zorba the Greek*, based on Kazantzakis's novel and directed by Michael Cacoyannis, who had been born in Cyprus and educated in England. The 1960s also saw the heyday of Greek popular music, with the *bouzouki*, an instrument traditionally beloved of the urban underclass, elevated by composers Manos Hadjidakis and Mikis Theodorakis into the vehicle for a musical style that would soon become a Greek trademark around the world. And in 1963, Greece received its first Nobel Prize—for literature, awarded to the poet George Seferis.[36]

But once again, just as had happened during the 1930s, economic and artistic innovation went hand in hand with political deadlock. By the middle of the decade, street demonstrations and politically motivated strikes were paralysing city life. An election due to be held in April 1967 was widely expected to result in victory for the Centre Left. On 21 April, nine days before polling day, a group of middle-ranking army officers seized power in a coup d'état. They relied on a plan that had been drawn up by the Americans to secure the country in the event of war with the Soviets. It worked with scarcely a hitch. Tanks replaced traffic in the streets. Parliament was dissolved and civil rights suspended. Dissidents were subjected to arbitrary arrest, torture, and long prison sentences. The music of Theodorakis, a known supporter of the banned Communist Party, was prohibited; another Communist, Yannis Ritsos, the most prolific and probably also the most popular Greek poet of the century, spent several years in internal exile on Aegean islands and under house arrest. According to the clumsy metaphor beloved of the military rulers, Greece had become a hospital patient strapped in a plaster cast as a necessary step to recovery. After six and a half years of this, the Yom Kippur War in the autumn of 1973 brought turmoil to the entire Western economy. Boom time for Greece was finally over.[37]

That November, a sit-in by students at the Athens Polytechnic drew thousands to the city centre to protest against the regime. In the early hours of Saturday, 17 November, a bloody crackdown began. Tanks, armed police, and soldiers were deployed against students and sympathisers whose only weapon was a short-wave radio station, that broadcast appeals for the regime to be overthrown and finally, desperately, for supplies of blood and bandages. Twenty-four demonstrators were killed that night; perhaps as many more by army sharpshooters in the streets during the days that followed. Hundreds were wounded. Thousands were either arrested or went into hiding. A week later, another coup d'état brought to power an even more hard-line faction within the military.[38]

The new rulers finally overreached themselves when they tried to extend their influence across the eastern Mediterranean to Cyprus. Back in the early 1950s, when Great Britain had started to withdraw from its imperial role overseas, the Greeks of Cyprus had petitioned for their island to become part of Greece. When that was rebuffed by a British Conservative government, the Greek Cypriots had taken matters into their own hands. A messy and sometimes brutal three-way conflict, involving Greece, Britain, and Turkey, had ended with an outcome that nobody had wanted, least of all the Greek Cypriots, when a newly created Republic of Cyprus became an independent member of the British Commonwealth in August 1960. Its first president was Archbishop Makarios, the charismatic head of the Orthodox Church on the island who had led the political wing of the struggle against the British for union with Greece.[39]

In July 1974, the military rulers of Greece staged a coup against the elected government of Cyprus. For several hours it appeared that Makarios had been killed. These actions were in flagrant violation of the treaty of independence, which was supposed to be guaranteed by Britain, Greece, and Turkey. After a daring escape from the ruins of the presidential palace in Nicosia, Makarios was flown to London by his old enemies, the British. But then the British government, led by Harold Wilson, declined to become involved.[40] Instead of a diplomatic initiative to restore the legitimate government of Cyprus, Turkey launched a massive air and sea assault on the island's north coast during the night of 19–20 July 1974. Faced with a war that they themselves had provoked, and could not possibly win, the military rulers in Athens panicked and stood down. Democracy was restored four days later. The first parliamentary elections in almost a decade were held in November. Shortly afterwards, for the second time in the country's history, a plebiscite abolished the monarchy, and the Kingdom of Greece became the Hellenic Republic, as it has remained ever since.

For the second time, too, since the ill-fated push into Anatolia in 1921, a military adventure by the Greek state had caused irreparable destruction to a portion of the wider Greek nation. More than a hundred thousand Greek Cypriots were either killed or forced from their homes in July and August 1974; the fate of many would never be known. This time there was no organised exchange of populations; tens of thousands of Greek Cypriots fled for their lives to the south of the island, and Turkish Cypriots to the north. No internationally agreed peace treaty has ever brought the war of that summer to an end. The line of control that still runs from west to east across the island of Cyprus is a ceasefire line, not a frontier. This was the price paid for the final healing of the wounds of divided Greece, that went all the way back to the second decade of the century.

15

NEW LEDGERS, NEW LEGENDS
1974–2021

A N UNINTENDED AND unforeseen consequence of the events
of 1974 was that from that time onwards there has been
not one but two Greek nation-states: the Hellenic Republic, with
Athens as its capital, and the Republic of Cyprus, with its capital
in Nicosia. Although the Cypriot constitution of 1960 is still legally in force and applies to the entire island, the reality since 1974
has been that the internationally recognised Republic of Cyprus,
which controls the south of the island, is a Greek-speaking state,
while the self-proclaimed Turkish Republic of Northern Cyprus, in
the north, is recognised only by Turkey. For thirty years, it was forbidden for Cypriots on either side to cross the ceasefire line; since
the opening of official crossing points in 2004, there has been little
mingling between ever more separate Greek and Turkish Cypriot
communities.[1]

Both republics (Greece and Cyprus) share the same national day
and national anthem. In the Republic of Cyprus, it is as common
to see the national flag of Greece flying on public buildings, and
even on churches, as the official flag that had been devised for the
island's independence. Subtle differences of emphasis, as well as
the system of government and a distinctive Cypriot accent, mark
the two nation-states off from one another. But in terms of policy,

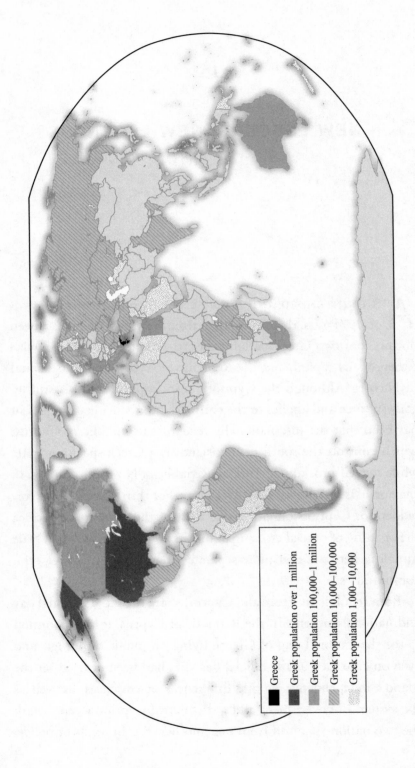

15. Countries of the world with the largest Greek populations today

Greece
Greek population over 1 million
Greek population 100,000–1 million
Greek population 10,000–100,000
Greek population 1,000–10,000

since 1974 (and in strong contrast to the decade before that), the two governments have tended to move in lockstep.

In the immediate aftermath of the events of that year, Athens and Nicosia both made great strides in developing and embedding their democratic institutions. Since that time, power has regularly changed hands after elections that have been fairly contested (as had all too rarely been the case in Greece before that), with a broad spectrum of political parties taking part. In Athens, a stable two-party system emerged. From the late 1970s until 2012, governments almost always alternated between the centre-right New Democracy, founded by Konstantinos Karamanlis, who became prime minister in 1974, and the Panhellenic Socialist Movement (known by the Greek acronym PASOK), led by Andreas Papandreou. From being a strongly left-wing populist movement in its early years, PASOK soon morphed into a centre-left party, close to the European mainstream, and was almost technocratic during the premiership of its second leader, Kostas Simitis, from 1996 to 2004. In Greece, the head of state is elected by parliament and the role is largely ceremonial. In Cyprus, on the other hand, the president has considerable executive powers and is directly elected. Since the time of Makarios, who died in 1977, presidents have been elected from political backgrounds ranging from the communist left to the nationalist right, and not necessarily aligned with the majority party in the House of Representatives.

Both Greece and Cyprus recovered quickly from the economic downturn of the mid-1970s and, in the case of Cyprus, from the far greater devastation caused by the Turkish invasion. Governments in Athens oversaw impressive growth from the 1980s until the first decade of the new century. But in hindsight, much of this would turn out to have been state-led. Patronage and tax breaks handed out by three PASOK governments in the 1980s and 1990s are often blamed for the financial crisis that would follow in 2010. But for several decades, Greeks in Greece had the experience of prospering, and the annual rate of growth was impressive. Standards of living had never been higher.[2]

All this went hand in hand with a geopolitical shift that affected both countries. The leadership of the United States in the Cold War meant that Greece since the late 1940s and Cyprus since independence in 1960 had looked first to America in international relations. But rightly or wrongly, since 1974, Greek public opinion has tended to blame US policy for the seven-year dictatorship in Greece and for what is often called the 'dismemberment' of Cyprus. As a result, both countries in the mid-1970s turned away from the United States and towards what was then the European Economic Community, the forerunner of today's European Union. Greece joined the EEC in 1981 as its tenth member, and the Eurozone, which shares the single currency, the euro, in 2001. Cyprus was one of a slew of smaller European states to join the EU in 2004, and it adopted the euro four years later.

This alignment has meant a great deal more than the technicalities of working with a supranational administration in Brussels and Strasbourg or the management and obligations of the single currency. Lifestyles in Greece became rapidly transformed during the 1980s. People stayed at home and watched television, newly opened up by the arrival of commercial channels which had been prohibited before. The traditional men-only *kapheneion*, where elderly denizens played backgammon, drank coffee, and disputed the contents of the daily newspapers, began to be displaced by smart bars where young people of both sexes would congregate. Not everybody was in sympathy with these changes, of course, and indeed the old ways have by no means disappeared. But in a more than superficial sense, since that time, Greece has become visibly more 'European'.

The physical landscape has been changing, too. Projects born in the late 1980s and funded by European programmes would go on to be completed during the next decade and a half. A long-awaited new Metro system for Athens opened in 2000, the new Eleftherios Venizelos International Airport in 2001. Thanks to a network of brand new motorways, carried on viaducts and through long tunnels, journey times from Athens to the provinces, or from the Adriatic port of Igoumenitsa on one side of the Pindos mountains to Thessalonica on the other, have been reduced from a whole day or more to just a few hours. Most spectacular of all is the Charilaos Trikoupis Suspension Bridge spanning the mouth of the Gulf of Corinth, almost three kilometres long, which opened to traffic in 2004.

Greek society began to change in the 1980s in other ways, too. These changes had less to do with European integration than with the advent of Greece's first socialist government, led by Andreas Papandreou, in 1981. Ironically enough, elected on a populist, anti-Europe programme that it would soon abandon, Papandreou's Panhellenic Socialist Movement (PASOK) would govern for seventeen of the next twenty-three years. Particularly during its first term, it introduced reforms that went far beyond legislative changes to begin to break down social prejudices that had remained unchanged for years, if not for centuries. For the first time, a women's movement played a visible part in public life. Adultery ceased to be a criminal offence. Gender equality was introduced into every aspect of civil society. Civil marriage was permitted, despite protests from the Orthodox Church, whose monopoly of authority on social matters would be challenged repeatedly, if often inconclusively, by successive governments. A national health service was created in 1983. Government spending on welfare increased by almost half. Huge investments were made in education, particularly in new and expanded universities and technical colleges all over Greece. Before long, almost all young Greeks would be participating in some form of higher education.[3]

THE ENDING OF the Cold War in 1989 brought changes of a different kind. For the first time in half a century, Greece was once again fully connected to its Balkan hinterland. Standards of living at the time were much higher in Greece than in any of the countries of the former Soviet bloc. As the country's northern neighbours scrambled to catch up with the capitalist economies of the West, Greek businesses found themselves at a natural advantage. On the other hand, large numbers of economic migrants began to arrive in Greece, particularly, and often illegally, from Albania. The social problems created at home threatened to outweigh the benefits abroad.

Greeks were spared the resurgence of vicious interethnic (actually, interreligious) warfare that ravaged the former Yugoslavia during the decade of the 1990s. But they were not unaffected. In a rare departure from the EU and NATO consensus, Greek public opinion, and even sometimes government policy, regularly aligned with the Orthodox Serbs and against the Catholic Croatians and the Muslims of Bosnia and Herzegovina. The most contentious issue, which first emerged at the end of 1991 and which would not be resolved until 2019, was over the name of the independent republic that broke away from Yugoslavia and claimed international recognition under the name of 'Macedonia'.

For as long as it had formed part of the Yugoslav federation, the existence of a 'Socialist Republic of Macedonia' beyond their northern border had been of no particular concern to Greeks. But for a foreign state to take a name that by this time almost all Greeks had come to regard as quintessentially and inalienably Greek was like a red rag to a bull. Worse, governments of the new republic in the 1990s adopted a flag based on the gold sunburst motif associated with ancient Macedonian monuments and most memorably depicted on the funeral casket that had contained the cremated remains of Philip II. Statues of Alexander the Great began to appear in Skopje, the republic's capital; tactless, if unrealistic, remarks by spokesmen for its government suggested that covetous eyes were being cast on Thessalonica as a gateway to the Aegean. All this was immediately seen by most Greeks as an existential threat.

Huge demonstrations of popular anger took place in Greek cities in 1992 and periodically thereafter, whenever a new twist brought the issue to the surface again. Thessalonica, Greece's second city and only fifty kilometres from the border, saw the most vociferous activity. And the popular outpouring was not confined to Greece. Nowhere was the issue more divisive than in Australia, where the descendants of immigrants from Yugoslavia, including many who now identified as Macedonians, clashed with Greek Australians in the streets of Melbourne and other cities. At issue was not the existence or the independence of the breakaway republic but its *name*. Feeling went right to the top of government, where a split over the issue was enough to bring down the New Democracy administration in 1993. Only in 2018 would a compromise solution be found and ratified on both sides a year later. Greece's northern neighbour is now officially known as 'North Macedonia'.[4]

'Macedonia is Greek. Read history' proclaimed lapel badges worn by ground staff at Greek airports in the 1990s. Of course, the ancestors of all the Slavonic languages, or dialects, spoken in the southern Balkans in modern times did not appear on the scene until almost a thousand years after the time of Philip II and Alexander. But the Athenian orator Demosthenes could not have disagreed more with the badge wearers, demonstrators, and politicians who pushed the issue to international prominence during three decades around the turn of the twenty-first century. One consequence of the dispute is that, since the 1990s, many Greeks have been sensitive to any questioning of the ethnic identity of the *ancient* Macedonians—the very issue that had provoked such heated debates in Athens almost two and a half thousand years ago.

IN AUGUST 2004, the Olympic Games were held in Athens for the second time. Once again, after a little over a century, the nation-state was on display before the eyes of the world. Despite much carping and doubting in advance, Greek state and private organisations proved themselves more than equal to the immense logistical challenges of hosting the modern Games. Infrastructure was ready on time, if only just. All over the country, public spaces, hotels, and venues had had a facelift for the occasion. In the centre of Athens, below the Acropolis, streets were pedestrianised and landscaped; those neoclassical buildings of the nineteenth century that had escaped the bulldozers of the twentieth were tastefully restored and repainted. The opening pageant that preceded the Games seamlessly presented vignettes from Greek history, from the mysterious marble figurines from the Cyclades that long predate the oldest evidence for the Greek language, down to the traditional music of the *bouzouki* and the paintings of the twentieth-century artist Yannis Tsarouchis. High above all floated a winged angel. Here was the elusive spirit of 'Greekness', that had been so anxiously sought back in the 1930s, made manifest and presented on the world stage using the latest in showbiz technology.

But Greece, as the poet Seferis had written back then, was 'still travelling'. Three years before the first Athens Olympics, held in 1896, the country had declared bankruptcy. Six years after the second Games, European governments and banks were reeling from the long-term effects of the global financial crisis of 2007 and 2008. In the spring of 2010, the PASOK government led by George Papandreou could no longer borrow enough to service its existing debts. Normally, in such circumstances, a government would default on part of its loans. Had that happened, it would have been the seventh time in the history of the Greek state. But Greece was now part of the Eurozone; a Greek default would have consequences for the rest of the EU and, beyond it, for the entire world banking system, that were literally unimaginable—because no one had thought to imagine them.[5]

As the crisis exploded across international markets, the cartoonists of the world's press delighted in poking fun at the hapless and incompetent heirs to a once-great civilisation. If the classical heritage had once served Greeks well in the early, formative stages of building a nation-state, it had now—and not for the first time—returned as a stick to beat them with. Ancient temples riven with cracks, a discus in the form of a one-euro coin being thrown into a dustbin by a naked athlete perched on a Doric column, a caricature of a *symposium* as depicted on an ancient vase: these were easy targets and all too recognisable.[6]

To avoid a formal bankruptcy, a system of bailouts for the beleaguered Greek government was devised. Greek elected politicians and officials had no more say in the arrangements hurriedly devised to 'rescue' them than they had had in determining the terms of their independence in the early 1830s. Known technically as 'memoranda of understanding', lifesaving loans from a 'troika' made up of two European institutions and the International Monetary Fund staved off a formal default and ensured that Greece did not crash out of the Eurozone, perhaps to bring the whole edifice down with it. Successive Greek governments received three such bailouts, in 2010, 2012, and 2015. But the price was to shrink the size of the Greek economy by a quarter; unemployment for several years stood at over 25 per cent, and more than double that among young adults. Between 2010 and the middle of the decade, Greece experienced what at the time was the largest downturn for a developed economy in peacetime anywhere in the world. Cyprus was not immune either, largely thanks to the exposure of its banks to Greek debt. Even more demanding terms were imposed on the government of Cyprus in return for a bailout in 2013, although there the recovery would follow much more quickly than in Greece.

In Greek towns and cities, suicide rates soared, shops and businesses closed. Long queues formed at soup kitchens set up by the Orthodox Church and public charities. Graffiti—sometimes sharply witty, sometimes expressing deep despair or defiance—sprawled over abandoned construction sites and the walls of homes and offices. Unable to find work at home, young graduates left the country in droves to seek work in other EU countries. In the first years, public anger several times spilled out onto the streets. In June 2011, three employees died inside a bank in central Athens when demonstrators set fire to it. Further violent demonstrations accompanied the signing of the second bailout in February 2012.

Even democratic institutions for a time looked fragile. An inconclusive parliamentary election in May that year was followed by a second, six weeks later. The centre-right New Democracy was able to form a government only thanks to the support of its rival PASOK and a small fringe party on the left. But a new force had emerged to lead the opposition and break the two-party consensus that had been stable for almost forty years. This was the Coalition of the Radical Left, known by its Greek acronym SYRIZA, a far-left party fighting on an avowedly populist platform. Also populist in its tactics was Golden Dawn, Greece's only fascist or neo-Nazi party. Openly linked to armed gangs and intimidation, its members sporting Nazi-style insignia and uniforms, and crudely racist in its public pronouncements, Golden Dawn entered parliament for the first time with almost half a million votes in 2012.[7]

Populist rhetoric swept the board three years later when Alexis Tsipras was elected to head a SYRIZA government in January

2015. Tellingly, this was in coalition with another fringe party that shared the same kind of populist platform, but this time belonged to the Far *Right* (though well short of the extreme position occupied by Golden Dawn, which all other parties shunned). For six months in 2015, relying on the defiant slogans of its election programme, the SYRIZA-led government embarked on a collision course with the European institutions and the International Monetary Fund, which were its only economic lifeline. In June, with the banks closed and the country only days away from formal bankruptcy and a catastrophic crash-out from the Eurozone, Tsipras called a referendum at only a week's notice. A majority voted to reject the terms laid down by the institutions. This was the moment when a populist government stared into the abyss and turned away from disaster at the last possible moment. A third (and, as it turned out, final) bailout was signed a few days later. And in September, Tsipras won a snap election, having shed the most extreme elements in his party. Greece's short-lived experiment with populist politics was over. During the next three and a half years, SYRIZA under Tsipras would tack—even if erratically—towards the centre-left mainstream.[8]

In the parliamentary election of July 2019, the pendulum swung back to New Democracy, which won a clear mandate under its new leader, Kyriakos Mitsotakis. The two-party system that had served the country so well for four decades was restored—with the formerly far-left SYRIZA now taking the place of PASOK as a more or less centre-left opposition. The extremist Golden Dawn failed to meet the threshold for representation in parliament. A year later, a five-year court case ended in October 2020 with the leader and the most prominent members of Golden Dawn convicted of running a criminal organisation in the guise of a political party. Six of them received jail terms of thirteen years—not for their political beliefs but for proven acts of violence and intimidation, including complicity in the notorious murder of the rap artist Pavlos Fyssas in 2013.[9]

Between 2012 and 2019, in no fewer than five general elections and one referendum, Greek voters tried every possible democratic route to solving the economic and social crisis of the decade. To what extent any or all of these governments can be credited with its eventual 'solution' is perhaps debatable. But by early in 2020, the crisis did finally seem to be at an end. And despite dire prognostications in many quarters, public order had not broken down. Greeks had turned their backs on the kind of populism that had been gaining ground in other parts of the world—from Turkey and Russia to the USA and even the UK. They had come through the crisis—thanks to reliance on the deeply traditional resource of the family and a quality of inner strength that can best be translated as 'endurance' or 'patient resignation'.[10]

And in the process they had not turned against the European Union or its institutions. Although opinion polls conducted since 2015 in Greece have shown a drop in public support for membership in the Eurozone, even at the nadir in 2017 it did not fall below 50 per cent. In the European elections of May 2019, only fringe parties supported a departure from the EU, and they attracted very few votes.[11] Neither in Greece nor in Cyprus has there been much public appetite for following the example of Brexit, despite having suffered what might be regarded as the severest provocations experienced anywhere in the Union. The geopolitical advantages of solidarity with the bloc still outweigh the claims of a more rigorously defined sovereignty in the minds of voters.

Nor, despite the intense pressures of the crisis decade, has Greece seen any sign of the breakaway movements that have been growing in some parts of Europe in recent years. Whether there remains any appetite for an eventual unification between the Republic of Cyprus and Greece must be a moot point. But in outlying regions within Greece which boast a strong regional identity, such as Crete, Macedonia, or Epiros, the overwhelming impetus over the last two hundred years has been to join with the national state and, once having joined, to stay joined. Greece has no equivalent to Catalonia or the Basque region within Spain, or Scotland within the United Kingdom.

EVEN WHILE THE crisis was at its height, other news was far more positive (and largely neglected by the world's media). Offshore, the extraordinary success story of Greek shipping continued unabated, even if with less of the glamour associated with an Onassis or a Niarchos. The Greek-owned cargo fleet is now reckoned to be the largest in the world, with a 17.3 per cent share of world tonnage recorded in 2018—a remarkable figure when set alongside Greece's share of world population, a mere 0.13 per cent.[12] And although these Greek-owned businesses remain as multinational as they always were, they have contributed spectacular benefits to Greeks worldwide, as well as to the infrastructure of the Greek state. Charitable foundations formed from the bequests of several leading shipowners of the postwar period, and bearing their names, disburse huge sums to support Greeks in need and to promote Greek culture and education, as well as for broader philanthropic purposes—while their assets remain, as ever, well beyond the reach of the Greek state.[13]

A specialist hospital for cardiac treatment, named after Alexander S. Onassis, the tycoon's son killed in an air accident in 1973, was opened in 1992. In 2010, just as the financial crisis was beginning to bite, the Onassis Foundation inaugurated a state-of-the-art centre for the performing arts in Athens. The Stavros Niarchos Foundation Cultural Center, funded from the estate of Onassis's great rival, was gifted to the Greek state and opened in 2017, on land near the sea at Phaleron that in ancient times had been used for public executions and more recently had been occupied by a race course. A beautifully landscaped park, with ponds and fountains, provides a stunning setting for the newly built and lavishly equipped home of the national opera company and the new National Library of Greece.

These achievements have been built upon Greek enterprise in faraway parts of the world. But the opposite process is also at work: Chinese firms have been investing heavily in infrastructure in both Greece and Cyprus. Part of the port of Piraeus is now Chinese-owned, and in November 2019 Greece joined China's controversial Belt and Road Initiative, which many see as an attempt to spread Chinese economic and political influence around the world. In Cyprus, wealthy Russian businessmen have been offered citizenship, which brings the benefit of free movement within the European Union, in return for inward investment in the Cypriot economy—although some restrictions were announced in autumn 2020. Arrivals at Larnaca International Airport in recent years have been greeted by glitzy advertising, apparently for real estate and business opportunities, with text entirely in either Russian or Chinese. These latest manifestations of globalisation are not universally welcomed. But they do show Greeks continuing to interact with all comers, wherever in the world they can reach, as they have done throughout all their long history.

Less controversial, though not without its attendant problems too, has been the tourist industry. From modest beginnings in the 1960s, when mass tourism was just beginning, annual numbers of tourist arrivals in Greece had topped thirty million by 2018—three times the country's population. Unlike the shipping business or (perhaps) inward investment from Russia or China, tourism is very much an onshore enterprise. Its benefits are immediate and obvious in terms of local infrastructure, employment opportunities, and revenue available to the Greek state through taxation. On the other hand, the impact on the landscape, ecology, and (as some have complained ever since the days of 1960s hippies) local standards of behaviour may be less beneficial. Mass tourism and its associated building projects have surely blighted the natural beauty of many a Greek island and coastline—though to a far less extent than in some other parts of the Mediterranean.

Until the Covid-19 pandemic struck early in 2020, the outlook for the economies of Greece and Cyprus, and for international Greek enterprise, was brighter than at any time for more than a decade.

In 2021, as Greece and Greeks worldwide commemorate two hundred years since the start of the Revolution that inaugurated the first Greek state, the pandemic is only one of several challenges that they face. And these are all of them as much global as they are local.

By the time the second wave of the virus began to sweep across Europe at the end of 2020, the two Greek-speaking states had fared relatively less badly than most of the rest of the continent. Some have put this down to climate—an unconscious echo, perhaps, of Winckelmann's explanation, in the eighteenth century, for the glories of classical sculpture. Others, more plausibly, have given the credit to governments which acted promptly and decisively in the early phase of the pandemic, then cautiously managed to save something of the summer tourist season, and with it their national economies, without at the same time importing dangerous levels of infection from abroad. It may also be relevant that both Greece and Cyprus have within living memory experienced curfews and restrictions on civil liberties far harsher and more rigorously enforced than any lockdown so far imposed, at least in the West, to combat Covid-19.

Other threats are of longer standing. Ever since deposits of crude oil were first discovered beneath the seabed off the northern Aegean island of Thasos at the end of 1973, Greece has resisted attempts by its neighbour Turkey to claim jurisdiction in and beneath the Aegean Sea and in the air above it. Successive governments on both sides have alternated between periods of tension and relative degrees of rapprochement. The spectre of armed conflict between the two NATO allies has returned roughly once per decade since 1976, when the leader of Greece's official opposition called for a Turkish exploration vessel to be torpedoed in the Aegean.

The discovery in 2011 of the Aphrodite oil field off the coast of Cyprus raised the stakes and brought in additional players, including Israel and Egypt. Further finds of oil and gas were made during 2019. When the Cyprus government granted a licence later that year for production to go ahead in its territorial waters, Turkey countered with new claims of its own. Since then, both republics, Greece and Cyprus, have watched with increasing anxiety as the policies of the Turkish president Recip Tayyip Erdoğan seek to extend his country's geopolitical influence in the region in ways that directly threaten their interests. The Greek and Cypriot governments continue to insist on an internationalist position and on finding solutions within the framework of existing maritime law, treaties, and a rule-governed international system. There is an obvious pragmatic rationale for this approach, given the strategic imbalance between the two sides; but the underlying principles can be traced back to the circumstances in which first Greece and, much later, Cyprus gained their independence. These principles are probably of greater long-term importance than the outcome of a spat over the exploitation of oil and gas at a time when most of the world's governments, and even leading oil companies, are moving away from dependence on carbon-based sources of energy in response to the greater threat from climate change.[14]

A challenge of a different kind, and quite new, at least in modern times, comes from inward migration. For centuries—indeed, quite possibly going back as far as the Bronze Age Mycenaeans—young Greeks had left their homeland in large numbers to seek their fortune elsewhere in the world. Now, since the early 1990s, the world has been coming to them.

The opening of the Cold War frontiers at the end of 1989 was only a beginning. By the turn of the new century, migrants and asylum seekers were reaching the country, via Turkey, from all over the Middle East, East Asia, and parts of Africa. Problems of housing, integration, exploitation of migrants by criminal gangs, and petty criminality followed, particularly in Athens and Thessalonica—conditions which may have contributed to the rise of Golden Dawn as a political force. Because a high proportion of these new immigrants were Muslim, a nation which had fought for its independence under the banner of Orthodox Christianity has now once again begun to find itself home to a significant and increasing Muslim population. It would take years of wrangling before the first official mosque to function in Athens in almost two hundred years opened its doors to worshippers in November 2020.

But nothing could have prepared the authorities for the mass arrivals into Greece of refugees fleeing wars and turmoil in Afghanistan, Syria, Iraq, Sudan, and even sub-Saharan Africa. This new crisis reached its peak in 2015, just at the time when the country was undergoing the most testing period of its domestic problems. In that year alone, over eight hundred thousand migrants, most of them in unseaworthy open boats, arrived on the Greek islands closest to Turkey. For the great majority, the goal was not to settle in Greece but to find asylum in the larger and more prosperous countries of the European Union. Then, in 2016, European states began to close their borders to migrants. The problem for Greece, as well as for the migrants themselves, became dramatically worse. At the time of writing, neither attempts by the institutions of the EU to share the burden among European states nor negotiations between the EU and Turkey have produced more than temporary, limited solutions. On Lesbos, the infamous Moria camp, built to house three thousand asylum seekers, had been packed with five times that number by the time it burned down in September 2020.[15]

Stories of traditional Greek warm-heartedness towards these new arrivals on their shores have given way to ominous signs of resentment at a problem that local or national governments cannot solve. Violence towards refugees on Lesbos and other islands is reported to be on the increase; public demands, demonstrations, and other forms of action have been growing on the most affected islands since the middle of the last decade. Today, Greece and Greeks find themselves on the front line (or one of the front lines) of a global problem that shows no sign of going away.

EPILOGUE

MORE THAN THREE and a half thousand years have passed since that imagined dawn over the Aegean with which this story began. In all that time, speakers of the Greek language have never ceased to reinvent themselves. There is every reason to suppose that they will go on doing so, in ways that we cannot imagine or predict, for long into the future.

Today, Greeks live and flourish on every inhabited continent. In 2011, Greece itself, according to the most recent census, was home to just under eleven million. The population of the Greek-speaking Republic of Cyprus at the same time was just over eight hundred thousand. No one knows for certain how many more people around the world speak Greek as a first or a heritage language or consider themselves to be of Greek descent. Communities of more than one hundred thousand can be found in the United States, Australia, South Africa, Argentina, Brazil, spread across several republics of the former Soviet Union, and (largely originating from Cyprus) Great Britain. A total figure of seven million, settled in 141 countries, has been hazarded. Even if these numbers are inflated, it is quite probable that up to half as many Greeks again live outside the Hellenic Republic as within its borders.[1] That is a very different ratio from the three-to-one that existed at the time when the Greek state was first created. But it is still an important reminder that the story of the Greeks is not just the story of Greece. And, since the nineteenth century, the dispersed Greek-speaking world once again has a geographical and emotional centre that most, if not all Greeks, irrespective of where they live, can identify with.

Constantinople as the centre of a world empire (once) and a universal church (still) retains its hold on the imagination and the loyalty of a majority of Greeks who maintain their links to the Orthodox branch of Christianity. But the political centre of the Greek-speaking world since the 1920s has been the national capital, Athens—which is also home to almost half the population of Greece. Greek communities around the world regularly lobby their own governments to support Greek interests in matters of foreign policy (and usually irrespective of whichever party is in power in Greece at the time). This has been most evident with the Greek American lobby in the United States, which scored notable successes particularly in the 1970s and 1980s. But it is a stance that has repeatedly been echoed around the world, to the extent that governments in both Greece and the Republic of Cyprus have come to rely on support from expatriate communities abroad.[2]

For these reasons, it does make sense, today, to talk of a Greek diaspora—meaning specifically the descendants of people who emigrated from the 'old' Greek-speaking world, as it was in the eighteenth century, to create new communities around the world in the nineteenth, twentieth, and—who knows?—perhaps also the twenty-first. Wherever these people are to be found, and regardless of the citizenship they hold, overwhelmingly they continue to think of themselves as Greek and to identify, to varying extents, with their idea of a Greek state to which they feel that they, too, belong. However divided Greece has been within itself at various times in its two-hundred-year history, no organised political alternative or rival to that state has ever emerged from the Greek diaspora—or, surely, is likely to. And although the old term of self-designation, *Romios*, can still be heard in certain contexts, every Greek, everywhere in the world, is today a Hellene in his or her own language.

Today, Astoria in the New York Borough of Queens is perhaps the biggest Greek village in the world. But Greek Americans who may now be of the fifth or sixth generation do not necessarily speak Greek well, or even at all. In the Australian states of New South Wales and Victoria during the 1970s and 1980s, government policy encouraged education in heritage languages. The children of Greek immigrants could take their lessons and exams at school in Greek; university courses in Modern Greek studies were full. But after changes in policy during the 1990s, these possibilities no longer exist. Third-generation Greek Australians are less likely to speak the language of their parents and grandparents, or to want to learn it.

It was ever thus. In centuries past, individuals and whole communities whose mother tongue was Greek might lose their language in favour of Latin, Arabic, Slavonic, Turkish, or French. English is only the most recent of these. But in every generation, at least as many kept faith with the language of their earliest years. And the centuries-old process of 'becoming Greek' has never quite ended either. For at least some of those who have arrived, fleeing persecution or hardship at home, landfall on a Greek island has been something more than a transitory step on a desperate, possibly unending journey. Hiva Panahi is a refugee from Iran who has made her home in Greece since 2000. A decade later, she was writing and publishing poems in Greek, as well as in her native Kurdish. This poem is called 'The Breath of the Olive Tree':

> *We the wandering*
> *We the barefoot*
> *We without space or country*
> *We the burnt and fiery winds*

We saw you, with those final breaths
That burned a piece of the sea.[3]

In these lines, a twenty-first-century refugee captures her first en-counter with an Aegean landscape that has been celebrated by trav-ellers, poets, and artists ever since Homer sang of the 'wine-dark sea' some thirty centuries ago—how else but in her newly adopted language, *Greek*.

ACKNOWLEDGEMENTS

This book would never have been written but for two people: my agent, the late Felicity Bryan, and Alex Bowler, who now oversees publishing at Faber. Back in 2016, Felicity was seeking a publisher for another book of mine. Among the rejection letters she passed on to me was one that said (in effect), 'Why doesn't he write the *whole* history of the Greeks?' The challenge had been thrown down. And no sooner had my earlier book gone to press than I began to flesh out the idea for *The Greeks*. I hadn't remembered where that rejection letter came from. But Felicity did. It came from Alex Bowler, who by then had recently taken up his post at Faber. The three of us met together only once, just after the contract had been signed. And this book is the result.

Felicity was the best agent any writer could wish for. Her loss to cancer at the age of seventy-four in June 2020 was felt throughout the publishing world, and there are many fitting tributes to her already in print. I had come to know Felicity relatively late in our respective careers. We met quite rarely (even before Covid-19 kept us all at home). But with her passing, I knew that I had lost a friend. Being a literary agent, for Felicity, was so much more than a business. She loved books and people; she knew what she liked, and she had the gift for making others as enthusiastic as she was.

Alex has stood by me from first to last, despite the responsibilities of a role that goes far beyond that of a commissioning editor. He was the first person to read the whole of this book in draft, and his observations and queries on the early chapters were full of insights that helped to guide me through the many thickets that lay ahead. I have also been fortunate in being able to call on friends who kindly read several chapters and generously gave me the benefit of their experience and expertise which goes far beyond my own: Professor John Bennet on the Mycenaean period and the dark age; Professor Paul Cartledge on ancient Greece; Assistant Professor Dionysios Stathakopoulos on the Byzantine millennium; and Dr John Kittmer, who served as British ambassador to Greece from 2013 to 2016, on the final chapters.

In preparing the book for press, I have benefited hugely from the encouragement and support of Brian Distelberg, editorial director at Basic Books, who commissioned the US edition. His colleague Emma Berry also contributed much thoughtful feedback. The near-final text was read, with a meticulous and sympathetic eye, by Eleo Carson on behalf of Faber, not once but twice. For whatever blemishes or omissions remain, I alone must take the blame.

For moral and practical support, I have accumulated debts too numerous to name. John Bennet not only gave expert advice, but as Director of the British School at Athens throughout the time that I was working on this project, he and his colleagues have given me their time, their friendship, and on numerous occasions, before the start of the Covid-19 pandemic, a roof over my head in the friendly and congenial atmosphere of the BSA, set in its delightful garden hidden away in the centre of dusty, noisy Athens. The School's administrator, Dr Tania Gerousi; the archivist, Amalia Kakissis; Vicki Tzavara in the front office; and Penny Wilson, the librarian until 2019—all went out of their way to assist me while I was writing this book.

I was fortunate, too, to enjoy the hospitality of the British Embassy in Athens, where Kate Smith, in post from 2017 to 2021, has also become a good friend. I thank the Greek ambassador to London during most of this period, Mr Dimitrios Caramitsos-Tziras, for many kindnesses. Professor Maria Georgopoulou and Professor David Holton helped with specific queries during lockdown, as did the Society for the Promotion of Hellenic Studies and the librarians of the collection that the society

Acknowledgements

shares with the Roman Society and the Institute for Classical Studies at the University of London.

At King's College London, Gonda Van Steen, my successor as Koraes Professor, has been generous with institutional and moral support whenever I needed it. Many others, whose names appear among the sources in the Notes at the end of the book, have contributed, too, not only through their published work but often through discussions and interactions that have taken place over many years, and helped to shape my thinking about the Greeks and the Greek-speaking world.

The book in its finished form owes a great deal to the superb professionalism of several people: Cecilia Mackay, the able and sympathetic picture researcher with whom it has been a pleasure to work for the second time; Fred Courtwright, who secured permissions to quote from material in copyright; Patti Isaacs, who drew the maps; and Christina Palaia, my copy editor at Basic Books. Special thanks for ensuring a smooth path to publication go to Carrie Plitt at the Felicity Bryan Agency in Oxford and her counterpart Zoë Pagnamenta in New York. It has been a pleasure, and at times even an education, to work with all of them. And the biggest thank-you of all goes to my wife, Fran, for—well—everything, but not least for her patient and eagle-eyed reading of so many different versions of *The Greeks*.

Roderick Beaton
Whitstable, Kent
March 2021

LIST OF ILLUSTRATIONS
AND PHOTO CREDITS

1. Gold funerary mask from Grave IV (Grave Circle A) at Mycenae, 16th century BCE. National Archaeological Museum, Athens, Department of Collection of Prehistoric, Egyptian, Cypriot and Near Eastern Antiquities. © Hellenic Ministry of Culture and Sports, Archaeological Receipts Fund (NAM inv. no. P 253).

2. Bronze Age fresco from Akrotiri on Thera (Santorini). West House, Room 5 (detail), 16th century BCE. Ephorate of Antiquities of the Cyclades. Photo: Picture Art Collection/Alamy.

3. Lyre Player and Bird Fresco from the Throne Room of Nestor's palace, Pylos, c. 1300 BCE. Watercolour reconstruction by Piet de Jong. Illustration from Mabel L. Lang, *The Palace of Nestor at Pylos in Western Messenia II: The Frescoes* (Princeton, NJ: University of Cincinnati and Princeton University Press, 1969). Reproduced by courtesy of The Department of Classics, University of Cincinnati.

4. Clay tablet PY Eq 213 inscribed in Linear B from the palace of Pylos, c. 1200–1180 BCE. National Archaeological Museum, Athens, Department of Collection of Prehistoric, Egyptian, Cypriot, and Near Eastern Antiquities. Photo: DEA/G. Dagli Orti/De Agostini/Getty Images. Caption information courtesy of John Bennet. Reproduced by permission of the Hellenic Ministry of Culture and Sports, Archaeological Receipts Fund.

5. Marble funerary statue of the Kore Phrasikleia, 550–540 BCE. National Archaeological Museum, Athens, Department of Sculpture

471

Collection. © Hellenic Ministry of Culture and Sports, Archaeological Receipts Fund (NAM inv. no. Γ 4889).

6. Phrasikleia Kore. Full polychromy restoration, displayed at *Gods in Color* exhibition at the Legion of Honor, San Francisco, 2017. Photo: Wikimedia Commons/R. Mathaler, CC BY-SA 4.0.

7. Marble funerary statue of the Kouros Kroisos, found at Anavyssos, Attica, c. 530 BCE. National Archaeological Museum, Athens, Department of Sculpture Collection. © Hellenic Ministry of Culture and Sports, Archaeological Receipts Fund (NAM inv. no Γ 3851).

8. Skyphos with scene of courtship by the Amasis Painter, c. 540 BCE. Musée du Louvre, Paris. Photo: © RMN–Grand Palais (Musée du Louvre)/Les frères Chuzeville.

9. Riace warrior, bronze, Statue A, c. 460 BCE. Museo Archeologico Nazionale, Reggio Calabria, Italy. Photo: Luisa Ricciarini/Bridgeman Images.

10. Salamis viewed from the Propylaea, Acropolis, Athens (Lucky/Alamy).

11. Marble relief (Block V) from the East Frieze of the Parthenon. © The Trustees of the British Museum, London.

12. Head of Philip II, King of the Macedonians, ivory carving from the Royal Tomb, Vergina, Greece, 4th century BCE. Archaeological Museum, Thessalonica. Photo: G. Dagli Orti/De Agostini/ Bridgeman Images.

13. Head of Alexander, 325–300 BCE, found at Giannitsa. Archaeological Museum, Pella. Ephorate of Antiquities of Pella, Hellenic Ministry of Culture and Sports. Photo: Ministry of Culture and Sports Archaeological Resources Fund.

14. Alexander confronts Darius III at the Battle of Issus (mosaic from Pompeii, 1st century CE). Museo Archeologico Nazionale, Naples. Photo: Zev Radovan/Bridgeman Images.

15. Panel thought to show the story of the Trojan Horse, Gandhara School, Pakistan, 2nd–3rd century CE. © The Trustees of the British Museum.

16. Portrait bust of Cleopatra VII, c. 40–30 BCE, Altes Museum, Berlin. Photo: Bridgeman Images.

17. Sphinx discovered in the submerged royal quarters of Alexandria's eastern harbour, 1st century BCE. National Museum of Alexandria, Egypt (283, SCA 450). Photo: Christoph Gerigk © Franck Goddio/ Hilti Foundation.

18. The Arch of Hadrian, Athens, photo by Braun, Clément & Cie, negative c. 1869; print c. 1890. J. Paul Getty Museum, Malibu, CA. 87.XM.99.3.

19. Jerash, Jordan. Photo: The author.

20. Marble relief representing part of a leg with an inscription dedicating it from Tyche to Asclepius and Hygieia as a votive offering. © The Trustees of the British Museum.

21. Papyrus 46, c. 175–225 CE, containing part of Saint Paul's First Letter to the Corinthians. Folio 40, beginning *1 Cor.* 2:3–3:5. Image courtesy of the University of Michigan Papyrology Collection.

22. Emperor Constantine, monumental head, 4th century. Capitoline Museums, Rome. Photo: Peter Horree/Alamy.

23. The interior of Hagia Sophia, Constantinople, from the western gallery. Image © Dumbarton Oaks, Image Collections & Fieldwork Archives, Washington, DC. Photo: Robert Ousterhout, BF.S.1979.10232.

24. Emperor Justinian, detail of mosaic dating from the 6th century, church of S. Apollinare Nuovo, Ravenna. Photo: Bible Land Pictures/ Alamy.

25. Mosaic panel depicting the Empress Theodora and her retinue, 547, from San Vitale, Ravenna. Photo: Wikimedia Commons/Petar Milošević.

26. Mosaic cross from the period of iconoclasm, apse of the Church of Saint Irene, Constantinople. Photo: Yasin Karabacak.

27. Late Byzantine icon (c. 1400) showing the 'Triumph of Orthodoxy', detail. © The Trustees of the British Museum.

28. Alexios I Komnenos, Byzantine school, 12th century. Biblioteca Apostolica Vaticana, Vatican City. Photo: Granger/Bridgeman Images.

29. John II Komnenos, Byzantine school, mosaic, 12th century from the east end, South Gallery, Hagia Sophia, Istanbul. Photo: G. Dagli Orti/De Agostini Picture Library/Bridgeman Images.

30. Manuel I Komnenos, Byzantine school. Facsimile of manuscript in the Biblioteca Apostolica Vaticana. Bibliothèque des Arts Decoratifs, Paris. Photo: De Agostini Picture Library/Bridgeman Images.

31. The sack of Constantinople in April 1204, miniature from *Croniques abrégies commençans au temps de Hérode Antipas* by David Aubert, 1401–1500, Bibliothèque de l'Arsenal, Paris. Ms-5090 réserve fol 205r (photo: BnF).

32. Theodore Metochites, donor portrait, c. 1316–1321, mosaic in the Kariye Camii (formerly Church of the Chora), Istanbul. Photo: Gezmen/Alamy.

33. Frankish warriors in the Peloponnese, detail from a historiated initial letter in Juan Fernández de Heredia, *The Chronicle of Morea*, c.1393. Biblioteca Nacional de España, Madrid, MS 10131, fol. 183r.

34. George Gemistos Plethon, detail from fresco, *The Cavalcade of the Magi*, 1459, by Benozzo Gozzoli. Palazzo Medici Riccardi, Florence. Photo: Bridgeman Images.

35. Sultan Mehmed II. Ottoman school, 15th–16th century. Topkapı Palace Library, Istanbul. Photo: Werner Forman/UIG/Leemage/Bridgeman Images.

36. The siege of Candia from the *Atlas Van Der Hagen*, pub. by N. Visscher, c. 1680. Photo: Koninklijke Bibliotheek, The Hague.

37. Phanariot with Armenian costume, 1818–1820, by Gerasimos Pizzamanos. Historical Archives, National Historical Museum, Athens.

38. The Caryatids, Saint Pancras Church, Euston Road, London. Photo: Michael Jenner/Alamy.

39. *The Reception of King Otto in Front of the Theseion, Athens*, by Peter von Hess, 1839. Neue Pinakothek, Munich. Photo: Leonard de Selva/Bridgeman Images.

40. Greek Independence Day, Sydney Opera House, Australia. Photo © Nick Bourdo.

41. *The Parthenon Eurozone*, cartoon, 2012. © Andy Davey.

42. *I wish you could learn something useful from the past*, street art by Dimitris Taxis, 2013, in Kerameikos, Athens. Photo: Julia Tulke, http://aestheticsofcrisis.org.

43. The new National Library of Greece, Stavros Niarchos Foundation Cultural Center, Athens, opened 2017. Photo: National Library of Greece. © NLG Nikos Karanikolas.

PERMISSIONS

Hesiod, excerpts from *Works and Days*, translated A. E. Stallings. Copyright © 2018 by A. E. Stallings. Used by permission of Penguin, an imprint and division of Penguin Random House UK.

Homer, excerpts from *The Iliad of Homer*, translated by Richmond Lattimore. Copyright 1951, © 2011 by The University of Chicago. Reprinted with the permission of The University of Chicago Press. Excerpts from *The Odyssey*, translated by Emily Wilson, Copyright © 2017 by Emily Wilson. Used by permission of W. W. Norton & Company, Inc.

Robin Lane Fox, excerpt from *Pagans and Christians*. Copyright © 1986 by Robin Lane Fox. Used by permission of Alfred A. Knopf, an imprint of the Knopf Doubleday Publishing Group, a division of Penguin Random House LLC and Penguin, a division of Penguin Random House UK. All rights reserved.

Excerpt from Romanos the Melodist from Paul Magdalino, "The history of the future and its uses: Prophecy, policy and propaganda" in Roderick Beaton and Charlotte Roueché (eds), *The Making of Byzantine History: Studies Dedicated to Donald M. Nicol* (Aldershot: Ashgate, 1993). Reprinted with the permission of Paul Magdalino.

Hiva Panahi, "The Breath of the Olive Tree," translated by Karen Emmerich, in Karen van Dyck (ed.), *Austerity Measures: The New Greek Poetry* (London: Penguin, 2016). Reprinted with the permission of the author, translator, and editors.

NOTES

References to Ancient Texts and Abbreviations Used in the Notes

Most of the ancient Greek (and Latin) texts referenced in the notes which follow have been translated many times. Older translations, out of copyright, are freely available to read on the internet; Greek texts can be found on sites such as Thesaurus Linguae Graecae (subscription required) or Perseus Digital Library: Greek and Roman Materials. Rather than full bibliographical details of any one edition or translation, in references I give only the author's name and the most commonly used English translation of the title. Where relevant, these are followed by the conventional numbering of books and lines (for verse) or paragraphs (for prose) common to all modern editions and most translations (without comma, to distinguish them from page numbers in all other references). For a small number of ancient works I use these standard abbreviations:

1 Macc.	First Book of Maccabees
2 Macc.	Second Book of Maccabees
Acts	*Acts of the Apostles* (New Testament)
Aesch. *Pers.*	Aeschylus, *The Persians*
Ath.Pol.	*The Constitution of the Athenians* (attributed to Aristotle)
Dio Cassius	Dion Kassios, *Roman History*
Diod.Sic.	Diodorus Siculus (of Sicily), *Library*

Fr(s).	(following an author's name, 'fragment(s)' followed by number)
Hdt.	Herodotus, *Histories*
Il.	Homer, *Iliad*
Isaiah	The Book of the Prophet Isaiah (Old Testament)
Justin	Justin, excerpts from the *Philippic Histories* by Trogus
Livy	Livy, *History of Rome from the Founding of the City*
Od.	Homer, *Odyssey*
Paul, *1 Cor.*	*First Epistle of Paul the Apostle to the Corinthians* (New Testament)
Paul, *Gal.*	*Epistle of Paul the Apostle to the Galatians* (New Testament)
Paus.	Pausanias, *Description of Greece*
Polyb.	Polybius, *Histories*
Thuc.	Thucydides, *History of the Peloponnesian War*
Xen. *Hell.*	Xenophon, *Hellenica*

Chapter 1: Of Ledgers and Legends

1. Bull leaping: Andrew Shapland, 'Jumping to Conclusions: Bull-Leaping in Minoan Crete', *Society and Animals* 21 (2013): 194–207. 'Lustral basins': Ellen Adams, *Cultural Identity in Minoan Crete: Social Dynamics in the Neopalatial Period* (Cambridge: Cambridge University Press, 2017), 54–62. Human sacrifice: Yannis Sakellarakis and Efi Sapouna-Sakellarakis, *Archanes: Minoan Crete in a New Light* (Athens: Ammos, 1997), 268–311. Ritual cannibalism: S. Wall, J. H. Musgrave, and P. M. Warren, 'Human Bones from a Late Minoan IB House at Knossos', *Annual of the British School at Athens* 81 (1986): 333–338.

2. On the unresolved issues surrounding the dating of this event, see Oliver Dickinson, 'The Aegean', in *The Cambridge World Prehistory*, 3 vols., ed. Colin Renfrew and Paul Bahn (Cambridge: Cambridge

University Press, 2014), 3.1860–1886 (see 1861); Cynthia Shelmerdine, 'Background, Sources, and Methods', in *The Cambridge Companion to the Aegean Bronze Age*, ed. Cynthia Shelmerdine (Cambridge: Cambridge University Press, 2008), 6; Adams, *Cultural Identity*, 4–8.

3. Jan Driessen and Colin Macdonald, *The Troubled Island: Minoan Crete Before and After the Santorini Eruption* (Liège and Austin: Université de Liège and University of Texas at Austin, 1997). On the geology of the eruption, see Christos Doumas, *Thera: Pompeii of the Ancient Aegean* (London: Thames & Hudson, 1983) and W. L. Friedrich, *Fire in the Sea, the Santorini Volcano: Natural History and the Legend of Atlantis*, trans. A. R. McBirney (Cambridge: Cambridge University Press, 1999); Dickinson, 'Aegean', 1873.

4. Louise Schofield, *The Mycenaeans* (London: British Museum Press, 2007), 28.

5. Most succinctly summarised in Geoffrey Horrocks, *Greek: A History of the Language and Its Speakers*, 2nd ed. (Medford, MA, and Oxford: Wiley Blackwell, 2014), 21. See also Daniel Pullen, 'The Early Bronze Age in Greece', in Shelmerdine, *Aegean Bronze Age*, 19–46 (see 38–41 for a summary of the main theories).

6. Colin Renfrew, *Archaeology and Language: The Puzzle of Indo-European Origins* (London: Jonathan Cape, 1987); Paul Heggarty and Colin Renfrew, 'Western and Central Asia: Languages', in Renfrew and Bahn, *Cambridge World Prehistory*, 3.1678–1699.

7. Schofield, *Mycenaeans*, 32–47.

8. See 'Palace of Nestor Excavations, Pylos, Greece, Featuring the Grave of the Griffin Warrior', http://www.griffinwarrior.org.

9. Pia de Fidio, 'Mycenaean History', in *A Companion to Linear B: Mycenaean Greek Texts and their World* [hereafter: *CLB*], 3 vols., ed. Yves Duhoux and Anna Morpurgo-Davies (Louvain-la-Neuve, Belgium: Peeters, 2008, 2011, 2014), 1.81–114 (see 88).

10. Jack Davis, 'Minoan Crete and the Aegean Islands', in Shelmerdine, *Aegean Bronze Age*, 186–208; Adams, *Cultural Identity*, 225–227.

11. Philip Betancourt, 'Minoan Trade', in Shelmerdine, *Aegean Bronze Age*, 209–229 (see 217); Janice Crowley, 'Mycenaean Art and

Architecture', in the same volume, 258–288 (see 260–261); Jack Davis and Sharon Stocker, 'The Gold Necklace from the Grave of the Griffin Warrior at Pylos', *Hesperia* 87, no. 4 (2018): 611–632.

12. Christos Doumas, *The Wall-Paintings of Thera* (Athens: The Thera Foundation, 1992), 47 and plates 26–29.

13. See (more cautiously) James Clinton Wright, 'Early Mycenaean Greece', in Shelmerdine, *Aegean Bronze Age*, 230–257 (see 251).

14. Adams, *Cultural Identity*, 54–62; J. A. MacGillivray, J. Driessen, and L. H. Sackett, *The Palaikastro Kouros. A Minoan Chryselephantine Statuette and Its Aegean Bronze Age Context* (London: British School at Athens, 2000); John Younger and Paul Rehak, 'Minoan Culture: Religion, Burial Customs, and Administration', in Shelmerdine, *Aegean Bronze Age*, 165–185 (see 170).

15. Yannis Galanakis, Efi Tsitsa, and Ute Günkel-Maschek, 'The Power of Images: Re-examining the Wall Paintings from the Throne Room at Knossos', *Annual of the British School at Athens* 112 (2017): 47–98; Mycenaean-style burials in the region of Knossos: Laura Preston, 'A Mortuary Perspective on Political Changes in Late Minoan II–IIIB Crete', *American Journal of Archaeology* 108 (2004): 321–348; Lesley Fitton, *Minoans* (London: British Museum, 2002), 189–191. Minoan customs: Adams, *Cultural Identity*, 219–221; Younger and Rehak, 'Minoan Culture', 170–173.

16. Laura Preston, 'Late Minoan II to IIIB Crete', in Shelmerdine, *Aegean Bronze Age*, 310–326; de Fidio, 'Mycenaean History', 90.

17. J. Driessen, 'Chronology of the Linear B Texts', *CLB* 1.69–79 (see 71–72, 76); J. Bennet, 'The Geography of the Mycenaean Kingdoms', *CLB* 2.137–168 (see 150). See also Ester Salgarella, *Aegean Linear Script(s): Rethinking the Relationship Between Linear A and Linear B* (Cambridge: Cambridge University Press, 2020).

18. John Bennet, 'Linear B and Homer', *CLB* 3.187–233 (see 203).

19. Driessen, 'Chronology', 77; C. Shelmerdine, 'Iklaina Tablet IK X1', in Pierre Carlier, *Études mycéniennes 2010* (Pisa: Fabrizio Serra, 2012), 75–77.

20. Shelmerdine, 'Background', 13.

21. Crowley, 'Mycenaean Art', 259; Stefan Hiller, 'Mycenaean Religion and Cult', *CLB* 2.169–211 (see 180 for lyre players at Thebes); Bennet, 'Linear B', 216–219.

22. Younger and Rehak, 'Minoan Culture', 169–170, 181, 183n11; Schofield, *Mycenaeans*, 89, 151, 168–169; Crowley, 'Mycenaean Art', 280.

23. Paul Halstead and John Barrett, eds., *Food, Cuisine and Society in Prehistoric Greece* (Oxford: Oxbow, 2004); Barbara Olsen, *Women in Mycenaean Greece: The Linear B Tablets from Pylos and Knossos* (London: Routledge, 2014).

24. Schofield, *Mycenaeans*, 78–79 (quoted); see also Sigrid Deger-Jalkotzy, 'Decline, Destruction, Aftermath', in Shelmerdine, *Aegean Bronze Age*, 387–414 (see 388–389); Oliver Dickinson, *The Aegean from Bronze Age to Iron Age* (London: Routledge, 2006), 36, 42.

25. Cynthia Shelmerdine and John Bennet, 'Mycenaean States: Economy and Administration', in Shelmerdine, *Aegean Bronze Age*, 289–309 (see 298–303). Defences at Pylos: Deger-Jalkotzy, 'Decline', 388, 408n9. On Thebes, see Vassilis Aravantinos, 'Mycenaean Thebes: Old Questions, New Answers', *Actes des journées d'archéologie et de philologie mycéniennes* 54 (2010): 51–72 (on fortifications, see 54).

26. John Bennet, 'Palaces and Their Regions: Geographical Analysis of Territorial Exploitation in Late Bronze Age Crete and Greece', *Pasiphae: Rivista di Filologia e Antichità Egee* 11 (2017): 151–173 (see 159–160, 168); see also Bennet, 'Geography', 148–157.

27. Gary Beckman, Trevor Bryce, and Eric Cline, *The Ahhiyawa Texts* (Atlanta, GA: Society of Biblical Literature, 2011), 61 (quoted), 63, 67–68, 101–122; Joachim Latacz, *Troy and Homer: Towards a Solution of an Old Mystery* (Oxford: Oxford University Press, 2004), 121–128.

28. E. Cline and S. Stannish, 'Sailing the Great Green Sea? Amenhotep III's "Aegean List" from Kom el-Hetan, Once More', *Journal of Ancient Egyptian Interconnections* 3, no. 2 (2011): 6–16; Latacz, *Troy*, 128–133; de Fidio, 'Mycenaean History', 96–98; Bennet, 'Geography', 158–162.

29. For the first possibility, see Jorrit Kelder, *The Kingdom of Mycenae* (Bethesda, MD: CDL Press, 2010). For the 'confederacy' alternative, first proposed by Christopher Mee, see Beckman et al., *Ahhiyawa Texts*, 4–6. For a range of views, see Jorrit Kelder and Willemijn Waal, eds., *From 'Lugal.gal' to 'Wanax': Kingship and Political Organisation in the Late Bronze Age Aegean* (Leiden: Sidestone, 2019).

30. Beckman et al., *Ahhiyawa Texts*, 269–270.

31. Beckman et al., *Ahhiyawa Texts*, 270–271, for text see 81, 95 ('Indictment of Madduwatta'); Kelder, *Kingdom*, 23–25.

32. Schofield, *Mycenaeans*, 102–115; Christopher Mee, 'Mycenaean Greece, the Aegean, and Beyond', in Shelmerdine, *Aegean Bronze Age*, 362–386 (364–365 quoted).

33. de Fidio, 'Mycenaean History', 93; L. García Ramón, 'Mycenaean Onomastics', *CLB* 2.213–251 (see 219–229).

34. Mee, 'Mycenaean Greece', 371–372; Latacz, *Troy*, 105–110, 118, 301.

35. Beckman et al., *Ahhiyawa Texts*, 269–270.

36. Thebes: Duhoux, 'Mycenaean Anthology', 381–389. Pylos: Sharon R. Stocker and Jack L. Davis, 'Animal Sacrifice, Archives, and Feasting at the Palace of Nestor', *Hesperia: The Journal of the American School of Classical Studies at Athens* 73, no. 2 (2004): 179–195; Paul Halstead and Valassia Isaakidou, 'Faunal Evidence for Feasting: Burnt Offerings from the Palace of Nestor at Pylos', in Halstead and Barrett, *Food*, 136–154. For alternative readings of the evidence, suggesting anxiety and preparation at Pylos, see Schofield, *Mycenaeans*, 143, 172–174; Deger-Jalkotzy, 'Decline', 389; Duhoux, 'Mycenaean Anthology', 335.

37. Colin Renfrew, 'Systems Collapse as Social Transformation: Catastrophe and Anastrophe in Early State Societies', in *Transformations: Mathematical Approaches to Culture Change*, ed. Colin Renfrew and Kenneth Cooke (New York: Academic Press, 1979), 481–506; Joseph Tainter, *The Collapse of Complex Societies* (Cambridge: Cambridge University Press, 1988).

38. Tainter, *Collapse*, 193, see also 4–5, 92, 110, 118–123.

39. Tainter, *Collapse*, 199–203.

40. See, most fully, Eric Cline, *1177 B.C.: The Year Civilization Collapsed* (Princeton, NJ: Princeton University Press, 2014).

41. The fullest ancient source is Plutarch, 'Life of Theseus' (written c. 100 CE). For modern reinterpretations of Minoan civilisation and related myths, see Nicoletta Momigliano and Alexandre Farnoux, eds., *Cretomania: Modern Desires for the Minoan Past* (Abingdon: Routledge, 2017); Nicoletta Momigliano, *In Search of the Labyrinth: The Cultural Legacy of Minoan Crete* (London: Bloomsbury, 2020).

42. Duhoux, 'Mycenaean Anthology', 262.

43. Momigliano, *In Search*, 190–196.

44. Sigmund Freud, *The Interpretation of Dreams*, trans. J. Strachey, Penguin Freud Library, vol. 4 (London: Penguin, 1991), 362–366.

45. See, for example, Natalie Haynes, *Pandora's Jar: Women in the Greek Myths* (London: Picador, 2020).

46. Freud himself thought there could be a historical connection between the two: Sigmund Freud, *Moses and Monotheism*, trans. J. Strachey, Penguin Freud Library, vol. 13 (London: Penguin, 1991), 312–313; Cathy Gere, *The Tomb of Agamemnon: Mycenae and the Search for a Hero* (London: Profile, 2006), 135–137; Nicoletta Momigliano, 'Introduction: Cretomania—Desiring the Minoan Past in the Present', in Momigliano and Farnoux, *Cretomania*, 1–14 (see 3, and chaps. 5 and 8 in that volume). No historical matriarchy: Younger and Rehak, 'Minoan Culture', 182.

47. Barry Strauss, *The Trojan War: A New History* (New York: Simon & Schuster, 2006), 7; Latacz, *Troy*, 283–287. For a useful summary, see Naoíse Mac Sweeney, *Troy: Myth, City, Icon* (London: Bloomsbury Academic, 2018), 32–35.

48. For the archaeology of Troy, see Mac Sweeney, *Troy*, 49–60. 'Traditional' date: Lowell Edmunds, 'Myth in Homer', in *A New Companion to Homer*, ed. Ian Morris and Barry Powell (Leiden and New York: Brill, 2011), 415–441 (see 434); Bennet, 'Linear B', 196.

49. Bennet, 'Linear B', 221–222.

50. See, for example, *Od.* 14.233–241; Hesiod, *Works and Days* 155–175.

Chapter 2: 'Homer's World, Not Ours'

1. Ian Morris, *Archaeology as Cultural History: Words and Things in Iron Age Greece* (Oxford: Blackwell, 2000), 206 (quoted); see also Anthony Snodgrass, *The Dark Age of Greece: An Archaeological Survey of the Eleventh to the Eighth Centuries* (Edinburgh: Edinburgh University Press, 1971), 2.

2. Southwestern Peloponnese: Pia de Fidio, 'Mycenaean History', in *A Companion to Linear B: Mycenaean Greek Texts and Their World*, ed. Yves Duhoux and Anna Morpurgo-Davies [hereafter: *CLB*], 3 vols. (Louvain-la-Neuve, Belgium: Peeters, 2008, 2011, 2014), 1.81–114 (see 103); see also Louise Schofield, *The Mycenaeans* (London: The British Museum Press, 2007), 170–185; Snodgrass, *Dark Age*, 364–367; Jonathan Hall, *A History of the Archaic Greek World, ca. 1200–479 BCE*, rev. ed. (Medford, MA, and Oxford: Wiley Blackwell, 2014), 60–62.

3. Ian Morris, 'Early Iron Age Greece', in *The Cambridge Economic History of the Greco-Roman World*, ed. Walter Scheidel, Ian Morris, and Richard Saller (Cambridge: Cambridge University Press, 2007), 211–241 (see 217); Lesley Fitton, *Minoans* (London: British Museum, 2002), 196.

4. Athens: Robin Osborne, *Greece in the Making, 1200–479 BCE* (London: Routledge, 1996), 47–48. Lefkandi: Osborne, *Greece*, 41–43; Ian Morris, 'Homer and the Iron Age', in *A New Companion to Homer*, ed. Ian Morris and Barry Powell (Leiden and New York: Brill, 2011), 535–559 (see 543–544); Morris, *Archaeology*, 218–221, 228–238; Hall, *History*, 62–63. Absence of exports from Lefkandi: Osborne, *Greece*, 43.

5. Morris, *Archaeology*, 198–201, 208–209; Morris, 'Early Iron Age', 234.

6. Geoffrey Horrocks, *Greek: A History of the Language and Its Speakers*, 2nd ed. (Medford, MA, and Oxford: Wiley Blackwell, 2014), 13–24; Hall, *History*, 44–56. For the suggestion, adopted here, that the dialects developed in situ *after* the Mycenaean collapse, see Oliver Dickinson,

The Aegean from Bronze Age to Iron Age (London: Routledge, 2006), 54, and, more theoretically, Jonathan Hall, *Ethnic Identity in Greek Antiquity* (Cambridge: Cambridge University Press, 1997), 153–170.

7. Susan Sherratt, 'Visible Writing: Questions of Script and Identity in Early Iron Age Greece and Cyprus', *Oxford Journal of Archaeology* 22, no. 3 (2003): 225–242 (see 225, 237).

8. Barry Powell, 'Homer and Writing', in Morris and Powell, *New Companion*, 3–32 (see 4–18); Osborne, *Greece*, 107–112; Hall, *History*, 56–59; James Whitley, *The Archaeology of Ancient Greece* (Cambridge: Cambridge University Press, 2001), 128.

9. See further the comparative tables in Osborne, *Greece*, 110–111 and Powell, 'Homer', 15. On the uniqueness of the invention, see Powell, 'Homer', 18.

10. This paragraph substantially follows Richard Janko, 'From Gabii and Gordion to Eretria and Methone: The Rise of the Greek Alphabet', *Bulletin of the Institute for Classical Studies* 58, no. 1 (2015): 1–32.

11. Sherratt, 'Visible Writing', 228. For the 'Cup of Philion', see Janko, 'Gabii', 3–6. 'Nestor's Cup': Powell, 'Homer', 23 (quoted, my translation); Osborne, *Greece*, 116–118.

12. Barry Powell, *Homer and the Origin of the Greek Alphabet* (Cambridge: Cambridge University Press, 1991), 119–186; Powell, 'Homer', 22–25. Words and images: John Bennet, 'Linear B and Homer', *CLB* 3.187–233 (see 219). Quoted: translator's introduction, in Hesiod, *Works and Days*, trans. A. E. Stallings (London: Penguin 2018), xxiv.

13. Janko, 'Gabii', 24–25, which slightly updates Richard Janko, *Homer, Hesiod and the Hymns: Diachronic Development in Epic Diction* (Cambridge: Cambridge University Press, 1982).

14. For the *Iliad*, see Joachim Latacz, *Troy and Homer: Towards a Solution of an Old Mystery* (Oxford: Oxford University Press, 2004), 187–192; for the *Odyssey*: *Od.* 1.91, 106, 133 (suitors, introduced at 1.245); 1.68–70 (Cyclops); 8.448 (Circe).

15. Richard Martin, 'Introduction to Richmond Lattimore's *Iliad*', in *The Iliad of Homer*, trans. Richard Lattimore (Chicago: University of

Chicago Press, 2011 [translation first published 1951]), 43; Powell, *Homer and the Origin*, 229.

16. See, for example, the proposals of Powell, *Homer and the Origin*, 221–237 and M. L. West, *The Making of the Iliad: Disquisition and Analytical Commentary* (Oxford: Oxford University Press, 2011).

17. Horrocks, *Greek*, 44–49; Geoffrey Horrocks, 'Homer's Dialect', in Morris and Powell, *New Companion*, 193–217 (on Mycenaean elements, see 201–203); C. J. Ruijgh, 'Mycenaean and Homeric Language', *CLB* 2.253–298.

18. Martin West, 'Homer's Meter', in Morris and Powell, *New Companion*, 218–237; Ruijgh, 'Mycenaean', 257–258; Bennet, 'Linear B', 215.

19. On the 'epic cycle', see, for example, Malcolm Willcock, 'Neoanalysis', in Morris and Powell, *New Companion*, 173–189 (see 175–176, 184–185). Ancient preference for the *Iliad*: Michael Haslam, 'Homeric Papyri and Transmission of the Text', in the same volume, 55–100 (see 56).

20. Oliver Taplin, 'Homer', in *The Oxford History of Greece and the Hellenistic World*, ed. John Boardman, Jasper Griffin, and Oswyn Murray (Oxford: Oxford University Press, 1991), 47–81 (see 47).

21. Robert Lamberton, 'Homer in Antiquity', in Morris and Powell, *New Companion*, 33–54.

22. Pantelis Michelakis and Maria Wyke, eds., *The Ancient World in Silent Cinema* (Cambridge: Cambridge University Press, 2013).

23. *Il.* 12.462–466, trans. Lattimore.

24. C. P. Cavafy, *The Collected Poems: Includes Parallel Greek Text*, ed. Anthony Hirst, trans. Evangelos Sachperoglou (Oxford: Oxford University Press, 2007), 36–39 (my translation).

25. *Il.* 5.304, 12.383, 12.449–462, 20.286. 'Age of heroes' (an expression not used by Homer): Hesiod, *Works and Days* 155–175.

26. Bennet, 'Linear B', 209.

27. Warrior Vase: *Il.* 13.132; Schofield, *Mycenaeans*, 120–121 and plate 68; Lefkandi: *Il.* 23.171–177 and Martin, 'Introduction', 36.

28. Chariots: Frank Stubbings, 'Arms and Armour', in *A Companion to Homer*, ed. Alan Wace and Frank Stubbings (London: Macmillan, 1962), 504–522 (see 521–522). Cremation: Dickinson, *Aegean from*

Bronze Age, 73, 180–181, 188–189. Conclusion: see, for example, Ian Morris, 'The Use and Abuse of Homer', *Classical Antiquity* 5, no. 1 (1986): 81–138; E. S. Sherratt, '"Reading the Texts": Archaeology and the Homeric Question', *Antiquity* 64 (1990): 807–824.

29. *Il.* 2.484–877 (2.485 and 487 quoted, trans. Lattimore).

30. Trojan allies: *Il.* 2.816–877; see also 1.38 (Tenedos); 9.128–129 (Lesbos); 21.141–143 and 154–158 (Paionia and River Axios). Olympus: Barbara Graziosi, *Homer* (Oxford: Oxford University Press, 2016), 49. See also (controversially), Latacz, *Troy*, 219–228.

31. G. S. Kirk, *The Iliad: A Commentary, Vol. 1: Books 1–4* (Cambridge: Cambridge University Press, 1985), 168–189, 237–240, 248–249, 262–263. For the most recent restatement of the argument that the origin of the 'Catalogue' is Mycenaean, see Latacz, *Troy*, 219–247. For a range of views and further reading, see Bennet, 'Linear B', 204, 205.

32. Thuc. 1.3; *Il.* 2.683–684; Jonathan Hall, *Hellenicity: Between Ethnicity and Culture* (Chicago: Chicago University Press, 2002), 53–54.

33. For the latter proposal, see E. S. Sherratt, 'The Trojan War: History or Bricolage?' *Bulletin of the Institute of Classical Studies* 53 (2010): 1–18; Naoíse Mac Sweeney, *Troy: Myth, City, Icon* (London: Bloomsbury Academic, 2018), 35–36.

34. David Konstan, '"To Hellenikon Ethnos": Ethnicity and the Construction of Ancient Greek Identity', in *Ancient Perceptions of Greek Ethnicity*, ed. Irad Malkin (Washington, DC: Center for Hellenic Studies, 2001), 29–50 (see 31–32). Hector and fatherland: *Il.* 12.243, 15.496–497, 17.157, 24.500. On language and identity in the *Iliad*, see *Il.* 2.867 and Hall, *Hellenicity*, 111–113.

35. *Il.* 1.493–611; Robert Parker, 'Greek Religion', in Griffin and Murray, *Oxford History*, 306–329 (see 306).

36. Respectively, *Il.* 9.411–416 (and see also Sarpedon's words at *Il.* 12.322–328); *Il.* 22.106–110, 22.305–306, trans. Lattimore. 'Generations of leaves': *Il.* 6.146–150, 21.464–466.

37. Graziosi, *Homer*, 81–91.

38. *Od.* 8.522–530, quoted from Homer, *The Odyssey*, trans. Emily Wilson (New York: W. W. Norton, 2018), and compare *Il.* 9.592–594.

39. *Il.* 11.670–760; *Od.* 21.17–33; *Od.* 24.357–360 (quoted), trans. Wilson.

40. *Od.* 9.252–256, trans. Wilson. The translator is unusually lenient towards this cannibal giant, see 'Introduction', 20–22. See also *Od.* 1.182–186, 8.161–165, 14.288–300, 15.415–484, 20.382–383. Phoenician traders, for once, get a good press at *Od.* 13.271–297.

41. *Od.* 17.288–290, trans. Wilson; see also *Il.* 19.162–163.

42. *Il.* 9.186–194 (189 quoted, trans. Lattimore); *Od.* 1.326–353, 1.369–371, 8.44–108, 8.255–368, 8.470–539, 9.5–11, 17.519–521, 22.330–377.

43. Hesiod, *Theogony* 22–34; Hesiod, *Theogony, Works and Days*, trans. M. L. West (Oxford: Oxford University Press, The World's Classics, 1988), 3. Compare *Il.* 1.1–7, 2.483–493, 2.761–762 and *Od.* 1.1–6.

44. Hesiod, *Works and Days*: respectively, 727–728, 177–178, 188–189, 575, trans. Stallings.

45. Anthony Snodgrass, *Archaic Greece: The Age of Experiment* (London: Dent, 1980), 20–24; Ian Morris, 'Early Iron Age', 211–241 (see 236); see also Brian Lavelle, *Archaic Greece: The Age of New Reckonings* (Medford, MA: Wiley Blackwell, 2020).

Chapter 3: Inventing Politics, Discovering the Cosmos

1. Robin Osborne, *Greece in the Making: 1200–479 BCE* (London: Routledge, 1996), 121–125, 197–200.

2. Plato, *Phaedo* 109b (my translation).

3. Osborne, *Greece*, 122, 179–180 (Spartan colonies); 129 ('every other year').

4. Jonathan Hall, *A History of the Archaic Greek World, ca. 1200–479 BCE*, 2nd ed. (Medford, MA, and Oxford: Wiley Blackwell, 2014), 97–100; Irad Malkin, *A Small Greek World: Networks in the Ancient Mediterranean* (Oxford: Oxford University Press, 2011), 162–164.

5. Malkin, *Small Greek World*, 4, 22, 158; Cyprian Broodbank, *The Making of the Middle Sea: A History of the Mediterranean from the*

Beginning to the Emergence of the Classical World (London: Thames & Hudson, 2013), 524–535.

6. Ian Morris, 'Early Iron Age Greece', in *The Cambridge Economic History of the Greco–Roman World*, ed. Walter Scheidel, Ian Morris, and Richard Saller (Cambridge: Cambridge University Press, 2007), 211–241 (see 241).

7. Aristotle, *Politics* 3.5.14.

8. Aristotle, *Politics* 3.5.13; Paul Cartledge, *Democracy: A Life*, 2nd ed. (Oxford: Oxford University Press, 2018), 15, 37–38; Paul Cartledge, *Thebes: The Forgotten City of Ancient Greece* (New York: Abrams, 2020), 66–67.

9. Mogens Hansen, *Polis: An Introduction to the Ancient Greek City-State* (Oxford: Oxford University Press, 2006), 11.

10. Aristotle, *Politics* 1.1.9 (Homer, *Iliad*, 9.63, trans. Lattimore).

11. 'Law of the city of Dreros, 650–600 BCE', in Charles Fornara, ed. and trans., *Translated Documents of Greece and Rome, Vol. 1: Archaic Times to the End of the Peloponnesian War* (Baltimore, MD: Johns Hopkins University Press, 1977; 2nd ed., 1983), 13; James Whitley, 'Literacy and Law-Making: The Case of Archaic Crete', in *Archaic Greece: New Approaches and New Evidence*, ed. Nick Fisher and Hans van Wees (London: Duckworth, 1998), 317–331.

12. Matthew Simonton, *Classical Greek Oligarchy: A Political History* (Princeton, NJ: Princeton University Press, 2017), 1, citing Pindar, *Pythian Odes* 2.86–88 (probably written shortly after 470 BCE). See also Hdt. 3.80–82 (written at least thirty years later, although referring—fictitiously—to an event in c. 522 BCE) and Cartledge, *Democracy*, 93–94.

13. Tyrants: Anthony Snodgrass, *Archaic Greece: The Age of Experiment* (London: Dent, 1980), 120–121; Osborne, *Greece*, 192–197; equality before law (*isonomia*): Cartledge, *Democracy*, 32, 55, 75.

14. Hall, *History*, 188.

15. Snodgrass, *Archaic Greece*, 42–47 (42 cited); Jonathan Hall, *Ethnic Identity in Greek Antiquity* (Cambridge: Cambridge University Press,

1997), 34–36; Catherine Morgan, 'Ethne, Ethnicity and Early Greek States, ca. 1200–480 BC: An Archaeological Perspective', in *Ancient Perceptions of Greek Ethnicity*, ed. Irad Malkin (Washington, DC: Center for Hellenic Studies, Harvard University, 2001), 75–112.

16. Paul Cartledge, *The Spartans: An Epic History* (London: Pan, 2013), 68 (prohibition on trade), 27, 39 (helots). Ratio: Hdt. 9.28; Simon Hornblower, *The Greek World, 479–323 BCE*, 4th ed. (Abingdon: Routledge, 2011), 11.

17. Hall, *History*, 243–251.

18. Cartledge, *Spartans*, 27–28, 32–34, 37, 57–68.

19. The primary sources are Hdt. 5.62–65 and *Ath.Pol.* 20–21. For modern assessments, see Osborne, *Greece*, 291–299; Hall, *History*, 235–243; Cartledge, *Democracy*, 58–75.

20. Malkin, *Small Greek World*, 32–33, 192–194.

21. Hdt. 1.141–151; Jonathan Hall, *Hellenicity: Between Ethnicity and Culture* (Chicago: Chicago University Press, 2002), 67–73.

22. Alcaeus, Fr. 112; Aristotle, *Politics* 3.5.14, 4.3.11.

23. Snodgrass, *Archaic Greece*, 97–104, 151–154.

24. Robert Parker, 'Greek Religion', in *The Oxford History of Greece and the Hellenistic World*, ed. John Boardman, Jasper Griffin, and Oswyn Murray (Oxford: Oxford University Press, 1991), 306–329.

25. Catherine Morgan, *Athletes and Oracles: The Transformation of Olympia and Delphi in the Eighth Century BC* (Cambridge: Cambridge University Press, 1990), 147, 203–205; Hall, *Hellenicity*, 134–168; Michael Scott, *Delphi and Olympia: The Spatial Politics of Panhellenism in the Archaic and Classical Periods* (Cambridge: Cambridge University Press, 2010), 256–273.

26. Hall, *Hellenicity*, 164–165; Scott, *Delphi*, 265.

27. Pindar, *Isthmian Odes* 2.23; see also Thuc. 5.49–50; Isocrates, *Panegyricus* 43; Judith Swaddling, *The Ancient Olympic Games* (London: British Museum, 1980), 11–12.

28. Osborne, *Greece*, 243–244; Morgan, *Athletes*, 212–223; Zinon Papakonstantinou, *Sport and Identity in Ancient Greece* (Abingdon: Routledge, 2019).

29. Modern opinion is divided on when a 'Hellenic' consciousness became established throughout the Greek-speaking world. Malkin (*Small Greek World*) argues for the eighth century BCE; the case for the fifth is made by Jonathan Hall, *Ethnic Identity, passim*. I follow the second approach here.

30. Archilochus, Frs. 32–46, trans. M. L. West, *Greek Lyric Poetry* (Oxford: Oxford University Press, 1994), 5–6.

31. The classic study is K. J. Dover, *Greek Homosexuality*, 3rd ed. (London: Bloomsbury, 2016), first published in 1978 and more recently challenged by James Davidson, *The Greeks and Greek Love: A Radical Reappraisal of Homosexuality in Ancient Greece* (London: Weidenfeld and Nicolson, 2007).

32. Sappho, Frs. 16, 31, trans. West, *Greek Lyric Poetry*, 37, 38–39. See further Jim Powell, *The Poetry of Sappho: An Expanded Edition, Featuring Newly Discovered Poems* (Oxford: Oxford University Press, 2019).

33. John Boardman, *Greek Sculpture: The Archaic Period*, 2nd ed. (London: Thames & Hudson, 1991), 18–21, 169–170.

34. Boardman, *Greek Sculpture*, 22, 66.

35. Cartledge, *Thebes*, 52–54 (author's translation) and plate 5; Robert Parker, 'Greek Religion', in Griffin and Murray, *Oxford History*, 306–329 (see 318).

36. Boardman, *Greek Sculpture*, 73 (author's translation) and fig. 108a; Mary Beard, *How Do We Look: The Eye of Faith* (London: Profile, 2018), 41–43, 82–84 and figs. 12, 37.

37. Robin Osborne, *The Transformation of Athens: Painted Pottery and the Creation of Classical Greece* (Princeton, NJ: Princeton University Press, 2018), 123; for rare exceptions, see 124–125 and figs. 5.1–5.2.

38. Snodgrass, *Archaic Greece*, 158, 187; John Boardman, *Early Greek Vase Painting* (London: Thames & Hudson, 1998), 263–266.

39. Osborne, *Transformation*, 25, 46–47, 126–128 and figs. 2.9, 5.3–5.4.

40. M. L. West, *Early Greek Philosophy and the Orient* (Oxford: Oxford University Press, 1971, reissued 2001); Jonathan Barnes, *Early Greek*

Philosophy (Harmondsworth: Penguin, 1987), 9–99; Osborne, *Greece*, 316 (on proof).

41. Xenophanes, Fr. B23 (quoted), B14, B15, trans. Barnes, *Early Greek Philosophy*, 95.

42. Heraclitus, Fr. 30, trans. G. S. Kirk, *Heraclitus: The Cosmic Fragments* (Cambridge: Cambridge University Press, 1954), 307; see also 284–287, 314–317; Barnes, *Early Greek Philosophy*, 18–19, 38–39.

43. Hdt. 1.6; Osborne, *Greece*, 344–347, 350; Malkin, *Small Greek World*, 40–41.

44. Hdt. 1.79–86, 1.154–176.

45. Hdt. 1.163–169; Herodotus, *The Histories*, trans. Aubrey de Sélincourt, rev. ed. (London: Penguin, 2003; translation first published 1954), 73 (quoted); Malkin, *Small Greek World*, 149–152.

46. Hdt. 5.28–38; Osborne, *Greece*, 318–322, 325; Fornara, *Translated Documents*, 45–46.

47. Hdt. 1.152–153.

48. Hdt. 5.73, trans. de Sélincourt, 338. For date and context of these events, see Osborne, *Greece*, 292–295; Cartledge, *Thebes*, 82–84.

49. Hdt. 5.97–103.

50. Hdt. 6.32, trans. de Sélincourt, 370; John Marincola, 'Notes', in Herodotus, *Histories*, 656–657; Osborne, *Greece*, 322–325.

51. Hdt. 5.100–106, trans. de Sélincourt, 354.

Chapter 4: The First World Wars and the 'Classical' Age

1 Hdt. 5.78–89, 6.87–94; Robin Osborne, *Greece in the Making, 1200–479 BCE* (London: Routledge, 1996), 325–328.

2. Hdt. 6.65–84; Cartledge, *The Spartans: An Epic History* (London: Pan, 2013), 95–96, 87–89; Osborne, *Greece*, 335–336.

3. Hdt. 6.48–49, 7.133, Herodotus, *The Histories*, trans. Aubrey de Sélincourt, rev. ed. (London: Penguin, 2003; translation first published 1954), 458 (quoted).

4. Hdt. 6.100–108; Cartledge, *Spartans*, 102.

5. Hdt. 6.109–117; Michael Llewellyn Smith, *Olympics in Athens 1896: The Invention of the Modern Olympic Games* (London: Profile, 2004), 179–191.

6. Osborne, *Greece*, 334–336; Cartledge, *Spartans*, 111–114.

7. Osborne, *Greece*, 331–333; Paul Cartledge, *Democracy: A Life*, 2nd ed. (Oxford: Oxford University Press, 2018), 70–73.

8. Plutarch, *Themistocles* 5–6, 22 (quoted), trans. Robin Waterfield in Plutarch, *Greek Lives* (Oxford: Oxford University Press, 1998), 86–87, 101. Herodotus covers only the initiatives of Themistocles in the final years of the decade (Hdt. 7.143–145; Osborne, *Greece*, 337).

9. Hdt. 7.89, 7.184–186; John Marincola, 'Notes', in Herodotus, *Histories*, 668n25, 668n27, 671n59; see also, for example, Osborne, *Greece*, 337.

10. Hdt. 7.157–167; Diod.Sic. 11.20–24; Osborne, *Greece*, 344–346.

11. Charles Fornara, ed. and trans., *Translated Documents of Greece and Rome, Vol. 1: Archaic Times to the End of the Peloponnesian War* (Baltimore, MD: Johns Hopkins University Press, 1977; 2nd ed., 1983), 59, reproduces the list inscribed on the base of the 'serpent column', originally set up at Delphi shortly after the end of the war and removed to Constantinople in the fourth century CE, where it can still be seen in central Istanbul's old Hippodrome. See also Herodotus (Hdt. 9.28–30, 9.81), whose narrative differs in some details from the list preserved on the column, and Osborne, *Greece*, 341–342.

12. Hdt. 7.176, 7.200.

13. Hdt. 8.53, trans. de Sélincourt, 517.

14. The fullest early account of the battle is Aesch. *Pers.* 353–470, on which see below. See also Hdt. 8.74–92.

15. Hdt. 9.13, 9.25–70, 9.90–105; Paul Cartledge, *After Thermopylae: The Oath of Plataea and the End of the Graeco–Persian Wars* (Oxford: Oxford University Press, 2013), 8, 88–121.

16. See, for example, Barry Strauss, *The Battle of Salamis: The Naval Encounter that Saved Greece—and Western Civilization* (New York: Simon & Schuster, 2004); Victor Davis Hanson, *Carnage and Culture:*

Landmark Battles in the Rise of Western Power (New York: Doubleday, 2001).

17. John Stuart Mill, 'Grote's *History of Greece I*', in *Essays on Philosophy and the Classics. Collected Works of John Stuart Mill*, ed. J. M. Robson (London: Routledge and Kegan Paul, 1978), 271–306 (see 273); Alexandra Lianeri, 'Historiography in Grote's *History*', in *Cultural Responses to the Persian Wars: Antiquity to the Third Millennium*, ed. Emma Bridges, Edith Hall and P. J. Rhodes (Oxford: Oxford University Press, 2007), 339. See also the same volume *passim* for many other examples.

18. Aesch. *Pers.* 807–808, 819–822.

19. Aesch. *Pers.* 790–794 (794 quoted, my literal translation).

20. Aesch. *Pers.* 241–242, 591–594, 402–405 (the last quoted, my translation).

21. Aristophanes, *Frogs* 1029–1030 (first performed in 405 BCE); Aristophanes, *Frogs and Other Plays*, trans. David Barrett (Harmondsworth: Penguin, 1964), 173.

22. Hdt. 1 (Preface). On known works written in prose before Herodotus, see Marincola, 'Introduction', in Herodotus, *Histories*, xix.

23. Jonathan Hall, *A History of the Archaic Greek World, ca. 1200–479 BCE*, rev. ed. (Medford, MA, and Oxford: Wiley Blackwell, 2014), 324.

24. Hdt. 1.1–4; Edith Hall, *Inventing the Barbarian: Greek Self-Definition Through Tragedy* (Oxford: Clarendon Press, 1989), 1–100; Kostas Vlassopoulos, *Greeks and Barbarians* (Cambridge: Cambridge University Press, 2013); Jonathan Hall, *History*, 308–310.

25. Hdt. 7.9, trans. de Sélincourt, 417–418.

26. Hdt. 8.22 (appeal to Ionians in Xerxes's fleet), 9.67 (Thebes), 9.12–13 (Argives, see also 7.148–152).

27. Hdt. 8.144 (my literal translation); compare 1.4, 1.86, 7.139, 7.145. For discussion of the passage in the wider context of national identity, see, for example, Samuel Huntington, *The Clash of Civilizations and the Remaking of World Order* (London: Simon & Schuster, 1997), 42; Anthony D. Smith, *The Cultural Foundations of Nations: Hierarchy, Covenant, and Republic* (Oxford: Blackwell, 2008), 57–58; Azar Gat, *The Long History and Deep Roots of Political Ethnicity and Nationalism*

(Cambridge: Cambridge University Press, 2013), 74. On the passage itself, see Jonathan Hall, *Ethnic Identity in Greek Antiquity* (Cambridge: Cambridge University Press, 1997), 44–47 and *Hellenicity: Between Ethnicity and Culture* (Chicago: Chicago University Press, 2002), 189–194; David Konstan, '"To Hellenikon Ethnos": Ethnicity and the Construction of Ancient Greek Identity', in *Ancient Perceptions of Greek Ethnicity*, ed. Irad Malkin (Washington, DC: Center for Hellenic Studies, 2001), 29–50 (see 32–34).

28. Aristotle, *Poetics* 1449b.

29. John Boardman, *Greek Sculpture: The Classical Period*, corrected ed. (London: Thames & Hudson, 1991), 33–50 (39 on individual nuances).

30. Mary Beard, *How Do We Look: The Eye of Faith* (London: Profile, 2018), 34. For the origin of civic statuary in the early fifth century BCE, see Boardman, *Greek Sculpture*, 24–26.

31. Boardman, *Greek Sculpture*, 52–54 and figs. 34–35, 38–39; Robin Osborne, *The Transformation of Athens: Painted Pottery and the Creation of Classical Greece* (Princeton, NJ: Princeton University Press, 2018), 240–242.

32. Osborne, *Transformation*, see, respectively, 114–115, 221–224 and fig. 9.6, 146–150, 83–84.

33. Osborne, *Transformation*, 209, 248–249, 252–253; Boardman, *Greek Sculpture*, 21.

34. Samantha Martin McAuliffe and John K. Papadopoulos, 'Framing Victory: Salamis, the Athenian Acropolis, and the Agora', *Journal of the Society of Architectural Historians* 71 (2012): 332–361; Johanna Hanink, *The Classical Debt: Greek Antiquity in an Era of Austerity* (Cambridge, MA: Harvard University Press, 2017), 42–44.

35. For the fullest accounts of the project, see Robin Frances Rhodes, *Architecture and Meaning on the Athenian Acropolis* (Cambridge: Cambridge University Press, 1995) and T. Leslie Shear Jr., *Trophies of Victory: Public Buildings in Periklean Athens* (Princeton, NJ: Princeton University Press, 2016).

36. Plato, *Apology* 38a (my translation).

37. Plato, *Theaetatus* 152a, citing Protagoras, and see also Plato, *Protagoras*; Peter Pormann, *The Cambridge Companion to Hippocrates* (Cambridge: Cambridge University Press, 2018).

38. Thuc. 1.76; Thucydides, *The Peloponnesian War*, trans. Martin Hammond, with Introduction and Notes by P. J. Rhodes (Oxford: Oxford University Press, 2009), 38 (translation slightly adapted), see also 2.36, 5.89.

39. Cartledge, *Democracy*, 105–122; P. J. Rhodes, *A History of the Classical Greek World, 478–323 BC*, 2nd ed. (Medford, MA, and Oxford: Wiley Blackwell, 2010), 61–67.

40. Rhodes, *History*, 59–61, 70–72; 64 (efficiency); Cartledge, *Democracy*, 114–116. For ancient assessments, see Thuc. 2.65; Plutarch, *Pericles* 9.

41. Thuc. 2.37, trans. Johanna Hanink, *How to Think About War: An Ancient Guide to Foreign Policy* (Princeton, NJ: Princeton University Press, 2019), 43, 45.

42. Simon Hornblower, *The Greek World, 479–323 BCE*, 4th ed. (Abingdon: Routledge, 2011), 121–128; Rhodes, *History*, 32. On resources, see Hornblower, *Greek World*, 127; Thuc. 1.141–142.

43. Thuc. 1.23, 1.88, trans. Hammond, 13, 43. For modern assessments, see Hornblower, *Greek World*, 108–115; Rhodes, *History*, 86–95; Donald Kagan, *The Peloponnesian War* (London: Harper Perennial, 2005), 41–54. For Spartan antipathy to 'democratic imperialism', see Victor Davis Hanson, *A War Like No Other* (New York: Random House, 2005), 13.

44. Thuc. 1.1; Kagan, *Peloponnesian War*, xxii; Paul Cartledge, *Thebes: The Forgotten City of Ancient Greece* (New York: Abrams, 2020), 132.

45. See Hanson, *War*, xvi, 3–4, 324; Hanink, *How to Think*, xv–xvi, xlviii–liv; Kagan, *Peloponnesian War*, xxiii; Cartledge, *Thebes*, 134.

46. Thuc. 2.48–54 (2.51 quoted, trans. Hammond, 98).

47. Thuc. 5.84–116 (116 quoted, trans. Hammond, 307).

48. Thuc. 6.31, trans. Hammond, 323; 7.16–17, 7.26–27; Kagan, *Peloponnesian War*, 267–268 (numbers).

49. Thuc. 6.18, trans. Hammond, 318.

50. Thuc. 8.18, trans. Hammond, 423; see also 8.43. For earlier negotiations, see Kagan, *Peloponnesian War*, 154–155; Thuc. 2.7, 2.67, 4.50 and, in 413–412 BCE, 8.5–6, 8.12.

51. Rhodes, *History*, 152, 172.

52. Diod.Sic. 13.98, trans. Kagan, *Peloponnesian War*, 458 (quoted). For the fullest early account of these events, see Xen. *Hell.* 1.6.24–1.7.34.

53. Xen. *Hell.* 2.2.3; Xenophon, *A History of My Times*, trans. Rex Warner, with introduction and notes by George Cawkwell (London: Penguin, 1979), 104.

54. Thuc. 5.26 and P. J. Rhodes, 'Introduction', in Thucydides, *Peloponnesian War*, xxv–xxviii; Xen. *Hell.* 2.2.23, trans. Warner, 108 (quoted, slightly adapted).

Chapter 5: Cultural Capital

1. Paul Cartledge, *Democracy: A Life*, 2nd ed. (Oxford: Oxford University Press, 2018), 224–225.

2. Paul Cartledge, *Thebes: The Forgotten City of Ancient Greece* (New York: Abrams, 2020), 167.

3. Xenophon, *Anabasis*; Xenophon, *The Persian Expedition*, trans. Rex Warner, with a new introduction by G. Cawkwell (Harmondsworth: Penguin, 1972).

4. Xen. *Hell.* 3.5.1–2; Xenophon, *A History of My Times*, trans. Rex Warner, with introduction and notes by George Cawkwell (London: Penguin, 1979), 174, and editor's note citing *Hellenica Oxyrrynchia* 7.5, an Athenian account contemporary with Xenophon's and known only from papyrus fragments, of unknown authorship; Simon Hornblower, *The Greek World, 479–323 BCE*, 4th ed. (Abingdon: Routledge, 2011), 220, 229.

5. Xen. *Hell.* 5.1.30–31; P. J. Rhodes, *A History of the Classical Greek World, 478–323 BC*, 2nd ed. (Medford, MA, and Oxford: Wiley Blackwell, 2010), 229–230; Hornblower, *Greek World*, 233. On the meaning and status of the term *autonomy* at this time, see Emily Mackil, *Creating a Common Polity: Religion, Economy, and Politics in the Making of the*

Greek Koinon (Berkeley: University of California Press, 2012), 92, 94, 115n17, 116n29.

6. Xen. *Hell.* 7.5.26, trans. Warner, 403.

7. Xen. *Hell.* 7.5.17, trans. Warner, 400; Paus. 9.15.4 (my translation), see also Pausanias, *Guide to Greece*, trans. Peter Levi, 2 vols. (Harmondsworth: Penguin, 1979), 1.339, and Paus. 8.11.5–9, trans. Levi, 2.398–399.

8. Xen. *Hell.* 7.5.27, trans. Warner, 403; Cawkwell, 'Introduction', in Xenophon, *History*, 7; see also Arnold Toynbee, *The Greeks and Their Heritages* (Oxford: Oxford University Press, 1981), 60, 66. For an opposite assessment, see Moses Finley, *The Use and Abuse of History*, rev. ed. (London: Chatto and Windus, 1986), 121–122; Jonathan Hall, *Ethnic Identity in Greek Antiquity* (Cambridge: Cambridge University Press, 1997), 227–228.

9. Cartledge, *Democracy*, 176–178.

10. Isocrates, *Antidosis* 1–10, written 354–353 BCE. On Plato, Isocrates, and the written word, see Andrea Wilson Nightingale, 'Sages, Sophists, and Philosophers: Greek Wisdom Literature', in *Literature in the Greek and Roman Worlds: A New Perspective*, ed. Oliver Taplin (Oxford: Oxford University Press, 2000), 156–191 (see 172–185); on the writing of speeches and the influence of the written versions, see also Chris Carey, 'Observers of Speeches and Hearers of Action: The Athenian Orators', in the same volume, 192–216 (see 215–216).

11. Isocrates, *Panegyricus* 185; trans. George Norlin, *Isocrates*, 3 vols. (London and New York: Loeb Classical Library, 1928), 1.239.

12. Isocrates, *Panegyricus* 81; Takis Poulakos, *Speaking for the Polis: Isocrates' Rhetorical Education* (Columbia: University of South Carolina Press, 1997), 84, 114n9.

13. Isocrates, *Panegyricus* 47–50 (50 quoted, my translation). See also *Antidosis* 299, in which Isocrates goes further, to imagine the whole of Greece as a city-state, with Athens as its sole 'city' and all the other *poleis* as mere villages by comparison, and Jonathan Hall, *Hellenicity: Between Ethnicity and Culture* (Chicago: Chicago University Press, 2002), 207–210, 219.

14. Robin Lane Fox, 'Philip of Macedon: Accession, Ambitions, and Self-Presentation', in *Brill's Companion to Ancient Macedon: Studies in the Archaeology and History of Macedon, 650 BC–300 AD*, ed. Robin Lane Fox (Leiden and Boston, MA: Brill, 2011), 335–366 (see 335–336), revising the commonly accepted 359 BCE.

15. Theopompus of Chios (fourth century BCE), cited in translation by Hornblower, *Greek World*, 268; Justin 9.8.10, trans. Ian Worthington, *Philip II of Macedonia* (New Haven, CT: Yale University Press, 2008), 195 (on this later Latin source see 212–13); Worthington, *Philip*, 4, 195, 201–203, 208.

16. Hornblower, *Greek World*, 275, 282.

17. Demosthenes, *Philippics* 3.30–31 (my translation); see also Ian Worthington, *Demosthenes of Athens and the Fall of Classical Greece* (Oxford: Oxford University Press, 2012), 220–223.

18. Worthington, *Demosthenes*, 265; Worthington, *Philip*, 166–167.

19. Isocrates, *Philip* 107–108, 154; M. B. Hatzopoulos, 'Macedonians and Other Greeks', in Lane Fox, *Companion*, 51–78 (see 67–69). See also Edward Harris, *Aeschines and Athenian Politics* (Oxford: Oxford University Press, 1995), 124–154.

20. Jonathan Hall, 'Contested Ethnicities: Perceptions of Macedonia Within Evolving Definitions of Greek Identity', in *Ancient Perceptions of Greek Ethnicity*, ed. Irad Malkin (Washington, DC: Center for Hellenic Studies, 2001), 159–186.

21. See Hatzopoulos, 'Macedonians'; Rhodes, *History*, 334–335; Hornblower, *Greek World*, 94–100. On personal names, see Miltiade Hatzopoulos, '"L'Histoire par les noms" in Macedonia', in *Greek Personal Names: Their Value as Evidence*, ed. Simon Hornblower and Elaine Matthews (Oxford: Oxford University Press, 2000), 99–117.

22. Hatzopoulos, 'Macedonia', 65–66. On Stageira, see Worthington, *Philip*, 75 and 254n5; Robin Lane Fox, 'Philip's and Alexander's Macedon', in Lane Fox, *Companion*, 367–391 (see 372).

23. Geoffrey Horrocks, *Greek: A History of the Language and Its Speakers*, 2nd ed. (Medford, MA, and Oxford: Wiley Blackwell, 2014), 73–80; Olivier Masson, 'Macedonian Language', in *The Oxford Classical*

Dictionary, 3rd ed., Simon Hornblower and Antony Spawforth (Oxford: Oxford University Press, 2003), 905–906 (4th ed., 2012, available online).

24. Demosthenes, *Philippics* 4.31–35; Worthington, *Demosthenes*, 224–227.

25. Lycurgus, *Against Leocrates* 1.50; Worthington, *Demosthenes*, 246–254; Worthington, *Philip*, 147–151; Cartledge, *Thebes*, 226–231.

26. There is no single surviving ancient source for these details, which have been pieced together by modern historians from several different sources. See Rhodes, *History*, 356–358; Hornblower, *Greek World*, 286–288; Worthington, *Demosthenes*, 255–259, 262–264; Worthington, *Philip*, 158–163.

27. Isocrates, 'Letter 3': 5 (my translation); see trans. Norlin, 3.402–407; Worthington, *Philip*, 167–170.

28. Worthington, *Demosthenes*, 48.

29. This and the previous paragraph are based closely on the two ancient sources for these events: Diod. Sic. 16.91–95 (written during the first century BCE) and Justin 9.6–7 (a later abridgement of a Latin history, also of the first century BCE). There are discrepancies between them in some details, which have been differently interpreted by modern historians. For the date (July or October), see A. B. Bosworth, *Conquest and Empire: The Reign of Alexander the Great* (Cambridge: Cambridge University Press, 1993), 23; Lane Fox, 'Philip's and Alexander's Macedon', 385. See also Paul Cartledge, *Alexander the Great: The Hunt for a New Past* (London: Pan Macmillan, 2005), 55–56, 63–65; Worthington, *Philip*, 172–193.

30. Justin 11.2.

31. Worthington lists the ancient sources (*Philip*, 269n45) and some modern approaches and contrasting verdicts (269–270n56). For the view that Alexander was not involved, with references to earlier scholarship on the subject, see Bosworth, *Conquest*, 25–26. Alexander's guilt has been proposed by Ernst Badian, 'The Death of Philip II', *Phoenix* 17 (1963), 244–250; and Worthington, *Philip*, 182–186.

32. Arrian, *Anabasis* 6.24.2–3, 7.1.4, 7.2.1, 7.28.2–3; for translation, see (respectively) Arrian, *The Campaigns of Alexander*, trans. Aubrey de Sélincourt, rev. with introduction and notes by J. R. Hamilton (Harmondsworth: Penguin, 1971), 335–336, 349, 350, 395–396.

33. Arrian, *Anabasis* 4.8–15, trans. de Sélincourt, 213–226; Plutarch, *Alexander* 48–55; Cartledge, *Alexander*, 263–265.

34. Manolis Andronikos, *Vergina: The Royal Tombs* (Athens: Ekdotiki Athinon, 1984), 62–78, 97–197, 226–233; for subsequent opinions and bibliography, see Worthington, *Philip*, 234–241.

35. Diod.Sic. 16.92.1, 17.3.1; Worthington, *Philip*, 187.

36. Diod.Sic. 17.4.4–7; Bosworth, *Conquest*, 189–194, 198.

37. Arrian, *Anabasis* 1.7.2, trans. de Sélincourt, 55 (quoted); Diod.Sic. 17.8–9; Plutarch, *Alexander* 11, trans. Robin Waterfield, *Plutarch: Greek Lives* (Oxford: Oxford University Press, 1998), 321.

38. Diod.Sic. 17.14–15; Plutarch, *Alexander* 11; Arrian, *Anabasis* 1.8–11; Bosworth, *Conquest*, 195–197; Cartledge, *Thebes*, 234–239.

39. Arrian, *Anabasis* 1.12.

40. Bosworth, *Conquest*, 35, 259, noting irreconcilable discrepancies in the extant ancient sources.

41. Arrian, *Anabasis* 1.16.7; Plutarch, *Alexander* 16.8 (my translation). The text is all but identical in both, and so must be presumed to be an accurate transcription.

42. Arrian, *Anabasis* 1.16, trans. de Sélincourt, 75; Cartledge, *Alexander*, 96–98.

43. Cartledge, *Alexander*, 45, 134–135.

44. Arrian, *Anabasis* 2.14.9, trans. de Sélincourt, 128.

45. Bosworth, *Conquest*, 75–79.

46. Arrian, *Anabasis* 3.15–17.

47. Respectively, Arrian, *Anabasis* 3.19; Plutarch, *Alexander* 37–38.

48. Arrian, *Anabasis* 5.26.2, trans. de Sélincourt, 293.

49. Hugh Bowden, *Alexander the Great: A Very Short Introduction* (Oxford: Oxford University Press, 2014), 84, 89–92.

50. J. R. Hamilton, 'Introduction', in Arrian, *Campaigns*, 30–32; Cartledge, *Alexander*, 75–76, 122–124.

51. On economic recovery, see Bosworth, *Conquest*, 204–205; on the building of the Theatre of Dionysus, see Johanna Hanink, *Lycurgan Athens and the Making of Classical Tragedy* (Cambridge: Cambridge University Press, 2014), 92–125; on the making of the Athenian 'brand', see the same work, 5–22, 230 (Athens as 'capital of theatre') and Johanna Hanink, *The Classical Debt: Greek Antiquity in an Era of Austerity* (Cambridge, MA: Harvard University Press, 2017), 32–69.

52. Armand Leroi, *The Lagoon: How Aristotle Invented Science* (London: Bloomsbury, 2014); Edith Hall, *Aristotle's Way: Ten Ways Ancient Wisdom Can Change Your Life* (London: Penguin, 2019).

53. Aristotle, *Nicomachaean Ethics* 10.7.8; Bosworth, *Conquest*, 278–290; Cartledge, *Alexander*, 215–227.

54. Mary Beard, *How Do We Look: The Eye of Faith* (London: Profile, 2018), 85–90; John Boardman, *Greek Art*, 4th ed. (London: Thames & Hudson, 1996), 160–164.

55. Bosworth, *Conquest*, 220.

56. Diod.Sic. 18.8.2–5; Bosworth, *Conquest*, 221.

57. Diod.Sic. 18.9.5, 18.10.2–3 (my translation).

58. Diod.Sic. 18.12–18; Cartledge, *Alexander*, 100–103; Cartledge, *Democracy*, 217.

59. Graham Shipley, *The Greek World After Alexander, 323–30 BC* (London: Routledge, 2000), 1; R. Malcolm Errington, *A History of the Hellenistic World, 323–30 BC* (Oxford: Blackwell, 2008), 8; Angelos Chaniotis, *Age of Conquests: The Greek World from Alexander to Hadrian 336 BC–AD 138* (Princeton, NJ: Princeton University Press, 2018), 1, 196–197.

Chapter 6: 'Becoming Greek'

1. The principal ancient source for these events is Diod.Sic. 18–20; see in English: Diodorus of Sicily, *The Library, Books 16–20: Philip II, Alexander the Great and the Successors*, trans. Robin Waterfield (Oxford: Oxford University Press, 2019), 179–423; the fullest modern account is

Robin Waterfield, *Dividing the Spoils: The War for Alexander the Great's Empire* (Oxford: Oxford University Press, 2011). For a succinct overview see Winthrop Lindsay Adams, 'The Hellenistic Kingdoms', in *The Cambridge Companion to the Hellenistic World*, ed. Glenn Bugh (Cambridge: Cambridge University Press, 2006), 28–51.

2. Ashoka inscription: translation and commentary in Susan Sherwin-White and Amélie Kuhrt, *From Samarkhand to Sardis: A New Approach to the Seleucid Empire* (London: Duckworth, 1993), 101–102. On the early Buddhist text, *Questions of King Milinda*, written in Pali, and its relation to Menander, the 'Indo-Greek king who ruled from 155–130 BCE, from a capital at Sagala (Sialkot)' in the Punjab, see Richard Stoneman, *The Greek Experience of India: From Alexander to the Indo-Greeks* (Princeton, NJ: Princeton University Press, 2019), 365–374.

3. John Boardman, *The Greeks in Asia* (London: Thames & Hudson, 2015), 82, 185. On Taxila and the history of these kingdoms, see 138–142; on coins, see 94–101. See also Stoneman, *Greek Experience*, 377–404.

4. Rachel Mairs, *The Hellenistic Far East: Archaeology, Language, and Identity in Greek Central Asia* (Oakland: University of California Press, 2014), xvii–xxii; for Greek texts with accompanying translations see 283–284 (cited in my own translation). See also Sherwin-White and Kuhrt, *Samarkhand*, 177–179; Boardman, *Greeks*, 83–86, and Peter Thonemann, *The Hellenistic Age: A Very Short Introduction* (Oxford: Oxford University Press, 2018), 1–3.

5. G. G. Aperghis, *The Seleukid Royal Economy: The Finances and Financial Administration of the Seleukid Empire* (Cambridge: Cambridge University Press, 2004), 37–38 (on Seleucia-on-the-Tigris); Sherwin-White and Kuhrt, *Samarkhand*, 149–159.

6. Sherwin-White and Kuhrt, *Samarkhand*, 142–148 (language and Berossus, 148 cited), 38–39, 154–155 (temple patronage); see also Paul Kosmin, *The Land of the Elephant Kings: Space, Territory, and Ideology in the Seleucid Empire* (Cambridge, MA: Harvard University Press, 2004), 113–114, 207–208.

7. Paul Kosmin, *Time and Its Adversaries in the Seleucid Empire* (Cambridge, MA: Harvard University Press, 2018), 21–26 and *passim*.

8. Strabo 17.1.6, cited and discussed by Sally-Ann Ashton, 'Ptolemaic Alexandria and the Egyptian Tradition', in *Alexandria: Real and Imagined*, ed. Anthony Hirst and Michael Silk (Aldershot: Ashgate, 2004), 15–40 (see 16–17).

9. Peter Clayton, 'The Pharos at Alexandria', in *The Seven Wonders of the Ancient World*, ed. Peter Clayton and Martin Price (London: Routledge, 2013), 138–157.

10. Franck Goddio, *Alexandria: The Submerged Royal Quarters* (London: Periplous, 1998); Ashton, 'Ptolemaic Alexandria'.

11. Herwig Maehler, 'Alexandria, the Mouseion, and Cultural Identity', in Hirst and Silk, *Alexandria*, 1–14. See also Graham Shipley, *The Greek World After Alexander, 323–30 BC* (London: Routledge, 2000), 214–215, 240–243.

12. G. E. R. Lloyd, *Greek Science After Aristotle* (London: Chatto and Windus, 1973), 3–8, 49–50, 75–85.

13. For the story of Ptolemaic patronage, see 'Aristeas to Philocrates' (2nd century BCE?), trans. M. Hadas in Michel Austin, *The Hellenistic World from Alexander to the Roman Conquest: A Selection of Ancient Sources in Translation*, 2nd ed. (Cambridge: Cambridge University Press, 2006), no. 261; James Carleton Paget, 'Jews and Christians in Ancient Alexandria: From the Ptolemies to Caracalla', in Hirst and Silk, *Alexandria*, 143–166 (see 149–151).

14. Ashton, 'Ptolemaic Alexandria'; Alan Bowman, *Egypt After the Pharaohs, 332 BC–AD 642* (London: British Museum, 1996), 168–169; R. Malcolm Errington, *A History of the Hellenistic World, 323–30 BC* (Oxford: Blackwell, 2008), 146–147; J. G. Manning, *The Last Pharaohs: Egypt Under the Ptolemies, 305–30 BC* (Princeton, NJ: Princeton University Press, 2010), 205–206.

15. Maehler, 'Alexandria', 6–7 ('cultural apartheid'); F. W. Walbank, *The Hellenistic World* (London: Fontana, 1992), 110, 214; Errington, *History*, 154–155. For an obsequious Greek response at the time, see Theocritus, *Idylls* 17.128–134.

16. 'A third century [BCE] description of central Greece', often attributed to Heracleides of Crete, trans. Austin in *Hellenistic World*, no. 101 (p. 198 cited); compare Strabo 17.1.6–10, describing Alexandria some three hundred years later (translated in the same volume, no. 292).

17. See, for example, Shipley, *Greek World*, 128–130; Paul Cartledge, *Democracy: A Life*, 2nd ed. (Oxford: Oxford University Press, 2018), 241–245.

18. Johanna Hanink, *Lycurgan Athens and the Making of Classical Tragedy* (Cambridge: Cambridge University Press, 2014), 225–243; N. J. Lowe, *Comedy (New Surveys in the Classics)* (Cambridge: Cambridge University Press, 2008), 63–80.

19. Walbank, *Hellenistic World*, 178–181; Shipley, *Greek World*, 176–191.

20. Diod.Sic. 20.54.1; for date, see Shipley, *Greek World*, 51.

21. Theocritus, *Idylls* 1.

22. Lloyd, *Greek Science*, 40–49 (40, 47 cited).

23. Polyb. 8.3–7; Polybius, *The Rise of the Roman Empire*, trans. Ian Scott-Kilvert, selected with an introduction by F. W. Walbank (London: Penguin, 1979), 364–368; Plutarch, *Marcellus* 14–17, 19.

24. For a Greek analysis, written while the historian was living as a hostage in Rome between 167 and 150 BCE, see Polyb. 6.11–58, trans. Scott-Kilvert, 311–352. For its limitations, and modern correctives, see Mary Beard, *SPQR: A History of Ancient Rome* (London: Profile, 2015), 184–192; Cartledge, *Democracy*, 247–263. On Polybius see further below.

25. Polyb. 1.3.3–4 (my translation); trans. Scott-Kilvert, 43; see also Polyb. 5.105.3–4, trans. Scott-Kilvert, 301; Angelos Chaniotis, *Age of Conquests: The Greek World from Alexander to Hadrian 336 BC–AD 138* (Princeton, NJ: Princeton University Press, 2018), 148–149.

26. Polyb. 18.45.9, 18.46.15, trans. Scott-Kilvert, 515 (slightly adapted), 517.

27. Shipley, *Greek World*, 380, citing Livy 42.51. See also Austin, *Hellenistic World*, no. 94.

28. Polyb. 29.27, trans. Austin, *Hellenistic World*, 374 (no. 211).

29. Thonemann, *Hellenistic Age*, 27. The view expressed here is closer to Walbank, *Hellenistic World*, 157–158. For the history of such institutions, see Emily Mackil, *Creating a Common Polity: Religion, Economy, and Politics in the Making of the Greek Koinon* (Berkeley: University of California Press, 2012).

30. Beard, *SPQR*, 212–213.

31. Paus. 7.16–17, trans. Austin, *Hellenistic World*, no. 100 (second century CE); Dio Cassius 21.72 (second to third century CE).

32. Walbank, *Hellenistic World*, 228, citing Hellanicus of Lesbos (fifth century BCE); Erich Gruen, 'Greeks and Non-Greeks', in Bugh, *Cambridge Companion*, 295–314 (see 300–302).

33. See, for example, Caroline Bishop, *Cicero, Greek Learning, and the Making of a Roman Classic* (Oxford: Oxford University Press, 2019).

34. Beard, *SPQR*, 170–172 (see 170, citing the second century BCE Latin author Porcius Licinius, as quoted by Aulus Gellius, *Attic Nights* 17.21); on this passage, see also Tim Whitmarsh, *Greek Literature and the Roman Empire* (Oxford: Oxford University Press, 2001), 9; see also Walbank, *Hellenistic World*, 247–249; Horace, *Epistles* 2.1, trans. Christopher Smart, *The Works of Horace*, rev. ed. (London: G. Bell, 1891), quoted.

35. Boardman, *Greeks*, 64–80; Sherwin-White and Kuhrt, *Samarkhand*, 84–90, 223–225.

36. Isaiah 43.1–3, 10–13; Seth Schwartz, *The Ancient Jews from Alexander to Muhammad* (Cambridge: Cambridge University Press, 2014), 24–29 (28 quoted).

37. Josephus, *Jewish Antiquities* 12.1–2 (first century CE); Simon Sebag Montefiore, *Jerusalem: The Biography* (London: Weidenfeld and Nicolson, 2011), 65–67.

38. 2 Macc. 4.10–13 (my translation); see also 1 Macc. 1.10–14, trans. Austin, *Hellenistic World*, no. 217; Josephus, *Jewish Antiquities* 12.5.1; Shipley, *Greek World*, 308; Schwartz, *Ancient Jews*, 41–42; Sherwin-White and Kuhrt, *Samarkhand*, 226–227.

39. 1 Macc. 1.44–56; 2 Macc. 6.1–9; Austin, *Hellenistic World*, no. 217; Shipley, *Greek World*, 309–310. For the voluntary submission of the

Samaritans of Mount Gerizim, see Josephus, *Jewish Antiquities* 12.5.5 and Sherwin-White and Kuhrt, *Samarkhand*, 229.

40. 2 Macc. 11.24–25; Shipley, *Greek World*, 311; Schwartz, *Ancient Jews*, 45.

41. Schwartz, *Ancient Jews*, 46–52. The *First Book of Maccabees* (1 Macc.) was written in the later first century BCE in either Hebrew or Aramaic and later translated into Greek, the version known today. The *Second* (2 Macc.), probably written some decades later, is a condensation of an older original and was written in Greek (Shipley, *Greek World*, 266; Austin, *Hellenistic World*, no. 216). Josephus, writing in Greek during the second half of the first century CE, under Roman rule, is the third principal source for these events.

42. Virgil, *Aeneid* 1.272; Beard, *SPQR*, 193–197.

43. Appian, *Mithridatic Wars* 4.22–23 (my translation); Shipley, *Greek World*, 389; Beard, *SPQR*, 270.

44. Appian, *Mithridatic Wars* 6.38, trans. Shipley, *Greek World*, 391 (slightly adapted), and see 472n62 for archaeological reports.

45. Shipley, *Greek World*, 393; Joel Allen, *The Roman Republic and the Hellenistic Mediterranean: From Alexander to Caesar* (Medford, MA: Wiley Blackwell, 2020), 179, 201, 207–208.

46. Plutarch, *Pompey* 45–46; Beard, *SPQR*, 273–278; Allen, *Roman Republic*, 229–230.

47. Shipley, *Greek World*, 212–213; Allen, *Roman Republic*, 188, 201–202.

48. Plutarch, *Antony* 54; C. P. Cavafy, *The Collected Poems: Includes Parallel Greek Text*, ed. Anthony Hirst, trans. Evangelos Sachperoglou (Oxford: Oxford University Press, 2007), 52–55 (my translation).

49. Shipley, *Greek World*, 397; Beard, *SPQR*, 340, 354; Allen, *Roman Republic*, 254–256.

Chapter 7: Rome's Greek Empire

1. Mary Beard, *SPQR: A History of Ancient Rome* (London: Profile, 2015), 384, 404–406. For the scandalous lives of the emperors, see

Suetonius, *The Twelve Caesars* (late first century CE); Tom Holland, *Dynasty: The Rise and Fall of the House of Caesar* (London: Little, Brown, 2015), 174–419.

2. Beard, *SPQR*, 480–483.

3. An exception in the east was the province of Dacia, the region of the Balkans to the north of the Danube, that was conquered by Trajan in the early first century CE. There, Latin was spoken (and Latin-derived Romanian still is, today). In the west, significant Greek-speaking communities existed at Rome, Carthage, and Lugdunum in Gaul (today's Lyon). On possible exceptions in Sicily and southern Italy, see next note.

4. Kathryn Lomas, *Rome and the Western Greeks, 350 BC–AD 200: Conquest and Acculturation in Southern Italy* (London and New York: Routledge, 1993), 96–97, 189–190. For the possibility of limited survival for Greek in Sicily until the fifth century, see Fergus Millar, *A Greek Roman Empire: Power and Belief Under Theodosius II (408–450)* (Berkeley and Los Angeles: University of California Press, 2006), 15; Roger Wilson, *Sicily Under the Roman Empire: The Archaeology of a Roman Province, 36 B.C.–A.D. 535* (Warminster: Aris and Phillips, 1989), 318.

5. Susan Alcock, *The Landscapes of Roman Greece* (Cambridge: Cambridge University Press, 1993), 168–169; Angelos Chaniotis, *Age of Conquests: The Greek World from Alexander to Hadrian 336 BC–AD 138* (Princeton, NJ: Princeton University Press, 2018), 281.

6. Simon Swain, *Hellenism and Empire: Language, Classicism and Power in the Greek World AD 50–250* (Oxford: Clarendon, 1996), 69; A. J. S. Spawforth, *Greece and the Augustan Cultural Revolution* (Cambridge: Cambridge University Press, 2012), 38–39; Greg Woolf, 'Becoming Roman, Staying Greek: Culture, Identity and the Civilizing Process in the Roman East', *Proceedings of the Cambridge Philological Society* 40 (1994): 116–143.

7. Chaniotis, *Age of Conquests*, 277, 283–288; Robin Lane Fox, *Pagans and Christians in the Mediterranean World from the Second Century AD to the Conversion of Constantine* (London: Penguin, 1988), 12–14. 'Long Hellenistic age': Chaniotis, *Age of Conquests*, 3 and *passim*; see also, argued on different grounds, Alcock, *Landscapes*, 218.

8. G. E. R. Lloyd, *Greek Science After Aristotle* (London: Chatto and Windus, 1973), 113–153 (113 quoted, see also 154, 177); 'Introduction', in Galen, *Method of Medicine, Books 1–4*, ed. and trans. Ian Johnston and G. H. R. Horsley (Cambridge, MA: Harvard University Press, Loeb Classics Series, 2011), xlix, on Galen's life see xii–xxiii.

9. Plutarch, *Moralia* 813D–813F, 824E–824F (my translation), cited and discussed in Alcock, *Landscapes*, 150; see also Paul Cartledge, *Democracy: A Life*, 2nd ed. (Oxford: Oxford University Press, 2018), 272. The essay is conventionally known by the Latin title *Praecepta gerendae reipublicae*, meaning roughly 'principles of statecraft'.

10. Andrew Erskine, 'Introduction', in Plutarch, *Hellenistic Lives*, trans. Robin Waterfield (Oxford: Oxford University Press, 2016), xii.

11. Geoffrey Horrocks, *Greek: A History of the Language and Its Speakers*, 2nd ed. (Medford, MA, and Oxford: Wiley Blackwell, 2014), 125–141; Swain, *Hellenism*, 1 (citing Philostratus, *Lives of the Sophists* 481), 6–21, 410 and *passim*.

12. Spawforth, *Greece*, 11–12, 271 (*Graecia vera*); 103–106 (Persian Wars); 31–32, 55, 241, 264–270 (Second Sophistic). On the image of Alexander from Augustus to the mid-third century, see Tony Spawforth, '"Macedonian Times": Hellenistic Memories in the Provinces of the Roman Near East', in *Greeks on Greekness: Viewing the Greek Past Under the Roman Empire*, ed. David Konstan and Suzanne Saïd (Cambridge: Cambridge Philological Society, Supplementary vol. 5, 2006), 1–26 (see 20–21, 25).

13. Chaniotis, *Age of Conquests*, 251–252, citing and translating *Inscriptiones Graecae* (Berlin: Berlin Academy of Sciences, 1873–), 7.2713; see also Spawforth, *Greece*, 236–238. For Nero's tour of Greece in 66–67 CE, see Edward Champlin, *Nero* (Cambridge, MA: Harvard University Press, 2003), 53–61. On the Corinth Canal, see Alcock, *Landscapes*, 141–142.

14. Spawforth, *Greece*, 249–264; Alcock, *Landscapes*, 166–168; Tim Whitmarsh, *Greek Literature and the Roman Empire: The Politics of Imitation* (Oxford: Oxford University Press, 2002), 24–25.

15. Lucian: Simon Goldhill, 'Introduction. Setting an Agenda: "Everything Is Greek to the Wise"', in *Being Greek Under Rome: Cultural Identity, the Second Sophistic and the Development of Empire*, ed. Simon Goldhill (Cambridge, Cambridge University Press, 2001), 1–23; Whitmarsh, *Greek Literature*, 122–128. Heliodorus, *Aethiopica* 10.41. Plutarch: Whitmarsh, *Greek Literature*, 116–118. See also Jonathan Hall, *Hellenicity: Between Ethnicity and Culture* (Chicago: Chicago University Press, 2002), 224–226.

16. Suzanne Saïd, 'The Rewriting of the Athenian Past: From Isocrates to Aelius Aristides', in Konstan and Saïd, *Greeks on Greekness*, 47–60; Clifford Ando, 'Imperial Identities', in *Local Knowledge and Microidentities in the Imperial Greek World*, ed. Tim Whitmarsh (Cambridge: Cambridge University Press, 2010), 17–45 (see 45); Chaniotis, *Age of Conquests*, 315–316.

17. Marcus Aurelius 9.29; Marcus Aurelius, *Meditations*, trans. Maxwell Staniforth (London: Penguin, 1964), 144. See also translator's introduction in the same volume, 7–8, 18–21, and Whitmarsh, *Greek Literature*, 216–225. The original Greek title of the work means *To Himself.*

18. See, for example, Graham Shipley, *The Greek World After Alexander, 323–30 BC* (London: Routledge, 2000), 105–106.

19. Lucretius, *De Rerum Natura* 3.830–977.

20. See, for example, Lane Fox, *Pagans*, 118–119, 151–153, 161–162; Chaniotis, *Age of Conquests*, 355–382.

21. On death: Lane Fox, *Pagans*, 95–98. Mysteries of Isis in the second century: Apuleius, *Metamorphoses* 11.21, trans. E. J. Kenney (Apuleius, *The Golden Ass* [London: Penguin, 1998], 207, quoted). See more generally Hugh Bowden, *Mystery Cults in the Ancient World* (London: Thames & Hudson, 2010).

22. Of the five Greek novels of this period which survive complete, the best known are Longus, *Daphnis and Chloe*; Achilles Tatius, *Leucippe and Cleitophon* (both written in the late second century CE); and Heliodorus, *Aethiopica*. The last has long been dated to the late fourth century, wrongly in my view. For the arguments supporting a date around

215 CE, much closer to the other novels and to the Second Sophistic, to which it clearly belongs, see Swain, *Hellenism*, 423–424; Lane Fox, *Pagans*, 137–138; Roderick Beaton, *The Medieval Greek Romance*, 2nd ed. (London: Routledge, 1996), 73–74, 241n16. See also Northrop Frye, *The Secular Scripture: A Study of the Structure of Romance* (Cambridge, MA: Harvard University Press, 1976).

23. Charles Freeman, *A New History of Early Christianity* (New Haven, CT, and London: Yale University Press, 2011), 18–19.

24. Paul, *1 Cor.* 4.15, 9.14 (probably the earliest uses of the word in this sense).

25. The regularly cited biographical details of Paul's origin come not from his own letters but from *Acts* (see 21.39, 22.28). For the inference that Paul's father had been a freed slave, with a modern assessment of Paul's background, see Freeman, *New History*, 48–49. On the importance of letters, see Richard Norris, 'The Apostolic and Sub-apostolic Writings: The New Testament and the Apostolic Fathers', in *The Cambridge History of Early Christian Literature*, ed. Frances Young, Lewis Ayres, and Andrew Louth (Cambridge: Cambridge University Press, 2004), 11–19 (see 11–12). On the language of early Christian texts, see Horrocks, *Greek*, 147–152.

26. Paul, *Gal.* 1.1, 1.4, 5.22–23, 5.14 (Authorized Version quoted).

27. Paul, *1 Cor.* 15.3–5, 15.52, 15.55 (quoted).

28. *Acts* 11.26, 28.30–31.

29. Tacitus, *Annals* 15.44, trans. J. Jackson (Loeb Classical Library, vol. 5, 1937), 283. On the fire, see Champlin, *Nero*, 121–126, 178–185.

30. Freeman, *New History*, 72–96 (see 82 on Luke); Geza Vermes, *Christian Beginnings: From Nazareth to Nicaea, AD 30–325* (London: Penguin, 2013), 115–133.

31. Celsus, *On the True Doctrine: A Discourse Against the Christians*, introduction and translation by R. Joseph Hoffman (Oxford: Oxford University Press, 1987).

32. Lane Fox, *Pagans*, 294–311; John Behr, 'Social and Historical Setting', in Young et al., *Cambridge History*, 55–70 (see 62–64).

33. See Lane Fox, *Pagans*, 317 for the 'guess' at 2 per cent in 250, but see also Averil Cameron, *The Mediterranean World in Late Antiquity, AD 395–700*, 2nd ed. (London: Routledge, 2012), 58–59 on the impossibility of making reliable estimates, even in the fourth and fifth centuries. For the lives and thought of second-century martyrs, see *The Apostolic Fathers, Early Christian Writings*, trans. Maxwell Staniforth, rev. with introduction and notes by Andrew Louth (London: Penguin, 1987).

34. The classic statement of Roman policy in the early second century is to be found in the brief exchange of letters on the subject between the emperor Trajan and his provincial governor in northern Anatolia, see Pliny the Younger, *Letters* 10.96–97. On martyrs and martyrdom, see Lane Fox, 419–492; Freeman, *New History*, 205–214. For second-century martyrs, see Eusebius, *Ecclesiastical History* 4.117–128.

35. Lloyd, *Greek Science*, 151, citing Galen, *On the Use of Parts* 3.20.

36. Cited in Lane Fox, *Pagans*, 169, for discussion see 168–177.

37. Ronald Heine, 'The Alexandrians', in Young et al., *Cambridge History*, 117–130; Freeman, *New History*, 175–195; Vermes, *Christian Beginnings*, 210–211, 213–215. On the language used by these third-century authors, see Horrocks, *Greek*, 155.

38. Beard, *SPQR*, 387, 420, 423–424.

39. Fergus Millar, *The Roman Empire and Its Neighbours*, 2nd ed. (London: Duckworth, 1981), 216–217, 239–248. See also Peter Brown, *The World of Late Antiquity, AD 150–750* (London: Thames & Hudson, 1971), 22–25; Averil Cameron, *The Later Roman Empire: AD 284–340* (London: Fontana, 1993), 3–11. End of 'epigraphic habit': Lane Fox, *Pagans*, 14, 573–575, 582–583; Brown, *World*, 66–67.

40. Beard, *SPQR*, 527–529 (527 quoted); Myles Lavan, 'The Spread of Roman Citizenship', *Past and Present* 229 (2016): 3–46. The explanation of the measure as a means to raise taxes was first proposed by the Greek historian Dio Cassius, in his universal history written shortly afterwards (Dio Cassius 78.9). See also Alex Imrie, *The Antonine Constitution, an Edict for the Caracallan Empire* (Leiden and Boston, MA: Brill, 2018).

41. Lane Fox, *Pagans*, 425 (on motives), 450–459, 550–554. The fullest ancient sources are Eusebius, *Ecclesiastical History* 7.10–12, and

Lactantius, *On the Deaths of the Persecutors* 4–5, both written about half a century afterwards, the former in Greek, the latter in Latin.

42. Eusebius, *Ecclesiastical History* 8.2, trans. G. A. Williamson and Andrew Louth (Eusebius, *The History of the Church*, rev. ed. [London: Penguin, 1989], 258–259); Lane Fox, *Pagans and Christians*, 592–595; Freeman, *New History*, 212.

43. Freeman, *New History*, 215–219 (percentage cited from 215). Lane Fox (*Pagans*, 592) suggests perhaps 'only 4 or 5 percent' by the end of the century.

44. Eusebius, *Life of Constantine* 3.13 (written shortly after 337); Eusebius, *Life of Constantine* (Oxford: Clarendon, 1999), trans. Averil Cameron and Stuart Hall, 265–266 (commentary).

45. Known as the 'Edict of Milan', versions are preserved by Lactantius (*On the Deaths* 48) and Eusebius (*Ecclesiastical History* 10.5). Both were written during the lifetime of Constantine. See also Timothy Barnes, *Constantine: Dynasty, Religion and Power in the Later Roman Empire* (Oxford: Blackwell, 2011), 93–94.

46. Eusebius, *Life* 1.28–29, trans. Cameron and Hall, 81, see also 204–210 for commentary. See also Peter Weiss, 'The Vision of Constantine', *Journal of Roman Archaeology* 16 (2003): 237–259 and discussion in Barnes, *Constantine*, 74–80.

47. Eusebius, *Life* 2.46, trans. Cameron and Hall, 111; for commentary, see 244; Barnes, *Constantine*, 110–111.

48. Eusebius, *Life* 4.62, trans. Cameron and Hall, 178.

49. For order as Constantine's overriding consideration, see Freeman, *New History*, 228, 237; Cameron and Hall, 'Introduction', 46. On the executions of Crispus and his stepmother Fausta in 326, see *The Prosopography of the Later Roman Empire*, 3 vols. (Cambridge: Cambridge University Press, 1971–1992), 1.233.

50. Paul Stephenson, *Constantine: Unconquered Emperor, Christian Victor* (London: Quercus, 2009), 305.

51. *Chronicon Paschale*, trans. Michael Whitby and Mary Whitby (Liverpool: Liverpool University Press, 1989), 17–18 (written c. 630);

Stephenson, *Constantine*, 190–211; Bettany Hughes, *Istanbul: A Tale of Three Cities* (London: Weidenfeld and Nicolson, 2017), 112–115.

Chapter 8: Becoming Christian

1. Eusebius, *Life of Constantine* 3.54; see also Timothy Barnes, *Constantine: Dynasty, Religion and Power in the Later Roman Empire* (Oxford: Blackwell, 2011), 111–113, 126–131 (following Eusebius); contrast Paul Stephenson, *Constantine: Unconquered Emperor, Christian Victor* (London: Quercus, 2009), 201–203.

2. Peter Brown, *The World of Late Antiquity, AD 150–750* (London: Thames & Hudson, 1971), 98–103 (98 quoted).

3. Averil Cameron, *The Mediterranean World in Late Antiquity, AD 395–700*, 2nd ed. (London: Routledge, 2012), 76–81; Charles Freeman, *A New History of Early Christianity* (New Haven, CT, and London: Yale University Press, 2011), 274–284 (281 on Pachomius).

4. G. W. Bowersock, *Julian the Apostate* (Cambridge, MA: Harvard University Press, 1978), 21–45.

5. Julian, *Oration* 7.217c; Wolf Liebeschuetz, *East and West in Late Antiquity: Invasion, Settlement, Ethnogenesis and Conflicts of Religion* (Leiden and Boston, MA: Brill, 2015), 333–334.

6. Stephen Mitchell, *A History of the Later Roman Empire, AD 284–641* (Oxford: Blackwell, 2007), 285–290; Bowersock, *Julian*, 16–17, 28–30; Brown, *World*, 93–94.

7. See farther Claudia Rapp, 'Hellenic Identity, *Romanitas*, and Christianity in Byzantium', in *Hellenisms: Culture, Identity, and Ethnicity from Antiquity to Modernity*, ed. Katerina Zacharia (Aldershot: Ashgate, 2008), 127–147; Anthony Kaldellis, *Hellenism in Byzantium: The Transformations of Greek Identity and the Reception of the Classical Tradition* (Cambridge: Cambridge University Press, 2007), *passim*. On education, see Cameron, *Mediterranean World*, 130–134.

8. Joseph Tainter, *The Collapse of Complex Societies* (Cambridge: Cambridge University Press, 1988), 128–152 and see Chap. 1 above; see also Walter Scheidel, *Escape from Rome: The Failure of Empire and*

the Road to Prosperity (Princeton, NJ: Princeton University Press, 2019), 127–131.

9. Fergus Millar, *A Greek Roman Empire: Power and Belief Under Theodosius II (408–450)* (Berkeley and Los Angeles: University of California Press, 2006), 13–14; Michael Kulikowski, *Imperial Tragedy: From Constantine's Empire to the Destruction of Roman Italy, AD 363–568* (London: Profile, 2019), 54 (gold).

10. Millar, *A Greek Roman Empire*, 2–4, 7, 14–15, 84–97; Cameron, *Mediterranean World*, 27–28, 176–181. See also Anthony Kaldellis, *Romanland: Ethnicity and Empire in Byzantium* (Cambridge, MA: Belknap, Harvard University Press, 2019), 85–94.

11. Freeman, *New History*, 238–253, 298–305 (on the Council of Chalcedon, see 303–305); Mitchell, *History*, 318–319.

12. Mitchell, *History*, 242; Cameron, *Mediterranean World*, 58–59.

13. Socrates, *Historia Ecclesiastica* 7.15, trans. J. Stevenson, cited in Cameron, *Mediterranean World*, 29.

14. Kulikowski, *Imperial Tragedy*, 168 ('jihadist terrorists'); Catherine Nixey, *The Darkening Age: The Christian Destruction of the Classical World* (London: Pan Macmillan, 2017), xix–xxi (Palmyra).

15. Olympic Games at Antioch: *The Chronicle of John Malalas* 17.13, trans. Elizabeth Jeffreys, Michael Jeffreys, and Roger Scott (Melbourne: Australian Association of Byzantine Studies, 1986), 236. On mimes and pantomimes: Ruth Webb, *Demons and Dancers: Performance in Late Antiquity* (Cambridge: Cambridge University Press, 2008); Ruth Webb, 'Mime and the Dangers of Laughter in Late Antiquity', in *Greek Laughter and Tears: Antiquity and After*, ed. Margaret Alexiou and Douglas Cairns (Edinburgh: Edinburgh University Press, 2017), 219–231 (see 228–229 for citations from Saint John Chrysostom, quoted). On survival of theatrical performances into the sixth century, see Brown, *World*, 180, 186; Cyril Mango, 'Daily Life in Byzantium', *Jahrbuch der Österreichischen Byantinistik* 31 (1981): 337–353 (see 341–344).

16. Robin Lane Fox, *Pagans and Christians in the Mediterranean World from the Second Century AD to the Conversion of Constantine* (London: Penguin, 1988), 495–507; Freeman, *New History*, 261–273.

17. For a highly coloured contemporary account, see Procopius, *Secret History* 7.1–29, trans. G. Williamson and Peter Sarris, rev. ed. (London: Penguin, 2007), 28–30. The standard modern treatment remains Alan Cameron, *Circus Factions: Blues and Greens at Rome and Byzantium* (Oxford: Clarendon, 1976).

18. *Chronicon Paschale*, trans. Michael Whitby and Mary Whitby (Liverpool: Liverpool University Press, 1989), 103–104; Malalas, *Chronicle* 17.1–2, trans. Jeffreys, 230–231; Peter Sarris, *Empires of Faith: The Fall of Rome to the Rise of Islam, 500–700* (Oxford: Oxford University Press, 2011), 135, 137; Peter Heather, *Rome Resurgent: War and Empire in the Age of Justinian* (Oxford: Oxford University Press, 2018), 83–85.

19. Malalas, *Chronicle* 18.1, trans. Jeffreys, 245 (on the author, see xxi–xxii); Procopius, *Secret History* 13.1–2, trans. Williamson and Sarris, 54. For contrasting opinions on the author and the nature of this work, see Averil Cameron, *Procopius and the Sixth Century* (London: Duckworth, 1985) and Anthony Kaldellis, *Procopius of Caesarea: Tyranny, History, and Philosophy at the End of Antiquity* (Philadelphia: University of Pennsylvania Press, 2004).

20. *Codex Justinianus* 1.1.1, trans. Mitchell, *History*, 270 (quoted), and see further 242–276; *The Novels of Justinian: A Complete Annotated English Translation*, ed. Peter Sarris, trans. J. D. Miller (Cambridge: Cambridge University Press, 2018), 439–440 (Novel 77), 929–932 (Novel 141) (homosexuality); Malalas, *Chronicle* 18.42, 18.47, trans. Jeffreys, 262, 264 (quoted).

21. Cameron, *Mediterranean World*, 136.

22. Procopius, *Wars* 1.24; *Chronicon Paschale*, trans. Whitby, 115–126; Sarris, *Empires*, 148–151; Heather, *Rome Resurgent*, 109–114.

23. Heather, *Rome Resurgent*, 120–123, 139–142, 164–179; Judith Herrin, *Ravenna: Capital of Empire, Crucible of Europe* (London: Allen Lane, 2020), 151–159. These events take up the greater part of Procopius, *Wars*, which remains the primary source.

24. Procopius, *Buildings* 1.2.9–12; Heather, *Rome Resurgent*, 181–182; Elena Boeck, *The Bronze Horseman of Justinian in Constantinople: The*

Cross-Cultural Biography of a Mediterranean Monument (Cambridge: Cambridge University Press, 2021).

25. Procopius, *Buildings* 1.1.30–54; Heather, *Rome Resurgent*, 192–195; Freeman, *New History*, 271–273.

26. Eusebius, *Oration in Praise of the Emperor Constantine* 1.6, delivered in the year 332 (my translation); I. A. Heikel, *Eusebius Werke, vol. 1* (*Die griechischen christlichen Schriftsteller* 7) (Leipzig: Hinrichs, 1902), 195–259.

27. Merle Eisenberg and Lee Mordechai, 'The Justinianic Plague: An Interdisciplinary Review', *Byzantine and Modern Greek Studies* 43 (2019): 156–180 (see 171–173 on climate); Sarris, *Empires*, 158–159 (158 quoted), 174–176; John Haldon, *The Empire That Would Not Die: The Paradox of Eastern Roman Survival, 640–740* (Cambridge, MA: Harvard University Press, 2016), 221. Devastation in 539: Procopius, *Wars* 2.4; *Secret History* 18.20–21.

28. Procopius, *Wars* 2.10.4 (my translation). For causes of this war, see *Wars* 2.1–3 (2.1 for Chosroes's accusation); Heather, *Rome Resurgent*, 218–219 (Antioch).

29. Procopius, *Wars* 2.23.17–18, 2.22.31, 2.22.33–34 (the last quoted, my translation); Sarris, *Empires*, 158–159; Kulikowski, *Imperial Tragedy*, 309–310. For global context, see Ian Morris, *Why the West Rules—For Now: The Patterns of History, and What They Reveal About the Future* (London: Profile, 2011), 346–347. On the number of victims, see Dionysios Stathakopoulos, *A Short History of the Byzantine Empire* (London: I. B. Tauris, 2014), 57, 78; see further Dionysios Stathakopoulos, *Famine and Pestilence in the Late Roman and Early Byzantine Empire* (Aldershot: Ashgate, 2004). Population of Constantinople in 540: Mark Whittow, *The Making of Orthodox Byzantium, 600–1025* (Basingstoke: Macmillan, 1996), 56.

30. Malalas, *Chronicle* 18.92, trans. Jeffreys, 286–287; Paul Magdalino, 'The History of the Future and Its Uses: Prophecy, Policy and Propaganda', in *The Making of Byzantine History: Studies Dedicated to Donald M. Nicol*, ed. Roderick Beaton and Charlotte Roueché (Aldershot:

Ashgate, 1993), 1–34 (see 6 for translated extract from Romanos, 'On the Ten Virgins', quoted, and 6–7 for popular attitudes in the 550s).

31. Herrin, *Ravenna*, 166–173, 188; for the origin of the imperial crown, see Malalas, *Chronicle* 13.8, trans. Jeffreys, 175.

32. Cameron, *Mediterranean World*, 172–173; Peter Frankopan, *The Silk Roads: A New History of the World* (London: Bloomsbury, 2015), 38–39, 54–55.

33. J. McCrindle, ed. and trans., *The Christian Topography of Cosmas* (London: Hakluyt Society, 1897), 367n7 (China); Cosmas Indicopleustes 2.147 (quoted, trans. McCrindle, 71).

34. Procopius, *Secret History* 12.14 (quoted, trans. Williamson and Sarris, 51–52); see also 18.1, 18.36–45. For the reading as satirical, I follow Heather, *Rome Resurgent*, 16–17.

35. Heather, *Rome Resurgent*, 330–331; Whittow, *Making*, 38–39, 42, 48, 68.

36. Theophylact Simocatta, *History* 8.6–8.13; trans. Michael Whitby and Mary Whitby (Oxford: Clarendon, 1986); *Chronicon Paschale*, trans. Whitby, 142–144. For these events as the start of the sequence that extends all the way to the end of the present chapter, see Whittow, *Making*, 69.

37. Whittow, *Making*, 73 ('civil war'); Sarris, *Empires*, 242–243; Walter Kaegi, *Heraclius, Emperor of Byzantium* (Cambridge: Cambridge University Press, 2003), 37–40.

38. *Chronicon Paschale*, trans. Whitby, 150–153, and see translators' note 423 on other early sources and the role of the Greens; Sarris, *Empires*, 244–245; Kaegi, *Heraclius*, 49–52.

39. Florin Curta, *The Edinburgh History of the Greeks, c. 500 to 1050. The Early Middle Ages* (Edinburgh: Edinburgh University Press, 2011), 16–21.

40. James Howard-Johnston, 'The Siege of Constantinople in 626', in *Constantinople and its Hinterland*, ed. Cyril Mango and Gilbert Dagron (Aldershot: Ashgate, 1985), 131–142 (for the events of the siege and original sources see 139–141); Kaegi, *Heraclius*, 132–138.

41. Howard-Johnston, 'The Siege', 141.

42. *The Chronicle of Theophanes*, trans. Harry Turtledove (Princeton, NJ: Princeton University Press, 1982), 16; Sarris, *Empires*, 250, 252–253, 258; Mitchell, *History*, 460; Kaegi, *Heraclius*, 129, see also 113–114 citing Heraclius's contemporary George of Pisidia.

43. Theophanes, *Chronicle*, trans. Turtledove, 29–30.

44. Sarris, *Empires*, 258, 260; Kaegi, *Heraclius*, 186, 194.

45. Kaegi, *Heraclius*, 205–207; P. J. Alexander, *The Byzantine Apocalyptic Tradition* (Berkeley: University of California Press, 1985), 38–51 (translation from Syriac of the 'Apocalypse of Pseudo-Methodius', including 'King of the Greeks'), 50 quoted, and 151–184 (discussion). See also the Latin 'Prophecy of the Tiburtine Sibyl', in Ernst Sackur, *Sibyllinische Texte und Forschungen: Pseudomethodius, Adso und tiburtinische Sibylle* (Halle an der Saale: Max Niemeyer, 1898), 177–187 ('king of the Romans'). For the possibility that the prophecy was inspired by Heraclius's action rather than the other way round, see Magdalino, 'The History', 19; Petre Guran, 'Genesis and Function of the "Last Emperor" Myth in Byzantine Eschatology', *Bizantinistica (Series 2)* 7 (2006), 273–303 (see 296–302).

46. Socrates, *Ecclesiastical History* 1.16; *Chronicon Paschale*, trans. Whitby, 17.

Chapter 9: 'The Eyes of the Universe'

1. John Haldon, *Byzantium in the Seventh Century: The Transformation of a Culture*, rev. ed. (Cambridge: Cambridge University Press, 1997), 53–74, 104–109 (on cities); John Haldon, *The Empire That Would Not Die: The Paradox of Eastern Roman Survival, 640–740* (Cambridge, MA: Harvard University Press, 2016), 32–52.

2. Florin Curta, *The Making of the Slavs: History and Archaeology of the Lower Danube Region, c. 500–700* (Cambridge: Cambridge University Press, 2001); Florin Curta, *The Edinburgh History of the Greeks, c. 500 to 1050. The Early Middle Ages* (Edinburgh: Edinburgh University Press, 2011), 48–109. Population: Averil Cameron, *The Byzantines* (Oxford: Blackwell, 2006), 32.

3. 'Systems collapse': Joseph Tainter, *The Collapse of Complex Societies* (Cambridge: Cambridge University Press, 1988), 151–152, 202–203. Byzantine 'dark age': Michael Whitby, *The Emperor Maurice and His Historian: Theophylact Simocatta on Persian and Balkan Warfare* (Oxford: Clarendon, 1988), 355–358; Haldon, *Byzantium*, 425–435.

4. Anthony Kaldellis, 'From "Empire of the Greeks" to "Byzantium": The Politics of a Modern Paradigm-Shift', in *The Invention of Byzantium in Early Modern Europe*, ed. Nathanael Aschenbrenner and Jake Ransohoff (Washington, DC: Dumbarton Oaks Center, 2021). See also Anthony Kaldellis, *Romanland: Ethnicity and Empire in Byzantium* (Cambridge, MA: Belknap, Harvard University Press, 2019), ix–xv; Claudia Rapp, 'Hellenic Identity, *Romanitas*, and Christianity in Byzantium', in *Hellenisms: Culture, Identity, and Ethnicity from Antiquity to Modernity*, ed. Katerina Zacharia (Aldershot: Ashgate, 2008), 127–147.

5. Peter Sarris, *Empires of Faith: The Fall of Rome to the Rise of Islam, 500–700* (Oxford: Oxford University Press, 2011), 284–286 (285 quoted, citing the *Armenian History Attributed to Sebeos*, trans. R. W. Thompson); Haldon, *Empire*, 42–43, 146.

6. Mark Whittow, *The Making of Orthodox Byzantium, 600–1025* (Basingstoke: Macmillan, 1996), 104, 193. See also Haldon, *Empire*, 293–294 and *passim*.

7. John Haldon, 'Greek Fire Revisited: Recent and Current Research', in *Byzantine Style, Religion and Civilization: In Honour of Sir Steven Runciman*, ed. Elizabeth Jeffreys (Cambridge: Cambridge University Press, 2006), 290–325.

8. *The Chronicle of Theophanes*, trans. Harry Turtledove (Princeton, NJ: Princeton University Press, 1982), 88–91; Haldon, *Byzantium*, 80–84; Haldon, *Empire*, 52–54; Si Shepard, *Constantinople AD 717–718: The Crucible of History* (Oxford: Osprey, 2020), 60–75; Philip Mansel, *Constantinople: City of the World's Desire, 1453–1924* (London: Penguin, 1997).

9. Ian Morris, *Why the West Rules—For Now: The Patterns of History, and What They Reveal About the Future* (London: Profile, 2011),

353–354, 356–363; Judith Herrin, *The Formation of Christendom*, 2nd ed. (London: Phoenix, 2001); Chris Wickham, *Framing the Early Middle Ages, 400–800* (Oxford: Oxford University Press, 2005).

10. Leslie Brubaker and John Haldon, *Byzantium in the Iconoclast Era, c. 680–850* (Cambridge: Cambridge University Press, 2011), 75–77; Theophanes, *Chronicle*, trans. Turtledove, 103.

11. Theophanes, *Chronicle*, trans. Turtledove, 96–97 (quoted), 103–104, 112–113.

12. Peter Brown, *The World of Late Antiquity, AD 150–750* (London: Thames & Hudson, 1971), 183 (changed attitude in seventh century); Whittow, *Making*, 142–143, 158 (divine favour).

13. Brubaker and Haldon, *Byzantium*, 2, 10.

14. Destruction of images (and limited extent): Brubaker and Haldon, *Byzantium*, 199–212; Robin Cormack, *Writing in Gold: Byzantine Society and Its Icons* (London: George Philip, 1985), 108–111, 142–143; Philipp Niewöhner, 'The Significance of the Cross Before, During, and After Iconoclasm: Early Christian Aniconism in Constantinople and Asia Minor', *Dumbarton Oaks Papers* 74 (2021): 185–242. Evidence of persecution: *Byzantine Defenders of Images: Eight Saints' Lives in English Translation*, ed. Alice-Mary Talbot (Washington, DC: Dumbarton Oaks Center, 1998); summary and discussion of the *Life of St Stephen the Younger*, written c. 807, in Cormack, *Writing*, 118–121.

15. Judith Herrin, *Women in Purple: Rulers of Medieval Byzantium* (London: Weidenfeld and Nicolson, 2001), 83–91; Brubaker and Haldon, *Byzantium*, 265–266.

16. Fall of Irene: Herrin, *Women*, 126–128. 'Theme system': Brubaker and Haldon, *Byzantium*, 744–755; see also Whittow, *Making*, 167–175 (167 for the belated military reform in relation to iconoclasm). Reconquest of Greece: Constantine Porphyrogenitus [909–959], *De administrando imperio*, Greek text ed. G. Moravcsik; English trans. R. J. H. Jenkins, rev. ed. (Washington, DC: Dumbarton Oaks Center, 1967), chaps. 49–50, pp. 228–231; Curta, *Edinburgh History*, 135–137.

17. Brubaker and Haldon, *Byzantium*, 6, 367–385.

18. Brubaker and Haldon, *Byzantium*, 398, 447–452 ('Triumph of Orthodoxy'); Herrin, *Women*, 202–213 (Theodora); Cormack, *Writing*, 141 (coins).

19. Photios, 'Sermon 17': 'On the inauguration of the image of the Virgin', cited in translation in Cormack, *Writing*, 150, and see 146–156 for context and discussion.

20. Whittow, *Making*, 136, citing *The Homilies of Photius, Patriarch of Constantinople*, trans. Cyril Mango (Cambridge, MA: Harvard University Press, 1958), 106–110.

21. Photios, 'Sermon 17', in Cormack, *Writing*, 149; Brubaker and Haldon, *Byzantium*, 271–275, 284–286, 774–788.

22. Anthony Kaldellis, *Streams of Gold, Rivers of Blood: The Rise and Fall of Byzantium, 955 A.D. to the First Crusade* (Oxford: Oxford University Press, 2017), xxvii.

23. Dmitri Obolensky, 'The Principles and Methods of Byzantine Diplomacy', in *Actes du XIIe Congrès international d'études byzantines, 1961*, vol. 2, ed. Georgije Ostrogorski (Belgrade: Naučno Delo, 1964), 52; Evangelos Chrysos, 'Byzantine Diplomacy, A.D. 300–800: Means and Ends', in *Byzantine Diplomacy*, ed. Jonathan Shepard and Simon Franklin (Aldershot: Variorum, 1992), 25–39 (see 28–29).

24. Chrysos, 'Byzantine Diplomacy'; Kaldellis, *Streams*, 9–10, citing Constantine Porphyrogenitus, *De Caerimoniis* 2.15 and Liutprand of Cremona, *Antapodosis* 6.5 (both tenth century).

25. Bettany Hughes, *Istanbul: A Tale of Three Cities* (London: Weidenfeld and Nicolson, 2017), 265, 268–272; Michalis Kordoses, Πρεσβείες μεταξύ Fu–lin (Βυζάντιο;) και Κίνας (Ioannina: Dodone, 1995).

26. Judith Herrin, *Byzantium: The Surprising Life of a Medieval Empire* (London: Allen Lane, 2007), 131–138, 215–216; Dionysios Stathakopoulos, *A Short History of the Byzantine Empire* (London: I. B. Tauris, 2014), 105–106.

27. The fullest account of these events, with references to the original sources, is Arnold Toynbee, *Constantine Porphyrogenitus and His World* (London: Oxford University Press, 1973), 582–591.

28. *Ioannis Scylitzes Synopsis Historiarum*, ed. J. Thurn (Berlin and New York: De Gruyter, 1973), 348–349 (late eleventh century). For modern discussions, see Paul Stephenson, *Byzantium's Balkan Frontier: A Political Study of the Northern Balkans, 900–1204* (Cambridge: Cambridge University Press, 2000), 71–74; Kaldellis, *Streams*, 120–127.

29. *Scylitzes*, 364 (my translation); Anthony Kaldellis, *The Christian Parthenon: Classicism and Pilgrimage in Byzantine Athens* (Cambridge: Cambridge University Press, 2009), 81–91.

Chapter 10: 'City of the World's Desire'

1. *The Itinerary of Benjamin of Tudela*, trans. Marcus Nathan Adler (London: Henry Frowde, 1907), 22–23; Philip Mansel, *Constantinople: City of the World's Desire, 1453–1924* (London: Penguin, 1997), 3.

2. Judith Herrin, *Byzantium: The Surprising Life of a Medieval Empire* (London: Allen Lane, 2007), 242–251 (242 citing Ioannes Tzetzes, *Epilogue to the Theogony*); Paul Magdalino, 'Hellenism and Nationalism in Byzantium', in Paul Magdalino, *Tradition and Transformation in Medieval Byzantium* (Aldershot: Ashgate, 1991), chap. XIV, pp. 5–6, 21, citing Eustathios, *Oration for the Emperor Manuel Komnenos* with commentary, both discussed by Anthony Kaldellis, *Hellenism in Byzantium: The Transformations of Greek Identity and the Reception of the Classical Tradition* (Cambridge: Cambridge University Press, 2007), 294.

3. Michael Psellos, *Chronographia*, translated as *Fourteen Byzantine Rulers* by E. R. A. Sewter (Harmondsworth: Penguin, 1966); Michael Jeffreys and Marc Lauxtermann, *The Letters of Psellos: Cultural Networks and Historical Realities* (Oxford: Oxford University Press, 2017). For a modern reassessment of the importance of Psellos, see Kaldellis, *Hellenism*, 191–226. Cultural and personal identity: Paul Magdalino, *The Empire of Manuel I Komnenos, 1143–1180* (Cambridge: Cambridge University Press, 1993), 394–395, 400–401, 409–410 ('Renaissance').

4. Roderick Beaton, *The Medieval Greek Romance*, 2nd ed. (London: Routledge, 1996), 52–88; *Four Byzantine Novels*, trans. with introductions and notes by Elizabeth Jeffreys (Liverpool: Liverpool University

Press, 2012). Satire: *Timarion*, trans. Barry Baldwin (Detroit, MI: Wayne State University Press, 1984). Epic: *Digenis Akritis: The Grottaferrata and Escorial Versions*, ed. and trans. Elizabeth Jeffreys (Cambridge: Cambridge University Press, 1998).

5. *Ptochoprodromos*, ed. Hans Eideneier (Heraklion: Crete University Press, 2012), 176 (my translation); see also Margaret Alexiou, 'Ploys of Performance: Games and Play in the Ptochoprodromic Poems', *Dumbarton Oaks Papers* 53 (1999): 91–109. On the language used here, see Geoffrey Horrocks, *Greek: A History of the Language and Its Speakers*, 2nd ed. (Medford, MA, and Oxford: Wiley Blackwell, 2014), 337–342.

6. Benjamin of Tudela, *Itinerary*, 20; Dionysios Stathakopoulos, *A Short History of the Byzantine Empire* (London: I. B. Tauris, 2014), 148–149.

7. The principal Greek source for these events is Michael Attaleiates, *History* 20–21, translated (with parallel Greek text) by Anthony Kaldellis and Dimitris Krallis (Cambridge, MA: Harvard University Press, 2012), 261–325; Anthony Kaldellis, *Streams of Gold, Rivers of Blood: The Rise and Fall of Byzantium, 955 A.D. to the First Crusade* (Oxford: Oxford University Press, 2017), 241–251.

8. Anna Komnene, *The Alexiad*, trans. E. R. A. Sewter, rev. with notes and introduction by Peter Frankopan (London: Penguin, 2009).

9. Peter Frankopan, *The First Crusade: The Call from the East* (London: Vintage, 2013), 57–70 (70 quoted); Kaldellis, *Streams*, 272–279.

10. Frankopan, *First Crusade*, 97–100 (99 quoted, citing the contemporary chronicle by Bernold of Constance); Kaldellis, *Streams*, 285–287. Church schism: Michael Angold, *Church and Society in Byzantium Under the Comneni, 1081–1261* (Cambridge: Cambridge University Press, 1995), 22–27.

11. Anna Komnene, *Alexiad* 10.5, trans. Sewter and Frankopan, 275 (quoted), see also 10.9.

12. Frankopan, *First Crusade*, 116.

13. Anna Komnene, *Alexiad* 10.9–11, trans. Sewter and Frankopan, 284–296; Frankopan, *First Crusade*, 132–133, 136; Kaldellis, *Streams*, 292–295, 296, 298–299 ('Byzantine imperial army').

14. Anna Komnene, *Alexiad* 10.8, trans. Sewter and Frankopan, 282–283 (crossbow); Frankopan, *First Crusade*, 66, 86, 140 (siege warfare).

15. Anna Komnene, *Alexiad* 11.2, trans. Sewter and Frankopan, 302 (quoted), 304; Frankopan, *First Crusade*, 139–142.

16. Anna Komnene, *Alexiad* 11.4–6, trans. Sewter and Frankopan, 306–315; Kaldellis, *Streams*, 297–301.

17. Holy war: Ioannis Stouraitis, '"Just War" and "Holy War" in the Middle Ages: Rethinking Theory Through the Byzantine Case-Study', *Jahrbuch für Österreichischen Byzantinistik* 62 (2012): 229–250; Frankopan, *First Crusade*, 202–206 (conclusion on Alexios's strategy). Quoted: Alexios I Komnenos, *The Muses* (1118), cited and translated in Magdalino, *Empire*, 28.

18. Magdalino, *Empire*, 41–42; Angeliki Papageorgiou, 'The Political Ideology of John II Komnenos', in *John II Komnenos, Emperor of Byzantium: In the Shadow of Father and Son*, ed. Alessandra Bucossi and Alex Rodriguez Suarez (Abingdon: Routledge, 2016), 37–52.

19. Jonathan Phillips, *The Second Crusade: Extending the Frontiers of Christendom* (New Haven, CT: Yale University Press, 2007), 171–175, 190–195; Elizabeth Jeffreys, 'The Comnenian Background to the *romans d'antiquité*', *Byzantion* 50 (1980): 112–131; Roderick Beaton, 'Transplanting Culture: From Greek Novel to Medieval Romance', in *Reading in the Byzantine Empire and Beyond*, ed. Teresa Shawcross and Ida Toth (Cambridge: Cambridge University Press, 2018), 499–513; Chrétien de Troyes, *Cligés*, in *Arthurian Romances*, trans. William Kibler (London: Penguin, 1991), 123–205.

20. Timothy Gregory, *A History of Byzantium*, 2nd ed. (Medford, MA, and Oxford: Wiley Blackwell, 2010), 315, citing *Nicetae Choniatae Historia*, ed. van Dieten (Berlin: De Gruyter), 108–109 [hereafter: Choniates, *History*]. For a translation of this work, see *O City of Byzantium: Annals of Niketas Choniates*, trans. Harry J. Magoulias (Detroit, MI: Wayne State University Press, 1984).

21. Michael Angold, *The Fourth Crusade: Event and Context* (London: Pearson Longman, 2003), 4 (competing modern assessments), 8–10, 42,

72, 99 (on Choniates); see also Alicia Simpson, *Niketas Choniates: A Historiographical Study* (Oxford: Oxford University Press, 2013).

22. For the role of the populace in Byzantine politics in general, see Anthony Kaldellis, *The Byzantine Republic: People and Power in New Rome* (Cambridge, MA: Harvard University Press, 2015), and specifically on these events: 112, 123–124, 129–130, 148–150, 161–162.

23. Michael Angold, *The Byzantine Empire, 1025–1204: A Political History* (London: Longman, 1984), 263–283. On separatism, see Jean-Claude Cheynet, *Pouvoir et contestations à Byzance (963–1210)* (Paris: Sorbonne, 1990), 110–156, 427–458.

24. See Angold, *Fourth Crusade*, 15; Jonathan Phillips, *The Fourth Crusade and the Sack of Constantinople* (London: Pimlico, 2005), 144–145 for citations from Geoffrey of Villehardouin and Robert Clari.

25. Phillips, *Fourth Crusade*, 168, 169, 315–316.

26. Angold, *Fourth Crusade*, 45–46 (Byzantine attitudes), 57, 75, 96, 98 (crusader intentions).

27. Angold, *Fourth Crusade*, 97–99; Phillips, *Fourth Crusade*, 221–241.

28. Choniates, *History*, 585 (my translation); trans. Magoulias, 322; Angold, *Fourth Crusade*, 100–101; Phillips, *Fourth Crusade*, 241–280.

Chapter 11: Hopeful Monsters

1. Jonathan Phillips, *The Fourth Crusade and the Sack of Constantinople* (London: Pimlico, 2005), xv; Michael Angold, *The Fourth Crusade: Event and Context* (London: Pearson Longman, 2003), 113–114.

2. Kenneth Setton, *Athens in the Middle Ages* (London: Variorum, 1975).

3. Averil Cameron, *The Byzantines* (Oxford: Blackwell, 2006), 192–193; Anthony Kaldellis, *Hellenism in Byzantium: The Transformations of Greek Identity and the Reception of the Classical Tradition* (Cambridge: Cambridge University Press, 2007), 308, 334–338; George Demacopoulos, *Colonizing Christianity: Greek and Latin Religious Identity in the Era of the Fourth Crusade* (New York: Fordham University Press, 2019), 5–9 and *passim*.

4. Adrian Hastings, *The Construction of Nationhood: Ethnicity, Religion and Nationalism* (Cambridge: Cambridge University Press, 1997); Joep Leerssen, *National Thought in Europe: A Cultural History* (Amsterdam: Amsterdam University Press, 2006), 25–51; Caspar Hirschi, *The Origins of Nationalism: An Alternative History from Ancient Rome to Early Modern Germany* (Cambridge: Cambridge University Press, 2012), 78–103 and *passim*.

5. Anthony Bryer, *The Empire of Trebizond and the Pontos* (London: Variorum, 1980).

6. Donald Nicol, *The Last Centuries of Byzantium 1261–1453*, 2nd ed. (Cambridge: Cambridge University Press, 1993), 10, 12–13; on Epiros, see more fully Donald Nicol, *The Despotate of Epiros*, 2 vols. (Cambridge: Cambridge University Press, 1957, 1984).

7. Michael Angold, *A Byzantine Government in Exile: Government and Society Under the Laskarids of Nicaea 1204–1261* (Oxford: Oxford University Press, 1975); Dimiter Angelov, *The Byzantine Hellene: The Life of Emperor Theodore Laskaris and Byzantium in the Thirteenth Century* (Cambridge: Cambridge University Press, 2019).

8. Nicol, *Last Centuries*, 31–33.

9. Nicol, *Last Centuries*, 41–42; Angold, *Fourth Crusade*, 148, 158, 160.

10. Nicol, *Last Centuries*, 33–37.

11. Nicol, *Last Centuries*, 41–71 (see 68–70 on 'Sicilian Vespers').

12. Nicol, *Last Centuries*, 72–89, 94–96 ('reign of terror', 95).

13. Angold, *Fourth Crusade*, 212; Kaldellis, *Hellenism*, 357–360.

14. Nicol, *Last Centuries*, 141–147, 170–172; Halil Inalcik, *The Ottoman Empire: The Classical Age 1300–1600* (London: Phoenix, 2000), 6–7; Caroline Finkel, *Osman's Dream: The Story of the Ottoman Empire, 1300–1923* (London: John Murray, 2005), 13–15.

15. George Akropolites, *The History*, Introduction, translation, and commentary by Ruth Macrides (Oxford: Oxford University Press, 2007); on Pachymeres and Gregoras (not translated into English), see Leonora Neville, *Guide to Byzantine Historical Writing* (Cambridge: Cambridge University Press, 2018), 237–248. On the fourteenth-century translation

of Aquinas by Demetrios Kydones, see Edmund Fryde, *Early Palaeologan Renaissance, 1261–c.1360* (Leiden and Boston, MA: Brill, 2000), 381–386.

16. Paul Underwood, ed., *The Kariye Djami, vol. 4. Studies in the Art of the Kariye Djami and Its Intellectual Background* (Princeton, NJ: Princeton University Press, 1975); Angold, *Fourth Crusade*, 222–223; Geoffrey Horrocks, *Greek: A History of the Language and Its Speakers*, 2nd ed. (Medford, MA, and Oxford: Wiley Blackwell, 2014), 213–214, 226–227, 268–271.

17. On versions and date of the (lost) original version, see Gill Page, *Being Byzantine: Greek Identity Before the Ottomans* (Cambridge: Cambridge University Press, 2008), 178–180, 303–304; Teresa Shawcross, *The Chronicle of Morea: Historiography in Crusader Greece* (Oxford: Oxford University Press, 2009), 42–52. Language: Horrocks, *Greek*, 349–357. Oral tradition: Michael Jeffreys, 'Formulas in the Chronicle of the Morea', *Dumbarton Oaks Papers* 27 (1975): 165–95, reprinted in Elizabeth and Michael Jeffreys, *Popular Literature in Late Byzantium* (London: Variorum, 1983); Shawcross, *Chronicle*, 118–119, 182–183. For the *Chronicle* as 'colonial discourse', see Demacopoulos, *Colonizing Christianity*, 103–121.

18. *The Chronicle of Morea*, ed. John Schmitt (London: Methuen, 1904) [parallel Greek text and English translation of versions H and P], H 724–726 (my translation); cited and discussed in Shawcross, *Chronicle*, 158.

19. *Chronicle*, ed. Schmitt, H 3991–3993 (my translation); cited and discussed by Shawcross, 208–209; Demacopoulos, *Colonizing Christianity*, 120.

20. Shawcross, *Chronicle*, 24–26, 238–259 (context for composition), 212–213 (disregard for the common people).

21. On the significance and probable date of the vernacular Greek translation of the Old French *Roman de Troie*, see Shawcross, *Chronicle*, 95–98; Elizabeth Jeffreys, 'Byzantine Romances: Eastern or Western?', in *Renaissance Encounters: Greek East and Latin West*, ed. Marina

Brownlee and Dimitri Gondicas (Leiden and Boston, MA: Brill, 2013), 221–237 (see 228–237).

22. The standard edition, with English translation, remains Leontios Machairas, *Recital Concerning the Sweet Land of Cyprus Entitled 'Chronicle'*, ed. and trans. R. M. Dawkins (Oxford: Clarendon, 1932). References to this edition in the following notes take the form of book number, followed by paragraph number. On language, see Horrocks, *Greek*, 362–366; Daniele Baglioni, 'Language and Identity in Late Medieval Cyprus', in *Identity / Identities in Late Medieval Cyprus*, ed. Tassos Papacostas and Guillaume Saint-Guillain (Nicosia: Cyprus Research Centre, 2014), 27–36.

23. Machairas, *Chronicle*, ed. Dawkins, 5.631, 5.674, 5.679 (on himself), 5.695–697, 5.700 (peasants' revolt and return of King Janus). On Machairas and his loyalties, see further Shawcross, *Chronicle*, 224–229, 234; Angel Nicolaou-Konnari, 'Alterity and Identity in Lusignan Cyprus from ca. 1350 to ca. 1450: The Testimonies of Philippe de Mézières and Leontios Makhairas', in Papacostas and Saint-Guillain, *Identity*, 37–66 (see esp. 58–59, 61–65).

24. Shawcross, *Chronicle*, 228–229.

25. On Epiros and the *Chronicle of the Tocco Family*, see Shawcross, *Chronicle*, 229–232; see below for the Despotate of the Morea in the fifteenth century and Chapter 12 for Venetian Crete in the sixteenth and seventeenth.

26. Nicol, *Last Centuries*, 205–208, 215. On the coronation and the fake jewels, see also C. P. Cavafy, 'Of Coloured Glass', in C. P. Cavafy, *The Collected Poems: Includes Parallel Greek Text*, ed. Anthony Hirst, trans. Evangelos Sachperoglou (Oxford: Oxford University Press, 2007), 152–153.

27. Nicol, *Last Centuries*, 241–247; Donald Nicol, *The Reluctant Emperor: A Biography of John Cantacuzene, Byzantine Emperor and Monk, c. 1295–1383* (Cambridge: Cambridge University Press, 1996).

28. Dirk Krausmüller, 'The Rise of Hesychasm', in *The Cambridge History of Christianity, Vol. 5: Eastern Christianity*, ed. Michael Angold (Cambridge: Cambridge University Press, 2006), 101–126.

29. Nicol, *Last Centuries*, 270–273 (mission of John V to Rome); Jonathan Harris, 'Being a Byzantine After Byzantium: Hellenic Identity in Renaissance Italy', *Kampos: Cambridge Papers in Modern Greek* 8 (2000): 25–44 (see 37 on transition from crusading to proto-nationalism).

30. Nicol, *Last Centuries*, 308–312 (309 quoted), 318; Donald Nicol, 'A Byzantine Emperor in England. Manuel II's Visit to London in 1400–1401', *University of Birmingham Historical Journal* 12 (1971): 204–225.

31. Nevra Necipoğlu, *Byzantium Between the Ottomans and the Latins: Politics and Society in the Late Empire* (Cambridge: Cambridge University Press, 2009), 149–183.

32. Nicol, *Last Centuries*, 230–231, 340–347; Necipoğlu, *Byzantium*, 235–284.

33. Respectively, George Gemistos Plethon, 'Memorandum to the Emperor Manuel', in *Παλαιολογικά και Πελοποννησιακά* [*Of the Palaiologans and the Peloponnese*], vol. 3, ed. Spyridon Lambros (Athens: Gregoriades, 1926), 249, 247 (my translation). The latter passage is cited and discussed in Niketas Siniossoglou, *Radical Platonism in Byzantium: Illumination and Utopia in Gemistos Plethon* (Cambridge: Cambridge University Press, 2011), 352.

34. Kaldellis, *Hellenism*, 371–379; Yannis Stouraitis, 'Reinventing Roman Ethnicity in High and Late Medieval Byzantium', *Medieval Worlds* 5 (2017): 85–88; see also Paul Magdalino, 'Hellenism and Nationalism in Byzantium', in Paul Magdalino, *Tradition and Transformation in Medieval Byzantium* (Aldershot: Ashgate, 1991), chap. XIV (see 12–18); Roderick Beaton, 'Antique Nation? "Hellenes" on the Eve of Greek Independence and in Twelfth-Century Byzantium', *Byzantine and Modern Greek Studies* 31, no. 1 (2007): 79–98 (see 87–95); and, more controversially, Anthony Kaldellis, *A New Herodotos: Laonikos Chalkokondyles on the Ottoman Empire, the Fall of Byzantium, and the Emergence of the West* (Washington, DC: Dumbarton Oaks Center, 2014), 222–228. For a partial precedent in the thirteenth century, see Angelov, *The Byzantine Hellene*.

35. Siniossoglou, *Radical Platonism*, 337–343; Teresa Shawcross, 'A New Lykourgos for a New Sparta: George Gemistos Plethon and the

Despotate of the Morea', in *Viewing the Morea: Land and People in the Late Medieval Peloponnese*, ed. Sharon Gerstel (Cambridge, MA: Harvard University Press, 2013). For summaries of Plethon's two memoranda on the Morea, see C. M. Woodhouse, *Georgios Gemistos Plethon. The Last of the Hellenes* (Oxford: Oxford University Press, 1986), 93–98, 102–109.

36. Nicol, *Last Centuries*, 353–359 (357 quoted); on the life and thought of Plethon, see most fully, in English, Woodhouse, *Plethon*, and Siniossoglou, *Radical Platonism*.

37. Nicol, *Last Centuries*, 361–368.

38. Nicol, *Last Centuries*, 370–371, 377–379; Michael Kordoses, 'The Question of Constantine Palaiologos' Coronation', in *The Making of Byzantine History: Studies Dedicated to Donald M. Nicol*, ed. Roderick Beaton and Charlotte Roueché (Aldershot: Ashgate, 1993), 137–141; Doukas, ed. Vasile Grecu, *Istoria turco-bizantină (1341–1462)*, chap. 37, paragraph 10 (quoted, my translation).

39. Nicol, *Last Centuries*, 380, citing Georgios Sphrantzes, *Chronicon Minus* and noting discrepancies in the primary sources.

40. Donald Nicol, *The Immortal Emperor: The Life and Legend of Constantine Palaiologos, Last Emperor of the Romans* (Cambridge: Cambridge University Press, 1992), 74–108.

41. Nicol, *Last Centuries*, 389–392; Philip Mansel, *Constantinople: City of the World's Desire, 1453–1924* (London: Penguin, 1997), 1 (quoted), citing Nicolò Barbaro, *Diary of the Siege of Constantinople*, trans. J. R. Jones (New York: Exposition, 1969). For the fullest account of these events, see Steven Runciman, *The Fall of Constantinople 1453* (Cambridge: Cambridge University Press, 1965).

Chapter 12: Between Two Worlds

1. Donald Nicol, *The Last Centuries of Byzantium 1261–1453*, 2nd ed. (Cambridge: Cambridge University Press, 1993), 391, 399–401.

2. See, most fully, Deno Geanakoplos, *Greek Scholars in Venice: Studies in the Dissemination of Greek Learning from Byzantium to Western*

Europe (Cambridge, MA: Harvard University Press, 1962); N. G. Wilson, *From Byzantium to Italy: Greek Studies in the Italian Renaissance*, 2nd ed. (London: Bloomsbury, 2017).

3. Wilson, *From Byzantium*, 47, 169, 178 (Byzantine education system), 28, 33, 36, 176 ('civic humanism').

4. Strabo and Columbus: Wilson, *From Byzantium*, 64–65. Byzantine prophecies: Nicol, *Last Centuries*, 411–412; Paul Magdalino, 'The History of the Future and Its Uses: Prophecy, Policy and Propaganda', in *The Making of Byzantine History: Studies Dedicated to Donald M. Nicol*, ed. Roderick Beaton and Charlotte Roueché (Aldershot: Ashgate, 1993), 1–34 (see 27–28).

5. Nicol, *Last Centuries*, 392–393; Petros Pizanias, *The Making of the Modern Greeks, 1400–1820* (Newcastle upon Tyne: Cambridge Scholars Publishing, 2020), 23–24, 29; Halil Inalcik, 'The Policy of Mehmed II Toward the Greek Population of Istanbul and the Byzantine Buildings of the City', *Dumbarton Oaks Papers* 23–24 (1969–1970): 229–249 (see 247 for the 1477 Ottoman census of households).

6. Inalcik, 'Policy', 233 (Mehmed's title); Caroline Finkel, *Osman's Dream: The Story of the Ottoman Empire, 1300–1923* (London: John Murray, 2005), 80, citing [Michael] Kritovoulos, *History of Mehmed the Conqueror*, trans. Charles Riggs (Princeton, NJ: Princeton University Press, 1954), 3, a work completed in 1467.

7. Halil Inalcik, *The Ottoman Empire: The Classical Age 1300–1600* (London: Phoenix, 2000), 78.

8. Inalcik, 'Policy', 240; Pizanias, *The Making*, 18.

9. Molly Greene, *The Edinburgh History of the Greeks, 1453 to 1768: The Ottoman Empire* (Edinburgh: Edinburgh University Press, 2015), 8–9, 24, 55.

10. N. M. Vaporis, *Witnesses for Christ: Orthodox Christian Neomartyrs of the Ottoman Period, 1437–1860* (Crestwood, NY: St. Vladimir's Seminary Press, 2000).

11. Inalcik, *Ottoman Empire*, 33–40; 41; Finkel, *Osman's Dream*, 108–138.

12. Greene, *Edinburgh History*, 91–93.

13. Noel Malcolm, *Agents of Empire: Knights, Corsairs, Jesuits and Spies in the Sixteenth-Century Mediterranean World* (Oxford: Oxford University Press, 2019), 160–167; Inalcik, *Ottoman Empire*, 41–42.

14. Chryssa Maltezou, 'The Historical and Social Context', in *Literature and Society in Renaissance Crete*, ed. David Holton (Cambridge: Cambridge University Press, 1991), 17–47 (see 19–25); Theocharis Detorakis, *History of Crete*, trans. J. C. Davis (Iraklion, Crete: privately published, 1994), 146–175; Sally McKee, *Uncommon Dominion: Venetian Crete and the Myth of Ethnic Purity* (Philadelphia: University of Pennsylvania Press, 2000), 168–171 and *passim*.

15. Geoffrey Horrocks, *Greek: A History of the Language and its Speakers*, 2nd ed. (Medford, MA, and Oxford: Wiley Blackwell, 2014), 392–398.

16. Maria Georgopoulou, *Venice's Mediterranean Colonies: Architecture and Urbanism* (Cambridge: Cambridge University Press, 2001), 22 (fortifications); Maltezou, 'Historical Context', 29–30; Nikolaos Panagiotakes, *El Greco—The Cretan Years*, trans. John Davis (Aldershot: Ashgate, 2009), 7 (change in Venetian policy).

17. Panagiotakes, *El Greco*, 9 (Jesuits); Geanakoplos, *Greek Scholars in Venice*, 60–61 (Greeks in Venice); Panagiotakes, *El Greco*, 1–12 (education), 4 (literacy).

18. Panagiotakes, *El Greco*, 29–33 ('eyewatering prices'), 79–82 (library).

19. David Holton, ed., *Literature and Society in Renaissance Crete* (Cambridge: Cambridge University Press, 1991): see, respectively, the chapters by Rosemary Bancroft-Marcus, 'The Pastoral Mode', 79–102; Alfred Vincent, 'Comedy', 103–128; Walter Puchner, 'Tragedy', 129–158; for English translation of four plays attributed to Chortatsis, see Georgios Chortatsis, *Plays of the Veneto-Cretan Renaissance*, vol. 1 [bilingual edition], trans. Rosemary Bancroft-Marcus (Oxford: Oxford University Press, 2013).

20. *Katzarapos*, in Georgios Chortatsis, *Plays*, 320–445 (this work is also known as *Katzourbos*); Markos Antonios Foskolos, *Fortounatos* [1655, in Greek], ed. Alfred Vincent (Heraklion, Crete: Society for

Cretan Historical Studies, 1980). No ancient Greek: Linos Politis, 'Introduction' [in Greek], in Georgios Chortatsis, *Κατζούρμπος: κωμωδία* [*Katzourbos: A Comedy*] (Heraklion, Crete: Society for Cretan Historical Studies, 1964), xxxvi, lvi.

21. David Holton, 'Romance', in Holton, *Literature*, 205–237; Roderick Beaton, '*Erotokritos* and the History of the Novel', *Kampos: Cambridge Studies in Modern Greek* 12 (2004): 1–25. For a verse translation, see Vitzentzos Kornaros, *Erotocritos*, trans. Theodore Stephanides (Athens: Papazissis, 1984); for a prose alternative, Vitsentzos Kornaros, *Erotokritos*, trans. Gavin Betts, Stathis Gauntlett, and Thanasis Spilias (Melbourne: Australian Association for Byzantine Studies, 2004).

22. Vitsentsos Kornaros, *Ερωτόκριτος, κριτική έκδοση* [*Erotokritos: Critical Edition*], ed. Stylianos Alexiou (Athens: Ermis, 1980), Part 1, lines 19–20, 25–26 (my translation).

23. *Erotokritos*, ed. Alexiou, Part 2, lines 319–320, 999–1000 (my translation). On the significance of this episode, see Holton, 'Romance', in Holton, *Literature*, 224–232.

24. Zuanne Papadopoli, *Memories of Seventeenth-Century Crete: L'Occio (Time of Leisure)*, [Italian text] edited with English translation by Alfred Vincent (Venice: Hellenic Institute of Byzantine and Post-Byzantine Studies, 2007), 44. For the author's life and background, see 'Introduction', 18, 19, 24–28, 30.

25. Papadopoli, *L'Occio*, trans. Vincent, 130–132, 138, 206–208.

26. Papadopoli, *L'Occio*, trans. Vincent, 68–72, 130.

27. Papadopoli, *L'Occio*, trans. Vincent, 210.

28. Maltezou, 'Historical Context', 42, citing in translation the report of Provveditore Generale Zuanne Mocenigo (1589) (quoted); Vincent in Papadopoli, *L'Occio* (commentary), 327, citing the same document.

29. David Holton, 'The Cretan Renaissance', in Holton, *Literature*, 1–16 (see 4–5).

30. Panagiotakes, *El Greco*, 11; William Prescott, *History of the Conquest of Peru*, 2 vols. (Philadelphia, PA: Lippincott, 1867), 1.263, 1.277–278, 2.228–229 (Pedro de Candia); Samuel Purchas, *Hakluytus Posthumus, or Purchas His Pilgrims* (Glasgow: Maclehose, 1906),

14.415–421 (first published 1625, reporting a meeting that took place in 1596); Peter Chimbos, 'The Greeks in Canada: An Historical and Sociological Perspective', in *The Greek Diaspora in the Twentieth Century*, ed. Richard Clogg (Basingstoke: Macmillan, 1999), 87–102 (see 100) (Juan de Fuca).

31. D. Eichholz, 'A Greek Traveller in Tudor England', *Greece and Rome* 16, no. 47 (1947): 76–84; George Seferis, Ένας Έλληνας στην Αγγλία του 1545' ['A Greek in England in 1545'] in Δοκιμές [*Essays*], vol. 2 (Athens: Ikaros, 1984), 101–111 (110 quoted, my translation). For the full text of Nikandros's three volumes of travels, see Nicandre de Corcyre, *Voyages*, ed. J.-A. de Foucault (Paris: Belles Lettres, 1962).

32. Greene, *Edinburgh History*, 36, 94–103 (101 quoted), 107.

33. David Holton, 'The Cretan Renaissance', 4–5 (Venice); Greene, *Edinburgh History*, 129–131 (Smyrna).

34. Finkel, *Osman's Dream*, 225–226.

35. Molly Greene, *A Shared World: Christians and Muslims in the Early Modern Mediterranean* (Princeton, NJ: Princeton University Press, 2000), 39–44; Detorakis, *History*, 237 (contemporary testimony), 185 (total population).

36. Detorakis, *History*, 238–242; Basil Gounaris, *'See How the Gods Favour Sacrilege': English Views and Politics on Candia Under Siege* (Athens: National Hellenic Research Foundation, 2012), 95–99 and *passim*.

37. Detorakis, *History*, 240–241; Marinos Tzane Bounialis, *Ο Κρητικός πόλεμος (1645–1669)* [*The Cretan War*], ed. Stylianos Alexiou (Athens: Stigmi, 1995), 433–436.

38. Detorakis, *History*, 242; Bounialis, *Cretan War*, 424, 485–488.

Chapter 13: 'Greek Revival'

1. Andrew Wheatcroft, *The Enemy at the Gate: Habsburgs, Ottomans and the Battle for Europe* (London: Bodley Head, 2008), 135–188, 228–229.

2. Molly Greene, *The Edinburgh History of the Greeks, 1453 to 1768: The Ottoman Empire* (Edinburgh: Edinburgh University Press, 2015), 131–132, 205–206; Christine Philliou, *Biography of an Empire:*

Governing Ottomans in an Age of Revolution (Berkeley: University of California Press, 2011), 8–10; Paschalis Kitromilides, *Enlightenment and Revolution: The Making of Modern Greece* (Cambridge, MA: Harvard University Press, 2013), 29–30.

3. Caroline Finkel, *Osman's Dream: The Story of the Ottoman Empire, 1300–1923* (London: John Murray, 2005), 302–303, 314, 319; Philip Mansel, *Constantinople: City of the World's Desire, 1453–1924* (London: Penguin, 1997), 150–151.

4. Finkel, *Osman's Dream*, 291–292, 336–338.

5. Greene, *Edinburgh History*, 131–132, 205–206; Philliou, *Biography*, 8–10; Kitromilides, *Enlightenment*, 29–30.

6. Philliou, *Biography*, 35–6; Kitromilides, *Enlightenment*, 31, 35.

7. John Penrose Barron, *From Samos to Soho: The Unorthodox Life of Joseph Georgirenes, a Greek Archbishop* (Oxford: Peter Lang, 2017), 154–155 (coffee houses), 158–182 (Greek church); Jonathan Harris, 'Silent Minority: The Greek Community of Eighteenth-Century London', in *Greek Diaspora and Migration since 1700: Society, Politics and Culture*, ed. Dimitris Tziovas (London: Routledge, 2009), 31–44; Richard Clogg, 'The Greek Diaspora: The Historical Context', in *The Greek Diaspora in the Twentieth Century*, ed. Richard Clogg (Basingstoke: Macmillan, 1999), 1–23 (see 1–2, 9–10 for Argentina, Bengal).

8. Thomas Gallant, *The Edinburgh History of the Greeks, 1768 to 1913* (Edinburgh: Edinburgh University Press, 2015), 14–15; Lucien Frary, *Russia and the Making of Modern Greek Identity 1821–1844* (Oxford: Oxford University Press, 2015), 20–27.

9. Vassilis Kardasis, 'Greek Diaspora in Southern Russia in the Eighteenth Through Nineteenth Centuries', in *Homelands and Diasporas: Greeks, Jews and Their Migrations*, ed. Minna Rozen (London: Bloomsbury, 2020), 161–167 (see 164); Gelina Harlaftis, *Creating Global Shipping: Aristotle Onassis, the Vagliano Brothers, and the Business of Shipping, c. 1820–1970* (Cambridge: Cambridge University Press, 2019), 35 ('deep-seagoing vessels'), 48–54 (Russian trade before 1830).

10. Olga Katsiardi-Hering, 'Central and Peripheral Communities in the Greek Diaspora', in Rozen, *Homelands*, 169–180 (see 174–175);

Traian Stoianovich, 'The Conquering Balkan Orthodox Merchant', *Journal of Economic History* 20 (1960): 234–313.

11. Paschalis Kitromilides, 'Diaspora, Identity, and Nation-Building', in Rozen, *Homelands*, 323–331 (see 324–327).

12. Philliou, *Biography*, 15–17, 38–40; Greene, *Edinburgh History*, 174–175.

13. See, for example, Joep Leerssen, *National Thought in Europe: A Cultural History* (Amsterdam: Amsterdam University Press, 2006), 82–89.

14. *Encyclopédie, ou Dictionnaire raisonné des sciences, des arts et des métiers* (Paris, 1751–1772), 5.635 ('enchaînement de connoissances'), 5.642 ('changer la façon commune de penser') (Diderot), 17.741 (Jaucourt) (my translation). Available online at http://enccre.academie -sciences.fr/encyclopedie/.

15. J. J. Winckelmann, *History of the Art of Antiquity*, trans. H. F. Mallgrave (Los Angeles: Getty, 2006; first published in German, 1764); citation from David Constantine, *In the Footsteps of the Gods: Travellers to Greece and the Quest for the Hellenic Ideal* (London: I. B. Tauris, 2011), 100–101. The argument briefly summarised here is made much more fully in Nasia Giakovaki, *Ευρώπη μέσω Ελλάδας: μια καμπή στην ευρωπαϊκή αυτοσυνείδηση, 17ος–18ος αιώνας* [*Europe via Greece: A Turning Point in European Consciousness, 17th–18th Centuries*] (Athens: Estia, 2006).

16. Matteo Zaccarini, 'The Athens of the North? Scotland and the National Struggle for the Parthenon, Its Marbles, and Its Identity', *Aevum* 92, no. 1 (2018): 179–195; Iain Gordon Brown, 'Edinburgh as Athens: New Evidence to Support a Topographical and Intellectual Idea Current in the Early Nineteenth Century', *Book of the Old Edinburgh Club, New Series* 15 (2019): 1–12. See more generally, J. Mordaunt Crook, *The Greek Revival: Neo-Classical Attitudes in British Architecture, 1760–1870* (London: John Murray, 1972).

17. On the history of the 'marbles' and controversy, see William St. Clair, *Lord Elgin and the Marbles*, 3rd ed., rev. (Oxford: Oxford University Press, 1998). On their reception in the early nineteenth century, see

the essays reprinted in William Hazlitt, *On the Elgin Marbles* (London: Hesperus, 2008); Frederic Will, 'Two Critics of the Elgin Marbles: William Hazlitt and Quatremère de Quincy', *Journal of Aesthetics and Art Criticism* 14, no. 4 (1956): 362–374.

18. Lord Byron, *Childe Harold's Pilgrimage*, Canto 2, stanzas 84–87 and 'Byron's Notes to Cantos I–II', section II (Athens, January 23, 1811); Roderick Beaton, *Byron's War: Romantic Rebellion, Greek Revolution* (Cambridge: Cambridge University Press, 2013), 23–29; Alexander Grammatikos, *British Romantic Literature and the Emerging Modern Greek Nation* (Cham, Switzerland: Palgrave Macmillan, 2018), 67–104.

19. Greene, *Edinburgh History*, 209; Konstantinos Staikos and Triantaphyllos Sklavenitis, *The Publishing Centres of the Greeks: From the Renaissance to the Neohellenic Enlightenment*, trans. David Hardy (Athens: National Book Centre of Greece, 2001); see also Philippos Iliou, *Ιστορίες του ελληνικού βιβλίου* [*Histories of the Greek Book*] (Heraklion, Crete: Crete University Press, 2005).

20. Kitromilides, *Enlightenment*, 63–88.

21. Kitromilides, *Enlightenment*, 76–81.

22. D. Katartzis, *Τα Ευρισκόμενα* [*Found Remains*], ed. K. Th. Dimaras (Athens: privately printed, 1970), 24 (my translation), on which see also Stratos Myrogiannis, *The Emergence of a Greek Identity (1700–1821)* (Newcastle upon Tyne: Cambridge Scholars, 2012), 102–103, and Kitromilides, *Enlightenment*, 142–154; Daniel Philippidis and Grigorios Konstantas, *Γεωγραφία νεωτερική: Περί της Ελλάδος* [*Modern Geography: On Greece*], ed. with introduction by Aikaterini Koumarianou (Athens: Ermis, 1970), 37, 38.

23. Alexis Politis, 'From Christian Roman Emperors to the Glorious Greek Ancestors', in *Byzantium and the Modern Greek Identity*, ed. David Ricks and Paul Magdalino (Aldershot: Ashgate, 1998), 1–14 (8 cited); Roderick Beaton, 'Antique Nation? "Hellenes" on the Eve of Greek Independence and in Twelfth-Century Byzantium', *Byzantine and Modern Greek Studies* 31, no. 1 (2007): 79–98 (see 80–87).

24. Paschalis Kitromilides, *Η Γαλλική Επανάσταση και η νοτιο-ανατολική Ευρώπη* [*The French Revolution and Southeastern Europe*], 2nd ed. (Athens: Poreia, 2000), 41–61.

25. Roderick Beaton, *Greece: Biography of a Modern Nation* (London: Allen Lane, 2019), 43–46, 53–68.

26. ʿ*Πατριαρχική διδασκαλία*ʾ ['Patriarchal Instruction'], 1797, in Adamantios Korais, *Άπαντα τα πρωτότυπα έργα, τόμ. Α´* [*Complete Original Works, Vol. 1*], ed. G. Valetas (Athens: Dorikos, 1964), 44–45 (my translation); for English translation and commentary, see Richard Clogg, ed. and trans., *The Movement for Greek Independence, 1770–1821: A Collection of Documents* (London: Macmillan, 1976; reprint, Hunstanton, UK: Witley Press, 2021), 56–64. See also Kitromilides, *Enlightenment*, 305–307.

27. Cited in Gavin Murray-Miller, *Revolutionary Europe: Politics, Community and Culture in Transnational Context, 1775–1922* (London: Bloomsbury, 2020), 121.

28. Ioannis Philemon, *Δοκίμιον ιστορικόν περί της Ελληνικής Επαναστάσεως* [*Historical Essay Concerning the Greek Revolution*], 4 vols. (Athens: Karyophyllis, 1859–1861), 1.47–68. More lurid versions of this plan were evidently in circulation for some time afterwards; see Thomas Gordon, *History of the Greek Revolution*, 2 vols. (Edinburgh: Blackwood, 1832), 1.180–181; George Finlay, *History of the Greek Revolution*, 2 vols. (Edinburgh: Blackwood, 1861), 1.122.

29. Ypsilantis's text, dated 24 February, which is equivalent to 8 March in the Western calendar, is available online at https://el.wikisource.org/wiki/Μάχου_υπέρ_πίστεως_και_πατρίδος (in Greek, my translation). Mavromichalis: cited in English in Gordon, *History*, 1.183.

30. Marios Hatzopoulos, 'From Resurrection to Insurrection: "Sacred" Myths, Motifs, and Symbols in the Greek War of Independence', in *The Making of Modern Greece: Nationalism, Romanticism, and the Uses of the Past (1797–1896)*, ed. Roderick Beaton and David Ricks (Farnham: Ashgate, 2009), 81–93.

31. Finlay, *History*, 1.189.

32. Beaton, *Greece*, 85–90.

33. William St. Clair, *That Greece Might Still Be Free: The Philhellenes in the War of Independence* (London: Open Book, 2008; first published 1972); Roderick Beaton, 'European Philhellenes', in *The Greek Revolution: A Critical Dictionary*, ed. Paschalis Kitromilides and Constantinos Tsoukalas (Cambridge, MA: Harvard University Press, 2021), 593–613. For philhellenism as a Europe-wide movement, see Denys Barau, *La Cause des Grecs, une histoire du mouvement philhellène (1821–1829)* (Paris: Honoré Champion, 2009).

34. Douglas Dakin, *The Greek Struggle for Independence, 1821–1833* (London: Batsford, 1973), 148–150 (Canning); Gary Bass, *Freedom's Battle: The Origins of Humanitarian Intervention* (New York: Vintage, 2009), 91–97 (95 cited); George Kaloudis, *Modern Greece and the Diaspora Greeks in the United States* (Lanham, MD: Lexington, 2018), 23–25.

35. J. M. Wagstaff, *Greece: Ethnicity and Sovereignty, 1820–1994. Atlas and Documents* (Archive Editions [Cambridge: Cambridge University Press], 2002), 141–145.

Chapter 14: European State, Global Nation

1. The standard treatment of this period remains John Petropulos, *Politics and Statecraft in the Kingdom of Greece, 1833–1843* (Princeton, NJ: Princeton University Press, 1968).

2. Eleni Bastéa, *The Creation of Modern Athens: Planning the Myth* (Cambridge: Cambridge University Press, 2000), 43–104; Yannis Hamilakis, *The Nation and Its Ruins: Antiquity, Archaeology, and National Imagination in Greece* (Oxford: Oxford University Press, 2007), 59–64, 94–98.

3. Kostas Kostis, *History's Spoiled Children: The Formation of the Modern Greek State*, trans. Jacob Moe (London: Hurst 2018; Greek original published in 2013), 108 (currency), 119 (universal male suffrage).

4. Elli Skopetea, Το «πρότυπο βασίλειο» και η Μεγάλη Ιδέα: όψεις του εθνικού προβλήματος στην Ελλάδα [*The 'Model Kingdom' and the*

Grand Idea: Aspects of the National Problem in Greece] (Athens: Polytypo, 1988), 162.

5. Michael Llewellyn Smith, *Olympics in Athens: 1896–2004* (London: Profile, 2004), 65–81, 94–97, 154–191; Alexander Kitroeff, *Wrestling with the Ancients: Modern Greek Identity and the Olympics* (New York: Greekworks.com, 2004), 25–26, 27–35, 48–50; Bastéa, *Creation*, 204–212.

6. Richard Clogg, *A Concise History of Greece*, 4th ed., rev. (Cambridge: Cambridge University Press, 2021), 313 (table 1: population statistics); Richard Clogg, 'The Greek Diaspora: The Historical Context', in *The Greek Diaspora in the Twentieth Century*, ed. Richard Clogg (Basingstoke: Macmillan, 1999), 1–23. The fullest study remains I. K. Hasiotis, *Επισκόπηση της ιστορίας της νεοελληνικής διασποράς* [*Survey of the History of the Modern Greek Diaspora*] (Thessaloniki: Vanias, 1993).

7. For a judicious sampling of original sources from the period, with commentary, see Alexis Politis, *Ρομαντικά χρόνια: ιδεολογίες και νοοτροπίες στην Ελλάδα του 1830–1880* [*Romantic Years: Ideologies and Mentalities in Greece, 1830–1880*] (Athens: Mnimon, 1993), 61–67. For an outsider's perception of attitudes in the 1870s, see Charles Tuckerman, *The Greeks of Today*, 2nd ed. (New York: Putnam, 1878; first ed., 1872), 123–124.

8. Gelina Harlaftis, *Creating Global Shipping: Aristotle Onassis, the Vagliano Brothers, and the Business of Shipping, c. 1820–1970* (Cambridge: Cambridge University Press, 2019), 4, 41, 158, 231, 262.

9. Harlaftis, *Creating*, 68, 92, 264–265 and *passim*.

10. Gelina Harlaftis, *A History of Greek-Owned Shipping: The Making of an International Tramp Fleet, 1830 to the Present Day* (Abingdon: Routledge, 2015; first ed., 1996), 41–44, 51–55; Colin Fenn and James Slattery-Kavanagh, *West Norwood Cemetery's Greek Necropolis: An Illustrated Guide* (London: Friends of West Norwood Cemetery, 2011).

11. Konstantinos Svolopoulos, *Κωνσταντινούπολη 1856–1908: η ακμή του Ελληνισμού* [*Constantinople 1856–1908: The Highpoint of Hellenism*] (Athens: Ekdotiki Athinon, 1994), 37–38 (population); Dimitri

Gondicas and Charles Issawi, eds., *Ottoman Greeks in the Age of Nationalism* (Princeton, NJ: Darwin Press, 1999).

12. Alexander Kitroeff, *The Greeks and the Making of Modern Egypt* (Cairo and New York: The American University in Cairo Press, 2019), 23–50, 67, 71–73.

13. E. M. Forster, 'The Complete Poems of C. P. Cavafy', in *The Mind and Art of C. P. Cavafy: Essays on His Life and Work* (Athens: Denise Harvey, 1983), 40–45 (44–45 quoted, essay first published 1951).

14. Gerasimos Augustinos, *Consciousness and History: Nationalist Critics of Greek Society, 1897–1914* (New York: Columbia University Press / *East European Quarterly*, 1977), 26, quoting (in translation) Neoklis Kazazis in *Ellinismos* 1 (1899): 7–8 (emphasis added).

15. Spyros Melas, *Η επανάσταση του 1909* [*The Revolution of 1909*] (Athens: Biris, 1957), 13, cited in translation in Michael Llewellyn-Smith, *Venizelos: The Making of a Greek Statesman, 1864–1914* (London: Hurst, 2021), 176.

16. Roderick Beaton, *Greece: Biography of a Modern Nation* (London: Allen Lane, 2019), 187–232; for a twenty-first-century reassessment, see Llewellyn-Smith, *Venizelos*.

17. Richard Hall, *The Balkan Wars, 1912–1913: Prelude to the First World War* (London: Routledge, 2002); Douglas Dakin, *The Unification of Greece 1770–1923* (London: Benn, 1972), 201–202.

18. Giorgos Mavrogordatos, *1915: ο Εθνικός Διχασμός* [*1915: The National Schism*] (Athens: Patakis, 2015), 93, 217, cited in translation in Beaton, *Greece*, 211 (emphases added).

19. On these events, from 1914 to 1923, see most fully in English: Michael Llewellyn Smith, *Ionian Vision: Greece in Asia Minor 1919–1922* (London: Hurst, 1998; first published 1973). See also Konstantinos Travlos, ed., *Salvation and Catastrophe: The Greek–Turkish War, 1919–1922* (London and New York: Lexington, 2020).

20. Dimitri Pentzopoulos, *The Balkan Exchange of Minorities and Its Impact upon Greece* (Paris and The Hague: Mouton, 1962; reprinted with a new introduction by Michael Llewellyn Smith, London: Hurst, 2002), 257–263; Renée Hirschon, ed., *Crossing the Aegean: An Appraisal*

of the 1923 Compulsory Population Exchange Between Greece and Turkey (Oxford: Berghahn, 2003). On the impact of the exchange, see Bruce Clark, *Twice a Stranger: Greece, Turkey and the Minorities They Expelled* (London: Granta, 2006). 'Outstanding success': Stathis Kalyvas, *Modern Greece: What Everyone Needs to Know* (Oxford: Oxford University Press, 2015), 76, 79.

21. George Seferis, 'In the Manner of G. S.', in Ποιήματα [*Poems*] (Athens: Ikaros, 2014), 99–101; George Seferis, Δοκιμές [*Essays*], vol. 1 (Athens: Ikaros, 1984), 102 (both my translation).

22. Nikos Kazantzakis, Βίος και πολιτεία του Αλέξη Ζορμπά [*Life and Times of Alexis Zorbas*] (Athens: Kazantzakis Editions, 1969), 178–179 (my translation); see also Nikos Kazantzakis, *Zorba the Greek*, trans. Peter Bien (New York: Simon & Schuster, 2014).

23. George Mavrogordatos, *Stillborn Republic: Social Coalitions and Party Strategies in Greece, 1922–1936* (Berkeley: University of California Press, 1983); John Koliopoulos, *Greece and the British Connection 1935–1941* (Oxford: Clarendon Press, 1977); Marina Petrakis, *The Metaxas Myth: Dictatorship and Propaganda in Greece* (London: I. B. Tauris, 2006).

24. Kitroeff, *The Greeks*, 1, 4, 8, 46–47.

25. Charles Moskos, 'The Greeks in the United States', in Clogg, *Greek Diaspora*, 103–119 (see 104); George Kaloudis, *Modern Greece and the Diaspora Greeks in the United States* (Lanham, MD: Lexington, 2018), 56, 76, 160–161.

26. Harlaftis, *Creating*, 39.

27. Mark Mazower, *Inside Hitler's Greece: The Experience of Occupation, 1941–44* (New Haven, CT, and London: Yale University Press, 1993), 41 and *passim*. See also Violetta Hionidou, *Famine and Death in Occupied Greece* (Cambridge: Cambridge University Press, 2006).

28. This paragraph draws extensively on Stathis Kalyvas, *The Logic of Violence in Civil War* (Cambridge: Cambridge University Press, 2006) (see especially 31) and by the same author, 'Red Terror: Leftist Violence During the Occupation', in *After the War Was Over: Reconstructing the Family, Nation, and State in Greece, 1943–1960*, ed. Mark Mazower

(Princeton, NJ: Princeton University Press, 2000), 142–183. See also Beaton, *Greece*, 278–285.

29. John Iatrides, *Revolt in Athens: The Greek Communist 'Second Round', 1944–1945* (Princeton, NJ: Princeton University Press, 1972); Lars Baerentzen, 'The Demonstration in Syntagma Square on Sunday the 3rd of December, 1944', *Scandinavian Studies in Modern Greek* 2 (1978): 3–52.

30. David Close, 'Introduction', in *The Greek Civil War, 1943–1950: Studies of Polarization*, ed. David Close (London: Routledge, 1993), 7–11 (statistics); Mazower, *Inside Hitler's Greece*, 235–261 (Holocaust); Giorgos Antoniou and A. Dirk Moses, eds., *The Holocaust in Greece* (Cambridge: Cambridge University Press, 2020).

31. E. A. Mantziris, 'The Greeks in South Africa', in Clogg, *Greek Diaspora*, 120–136; Nicholas Doumanis, 'The Greeks in Australia', in the same volume, 58–86; see also Joy Damousi, *Memory and Migration in the Shadow of War: Australia's Greek Immigrants After World War II and the Greek Civil War* (Cambridge: Cambridge University Press, 2015).

32. David Close, *Greece Since 1945: Politics, Economy and Society* (London: Longman, 2002), 52, 48 (statistics); see also Mazower, *After the War Was Over*.

33. Harlaftis, *History*, 226–245.

34. Harlaftis, *Creating*, 172–186.

35. Gelina Harlaftis, *Greek Shipowners and Greece, 1945–1975* (London: Bloomsbury, 2015), 9–23; Harlaftis, *Creating*, 231–232, 255, 259, 261, 263, 271–272, 279–284.

36. Vrasidas Karalis, *A History of Greek Cinema* (New York and London: Continuum, 2012), 79–80; Achilleas Hadjikyriacou, *Masculinity and Gender in Greek Cinema, 1949–1967* (London: Bloomsbury Academic, 2013), 66–67; Dimitris Papanikolaou, *Singing Poets: Literature and Popular Music in France and Greece* (London: Legenda, 2007).

37. C. M. Woodhouse, *The Rise and Fall of the Greek Colonels* (London: Granada, 1985); Othon Anastasakis and Katerina Lagos, eds., *The Greek Military Dictatorship: Revisiting a Troubled Past, 1967–1974* (New York and Oxford: Berghahn, 2021).

38. Kostis Kornetis, *Children of the Dictatorship: Student Resistance, Cultural Politics, and the 'Long 1960s' in Greece* (New York and Oxford: Berghahn, 2013), 251–280.

39. See most fully Robert Holland, *Britain and the Revolt in Cyprus, 1954–1959* (Oxford: Clarendon Press, 1998).

40. Alexandros Nafpliotis, *Britain and the Greek Colonels: Accommodating the Junta in the Cold War* (London: Bloomsbury, 2013), 233–237.

Chapter 15: New Ledgers, New Legends

1. James Ker-Lindsay, *The Cyprus Problem: What Everyone Needs to Know* (Oxford: Oxford University Press, 2011); Roderick Beaton, *Greece: Biography of a Modern Nation* (London: Allen Lane, 2019), 346, 370–373.

2. David Close, *Greece Since 1945: Politics, Economy and Society* (London: Longman, 2002), 161–162, 178–182; Stathis Kalyvas, *Modern Greece: What Everyone Needs to Know* (Oxford: Oxford University Press, 2015), 140–151.

3. Richard Clogg, ed., *Greece, 1981–89: The Populist Decade* (Basingstoke: Macmillan, 1993).

4. Thanos Veremis, *A Modern History of the Balkans: Nationalism and Identity in Southeast Europe* (London: I. B. Tauris, 2017), 143–152; Loring Danforth, *The Macedonian Conflict: Ethnic Nationalism in a Transnational World* (Princeton, NJ: Princeton University Press, 1997), 202–212.

5. George Papaconstantinou, *Game Over: The Inside Story of the Greek Crisis* (English edition privately published, 2016), 30–40.

6. Johanna Hanink, *The Classical Debt: Greek Antiquity in an Era of Austerity* (Cambridge, MA: Harvard University Press, 2017), 215–229.

7. Sofia Vasilopoulou and Daphne Halikiopoulou, *The Golden Dawn's 'National Solution': Explaining the Rise of the Far Right in Greece* (New York: Palgrave Macmillan, 2015).

8. Beaton, *Greece*, 389–398; Yanis Varoufakis, *Adults in the Room: My Battle with Europe's Deep Establishment* (London: Bodley Head,

2017); Viktoria Dendrinou and Eleni Varvitsioti, *The Last Bluff: How Greece Came Face-to-Face with Financial Catastrophe and the Secret Plan for Its Euro Exit* (Athens: Papadopoulos, 2019), 129–310. For an intellectual assessment from within SYRIZA, see Costas Douzinas, *Syriza in Power* (Cambridge: Polity, 2017).

9. *The Guardian* (23 October 2020), 30–31 and online.

10. Among many accounts and analyses of the crisis, see Dimitris Tziovas, ed., *Greece in Crisis: The Cultural Politics of Austerity* (London: I. B. Tauris, 2017).

11. See the website of the European Parliament: parliamentary elections 2019, national breakdown of results: www.europarl.europa.eu /election-results-2019/en.

12. Gelina Harlaftis, *Creating Global Shipping: Aristotle Onassis, the Vagliano Brothers, and the Business of Shipping, c. 1820–1970* (Cambridge: Cambridge University Press, 2019), 1, 7, see also 122–123, 263, 284; 'Greece Demographics', Worldometer, www.worldometers.info /demographics/greece-demographics/ (accessed 15 February 2021).

13. Gelina Harlaftis, *Greek Shipowners and Greece, 1945–1975* (London: Bloomsbury, 2015), 9–23; Harlaftis, *Creating*, 231–232, 255, 259, 261, 263, 271–272, 279–284.

14. Simone Tagliapietra, *The Politics and Economics of Eastern Mediterranean Gas* (Leuven, Netherlands: Claeys and Casteels, 2017); 'The First Natural Gas Field in Cyprus', Delek Drilling, www.delekdrilling.com /project/aphrodite-gas-field.

15. Jonathan Clayton and Hereward Holland, ed. Tim Gaynor, 'Over One Million Sea Arrivals Reach Europe in 2015', UNHCR, 30 December 2015, www.unhcr.org/uk/news/latest/2015/12/5683d0b56 /million-sea-arrivals-reach-europe-2015.html; Marie Doutrepont, *Moria: Chroniques des limbes de l'Europe* (Brussels: 180° Editions, 2018).

Epilogue

1. See the websites of the Hellenic Republic and Republic of Cyprus for results of the 2011 census in each country: www.statistics.gr

/en/2011-census-pop-hous; www.cystat.gov.cy/mof/cystat/statistics.nsf /populationcondition_22main_en/populationcondition_22main_en ?OpenForm&sub=2&sel=2. For Greeks outside Greece and Cyprus, see John Koliopoulos and Thanos Veremis, *Greece: The Modern Sequel* (London: Hurst, 2002), 211; Richard Clogg, *A Concise History of Greece*, 4th ed., rev. (Cambridge: Cambridge University Press, 2021), 228, 276 (estimated numbers and comment); Richard Clogg, 'The Greek Diaspora: The Historical Context', in *The Greek Diaspora in the Twentieth Century*, ed. Richard Clogg (Basingstoke: Macmillan, 1999), 1–23 (see 14) (countries).

2. Orthodox Church: Paschalis Kitromilides, *Religion and Politics in the Orthodox World: The Ecumenical Patriarchate and the Challenges of Modernity* (London and New York: Routledge, 2019). Greek American lobby: George Kaloudis, *Modern Greece and the Diaspora Greeks in the United States* (Lanham, MD: Lexington, 2018), 186–196.

3. Translated by Karen Emmerich, in Karen van Dyck, ed., *Austerity Measures: The New Greek Poetry* (London: Penguin, 2016), 410–411.

FURTHER READING

The Long View

Doumanis, Nicholas. *A History of Greece*. Basingstoke: Macmillan, 2010.

Gallant, Thomas (general editor). *The Edinburgh History of the Greeks* (Edinburgh: Edinburgh University Press). Of ten volumes announced only three have so far been published, covering the periods c. 500 CE–1050 (2011), 1453–1768 (2015), and 1768–1913 (2015).

Horrocks, Geoffrey. *Greek: A History of the Language and Its Speakers*. 2nd ed. Medford, MA, and Oxford: Wiley Blackwell, 2014.

Thomas, Carol. *Greece: A Short History of a Long Story, 7000 BCE to the Present*. Malden, MA, and Oxford: Wiley Blackwell, 2014.

In Greek, the classic treatment is the six-volume *History of the Greek Nation* by Konstantinos Paparrigopoulos, published between 1860 and 1877. Among the many successors to this work is the multiauthor *Greek History*. 2nd ed. [in Greek]. Athens: Ekdotiki Athinon, 2007.

Mycenaeans and Minoans

Cline, Eric, ed. *The Oxford Handbook of the Bronze Age Aegean (ca. 3000–1000 BC)*. Oxford: Oxford University Press, 2012.

Fitton, Lesley. *Minoans*. London: British Museum Press, 2002.

Mac Sweeney, Naoíse. *Troy: Myth, City, Icon*. London: Bloomsbury Academic, 2018.

Schofield, Louise. *The Mycenaeans*. London: British Museum Press, 2007.

Shelmerdine, Cynthia, ed. *The Cambridge Companion to the Aegean Bronze Age*. Cambridge: Cambridge University Press, 2008.

Watrous, L. Vance. *Minoan Crete: An Introduction*. Cambridge: Cambridge University Press, 2021.

The Dark Age and Archaic Greece

Graziosi, Barbara. *Homer*. Oxford: Oxford University Press, 2016.

Hall, Jonathan. *A History of the Archaic Greek World, ca. 1200–479 BCE*. Rev. ed. Malden, MA, and Oxford: Wiley Blackwell, 2014.

Hansen, Mogens. *Polis: An Introduction to the Ancient Greek City-State*. Oxford: Oxford University Press, 2006.

Lavelle, Brian. *Archaic Greece: The Age of New Reckonings*. Medford, MA: Wiley Blackwell, 2020.

Morris, Ian, and Barry Powell, eds. *A New Companion to Homer*. Leiden and New York: Brill, 2011.

Osborne, Robin. *Greece in the Making, 1200–479 BCE*. London: Routledge, 1996.

The Classical Heyday

Cartledge, Paul. *Democracy: A Life*. 2nd ed. Oxford: Oxford University Press, 2018.

———. *The Spartans: An Epic History*. London: Pan, 2013.

———. *Thebes: The Forgotten City of Ancient Greece*. New York: Abrams, 2020.

Holland, Tom. *Persian Fire: The First World Empire and the Battle for the West*. London: Little, Brown, 2005.

Hornblower, Simon. *The Greek World, 479–323 BCE*. 4th ed. Abingdon: Routledge, 2011.

Kagan, Donald. *The Peloponnesian War*. London: Harper Perennial, 2005.

Rhodes, P. J. *A History of the Classical Greek World, 478–323 BC.* 2nd ed. Medford, MA, and Oxford: Wiley Blackwell, 2010.

The Rise of the Macedonians and Alexander the Great

Anson, Edward. *Philip II, the Father of Alexander the Great: Themes and Issues.* London: Bloomsbury, 2020.

Bosworth, A. B. *Conquest and Empire: The Reign of Alexander the Great.* Cambridge: Cambridge University Press, 1993.

Bowden, Hugh. *Alexander the Great: A Very Short Introduction.* Oxford: Oxford University Press, 2014.

Cartledge, Paul. *Alexander the Great: The Hunt for a New Past.* London: Pan Macmillan, 2005.

Lane Fox, Robin. *Alexander the Great.* London: Penguin, 1973.

Worthington, Ian. *Demosthenes of Athens and the Fall of Classical Greece.* Oxford: Oxford University Press, 2012.

———. *Philip II of Macedonia.* New Haven, CT: Yale University Press, 2008.

The Hellenistic World

Allen, Joel. *The Roman Republic and the Hellenistic Mediterranean: From Alexander to Caesar.* Medford, MA: Wiley Blackwell, 2020.

Boardman, John. *The Greeks in Asia.* London: Thames & Hudson, 2015.

Chaniotis, Angelos. *Age of Conquests: The Greek World from Alexander to Hadrian 336 BC–AD 138.* Princeton, NJ: Princeton University Press, 2018.

Errington, R. Malcolm. *A History of the Hellenistic World, 323–30 BC.* Oxford: Blackwell, 2008.

Manning, J. G. *The Last Pharaohs: Egypt Under the Ptolemies, 305–30 BC.* Princeton, NJ: Princeton University Press, 2010.

Shipley, Graham. *The Greek World After Alexander, 323–30 BC.* London: Routledge, 2000.

Stoneman, Richard. *The Greek Experience of India: From Alexander to the Indo-Greeks*. Princeton, NJ: Princeton University Press, 2019.

Thonemann, Peter. *The Hellenistic Age: A Very Short Introduction*. Oxford: Oxford University Press, 2018.

The Roman Empire and Early Christianity

Barnes, Timothy. *Constantine: Dynasty, Religion and Power in the Later Roman Empire*. Oxford: Blackwell, 2011.

Beard, Mary. *SPQR: A History of Ancient Rome*. London: Profile, 2015.

Fox, Robin Lane. *Pagans and Christians in the Mediterranean World from the Second Century AD to the Conversion of Constantine*. London: Penguin, 1988.

Freeman, Charles. *A New History of Early Christianity*. New Haven, CT, and London: Yale University Press, 2011.

Spawforth, A. J. S. *Greece and the Augustan Cultural Revolution*. Cambridge: Cambridge University Press, 2012.

Vermes, Geza. *Christian Beginnings: From Nazareth to Nicaea, AD 30–325*. London: Penguin, 2013.

Whitmarsh, Tim. *Greek Literature and the Roman Empire: The Politics of Imitation*. Oxford: Oxford University Press, 2002.

From the Roman Empire to the Byzantine (Late Antiquity)

Brown, Peter. *The World of Late Antiquity, AD 150–750*. London: Thames & Hudson, 1971.

Cameron, Averil. *The Mediterranean World in Late Antiquity, AD 395–700*. 2nd ed. London: Routledge, 2012.

Haldon, John. *The Empire That Would Not Die: The Paradox of Eastern Roman Survival, 640–740*. Cambridge, MA: Harvard University Press, 2016.

Heather, Peter. *Rome Resurgent: War and Empire in the Age of Justinian*. Oxford: Oxford University Press, 2018.

Kulikowski, Michael. *Imperial Tragedy: From Constantine's Empire to the Destruction of Roman Italy, AD 363–568*. London: Profile, 2019.

Mitchell, Stephen. *A History of the Later Roman Empire, AD 284–641*. Oxford: Blackwell, 2007.

Sarris, Peter. *Empires of Faith: The Fall of Rome to the Rise of Islam, 500–700*. Oxford: Oxford University Press, 2011.

The Byzantine Empire and the Crusades

Angold, Michael. *The Fourth Crusade: Event and Context*. London: Pearson Longman, 2003.

Brubaker, Leslie, and John Haldon. *Byzantium in the Iconoclast Era, c. 680–850*. Cambridge: Cambridge University Press, 2011.

Cameron, Averil. *The Byzantines*. Oxford: Blackwell, 2006.

Frankopan, Peter. *The First Crusade: The Call from the East*. London: Vintage, 2013.

Herrin, Judith. *Byzantium: The Surprising Life of a Medieval Empire*. London: Allen Lane/Penguin, 2007.

Kaldellis, Anthony. *Streams of Gold, Rivers of Blood: The Rise and Fall of Byzantium, 955 A.D. to the First Crusade*. Oxford: Oxford University Press, 2017.

Phillips, Jonathan. *The Fourth Crusade and the Sack of Constantinople*. London: Pimlico, 2005.

Stathakopoulos, Dionysios. *A Short History of the Byzantine Empire*. London: I. B. Tauris, 2014.

Aftermath of the Fourth Crusade and the Early Ottoman Period (to 1669)

Demacopoulos, George. *Colonizing Christianity: Greek and Latin Religious Identity in the Era of the Fourth Crusade*. New York: Fordham University Press, 2019.

Finkel, Caroline. *Osman's Dream: The Story of the Ottoman Empire, 1300–1923*. London: John Murray, 2005.

Greene, Molly. *The Edinburgh History of the Greeks, 1453 to 1768: The Ottoman Empire*. Edinburgh: Edinburgh University Press, 2015.

Holton, David, ed. *Literature and Society in Renaissance Crete*. Cambridge: Cambridge University Press, 1991.

Inalcik, Halil. *The Ottoman Empire: The Classical Age 1300–1600*. London: Phoenix, 2000.

Nicol, Donald. *The Last Centuries of Byzantium 1261–1453*. 2nd ed. Cambridge: Cambridge University Press, 1993.

Pizanias, Petros. *The Making of the Modern Greeks, 1400–1820*. Newcastle upon Tyne: Cambridge Scholars Publishing, 2020.

Wilson, N. G. *From Byzantium to Italy: Greek Studies in the Italian Renaissance*. 2nd ed. London: Bloomsbury, 2017.

Greeks and Greece in Modern Times

Beaton, Roderick. *Greece: Biography of a Modern Nation*. London: Allen Lane/Penguin, 2019.

Brewer, David. *The Flame of Freedom: The Greek War of Independence, 1821–1833*. London: John Murray, 2001.

———. *Greece: The Decade of War: Occupation, Resistance and Civil War*. London: I. B. Tauris, 2016.

Clogg, Richard. *A Concise History of Greece*. 4th ed. rev. Cambridge: Cambridge University Press, 2021.

Kalyvas, Stathis. *Modern Greece: What Everyone Needs to Know*. Oxford: Oxford University Press, 2015.

Kitromilides, Paschalis. *Enlightenment and Revolution: The Making of Modern Greece*. Cambridge, MA: Harvard University Press, 2013.

Kostis, Kostas. *History's Spoiled Children: The Formation of the Modern Greek State*. Translated by Jacob Moe. London: Hurst, 2018.

Llewellyn-Smith, Michael. *Venizelos: The Making of a Greek Statesman, 1864–1914*. London: Hurst, 2021.

Mazower, Mark. *The Greek Revolution: 1821 and the Making of Modern Europe*. London: Allen Lane, 2021.

Further Reading

St. Clair, William. *That Greece Might Still Be Free: The Philhellenes in the War of Independence.* London: Open Book, 2008; first published 1972.

Thomas, Gallant. *Modern Greece: From the War of Independence to the Present.* 2nd ed. London: Bloomsbury, 2016.

Tziovas, Dimitris. *Greece from Junta to Crisis: Modernization, Transition and Diversity.* London: I. B. Tauris, 2021.

Veremis, Thanos. *A Modern History of the Balkans: Nationalism and Identity in Southeast Europe.* London: I. B. Tauris, 2017.

INDEX

Index

Index

Index

Index

Index

Index

Index

Index

Index

Index

Index

Index

Index

Index

Index

Index

Index

Roderick Beaton

Roderick Beaton is an emeritus professor at King's College London and Commander of the Order of Honour of the Hellenic Republic. One of his recent books, *Greece: Biography of a Modern Nation*, was shortlisted for the Cundill History Prize and won the prestigious Runciman Award, making him a four-time winner. He lives in Kent, England.